Opinions Throughout History

Immigration

Opinions
Throughout
History

Immigration

Micah L. Issitt

Grey House
Publishing

PUBLISHER:	Leslie Mackenzie
EDITORIAL DIRECTOR:	Laura Mars
PROJECT EDITOR:	Betsy Maury
MARKETING DIRECTOR:	Jessica Moody
PRODUCTION MANAGER:	Kristen Hayes

Grey House Publishing, Inc.
4919 Route 22
Amenia, NY 12501
518.789.8700
Fax 518.789.0545
www.greyhouse.com
e-mail: books@greyhouse.com

Publisher's Cataloging-In-Publication Data
(Prepared by The Donohue Group, Inc.)

Names: Issitt, Micah L.
Title: Immigration / Micah L. Issitt.
Description: Amenia, NY : Grey House Publishing, [2018] | Series: Opinions throughout history | Includes bibliographical references and index.
Identifiers: ISBN 9781682177228 (hardcover)
Subjects: LCSH: United States--Emigration and immigration--History--Sources. | Emigration and immigration law--United States--Sources. | National characteristics, American--Sources.
Classification: LCC JV6450 .I87 2018 | DDC 325.73--dc23

Table of Contents

30. The Fight for American Ideology

31. Open or Closed

Publisher's Note

Opinions Throughout History: Immigration is the second title in a new series from Grey House Publishing. Single, in-depth volumes are designed to follow the path of public opinion on current, controversial topics as they have evolved throughout history. Each volume includes a range of primary and secondary source documents, including newspaper and magazine articles, speeches, court decisions, and other legislation. These documents are accompanied by expert commentary and analysis to guide the reader through the process of understanding how each document contributed to, or is a reflection of, changing attitudes on important issues of public interest.

Opinions throughout History: Immigration starts with a detailed, 12-page *Introduction,* that follows immigration throughout history, what it means to be an American, and why it's important. This is followed by a comprehensive *Timeline* of significant events related to immigration, and 30 related documents, arranged in chronological order. Most of them are reprinted in their entirety, and are clearly distinguished by a shaded title bar. Often, the document is broken up into sections to better demonstrate the points discussed in the 1,500 words of analysis and commentary that accompany it, detailing the significance of the document and how it reflects the ongoing tension between opposing priorities of immigration in America.

The time period covered is sweeping. The content starts with the *1798 Treaty With the Delawares*, which established a nation-to-nation relationship between European colonists (the first immigrants) and various indigenous American societies, and ends with the Smithsonian article, *"America's True History of Religious Tolerance."* Each chapter starts with a valuable *Introduction* and list of *Topics Covered,* and ends with a *Conclusion, Discussion Questions,* and *Works Used.* Each chapter is further enhanced by photos and other images, quotations, and sidebars. Footnotes referenced in the text begin on page 583.

Back matter includes *Historical Snapshots* that provide broad overviews of political, social and cultural developments that give the reader an understanding of the political and social climate of the time. Also included is a list of *Primary and Secondary Sources* that appear in this volume, and a *Glossary* of terms frequently used when discussing immigration. A *Bibliography* and detailed *Index* complete the volume.

The first title in this series is *Opinions Throughout History: National Security vs. Civil & Privacy Rights.* Following this second volume on *Immigration* are works that tackle *Gender Roles* and *Drug Use & Abuse.*

Introduction

Opinions Throughout History: Immigration does not cover, as many books about immigration do, the "immigrant experience," which typically involves exploring the lives and experiences of immigrants who have come to the United States and struggled with cultural differences and assimilation. Nor does it detail the proportions of immigrants coming to the United States from different countries, or the global issues that lead to surges of immigration.

Rather, *Opinions Throughout History: Immigration* traces the history of immigration in the United States from the eighteenth century to present day, and examines, through analysis of primary and secondary documents, how immigration policy and activism relate to public opinion. This work is about how opinions and ideas shaped and continue to shape the history of immigration and, as such, focuses on the power of ideologies, prejudices, attitudes, fears, and hopes that shape the immigrant debate.

Preserving Identity

It is common for politicians and social activists to refer to America as a "nation of immigrants," or as a "melting pot," and this reflects the importance of immigration and the blending of cultures in the nation's history. At any moment in any society, however, there is typically one group, whether political, racial, ethnic, religious, or otherwise, that is dominant, meaning that the group has an outsized influence on law, policy, and popular culture. In the United States, the dominant group has always consisted of white, Christian (usually Protestant) males, of Western or Northern European descent. This is still largely the case, but is rapidly changing, and will not be the case in the future. A majority of children living in the United States in 2018 are not white and so, in coming years, America will no longer be a white-majority nation. The history of immigration policy documents the efforts of the dominant group to preserve their perceived identity by restricting access to one or more "outsider" groups.

Immigrant groups that have been targeted for exclusion include Catholics, Irish, Anarchists, Communists, Socialists, Jews, Eastern Europeans, Asians, Southeast Asians, Africans, and Muslims. In every era, there is at least one group that is considered by immigration opponents as the primary foreign threat of the day. Which group is targeted depends on a variety of factors and may be based on different justifications but always also on fear. In the 1800s, there was a common saying among some European immigrants that "America beckons, but Americans repel." This statement reflects the true nature of America's diverse and conflicted society. Americans are always excluding *and* embracing, resisting *and* accepting, attacking *and* defending, and all of this is essential to America's evolution, as a nation, and evolving embodiment of the nation's fundamental ideals and identity.

Understanding American Identity

Being American is not so much a state of *being* as it is an active, ongoing process. The foundational laws and documents of the United States possess an inherent mutability, or lack of specificity, which provides the capability for evolution and response to current issues. This helps redefine the nation's identity over time, an ongoing process that demonstrates that being American exists on two levels: subjective and objective.

Subjective Americans

What it means to be American is, on one level, a personal concept that exists in every American's mind, and there are no right or wrong answers. When trying to determine whether or not a group or an idea "fits" with American identity or culture, what is actually being measured is the weight of public opinion AND the power that each group of Americans commands. Looking at some current controversies shows how this works:

Gun Control: As of 2017, more than 60 percent of Americans think gun laws should be stricter, whereas only 33 percent want gun laws to stay the same.[1]

DREAMers (undocumented aliens who were brought to the United States as children): As of 2017, 86 percent of Americans support allowing the DREAMers to become American citizens or to have permanent legal status.[2]

Despite majority support for stronger gun laws, and *overwhelming* support for the DREAMers, the power in American society is not behind the majority in either case, but behind the minority.

Whether or not a group gains or loses political power depends on a number of factors:
1. Can the group generate revenue to purchase the support of politicians, pundits, and lobbyists?
2. Is the group cohesive enough to influence politicians by providing or withdrawing political support?
3. Are the people within a group willing to vote based on their beliefs regarding a single issue or debate?

The evolution of America is not a matter of public opinion, but of the degree to which groups of Americans, focused on individual issues, can *concentrate* their political power. This often comes down to the ability to marshal economic influence and this is why the wealthy, despite constituting a vanishingly small percentage of Americans, exert far more influence over politics than the rest of the country. Wealthy or not, if a group can gather power and influence, they can push the evolution of the country in *any* direction.

America could be or could *become* anything, even a communist nation or a monarchy, and it would still be America so long as enough of the people, commanding sufficient power and influence, wanted the nation to become so.

Objective Americans

Being American is something that can be determined objectively because the laws and constitutional principles of American society have defined American citizenship. More than this, those same laws say that any person who is an American citizen *is* American. This is not a subjective assessment, it is a function of the U.S. Constitution.

In 2018, America is black, white, Asian, Indigenous, Muslim, Christian, Jewish, Buddhist, Sikh, Hindu, Satanist, Anarchist, Communist, Socialist, Capitalist, Homosexual, Heterosexual, Cisgender, Transgender, and many other things. That America *is* these things in the present is not optional, though this can change over time. With sufficient public support and political power, any of these various American groups could be legally and constitutionally prohibited and so would no longer be *legally or constitutionally* American.

Each American can define American identity in his or her own mind but does not have the legal right to define this for all Americans. Constitutionally this power belongs to the *people*, not a person, and it is only through collective action urging laws and constitutional amendments that the objective level of American identity can be changed.

Conservative or Liberal: The Name Game

People are not generally either conservative or liberal, but rather, most people are conservative in some ways and liberal in others. Politicians and political movements can be described as conservative or liberal because such a designation describes the overall political aims of the movement, but not the subtlety of the feelings possessed by people within those same movements. Political labels are typically prejudicial and do not reflect the nuanced views that many people hold.

Some examples of ideology in immigration policy are as follows:
1. Those who believe in open immigration, without restriction, might be called liberal, because they emphasize liberty and downplay tradition.
2. Those who believe immigration should be restricted or at least kept at the same level, might be called conservative, because they are trying to preserve American society as it exists or how it was in a past state.
3. A person who believes immigration policy should be used to help the less fortunate or as a tool for egalitarian goals might be called progressive.
4. A person who believes that immigration laws should be based on the 1924 Immigration Act might be called a traditionalist or anti-Modernist.
5. A person who believes that only white people should be allowed to migrate to the United States would most likely be considered racist.

What Is Conservatism?

Conservatism is an ideology based on the desire to protect and preserve aspects of one's culture. Conservatives are not always racist or xenophobic, but these views are more common in conservatism because xenophobia and racism are also based on a desire to protect or preserve aspects of culture. People are xenophobic because they fear what outside or alien influence will do to them and their culture. People are racist because they believe that races have different values and qualities and fear what people of other races will do to their identity and culture.

Conservative Differences with Progressivism

Every society needs both conservatism and progressivism. Progressivism is needed to drive evolution and identify issues hindering the process of expanding the benefits of society to the greatest number of people as possible. Conservatism preserves perceptively beautiful or beneficial aspects of society, and calls attention to the marginalization of those whose lifestyles and worldviews are tied to facets of society that may be threatened by the nation's progress.

Without progressivism, societies stagnate, and without conservatism, societies rapidly develop beyond the capabilities of many to adjust.

A Dysfunctional Two-Party System

Because the United States has an artificially simplistic two-party system, all types of right-wing ideals are lumped into one of the two parties whereas all progressive or left-wing ideologies are lumped together in the other. There is little room for the nuances that are more natural to people's belief systems.

Modern members of the Republican Party sometimes like to remind people that Abraham Lincoln was Republican. This is true, but also misleading. In Lincoln's time, the Republican Party was progressive and more liberal and the Democrats were conservative and typically nativist. This changed in the mid-twentieth century when the Democratic Party began to focus on minority rights and the Republican Party came to represent the conservative, more traditionalist demographic. That is how it remains in 2018, with the Republican

Party serving as a catchall for conservative ideals and the Democrats serving as a similarly nebulous blend of liberal and progressive ideals.

The two-party system doesn't reflect the way that many people actually think or feel about issues and this is likely one reason why, over time, satisfaction with the political parties has declined. In the 1950s, more than 70 percent of Americans trusted their government all or most of the time, but this percentage fell to only 18 percent by 2017, the lowest level of trust in government ever recorded.[3] A person who votes Republican because he or she doesn't like the spending policies of Democratic candidates is, therefore, forced to support all of the other ideals that have been folded into the Republican Party's platform, such as opposition to abortion, opposition to gay rights, opposition to immigration, etc. To make matters worse, many Americans embrace tribalism to a high degree, adhering to party lines with little or no effort to make independent decisions on politics.

Immigration Policy Leans Heavily Conservative

In the United States, immigration policy is almost *always* conservative, with shorter periods of intervening progressivism that typically lead to a strong conservative backlash. This is logical, because immigration policy determines how a society's racial and ethnic balance changes or is maintained over time. Conservatives take the lead in immigration reform movements because the desire to resist ethnic or racial changes to the nation's composition is conservative by nature. Even when one ideological strategy dominates, there are usually (but not always) compromises between the two sides, but this often does not reflect the variety of ways that people felt about these laws either in the present or in history.

Immigration Concerns are Universal

Racism and xenophobia are universal to humanity and are expressed in every culture. The opposing ideals—tolerance and xenophilia—are also instinctual and are found in every society. Whether a majority gravitates towards racism or tolerance, or towards xenophobia or xenophilia, depends on a variety of factors, such as familiarity, stability, and overall satisfaction with one's society and quality of life. It is important to understand that the values associated with such concepts are *subjective* and *not* absolute.

Constant—and True—Immigration Concerns

Those who oppose immigration or want to reduce the number of immigrants who come to the United States each year, typically cite one of several common claims as reasons:

1. Immigrants take jobs and resources from American workers.
2. Immigrants bring crime or are more likely to be criminal.
3. Immigrants do not share American values and so are dangerous.
4. Immigrants do not assimilate into American society.

These arguments have remained basically unchanged from the very beginning of American debates about immigration. These exact same arguments were made about Chinese, Japanese, Southeast Asian, Irish, Mexican, Central American, Catholic, Communist, and Anarchist immigrants at different points in history. Although all the concerns listed above are based on legitimate fears, the claim that immigrants pose any of these dangers has been highly exaggerated in history and in the present debate.

Decades of research indicate that fears about Chinese immigrants were exaggerated in 1880 just as fears of Mexican immigrants are exaggerated in 2018. Over time, as the immigrant threat in each generation fails to produce a demonstrable threat to American lives, increasingly more Americans gravitate away from the most extreme fears of anti-immigration advocates.

Immigrants also make contributions to American society that some Americans value. For instance, the American Community Survey (a bipartisan group of mayors and business leaders) reported that immigrants contribute $105 billion in state and local taxes each year, and $224 billion in federal taxes. Constituting some 13 percent of the population, immigrants contribute 15 percent of the nation's entire economic output, meaning that immigrants are among the most productive and economically beneficial sectors of the American population.[4] The contribution of immigrants to America's growth has also been well documented in historical research. Immigrants were absolutely essential to the nation's growth during the industrial revolution and to the building of the continental railroad. Economists and historians agree that without the "golden era of mass migration," America's industrial revolution would not have been nearly as successful and the United States would probably not now be the world's largest economy.

Outside of the well-documented economic benefits of America's immigration system a large and growing majority of Americans place value on cultural diversity, and many in this group list diversity as one of the chief benefits of immigration. In 2017, Pew Research found that 64 percent of Americans reported that the increasing number of people from different races, ethnic groups, and nationalities makes the United States a better place to live. About 29 percent of respondents felt that diversity made little difference, whereas only 5 percent thought that diversity makes the country a worse place to live. Among Americans with a postgraduate degree, the percentage who believe diversity makes the country a better place to live increases to an overwhelming 79 percent, with only 3 percent believing diversity makes the country worse. Even among Americans identifying as "conservative," 45 percent believe that diversity makes the country better, while 38 percent think it makes no difference, and only 10 percent deem it makes the country worse.[5]

A Significant Shift Occurs

Americans are still, in general, suspicious and resistant to immigration overall, but there has been a significant shift towards the belief that diversity and immigration are good for America. For instance, in 2017 although Pew Research found that 65 percent say immigrants strengthen America because of their hard work and talents, in 1994, when Pew asked the same question, 63 percent believed that immigrants were a burden on society, and only 31 percent believed that they strengthened the country.

Liberals and progressives have seen the biggest change in attitudes about immigration, developing positive views of immigrants and diversity in general more rapidly and completely than conservatives, but the shift towards a more positive view of immigrants and immigration crosses partisan lines. In general, American evolution has been towards progressivism, though at each era this push is tempered by conservative resistance. Therefore, the conservative concerns may remain more or less similar from generation to generation, while there is a broader softening of attitudes about these threats as society becomes increasingly liberal and less frightened of outsider influence.[6]

Not Reflected in the Halls of Power

In 2017, Americans had the most positive attitudes about immigrants overall ever recorded. However, with the election of President Donald Trump the power base now holds views on immigration that are out of step with the majority of Americans.

President Trump has proposed ideologically polarized immigration policies and Trump's election and presidency reflect the increasing intransigence of those who adhere closely to ideological extremes. In 2017, polls found the lowest level of trust in government ever recorded among the public. Whereas a Republican like Ronald Reagan was able, in some ways, to breach this divide and create compromise, politicians in 2018 are less willing or less capable of doing so. American attitudes about immigrants and immigration are changing, but politicians, in their struggle for support in a polarized environment, are increasingly standing to the periphery of American culture, rather than in the center.

Ultimately, the anti-modernist moment in immigration policy promoted by Trump is unlikely to affect the momentum of public opinion, which has always been a slow, moderate march towards progress and liberalism, though always assuaged by conservative temperance. If anything, the more politicians stretch to the far right or far left the less relevant they become to the nation's cultural evolution.

Works Used

Clement, Scott and David Nakamura. "Survey finds strong support for 'dreamers'." *The Washington Post*. Washington Post, Co. 25 Sept. 2017.

"Guns." *Gallup News*. Gallup, Inc. 2018.

"In First Month, Views of Trump Are Already Strongly Felt, Deeply Polarized." *Pew Research Center*. 16 Feb. 2017.

"Is Trump A Racist?" *Rasmussen Reports*. Rasmussen Reports, LLC. 18 Jan. 2018.

"Public Trust in Government: 1958–2017." *Pew Research*. Pew Research Center. U.S. Politics and Policy. 3 May 2017.

"The Partisan Divide on Political Values Grows Even Wider," *Pew Research*. 5 Oct. 2017.

Tan, Avianne. "Without immigrants, the US economy would be a 'disaster,' experts say." *ABC News*. ABC. 16 Feb. 2017.

Historical Timeline

1492: Christopher Columbus arrived in the United States during an effort to reach India, mistakenly named the native residents he encountered "Indians"

1606: Colony of Virginia was founded, becoming the anchor for later European immigration to North America

1614: The Chickahominy Treaty between the Virginia colony and a branch of the Pequot nation established the sovereignty of the Virginia Colony through a mutual defense treaty with the Pequot

1722: The Great Treaty of 1722 became the first ratified treaty in U.S. history between the colonies of New York, Virginia, and Pennsylvania and the Five Nations (Mohogs, Oneydes, Onondages, Cayauges, and Sinnekees)

The treaty helped to defend the colonies against the encroachment of Spanish and French colonists

1775: The American Revolution began with the Thirteen Colonies fighting for independence from the British monarchy

1776: The Declaration of Independence was signed

1778: The United States ratified the Treaty with the Delawares between the U.S. government and the Delaware Nation, the first nation-to-nation treaty recognizing the sovereignty of the United States government

State legislatures ratified the U.S. Constitution, establishing the basic precedent for all future constitutional law

Legislators immediately began debating a series of amendments further defining the powers of the branches of the government and the rights of citizens

1790: The United States passed the Uniform Rule of Naturalization, the nation's first naturalization law; this law stated that any free white person who had resided in the nation for two years and who appeared before any court and was found to be of "good character," had the right to become a citizen

1791: The U.S. Congress ratified the Bill of Rights, creating the first 10 amendments to the United States Constitution

The Haitian Revolution began in Haiti and led to a mass migration of Spanish colonists and African slaves into Louisiana

1794: The U.S. government and the Six Nations signed the Calico Treaty, which became one of the longest lasting indigenous American treaties in U.S. history, still in effect as of 2018: The "XYZ affair," between the United States and the French Revolutionary government led to the possibility of a war with France and instigated the nation's first anti-immigration movement

1798: Congress passed the Alien and Sedition Acts under President John Adams, which placed new, more stringent limitations on immigration overall and changed the residency requirements for naturalization from 2 to 14 years

The laws also established the power of the federal government to conduct deportations of any alien considered dangerous to the U.S. government

1802: The Naturalization Law eliminated the 14-year waiting period of the Alien and Sedition Acts, as well as many of the other controversial provisions of the former law and established a 5-year residency requirement for obtaining citizenship

1804: The Women and Children of Declarant law was the first law regarding the citizenship of women, establishing that a foreign-born woman could become a citizen if married and if the woman's husband was himself eligible for citizenship

1845: The Great Famine in Ireland motivated a surge in Irish immigration to the United States, resulting in the birth of the Know Nothing political party and the Order of the Star-Spangled Banner (OSSB), nativist organizations that opposed Irish and Catholic immigration

1848: The Women's Suffrage movement developed through the Seneca Falls convention organized by Susan B. Anthony and Elizabeth Cady Stanton

Gold was discovered in California leading to a mass migration of native and foreign-born towards the west coast to participate in what became known as the "gold rush"

1850: After an influx of Chinese migrants began arriving in the United States to work as miners, an anti-Chinese movement emerged among the mining communities in California and elsewhere on the west coast

1855:

The California State Government passed the "Foreign Miners Tax," which charged a fee to foreign-born workers in the mining industry and was specifically meant to discourage Chinese migration

The Naturalization Act of 1855 established that any child born to a male U.S. citizen, even if born outside of the United States is considered a citizen by birth

The Naturalization Act further established that a foreign-born woman could gain citizenship status through marriage to a U.S. citizen

1862:

The Homestead Act granted federally owned land to individuals and families agreeing to develop the property, located primarily in the then western frontier of the nation

The Homestead Act encouraged a wave of immigration with foreign-born settlers applying for homesteading licenses as a path to full citizenship

California passed the Anti-Coolie Act that discouraged Chinese migration through a tax placed on any worker from the "Mongolian race" wishing to work in the state

The U.S. Congress passed a similar act that same year (An Act to Prohibit the 'Coolie Trade' by American Citizens in American Vessels), also intended to discourage Chinese migration

1864:

The Act to Encourage Immigration became the nation's first and only law specifically designed to increase immigration rates as Abraham Lincoln and the Union congress hoped to use immigrants to bolster the Union armies during the U.S. Civil War

The act was successful, resulting in an influx of new immigrants, many of whom became homesteaders while others fought in the Civil War as a stepping stone towards citizenship

1865: The Thirteenth Amendment to the U.S. Constitution formally abolished the institution of slavery under U.S. law

The Central Pacific Railroad company, under Director Charles Crocker, began importing Chinese laborers to fill shortages on the company's railroad program

The arrival of Chinese indentured laborers led to an anti-Chinese movement in the western United States

1868: The Fourteenth Amendment to the U.S. Constitution was passed and guarantees all citizens the right to due process under the law

1870: The Naturalization Act of 1870 extended the freedom to become a naturalized citizen to individuals of African nativity or descent, becoming the first U.S. law to open the naturalization process to nonwhite individuals

1874: In *Minor v. Happersett* the U. S. Supreme Court ruled that the right to vote is not a right of citizenship thus denying the right to vote to women and limited the voting rights to African Americans

1875: In *Henderson v. Mayor of New York*, the U. S. Supreme Court ruled that the State cannot regulate immigration through tax laws, as such laws constitute the regulation of foreign commerce, which is a power exclusive to the federal government

1876:   In *Chy Lung v. Freeman,* the first time that a Chinese litigant appeared in the U.S. courts, the U. S. Supreme Court ruled against a California law meant to discourage immigration by giving state authorities the power to reject prostitutes or "lewd" persons

1882:   The Chinese Exclusion Act formally prohibit the migration of Chinese people to the United States for 10 years

The law was renewed in 1892 and was eventually made permanent

The Chinese Exclusion Act was the first U.S. law to specifically prohibit the immigration of a racial or ethnic group

The law, heavily influenced by the pseudoscience of eugenics, also prohibited the immigration of individuals with physical or mental infirmities or disabilities

1886:   In *Yick Wo v. Hopkins* the U.S. Supreme Court ruled that the Fourteenth Amendment guarantees equal protection regardless of race and gender

The government of France gave the Statue of Liberty to the U.S. government, symbolizing both nation's shared commitment to freedom and democracy and opposition to slavery

The statue later became a symbol of American immigration due to its proximity from New York's famous immigration facilities

1891: The 1891 Immigration Law transferred all power to regulate immigration from the states to the federal government

Before the law, the federal government claimed exclusive power to regulate naturalization, while states were permitted to regulate immigration

1892: The first federal immigration center was established on Ellis Island in New York Harbor

The facility became symbolic of the "golden age of mass migration" that saw millions of European immigrants arriving in the United States between the 1850s and the 1920s

1903: Congress passed a new immigration law that officially enabled the federal government to ban individuals because of ideology

The law, called the Anarchist Exclusion Act, specifically prohibited the immigration of anarchists from Europe and was inspired primarily by the 1901 assassination of William McKinley by a native-born man with ties to the nation's labor movement anarchist movement

1910: A second federal immigration center was established on Angel Island in San Francisco Bay

The facility became famous as a detention center for Chinese and other ethnic migrants attempting to enter the United States through the west coast

1917:   The 1917 Immigration Act was passed as the United States entered World War I, restricting immigration from Central, Southern, and Eastern Europe

The 1917 Immigration Act also expanded on the Chinese Exclusion Act by barring immigration to any individual from the Asiatic Barred Zone, including most of Asia as well as the Arabian Peninsula and Polynesia

The United States entered World War I after German submarines were linked to an attack on the British freighter *Lusitania*, which was transporting U.S. citizens

1921:   The Emergency Quota Act or National Origins Act of 1921 restricted immigration from any country to 3 percent of the total number of foreign-born persons from that same country living in the nation as of the 1910 U.S. Decennial Census

The act was intended to limit the immigration of Jewish refugees in the wake of World War I and to maintain the proportion of ethnicities within the nation

1922:   In *Ozawa v. United States* a foreign born Japanese resident challenged the federal government's naturalization laws

The Supreme Court ruled that the U.S. government had the right to restrict naturalization based on race or ethnicity

1924:   The Immigration Act of 1924, also known as the Johnson-Reed Act, made the national origins quota systems established first in the 1921 Emergency Quota Act permanent

According to the act, immigration from each nation was limited to 2 percent of the population from that nation living in the nation as per the 1890 U.S. Census report

The law also formally banned the immigration of Japanese people, who had been one of the only Asian ethnicities not previously barred from migrating into the country

1926: The Cristero War in Mexico resulted in a surge of Mexican migrants entering the United States and motivated the nation's first anti-Mexican immigrant movement

1929: The Great Depression, the most long-lasting and devastating economic depression in U.S. history began.

The depression heightened anti-immigrant and anti-migrant sentiment, deepening the anti-Mexican migrant and labor movement in the southwest and western United States

1930: The Mexican Repatriation movement began, during which time state and federal immigration authorities expelled more than 1 million Mexican migrants, immigrants, and Mexican-American citizens, from the United States into Mexico

The actions of the governmental agencies involved was later seen as unconstitutional with reparations paid to some of the Mexican-Americans who were expelled due to racial prejudice during the depression

1942: President Franklin Roosevelt signed Executive Order 9066 permitting the government to forcibly intern

Japanese-Americans and Japanese immigrants living in the United States

The Bracero Program, created under Executive Order 8802, was established, bringing thousands of temporary Mexican migrants into the United States to work in the agriculture industry

The Bracero Program resulted in an increase in illegal migration from Mexico and this gradually led to the growth of the anti-Mexican immigration movement

1943:   The Magnusson Act of 1943 officially ended Chinese exclusion, permitting Chinese individuals to both migrate or immigrate to the United States and to become U.S. citizens through the naturalization process

The law officially made individuals of Chinese descent the first nonwhite group allowed to become naturalized citizens

1944:   In *Korematsu v. United States*, the U.S. Supreme Court ruled that the Japanese internment program did not violate the constitutional rights of Japanese citizens

1945:   An Executive Order issued by President Harry Truman resulted in 23,000 Jewish refugees being allowed to relocate to the United States in 1946:

1948:   The Displaced Persons Act amended U.S. law regarding the immigration of refugees and largely restricted refugees from Central, Southern, and Eastern Europe from immigrating to the United States

After two years of campaigning by Truman and

supporters of Jewish refugees, the Displaced Persons Act was amended in 1950, enabling an additional 200,000 Jewish refugees to come to the United States.

1950: The Korean War began, marking the beginning of the Cold War era of U.S. history

Senator Joseph McCarthy delivered a shocking speech claiming that more than 200 communist spies had infiltrated the U.S. government

1951: The Bracero Bill provided new federal oversight to a system bringing temporary Mexican migrants to the United States

The bill increased migrant labor but also increased unauthorized migration, which strengthened the anti-Mexican immigration movement

1952: The McCarran-Walter Act continued the national quota system and ended the exclusion of immigrants from the Asiatic Barred Zone

Under McCarran-Walter, immigration restrictions were strengthened to preserve the proportions of races and ethnicities living in the United States

President Truman vetoed the McCarran-Walter Act, seeing it as prejudicial, but Congress voted to override the veto, enabling the quota system to continue

1954: The U.S. federal government began "Operation Wetback," a deportation program meant to reduce illegal immigration from Mexico

The program was unsuccessful, ultimately resulting in increasing illegal immigration across a broader portion of the Mexico–U.S. border

1955:   The Vietnam Conflict began, becoming the second major proxy war of the Cold War era

1964:   The Civil Rights Act was passed by Congress, officially ending racial segregation and prohibiting discrimination because of race, color, religion, sex, or national origin. The act also mandated equal access to all publicly owned property and facilities

1965:   The Hart-Celler Act (also known as the Immigration and Nationality Act of 1965) officially ended the national quota system, creating a uniform immigration limit system that permitted individuals of any race or ethnicity to immigrate to the United States

Though not considered the most controversial bill passed in the year, the Hart-Celler Act resulted in a massive increase in immigration from Asia, India, and Africa, fundamentally changing the racial composition of the United States

The U.S. Congress passed the Voting Rights Act, which prohibited discrimination in voting based on color, race, ethnicity, or gender

1975:   The Vietnamese refugee crisis—more than 130,000 Southeast Asian refugees were stranded on boats, nationless, after fleeing Vietnam following the fall of Saigon

1980:   The Mariel Boatlift, in which more than 120,000 refugees fled the communist regime in Cuba, resulted in a major immigration controversy in the United States

The migration of so many Cubans into Florida put a strain on the Florida economy and job market and later became an example of the dangers of refugee immigration frequently cited by anti-immigration activists

The Carter administration passed the Refugee-Act, giving the federal government the power to expand immigration quotas in order to admit refugees and changed the governmental classification of refugees to be in keeping with the definition of refugee in the 1951 United Nations on Human Rights and the 1967 Protocol on Refugees

1982:   The *Plyler v. Doe* the U.S. Supreme Court established that undocumented children would still be allowed access to the U.S. public school system despite their status

1985:   Federal courts in Texas heard cases involving a religious "Sanctuary Movement" that helped Central American migrants unable to obtain federal refugee status because of the U.S. federal activities in Central America

This became part of the "contra" controversy of the Reagan administration in which the administration was accused of fomenting civil war in Central American by funding forces opposed to communism This was a precursor to the "Sanctuary Cities" movement of 2017–2018

1986:   The Simpson-Mazzoli Act provided an amnesty program for 3 million Mexican migrants living illegally in the United States and also established a new border control program that ultimately failed to decrease unauthorized migration

1990: The Immigration Act of 1990 established a federal diversity lottery system distributing 50,000 visas to individuals from countries underrepresented in the United States

The Immigration Act also established the H-1B visa program, a temporary worker program that enabled U.S. tech and other companies to recruit high-skilled migrants to work in the medical, engineering, technology, and other industries

The Immigration Act of 1990 also removed the "ideological prohibitions" against immigrants connected to allegedly dangerous ideologies like socialism, communism, and anarchism

2001: The September 11 terrorist attacks resulted in Congress authorizing the Bush Administration to utilize military methods to combat terrorism

The Transportation Security Administration (TSA) was established, creating the "No Fly" and "Selectee" lists that limited the right to travel on airplanes in the United States, creating concern about due process protections

2002: The Bush administration created the Department of Homeland Security (DHS) that established the National Security Entry-Exit Registration System (NSEERS) targeting individuals from Muslim-majority countries for extra scrutiny by the FBI and DHS

2003: The Bush Administration established a new immigration and deportation bureau, the Immigration and Customs Enforcement (ICE) division under the auspices of the DHS

The ICE bureau consolidated authorities formerly distributed to several other departments, including the Immigration and Naturalization Service, the Customs Service, the Federal Protective Service, and the Federal Air Marshalls Service

2006: The Bush Administration passed the Secure Fence Act, which calls for the construction of a border security fence between Mexico and the United States

2013: President Barack Obama established the Deferred Action for Childhood Arrivals (DACA) by Executive Order, granting temporary protection from deportation to individuals brought to the United States illegally as children and have since grown in U.S. culture but without citizenship status and associated benefits

2017: President Donald Trump canceled the DACA Executive Order established by former President Obama in hopes of using the fate of undocumented childhood arrivals as leverage to force his political opponents to support his border wall proposal

2017: Trump announced plans to complete a border wall between the United States and Mexico, which was one of the proposals that Trump made during his presidential campaign

The Trump administration attempted on three occasions

to establish, via Executive Order, a travel ban on individuals from Muslim majority countries

Introduction

The document that starts off this volume is the text of the 1778 Treaty With the Delawares, which established a mutual nation-to-nation relationship between the new United States government and the Delaware Nation. In the 1770s, the fledgling U.S. government was under threat from the English monarchy, and the treaties with indigenous American societies were essential to the nation's survival and eventual victory in the independence struggle.

The nation-to-nation relationship between the United States and various indigenous American societies is still in place, meaning that the United States is not only home to one nation, but many. And indeed, our ancestors were the first immigrants to call this country home. Despite the current debate, immigration created this country hundreds of years ago and has been part of this country's history ever since.

As this document demonstrates, long before the Declaration of Independence, or the Bill of Rights, the foundations of American law were already being established through a series of treaties between indigenous American societies and the European colonies that developed along the nation's eastern coast. This chapter explores how treaties were used to establish legal ownership or sovereignty for the colonies on the East Coast and to secure the help and assistance of indigenous Americans in protecting the colonists against hostile indigenous societies and rival colonies supported by other colonial powers. These treaties thus determined the extent of claims made by the French, Spanish, Dutch, or English powers across the Atlantic to portions of North America.

Topics covered in this chapter include:
- Indigenous American society
- The American Revolution
- Sovereignty
- Treaty law
- Cultural assimilation
- Colonial era
- Racism and Xenophobia

This Chapter Discusses the Following Source Document:
"Treaty With the Delawares: 1778." *Yale University*. Avalon Project. Lillian Goldman Law Library. 2008.

From Immigration to Sovereigns
The United States Before Nationhood

In the beginning of the United States, the Americans were indigenous, and the immigrants were white. The white Europeans didn't see themselves as immigrants, of course, but as explorers, adventurers, or political/religious refugees. However, as what is now the United States already had a population in the millions, including hundreds of different languages and cultural traditions tens of thousands of years old, the new European arrivals certainly fit any definition of "immigrant" produced since. The colonists who arrived on American shores were searching for a new life and the chance to leave the inequities of monarchic Europe behind them. Their historic journey, and struggle to build their fledgling community, has been romanticized in the vein of the great European epics, as a quest endowed by God that led to the foundation of a new world. In reality, the foundation of the United States was accomplished by violence and persecution, and there is no historical evidence that refutes this.

Establishing Sovereignty

Sovereignty is a governmental/political concept that reflects both territoriality and cooperative communality. In short, sovereignty refers to the degree to which a government, or leader, has the right to dictate rules for a specific territory, or, more simply, the degree of ownership a person or government has over the physical land that that person controls. In international law, sovereignty is a special type of ownership that gives a government or leader the right to negotiate on behalf of a territory with other sovereign powers. Treaties are, therefore, the substrate of sovereignty.

Over the first hundred years of colonization, America became a British colony, though Britain's ownership was contested by the French, with the colonists, and the unfortunate indigenous population, caught between these powers. America was a proxy battleground in which powerful monarchies funded groups of native inhabitants and groups of colonists against one another as part of their broader colonial machinations. Europeans transitioned from explorers to landowners and saw themselves as rightful sovereigns of the lands they claimed. The colonies developed from little more than encampments to burgeoning city states with their own governments. Part of this effort involved forming treaties with foreign governments, other territories, and with the indigenous populations living in the nation.

It Begins in Violence

The Colony of Virginia was the first permanent English settlement in the United States. They arrived in 1606 and found a spacious and resource-rich landscape. Had they arrived a century earlier, they might have discovered a far more populous world, but diseases brought by earlier waves of Europeans had already killed millions of the region's indigenous inhabitants. The first Virginia colonists discovered whole ghost towns filled with skeletonized bodies, the result of the mass plague that swept across the region after Columbus' visit in 1492.

At first, the fledgling colonies were barely able to survive, and most would not have done so if not for the help of the Pequot people living in that area. Indigenous Americans taught the Pilgrims how to grow local crops and what resources to gather and showed them how to make and use fish-based fertilizer on their crops. Historians believe that the shared meal that gave rise to the legend of Thanksgiving probably happened in September or October of 1621, after the Pilgrims had, with the help of their indigenous neighbors, completed their first successful harvest and invited a group of Pequot to dine with them.

Over the next year, tensions began to rise. No historian would be accurate if he or she were to describe the violence that followed as being entirely the fault of either the indigenous inhabitants or the colonists. For many years, history books in the United States held that the peaceful

colonists had been attacked by the native inhabitants and so had to fight back. This is inaccurate. Tensions built slowly over the first few years of colonization. As the Pilgrims expanded, they encountered xenophobia from indigenous people who objected to the colonists encroaching on their territory. Keep in mind, they had controlled the region for thousands of years and so were well within their rights to resist colonial expansion. There are documented incidents of Pequot natives killing European traders and hunters, and there are also documented instances where traders and hunters killed Pequot.

Harvard University historian Bernard Bailyn has found, in his research, that the difference between the two groups was in the style of warfare that they understood. The Pequot engaged in frequent fighting among the various groups within the larger nation, but such fights were handled within a long-established system that included rules of decorum. For one thing, noncombatants were not supposed to be hurt; and it was customary, in some cases, for orphaned children to be the responsibility of the group that killed the orphan's parents. The colonists had absorbed a very different attitude, in part because of their religious beliefs. Christianity has, over the course of history, been one of the influences behind popular movements against racism and violence and towards taking care of the less fortunate. Love is everywhere in biblical scripture, including love and peace towards one's neighbors. However, biblical scripture also tells believers that it is not only okay, but in many ways encouraged, to strike violently at the forces of evil, which are to be permanently extinguished from the Earth as part of God's plan for humanity. The problem was, the Pilgrims believed that the Pequot natives they encountered were "savage" and "uncivilized," as demonstrated by their writings from the period. Over time, as fear and xenophobia grew, they began to see the Pequot as potentially evil and satanic.

The year after the now famous Thanksgiving meal, the better-armed Pilgrims ambushed and massacred a Pequot village of some 800 residents, killing men, women, children, and infants with impunity. This violent event was recorded in the diaries of those who took part, some of whom described the savagery of the attack quite clearly. The new European style of warfare being introduced to the Pequot was so anathema to their society that they were afraid and did not mount an effective resistance. As a result, the religious zealots now known as the Pilgrims grew and deepened their hold on the region. In an interview with Bailyn, Ron Rosenbaum (*Smithsonian Magazine*) indicated that Bailyn found evidence of such ferocious violence during the Pilgrim era that he titled his book about this preliminary period in America's history, *The Barbarous Years: The Peopling of British North America: The Conflict of Civilizations, 1600-1675*, saying of these tumultuous times, "Death was everywhere."[1]

Trick or Treaty

The now famous 1614 Treaty between the Chickahominy people and the Virginia colony brought an end to the First Anglo-Powhatan War (1610–1614). At the time, the European colonists were severely outnumbered by the Chickahominy people and thus, the treaty likely saved the colony from extinction. However, the growth of the English population and attacks on indigenous natives led to a breakdown in relations, and the Second Anglo-Powhatan War (1622). Another peace treaty was established in 1632, with a Third Anglo-Powhatan War breaking out in 1644, which ended with the Treaty of 1646, followed by Bacon's Rebellion, an internal power struggle for control of the lucrative fur trade. Then there was the 1677 Treaty of Middle Plantation, the 1679 Albany Conference, the 1684 Albany agreement, the 1701 Deed or Nanfan Treaty, and so on.[2]

The broad reading of European-indigenous relations reveals that few of the treaties established were honored in their entirety. Shortly after a treaty was established, European colonists began spreading into new areas,

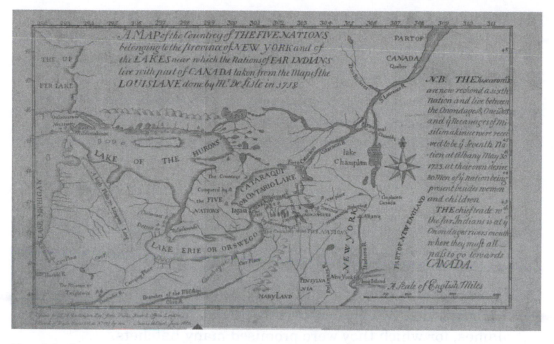

Map of the Country of the Five Nations, 1730, via Wikimedia Commons

taking more resources, and muscling native hunters out of their territories. Fighting would ensue, followed by another treaty. Although both groups occasionally violated the terms of these treaties, the colonists were far more egregious in their tendency to violate the treaties they created. The history of U.S.-indigenous relations can be traced along a series of broken treaties extending all the way to the 2017 controversy surrounding the Dakota Access Pipeline (DAPL), in which a coalition of tribes including the Standing Rock Sioux argue that federal claims on the region violate the 1868 Treaty of Fort Laramie.[3]

These treaties were tools of colonization, stemming the tide of rebellion and organized resistance and allowing the colonies to grow and trade, protected by alliances with the indigenous nations that allowed them to resist violence from other indigenous groups as well as competing colonial settlements. The first known territorial treaty between the Jamestown colony and the Chickahominy tribe, which was never written down, included the following provisions:

- To relinquish their name and to be known as Englishmen, or "Tassantasses;"
- To refrain from killing English men or their cattle and to return any trespassers, for which they were to be rewarded;
- To provide 300 bowmen for defense of the region against invasion (by the Spanish);
- To refrain forever from breaking down a paled area or invading a town;
- To announce their presence before entering an English area. Canoes encountering English vessels would be allowed to pass as "Chickahominy Englishmen;"
- To send 500 fighting men (or as many fighting men as they had) each carrying two bushels of corn annually as tribute to King James, for which they were promised many hatchets.[4]

It is important to note that one of the provisions of the treaty was that the Chickahominy participating would essentially give up their indigenous identity, and would then be known as "Englishmen," or "Tassantasses." The Chickahominy natives who participated in the 1614 negotiations were voluntary English subjects, but this marked the beginning of a long history of forced assimilation. Increasingly, as the colonies grew and became more powerful, the treaties between colonists and the indigenous Americans forced the natives to relinquish their cultural identity and to adopt English customs and law. Essentially, the treaties were not only used to prevent warfare and to secure resources, but also to enshrine European racial and cultural superiority in the legal history of the era.

The first ratified treaty on record, known as the Great Treaty of 1722, between the Five Nations (Mohogs, Oneydes, Onondages, Cayauges, and Sinnekees) with the Colonies of New York, Virginia, and Pennsylvania, specifically called for the indigenous populations to avoid relations

with the French colonies in Canada and to, as is written several times in the transcript of the treaty, "…depend entirely on the English & cleave close to them."[5] Contests between would-be colonial powers gave way to a contest for power between the fledgling independence movement and the British monarchy. Again, treaties with indigenous Americans were used as a tool to consolidate power and to defray or delay fighting between the colonists and their indigenous neighbors, to allow the revolutionaries to concentrate on their effort to break free of the British yoke.

After 1776, the United States was a nation, and the treaties that were formed thereafter were between the United States as a nation and their neighboring indigenous nations. Treaties with the remaining indigenous inhabitants were thus the first expression of the new government's sovereignty. The following transcript is one of the first treaties negotiated with an indigenous nation following the 1776 Declaration of Independence. It is clear from the text of the treaty, that the colonial framers had clear intentions: to secure the assistance of the region's indigenous nations and to deny this assistance to the English.[6]

TREATY WITH THE DELAWARES
1778
Source Document

Articles of agreement and confederation, made and, entered; into by, Andrew and Thomas Lewis, Esquires, Commissioners for, and in Behalf of the United States of North-America of the one Part, and Capt. White Eyes, Capt. John Kill Buck, Junior, and Capt. Pipe, Deputies and Chief Men of the Delaware Nation of the other Part.

ARTICLE I.
That all offences or acts of hostilities by one, or either of the contracting parties against the other, be mutually forgiven, and buried in the depth of oblivion, never more to be had in remembrance.

ARTICLE II.
That a perpetual peace and friendship shall from henceforth take place,

Treaty With the Delawares
continued

and subsist between the contracting parties aforesaid, through all succeeding generations: and if either of the parties are engaged in a just and necessary war with any other nation or nations, that then each shall assist the other in due proportion to their abilities, till their enemies are brought to reasonable terms of accommodation: and that if either of them shall discover any hostile designs forming against the other, they shall give the earliest notice thereof that timeous measures may be taken to prevent their ill effect.

ARTICLE III.

And whereas the United States are engaged in a just and necessary war, in defence and support of life, liberty and independence, against the King of England and his adherents, and as said King is yet possessed of several posts and forts on the lakes and other places, the reduction of which is of great importance to the peace and security of the contracting parties, and as the most practicable way for the troops of the United States to some of the posts and forts is by passing through the country of the Delaware nation, the aforesaid deputies, on behalf of themselves and their nation, do hereby stipulate and agree to give a free passage through their country to the troops aforesaid, and the same to conduct by the nearest and best ways to the posts, forts or towns of the enemies of the United States, affording to said troops such supplies of corn, meat, horses, or whatever may be in their power for the accommodation of such troops, on the commanding officer's, &c. paying, or engageing to pay, the full value of whatever they can supply them with. And the said deputies, on the behalf of their nation, engage to join the troops of the United States aforesaid, with such a number of their best and most expert warriors as they can spare, consistent with their own safety, and act in concert with them; and for the better security of the old men, women and children of the aforesaid nation, whilst their warriors are engaged against the common enemy, it is agreed on the part of the United States, that a fort of sufficient strength and capacity be built at the expense of the said States, with such assistance as it may be in the power of the said Delaware Nation to give, in the most convenient place, and advantageous situation, as shall be agreed on by the commanding officer of the troops aforesaid, with the advice and concurrence of the deputies of the aforesaid Delaware Nation, which fort shall be garrisoned by such a number of the troops of the United States, as the commanding officer can spare for the present, and hereafter by such numbers, as the wise men of the United States in council, shall think most conducive to the common good.

continued

ARTICLE IV.

For the better security of the peace and friendship now entered into by the contracting parties, against all infractions of the same by the citizens of either party, to the prejudice of the other, neither party shall proceed to the infliction of punishments on the citizens of the other, otherwise than by securing the offender or offenders by imprisonment, or any other competent means, till a fair and impartial trial can be had by judges or juries of both parties, as near as can be to the laws, customs and usages of the contracting parties and natural justice. The mode of such trials to be hereafter fixed by the wise men of the United States in Congress assembled, with the assistance of such deputies of the Delaware nation, as may be appointed to act in concert with them in adjusting this matter to their mutual liking. And it is further agreed between the parties aforesaid, that neither shall entertain or give countenance to the enemies of the other, or protect in their respective states, criminal fugitives, servants or slaves, but the same to apprehend, and secure and deliver to the State or States, to which such enemies, criminals, servants or slaves respectively belong.

ARTICLE V.

Whereas the confederation entered into by the Delaware nation and the United States, renders the first dependent on the latter for all the articles of clothing, utensils and implements of war, and it is judged not only reasonable, but indispensably necessary, that the aforesaid Nation be supplied with such articles from time to time, as far as the United States may have it in their power, by a well-regulated trade, under the conduct of an intelligent, candid agent, with an adequate salary, one more influenced by the love of his country, and a constant attention to the duties of his department by promoting the common interest, than the sinister purposes of converting and binding all the duties of his office to his private emolument: Convinced of the necessity of such measures, the Commissioners of the United States, at the earnest solicitation of the deputies aforesaid, have engaged in behalf of the United States, that such a trade shall be afforded said nation conducted on such principles of mutual interest as the wisdom of the United States in Congress assembled shall think most conducive to adopt for their mutual convenience.

ARTICLE VI.

Whereas the enemies of the United States have endeavored, by every artifice in their power, to possess the Indians in general with an opinion,

Treaty With the Delawares
continued

that it is the design of the States aforesaid, to extirpate the Indians and take possession of their country to obviate such false suggestion, the United States do engage to guarantee to the aforesaid nation of Delawares, and their heirs, all their territorial rights in the fullest and most ample manner, as it bath been bounded by former treaties, as long as they the said Delaware nation shall abide by, and hold fast the chain of friendship now entered into. And it is further agreed on between the contracting parties should it for the future be found conducive for the mutual interest of both parties to invite any other tribes who have been friends to the interest of the United States, to join the present confederation, and to form a state whereof the Delaware nation shall be the head, and have a representation in Congress: Provided, nothing contained in this article to be considered as conclusive until it meets with the approbation of Congress. And it is also the intent and meaning of this article, that no protection or countenance shall be afforded to any who are at present our enemies, by which they might escape the punishment they deserve.

In witness whereof, the parties have hereunto interchangeably set their hands and seals, at Fort Pitt, September seventeenth, anno Domini one thousand seven hundred and seventy-eight.

Andrew Lewis, [L. S.]
Thomas Lewis, [L. S.]
White Eyes, his x mark, [L. S.]
The Pipe, his x mark, [L. S.]
John Kill Buck, his x mark, [L. S.]

In presence of-

Lach'n McIntosh, brigadier-general, commander the Western Department.
Daniel Brodhead, colonel Eighth Pennsylvania Regiment,
W. Crawford, collonel,
John Campbell,
John Stephenson,
John Gibson, colonel Thirteenth Virginia Regiment,
A. Graham, brigade major,
Lach. McIntosh, jr., major brigade,
Benjamin Mills,
Joseph L. Finley, captain Eighth Pennsylvania Regiment,
John Finley, captain Eighth Pennsylvania Regiment.

The treaty with the Delaware people was one of many similar agreements entered by the fledgling American government as they struggled against the British, and, after the American Revolution, as they endeavored to prevent foreign powers from using native inhabitants to molest or undermine the new union. Of the treaties formed, most were changed, altered, or in other ways abandoned, and such changes, in general, meant that the indigenous people lost land, rights, and access to resources. However, some of the treaties endured, even into the twenty-first century.

Simon van de Passe, via Wikimedia Commons

Still a Nation of Treaties

In 1794, George Washington dispatched postmaster Timothy Pickering to renew a peace treaty with the Haudenosaunee (Six Nations), a confederation of indigenous people that included the Cayuga, Mohawk, Oneida, Onondaga, Seneca, and Tuscarora peoples. The treaty established a permanent promise of peace between the Six Nations and the newly emerging United States government. The democratic confederacy of the Six Nations was, in fact, one of the foundational inspirations for the United States style of representative democracy and Washington, especially, had a fondness and appreciation for the Six Nations people and their complex representative government.

According to the treaty, part of the United States was to remain the property of the Six Nations people, and the U.S. government agreed to pay $10,000 plus annual payments of $4500 in goods. Washington had a

Davy Crockett, by Chester Harding (1792-1866), via Wikimedia Commons

commemorative wampum (beaded belt) made for the occasion, featuring 13 figures representing the colonies at the time and the Six Nations. The Calico Treaty (also known as the Pickering Treaty and the Treaty of Canandaigua) is one of the first treaties that the U.S. government entered and is still in force as of 2018. Representatives of the Six Nations still have the original wampum commissioned by Washington in their possession and each year in July, the Bureau of Indian Affairs sends a symbolic yard of cloth per tribal citizen to the members of the tribes, as per the original agreement. Kevin Gover, a member of the Pawnee Nation and curator at the National Museum of the American Indian, said of the continued observance of the nation's early treaties:

_____ *"These tribal-federal treaties were critical to a very fragile, young American nation, helping to secure the borders from European competitors. They created a nation-to-nation relationship that lasts until this day. Even though it has its ups and far too many downs, it is still there, and the opportunity is still there for the U.S. and the Indian nations to thrive together."*[7]

The fact that the U.S. government frequently reneged or altered their treaties at the expense of America's indigenous inhabitants has become familiar in American culture. This revision is a step towards righting one of the many wrongs delivered against the nation's indigenous peoples, the grossly biased depiction of history that portrays the colonists as peaceable, honest in their dealings, or in any way justified in the many crimes committed against America's first inhabitants and sovereigns.

The oft-retold story of Pocahontas, a young native woman who legend says saved a white colonist, John Smith, later marrying him, and then became a symbol of peace between her people and the colonists, is an example of how the history of U.S. relations with indigenous Americans has been revised to portray the colonists in a far more beneficent light.

Pocahontas's actual name was Matoaka and she was the daughter of the powerful chief Powhatan. The myth says that, after saving colonist John Smith from execution at the hands of her father, she helped broker the 1614 Treaty with the Chickahominy, married Smith, embraced Christianity, and lived with her husband in England. Historians have since determined that Matoaka was never married to or involved with John Smith and did not save his life (being only 9 or 10 years old at the time Smith claimed to have been saved by her intervention). In fact, John Smith was never actually going to be executed by Powhatan, but simply told the story that way in his highly fictionalized memoir.

Matoaka was kidnapped by the English as a way to control her father Powhatan and was raped and impregnated while in captivity. She was married to tobacco farmer John Rolfe, who used the marriage to secure a tobacco growing alliance with the native population. She was forced to wear English clothes and was taken to England where she was paraded to royalty and other elites. Historians have found evidence that she was not a willing participant, never embracing Christianity and frequently ripping off the English clothing she was forced to wear. Given the name

"Rebecca Rolfe," some historians believed she was brought to England to reassure members of the elite who had become concerned that the indigenous Americans were being abused. It is now believed she was murdered, possibly poisoned, at around 20 years old, though the reasons for this have been lost to history.[8]

For all the patriotic splendor that Americans, looking through the distorted goggles of history, have found in the early history of the nation—the struggle to establish the first colonies, the contest between colonial powers, and the independence struggle culminating in the American Revolution—this same history is also one of exploitation and violence. The indigenous Americans were the victims of a familiar process called "dehumanization," in which one group or type of people imagines, describes, and comes to believe that another group is less evolved, less human, less civilized, and, therefore, less deserving of empathy and respect.

The colonists merely wanted land and the freedom to build a new society. The American people living in this era had been conditioned to see themselves as superior, and research demonstrates that the white colonists were bombarded with depictions of indigenous Americans as dangerous heathens who practiced all manner of behaviors seen as un-Christian and immoral, like cannibalism and strange sexual activities. It is impossible to know how widespread this belief was, but dissenting voices were rare and certainly in the minority. Over time, there was a movement that emerged to protest the nation's treatment of indigenous Americans, but this movement was not powerful enough to oppose those who saw the displacement and, at times, extinction of indigenous Americans as necessary for the nation's growth and economic prosperity. President Andrew Jackson, who built his reputation as an "Indian fighter," was one of the most egregious. In 1830, Jackson passed the Indian Removal Act, which gave the federal government the right to conduct ethnic cleansing in the area west of the Mississippi River that was then the frontier of the American nation. The debate over this was significant and there were many

THE AMERICAN GENOCIDE DEBATE

Historians are in the process of debating whether or not the persecution of Indigenous Americans was a form of genocide. The term "genocide" was invented in 1944 by Polish-Jewish lawyer Raphael Lemkin in a book documenting Nazi policies with regard to the Jewish people and other ethnic groups of Europe. Lemkin invented the term by combining the Greek word "geno," meaning "race or tribe," and "-cide," which is a Latin term that means killing. Lemkin's term became part of the 1948 United Nations Universal Declaration of Human Rights. As per the Convention, genocide is described as any violent act committed with the intent to destroy, in whole or in part, a national, ethnical, racial, or religious group[11].

Using the above definition, some scholars have found that the persecution of Indigenous Americans was, in some cases, genocidal. For instance, California's first civilian Governor, Peter H. Burnett, authorized a campaign to exterminate the Yana people of Central California, stating of this effort, "a war of extermination will continue to be waged…until the Indian race becomes extinct." In 1851 and 1852, California State conducted state-sponsored "Indian hunts" using armed militia who were paid based on the number of Indian scalps that they could deliver. This campaign was, in part, funded by the federal government because the Yana were seen as a threat to settlers and immigrants during westward expansion. Genocide scholars Jurgen Brauer and Raul Caruso write of this campaign, "One can hardly be clearer about the deliberateness of the intent and the genocidal choice made."[12]

who opposed the idea, including famed American pioneer Davy Crockett, who had come to respect and admire the indigenous natives he had known. At the congressional debate over the proposed act, Massachusetts Representative Edward Everett gave an opposing speech that was surprisingly prescient:

"The evil, Sir, is enormous; the inevitable suffering incalculable. Do not stain the fair fame of the country.... Nations of dependent Indians, against their will, under color of law, are driven from their

homes into the wilderness. You cannot explain it; you cannot reason it away. . . . Our friends will view this measure with sorrow, and our enemies alone with joy. And we ourselves, Sir, when the interests and passions of the day are past, shall look back upon it, I fear, with self-reproach, and a regret as bitter as unavailing."[9]

Many of the nation's treaties with indigenous nations were undertaken in earnest but have since served as a written record of the exploitation of America's native population. Though difficult, it is a history that all Americans should attempt to understand. Speaking at a National Archives exhibit of U.S. treaties with indigenous Americans in 2015, curator Suzan Shown Harjo of the Cheyenne and Hodulgee Muscogee nations said,

"The people who are citizens of the U.S., these are your treaties. They aren't just the Indians' treaties. No one gave us anything. No one was dragging any land behind them when they came here. This was our land."[10]

Legacy of the Americans

One of the results of the misrepresentation of indigenous Americans in American popular culture is the misconception that there was a singular "Indian" culture. While some groups might share a language or other cultural characteristics, often indigenous American nations were and are as different from one another as any modern country differs from another. Europe provides a metaphor. Like the neighboring nations of Germany and France, two indigenous peoples living prior to European arrival often had their own unique governments, languages, religion, and cultural customs. In short, America before Europeans was not home to a native

American culture, but rather, it was home to *hundreds* of cultures, each unique and many of which are now extinct.

Indigenous Americans are still part of American society and are still separate but connected nations *inside* the American nation. Many aspects of U.S. culture familiar to Americans in the 21st century are, in fact, the remnants of Indigenous American influence. Indigenous Americans were the first to grow (and taught European colonists how to grow) potatoes, beans, corn, peanuts, pumpkins, tomatoes, squash, peppers, nuts, melons, and sunflower seeds. They invented lacrosse, hockey, canoeing, tug-of-war, relay races, and many other games still played in the United States and considered "American." The English language in the United States is littered with Indigenous words like hammock, skunk, mahogany, hurricane, barbeque, bayou, chipmunk, opossum, pecan, raccoon, chili, coyote, tomato, tobacco, cashew, and cannibal and 26 of the 50 states in the union have names taken from Indigenous tribes or words.

In fact, the United States owes far more to Indigenous American culture than is generally known. On October 5, 1988, the United States Senate adopted an official resolution that stated the following:

> _____ *To acknowledge the contribution of the Iroquois Confederacy of Nations to the development of the United States Constitution and to reaffirm the continuing government-to-government relationship between Indian tribes and the United States established in the Constitution.*
>
> *Whereas the original framers of the Constitution, including, most notably, George Washington and Benjamin Franklin, are known to have greatly admired the concepts of the Six Nations of the Iroquois Confederacy.*

> *Whereas the confederation of the original Thirteen Colonies into one republic was influenced by the political system developed by the Iroquois Confederacy as were many of the democratic principles which were incorporated into the Constitution itself...*[13]

This document shows that *even* the U.S. Constitution and the unique American style of democracy itself were not solely white or European inventions but were a blend of European and Indigenous American ideals and beliefs. The Iroquois Confederacy was group of five (later six) nations governed by elected leaders that created a complex system of laws and treaties subject to democratic referendums, with any treaty or law only accepted if 75 percent of men AND 75 percent of women agreed. It was a democratic republic that bound together different people with different languages and customs based on shared interests and the desire for peace and this appealed to the founding fathers so much that it became part of American society then and forever.

As America progressed from colonies to a nation, Americans began seeing themselves as the rightful owners of the United States, rather than as having to share the land they claimed with the region's indigenous nations. They had thus transitioned from immigrants to sovereigns and began the process of deciding who should be allowed to be part of the nation they had created and what kind of culture would characterize American identity. The debate over Indian Removal shows that this was never a one-sided issue. Even then, there was disagreement over what the nation should be and what kind of people should be allowed to be part of it. This same debate is present in all immigration policy and law going forward.

CONCLUSION

The treaties between the colonies and later between the U.S. government and the indigenous nations of North America were the key to the independence struggle and remained an important political tool for the entirely of the nation's existence. However, the U.S. government did not adhere to the pacts established with America's indigenous people as the desire for land and resources, coupled with racism, precipitated a repeated pattern that continues today, as demonstrated by the Dakota Access Pipeline controversy of 2017, in which the Trump administration violated the 1868 Treaty of Fort Laramie to seize land legally belonging to an indigenous American nation.

DISCUSSION QUESTIONS

- Are indigenous Americans still stereotyped in American culture? Explain.
- Do the treaties with indigenous Americans presented in this chapter demonstrate prejudice? Explain.
- What does the idea "nation-to-nation relationship" mean regarding indigenous Americans?
- How do these treaties represent an attempt to assimilate indigenous Americans into U.S. culture?

Works Used

Brauer and Caruso, "For Being Aboriginal," in Anderton, C.H. and Jurgen Brauer, eds. *Economic Aspects of Genocides, Other Mass Atrocities, and their Prevention*. New York: Oxford UP, 2016. p. 293.

Capriccioso, Rob. "Illuminating the Treaties That Have Governed U.S.-Indian Relationships." *Smithsonian*. Smithsonian Institution. 21 Sept. 2014.

"Conference between Governor Burnet and the Indians." *University of Nebraska, Lincoln*. Early Recognized Treaties with American Indian Nations.

Grizzard, Frank E. Jr., and D. Boyd Smith. *Jamestown Colony: A Political, Social, and Cultural History*. Santa Barbara, CA: AB-CLIO, Mar. 2007.

"Historical Record: 1614 Treaty." *Charlescity*. Natives in the Landscape. Charles City County. 2006.

Kimmel, Lauren. "Does the Dakota Access Pipeline Violate Treaty Law?" *Michigan Journal of International Law*. Vol. 38, 17 Nov. 2016.

Rosenbaum, Ron. "The Shocking Savagery of America's Early History." *Smithsonian*. Smithsonian Institution. 21 Feb. 2013.

Schilling, Vincent. "The True Story of Pocahontas: Historical Myths Versus Sad Reality." *Indian Country*. Indian Country Media Network. 8 Sept. 2017.

"Statements from the Debate on Indian Removal." *Columbia University*.

"Treaty With the Delawares: 1778." *Yale Law School*. Lillian Goldman Law Library.

Wade, Lisa. "US Schools are Teaching Our Children that Native Americans are Dead." *PS Mag*. Pacific Standard. Dec 3, 2014.

Wang, Hansi Lo. "Broken Promises On Display At Native American Treaties Exhibit." *NPR*. National Public Radio. 18 Jan. 2015.

"What is Genocide?" *USHMM*. United States Holocaust Memorial Museum. Holocaust Encyclopedia. 2017.

Introduction

As discussed in Chapter 1, several years after the signing of the Treaty With the Delawares, that established the nation-to-nation relationship between indigenous Americans and the Federal government, the United States began efforts to determine how to regulate the flow of foreign arrivals into the United States. This effort was informed by the American Revolution (1775–1783) and the Declaration of Independence (1776) and then in the debates that led to the drafting and ratification of the U.S. Constitution (1789). The year after the Constitution was adopted, the nation adopted its first immigration law, the Uniform Rule of Naturalization (1790), establishing the initial rules for how a foreign-born person would be allowed to become a United States citizen.

The document discussed in this chapter is the full text of the 1790 Uniform Rule of Naturalization, a concise law determining that any free white person who lived in the nation for at least two years could become a citizen so long as they appeared in any court and were judged to be of good character. The simplicity of the law reflects an American culture that had not yet begun to contend with many of the issues that would later define the nation's immigration debates, as well as the effort to extend the founding principles of the Declaration of Independence and U.S. Constitution to the citizenship process.

Topics covered in this chapter include:
- Indigenous American society
- The American Revolution
- Constitutional law
- Institutionalization of racism
- Centralization of political power
- Naturalization law
- George Washington Administration

Becoming American
The Naturalization Process (1790-1798)

America was born when the Thirteen Colonies controlled by radical militants fought a centuries old power for control of a burgeoning agricultural empire fueled by slavery and the exploitation of the indigenous culture. The American Revolution (1775–1783) established sovereignty for the Thirteen Colonies, and with this began a long-term process of building the machinery of the central government from the remnants of the colonial administrations then in place. Part of this effort involved determining how the benefits of citizenship would be bestowed upon all those already living in the United States and those who wished to join in the new, governmental experiment taking place. This meant building the nation's first immigration laws, deciding the rules, laws, and customs that would govern the process of becoming American.

One Tyranny Ends and Another Begins

The American Revolution (1775–1783) is typically seen as the beginning of the American experiment, but it was also the culmination of more than a century of evolution. The American colonies started as an outgrowth of England and, for many years, wealthy elites in Europe profited from the labor and struggles of the American colonists, but provided (at least in the Patriots' eyes) little in return. It was unfair taxation that became the sticking point in the conflict, with the British government attempting to balance their growing colonial expenditures by increasing taxation among their colonies.

In 1776, the year that the Thirteen Colonies officially declared their independence from England, the fledgling United States was already becoming a blend of cultures. Nearly 85 percent of the colonists in 1776 were British or from one of the British colonies (Wales, Ireland, Scotland), whereas 10 percent were German, 4 percent were Dutch, and 2 percent

Signing of the Declaration of Independence, by John Trumball, via Wikimedia Commons

were French.[14] A new identity was beginning to emerge, representing the ways that European cultural and social traditions had changed from exposure to the rugged landscape of the Americas. Before the first musket ball was fired, the colonists were already becoming something different, but it wasn't until the revolution that they declared themselves Americans.

The Declaration of Independence (1776) expressed the ideological underpinnings of the American Revolution. Not only were the Patriots fighting against an exploitative colonial power, but they were fighting against the very idea of the hierarchies of power and wealth that propped up such regimes around the world. As Thomas Jefferson wrote eloquently:

> *"We hold these Truths to be self-evident, that all Men are created equal, that they are endowed by their Creator with certain unalienable Rights, that among these are Life, Liberty, and the Pursuit of Happiness."*

However, the inequities and stratification of European society endured the flames of the revolution. The Patriots of the Thirteen Colonies saw themselves as united against tyranny, but had become a tyrannical force in their own right. In general, the colonists were wealthier than their European counterparts, and income inequality (a severe crisis in the United States of the 2010s) was already emerging. In 1774, the top 1 percent of

American citizens controlled nearly 7 percent of the nation's wealth, and this wealthy elite profited not only from the underpaid work of whites, but also from the African slave trade.

In 1776, 20 percent of those living in the colonies were slaves, and it would be many years before the U.S. government would try to address the inherent inequity of this economic system. There is no justification for slavery that will meet with the approval of modern Americans. Those Africans brought to the nation were treated like human-shaped beasts of burden, dehumanized to such a degree that violence against them was no more prohibited than against a farm animal.[15] However, even then, some Americans already had strong moral objections.

Historians have discovered evidence that Thomas Jefferson, in writing the Declaration, originally wanted to blame King George III for African slavery, calling it a "cruel war against human nature." Jefferson's objections were overruled and the statement was left out, but it is interesting to imagine how American history might have differed had the framers agreed that slavery was immoral this early in history. This did not happen because the wealthy were already dependent on slavery and would not have been nearly as wealthy had they been forced to pay for the labor they were using to increase their wealth. It would take a civil war, a labor movement, and a civil rights movement to upend the system that was already in place in the Thirteen Colonies and that created a hierarchy of value that divided America's racial minorities from white society.

The language of those foundational documents also clearly establishes the racial hierarchies that came to dominate American society into the twenty-first century. For instance, in the Declaration of Independence, the founders provide a list of complaints against King George III, essentially restating the reasoning behind their desire for separation. The very last of these complaints reads:

_____ *"He has excited domestic insurrections amongst us, and has endeavored to bring on the inhabitants of our frontiers, the merciless Indian savages, whose known rule of warfare, is undistinguished destruction of all ages, sexes, and conditions."*[16]

_____

The very document that states "all Men are created equal," also refers to an entire population of indigenous inhabitants as "savages," and thus these people were *legally* "savages" in the U.S. government from this moment on. It is also worth pointing out that the indigenous people rarely practiced warfare that targeted men, women, and children, though this did occur. Depicting them as such was, even in 1776, political rhetoric and what might today be called "fake news," designed to make King George seem evil. In the American Revolution, the indigenous Americans were caught between two powers, unable to win no matter which they backed. Nevertheless, many indigenous Americans fought alongside the Patriots and against the British, whereas others remained faithful to the British, having signed treaties in good faith with the British colonial government.

Of the fate of indigenous Americans in the American Revolution, historian Colin G. Calloway writes:

_____ *"Indians fought in the Revolution for Indian liberties and Indian homelands, not for the British empire. But the image of Indian participation presented in the Declaration of Independence prevailed: most Americans believed that Indians had backed monarchy and tyranny. A nation conceived in liberty need feel no remorse about dispossessing and expelling those who had fought against its birth."*[17]

_____

The Right to Become American

The year 1790 was an important one in the United States. President George Washington gave the nation's first State of the Union Address, Thomas Jefferson became the first Secretary of State, and the Supreme Court of the United States met for the first time in New York City. The Thirteen Colonies were flying under the Betsy Ross flag featuring a circle of thirteen stars (one for each colony) against the red and white stripes signifying valor and purity, and the framers were engaged in the exciting process of creating the legislative, judicial, and executive branches of the government.

A BILL to establish an uniform Rule of Naturalization, and to enable Aliens to hold Lands under certain Restrictions.

Sect. 1st BE IT ENACTED BY THE SENATE AND HOUSE OF REPRESENTATIVES OF THE UNITED STATES OF AMERICA IN CONGRESS ASSEMBLED, That any alien, other than an alien enemy, being a free white person, who shall have resided within the limits and under the jurisdiction of the United States for the term of TWO YEARS, may be admitted to become a citizen thereof, on application to any common law court of record in any one of the States wherein he shall have resided for the term of ONE YEAR at least, and making proof to the satisfaction of such court, that he is a person of a good character, and taking the oath or affirmation prescribed by law to support the Constitution of the United States, which oath or affirmation such court shall administer, and the clerk of such court shall record such application and the proceedings thereon; and thereupon such person shall be considered as a citizen of the United States. And the children of such person so naturalized, dwelling within the United States, being under the age of twenty-one years at the time of such naturalization, shall also be considered as citizens of the United States. And the children of citizens of the United States, that may be born beyond sea, or out of the limits of the United States, shall be considered as natural born citizens.

PROVIDED, That the right of citizenship shall not descend to persons whose fathers have never been resident in the United States:

PROVIDED ALSO, That no person heretofore proscribed by any State shall be admitted a citizen as aforesaid, except by an Act of the Legislature of the State in which such person was proscribed.

[NEW-YORK, PRINTED BY THOMAS GREENLEAF.]

Uniform Rule of Naturalization, 1790, Library of Congress

That same year, the new nation tackled immigration for the first time, with the Uniform Rule of Naturalization, established on March 26, 1790. This law determined who, from among the many multitudes of the world, was eligible to become a citizen of the new republic.

UNIFORM RULE OF NATURALIZATION
March 26, 1790
Source Document

Be it enacted by the Senate and House of Representatives of the United States of America in Congress assembled, That any alien, being a free white person, who shall have resided within the limits and under the jurisdiction of the United States for the term of two years, may be admitted to become a citizen thereof, on application to any common law court of record, in any one of the states wherein he shall have resided for the term of one year at least, and making proof to the satisfaction of such court, that he is a person of good character, and taking the oath or affirmation prescribed by law, to support the constitution of the United States, which oath or affirmation such court shall administer; and the clerk of such court shall record such application, and the proceedings thereon; and thereupon such person shall be considered as a citizen of the United States. And the children of such persons so naturalized, dwelling within the United States, being under the age of twenty-one years at the time of such naturalization, shall also be considered as citizens of the United States. And the children of citizens of the United States, that may be born beyond sea, or out of the limits of the United States, shall be considered as natural born citizens: *Provided,* That the right of citizenship shall not descent to persons who fathers have never been resident in the United States: *Provided also,* That no person heretofore proscribed by any state, shall be admitted a citizen as aforesaid, except by an act of the legislature of the state in which such person was proscribed.[18]

The Uniform Rule of Naturalization was short and concise, which contrasts mightily with the lengthy and complex immigration laws of future generations, and this reflects the relative simplicity of immigration politics at the time. The rules were comparatively simple, requiring that a person reside in the nation for two years and appear before any court, which had

the authority to determine if the person was of "good character." The text of the law also makes it quite clear that women and racial minorities are excluded from citizenship. This is the first immigration document to tie American citizenship with a specific gender and race and the legacy of this law and others that followed helped to deepen America's gender and racial hierarchies.

THE CREOLIZATION OF LOUISIANA

One exception to the general white Europeans only pattern of immigration in the 1790s came after the Haitian Revolution began in 1791. The thirteen-year independence war fought in the former French colony resulted in the first black republic in the western hemisphere, and changed the demographics of the American south, particularly the future state of Louisiana. At the time, Louisiana was a Spanish colony, and the Spanish, fearing the unchecked growth of the black population, had banned entry to any individuals of African or West Indian descent. However, the Haitian revolution resulted in a mass exodus of French (the colonial rulers of Haiti at the time), free blacks, and West Indian slaves from Saint Dominque to New Orleans. Spain ceded control of Louisiana to France in 1800, and France sold Louisiana to the United States in 1803, leaving the mixed community of former free blacks, descendants of French colonists, and African and West Indian slaves to create one of the most unique and ethnically diverse communities in the United States.[19]

The Nature of Being American

Immigration was key to the American Revolution because it was the flow of religious and political radicals into the pre-united colonies that fueled the revolutionary councils and manned the militias that enabled the nation to achieve independence. These political radicals viewed immigration through much the same high-minded ideological lens that would dominate immigration rhetoric for centuries after the nation won its independence. For instance, in a 1776 issue of the now famous publication *Common Sense*, former immigrant Thomas Paine wrote,

> *"Europe, and not England, is the parent country of America. This new world hath been the asylum for the persecuted lovers of civil and religious liberty from every part of Europe. Hither have they fled, not from the tender embraces of the mother, but from the cruelty of the monster; and it is so far true of England, that the same tyranny which drove the first emigrants from home, pursues their descendants still."*[20]

However, though immigration had been a cornerstone of the revolution, it was a relatively minor concern for the U.S. government between the 1790s and the 1820s, in part because the flow of immigrants was slow. Roughly 6,000 immigrants arrived on the nation's shores each year. Of those that arrived between 1790 and 1820, nearly 50,000 were of Scotch-Irish descent, whereas 45,000 were English, 40,000 were French, 25,000 were German, and 25,000 came from Ireland. The growth of the slave population was far more rapid, with nearly 85,000 slaves brought to the nation during this same period. As the Africans brought as slaves were not considered Americans, citizens, or even humans, immigration to that point had created a melting pot, but one filled (officially) only with European ingredients.[21]

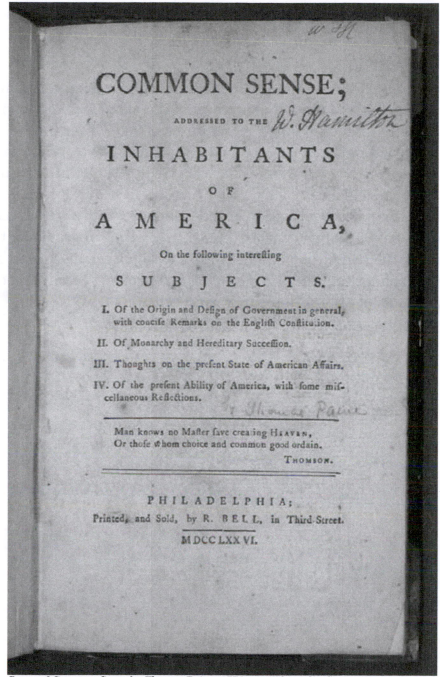

Cover of *Common Sense* by Thomas Paine, 1776, via Wikimedia Commons

CONCLUSION

There is scant evidence from the Revolutionary War demonstrating how Americans of the era felt or were thinking about immigration because of the number of other, more pressing issues that the colonists-turned-national-citizens had to consider. Developing the government was the chief concern, as reflected by the relatively minor weight that the legislature gave to the nation's first immigration policy. Following the Declaration of Independence, there was also a widespread belief that the nation needed new waves of immigrants to help bolster the population against future foreign threats as well as an ideological belief that others (at least British people) seeking freedom and independence from European tyranny should be welcomed as ideological allies in the building of the nation.

DISCUSSION QUESTIONS

- What is the difference between naturalization and immigration?
- Was the Declaration of Independence prejudiced by modern standards? Explain.
- How might the United States be different if the U.S. Constitution had banned slavery? Explain.
- How would you define tyranny? Give an example from the modern world.

Works Used

"A Century of Lawmaking for a New Nation: U.S. Congressional Documents and Debates, 1774–1875." *Library of Congress*. 2016.

Calloway, Collin G. "American Indians and the American Revolution." *National Park Service*. U.S. Department of the Interior. Dec. 2008.

"Declaration of Independence: A Transcription," *National Archives*. U.S. National Archives. 26 June 2017.

"Immigration Timeline." *Liberty Ellis Foundation*. The Statue of Liberty—Ellis Island Foundation, Inc. 2017.

Mirrer, Louise. "As American as the Haitian Revolution." *Huffington Post*. Huffington Post. 17 Jan. 2018.

Paine, Thomas. "Thoughts on the Present State of American Affairs." *Common Sense*. Independence Hall Association. 2018.

Smith, Daniel Scott. "The Demographic History of Colonial New England." *Journal of Economic History*, Cambridge UP Vol. 32, No. 1, Mar. 1972: pp. 165–83.

Weissmann, Jordan. "U.S. Income Inequality: It's Worse Today Than It Was in 1774." *The Atlantic*. Atlantic Monthly Group. 19 Sept. 2012.

Introduction

This chapter explores the history surrounding the nation's first anti-immigrant movement in the late 1790s and early 1800s, resulting from a prevailing fear of an impending war with France. This fear led to a series of restrictionist immigration policies designed to limit the number of new people allowed to become American out of concern over sedition and espionage. Alexander Hamilton, himself an immigrant, became the leader of the anti-immigrant movement and one of the founders of the Federalist Party that supported a strong central government isolated from much of the rest of the world to be better protected from foreign threats.

The documents analyzed in this chapter are the Naturalization Act and the Alien and Friends Acts, all passed in 1798 and all motivated by an emerging nativist movement that feared immigration and sought to reserve the benefits of U.S. citizenship for those born on American soil. All of the laws enacted by the Federalists in 1798 were meant to limit immigration, to enhance national security, and to provide legal protection for the economic and ethnic hierarchies of power that were beginning to define the way that some Americans saw the nation's culture.

Topics covered in this chapter include:
- Nativism
- United States foreign relations
- The Federalist Party
- Alexander Hamilton
- Ethnic prejudice
- Naturalization law
- Immigration law
- National security policies
- John Adams Administration

This Chapter Discusses the Following Source Documents:

"1798 Alien Enemies Act." *UWB*. University of Washington-Bothell Library. US Immigration Legislation Online. Session II, Chap. 66, Statute 570. 5th Congress; 6 July 1798.

"1798 Naturalization Act." *UWB*. University of Washington-Bothell Library. US Immigration Legislation Online. Session II, Chap. 54, Statute 566. 5th Congress, 17 June 1798.

Friends and Enemies
Immigration and National Security Collide (1798)

Four laws, all passed in 1798, set the path not only for America's immigration policy in general, but also for the way that immigration could be curtailed in cases of national emergency or impending war.

There are direct parallels between the immigration debate of 1798 and the immigration debate of 2017–2018, as the Trump Administration's proposals for a ban on Muslim immigration, a Border Wall between the United States and Mexico, and, in favor of more limited immigration of non-white foreigners in general, echo the same concerns and justifications raised by members of the 1798 Congress. Then, as in 2017–2018, legislators and politicians used the fear of an impending war (with France) as justification for new immigration restrictions as well as laws that increased the power of the federal government to prohibit and prevent the development of internal movements that might delegitimize or compromise the central government.

America's First Anti-Immigrant Movement

Though they weren't Americans before 1776, the descendants of the nation's early colonies and those who fought in the American Revolution quickly began to see themselves as the "real Americans," whereas the immigrants coming to the nation after the war, were increasingly seen as opportunists coming to reap the riches of the society they had created.

Alexander Hamilton, considered one of the founding fathers of the United States, was himself an immigrant, born on the British Leeward Islands to an unwed mother and abandoned, only to be adopted by a wealthy merchant. Sent to New York by his adopted father to receive an education, Hamilton became a major figure in the American Revolution and was known as a strong proponent of central government authority. His status as an immigrant was part of the reason Hamilton was chosen as

Cartoon of the XYZ Affair, considered to be America's first anti-immigration movement, via Wikimedia Commons

the subject for the widely-lauded musical *Hamilton* (2015). Lines like, "Immigrants: We get the job *done*!" from the musical reveal the underlying social justice goals of the production, and also portray Hamilton as fore-word-thinking people's (and immigrant's) hero.

In reality, Hamilton was far from a man of the people. Raised rich, despite having been orphaned as a child, Hamilton developed into an economic elitist who cared little for income equality, the plight of the lower class, or of slaves and other races persecuted under the new republic. He was also an anti-immigrant ideologue responsible for starting one of the nation's first anti-immigration movements.[22]

George Mason University historian Phillip Magness writes of Hamilton, in his essay "Alexander Hamilton as Immigrant,"

"Measured in three dimensions—his use of political attacks on immigrant contemporaries, his role in the Alien and Sedition Acts, and his adoption of an aggressive anti-immigration position at the outset of the Jefferson presidency—Alexander Hamilton's political career might legitimately be characterized as a sustained drift into nationalistic xenophobia."[23]

Although there are no public opinion polls from the 1790s to demonstrate how the average American citizen felt about immigrants, historians surveying the documents and records of the era report that nationalism and anti-immigrant attitudes were on the rise. At the time, anti-immigrant sentiment was directed at two categories of immigrants: the Irish and the French. In part, these attitudes were motivated by xenophobia and religious intolerance, with Americans (predominantly Protestant) objecting to what was sometimes called the "Catholicization of America" through the influx of Catholic immigrants from Ireland.

Anti-French sentiment of the era was more a matter of national insecurity. The French Revolution (1789–1799) resulted in the end of the Kingdom of France and the beginning of the French Revolutionary Government. Americans watching from abroad saw how France used espionage and hidden actors to weaken their targets before invasion and many feared that the French, who had ambitions in the new world as well, might try the same tactic against the newly emerging American republic. Fear of spies and saboteurs, therefore, motivated a strong anti-French sentiment among the American public and political body.

In 1794, The Directory (the French Revolutionary Government) issued an order allowing their naval forces to seize American merchant ships, the result of financial difficulties in funding the nation's many overseas wars. John Adams (second president of the United States) sent three envoys to restore peace, Elbridge Gerry, Charles Cotesworth Pinckney, and John Marshall, but the three representatives were refused access to Foreign Minister Charles Maurice de Talleyrand, and instead were met by a series of intermediaries, Nicholas Hubbard, Jean Hottinguer, Pierre Bellamy, and Lucien Hauteval, later known as W, X, Y, and Z, respectively. The "alphabet envoys" told the American representatives that France would agree to their demands in return for a bribe to Talleyrand directly, and a low-interest loan to the French government.

The XYZ affair, as it came to be known, was a major controversy, and John Adams began preparations for war. The period from 1798 to 1800 is sometimes called the Quasi-War with France, though open military engagement never occurred. It was a cold war of economic weaponry that ultimately ended in a new peace agreement but forever altered American democracy.[24]

With the threat of a war with France looming, America's political parties began taking shape. On one hand there were the Federalists, led by Alexander Hamilton, who favored a strong central government to provide a robust defense against foreign threats. State sovereignty was one of the first political controversies to emerge after the revolution and has remained a topic of legislative and political disagreement to the modern day. The Democratic Party of the era, championed by Thomas Jefferson, was skeptical of creating a strong central government, fearing that this could lead to tyranny, much like the governments that the Patriots struggled to escape in the revolution. Jefferson and the other Democrats thus championed state sovereignty and the rule of the common people, whereas the Federalists fought for stronger centralized power and a meritocracy in which the educated elite would be the primary source of political influence. In 1798, the potential war with France created sufficient paranoia and fear to give the Federalists an advantage with the public and in the legislature.[25]

The Alien and Sedition Acts (1798)

The brief dominance of Hamilton's Federalists led to the passage of four landmark pieces of legislation, collectively known as the Alien and Sedition Acts of 1798. The Sedition Act of 1798 made it illegal for any individual to:

_____ *"...write, print, utter or publish, or shall cause or procure to be written, printed, uttered or published, or shall knowingly and willingly assist or aid in writing, printing, uttering or publishing any false, scandalous and malicious writings or writings against the government of the United States, or either house of Congress of the United States, or the President of the United States, with intent to defame the said government, or either house of the said Congress, or the said President, or to bring them, or either of them, into contempt or disrepute; or to excite against them, or either or any of them, the hatred of the good people of the United States, or to stir up sedition within the United States, or to excite any unlawful combinations therein, for opposing or resisting any law of the United States, or any act of the President of the United States...shall be punished by a fine not exceeding two thousand dollars, and by imprisonment not exceeding two years."*[26]

_____

Essentially, the Sedition Act made it illegal to criticize the president, Congress, or any law. Enforcing such a law would be highly unlikely in the twenty-first century, because decades of social evolution have established Free Speech (the First Amendment to the U.S. Constitution) as a cornerstone of American democracy. Furthermore, the freedom to question, criticize, or even peaceably oppose the government was (even in 1798) considered a key factor in America's unique brand of democracy, and it was only in the wake of a national crisis and perceived impending war with France that such a law was able to pass through the legislature.

The other three laws comprising the 1798 Alien and Sedition Acts concerned immigration directly and were designed, by Hamilton and the other Federalists, to drastically slow, or even stop new immigration, while also giving the government powers to eliminate non-Americans in the nation's midst. First among the laws meant to achieve this was the Naturalization Act of 1798, which, compared to the nation's first immigration law, the Uniform Rule of Naturalization in 1790, marked a major step towards nationalism and isolationism.

NATURALIZATION ACT
1798
Source Document

SECTION I. *Be it enacted by the Senate and House of Representatives of the United States of America in Congress assembled*, That no alien shall be admitted to become a citizen of the United States, or of any state, unless in the manner prescribed by the act, instituted "An act to establish an uniform rule of naturalization; and to repeal the act heretofore passed on that subject," he shall have declared his intention to become a citizen of the United States, five years, at least, before his admission, and shall, at the time of his application to be admitted, declare and prove, to the satisfaction of the court having jurisdiction in the case, that he has resided within the United States fourteen years, at least, and within the state or territory where, or for which such court is at the time held, five years, at least, besides conforming to the other declarations, renunciations and proofs, by the said act required, any thing therein to the contrary hereof notwithstanding: Provided, that any alien, who was residing within the limits, and under the jurisdiction of the United States, before . . . [January 29, I795}] . . . may, within one year after the passing of this act—and any alien who shall have made the declaration of his intention to become a citizen of the United States, in conformity to the provisions of the act [of Jan. 29~~ I795]} may, within four years after having made the declaration aforesaid, be admitted to become a citizen, in the

continued

manner prescribed by the said act, upon his making proof that he has resided five years, at least, within the limits, and under the jurisdiction of the United States: And provided also, that no alien, who shall be a native, citizen, denizen or subject of any nation or state with whom the United States shall be at war, at the time of his application, shall be then admitted to become a citizen of the United States.

SEC. 4. And be it further enacted, That all white persons, aliens, (accredited foreign ministers, consuls, or agents, their families and domestics, excepted) who, after the passing of this act, shall continue to reside, or who shall arrive, or come to reside in any port or place within the territory of the United States, shall be reported, if free, and of the age of twenty-one years, by themselves, or being under the age of twenty-one years, or holden in service, by their parent, guardian, master or mistress in whose care they shall be, to the clerk of the district court of the district, if living within ten miles of the port or place, in which their residence or arrival shall be, and otherwise, to the collector of such port or place, or some officer or other person there, or nearest thereto, who shall be authorized by the President of the United States, to register aliens: And report, as aforesaid, shall be made in all cases of residence, within six months from and after the passing of this act, and in all after cases, within forty-eight hours after the first arrival or coming into the territory of the United States, and shall ascertain the sex, place- of birth, age, nation, place of allegiance or citizenship, condition or occupation, and place of actual or intended residence within the United States, of the alien or aliens reported, and by whom the report is made. . . And the clerk of each district court shall, during one year from the passing of this act, make monthly returns to the department of State, of all aliens registered and returned, as aforesaid, in his office.

SEC. 5. And be it further enacted, That every alien who shall continue to reside, or who shall arrive, as aforesaid, of whom a report is required as aforesaid, who shall refuse or neglect to make such report, and to receive a certificate thereof, shall forfeit and pay the sum of two dollars; and any justice of the peace, or other civil magistrate, who has authority to require surety of the peace, shall and may, on complaint to him made thereof cause such alien to be brought before him, there to give surety of the peace and good behaviour during his residence within the United States, or for such term as the justice or other magistrate shall deem reasonable, and until a report and registry of such alien shall be made, and a certificate

Naturalization Act
continued

thereof, received as aforesaid; and in failure of such surety, such alien shall and may be committed to the common goal, and shall be there held, until the order which the justice or magistrate shall and may reasonably make, in the premises, shall be performed. And every person, whether alien, or other, having the care of any alien or aliens, under the age of twenty-one years,-or of any white alien holden in service, who shall refuse and neglect to make report thereof, as aforesaid, shall forfeit the sum of two dollars, for each and every such minor or servant, monthly, and every month, until a report and registry, and a certificate thereof, shall be had, as aforesaid.

APPROVED, July 18, 1798.[27]

Whereas, under the Uniform Rule for Naturalization of 1790, a free white male was eligible for citizenship after being in the nation for two years and appearing before any state court, the 1798 law was far more severe, changing the residency requirements to fourteen years, which virtually guaranteed that few, if any, immigrants would become full citizens in the short term. The 1798 law also required anyone who wanted to become a citizen to submit formal notification of their intention to attain citizenship five years before appearing in court to obtain permission. Further, the law changes the authority responsible for approving citizenship from the courts at large to the federal courts, which were dominated by Federalist-appointed judges. Thus, the Naturalization Act gave the Federalists direct influence over who could become citizens, a barrier that they hoped could ferret out spies and saboteurs.

The next in the quartet of anti-immigrant laws was the 1798 Alien Friends Act, which granted power to the President of the United States to, at any time of his choosing, deport any alien deemed dangerous to the union. The goal of the act was to make it legal to throw spies and dissidents out

of the country. The act also contained a records provision under which the federal government required all aliens to register with the state. This, they hoped, would make it easier to monitor the alien population and potentially to identify dangerous individuals for deportation. The following excerpt explains the purpose of the law:

AN ACT CONCERNING ALIENS
1798
Source Document

SECTION 1. *"Be it enacted by the Senate and House of Representatives of the United States of America in Congress assembled,* That it shall be lawful for the President of the United States at any time during the continuance of this act, to *order* all such *aliens* as he shall judge dangerous to the peace and safety of the United States, or shall have reasonable grounds to suspect are concerned in any treasonable or secret machinations against the government thereof, to depart out of the territory of the United States, within such time as shall be expressed in such order, which order shall be served on such alien by delivering him a copy thereof, or leaving the same at his usual abode, and returned to the office of the Secretary of State, by the marshal or other person to whom the same shall be directed. And in case any alien, so ordered to depart, shall be found at large within the United states after the time limited in such order for his departure, and not having obtained a license from the President to reside therein, or having obtained such *license* shall not have conformed thereto, every such alien shall, on conviction thereof, be imprisoned for a term not exceeding three years, and shall never after be admitted to become a citizen of the United States."[28]

Finally, the fourth law of the quartet was designed specifically for war time national security, providing the federal government with the power to immediately arrest, hold, and deport aliens from nations with which the United States was currently at war. This is essentially the same justification that was used to arrest and detain thousands of Japanese-Americans and immigrants during World War II, demonstrating how little changed

An Act Concerning Aliens, 1798, Library of Congress

between 1798 and the 1940s, at least in terms of how Americans react when they feel threatened. As the United States was contemplating a potential war with France at the time of the law's passage, the law might have applied to thousands of French aliens then living in the nation. The following excerpt provides the basic aims of the act:

AN ACT RESPECTING ALIEN ENEMIES
1798
Source Document

SECTION 1. *"Be it enacted by the Senate and House of Representatives of the United States of America in Congress assembled,* That whenever there shall be a declared war between the United States and any foreign nation or government, or any invasion or predatory incursion shall be perpetrated, attempted, or threatened against the territory of the United States by any foreign nation or government, and the President of the United States shall make public proclamation of the event, all natives, citizens, denizens, or subjects of the hostile nation or government being males of the age of fourteen years and upwards, who shall be within the United States, and not actually naturalized, shall be liable to be apprehended, restrained, secured and removed, as alien enemies..."

The Alien and Sedition Acts were a major turning point in U.S. immigration policy and philosophy. In some ways, the Federalists were taking positions similar to what might be associated with the U.S. Republican Party or more general conservative movement. However, the label "conservative" had little meaning at the time, as the history of the nation was so limited that there was little to conserve. The Democrats of the time also had much in common with conservatives of later eras in that they were trying to uphold states' rights, thus preserving (or *conserving*) the system that evolved out of the original colonial arrangement in which each colony was essentially its own sovereign state.

However, like the conservative movement of the twenty-first century, the Federalists were motivated by fear, nationalism, xenophobia, and prejudice against other nationalities. Federalist politicians were quick to call out signs of possible treason or sedition and even believed that Thomas Jefferson's inner circle of acquaintances and associates might contain French spies.

The Alien and Sedition Acts were essentially aimed at making life more difficult for immigrants and perspective immigrants such that they might choose to leave on their own or choose not to immigrate at all. Many did, with French aliens leaving in large numbers as they expected deportation might be coming soon, and thus fueling the growth of French Canada. The Alien and Sedition Acts created the nation's first legal deportation system, as well as other penalties for those who refused to abide by an order to leave the nation, but the provisions of the four laws provided no due process. Under the Alien and Sedition Acts, there was no system for the accused to petition the government nor limit on the government's abilities to arrest, detain, or deport any individual labeled a threat.

The fear that generated the Alien and Sedition Acts faded as it became clear that the United States was going to avoid war with France. In 1799, President Adams announced that he was going to resolve the crisis with France diplomatically, rather than militarily, and this weakened the Federalist cause considerably, as well as Adams' position within the party. As fear of war abated, the American public had little interest in Federalist saber-rattling. Interestingly, Adams, who was then maligned by former allies in the Federalists, made the choice to sacrifice his own political power, and likely his future career, to avoid war.[29]

Focus on immigration shifted many times over the first half of the nineteenth century. The Naturalization Law of 1802 formally eliminated the 1798 laws 14-year waiting period for citizenship eligibility, reducing the requirements to five years. However, anti-immigrant sentiment spread, motivated less by fear of war or sabotage, and, instead, by a quasi-religious nationalism that led to an anti-Catholic and anti-Irish movement.

CONCLUSION

Developed during a time when Americans were concerned about an impending war, the passage of the 1798 immigration and naturalization laws also demonstrate how attitudes and approaches to foreign policy and immigration can dramatically change when American politicians and/or the public perceive a threat to national security. The campaigns by the Federalists were a major factor in changing public opinion against immigration in the 1790s, but this was a short-lived movement. Many Americans still felt culturally linked to the European nations of their ancestors; and when the threat of war faded, groups of Americans identifying with these ethnic identities, like British-Americans, French-Americans, and German-Americans, more often favored liberalization of immigration, at least as far as admitting more of their specific "type" to become U.S. citizens.

DISCUSSION QUESTIONS

- What modern political party is most similar to the Federalist Party? Explain.
- Should the U.S. government favor native-born citizens over foreign-born citizens? Why or why not?
- The Sedition Act made it illegal to criticize the president; could such a law be adopted in modern America? Why or why not?
- Other than that discussed in this chapter, what is another example of how national security affects immigration policies?

Works Used

Anderson, Stuart. "When Criticizing The President Was Against The Law." *Forbes*. Forbes, Inc. 17 Dec. 2016.

"1798 Alien Enemies Act." *UWB*. University of Washington-Bothell Library. US Immigration Legislation Online. Session II, Chap. 66, Statute 570. 5th Congress; 6 July 1798.

"1798 Naturalization Act." *UWB*. University of Washington-Bothell Library. US Immigration Legislation Online. Session II, Chap. 54, Statute 566. 5th Congress, 17 June 1798.

"A Century of Lawmaking for a New Nation: U.S. Congressional Documents and Debates, 1774 – 1875." *Library of Congress*. Statutes at Large. 5th Congress, 2nd Session. 2016.

Boyd, Eugene. "American Federalism, 1776 to 1997: Significant Events." Library of Congress. Congressional Research Service. 1997.

Frank, Jason, and Isaac Kramnick. "What 'Hamilton' Forgets About Hamilton." *New York Times*. New York Times, Co. 10 June 2016.

Magness, Phillip W. "Alexander Hamilton as Immigrant: Musical Mythology Meets Federalist Reality." *Independent Review*. The Independent Institute, Vol. 21, No. 4, Spring 2017.

"The XYZ Affair and the Quasi-War with France, 1798–1800." *Office of the Historian*. U.S. Department of State. 2016.

Introduction

Whereas the 1790s saw the nation's first major anti-immigration movement, the first half of the nineteenth century saw a nation deeply divided on the issue. On one hand, millions of European immigrants eagerly flocked to take advantage of the nation's material riches and open landscape ripe for exploitation and development, while the deepening of economic inequality led to an increasing nativist campaign against immigrants in general.

This chapter looks at one of the strongest branches of nativist sentiment in this period, the anti-Catholic and anti-Irish movement that sought to limit the immigration of individuals seen as ideologically or ethnically inferior and detrimental to American society.

America's anti-Irish period has been well documented and explored, in part because of the interest in this subject by the sizable proportion of Americans who continue to identify with their Irish heritage. The source for this chapter is a 2015 article by journalist Dara Lind in *Vox* magazine, "Why historians are fighting about 'No Irish Need Apply' signs—and why it matters." Lind explores different views on the history of anti-Irish attitudes in 1800s America and explores how these attitudes contribute to modern American identity and prejudice.

Topics covered in this chapter include:
- Nativism
- Ethnic prejudice
- Religious intolerance
- Anti-Catholic sentiment
- Anti-Irish sentiment
- Ethnic riots
- Know Nothing Party
- American Secret Societies

This Chapter Discusses the Following Source Document:
Lind, Dara. "Why Historians are Fighting About 'No Irish Need Apply' Signs—and Why it Matters." *VOX*. Vox Media. 4 Aug. 2015.

The Green Menace
The Know-Nothings and the Nativist Movement (1800-1850s)

From 1800 to 1850, immigration reform shifted towards nationalism and nativism, and the chief target were Irish immigrants, long the most maligned ethnic group of the British empire.

Anti-Irish sentiment in the United States was an outgrowth of centuries-old British prejudice. Within the United Kingdom, the Irish had long been stereotyped as lazy, unhygienic, and uncivilized. The fact that the Irish rebelled violently against British rule, and that their rebellion was organized through the island's predominant Catholic faith, also created a stereotype of Catholicism as a radical, potentially dangerous branch of Christian theology. One of the earliest academic texts on the Irish landscape, wildlife, and culture was *Topographia Hibernica*, written by Gerald of Wales in the 1180s. The book has become famous, however, for the author's inflammatory and dehumanizing depictions of the Irish as a wholly uncivilized, immoral, and largely inhuman race. In a 1995 academic study of the book, Professor David Rollo writes:

Uncle Sam's Youngest Son, Citizen Know Nothing, representing the nativist ideal of the Know Nothing Party, by Sarony & Co., via Wikimedia Commons

_____ *"...if his (Gerald of Wales) ethnological remarks are given any credit, then it must be assumed that the twelfth-century Irish were indeed scrofulous barbarians notable for their addiction*

to unbounded turpitudes of lust, for these ostensible monsters of perversion allegedly practiced incest, granted bestiality a ritualistic function in ceremonies of kingship, and idiosyncratically displayed the stigmata of hermaphroditism as the physical consequences of their ethnic deviance..."[30]

Students of history will notice that whenever a dominant group is fearful of an outsider group, it is common for the out group to be depicted as animalistic and sub-human. One popular way to do this in 1800s America was to show Irish people looking like apes, and specifically the gorilla (*Gorilla gorilla*), because this led to the allegedly-clever play on Irish names, "G. O'Rilla," as in "O'Reilly" or "O'Rourke." The "O" at the beginning of many Irish surnames means "descendant of," and this lent an extra-layer of insult to the "G. O'Rilla" epithet.

There has been considerable debate about how widespread anti-Irish prejudice was in the United States in the early 1800s, but the existence of political groups and rallies against Irish immigration indicate that it was a popular movement, especially in New York, Philadelphia, and other large cities. The Irish of the 1800s were poor, and Ireland as a whole was impoverished. When Irish immigrants came to the United States, they were often willing to take low-paying, unskilled jobs and thus competed with poor Protestants seeking the same jobs. Thus, the Irish were maligned for stealing jobs from "real" Americans.

A Brief Description of Nativism

In the writings of the era, white Protestant men often called themselves "native Americans," signifying that they were native-born and *not* immigrants. Thus, anti-Irish prejudice was the beginning of America's oldest immigration movement, nativism, in which politicians, activists, and lobbyists protested immigration as a way to preserve the dominance of their

"type" within society and to preserve the benefits of the nation for those like them. American nativism, then and now, exists on three basic levels: economic, ethnic, and protectionist.

Economic Nativism

The economic dimension of nativism is about preserving jobs or access to resources for the native-born. This dimension develops primarily because immigrants were typically willing to work for less than native-born inhabitants and so were creating unfair competition for jobs.

Ethnic Nativism

On the ethnic level, nativists typically depict members of one or more outsider groups as somehow inherently inferior to the native-group. Irish were, therefore, seen as unhygienic and of low-morals, and these prejudices fueled the belief that they should be prohibited.

Protectionism

On the protectionist level, nativists often target individuals coming from countries that had revolutions or uprisings. This was the tactic taken by nativist Alexander Hamilton in the 1790s, when he wanted to ban French and Irish immigration on the basis of the fact that both groups had been involved in revolutionary uprisings in their native nations. Hamilton feared that the Irish and French would become spies and saboteurs in the United States. Some believed, at the time, that the tendency towards anti-government rebellion was an innate characteristic of some ethnicities whereas others believed that these characteristics were learned in a native country and then carried into the United States.

Nativism = Prejudice

Politicians sometimes try to portray nativism as logical or intellectual. For instance, the modern nativist movement, under Donald Trump's "America First" slogan, is not really substantially different from Hamilton's Federalist nativism in the 1790s. Then, as now, only certain groups are targeted for prohibition and these groups are *always* ones that are also depicted as inferior culturally or racially. Thus, when Donald Trump insinuates that Mexican immigrants are primarily only those Mexicans who are criminals, rapists, or drug dealers, this is racial and ethnic prejudice. Students of history will find that there are no nativist movements that are not also prejudiced by views of a certain race or ethnicity. The primary goal of nativism is to protect one's culture and identity by making sure that people who are in one's own group (ethnic, racial, etc.) remain dominant in American society.

In a 2017 article in *The Atlantic*, journalist Uri Friedman interviews political scientists and historians and develops a definition of "nativism" as a form of "xenophobic nationalism," or "majority-ethnic nationalism." It is a mindset that seeks to protect a perceived or existing "demographic predominance" in a specific territory. Nativists thus spend much of their time defining outsiders and non-natives but are less specific when it comes to defining themselves.

The designation of an "other" also serves the native by creating an unstated inverse. In the words of political scientist Cas Mudde (as told to Uri Friedman of *The Atlantic*):

> *"The other is barbarian, which makes you modern. The other is lazy, which makes you hardworking. The other is Godless, which makes you God-fearing."*[31]

The Nativist Movement of Knew Nothing

Evidence of anti-Irish prejudice in the 1800s is notable in the now-famous signs that some businesses hung refusing to hire or to let or rent rooms to Irish or Catholic tenants. The *New York Times* found that an advertisement for a servant girl posted in the newspaper in

Depicting the More Free Than Welcome sentiment of the Nativist
Movement, by Currier & Ives, 1855, Library of Congress

1854 was the first time that the phrase "No Irish need apply" was seen in print. The phrase, "No Irish need apply" or "Irish need not apply," or other variations, appeared at least 29 times in *New York Times* classified ads from this period. Prejudice against the Irish also came in a more covert form. Many ads would specify a "Protestant" man or woman was wanted for a job or when offering a rental property, thus excluding the predominantly Catholic Irish without needing to specify.[32]

In *The Faithful: A History of Catholics in America*, historian James M. O'Toole describes a sign posted anonymously on a newly opened Catholic church in Connecticut, by a person who called him or herself "A True American," that read:

_____ *"Be it known...all Catholics and all persons in favor of the Catholic religion are a set of vile imposters, liars, villains and cowardly cut throats..."*[33]

The Great Famine in Ireland (1845–1849) was an agricultural disaster in which a disease known as potato blight destroyed the Irish potato crops for several years. With nearly one-third of Irish farmers dependent on potato agriculture, as many as one million Irish died of hunger, even though Ireland was under the protection and management of Britain, the world's richest nation at the time. The British government's failure to help the Irish was the beginning of Irish nationalism, but it also led to a mass migration out of Ireland, with hundreds of thousands fleeing to the United States.[34] Between 1845 and 1854, 2.9 million immigrants came to America, many from Ireland or Germany, and many of whom were Catholic. The native Anglo-protestant majority felt like they were losing their dominance in society and thus identity, and began to gather into increasingly hostile nativist groups.

In the 1840s, a secret society known as the Order of the Star-Spangled Banner (OSSB) spread through America's cities. Membership was limited to individuals of pure-blooded Anglo-Saxon heritage and Protestants and the group developed many secret rituals, passwords, and special handshakes to encrypt their secret meetings and prevent infiltration by outsiders. When asked about their membership or the activities of the society, they would claim to "know nothing."

This secret society gave rise to America's first legitimate third-party, called the American Party, but more generally known, in reference to the secrecy of the OSSB, as the "Know-Nothings." One of the party's official mottos was "Americans Shall Rule America."[35]

The Know-Nothings weren't very successful at the highest levels of politics, but a number of local and city officials were representatives of the party. At the street level, tensions between Protestants and Catholics devolved into violence on a number of occasions. In 1844, a riot broke out in the Philadelphia neighborhood of Kensington, a hotbed for Irish immigration, after a false rumor spread through the city's Protestant commu-

nities that a local Irish-Catholic was trying to force the schools to stop conducting daily prayers. At least thirty houses, numerous businesses, local schools, and St. Michael's church and the Sisters of Charity Seminary were destroyed by mobs of angry Anglo-Protestants.[36] Another violent conflict occurred in Saint Louis, Missouri, when mayoral incumbent, and nativist Luther Kennett claimed that his opponent, Thomas Hart Benton was courting illegal immigrant votes in the mayoral election of 1854, which is eerily similar to Donald Trump's claims that millions of illegal immigrants were going to vote for Hillary Clinton in the 2016 elections and his suggestion that the people

Cartoon of the Irish way of doing things, by Thomas Nast, 1871, via Wikimedia Commons

would "do something about it." Kennett's false claims led to fighting in the streets and after a skirmish led to one Anglo-Protestant being stabbed by a young Irish immigrant, a mob of nativists killed at least 10 people and destroyed 93 Irish houses and businesses along the city's riverfront.[37]

Nativism's violent street-level manifestations were occurring while the Know-Nothing party consolidated local power to exert national political influence. Like the Federalist anti-immigrant movement of the 1790s, the Know-Nothings hoped to pass laws that would make it extremely difficult for immigrants to become citizens. They proposed a 21-year residency requirement for those who wanted to become citizens, as well as new immigration laws that would permit the government to deport "beggars" and "criminals," mandatory Bible reading (from the Protestant King James Bible) in schools, and a complete prohibition on Catholic politicians in any public office.

The Political Utility of Anti-Irish History

In his seminal 1965 book *A Nation of Immigrants*, former President (and Irish-Catholic) John F. Kennedy wrote:

> _____ *"The Irish were the first to endure the scorn and discrimination later to be inflicted, to some degree at least, on each successive wave of immigrants by already settled 'Americans'."*[38]

Kennedy, being the first Catholic president, sought to use the well-known example of anti-Irish sentiment to formulate an argument against all forms of anti-immigrant prejudice. In Kennedy's estimation, the nation was a melting pot made stronger by the inclusion of individuals from different cultures, religions, and backgrounds. However, was the plight of the Irish comparable to the plight of other marginalized groups in the nation? To women? To African Americans? To Jewish immigrants?

In this 2015 article in *Vox*, journalist Dara Lind describes an academic debate about whether "No Irish Need Apply" signs were rare or common in the era and whether the history of anti-Irish prejudice has been appropriately portrayed as part of the nation's immigration history:

WHY HISTORIANS ARE FIGHTING ABOUT "NO IRISH NEED APPLY" SIGNS—AND WHY IT MATTERS
by Dara Lind
Vox, August 4, 2015
Source Document

The image of a "No Irish Need Apply" sign has become a stand-in for an entire narrative about how immigrants are treated in America. It's also the subject of a surprisingly heated academic fight.

continued

In one corner, arguing that an Irish immigrant in mid-19th-century America was relatively unlikely to run into "No Irish Need Apply" postings, is a tenured but ideologically iconoclastic historian. In the other, arguing that they were a lot more widespread, is a 14-year-old with excellent archival research skills.

There's a reason (beyond academic infighting) that the question of whether the symbolic "No Irish Need Apply" sign was exaggerated—and with it, the scope of anti-Irish discrimination during the first big wave of Irish Catholic immigration to the US—is still being fought over almost 200 years later. That's because of the sign's symbolism. When politicians or others refer to "No Irish Need Apply" signs, here's what they're saying: every new immigrant group that's come to the United States has faced discrimination from natives. But over time, the immigrant group has fought back against discrimination and won and has assimilated into broader American society—to the point that it becomes hard to imagine they ever would have been oppressed to begin with.

As it was with the Irish in the 19th century, the story implies, so it will be with Latino and Asian immigrants today.

So the controversy over "No Irish Need Apply" signs ask the same questions that have been raised for every single group of immigrants since then: are they really being discriminated against in material ways, like work and housing, or are they just the victims of prejudiced attitudes? And if they react by thinking of themselves as underdogs, are they acknowledging the truth, or making themselves into victims?

What's clear, through the controversy, is that Irish Americans chose to identify with the narrative the sign represents. And it's made them a continued ally for immigrants—both Irish and not—straight through to the 21st century.

The case that No Irish Need Apply was less common than you think

In 2002, historian Richard Jensen published a takedown of "No Irish Need Apply," calling it "a myth of victimization." Jensen looked through newspaper classified ads from the 1850s to the 1920s and found, he wrote, that only about two ads per decade told Irish men not to apply. (It was more common for ads for domestic workers to specify no Irish or, more frequently, no Catholics.) Furthermore, Jensen wrote, "there is no evidence for any printed NINA signs in America, or for their display at places of employment

Why Historians are Fighting About "No Irish Need Apply" Signs—And Why it Matters
continued

other than private homes."

But that left Jensen with a tricky question to answer: how on earth did "No Irish Need Apply" become part of Irish Americans' collective memory? His alternative theory: because of a song.

Anti-Irish discrimination *was* rampant in Britain, and a song became popular there in the 1850s called "No Irish Need Apply." The song hopped the pond to America—in at least two different versions. In one version, printed in Philadelphia, the narrator recalls being discriminated against in London—but says now that she's in "the land of the glorious and free," she's sure Americans will be more welcoming to her. In the other version, printed in New York, the narrator sees a "No Irish Need Apply" ad *in America*—and proceeds to seek out the proprietor and beat him up. Guess which version became wildly popular.

Jensen believed that in America, it was the song that popularized the phrase—not the other way around.

Were Irish Americans stuck in a "culture of victimhood"?

There's plenty of evidence that "native Americans" considered Irish Catholics to be inferior. (Irish Protestants, on the other hand, didn't come in for the same prejudice—and in fact, many of them joined the nativist Know-Nothing Party in the 1830s to protest the arrival of their Catholic counterparts.) But did that prejudice turn into outright discrimination against Irish immigrants? Or have Irish Americans been holding on to the "myth of victimization"?

In other words: was America in the mid-19th century like some say America is today, with some people saying unpleasant things about other ethnic groups but very little widespread oppression? Or was it like another view of 21st-century America, with systemic racism that has material effects on people's lives?

Did anti-Irish attitudes stay on magazine covers, or move into the workplace? Jensen's in the first camp. As a result, his attitude toward the Irish of the 19th century sounds a bit like conservatives blaming a "culture of victimhood" for the problems facing nonwhites today:

> When Protestants denied NINA that perhaps just reinforced the Irish sense of conspiracy against them (even today people who deny NINA are suspected

continued

of prejudice.) The slogan served both to explain their poverty and to identify a villain against whom it was all right to retaliate on sight—a donnybrook for the foes of St. Patrick. The myth justified bullying strangers and helped sour relations between Irish and everyone else. The sense of victimhood perhaps blinded some Irish to the discrimination suffered by other groups.

Other historians think Jensen overstates his case when he says there was no widespread job discrimination against Irish Catholics. And there's suspicion that Jensen has an axe to grind, since his characterization of Irish Americans as self-aggrandizing drama queens sounds a little like some conservative characterizations of other ethnic minorities.

But he's not the only one saying racial discrimination wasn't as big a factor in mid-19th-century Irish-American life as people tend to think. Historians of Irish Americans have turned away from the idea that Irish immigrants were considered "not white" when they came to the US, and became "white" via assimilation (and by oppressing African Americans). In the words of historian Kevin Kenny, the "whiteness" question "obscured more than it clarified." And labor historians have suggested that at least part of

what looks like oppression based on ethnicity was in fact oppression based on class: 'Irish workers were certainly exploited,' in Kenny's words, "but they did not suffer from racism."

The case that NINA notices were everywhere, if you knew where to look for them

Other historians protested that anti-Irish discrimination was widespread, but didn't contest Jensen's findings about NINA signs. A couple of them even corroborated his conclusions. For what it's worth, when I originally wrote this article, I did some follow-up research of my own in the Library of Congress' digitized newspaper database—and found, similar to Jensen, that there weren't any more than two wanted ads per decade that specified "No Irish Need Apply."

But the problem was that the databases being used just weren't complete enough. In spring 2015, Rebecca Fried, a 14-year-old whose father had brought home the article from work, checked out Jensen's claims. She found much more evidence of "No Irish Need Apply" notices than Jensen's article had allowed.

Fried turned up about 50 businesses putting "No Irish Need Apply" in their newspaper ads between 1842 and 1903. The notices were especially popular in New York (which had "No

Why Historians are Fighting About "No Irish Need Apply" Signs—And Why it Matters
continued

Irish Need Apply" ads for 15 businesses in 1842–1843 alone, and 7 after that) and Boston, which had NINA ads for 9 businesses. Of course, these were also the centers of Irish immigrant settlement at the time. And she found several news reports that mentioned "No Irish Need Apply" signs—the ones that Jensen said there was no evidence to believe ever existed—being hung at workplaces, as well as public accommodations.

So while Jensen's research turned up about 2 ads a decade, Fried's turned out closer to one a year—although that varied a lot depending on where and when you were.

This obviously doesn't cover every newspaper published during the period. But it's hard to tell how to extrapolate it. Databases like the Library of Congress', which really *don't* have many "No Irish Need Apply" ads, are obviously incomplete—but so are databases that do have them. What's most representative of all newspapers of the time?

There's a pretty spirited academic back-and-forth between Fried and Jensen about Fried's findings, as covered in this article in the *Daily Beast*. Jensen points out that any given

Irish immigrant, on any given day, was unlikely to open a newspaper and see a "No Irish Need Apply" ad—which may very well still be true. But Fried argues that the point is that they did, in fact, exist—and so it makes sense that they'd become part of how Irish Americans understand their role in American history.

Discrimination was real—but memory has outlasted it

Three things are clearly true. There was obviously widespread prejudice against Irish Catholics during the mid-19th-century wave of immigration to the US, and that prejudice led to actual discrimination in at least some cases (and, probably, fairly often).

The second truth is that Irish Americans have been *resisting* discrimination for as long as they've been experiencing it. Alongside the want ads requesting "No Irish Need Apply" that Fried found were reports of Irish workers filing libel lawsuits, holding protests, or even going on strike in response to such ads. Those reports are almost as old as the first NINA ads that Fried found. And that's not to mention jokes that both Fried and I found in our research that would be reprinted from one paper to another, using "No Irish Need Apply" as a

continued

springboard for humor: one common joke involved an Irishman, with an exaggerated accent, pretending to be French to get around the sign.

That last category included several papers reprinting the lyrics of one version or another of the "No Irish Need Apply" song that Jensen says was so important. And remember, the version of the song that became popular wasn't the one in which coming to America was a happy ending; it was the version in which, even in America, there were bigots who needed to get beaten up. Fighting back was as much a part of Irish American history, as remembered by Irish Americans, as being held down.

But here's the third truth: memory of "No Irish Need Apply" has long outlasted actual anti-Irish discrimination. Many of the people who claimed to have seen NINA signs almost certainly didn't —just like some of the places that claim "George Washington Slept Here." The late Senator Ted Kennedy used to talk about seeing "No Irish Need Apply" signs growing up; Kennedy was not only born in 1932, several decades after anti-Irish prejudice had peaked, but he also grew up in an upper-class neighborhood where (in Jensen's opinion) he was unlikely to run across any stores that might have posted NINA signs. And replica signs, like the one on top of this article, are so popular that maybe they really are more common than real signs ever were.[39]

Jensen might argue that this is because of the "myth of victimization"— what other pundits might call a "culture of victimhood." But historians have floated another idea: that Irish Americans, more than any other immigrant group, saw themselves as exiles from their home country, rather than as people who were choosing to come to the US for a better life.

The "exile hypothesis" painted this as a bad thing: Irish immigrants were mostly powerless in the face of historical forces, both in Ireland and in the US. But just as the exile hypothesis was becoming popular, in the mid-1980s, another wave of Irish immigrants were coming to the US — and the reaction to them made it clear there was a substantial upside to Irish Americans continuing to identify with victims.

How the Irish still shape immigration policy

During the 1980s, tens of thousands of Irish immigrants came to the US— many of them coming on student or tourist visas and then staying after those visas expired. Irish Americans welcomed the new unauthorized immigrants—their Irishness mattered more than their legal status. And because Irish Americans had political

Why Historians are Fighting About "No Irish Need Apply" Signs—And Why it Matters
continued

power, politicians set about to fix the immigration system so it would be easier for Irish immigrants to come the right way.

In 1990, Congress passed an Immigration Act—championed by none other than Senator Ted Kennedy himself. The law created a new visa lottery, which is today called the "diversity visa"—it gives visas to people from countries that don't otherwise send many immigrants to the US. But for the first three years of its existence, the law required that 40 percent of the visas—called "Donnelly visas"—needed to go to Irish immigrants. Furthermore, an additional temporary program gave "Morrison visas" to Irish immigrants for the three years after the law passed. (Both visas were named after the Irish-American members of Congress who had championed them.) Between the two visas, most of the unauthorized Irish immigrants in the US were able to achieve legal status.

Today, the Irish aren't among the top 25 countries for unauthorized immigrants living in the US. (The only European country that cracks the top 25 is Poland.) But Irish Americans and Irish immigrants maintain an outsize presence in arguing for immigration reform to give legal status and citizenship to unauthorized immigrants. (The Irish Lobby for Immigration Reform has been a presence in New England and Washington for nearly a decade, since the beginning of the current reform fight.) And even the Irish government praised President Barack Obama for his executive actions last November, allowing millions of unauthorized immigrants to apply for protection from deportation and work permits.

Ostensibly, groups like the Irish Lobby are fighting on behalf of the 50,000 unauthorized Irish immigrants. But they're putting in more effort than, say, Polish groups, despite having less of a direct stake in the outcome of reform. And Irish-American politicians continue to draw a direct line from the memory (founded or not) of "No Irish Need Apply" signs from 150 years ago to the unauthorized immigrants in the shadows today.

Here's another version of the "No Irish Need Apply" song. In this version, the narrator takes a deep breath and decides not to beat up the proprietor. Instead, he educates him: "Your ancestors came over here like me, to try to make a living in this land of liberty." That's the role the Irish play in today's immigration debate—except now, they

continued

are both the "ancestors" and the new immigrants trying to make good.

Americans living in the 1840s, especially in the nation's largest cities, felt like they faced a lot of problems: insufficient pay, too much crime, and a lack of jobs. These problems were difficult to manage for politicians of the era and the contemporary Democratic and Federalist parties had no satisfying answers to these pervasive problems. The Know-Nothings approached this by preying on the ingrained prejudices of their constituents, and thereby used Irish immigrants as a scapegoat for a variety of social and societal ills.

The Know-Nothing party fell out of favor in the late 1950s as events elsewhere in the country brought slavery to the forefront of the national debate. Faced with an increasingly powerful abolitionist movement that was busy calling attention to the systematic dehumanization and exploitation of African Americans, Irish Catholics no longer seemed a key enemy of the "real" American people. The Know-Nothings weren't offering anything to the abolition debate that wasn't already being said by other nativists in the Federalist camp, and so the Know-Nothings fell by the wayside.

This bronze sculpture by Glenna Goodacre is the centerpiece of the Irish Memorial in Philadelphia, Pennsylvania, which also includes plaques detailing the history of the 1840's Irish Famine and the resulting wave of Irish immigrants to the U.S., via Wikimedia Commons

It cannot be legitimately argued that the prejudice levied at Catholics or the Irish is in any way similar to the prejudice then (or now) directed at African Americans, indigenous Americans, Asians, or, to a lesser extent, Jewish people. There are levels of "otherness" and individuals at each level suffer from a different set of limitations and prejudice. Over time, the blending of white Europeans simply made all white Europeans white, with nationalistic differences quickly fading away. This was not the case for African Americans, Latino and Hispanic Americans, and Asian Americans whose more obvious differences made them the target of a far more violent kind of prejudice.

CONCLUSION

Irish-Americans and Irish immigrants continue to play a key role in the pro-immigrant lobby, in part because of the historic abuse directed at the Irish people as one of Europe's most marginalized white subgroups. It is clear from historic records that anti-Irish sentiment and anti-Catholic sentiment were not just a political tool but widespread among the public as well. The riots and violence between Irish-Americans and British-Americans were motivated by the "fake news" of the era, in the form of rumors, public posters and flyers, and political speeches connecting Irish and Catholic immigrants with job losses for other Americans and with a perceived threat to developing American identity and culture, which many Americans then believed should remain largely British and Protestant.

DISCUSSION QUESTIONS

- Was the prejudice against the Irish the same as prejudice against African Americans? Why or why not?
- Was the anti-Catholic movement an example of religious intolerance? Did this movement violate the First Amendment right to freedom of religion?
- Was the anti-Catholic movement of the 1800s different from the anti-Muslim movement of the twenty-first century? How?
- How did the anti-Irish movement relate to the idea of "majority-ethnic nationalism"?

Works Used

Boissoneault, Lorraine. "How the 19th-Century Know-Nothing Party Reshaped American Politics." *Smithsonian*. Smithsonian Institution. 26 Jan. 2017.

Bulik, Mark. "1854: No Irish Need Apply." *Times Insider.* New York Times, Co. 8 Sept. 2015.

Donnelly, Jim. "The Irish Famine." *BBC*. BBC History. 17 Feb. 2011.

Friedman, Uri. "What Is a Nativist?" *The Atlantic*. Atlantic Monthly Group. 11 Apr. 2017.

Hingston, Sandy. "Bullets and Bigots: Remembering Philadelphia's 1844 Anti-Catholic Riots." *Philadelphia*. News & Opinion. 17 Dec. 2015.

Lind, Dara. "Why historians are fighting about 'No Irish Need Apply' signs—and why it matters." *VOX*. Vox Media. 4 Aug. 2015.

Moses, Paul. "Irish-Americans: Remember from whence you came." *CNN*. CNN. 16 Mar. 2017.

O'Neil, Tim. "A look back—Irish immigrants fight back in 1854 nativist riots." *St. Louis Post Dispatch*. STL Today. 8 Aug. 2010.

O'Toole, James. *The Faithful: A History of Catholics in America*. Cambridge, MA: Harvard UP, 2009, p. 89.

Rollo, David. "Gerald of Wales' 'Topographia Hibernica': Sex and the Irish Nation." *The Romantic Review*. Vol. 86, No. 2. March 1995.

Introduction

This chapter explores the way that early immigration and naturalization laws reflected and deepened gender inequality for both native-born and foreign-born women in the United States.

The document for this chapter is the 1855 naturalization law, entitled "An Act to Secure the Right of Citizenship to Children of Citizens of the United States born out of the Limits Thereof." This law resulted in establishing two important consequences: individuals born out of the country to U.S. citizens would still be citizens of the nation, and men and women who married U.S. citizens would also be afforded citizenship status. Allowing individuals born out of the country to become citizens through marriage led to the most familiar type of naturalization fraud in the United States, "green card" marriages.

Topics covered in this chapter include:
- Gender inequality
- Naturalization law
- Family-based immigration
- Green card marriages
- Women's Suffrage Movement
- Anti-Women's Suffrage Movement
- Anti-Slavery Movement
- Franklin Pierce Administration

This Chapter Discusses the Following Source Document:
"An Act to Secure the Right of Citizenship to Children of Citizens of the United States born out of the Limits Thereof." *LOC*. Library of Congress. Thirty-Third Congress. Sess. II. 1855. 2018.

Marrying Citizenship
Women and Immigrants' Rights (1850-1855)

The United States is a descendant of what is now called "Western philosophy," a branch of civic, legal, and philosophical heritage that can be traced back to before the dawn of Christianity, through the Roman and Greek republics, and, from there, all the way back to the tribal customs of the pre-nationhood peoples who built the first European and Mediterranean societies. This is a legacy that produced the ideals of representative democracy and the rule of the people, but also one that embraced, systematized, and normalized the marginalization and, at times, ownership of women and members of non-white races.

In the United States there have been two broad movements against the ancient hegemony of male dominance: Women's Suffrage, which was the movement to secure the right to vote and thus the fundamental privileges of citizenship for women, and the Women's Rights Movement, which can be described as the ongoing effort to address the systemic marginalization of women in American culture. Both movements challenged the existing hierarchies of power, threatened the hegemony of powerful men, and so met with resistance ranging from popular dismissal to pseudoscientific claims that women lacked the capacity (intellectual and/or emotional) to participate in the political process.

Women's rights and immigrants' rights are closely tied together. There are few sources of data to indicate how many women immigrants arrived in the United States prior to the late 1800s, but popular histories of the late 1700s and early 1800s indicate that there were many foreign-born women living unmarried or widowed, often with children, within the United States. The struggle for women's rights in the broader sphere would, therefore, have a major impact on the large population of foreign-born women who, by having few connections within the United States, were even more marginalized than the native-born women living through an era of extreme gender-inequity.

The First Women's Immigration Law

The nation's first immigration law, the Uniform Rule of Immigration did not specify "males" when it described the citizenship process. Likewise, the 1795, and 1802 reiterations of the naturalization process did not specify that the individual needed to be male (though the laws *did* specify that the individual needed to be white). Until the 1800s, therefore, there were no specific immigration provisions that applied directly to the naturalization of women.

The first immigration law that applied directly to immigrant women was adopted on March 26, 1804 and known as the Women and Children of Declarant law, Section 2168. The text of the law reads:

> *"When any alien, who has complied with the first condition specified in section twenty-one hundred and sixty-five, dies before he is actually naturalized, the widow and the children of any such alien shall be considered as citizens of the United States, and shall be entitled to all rights and privileges as such, upon taking the oaths proscribed by law."*[40]

The 1804 law tied women's naturalization to the naturalization of their male spouses and extended the rights and privileges of citizenship only to those who arrived married and whose husbands had at least begun the process of naturalization prior to the woman becoming widowed. Little has been written about the 1804 law or the debate about immigrant women in the period, and it appears that the issue was a relatively low priority both for legislators and the public. It is likely that the problem of widowed women with children, whose husbands died before obtaining citizenship, or during the five-year wait for naturalization, motivated a short, succinct

law to address the problem. It would be more than 50 years before the legislature would again pass any law respective of women immigrants.

The Suffrage Movement Begins

One reason why the naturalization of women wasn't considered a major issue was because women had few recognized rights. They were unable to vote until the passage of the Nineteenth Amendment, and were unable to own property and thus, naturalization conferred few benefits. The suffrage movement sought to address one of these inequities by granting women the right to vote, which would then become a right of citizenship that would be gained by any woman who became naturalized.

Lucretia Mott, by Joseph Kyle (1815-1863), Smithsonian National Portrait Gallery, via Wikimedia Commons

The Suffrage movement grew from a number of smaller, local, and grass roots women's rights movements that sprung up across the United States and coalesced into a national movement in the mid-nineteenth century, inspired by the anti-slavery movement of the era. Women played a key role in the abolition movement, and many saw both as human rights and social justice issues and so felt that the two groups should work together to achieve parity with the white males who dominated society. At a major Anti-Slavery Convention held in 1840, activists Elizabeth Cady Stanton and Lucretia Mott were offended when they were told they had to sit in a women's-only section that was strategically placed out of view of the men attending the conference. The men organizing and leading the convention had misgivings about women taking an active role and were trying to downplay the presence of women to avoid any controversy. This slight inspired Mott and Stanton to hold their *own* convention, one led entirely by women and focused specifically on women's rights and suffrage.[41]

Pioneer women's rights advocates Susan B. Anthony and Elizabeth Cady Stanton then organized the first national women's rights convention in 1848 in Seneca Falls, New York, which, though it was not the first women's rights meeting in the United States, nor even the first organized by Stanton and Anthony, left a lasting impression on those involved, signifying the beginning of something bigger. At this historic meeting, the women involved drafted a Declaration of Sentiments, based on the Declaration of Independence, that listed the ways in which women were marginalized in society at the time.

_____ *"The history of mankind is a history of repeated injuries and usurpations on the part of man toward woman, having in direct object the establishment of an absolute tyranny over her. To prove this, let facts be submitted to a candid world.*

He has never permitted her to exercise her inalienable right to the elective franchise.

He has compelled her to submit to laws, in the formation of which she had no voice.

He has withheld from her rights which are given to the most ignorant and degraded men—both natives and foreigners.

Having deprived her of this first right of a citizen, the elective franchise, thereby leaving her without representation in the halls of legislation, he has oppressed her on all sides.

He has made her, if married, in the eye of the law, civilly dead."[42]

Though it took many more years for women's rights to gain federal traction, the growing women's rights movement did find allies in state governments. In the same year that Anthony and Stanton held their convention, for instance, New York State became the first state to pass a law that allowed married women to own property.[43] As the Suffrage Movement gained steam, opposition to the movement increased, not only from men, but from women's anti-Suffrage groups that campaigned against voting rights. One such group, the National Association OPPOSED to Woman Suffrage published a pamphlet warning against suffrage in the 1910s that provided tips for various home keeping activities, mixed in with not-so-subtle anti-Suffrage messages, including such tips as:

> *"You do not need a ballot to clean out your sink spout. A handful of potash and some boiling water is quicker and cheaper."*

> *"Control of the temper makes a happier home than control of elections."*

After the list of household recommendations, the pamphlet concludes:

> *"There is, however, no method known by which mud-stained reputations may be cleansed after bitter political campaigns."*[44]

Before the Green Card

In 1855, Congress passed the second-ever immigration law specifically pertaining to the immigration of women, in a set of laws meant to benefit the immigrant children and wives of citizens. Entitled, *An Act to secure the Right of Citizenship to Children of Citizens of the United States born out of the Limits Thereof.*

AN ACT TO SECURE THE RIGHT OF CITIZENSHIP TO CHILDREN OF CITIZENS OF THE UNITED STATES BORN OUT OF THE LIMITS THEREOF
Source Document

"That persons heretofore born, or hereafter to be born, out of the limits and jurisdiction of the United States, whose fathers were or shall be at the time of their birth citizens of the United States, shall be deemed and considered and are hereby declared to be citizens of the United States: *Provided, however*, that the rights of citizenship shall not descend to persons whose fathers never resided in the United States.

And be it further enacted, That any woman who might lawfully be naturalized under the existing laws, married, or who shall be married to a citizen of the United States, shall be deemed and taken to be a citizen."[45]

The 1855 act was the start of two famous features of the U.S. immigration system; 1) that citizens born to American citizens, even when born abroad, are full citizens of the United States from birth, with no restrictions and, 2) that women could essentially gain citizenship by marriage. Combined with the 1804 law, this meant that a woman who married a U.S. citizen was also a U.S. citizen, and, even if her marriage was later dissolved, would remain a citizen. At the time, because the women's rights movement was still in its infancy, being a naturalized citizen may have carried few benefits and so, as in previous years, the issue wasn't much discussed or controversial. However, as the women's rights movement began to achieve victories, the rights of citizenship for women became more pronounced, thus making naturalization a more attractive option for foreign-born women.

The naturalization law of 1855 was, therefore, the first piece of a well-known form of immigration fraud: the "green card" marriage, named after the pea-green resident alien cards given out in the 1940s. Green card fraud may take a variety of forms, but typically involves a woman or man seeking to marry a U.S. citizen to gain citizenship status and access to the benefits thereof. In some

Emigrants Below Deck on the "Northern Star", 1869

Immigrants below deck on the *Northern Star*, 1869, bound for America, iStock

cases, a woman may use deception to enter into a green card marriage whereas, in other cases, a man and woman may agree to engage in the deception together, entering a fake marriage to secure citizenship for one of the two parties involved.

Despite the potential for fraud, the United States has maintained laws that allow citizenship by marriage as such laws are typically defended as being representative of the American commitment to family and the institution of marriage. Likewise, the children of U.S. citizens born abroad, if the relationship could be firmly established, have always been afforded U.S. citizenship and this, too, has been maintained as signifying the American commitment to family and the welfare of children. As America moved through the 1850s and into the difficult decade of the Civil War, however, women's rights took second stage to the other civil rights war that had been brewing for years, the effort to end the institution of slavery.

CONCLUSION

The Women's Suffrage movement was closely aligned with the Anti-Slavery movement as activists in both camps saw significant overlaps between the marginalization of African Americans and that of women of every race. Laws regarding women and citizenship were practical consequences of the traditionalist view of women in American society. The rights of a married woman were subsumed by the rights of her husband, while the unmarried women had no status. Early gender-based immigration and naturalization laws were only meant to extend certain rights and citizenship protections to women who were widowed and, thus, lost their marriage-based status. These laws unwittingly led to one of America's oldest forms of immigration fraud, later called "green card marriages."

DISCUSSION QUESTIONS

- Are green card marriages ever morally acceptable? Explain.
- Is gender equality still a significant issue in the United States? Provide some examples to defend your position.
- In what ways were the Women's Suffrage and Anti-Slavery movements alike? In what ways were the two movements different?
- Are there any valid arguments that could be used to deny women the right to vote? Explain.

Works Used

"An Act to Secure the Right of Citizenship to Children of Citizens of the United States born out of the Limits Thereof." *Library of Congress*. Thirty-Third Congress. Sess. II. 1855. PDF. 2018.

Barkhorn, Eleanor. "'Vote No on Women's Suffrage': Bizarre Reasons For Not Letting Women Vote." *The Atlantic*. Atlantic Monthly Group. 6 Nov. 2012.

Blakemore, Erin. "Five Things to Know About the Declaration of Sentiments." *Smithsonian*. Smithsonian Institution. 8 June 2016.

"Declaration of Sentiments and Resolutions: Woman's Rights Convention, Held at Seneca Falls, 19–20 July 1848." *ECSSBA*. Elizabeth Cady Stanton & Susan B. Anthony Papers Project. Rutgers University. 2010.

LeMay, Michael C., and Elliott Robert Barkan. *U.S. Immigration and Naturalization Laws and Issues: A Documentary History*. Westport, CT: Greenwood P, 1999.

"Married Women's Property Laws." *Library of Congress*. American Women. 2018.

Introduction

While the first half of the 1800s saw the emergence of the nation's first anti-immigration movements, the U.S. Civil War (1861–1865) resulted in a new era in immigration with the Union states openly courting immigrants to support their side in the war.

This chapter explores the way that the Civil War influenced federal immigration policy and the role that immigrants and immigration played in this devastating chapter in American history. The document for this chapter is the 1864 immigration law, entitled "An Act to Encourage Immigration," which was the first and only time the central government enacted a law explicitly aimed at actively attracting immigrants to come to the United States. This law, along with the Homestead Act, which granted federal land to individuals and families who agreed to move into the American frontier, gave the Union Army a significant advantage in the war and solidified foreign-born support behind the Union cause.

Topics covered in this chapter include:

- U.S. Civil War
- Slavery in the United States
- Abraham Lincoln Administration
- Institutional racism
- Westward expansion
- State's rights
- Confederate history
- Confederate monuments debate
- Immigrants in the U.S. Armed Forces

This Chapter Discusses the Following Source Document:
"An Act to Encourage Immigration." *New York Times*. New York Times, Co. 3 Aug. 1864.

Encouraging Immigration
The Civil War and the Nation's First and Only Pro-Immigration Period (1860–1864)

The onset of the American Civil War brought about fundamental changes to American immigration policy and the attitudes of Americans towards immigrants of various ethnicities and backgrounds. The anti-immigrant and anti-Irish nativist movement of the 1840s and early 1850s was completely swept aside as the issue of slavery permeated the nation's media and popular culture. As new battle lines were drawn, creating new insider and outsider groups, the identity of the American people changed. Friends became enemies and enemies became friends as Americans, from various backgrounds and ethnicities once seeing each other as on opposing sides, were united behind common causes that would define American identity moving forward.

Confederate Mythology

In 2017, a movement spread across a number of American cities calling for the removal of Confederate statues and monuments from public land. This inspired outrage from neo-Confederate enthusiasts, white nationalists, and Civil War history buffs who insist that such monuments are representative of Southern heritage and history, and not of slavery. Even President Trump spoke out on the issue, siding with those who believe such monuments are historic emblems and not symbols of America's racist heritage.

Ask a Confederate history buff about the Civil War, and you might be told that the war itself was not really about *slavery* but about economics or the debate over federal authority vs. state's rights. Such a view depicts the supporters of the Confederacy as people very similar to modern conservatives, who objected to the "tyranny" or "corruption" of big government.

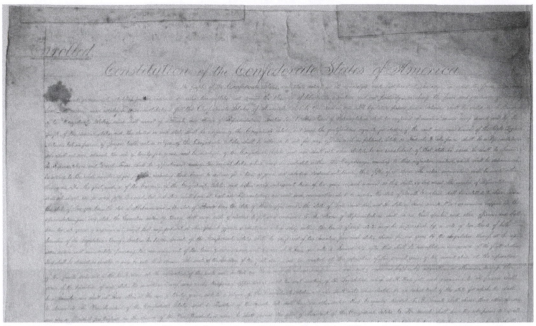

Constitution of the Confederate States of America, 1861, University of Georgia Library, via Wikimedia Commons

The idea that the Civil War was not really about slavery is the result of a long-term, purposeful campaign to revise history so as to defang criticisms of the Confederacy and to enable Americans to have "Southern pride" freed from the guilt that such pride was pride in a systematically racist institution that actually sought to secede from the union rather than abandoning the indefensibly inhuman, yet ultimately very profitable, slavery industry. This effort has been very successful as demonstrated by a study by James W. Loewen of the Southern Poverty Law Center in 2011, which found that 55–75 percent of American teachers, across regions and racial lines, stated that "state's rights" was the primary reason for the Civil War, rather than slavery.[46]

The state's rights argument is historically inaccurate. For one thing, the Southern Constitution written when the South seceded from the nation established a federal law (for their new federation) to protect the institution of slavery.

As written in the 1861 Constitution:

> *"In all such territory the institution of negro slavery, as it now exists in the Confederate States, shall be recognized and protected by Congress and the Territorial government."*[47]

Essentially, Southern secessionists didn't believe that the issue should be left up to the states and decided to make the legality of slavery a federal mandate. The declaration of secession for the state of Texas is even more explicit as to the actual causes and motivations of the war:

> *"We hold as undeniable truths that the governments of the various States, and of the confederacy itself, were established exclusively by the white race, for themselves and their posterity; that the African race had no agency in their establishment; that they were rightfully held and regarded as an inferior and dependent race, and in that condition only could their existence in this country be rendered beneficial or tolerable."*[48]

Thus, the Civil War was *primarily* about slavery as from that, other contentions arose—namely, economic survival, state's rights, and the ability of a divided house to stand. The South was so economically dependent on slavery as an institution that the threat of abolition motivated them to secede rather than face the end of their culture, their economic power, and the identity they had created over more than a century of legal exploitation and systemic racism. To counter critics who took moral umbrage to slavery as an institution, slave owners and lobbyists for the industry engaged in a long-term campaign of propaganda and pseudoscientific misinformation arguing that black people were unable to care for themselves and that slavery was a benevolent institution that provided for the biologically inferior and incapable. In essence, slavery, and the Southern economy, was under threat, and the propagandistic dehumanization campaign intensified to defend it.[49]

So, although there were other issues at play, slavery was at the heart of the war. Furthermore, every representation of the Confederate states, be it the Confederate flag, busts or statues of Confederate leaders, or even the more generalized plaques and statues commemorating the many former citizens of the United States who died fighting for their morally bereft and ultimately failed cause, are also representations of the inherently racist ideology that underpinned slavery as an institution.

Homesteads Provide a Path to Citizenship

The Civil War had a major impact on immigration policy. The Southern states had long been anti-immigrant for very practical reasons. Most immigrants settled in the North, both because that is where European immigrants typically arrived and because there were more jobs in the Northern cities. Moreover, there were nationalist communities that could help newly arriving immigrants to assimilate. But it was also true that the majority of new European immigrants were sympathetic to the abolitionist movement. This was, in part, because many of those same European countries from which the immigrants were coming had already been through anti-slavery movements that resulted in the abolition of slavery. Slavery was

John Bakken, son of Norwegian immigrants who homesteaded and built this sod house, with wife Marget and children Tilda and Eddie, Milton, North Dakota, 1898, via Wikimedia Commons

Certificate of the first homestead according the Homestead Act, given to Daniel Freeman, Beatrice, Nebraska, 1963, via Wikimedia Commons

abolished in the British Empire as a whole in July of 1833, but had been prohibited in part for 20 years already. So, many of the newly arriving British immigrants to the United States had already come to see slavery as an uncivilized and unsavory practice. Southerners were, therefore, passionately anti-immigrant in part because they knew that the growth of the North would mean a stronger anti-slavery movement.

The first legislative effort undertaken after the war began that directly impacted immigration was the Homestead Act of 1862, a land law that distributed publicly owned lands to private individuals and families.

The Civil War came at a time when the American economy was changing, from a primarily agrarian economy to an industrial economy. This march towards industrialization would ultimately make America one of the world's great powers by the beginning of the twentieth century, but, in the 1850s and 60s, the economies of the North and South were diverging. At the time, the South produced about 29 percent of the entire global cotton supply, the source of the riches enjoyed by the South's elite families, but not, of course, by the laborers responsible for making this harvest happen each year. The cotton crop was the most valuable export in the United States and was worth more, in 1840, than all the nation's other exports combined, but the South had little in the way of manufacturing capabilities. For instance, according to research collected by the National Park Service, the North produced 3,200 firearms to every 100 produced in the South, as well as 17 times more cotton textiles, 30 times more leather goods, and 20 times more iron. Only about 40 percent of Northern residents were employed in agriculture in 1860, compared to 84 percent of Southern citizens.[50] Southerners in Congress had long lobbied against any legislation that would have provided an advantage to Northern industrialists or farmers, seeking to preserve the South's dominance of the agricultural industry.

When the war broke out, Southerners and many pro-slavery Democrats of the era left Congress to join the newly formed Southern states and thus, the Republicans and central-government friendly Democrats who remained, had an opportunity to create a new economic and social model for the future. Recognizing the need to create a new agricultural base, Congress passed the Homestead Act of 1862, which provided a free land title (up to 160 acres) on federally-owned land outside the original 13 colonies, to any person willing to live on and cultivate the land for at least five years. The South had opposed similar measures in the past, because they felt it would limit their capability to expand slavery into the new territories settled by the new wave of "free-soiler" farmers. For instance, the House of Representatives passed proposals for a similar Homestead law in 1852, 1854, and 1859, but, in each case the Senate, which was dominated by Southern politicians, rejected the proposal.

On February 12, 1861, just after winning the election to the presidency, Abraham Lincoln addressed the Homestead Act in a speech given to the

German Club of Cincinnati, Ohio:

> _"...I hold that while man exists, it is his duty to improve not only his own condition, but to assist in ameliorating mankind; and therefore, without entering upon the details of the question, I will simply say, that I am for those means which will give the greatest good to the greatest number. In regard to the Homestead Law, I have to say that in so far as the Government lands can be disposed of, I am in favor of cutting up the wild lands into parcels, so that every poor man may have a home."_[51]

Whether or not immigrants were the intended beneficiaries of the Homestead Act, many immigrants seized the opportunity as the provisions of the act essentially made federal homesteading an automatic path to citizenship for those willing to take on the challenge. Debates in the 37th Congress make it clear that encouraging immigrants to become homesteaders was, in fact, one of the intended goals of the bill. The language of the law stated specifically that applicants for plots under the law had to either be citizens OR declare their intention to become so. Within the first month after the bill was signed into law, tens of thousands of homestead claims were filed, many by immigrants.

Calling on Immigrant Soldiers

Though it may come as a surprise given the nation's mythological history as the "land of immigrants," the Civil War was the first and only time in American history that the government passed a law meant to actively encourage immigration.

NOT WANTED

Uncle Sam behind a fence with immigrants "Rome," "Rum," and "Red" on the other side, via Wikipedia

In an 1855 letter written to friend Joshua F. Speed, after Speed asked Lincoln about his opinion on the Know-Nothing party, Lincoln's response helped illustrate his attitude vis-à-vis the broader immigrant issue:

_____ *"I am not a Know-Nothing. That is certain. How could I be? How can anyone who abhors the oppression of negroes, be in favor of degrading classes of white people? Our progress in degeneracy appears to me to be pretty rapid. As a nation, we begin by declaring that 'all men are created equal.' We now practically read it 'all men are created equal, except negroes.' When the Know-Nothings get control, it will read 'all men are created equal, except negroes, and foreigners, and Catholics.' When it comes to this I should prefer emigrating to some country where they make no pretense of loving liberty—to Russia, for instance, where despotism can be taken pure, and without the base alloy of hypocrisy."*[52]

_____

Lincoln personally championed the 1864 Act to Encourage Immigration as the first step towards a more egalitarian and diverse future for the nation. On December 8, 1863, speaking to the 37th Congress, Lincoln gave a speech recommending his proposed immigration bill, saying:

_____ *"I again submit to your consideration the expediency of establishing a system for the encouragement of immigration. Although this source of national wealth and strength is again flowing with greater freedom than for several years before the insurrection occurred, there is still a great deficiency of laborers in every field of industry, especially in agriculture and in our mines, as well as of iron and*

coal as of the precious metals. While the demand for labor is thus increased here, tens of thousands of persons, destitute of remunerative occupation, are thronging our foreign consulates and offering to emigrate to the United States if essential, but very cheap assistance, can be afforded them. It is very easy to see that under the sharp discipline of Civil War, the Nation is beginning a new life. This noble effort demands the aid and ought to receive the attention and support of the Government."[53]

The legislature was swayed by Lincoln's campaign, recognizing both the need for laborers in the present and the future need for laborers to make up the deficit that would exist in the South after the end of slavery. The bill, An Act to Encourage Immigration, was passed on March 2, 1864.

AN ACT TO ENCOURAGE IMMIGRATION
Source Document

Be it enacted by the Senate and House of Representatives of the United States of America in Congress assembled, That the President of the United States is hereby authorized, by and with the advice and consent of the Senate, to appoint a Commissioner of Immigration, who shall be subject to the direction of the Department of State, shall hold his office for four years, and shall receive a salary at the rate of $2,500 a year. The said Commissioner may employ not more than three clerks, of such grade as the Secretary of State shall designate, to be appointed by him, with the approval of the Secretary of State, and to hold their offices at his pleasure.

SEC. 2. And be it further enacted, That all contracts that shall be made by emigrants to the United States in foreign countries, in conformity to regulations that may be established by the said Commissioner, whereby emigrants shall pledge the wages of

An Act to Encourage Immigration
continued

their labor for a term not exceeding twelve months to repay the expenses of their emigration, shall be held to be valid in law, and may be enforced in the courts of the United States, or of the several States and Territories; and such advances, if so stipulated in the contract, and the contract be recorded in the Recorder's office in the county where the emigrant shall settle, shall operate as a lien upon any land thereafter acquired by the emigrant, whether under the Homestead Law when the title is consummated or on property otherwise acquired, until liquidated by the emigrant; but not being herein contained shall be deemed to authorize any contract contravening the Constitution of the United States or creating in any way the relation of Slavery or servitude.

SEC. 3. And be it further enacted; That no emigrant to the United States who shall arrive after the passage of this act shall be compulsively enrolled for military service during the existing insurrection, unless such emigrant shall voluntarily renounce under oath his allegiance to the country of his birth and declare his intention to become a citizen of the United States.

SEC. 4. And be it further enacted, That there shall be established in the City of New-York an office to be known as the United States Emigrant Office; and there shall be appointed, by and with the advice and consent of the Senate, an officer for said City, to be known as Superintendent of Immigration, at an annual salary of two thousand dollars; and the said Superintendent may employ a clerk of the first class; and such Superintendent shall, under the direction of the Commissioner of Immigration, make contracts with the different railroads and transportation companies of the United States for transportation tickets, to be furnished to such immigrants, and to be paid for by them, and shall, under such rules as may be prescribed by the Commissioner of Immigration, protect such immigrants from imposition and fraud, and shall furnish them such information and facilities as will enable them to proceed in the cheapest and most expeditious manner to the place of their destination. And such Superintendent of Immigration shall perform such other duties as may be prescribed by the Commissioner of Immigration: Provided, That the duties hereby imposed upon the Superintendent in the City of New-York shall not be held to affect the powers and duties of the Commissioner of the Immigration of the State of New-York. And it shall be the duty of said Superintendent in the City of New-York, to see that the provisions of the

continued

act commonly known as the Passenger Act, are strictly complied with, and all breaches thereof punished according to law.

SEC. 5. And be it further enacted. That no person shall be qualified to fill, any office under this act who shall be directly or indirectly interested in any corporation having lands for sale to immigrants, or in the carrying or transportation of immigrants, either from foreign countries to the United States and its Territories or to any part thereof, or who shall receive any fee or reward, or the promise thereof, for any service performed or any benefit rendered to any person or persons in the line or his duty under this act. And if any officer provided for by this act shall receive from any person or company any fee or reward, or promise thereof, for any services performed or any benefit rendered to any person or persons in the line of his duty under this act, he shall, upon conviction, be fined one thousand dollars or be imprisoned, not to exceed three years, at the discretion of a court of competent jurisdiction, and forever after be ineligible to hold any office of honor, trust, or profit in the United States.

SEC. 6. And be it further enacted, That said Commissioner of Immigration shall, at the commencement of each annual meeting of Congress, submit a detailed report of the foreign immigration during the preceding year, and a detailed account of all expenditures under this act.

SEC. 7. And be it further enacted, That the sum of twenty-five thousand dollars, or so much thereof as may be necessary, in the judgment of the President, is hereby appropriated, out of any money in the treasury not otherwise appropriated, for the purpose of carrying the provisions of this act into effect.

APPROVED, July 4, 1864.[54]

The brief pro-immigration surge of the Civil War did not endure when the war came to an end, and no future administration ever made so direct an effort to attract immigrants to the nation. However, the Act to Encourage Immigration had some lasting effects in that many immigrants answered the call, diversifying the immigrant communities in America's cities and bolstering support for immigrants in subsequent years.

The Union won the Civil War and slavery was abolished, but the victory came at a terrible cost. Current research suggests that as many as 750,000 died in the Civil War, which is more than the number of Americans who died in every subsequent war combined (around 640,000). In the aftermath, a massive swath of the nation lay destitute and destroyed, and the process of rebuilding the nation lasted for decades and transformed America's cultural and political landscape.[55] Not only did the Civil War benefit immigrants in many ways, but immigrants were also key to the Union victory.

In 1860, about 13 percent of the U.S. population was foreign born, similar to the proportion in 2018, but the proportion of foreign-born in the North was much higher. One in four Union soldiers was an immigrant, nearly 543,000 of the estimated 2 million. Another 18 percent of those had at least one foreign-born parent and thus, immigrants and second-generation immigrants composed some 43 percent of the Union's forces.[56] Though popular history tends to portray the war as a struggle between "brothers," the contribution of new arrivals, and of those who arrived when the war was already underway, cannot be overstated. Without immigrants, including those that came in droves after Lincoln's Homestead Act and the Act to Encourage Immigration opened the door to more immigrants than ever before, the Union would not have won the war and the nation would now be a very different place.

CONCLUSION

The Civil War led to a shift in public opinion against the institution of slavery, but not necessarily towards the belief that African Americans and white Americans should be treated equally under the law. Moving forward, however, the fact that the nation adopted an official anti-slavery policy complicated the campaign of those many politicians who continued to believe that the benefits of citizenship should be distributed differently among the nation's ethnic and racial groups. The short-lived effort to attract immigrants to the United States to bolster the northern armies and support for the Union led to a mass overseas marketing campaign portraying the United States as a land of unparalleled opportunity. The immigrant communities that evolved after the Civil War thus facilitated more immigration from Europe, while nativists began focusing, increasingly, on using immigration policy to control the nation's ethnic and racial composition.

DISCUSSION QUESTIONS

- Are Confederate monuments symbolic of slavery? Why or why not?
- How is the Republican Party of the twenty-first century different from the Republican Party when Abraham Lincoln was in office? How are the two parties similar?
- Why did members of the confederate states oppose immigration?
- Does institutional slavery still play a role in the status of African Americans? Why or why not?

Works Used

"A Brief History." Overview of Slavery in the United States. Civil War Trust. 2018, www.civilwar.org/learn/articles/slavery-united-states.

"An Act to Encourage Immigration." *New York Times*. New York Times Co. 3 Aug. 1864.

Arrington, Benjamin T. "Industry and Economy during the Civil War." *NPS*. National Park Service. 2017.

"Confederate States of America—A Declaration of the Causes Which Impel the State of Texas to Secede from the Federal Union." *Yale Law School*. Lillian Goldman Law Library. The Avalon Project. Documents in Law, History, and Diplomacy. 2008.

"Constitution of the Confederate States; March 11, 1861." *Yale Law School*. Lillian Goldman Law Library. The Avalon Project. Documents in Law, History, and Diplomacy. 2008.

Doyle, Don H. "The Civil War Was Won by Immigrant Soldiers." *Time*. Time Inc. 29 June 2015.

Flanagin, Jake. "For the last time, the American Civil War was not about states' rights." *Quartz*. Atlantic Media. 8 Apr. 2015.

Gugliotta, Guy. "New Estimate Raises Civil War Death Toll." *New York Times*. 2 Apr. 2012.

Hing, Bill Ong. *Defining America Through Immigration Policy*. Philadelphia, PA: Temple UP, 2012. p. 21.

Lincoln, Abraham. "Speech to Germans at Cincinnati, Ohio." In Smith, Steven B. ed. *The Writings of Abraham Lincoln*. New Haven, CT: Yale UP, 2012.

"Lincoln on the Know-Nothing Party." August 24, 1844: Letter to Joshua F. Speed. *NPS*. National Park Service. 10 Apr. 2015.

Introduction

Whereas the federal government encouraged higher levels of immigration during the Civil War to build a stronger army, during the "reconstruction period" that followed the war, marked by the effort to reintegrate the southern and northern states, immigration priorities were changing again. The return of nativist southern politicians to Congress resulted in a stronger anti-immigration movement and debates over how to change immigration laws to reflect the abolishment of slavery.

The source for this chapter includes excerpts of the 1870 Naturalization Act, which, for the first time in history, enabled nonwhite individuals to become naturalized citizens of the United States. Prior to this, the immensely impactful Fourteenth Amendment already fundamentally changed U.S. immigration law by establishing that all persons born or naturalized in the United States were permanent citizens, no matter where they lived. The amendment also gave the federal government sole power to determine who could become citizens and prohibited any state government from restricting citizenship. The 1870 Naturalization Act followed logically from this, asserting that, because persons of African descent were now U.S. citizens, it was now legal for immigrants of African descent to *become* citizens. This did not make a significant difference at the time, as few new African immigrants came to the United States, but it was a major factor in later efforts to limit the immigration of nonwhite persons into the United States.

Topics covered in this chapter include:
- U.S. Civil War
- Reconstruction Period
- Fourteenth Amendment

- Thirteenth Amendment
- Women's Suffrage
- Women's Rights
- State's rights
- Naturalization Law

This Chapter Discusses the Following Source Document:
"An Act to Amend the Naturalization Laws and to punish Crimes against the same, and for other Purposes." *LOC*. Library of Congress. Forty-First Congress, Sess. II. 2018.

The Color of Citizenship
Post-War Immigration Policy (1870–1875)

In the wake of the Civil War, as America struggled through the difficult Reconstruction Period, the nation faced an advanced citizenship challenge, transitioning millions of former slaves into citizenship while redefining the nation's economic identity.

At the time, immigration laws fell under the authority of two separate domains: immigration and nationality. Immigration policy governed the economic and procedural practices surrounding the act of immigration itself, whereas nationality law, drafted by a separate congressional committee, set rules about naturalization and citizenship.

That the Southern states had always been big on state's rights is true, and this was because the Southern states feared that a stronger central government would outlaw slavery. They thus argued, for years, that the central government didn't have this authority and that only a state government could decide to abolish immigration. With the South temporarily absent from the legislature, the federal government expanded its powers and, specifically, passed laws stating that no state government could pass laws that violated citizenship rights as defined by the central government. In the 1870s, Congress and the courts struggled to determine how changes in nationality law, brought about by the Fourteenth Amendment (1868) and the end of slavery would impact immigration.

A New Era in Citizenship

Although the Thirteenth Amendment abolished slavery as a whole, across the entire nation, it was the Fourteenth Amendment that made the former slaves into citizens. The Fourteenth Amendment to the U.S. Constitution, passed in 1868, affected both nationality and immigration policy. Section 1 of the Amendment contained four clauses, known as the Citizenship Clause, the Privileges and Immunities Clause, the Due Process Clause, and the Equal Protection Clause, which collectively altered the course of American history with regard to racial equality.

Collectively, the four clauses of the Fourteenth Amendment are among the most debated and legislated principles of American political philosophy. The four clauses of the first section were used to argue against segregation in schools, reproductive rights laws, gender discrimination, and racial quota systems used in both immigration and education. The four clauses also placed significant restrictions on the states, creating a new balance between the federal and state governments. Moving forward, the Fourteenth Amendment essentially made the Bill of Rights applicable to all states and abolished all state laws that altered the rights therein expressed.

This, of course, did not end racism, nor did it end the efforts of politicians to legalize racism in one way or another. Moving forward, states would argue that keeping the peace or protecting national security, or protecting the economic welfare of the poor or middle class were justifications for passing laws allowing businesses and people to exclude others based on race.

Citizenship Clause

"All persons born or naturalized in the United States, and subject to the jurisdiction thereof, are citizens of the United States and of the state wherein they reside."

Privileges and Immunities Clause

"No state shall make or enforce any law which shall abridge the privileges or immunities of citizens of the United States;"

Due Process Clause

"nor shall any state deprive any person of life, liberty, or property, without due process of law;"

Equal Protection Clause

"nor deny to any person within its jurisdiction the equal protection of the laws."[57]

What About Black Immigrants?

With citizenship extended to the children of former slaves, there was still a serious question unanswered: the citizenship status of black immigrants

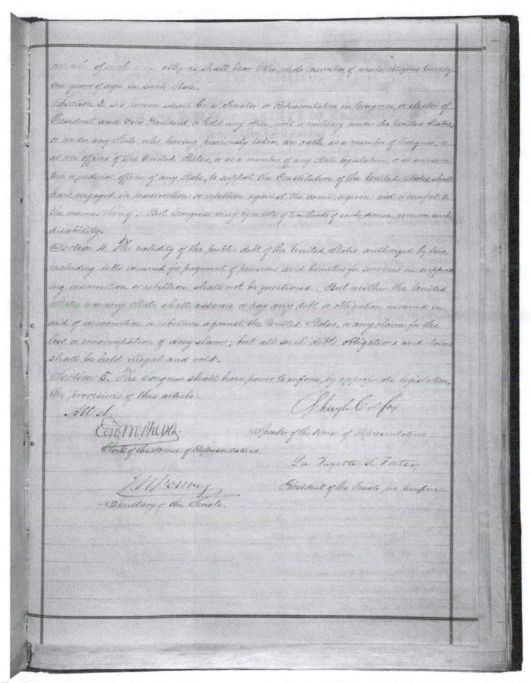

The Fourteenth Amendment, representing a new era in citizenship, U.S. National Archives, via Wikimedia Commons

not born in the United States. Until the Civil War, only white males were allowed to become citizens. The Fourteenth Amendment left the nation in a logical bind, therefore, as extending citizenship to former slaves and the children of slaves was incongruous with a broader naturalization policy that only enabled white males to become citizens.

The Naturalization Act of 1870 contained one clause, isolated in the last section of the bill, that fundamentally changed U.S. immigration policy as it had existed since the 1790 Uniform Rule of Naturalization. This ground-breaking change to U.S. immigration philosophy came at the tail end of an otherwise routine piece of legislation that strengthened penalties for immigration fraud.

Section one of the bill provided a term of 1 to 5 years imprisonment and a fine of up to $1000 for anyone who violated oaths, affirmations, or affidavits made with regard to naturalization of aliens. This was intended to end fake naturalization scams and other types of naturalization fraud.

Section two, the longest and most complex of the bill, also dealt with immigration fraud, in the typical, impenetrable legal language of the era:

THE NATURALIZATION ACT OF 1870
Source Document Excerpt

Sec. 2. And be it further enacted, That if any person applying to be admitted a citizen, or appearing as a witness for any such person, shall knowingly personate any other person than himself, or falsely appear in the name of a deceased person, or in an assumed or fictitious name, or if any person shall falsely make, forge, or counterfeit any oath, affirmation, notice, affidavit, certificate, order, record, signature, or other instrument, paper, or proceeding required or authorized by any law or act relating to or providing for the naturalization of aliens; or shall utter, sell, dispose of, or use as true or genuine, or for any unlawful purpose, any false, forged, ante-dated, or counterfeit oath, affirmation, notice, certificate, order, record, signature, instrument, paper, or proceeding as aforesaid; or sell or dispose of to any

continued

person other than the person for whom it was originally issued, any certificate of citizenship, or certificate showing any person to be admitted a citizen; or if any person shall in any manner use for the purpose of registering as a voter, or as evidence of a right to vote, or otherwise, unlawfully, any order, certificate of citizenship, or certificate, judgement, or exemplification, showing such person to be admitted to be a citizen, whether heretofore or hereafter issued or made, knowing that such order or certificate, judgement, or exemplification has been unlawfully issued or made; or if any person shall unlawfully use, or attempt to use, any such order or certificate, issued to or in the name of any other person, or in a fictitious name, or the name of a deceased person; or use, or attempt to use, or aid, or assist, or participate in the use of any certificate of citizenship, knowing the same to be forged, or counterfeit, or ante-dated, or knowing the same to have been procured by fraud, or otherwise unlawfully obtained; or if any person, and without lawful excuse, shall knowingly have or be possessed of any false, forged, ante-dated, or counterfeit certificate of citizenship, purporting to have been issued under the provisions of any law of the United States relating to naturalization, knowing such certificate to be false, forged, ante-dated, or counterfeit, with intent unlawfully to use the same; or if any person shall obtain, accept, or receive any certificate of citizenship known to such person to have been procured by fraud or by the use of any false name, or by means of any false statement made with intent to procure, or to aid in procuring, the issue of such certificate, or known to such person to be fraudulently altered or ante-dated; or if any person who has been or may be admitted to be a citizen shall, on oath or affirmation, or by affidavit, knowingly deny that he has been so admitted, with intent to evade or avoid any duty or liability imposed or required by law, every person so offending shall be deemed and adjudged guilty of felony, and, on conviction thereof, shall be sentenced to be imprisoned and kept at hard labor for a period not less than one year nor more than one thousand dollars, or both such punishments may be imposed, in the discretion of the court, And every person who shall knowingly and intentionally aid or abet any person in the commission of any such felony, or attempt to do any act hereby made felony, or counsel, advise, or procure, or attempt to procure the commission thereof, shall be liable to indictment and punishment in the same manner and to the same extent as the principal party guilty of such felony, and such person may be tried and convicted thereof without the previous conviction of such principal.

The Fifth and Sixth Section of the bill created a municipal system to protect against voting fraud, including ordering the circuit courts in cities with more than 20,000 residents to appoint two individuals, residents of the city, one from each party, to oversee elections and vote counting. The provision was intended, in part, to address the voting rights issues that Congress knew would arise as the freed black population began to express their newly acquired citizenship in upcoming elections.

But, it was the Seventh Section of the bill that had the most lasting impact on immigration policy, stating simply:

THE NATURALIZATION ACT OF 1870
Source Document Excerpt

Sec. 7. And be it further enacted, That the naturalization laws are hereby extended to aliens of African nativity and to persons of African descent.[58]

That such a momentous change was expressed in so simple a manner might seem strange, but, the underlying principles of the clause were also fairly straightforward. From that moment on, citizenship was not only available for African slaves and their children, but to all people of African descent, whether born in the United States or abroad. This did not fundamentally change the racial mix of America's immigrants, however, because, for many years few African natives chose to migrate to the United States. That this did not occur makes sense as those who did still faced extreme prejudice and even violence in many parts of the country from the many white Americans who feared and thus were hostile to Africans as well as African Americans.

Inequality Endures

The Fourteenth Amendment was a major victory for the abolitionists and, of course, the former slaves and their children who glimpsed, for the first

time, a more egalitarian potential future within the United States. However, the Fourteenth Amendment failed to extend the promise of citizenship to others who had likewise been marginalized under the existing hegemony and, at least in one case, appeared to make matters worse.

Women's rights was a slow-burning background movement in the United States for many years and intensified in the urban expansion of the mid-1800s. In general, the women's suffrage movement (women's right to vote) and broader women's rights movement took a back seat to abolition during the Civil War. Many women who had aims of gender equality saw parallels with the way that women and African Americans had been denied rights and feminists played an important role in the aboli-

Elizabeth Cady Stanton, via Wikimedia Commons

tionist movement that achieved a major success with the Thirteenth and Fourteenth Amendments. However, pioneer women's suffrage advocates like Susan B. Anthony and Elizabeth Cady Stanton were among a group of women who lobbied against the Fourteenth Amendment when the text of the bill was revealed. Their objection was based on the Second Section of the Fourteenth Amendment, which concerned voting rights, and said:

> *"...the right to vote at any election for the choice of electors for President and Vice President of the United States, Representatives in Congress, the Executive and Judicial officers of a State, or the members of the Legislature thereof, is denied to any of the male inhabitants of such State, being twenty-one years of age, and citizens of the United States, or in any way abridged, except for participation in*

rebellion, or other crime, the basis of representation therein shall be reduced in the proportion which the number of such male citizens shall bear to the whole number of male citizens twenty-one years of age in such State."[59]

The second section of the Fourteenth Amendment was the first time the word "male" had been introduced to the Constitution, and women's rights activists like Anthony and Stanton felt betrayed by the overt insult of dividing the populace by gender even as the new amendment opened up the possibility of equality for African men. This drove a wedge between former allies, with the suffragettes accusing male supporters of the Fourteenth Amendment of betraying the spirit of their shared battle over the past decade, and Fourteenth Amendment supporters feeling that the feminists had betrayed the cause of racial equality. In 1869, the year after the Fourteenth Amendment was ratified, Stanton and Anthony split from the American Equal Rights Association, which had advocated both for women's and black people's rights, to found the National Woman Suffrage Association. They also used their new association to create and publish a new women's rights publication, *The Revolution*, each issue of which bore the tagline, "Men, their rights and nothing more; women, their rights and nothing less!"[60]

Stanton and Anthony also broke from their former allies over the Fifteenth Amendment, a simple modification to the Constitution framed in the following way:

"The right of citizens of the United States to vote shall not be denied or abridged by the United States or by any State on account of race, color, or previous condition of servitude."[61]

Again, Stanton, Anthony and their supporters opposed the amendment because it did not also specify that rights could not be abridged for persons of any sex or gender. In 1871 and 1872, women attempted to vote despite state laws prohibiting the practice. It was part of a strategy known as the New Departure, in which the women hoped to challenge state laws using the Equal Protection Clause of the Fourteenth Amendment.

Virginia Minor was one of those pioneering women who attempted to vote in 1872 in her home state of Missouri. Minor was denied and sued the state, taking the issue all the way to the Supreme Court where, in 1874, the Supreme Court was asked to rule on whether or not the Equal Protection Clause necessitated providing women citizens with the right to vote.

The U.S. Supreme Court under Chief Justice Morrison Waite heard the case in 1874 (*Minor v. Happersett*) and ruled that the Constitution did not guarantee the right to vote to citizens, and thus that the Fourteenth Amendment did not extend this right to all citizens unless empowered to vote by other laws. The court's ruling in *Minor v. Happersett* was a major blow to the women's rights movement of the time and essentially demonstrated that the New Departure strategy had failed. Though the Supreme Court refused to recognize voting rights as a function of basic citizenship, the Fourteenth Amendment had established this connection, but only for males. Undeterred, the Suffragist movement only intensified after their demoralizing defeat with regard to the Fourteenth and Fifteenth Amendments, though their ultimate victory was still half a century away.[62]

CONCLUSION

While the 1870 naturalization law opened citizenship to persons of African descent, the language of the law and the amendments that preceded it dealt a blow to women's rights advocates as, for the first time, the law said that citizenship rights were only available to "males" of white or African descent. Women's rights supporters, who had been an active and important group in the anti-slavery movement, therefore, campaigned against the Fourteenth and Fifteenth Amendments and the 1870 Naturalization Law, arguing that the laws and amendments should not be used to exclude women from citizenship rights.

In terms of public opinion, the end of slavery was very contentious. The anti-slavery movement had, for several decades, been trying to influence public opinion through pamphlets and informational brochures criticizing slavery as an immoral institution, and a majority of Americans approved of the abolishment of legal slavery. However, there was no similar majority in favor of integrating white and African American society. The end of slavery was, therefore, the beginning of "segregation," a long-term cultural and legal effort to limit the rights and citizenship benefits afforded to African Americans motivated by those who felt integration would damage or negatively impact white society.

DISCUSSION QUESTIONS

- How does the Fourteenth Amendment affect state's rights?
- What did Section 2 of the 1870 Naturalization Act indicate about the concerns of politicians regarding immigration at the time?
- Should voting rights be a fundamental right of U.S. citizenship? Why or why not?
- Are there any modern issues that concern the Fourteenth Amendment? If so, explain how these issues relate to the four clauses of the amendment presented in the article.

Works Used

"Amendment XIV." *Cornell*. Cornell Law School. U.S. Constitution. LII. 2018.

"Amendment XV." *Cornell*. Cornell Law School. U.S. Constitution. LII. 2018.

"An Act to amend the Naturalization Laws and to punish Crimes against the same, and for other Purposes." *LOC*. Library of Congress. Forty-First Congress, Session II. PDF. 2018.

Dudden, Faye E. *Fighting Chance: The Struggle Over Woman Suffrage and Black Suffrage in Reconstruction America*. New York: Oxford UP, 2011.

Kelly, Gary, Christine Bold, and Joad Raymond, Eds. *The Oxford History of Popular Print Culture: Volume Six: US Popular Print Culture 1860–1920*. New York: Oxford UP, 2012.

"Minor v. Happersett." Cornell. Cornell Law School. Supreme Court. LII. 2018.

Introduction

At the end of the Civil War, the United States engaged in the largest and most ambitious infrastructure project in the nation's history: the building of the Transcontinental Railroad. Millionaire industrialists whose companies worked on the railroad wanted cheap labor and the end of slavery meant that a new source of labor was needed. Companies, therefore, encouraged a wave of immigrants from Ireland and China, who were willing to enter into exploitative labor contracts and to accept substandard wages. This led to conflict in the nation's labor classes and, ultimately, to a virulent anti-Chinese movement that spread across the United States.

The majority of Asian immigrants came to the west coast and, specifically, California and so California became the focal point for the nation's anti-Chinese immigration movement. Despite facing prejudice and violence, thousands of Chinese laborers came to the United States and played an important role in building the nation's west coast cities and infrastructure. The source for this chapter is a 2016 article by Jeffrey Bolognese in *Medium*, "3 Reasons Why Chinese Workers Were the MVP's on the Transcontinental Railroad," exploring the contributions of Chinese immigrant workers to the nation's westward expansion.

Topics covered in this chapter include:
- Westward expansion
- Racial prejudice
- Anti-Asian prejudice
- The Transcontinental Railroad
- Income inequality
- Labor rights
- Unauthorized immigration
- Nativism

Railroad Chinese coolie (unskilled, non-white, indentured laborer), via Wikimedia Commons

This Chapter Discusses the Following Source Document:
Bolognese, Jeffrey. "3 Reasons Why Chinese Workers Were the MVP's on the Transcontinental Railroad." *Medium*. SASEprints. Society of Asian Scientists and Engineers. May 20, 2016.

The East in the West
Railroads, Coolies, and Racism (1800–1868)

The nativist movement against Irish and Catholic immigration in the mid-1800s was based on lingering European tribalism and prejudice. Politicians like Alexander Hamilton stoked these prejudices to build support for the Federalist Party and their isolationist vision for America. A far more long-lasting and violent prejudice developed targeting Asian, and especially Chinese, immigrants in the 1800s. Whereas anti-Irish prejudice was quickly subsumed in America's early melting pot that created a more uniform whiteness out of a European stew, members of other races were excluded from this admixture, and the differences perceived by white Americans between themselves and other races was fuel for an altogether more lasting racism that continues to pervade American culture.

To white Americans in the 1800s, Chinese people must have seemed very alien. Their language was strange and tonal, differing markedly from America's Germanic phonemes. The Chinese weren't Christian, and the way in which they engaged with their strange, heathen religions was not similar to how Christians practice theirs. But most importantly, they looked different, with unique skin tones, bone structures, and differently shaped features. As with the Irish in the mid-1800s, and the freed blacks in the 1870s, Chinese immigrants that came to America in the 1800s were, on the whole, very poor and willing to endure abject poverty for the chance at a job that might lead to a new, and better life for them and their families. In every era, it is the most destitute immigrants who become the target of America's anti-immigration movement du jour. This was true of the Irish, when almost all immigrants were European, and it was true of the Chinese during the gold rush and westward expansion.

Replacing Slavery

The institution of slavery in the southern states provided farmers who settled there with a major economic advantage as they profited from free labor to grow their interests. Slavery created a generation of land-owning gentry out of what might have been under other circumstances struggling farmers working smaller fields and collecting smaller profits. Agricultural production would have grown at a far slower rate had plantation owners not used slaves as the workforce to develop the land.

America has long been called a "land of opportunity," and this is sometimes attributed to the unique nature of America's political system. It was not, however, the politics or ideals of the nation that attracted immigrants in the 1800s but rather the simple fact that America was a massive, resource rich country with a growing economy whereas much of the rest of the world had already been occupied and developed for so many hundreds of years that opportunities for accruing wealth were harder to attain. The wealth of America was also the product of slave labor, which drove the American economy much further and faster than was possible in nations that outlawed or never undertook the practice. This rapid economic growth, however, also had a downside. As more and more Americans climbed the socioeconomic ladder, many were left behind, qualified only for low-paying jobs. This pattern has remained largely unchecked over the entire course of American history and is the root cause of the nation's severe income inequality in the twenty-first century. For those white Americans in each generation who lack the education, training, or social/political connections to be mobile (economically), job opportunities become increasingly rare and they are forced to compete with immigrant laborers for whom even low-paying American jobs are far more lucrative and sustaining than what was available in their native countries.

Now, because slavery was always morally controversial and because many states outlawed slavery long before the Civil War created a federal prohibition, there was a strong demand in many states, especially anti-slave states, for low-paid labor. On the Pacific site of the United

States, Chinese "coolies" seemed to fit this bill. Coolie is a term used by the British to describe unskilled, non-white, indentured laborers within Britain's colonial territories. The term came from India, where the term coolie refers to a person who carries another person's baggage. In the United States, the term became an ethnic slur used primarily to refer to Chinese immigrants who came to the United States looking for work.

An indentured servant is a person under contract to work for another person for a certain period, in return either for providing passage to a new country, or for housing and the basic resources needed to live in a specific place. In the 1800s, indentured servitude was legal in the United States and the system worked like this: a company or individual offered a laborer room, board, and a low wage in return for the worker signing a typically long-term contract (usually 5 or more years). In the mid-1800s, as American companies were working to build the railroads that crisscrossed the American west, many of the states had no slaves and so contracted indentured Chinese and Irish laborers for the difficult and often dangerous task of building the infrastructure of the railroad system. These laborers were horrendously exploited in the same way as indentured servants had been exploited for thousands of years. The employers paid their servants too little to build the wealth required to leave the system and so at the end of their contracts, they faced homelessness and destitution or signed another contract. Indentured servitude is essentially economic slavery without physical ownership of the servants involved.[63]

Chinese participation in the transcontinental railroad began in earnest with an 1865 experiment by Central Pacific Railroad company (CPRR) director Charles Crocker. Crocker and the company needed 5,000 laborers, but their advertisements resulted in only a few hundred white applicants. Furthermore, the Western Gold Rush was on, and many who traveled to the west to work on the railroads left the difficult job to become precious metal prospectors from Nevada to California. Central Pacific was

From *Views of the Chinese*, published in *The Graphic* and *Harper's Weekly*, via Wikimedia Commons

facing a severe labor shortage and so Crocker hired 50 Chinese workers, from among the population of some 50–60,000 then living in California. Beginning in July of 1865, Crocker began hiring workers directly from China, shipping in boats filled with eager laborers who agreed to unfavorable contracts to secure immigration. By 1867, 80 to 90 percent of the Central Pacific workforce was Chinese, and the remaining were Irish (a group still maligned at the time as Europe's lowest-class immigrants). [64]

Central Pacific benefitted from imported Chinese labor in numerous ways. For one thing, Chinese laborers were paid between $20 and $30 per month, as opposed to the $40 per month for white laborers. As immigrants who could not become naturalized citizens, Chinese people had no federal protections and so could legally be arrested, whipped, and beaten if they tried to leave their jobs. In general, Chinese railroad workers worked longer hours and for far less pay than the average white worker in the same job. The most dangerous jobs were also typically

given to Chinese laborers, and legend has it this was the origin of the slur "Chinaman's chance," meaning a very slim chance of succeeding (perhaps more accurately, *surviving*), a certain job.[65]

Labor Versus Ownership

The wealthy American industrialists and agriculturalists who helped build the American west also created the mythos of the American dream. Rising from rags to riches became the story sold to the world to promote the patriotic American experiment. This myth was created by the winners of the economic race and so is framed in such a way as to deify business itself and the corporate-friendly mindset allegedly fueling America's unparalleled opportunities. Commensurate with this was another of America's characteristic economic idiosyncrasies, an outright phobia of regulation. Regulation was (and is still) seen as an affront in a nation that idolizes liberty and efforts to regulate businesses are often opportunistically called "authoritarian," which enables opponents of regulation to argue that such measures are the beginning of a slippery slope that leads directly back to King George III and the inherent injustice of Europe's monarchies.[66]

America's business elite enthusiastically supports a reading of history in which resistance to regulation and the glories of the free market create a uniquely competitive and thus creative business environment and, more importantly, that this is *the* key ingredient to the American success story. Although the free market does, in many cases, support and encourage competitive innovation, this is not why America was a land of opportunity, but rather, it was the exploitation of slaves and then the working class, combined with the fact that the United States is a huge, resource rich nation, that created the many American success stories still celebrated in schools and in patriotic explorations of American history.

Consider that the second most economically-powerful nation in the world in 2018 is China, but that China, unlike the United States, is not a free-market, capitalist system and so the growth of the Chinese economy, relative to other nations, cannot be explained as a product of the inherent superiority of capitalism. Like the United States, China is a large, resource rich nation in which politicians and a cadre of elites exploit the poor and working class. This comparison thus shows that initial wealth, in terms of resources, and the willingness to exploit labor are among the most important ingredients for achieving economic dominance on a global scale. The United States, like China, has always had a wealth of physical resources and a population of laborers who could be exploited by a relatively small elite and thus, both nations emerged as the most powerful economic forces in the world.

As American companies began importing Chinese laborers into the west, economic competition between those laborers and poor white workers inspired a vitriolic anti-Chinese movement. The true villains in this long-lasting racial feud were the companies that hired immigrant laborers. The Central Pacific Railroad company, for instance, shifted to Chinese laborers because they were unable to attract a sufficient white workforce, but this was because the company did not want to pay wages or benefits sufficient to make the jobs they were offering lucrative or even sustainable. A pro-business critic might argue that railroad executive Charles Crocker was simply making smart business decisions, operating in the best interests of his company and ultimately all the workers that depended on his company, by doing his best to make the company profitable. Consider however, that Crocker died with a *personal* net worth of $20 million, the equivalent of nearly half a billion in 2018, and it's easy to imagine that the $40 per month the company was offering to white workers was (in the least judgmental terms) exploitative.

Like the Irish of the same period and Mexican migrants in 2018, Chinese coolies were accused of "stealing" jobs that would otherwise go to white workers. This belief pervaded anti-Chinese sentiment throughout the nineteenth and early twentieth centuries. In 1905, as the controversy

surrounding Chinese immigration had become a federal issue, President Theodore Roosevelt stated in a speech that Chinese immigrants were undesirable because of the low wages they were willing to accept and the conditions in which they were willing to live.[67]

Consider the implications Roosevelt's assertion, that a class of people so desperate for opportunity that they were willing to live in squalid conditions (necessitated by their low wages) to accept unsustainable pay, work longer hours, and to endure racism, prejudice, and sometimes violence, were to blame for the plight of America's working class, and *not* the companies that chose low-cost indentured servants to white workers or the government that refused to anger corporate lobbyists and campaign contributors to regulate those same businesses.

Were the Chinese really willing to accept the conditions and paltry pay offered to them in the United States? In many cases, yes, but Chinese workers also staged the largest labor strike in the nineteenth century, when, on June 25, 1867, as many as 5,000 workers from the Central Pacific Railroad went on strike to protest low wages and long hours. The specific demands from the strikers including a raise in wages from $31 to $40 per month, an 8-hour workday, less time in the tunnels and working on other especially dangerous jobs, and the elimination of the "right to whip them or restrain them" from seeking other employment. In essence: basic workers' or human rights. Crocker refused to negotiate and instead cut off all food and water from the workers until they gave up.[68] The strike would seem to demonstrate that, contrary to the popular stereotype, Chinese coolies weren't at all satisfied with the plight they needed to endure to get their feet in the door, and many likely found the experience of American immigration lacking considerably from the myths they'd heard abroad.

The Dehumanization Machine

Chinese laborers helped build the American west. They played a major role in founding cities across the Pacific Coast, and the legacy of these early enclaves of Chinese immigrants is still present in the nation's Chinatowns, created as Chinese immigrants (excluded from white society of the day) founded their own neighborhoods for mutual protection and cooperation.[69] For most of U.S. history, however, the role of the Chinese in American history and in the westward expansion, in particular, was relegated to a few obligatory paragraphs in every standard text on history. The fullness and richness of the Chinese contribution was often overlooked. Not only were Chinese laborers essential to the railroad, but the entire culture of the western United States is tied to Chinese immigration. Chinese immigrants, for instance, were largely responsible for building the famous Sonoma wineries in California, until the growing racism of the region's white residents essentially pushed the laborers out of wine country, and largely erased their contribution from history.[70]

In this article from *Medium*, author Jeffrey Bolognese discusses some of the reasons that Chinese laborers were so essential to the completion of the transcontinental railroad.

Doyers Street in 1898, still the center of New York City's Chinatown, via Wikimedia Commons

3 REASONS WHY CHINESE WORKERS WERE THE MVP'S ON THE TRANSCONTINENTAL RAILROAD

by Jeffrey Bolognese

Medium

Source Document

In the US, May is recognized as Asian American Pacific Islander Heritage Month (AAPIHM). The selection of this month to recognize Asian Americans is linked to one of the greatest engineering achievements of the 19th Century: The completion of the 1,776 mile Transcontinental Railroad on May 10th, 1869. The success of that engineering marvel would not have been possible without the sacrifices of some 10,000–15,000 Chinese immigrants who dug tunnels, built bridges, and laid track from Sacramento, CA to Promontory Summit, UT. The story of how they became part of that chapter of American history and their amazing accomplishments demonstrate that those Chinese workers were true MVP's of the Transcontinental Railroad.

An Unlikely Workforce

The Transcontinental Railroad was built by two companies working from opposite sides of the US with plans to meet in the middle: The Union Pacific began working in Omaha, Nebraska and laid track to the west. The Central Pacific Railroad started in California and worked east. As the work started in 1865, the Central Pacific (CP) had need of 4000 workers for their task. Due to labor shortages, the CP could only manage to hire and retain about ¼ of that number. Most of those workers were Irish immigrants from the East Coast of the US. In an attempt to bolster the workforce, Charles Crocker, who managed construction for the Central Pacific, suggested taking advantage of a largely untapped workforce: Chinese immigrants. Thousands of Chinese had come to California in the 1850's to try and strike it rich in the California gold rush. Like the majority of prospectors, most were unsuccessful and forced to take other jobs to survive.

Crocker's suggestion faced stiff resistance from others on the Central Pacific. Most thought the Chinese to be unreliable workers and not strong enough to handle the hard labor needed to build the railroad. To counter that argument, Charles Crocker was said to have retorted, "the Chinese made the Great Wall, didn't they?" Central Pacific executives reluctantly agreed and brought on a small number of Chinese to replace striking Irish railroad workers. The Chinese proved to be excellent workers, excelling at all jobs. The Central Pacific hired

3 Reasons Why Chinese Workers Were The MVP's on the Transcontinental Railroad
continued

more Chinese and began recruiting even more from mainland China. By 1868 some 12,000 Chinese were on the payroll making up 80% of the Central Pacific's workforce.

Based on those numbers alone, the Chinese were clearly a critical part of building the railroad. But that's only part of the story. Consider these three examples of how those Chinese immigrants showed that they were true MVP's.

1) Tunnelling with Explosives

The route from West to East carved out by the Central Pacific required workers to lay track through the Sierra Nevada mountains. That meant carving grades, building bridges, and blasting tunnels. In all, they dug 11 tunnels through the mountains, enduring harsh conditions, backbreaking work, and fierce winter storms that left 18 feet of snow on the summits. Digging through the granite mountains required use of explosives which were mainly handled by the Chinese workers. At times, workers were lowered down the sheer mountain faces on ropes, reportedly in baskets, to drill holes and set explosives. The Chinese workers appeared fearless when confronted by the staggering heights of the mountains or working with dangerous black powder.

Later on, black powder explosives were replaced by more powerful, but much more temperamental, nitroglycerin. The work was hazardous and without the patience and expertise in handling explosives brought by the Chinese workers, traversing the Sierra Nevada mountains would have taken much longer and probably cost the lives of many more workers.

2) Diet and Hygiene

More than 100 years before the term "wellness" entered the corporate vocabulary, Chinese railroad workers demonstrated the value of self-care in creating an efficient workforce. Healthy diet and hygiene practices were a significant factor in the success of the Chinese workers. Unlike the other workers on the Central Pacific, the Chinese had food brought in specifically for them. Their diet was much more varied than the meat, beans and potatoes which was the staple diet of the other workers. The Chinese workers arranged to have items such as rice, dried vegetables, dried oysters, dried abalone fish, pork, poultry, and of course tea, brought to the work site. Because the Chinese workers drank boiled tea instead of untreated water, they were much less susceptible to dysentery and other diseases that were constant threats to the workers

continued

on both routes of the Transcontinental Railroad. Food was so important to the Chinese workers that their cooks were often paid more than typical laborers. The Chinese also had hot water ready for them after their work shifts so that they could bathe and change into clean clothes before their evening meal. Chinese physicians were available at work sites to tend to the physical health of the workers, and Buddhist shrines and joss houses were erected to address spiritual health.

Those "wellness" perks were not free, though. Unlike the white workers whose board was included, the cost of food for the Chinese workers was taken from their already low salaries.

3) Ten Mile Day

One of the most amazing accomplishments of the Central Pacific workers started as a bet. The Union Pacific (the company laying track from the east) and Central Pacific teams had a running competition as to which team could lay the most track in one day. Union Pacific workers laid 6 miles of track in one day, then Central Pacific workers put down 7 miles of track. The Union Pacific next beat that record by ½ mile. Charles Crocker of the Central Pacific made the bold claim that his workers could lay 10 miles of track in one day. Union Pacific Railroad Vice President, Thomas Durant, reportedly wagered $10,000 that they couldn't, and the race was on.

The Central Pacific crews worked with assembly line efficiency. Starting at 7am, eight Irish workers and some 4000 Chinese began laying track. They worked at an astonishing rate of almost one mile an hour. A correspondent for a San Francisco newspaper timed the track layers. He wrote: *"I timed the movement twice and found the speed to be as follows: The first time 240 feet of rail was laid in one minute and twenty seconds; the second time 240 feet was laid in one minute and fifteen seconds. This is about as fast as a leisurely walk and as fast as the early ox teams used to travel over the plains."*

By 7pm they were done, and had set down 10 miles and 56 feet of new track. By the end of that 12 hours, each rail handler had lifted 125 tons of iron.

Nameless Heroes

Sadly the names of the majority of the Central Pacific's Chinese laborers are lost to history as most were not listed in the company's payroll. Only the eight Irish workers from the "Ten Mile Day" were specifically recognized by name. In spite of the fact that over 2/3rds of the Central Pacific work crew were Chinese, they are largely absent from pictures showing the celebration of the "golden spike" completing the Transcontinental Railroad. To add

3 Reasons Why Chinese Workers Were The MVP's on the Transcontinental Railroad
continued

injury to insult, many of those same Chinese workers faced discrimination and hostility as an anti immigration sentiment grew in US. Less than 20 years after the completion of the Transcontinental Railroad, Congress passed the Chinese Exclusion Act of 1882 which effectively barred immigration from China until 1943.

In 2014, the Department of Labor tried to help right some of those wrongs and recognized the contributions of those thousands of Chinese railroad workers by inducting them into their "Hall of Honor." The citation commends the Chinese workers saying, *"Their efforts, which connected the western United States to the eastern United States, laid the foundation for the extraordinary economic prosperity enjoyed by the United States in the years that followed."*

As we recognize the contributions of Asian Americans and Pacific Islanders this month take some time to remember and honor the thousands of Chinese immigrants who risked life and limb to construct an engineering marvel that spanned a continent. Their sacrifices helped to link this country together in a way that has allowed generations of Americans to dream of even greater achievements and lay down their own tracks toward the future. [71]

As competition between white and Chinese laborers intensified, racial stereotypes flourished. It is often difficult for those living in the twenty-first century United States to understand how racism in the past could have been so explicit and overtly hostile. Depictions of Chinese people with extreme exaggerated features, including slit-eyes, buck teeth, and top-tail haircuts dressed in robes were common in the 1800s anti-Chinese movement. Chinese people were sometimes depicted as animalistic, a tactic known as dehumanization, in which a person, organization, or political group promotes a dehumanized impression of another group or individual such as to make it easier for their supporters to openly hate and revile the target without empathy or humanitarian impulses.

The term "race baiting" is used to describe situations in which an individual, company, or political group plays on racial differences, stereotypes, and fears to gain a political advantage. It is a venerable strategy in global politics, predating democracy itself. Newspapers, politicians, and white labor leaders of the era engaged in flagrant race baiting in their effort to turn public opinion against Chinese immigrants. For instance, newspaper journalists of the era called it the "yellow peril" or "yellow terror," in reference to the stereotypically "yellow skinned" depiction of Asian people. Propaganda and political cartoons at the time created associations between the Chinese and rape, sexual perversion, and violence, such as an 1899 editorial cartoon entitled "The Yellow Terror in all his Glory," which depicts a grotesquely racialized Chinese man with a knife in his mouth, a smoking gun in one hand and a smoking torch in the other standing over the body of a bloody white woman. The poster thus implies that the Chinese are violent and savage and further, that they pose a danger to American women, thus playing on the instinctual competitive impulse of white men and their protective instincts vis-à-vis the women of their race.[72]

"Yellow Terror in all its Glory," 1899, shows Qing Dynasty Chinese man, literally armed to the teeth, defeating Western European colonialism, represented by fallen white woman, via Wikimedia Commons

The popular poem turned song known as "The Heathen Chinee," tells the story of a Chinese man cheating two white men in a card game. The "heathen" is called "Ah Sin," which highlights his non-Christian and, therefore, "sinful" heritage while, as a bonus, making fun of the strange, alien names used by the Chinese people. The character Ah Sin is depicted as deceitful, untrustworthy, dishonest, and villainous using his long sleeves and inscrutable face to pull a con on his trusting white opponents. However, a telling stanza in the song reveals the actual motivation behind the racial revulsion that the poem expresses:

_____ *"Then I looked up at Nye,*

And he gazed upon me;

And he rose with a sigh,

And said, "Can this be?

We are ruined by Chinese cheap labor,"—

And he went for that heathen Chinee."[73]

_____

It may be pleasant and comforting for some to imagine that such overt racism is a feature of the past that has no place in modern society. Enter Michigan GOP politician Pete Hoekstra who produced an ad for his 2012 senate race, shown during the Super Bowl in Michigan, in which Chinese-American actress Lisa Chan, pretending to speak to the audience from rural China, praises Hoekstra's Democratic opponent Debbie Stabenow for allegedly weakening the American economy. In the ad, the actress calls Stabenow "Debbie Spend-it-now," in a play on words that lacks both wit and subtlety. Speaking in what many described as an extremely racist stereotypical "Chinese" accent, the Chinese woman claims of Stabenow, "You borrow more and more from us. Your economy get very weak. Ours get very good. We take your jobs."[74]

Chan publicly apologized for her role in the ad, recognizing that she had essentially helped to deepen racist depictions of Asian identity, whereas Hoekstra defended the ad as necessary to highlight Stabenow's bad spending practices. Hoekstra lost the election and was absent from politics for several years but was chosen by Donald Trump to serve as the United States Ambassador to the Netherlands.

CONCLUSION

Historians are unclear how widespread racism against Chinese people was in the 1800s, though posters, songs, and other publications containing racist depictions of Chinese people were common, and this indicates that such beliefs were also not uncommon. The voices of those expressing extreme racial prejudice towards Chinese people are amplified in history by the fact that this lobby gained political power in the era, but this does not necessarily mean that there was not a significant minority who opposed these same policies and attitudes.

DISCUSSION QUESTIONS

- Was the 2012 advertisement by Republican Pete Hoekstra prejudiced? Why or why not?
- Does dehumanization contribute to racial violence? Why or why not?
- What are some examples of the contribution of Chinese immigrants to American culture?
- Is there a modern group of immigrants that face similar attitudes and prejudice as Chinese immigrants in the 1800s? If so, how is the modern situation similar or different?

Works Used

Ambrose, Stephen E. *Nothing Like It in the World: The Men Who Built the Transcontinental Railroad.* New York: Touchstone Books, 2000, pp. 230–242.

Bolognese, Jeff. "3 Reasons Why Chinese Were the MVPs on the Transcontinental Railroad." *Medium.* SASEprints. Society of Asian Scientists and Engineers, 20 May 2016.

Chang, Gordon H. and Shelley Fisher Fishkin. "'The Chinese Helped Build America'." *Forbes.* Forbes Inc. 12 May 2014.

Cottle, Michelle. "Hoekstra Ad Revives Anti-Asian Strain in American Politics." *Newsweek.* Newsweek, LLC. 13 Feb. 2012.

Fuchs, Chris. "150 Years Ago, Chinese Railroad Workers Staged the Era's Largest Labor Strike." *NBC News.* NBC Universal. 21 June 2017.

Gandhi, Lakshmi. "A History Of Indentured Labor Gives 'Coolie' Its Sting." *NPR.* National Public Radio. 25 Nov. 2013.

Goyette, Braden. "How Racism Created America's Chinatowns." *Huffington Post.* Huffington Post. 6 Dec. 2017.

Harte, Bret. "The Heathen Chinee" (formerly "Plain Language from Truthful James."). The Overland Monthly Magazine. (Sept. 1879). *Mark Twain Library*. University of Virginia.

Hollender, Jeffrey, and David Levine. "Huffpo: The Harms of Regulation Phobia." American Sustainable Business Council, *Huffington Post*. Huffington Post. 2 June 2011.

Lynch, Grace Hwang. "Chinese Laborers Built Sonoma's Wineries. Racist Neighbors Drove Them Out." *NPR*. National Public Radio. 13 July 2017.

Roosevelt, Theodore. *A Square Deal*. Allendale, NJ: The Allendale Press, 1906.

Singh, Minal. "A Chinaman's chance: The immigrant's journey—Eric Liu on race, immigration, and citizenship." *Asian Weekly*. 30 Jan. 2015.

Weiner, Rachel. "Pete Hoekstra's China ad provokes accusations of racism." *The Washington Post*. Washington Post co. 6 Feb. 2012.

THE CHINESE PROBLEM GOES FEDERAL
Racism Becomes Federal Law (1860–1890)

Introduction

This chapter explores the anti-Chinese movement that emerged in the mid-1800s. Whereas, in the previous chapter we discussed how anti-Chinese prejudice and racism motivated violence against Chinese communities, in the 1870s and 1880s state governments began addressing the issue with new legislation designed to restrict or reduce Chinese immigration. Some of these laws conflicted with constitutional law and raised concerns involving the balance of power between the states and the federal government. The anti-Chinese lobby then became more powerful in Congress, leading to federal efforts to address the issue.

The source for this chapter is the 1882 Chinese Exclusion Act, marketed to the American people as a temporary 10-year ban on the import of Chinese laborers. The ban was temporary, rather than permanent, because the nation's treaties with China prohibited a permanent ban but allowed temporary restrictions. The Chinese government objected to the ban, but the anti-Chinese movement had support across economic and political lines and so held sway over the legislature. As a result, Chinese Exclusion was not only adopted but was later extended and finally made permanent, leading to more than 60 years of legal prohibitions against Chinese immigration.

Topics covered in this chapter include:
- Westward expansion
- Racial prejudice
- Anti-Asian prejudice
- The Transcontinental Railroad
- Income inequality
- Labor rights
- Unauthorized immigration

- The Fourteenth Amendment
- U.S.-Sino Foreign Relations
- Rutherford B. Hayes Administration
- Abraham Lincoln Administration

This Chapter Discusses the Following Source Document:
"Transcript of the Chinese Exclusion Act (1882)." *Our Documents*.
   The U.S. National Archives. 2018.

The Chinese Problem Goes Federal
Racism Becomes Federal Law (1860–1890)

In the late 1800s, tensions between low-wage white workers and Chinese workers in the American west became the nation's most controversial political issue. Race-baiting politicians seized on prejudices in the white working class to propel their political careers and the anti-Chinese sentiment sweeping through the west thus began to dictate public policy at the federal level.

California Legislates Racial Tension

Legislative efforts to restrict Chinese immigration began in the California State Government, with the 1850 Foreign Miner's Tax, which charged a $20 per month fee to miners of foreign descent who wished to mine gold or silver in the state. The law was intended to discourage Chinese laborers from gold mining, but was poorly written, applying the tax to all foreign-born miners. Thus, protests from Irish, English, and other foreign-born white miners resulted in the law being abandoned, but recreated in 1852 in an altered form, taxing all those who could not, in principle, become naturalized citizens, which, at the time applied to the Chinese (as well as foreign-born Africans and Mexicans). The law was in effect until 1870, though it no longer applied to Africans after the Civil War. However, the law wasn't necessary for most of that time, as the majority of Chinese miners were run out of California's mining territory by vigilante groups of white nativists in the 1860s.[75]

In 1852, the same year that the new foreign miner's tax was enacted, a series of anti-Chinese riots in the city of Yuma forced out some 20,000 Chinese miners who had been working in the area. In her book, *Driven Out: The Forgotten War Against Chinese Americans*, historian Jean Pfaelzer writes of this period in American history:

_____ *"...the white miners drank, gambled, and condemned the capitalists, shipowners, and merchants who profited by transporting or hiring Chinese laborers. But closer at hand were the Chinese themselves."*
_____

Of the riots that targeted the miners, she writes:

_____ *"In Sonora, harassing the local Chinese had become a "traditional sport." White miners rushed the Chinese camps at midnight, firing pistols to wake the sleeping miners and plundering their tents and cabins. They looted a large Chinese claim along the Yuba River, set fire to the building, and declared themselves new owners by right of possession. The legal system didn't blink; a few white friends of the Chinese tried to bring a lawsuit against the vigilantes, but the Chinese were not allowed to testify and it failed."*[76]
_____

By the 1860s, vigilante attacks and abuse had driven Chinese miners from all but the least desirable mining claims across much of California. However, a new problem was developing as wealthy industrialists were beginning to recognize the economic benefit of shipping in Chinese laborers to work on the railroads. To protect the interests of "free white labor," the California state government passed the Anti-Coolie Act of 1862.

The California Anti-Coolie act attempted to discourage Chinese immigration through a new tax, known as the Chinese Police Tax, which charged any person of the "Mongolian race, of the age of eighteen years and upwards..." a tax of $2.50 per month to hold a business license of any kind in the state. Interestingly, the law exempted Chinese involved exclu-

sively in the manufacture of sugar, rice, coffee, and tea, thus attempting to avoid angering agriculturalists who depended on Chinese labor, while targeting Chinese entrepreneurs and those who worked in contested fields, such as railroad labor and mining. The law was thus carefully worded to specifically prohibit Chinese people from owning their own businesses or participating in businesses that appealed to white laborers, but not from being involved in other businesses in which white labor had little interest.[77]

By the 1860s, as America entered the Civil War and the Union was struggling to maintain the support of citizens in the Western Territories, federal politicians got on board with the anti-Chinese movement even though the issue was, at best, a minor priority for East Coast Americans. In 1862, with the Civil War underway, Congress courted the continued support of conservative nativists in the West by adopting their own version of the Anti-Coolie act, known as "An Act to prohibit the 'Coolie Trade' by American Citizens in American Vessels." The law specifically targeted shipowners who brought Chinese laborers to the United States, thereby attempting to cut off the supply of foreign labor and convince native companies to return to white laborers, and, therefore, answer the concerns of the white-labor movement in the west.

> _____ *"Be it enacted by the Senate and House of Representatives of the Unites States of America in Congress assembled, That no citizen or citizens of the United States, or foreigner coming into or residing within the same shall, for himself or for any other person whatsoever, either as master, factor, owner, or otherwise, build, equip, load, or otherwise prepare, any ship or vessel, or any steamship or steam-vessel, registered, enrolled on licenses, in the United States, or any port within the same, for the*

> *purpose of producing from China, or from any port or place therein, or from any other port or place the inhabitants or subjects of China, known as 'coolies,' to be transported to any foreign country, port, or place whatever, to be disposed of, or sold, or transferred, for any term of years or for any time whatever, as servants or apprentices, or to be held to service or labor."* [78]

Reason Rises but Racism Wins

In the wake of the Civil War, the federal government briefly lost its taste for prohibiting Chinese immigration. China and the United States had long had a tense relationship, especially after the Opium Wars of the 1850s and 60s, during which time U.S. policy towards the nation bordered on openly hostile. Persecution of Chinese immigrants eroded relations further and when, in 1861, President Lincoln appointed Anson Burlingame as the U.S. envoy to China's Qing Empire, Burlingame took the opportunity to try a new, more diplomatic and cooperative approach with China. In many ways, Burlingame's friendly and productive negotiations abroad contrasted with the often-violent Chinese-American relationship back home. This is because the U.S. government was essentially caught between the need for productive international trade with nations like China, on one hand, and the increasingly violent anti-Chinese movement on the West Coast on the other.

In the wake of the Civil War, with the union struggling to grow the nation's economy after the loss of the nation's slave labor population, Burlingame convinced Congress to temporarily abandon the anti-Chinese political movement in favor of a stronger diplomatic relationship. The Burlingame or Burlingame-Seward Treaty of 1868 gave the United States a special and very lucrative trade arrangement, with each named as the other's

The San Francisco Call demonstrates the strong sentiment against Chinese immigrants, Library of Congress, via Wikimedia Commons

"Most Favored Nation" (MFN) for trade, but with the controversial agreement that neither nation would restrict immigration from members of the other.

The Burlingame-Seward Treaty angered conservative nativists who were using public racism against the Chinese as leverage for their political careers. Burlingame, for his part, having spent time in China, had developed an affinity for Chinese culture and a far more nuanced and realistic view of the Chinese people as a whole. To the angry white nativists at home, whose view of China had been colored by the propagandistic rhetoric of the day, the treaty was a betrayal.[79]

In retrospect, Burlingame's treaty with China was well ahead of its time. The bureaucrats of the Qing Empire were so impressed with his diplomacy that he was given an honorary rank in the empire after his untimely death in 1870, when he was not yet 50 years old. The Burlingame Treaty made things worse in some ways, as it encouraged Chinese immigration and thus exacerbated tensions between whites and Chinese on the west coast. Conservatives began gaining power in the legislature, after the return of southern nativists, and pushed for changes to the Burlingame Treaty, but it took years for these changes to be realized.[80]

In many ways, the anti-Chinese movement of the late 1800s was America's most successful white nationalist movement after slavery. With more and more pressure on the federal government to do something about Chinese labor competition and other claims of unsavory behavior, federal legislators were in a bind, with national interests on one hand and nativist sentiment on the other. Congress attempted to ban Chinese immigration in the 1870s, but the bill was rejected by President Rutherford B. Hayes on the basis that Congress could not create a law that violated international treaties. In 1880, the United States renegotiated the Burlingame Treaty through U.S. diplomat James Burrill Angell. The Angell Treaty of 1880 (formally known as the Treaty Regulating Immigration from China)

gave the United States the right to *temporarily limit* or *suspend* immigration, but not the power to prohibit immigration.

The Angell treaty gave anti-immigration ideologues the power that they needed and, in 1882, Congress passed the Chinese Exclusion Act, which suspended immigration of Chinese laborers for 10 years. It was the first act in American history to place broad limits on immigration and among the most overtly racist laws ever passed by the American Congress.

THE CHINESE EXCLUSION ACT
Source Document Excerpt

Be it enacted by the Senate and House of Representatives of the United States of America in Congress assembled, That from and after the expiration of ninety days next after the passage of this act, and until the expiration of ten years next after the passage of this act, the coming of Chinese laborers to the United States be, and the same is hereby, suspended; and during such suspension it shall not be lawful for any Chinese laborer to come, or having so come after the expiration of said ninety days to remain within the United States.

SEC. 2. That the master of any vessel who shall knowingly bring within the United States on such vessel, and land or permit to be landed, any Chinese laborer, from any foreign port or place, shall be deemed guilty of a misdemeanor, and on conviction thereof shall be punished by a fine of not more than five hundred dollars for each and every such Chinese laborer so brought, and may be also imprisoned for a term not exceeding one year.

SEC. 3. That the two foregoing sections shall not apply to Chinese laborers who were in the United States on the seventeenth day of November, eighteen hundred and eighty, or who shall have come into the same before the expiration of ninety days next after the passage of this act, and who shall produce to such master before going on board such vessel, and shall produce to the collector of the port in the United States at which such vessel shall arrive, the evidence hereinafter in this act required of his being one of the laborers in this section mentioned; nor shall the two foregoing sections apply to the case of any master whose vessel, being bound to a port not within the United States, shall come within the jurisdiction of the United States by reason of being in distress or in stress of weather, or touching at any port of the United States on its voyage to any

The Chinese Exclusion Act
continued

foreign port or place: Provided, That all Chinese laborers brought on such vessel shall depart with the vessel on leaving port.

SEC. 4. That for the purpose of properly identifying Chinese laborers who were in the United States on the seventeenth day of November eighteen hundred and eighty, or who shall have come into the same before the expiration of ninety days next after the passage of this act, and in order to furnish them with the proper evidence of their right to go from and come to the United States of their free will and accord, as provided by the treaty between the United States and China dated November seventeenth, eighteen hundred and eighty, the collector of customs of the district from which any such Chinese laborer shall depart from the United States shall, in person or by deputy, go on board each vessel having on board any such Chinese laborers and cleared or about to sail from his district for a foreign port, and on such vessel make a list of all such Chinese laborers, which shall be entered in registry-books to be kept for that purpose, in which shall be stated the name, age, occupation, last place of residence, physical marks of peculiarities, and all facts necessary for the identification of each of such Chinese laborers, which books shall be safely kept in the custom-house;

and every such Chinese laborer so departing from the United States shall be entitled to, and shall receive, free of any charge or cost upon application therefor, from the collector or his deputy, at the time such list is taken, a certificate, signed by the collector or his deputy and attested by his seal of office, in such form as the Secretary of the Treasury shall prescribe, which certificate shall contain a statement of the name, age, occupation, last place of residence, persona description, and facts of identification of the Chinese laborer to whom the certificate is issued, corresponding with the said list and registry in all particulars. In case any Chinese laborer after having received such certificate shall leave such vessel before her departure he shall deliver his certificate to the master of the vessel, and if such Chinese laborer shall fail to return to such vessel before her departure from port the certificate shall be delivered by the master to the collector of customs for cancellation. The certificate herein provided for shall entitle the Chinese laborer to whom the same is issued to return to and re-enter the United States upon producing and delivering the same to the collector of customs of the district at which such Chinese laborer shall seek to re-enter; and upon delivery of such certificate by such Chinese laborer to the collector of customs at the time of re-entry in the

continued

United States said collector shall cause the same to be filed in the custom-house anti duly canceled.

SEC. 5. That any Chinese laborer mentioned in section four of this act being in the United States, and desiring to depart from the United States by land, shall have the right to demand and receive, free of charge or cost, a certificate of identification similar to that provided for in section four of this act to be issued to such Chinese laborers as may desire to leave the United States by water; and it is hereby made the duty of the collector of customs of the district next adjoining the foreign country to which said Chinese laborer desires to go to issue such certificate, free of charge or cost, upon application by such Chinese laborer, and to enter the same upon registry-books to be kept by him for the purpose, as provided for in section four of this act.

SEC. 6. That in order to the faithful execution of articles one and two of the treaty in this act before mentioned, every Chinese person other than a laborer who may be entitled by said treaty and this act to come within the United States, and who shall be about to come to the United States, shall be identified as so entitled by the Chinese Government in each case, such identity to be evidenced by a certificate issued under the authority of said government, which certificate shall be in the English language or (if not in the English language) accompanied by a translation into English, stating such right to come, and which certificate shall state the name, title or official rank, if any, the age, height, and all physical peculiarities, former and present occupation or profession, and place of residence in China of the person to whom the certificate is issued and that such person is entitled, conformably to the treaty in this act mentioned to come within the United States. Such certificate shall be prima-facie evidence of the fact set forth therein, and shall be produced to the collector of customs, or his deputy, of the port in the district in the United States at which the person named therein shall arrive.[81]

The burgeoning friendship between the United States and China engendered during the 1850s ended with the Chinese Exclusion Act of 1882. The Chinese government considered the act an insult, but American politicians of the era were either believers in the prejudiced rhetoric themselves, or too indebted to the anti-Chinese lobby to be swayed by international objections. Ten years later, with the same sentiment still pervasive, Congress renewed the prohibition again and even expanded it to apply to Hawaii and the Philippines. Later Chinese Exclusion was simply made permanent. There were anti-American boycotts in China that lasted for five months in the early 1900s, after the prohibition of immigrants to the Philippines and Hawaii.[82] All told, exclusion lasted for nearly a century, and Chinese–U.S. relations did not improve markedly during this time.

A Lonely Win for Equal Rights

Chinese prejudice also had one important repercussion that became a major milestone for those who value equal rights. In 1886, the U.S. Supreme Court heard the case of *Yick Wo v. Hopkins* regarding a California law that prohibited laundromats from occupying wooden buildings. The city had 320 laundries, 310 of which were in wooden buildings and 240 of which were owned by Chinese immigrants. Sheriff Peter Hopkins of San Francisco, however, only targeted Chinese laundry owners and did not apply the law to the 79 white males who owned laundries in wooden buildings as well. A laundry owner named Lee Yick led a group of Chinese entrepreneurs who sued the state. The state courts backed the Sheriff, including the State Supreme Court, but Lee pressed the case on, reaching the U.S. Supreme Court in 1886.[83] The U.S. Supreme Court ruled that the law had been applied in violation of the Fourteenth Amendment guaranteeing equal protection and thus struck down the California law.

This victory was a major moment in Supreme Court history, establishing an extremely important precedent regarding the application of the Fourteenth Amendment with regard to both immigrants and individuals of different races and genders. The case brought by Lee is, therefore, studied as part of the history of constitutional law and equal protection. In an ironic historical twist, the case is known as *Yick Wo v. Hopkins* because the courts in California and the Sheriff believed that the primary plaintiff's

name was the same as the name of his business, Yick Wo Laundry, when, in fact, the man's name was actually *Lee Yick*.

Cartoon depicting the unfair attempt by California law to shut down Chinese laundries. The Supreme Court decided, in 1886, that the law was in violation of the 14th Amendment, via Wikimedia Commons

CONCLUSION

U.S.–Chinese relations remain a source of controversy in the twenty-first century as the two nations compete for economic dominance. Public opinion polls taken in 2017 indicate that more than half of Americans have a negative view of China as a nation, but that the perception of China has been gradually improving in the twenty-first century. Though there were no public opinion polls measuring attitudes about Chinese immigration in the 1880s, the Chinese Exclusion Act had majority support in Congress. Some supported the Chinese Exclusion Act out of the belief that doing so would protect native-born workers, but racial prejudice was always at the root of the movement. There were no similar efforts to prohibit Mexican or Irish immigration, for instance, though these groups of immigrants were also willing to work for lower wages and so competed with native-born laborers for jobs on the railroads and in America's factories and farms.

DISCUSSION QUESTIONS

■ Was the Chinese Exclusion Act of 1882 based on racial prejudice? Explain.

■ How did anti-Chinese prejudice lead to a new civil rights precedent in the Yick Wo case?

■ Why was the Chinese Exclusion Act of 1882 a temporary law?

■ Are any modern political movements similar to the anti-Chinese movement of the 1800s? Explain.

Works Used

"An Act to prohibit the 'Coolie Trade' by American Citizens in American Vessels." *LOC*. Library of Congress. Thirty-Seventh Congress, Session II. 1862. 2018. PDF.

Arnesen, Eric. *Encyclopedia of U.S. Labor and Working-Class History, Volume 1*. New York: Routledge P, 2007.

"California's Anti-Coolie Act of 1862." *SDSU*. San Diego State University. Department of Political Science. 2016.

"Chinese Immigration and the Chinese Exclusion Acts." *Department of State*. Office of the Historian.

Jue, Stanton. "Anson Burlingame, an American Diplomat." *UNC*. American Diplomacy. University of North Carolina, Chapel Hill. September 2011.

Pfaelzer, Jean. *Driven Out: The Forgotten War Against Chinese Americans*. Berkeley, CA: U of California P, 2008.

"The Burlingame-Seward Treaty, 1868." *U.S. Department of State*. Office of the Historian. Milestones. 2016.

"The Strange Case of the Chinese Laundry." *Thirteen*. Freedom: A History of the U.S. PBS. 2002.

"Transcript of the Chinese Exclusion Act (1882)." *Our Documents*. The U.S. National Archives. 2018.

Introduction

While the previous two chapters demonstrated how the anti-Chinese movement began and spread and how this resulted in the first federal legislation restriction immigration based on race, this chapter looks at how the anti-Chinese movement continued to play a major role in shaping immigration policy after Chinese exclusion was adopted as federal law. As state governments attempted to address the anti-Chinese movement demands by establishing new state laws to discourage Chinese migration, such efforts were controversial because they impacted the federal government's diplomatic arrangements.

The source for this chapter is a 2012 *Slate Magazine* article by journalist Paul A. Kramer, "The Case of the 22 Lewd Chinese Women," exploring the history and legacy of the Supreme Court case of *Chy Lung v. Freeman*. The case involved a California state law that allowed state immigration authorities to impose a monetary penalty on ships transporting Chinese women suspected of prostitution. One of the primary concerns regarding state-efforts to tax ships carrying immigrants was that such laws affected the economic relationship between two nations and thus had potential diplomatic consequences. This was one of the primary motivations for the decision, in 1891, to grant sole power to regulate immigration to the federal, rather than the state governments.

Topics covered in this chapter include:
- State's rights
- Foreign Commerce Law
- Anti-Chinese sentiment
- Racial prejudice
- Federal immigration authority
- United States Supreme Court cases

This Chapter Discusses the Following Source Document:
Kramer, Paul A. "The Case of the 22 Lewd Chinese Women." *Slate*.
   The Slate Group. 23 Apr. 2012.

Centralizing Immigration Policy
The Birth of the INS (1824–1891)

The late 1800s was a transformative time in America. The post-Civil War economy was booming as the Industrial Revolution reached its peak in America's cities. Meanwhile, the effects of the Homestead Act (1862) and other programs meant to encourage westward migration had born lucrative fruit, and the vast western frontier created a new source of work, wealth, and growth for the nation's economy. This period, known as the Gilded Age, was a time of prosperity for the wealthy, white elite who owned the vast share of American wealth and this same economic boom led to what has been called the "golden age of mass migration."[84]

Rapid industrial growth created a serious need for laborers and America's business leaders actively courted immigrants to fill this need. This sparked tension with white nativists who believed the benefits of American growth should be conserved for "real" Americans (Anglo-Americans). The push and pull—demand for immigrant labor versus nativist resistance—made it clear as America entered the late 1880s that a new approach to immigration policy was becoming necessary.

Challenging State Authority

Throughout American history, there have been many key debates and social/political controversies in which the balance of power between the federal government and the states was a central factor. In the 2010s, issues like gun rights/control, the legality of various types of recreational substances, and abortion law reflect the push and pull between federal and state governments. Supporters of states' rights typically argue that state and local governments are more responsive to the immediate needs and will of the populace and that the federal government is too removed to effectively legislate on regional issues. This argument has logical merit in that the federal government must be responsible to the broader needs

Angel Island Immigration Station in California, c. 1915, by J.D. Givens, Library of Congress

of the public and so cannot as readily pass laws or remove laws pertaining to regional concerns. When it comes to immigration issues, states that serve as primary ports for immigrants, like New York, California, and Louisiana, have different needs than the general public. Thus, there have always been legislators, lobbyists, and immigration advocates who believe the states can legislative more effectively on immigration than the federal government.

Problems with state laws arise when a state or other local government bends to the will of the public in such a way as to create a policy that has broader implications for national commerce, or laws regarding rights, citizenship, and privileges. Until the 1880s, the federal government's primary role in immigration policy was in setting the rules for naturalization. Beyond that, it was the states and state laws that determined the logistical and legal processes involved in immigration. This meant that coastal states, like San Francisco and New York, were the primary agents for determining how immigrants would be filtered into the nation. Two U.S. Supreme Court cases in the 1870s helped demonstrate the problems with the state-oriented approach.

In the 1875 case of *Henderson v. Mayor of New York*, the British owners of the steamship *Ethiopia* sued the state of New York over a law that required shipmasters to provide a monetary guarantee on passengers

brought to the state. The law passed in 1824 under the title, "An Act concerning passengers in vessels coming to the Port of New-York."[85] The Supreme Court ruled in the case, that the tax imposed on foreign ships constituted the "regulation of foreign commerce," which is a power given exclusively to the federal government via the U.S. Constitution, and thus the law was invalidated.

The port tax law enacted by the state of New York was an effort to limit immigration by making it prohibitively expensive for shipowners to bring immigrants to the state. With a huge population of immigrants at the time, the chief issue in New York concerned the poor, and especially nonwhite poor, who some felt would become wards of the state, leeching resources and tax monies contributed by American workers. This is, in fact, still one of the biggest arguments against allowing immigrants, especially the poor and economic refugees, into the United States. On the plus side, for the city and state of New York, monetary penalties levied against ships wishing to dock and transport passengers would provide a tidy sum for the state. The law was ruled unconstitutional not because of why the law was enacted, but solely because it constituted a commercial penalty on foreign individuals and shipmasters and so effected the broader foreign commerce of the nation.[86]

The *Henderson v. Mayor of New York* case was a blow to states hoping to levy taxes on ships to discourage immigration, but it was the case of *Chy Lung v. Freeman* decided by the Supreme Court that same year, that had the most significant impact on the balance of state and federal power in immigration. The case was similar to *Henderson v. Mayor of New York* in that it involved a California law requiring shipmasters to pay a fine to cover the cost of caring for passengers that would require state support or maintenance.

In the *Chy Lung* case, The California State commissioner of Immigration, Rudolph Piotrowski, inspected an American steamship called the *Japan*, carrying 600 passengers, nearly all of whom were Chinese. Anti-Chinese sentiment was a trend in California at the time as poor-white laborers and their advocates blamed Chinese laborers for taking jobs that might otherwise be available for white Americans. At the time, most Chinese immigrants had been male, but those immigrants were beginning to pay for their wives and children to join them in America.

The State of California did not try to stop this, but had passed a law prohibiting the import of prostitutes or women of low-moral character. After examining the *Japan* in 1874, Piotrowski determined that 22 of the women on board were suspicious, traveling without husbands or children, and thus, Piotrowski ordered the shipmaster to pay a $500 bond per woman to allow them to disembark. The shipmaster refused and Chy Lung and the other women were detained aboard the ship. The media of the era described them as "lewd and debauched," though there was never any proof that any of the women were prostitutes.

In this 2012 article in *Slate* magazine, legal journalist Paul Kramer describes the Chy Lung case in relation to a 2012 Supreme Court case involving a series of 2010 state laws in Arizona intended to prohibit legal immigration into the states that critics believed violated federal protections regarding due process in excess of what federal immigration regulations allowed.

THE CASE OF THE 22 LEWD CHINESE WOMEN

by Paul A. Kramer

Slate Magazine, April 23, 2012

Source Document

When Arizona's notorious immigration law passed two years ago—seemingly out of nowhere—supporters said the measure would merely "mirror" and "assist" federal immigration enforcement. S.B. 1070, which comes before the U. S. Supreme Court this week, in fact contained harsh new criminal penalties against immigrants in an effort to achieve "attrition through enforcement," as the state of Arizona puts it. (Or, as Mitt Romney has called it, self-deportation.) The Supreme Court will consider the four provisions of S.B. 1070 blocked by a federal district judge in July 2010: provisions that require state and local police to try to determine the immigration status of anyone detained if reasonable suspicion exists that they are in the United States illegally; that criminalize an immigrant's failure to register with the federal government and carry a registration card; that make it illegal for undocumented immigrants to work or solicit work; and that permit state and local police to arrest immigrants without warrants if there is probable cause to deport them because they have committed a crime. At stake is whether federal law trumps—and thus invalidates—these contested elements of state law.

Laws like Arizona's have become familiar as Alabama, Georgia, Indiana, South Carolina, and Utah have passed versions of immigration control. At first, these moves by the states were surprising because federal primacy over immigration policy had gone virtually undisputed over the previous 100 years. Go back further in time, however, and you see that American society has gone the way of state-based crackdowns on immigration before. About a century and a half ago, for example, California set out to seal its borders against unwelcome arrivals. As today, the state's immigration code met legal challenges, and the resulting Supreme Court decision helped firmly establish federal authority over immigration. One critical case involved 22 Chinese women who were identified by a California official as "lewd"—i.e., prostitutes—and barred from entering the United States under state law. Its story shows how 19th-century Supreme Court justices came to disapprove mightily of state efforts to regulate immigration.

The Case of the 22 Chinese Women, as it became known, began at 1 p.m. on Monday, Aug. 24, 1874, when California's commissioner of

The Case of the 22 Lewd Chinese Women
continued

immigration, Rudolph Piotrowski (himself an immigrant, from Poland), boarded the American steamer *Japan*, recently docked at San Francisco harbor, and inspected its passengers. The ship had set out from Hong Kong, and nearly all of the 600 people aboard were Chinese. Finding 22 of the female passengers suspicious—because they were traveling without husbands or children and their replies to his questions about their domestic circumstances were "perfectly not satisfactory"—he commanded the ship's master to pay a bond of $500 for each woman to disembark. When the master refused, Piotrowski ordered the women detained onboard and forcibly returned to Hong Kong on the ship's next voyage. They were, he said, "lewd."

No one ever determined whether or not the women were prostitutes, but the answer mattered a great deal. California law required any ship's master transporting "lewd and debauched women" to pay $500 bonds to the commissioner of immigration. As it happened, California officials did not work very hard to distinguish between "lewd and debauched" women and Asian women. The state had spent the previous decades implementing laws that extorted the Chinese with the goal of expelling them. A Foreign Miner's Tax directed at Chinese miners had siphoned off roughly one-half their earnings; a Chinese Police Tax had been charged to most persons "of the Mongolian race." Chinese adults were prohibited from testifying against whites in criminal or civil cases and Chinese children denied access to the state's public schools. The Chinese, it was said, were arriving in overwhelming numbers to take jobs that, however low-paying, back-breaking, and life-threatening, belonged to Americans, and their "alien" language and culture threatened American morality and civilization.

Some anti-Chinese laws proved vulnerable when brought before the California Supreme Court. Meanwhile, by the 1870s the federal government was gathering strength as it re-engineered the South. "States' rights" was, for a long moment anyway, the shrill cry of beaten slaveholders. By the middle of the decade, expanding federal authority and the remaining California laws aimed at driving out or subordinating the Chinese were headed for a direct collision.

The day after Piotrowski ordered the detention of the 22 women, someone—likely Chinese merchants—retained lawyers for them. At the four-day trial in San Francisco, the two sides grappled over state and federal power, the women's rights, and about what a quick inspection through an interpreter

continued

could and could not tell you about an immigrant. The state argued that California had a right to protect itself against "pestilential immorality." The women's lawyers countered that their clients had certificates of transit and rights under the United States' treaty with China, which guaranteed the "inherent and inalienable right of man to change his home and allegiance." Called to the witness stand, the women protested their innocence; many insisted they had husbands, some in China and some in the United States. When a woman named Ah Fook, who told the court she had traveled to San Francisco with her sister in search of sewing work, burst into tears, insisting on her "good intention," the other women joined her, "making the room echo with their cries and screams." The bewildered judge hurriedly left the bench and the women were temporarily removed from the chamber.

As the trial progressed, lewdness proved to be soft legal ground upon which to build a barrier between legal and illegal immigration. A missionary testified that dissolute women in China wore a "flowered, gaudy kind of clothing," but other witnesses disagreed. Judge Robert F. Morrison, noting the looseness of the women's attire, decided that there would be "no indelicacy or impropriety in gazing down their sleeves." The women's lawyer "performed the operation" upon several of them, finding that all wore "some dress of gaudy color and material beneath their outer garment." Lewdness was apparently a matter for eyeball jurisprudence.

Morrison ruled against the women: They were "lewd," he said, and the state's codes legitimately aimed to preserve California's "well-being and safety." But the fight was not over. The women went to the California Supreme Court, which heard the case the following week. They lost again. They sought relief from the Circuit Court for the District of California and here, they triumphed. The court's decision was somewhat startling. In his September 1874 opinion in the case, Justice Stephen Field (a Supreme Court justice who was hearing lower-court cases, a practice at the time), recognized that state governments could invoke "the sacred law of self-defense"—the power to exclude convicts, lepers, those afflicted with incurable disease, and others likely to become public charges. But states' power in this arena was tightly restricted in light of the federal powers. "Whatever outside of the legitimate exercise of this right affects the intercourse of foreigners with our people," he wrote, "their immigration to this country and residence therein, is exclusively within the jurisdiction of the general government, and is not

The Case of the 22 Lewd Chinese Women
continued

subject to state control or interference." Field saw state immigration laws as atavistic holdovers from slavery, when governments had sought to "exclud[e] free negroes from their limits." And he noted that "the most serious consequences," including war, might result from a state government's abuse of foreign nationals. Instead of remaining hostage to codes that protected states from free black people, the law needed to protect the nation from unruly states. Finally, Field argued that the California statute violated the women's rights under the U.S. treaty with China, the recently passed Fourteenth Amendment, and an 1870 federal law that blocked states from imposing "onerous" conditions on a singled-out group of immigrants.

San Francisco's anti-Chinese press was outraged; would the U.S. Supreme Court sustain what the *Examiner* called "the monstrous perversion of law"? Field wondered, too. In announcing his decision, he suggested that the government take the case to the Supreme Court. The case, now called *Chy Lung v. Freeman*, was argued in 1876 and marked the first time that a Chinese litigant appeared before the United States' highest court.

In its ruling in March, the Supreme Court upheld the women's victory, flattening California's statute with language that bordered on the incredulous. For Justice Samuel Miller, who wrote the decision, the law was wrongheaded for three distinct reasons. First, it swelled a petty state official like Piotrowski with an arbitrary and potentially tyrannical power that, in practice, would create "systematic extortion of the grossest kind." As he put it, "Whether a young woman's manners are such as to justify the commissioner in calling her lewd may be made to depend on the sum she will pay for the privilege of landing." Second, the law led to rushed, shallow profiling. "The commissioner has but to go aboard a vessel filled with passengers ignorant of our language and our laws," Miller wrote, "and without trial or hearing or evidence, but from the external appearances of persons with whose former habits he is unfamiliar, to point with his finger … and say to the [ship's] master, 'These are idiots, these are paupers, these are convicted criminals, these are lewd women, and these others are debauched women.'" Finally, the law granted California the license to deflate the United States' global standing or even prompt retaliation. If state governments had the power to deny immigrants entry, the court found, "a single State [could], at her pleasure, embroil us in disastrous quarrels with other nations."

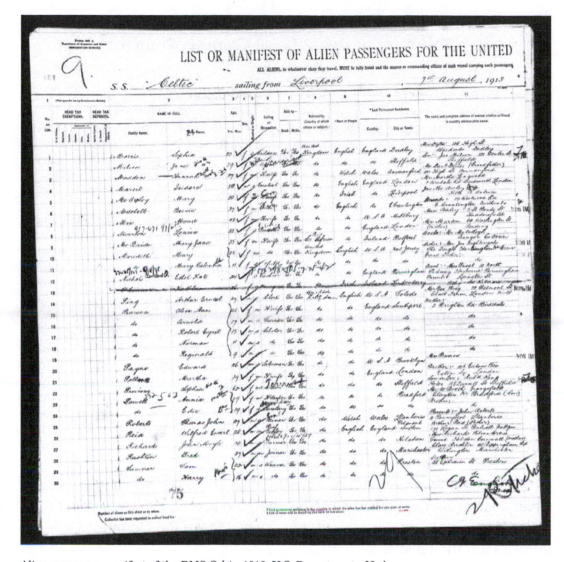

Alien passenger manifest of the *RMS Celtic*, 1913, U.S. Department of Labor

The Case of the 22 Lewd Chinese Women
continued

A legislative recipe for extortion; a capricious exercise of perception and power; a dangerous usurpation of federal control: What was not wrong with California's immigration law? "It is idle to pursue the criticism," Miller concluded. The statute was "in conflict with the Constitution of the United States, and therefore void."

Federal authority over immigration did not guarantee justice. Congress went on to bar the immigration of Chinese laborers in 1882. Still, the Supreme Court's decision in *Chy Lung v. Freeman* stands as a rebuke to Arizona today. Like California's lewdness code, S.B. 1070 calls for hasty estimates by government officials based on "the external appearances of persons," rather than judgments based on "trial or hearing or evidence," as Miller put it. The law extends a state government's power "far beyond what is necessary, or even appropriate" to protect state residents. And it is a state law that impinges on international affairs, "whose enforcement renders the general government liable to just reclamations."

In his 1874 opinion, Justice Field, for his part, warned that the regulation of immigration by state-level authorities would inevitably lead to superficial profiling and the abuse of power. If states could take it upon themselves to deny immigrants the right to enter the country merely on suspicion of law-breaking or immorality, he prophesied, "a door will be opened to all sorts of oppression." One hundred and thirty-eight years later, Arizona and a handful of other states have opened that door. It is now the Supreme Court's job to close it.[87]

In *Chy Lung v. Freeman*, the court ruled against the California state law. Chief Justice Samuel Freeman Miller cited the text of the law, which he called a "...most extraordinary statute," which gave the Commissioner of Immigration the task:

_____ *"to satisfy himself whether or not any passenger who shall arrive in the state by vessels from any foreign port or place (who is not a citizen of the United States) is lunatic, idiotic, deaf, dumb, blind, crippled or infirm, and is not accompanied by*

relatives who are able and willing to support him, or is likely to become a public charge, or has been a pauper in any other country, or is from sickness or disease (existing either at the time of sailing from the port of departure or at the time of his arrival in the state) a public charge, or likely soon to become so, or is a convicted criminal, or a lewd or debauched woman."

To the validity of this statute, Justice Miller said,

"It is hardly possible to conceive a statute more skillfully framed, to place in the hands of a single man the power to prevent entirely vessels engaged in a foreign trade, say with China, from carrying passengers, or to compel them to submit to systematic extortion of the grossest kind.

The commissioner has but to go aboard a vessel filled with passengers ignorant of our language and our laws, and without trial or hearing or evidence, but from the external appearances of persons with whose former habits he is unfamiliar, to point with his finger to twenty, as in this case, or a hundred if he chooses, and say to the master, 'These are idiots, these are paupers, these are convicted criminals, these are lewd women, and these others are debauched women.'"

Miller then weighed in on the balance of powers:

"The passage of laws which concern the admission of citizens and subjects of foreign nations to our shores belongs to Congress, and not to the states.

It has the power to regulate commerce with foreign nations; the responsibility for the character of those regulations and for the manner of their execution belongs solely to the national government. If it be otherwise, a single state can at her pleasure embroil us in disastrous quarrels with other nations."[88]

The Birth of the Immigration and Naturalization Service

The court's ruling that the states did not have the power to use taxes to deter immigration was a major defeat for nativists and anti-immigrant activists. However, these movements held so much sway in the 1880s that the federal government invalidated those two Supreme Court cases in 1882. This came in two forms, first in the form of the Chinese Exclusion Act, which entirely prohibited the immigration of Chinese people and also prohibited the immigration of any individuals who it was believed might become wards of the state. This included idiots (people of low intelligence), insane persons, and former convicts. In addition, any individual whose ticket was paid for by another was barred from entry, as it had been argued that America only wanted those who could pay their own way and so were less likely to need state assistance after their arrival.[89]

However, even after the 1882 Immigration Act and Chinese Exclusion Act reflected the nativist and white nationalist lobbies of the era, conflicts between state and federal policies continued to occur. In 1891, as the legislature debated a new era of immigration reform, it was decided to transfer all power to regulate immigration to federal authorities. This included the power to detain, deport, register, and monitor immigration as a whole and was the beginning of the modern immigration system. The legacy of the 1891 act is manyfold, including the establishment of the Immigration and Naturalization Service (INS) and, the development of two federal immigra-

tion stations, one in New York and one in California, that became symbolic (in very different ways) for America's hallowed role as a home for the world's freedom-seeking refugees.[90]

Early officers of San Francisco's Six Companies, also known as the Chinese Consolidated Benevolent Association, wearing changshans, the traditional power suit, via Wikimedia Commons

CONCLUSION

The Golden Age of Mass Migration saw millions of European immigrants arriving in the United States, fueling the industrial revolution, westward expansion, and building hundreds of new towns and communities across the United States, but also leading to increasing tensions between native-born Americans and foreign-born arrivals. This era thus led both to persistent negative views of immigrants and the broader American pride in the nation's immigrant heritage. After the federal government took control of immigration policy, federal immigration centers were established. These facilities became emblematic of American immigration and ultimately played a role in fostering a more positive view of America's immigration history, though this attitude developed slowly, and immigration policy was more often dominated by those who saw immigration as a threat.

DISCUSSION QUESTIONS

- Did racial prejudice influence the situation that led to the Chy Lung case? Explain.
- Was the federal government justified in taking over control of immigration authority? Why or why not?
- What are the negatives and positives of allowing state laws to affect foreign commerce between two nations?
- Nativists often refer to "real" Americans. How would you define a "real" American? Are there some Americans who do not fit into this group?

Works Used

"1882 Immigration Act." *Library UWB*. University of Washington-Bothell Library. PDF. 2018.

"Chy Lung v. Freeman." *FindLaw*. Thomson Reuters. 2018.

Golden, Ian, Geoffrey Cameron, and Meera Balarajan, *Exceptional People*: *How Migration Shaped Our World and Will Define Our Future*. Princeton UP, 2011, p. 58.

"Henderson v. Mayor of City of New York." *FindLaw*. Thomson Reuters. 2018.

Kramer, Paul A. "The Case of the 22 Lewd Chinese Women." *Slate*. The Slate Group. 23 Apr. 2012.

Laws of the State of New-York, Relating particularly to the City of New-York. New York: Gould and Banks, 1833, pp. 567–68.

"Origins of the Federal Immigration Service." *USCIS*. U.S. Citizenship and Immigration Services, Department of Homeland Security. 4 Feb. 2016.

Introduction

This chapter explores how America's immigration identity changed after a federal immigration law in 1891 placed all immigration authority under the control of the federal government. This resulted in the establishment of the now famous Ellis Island immigration facility in New York harbor and the now infamous Angel Island facility in San Francisco Bay. The Ellis Island facility became the source of cherished stories about the struggles of the nation's European migrants, while Angel Island became a lesser-known focal point for the prevention of illegal Chinese immigration.

The source for this chapter is the poem "The New Colossus," by Jewish-American, New York poet Emma Lazarus. Lazarus, whose poem was written for a fundraiser aimed at helping to pay to have the Statue of Liberty erected, imagined the statue representing a goddess staring out to the ocean, beckoning refugees to the nation's shores and so later became entwined with the nation's legacy as an immigrant nation and a nation that would welcome the oppressed.

Topics covered in this chapter include:
- Federal immigration authority
- Federal immigration centers
- New York immigration culture
- Anti-Chinese sentiment
- Racial prejudice in immigration

This Chapter Discusses the Following Source Document:
"The New Colossus—full text." *NPS*. National Park Service. Statue of Liberty. 3 Aug. 2017.

Symbolizing Immigration
The Federal Immigration Centers (1892–1910)

One of the most lasting legacies of the 1891 Immigration Law that transferred all immigration authority from the states to the federal government was the establishment of two federal immigration stations, the now famous Ellis Island (1892) in New York, and the not-so-well-known Angel Island (1910) in California. These institutions became emblematic of American immigration in different ways. Whereas Ellis Island became enshrined in popular lore as the touchstone of America's embrace of Europe's political refugees, Angel Island represents the legacy of American prejudice and xenophobia—two sides of America's troubled immigration history separated by the body of the nation and representing vastly different views on what immigration means and what role it plays in America's legacy.

The first building on Ellis Island, c. 1892, via Wikimedia Commons

Ellis Island

Ellis Island has long been a landmark not only of immigration into the United States, but also of New York's role in the immigration process. The muddy rocks that became Ellis Island were located above tidal flats comprising the western edge of New York Harbor. It was prime oyster hunting ground in the era before it was developed and had been known as *Kioshk*, or "Gull Island," to the Mohegan Nation because of the concentration of gulls that gathered to feed on the oysters exposed on the rocky flats at low-tide. The colonial government of New Amsterdam called it Oyster Island after purchasing the island from the Mohegan Nation in 1630. In the 1700s, the island changed hands several times and several high-profile executions were held there, including the execution of an infamous pirate whose name has been recorded as "Anderson," using a gibbet, or "gallows tree," and so the island was known, for a time in the 1700s, as Gibbet Island. The island was bought by merchant Samuel Ellis in the 1770s and so, when it was ceded to the federal government in 1808 for use as the site of a new military outpost, Fort Gibson (completed in 1812), the island came to be called Ellis Island.[91]

The federal government decided to use Ellis Island as the site of a new federal immigration station after the Immigration Law of 1891 transferred immigration authority to the federal government. The facility opened on January 1, 1892 and was a modern, innovative structure reportedly built entirely from Georgia pine.

A teenage Irish immigrant named Annie Moore, accompanied by two younger brothers, became the first to be processed at the facility and was thereafter enshrined in the lore of American immigration. Moore was later memorialized by bronze statues both in New York Harbor and in Ireland, and became the subject of many stories, written accounts, songs, and anecdotes of the era. In an article commemorating the historic opening of the facility, the *New York Times* described how the superintendent of

immigration presented the young woman with a $10 gold coin that Moore told *Times* reporters she would keep in honor of that historic moment when she and her brothers reached the promised land. The story of her life, as typically told, was that she and her family traveled west, reaching Texas, where Moore eventually married a wealthy Irish-American farmer. Later researchers discovered that this story was largely inaccurate, because the life of the original Annie Moore had become entangled with another Annie Moore, who was the one who lived in Texas. The original Annie Moore moved to the Lower East Side of Manhattan, married a clerk at a local bakery, had 11 children (five of whom survived to adulthood) and lived in relative poverty before dying of heart failure in 1924, at age 47.[92]

Approximately 12 million immigrants were processed through Ellis Island between 1892 and 1912, but this number does not reflect the actual number of immigrants arriving in the nation. Immigrants arriving in First Class were not required to submit to processing and so those recorded represent the poorer immigrants who had traveled in third-class or steerage aboard the boats that provided Atlantic passage. This fact reflects

Ellis Island in 1905, by A. Coeffler, via Wikimedia Commons

the prevailing philosophy of immigration at the time, that America wanted only self-sufficient immigrants who would provide a boon, rather than a drain, on the American economy and this remained a cornerstone of conservative immigration policy into the twenty-first century.

In 1897, the entire wooden facility at Ellis Island burned to the ground. Though no one was killed, the fire plagued researchers and academics studying immigration for many years as it resulted in the loss of many immigration records stretching back to the 1850s. The facility was rebuilt using far less wood and opened its doors in 1900, processing 2,241 immigrants that year.[93]

Immigration continued to increase during the first decade of the 1900s because of the industrial revolution that peaked in the early 1900s and created a massive nationwide demand for laborers. The busiest year in American immigration history while Ellis Island was in use came in 1907, with 1.25 million immigrants arriving that year. The Ellis Island facility processed 11,747 immigrants on a single day, April 17, 1907, which was the busiest day in the history of the facility that typically saw an average of 5,000 immigrants per day.[94]

Immigrants on bridge from Ellis Island, via Wikimedia Commons

European immigrants came to the United States for a variety of reasons and the experiences of these immigrants became part of the nation's history and mythology. Over time, Ellis Island transformed New York City's view of immigration, becoming a point of pride for many in the city and a symbol of the city and state's essential role in the industrial revolution.

In the 1890s and early 1900s, the Statue of Liberty became a beacon of American immigration, representing the emotional impact of seeing the first glimpse of the statue by the tired and weary passengers who had finally finished their difficult oceanic passage to the new world. However, the statue didn't originally have anything to do with immigrants at all.

The Statue of Liberty was given to the United States by the government of France in 1886 to commemorate both nations' commitment to democracy and rejection of slavery, but this gift also required a significant investment from Americans to help transport and erect the statue. At an 1883 fundraiser for the completion of the Statue of Liberty, an upper-class Jewish New York resident, Emma Lazarus, wrote a poetic myth about the woman that the statue depicted, imaging her as a goddess called the "Mother of Exiles," lighting the way to the poor and tired with her lamp. Lazarus was a proponent of refugee immigration before it became part of America's official immigrant policy, and she was especially concerned for the plight of Russian Jewish immigrants. A mass influx of those same immigrants was one of the main reasons that 1907 was the busiest day in Ellis Island history.[95]

Lines from Lazarus' poem, entitled "The New Colossus," were eventually included in a plaque at the base of the statue: Though not originally intended to symbolize immigration or America's welcoming of refugees, these became the legacies of Ellis Island *and* the Statue of Liberty in America's mythopoetic construction of its history. To be sure, Ellis Island was a focal point for a period in American history that created the "melting pot" of American society, though it was not then, and wouldn't be for many years, a beacon to the poor or yearning from anywhere other than Europe. This legacy is preserved on the other side of the country, in California's Angel Island.

THE NEW COLOSSUS
by Emma Lazarus
Source Document

"Not like the brazen giant of Greek fame,
With conquering limbs astride from land to land;
Here at our sea-washed, sunset gates shall stand
A mighty woman with a torch, whose flame
Is the imprisoned lightning, and her name
Mother of Exiles. From her beacon-hand
Glows world-wide welcome; her mild eyes command
The air-bridged harbor that twin cities frame.
"Keep, ancient lands, your storied pomp!" cries she
With silent lips. "Give me your tired, your poor,
Your huddled masses yearning to breathe free,
The wretched refuse of your teeming shore.
Send these, the homeless, tempest-tost to me,
I lift my lamp beside the golden door!"[96]

Emma Lazarus, by T. Johnson and W. Kurtz, via Wikimedia Commons

Immigrant Detention: The Legacy of Angel Island

The vast influx of immigrants during the golden age of mass migration spawned many stories of American immigrant life. Poems, plays, and songs reflect the difficulties and triumphs of immigrants struggling to escape economic stagnation abroad and attracted by advertisements and stories, some true others heartily exaggerated, about the possibilities in the new world. These stories were propelled by the Industrial Revolution, which created so many jobs that America desperately needed the immigrants who answered the call and came to the United States. Between 1849, when gold

was discovered in California, and 1882, thousands of Chinese immigrants came to the nation known in Chinese lore as "Gold Mountain," hoping to earn their fortunes. The Chinese economic system of the era had little room for mobility and many were born into serfdom. The promises of the "new world's" mineral riches represented the opportunity to escape from the confines of China's imperial castes and for many poor Chinese workers, this was an opportunity that they could not refuse.

As Ellis Island grew into the famed port of harbor and hope for immigrants arriving over the Atlantic, most Chinese migrants arrived in the United States over the Pacific Ocean. For this reason, the west coast had a very different immigrant culture and became the focal point for a national anti-Chinese movement that eventually swept across the country in the 1870s, resulting in the Chinese Exclusion Act of 1882, which banned the immigration of Chinese migrants entirely.

Despite the ban, over the course of the 1890s and early 1900s, hundreds of Chinese migrants still tried to enter the United States. This continued to occur for two reasons; first, because American businesses were still hiring Chinese workers despite the ban, and second, because American immigration law, as it was written, meant that Chinese people born in the United States were citizens, even if they could no longer migrate to the country or become *naturalized* citizens. Therefore, these Chinese-Americans, born into citizenship, were still allowed to bring children and wives from overseas. This led to an immigrant black market in which prospective Chinese immigrants adopted fake names or tried, in other ways, to smuggle themselves in despite the ban. Known as the "paper sons and daughters," these prospective immigrants risked much to immigrate, and the stories of their experiences are an important part of America's immigration history even as, on the other side of the nation, Ellis Island was creating a proud legacy in a vastly different direction.

Chinese exclusion made processing immigrants far more complex in California and, for two decades after the Exclusion Act was made into law, those who came to the west coast were often confined to the ships that brought them, sometimes for months. The Chinese government petitioned the U.S. government to address this human rights issue and the Bureau of Immigration set about creating a new, larger facility for immigrants to the west coast. The result was a facility on the northeastern edge of the largest island in the San Francisco Bay, Angel Island. Like Ellis Island, the choice of an offshore facility was deemed appropriate and favorable as it would enable immigration authorities to quarantine individuals who might have communicable diseases and because the facility was distant enough from the mainland to prevent immigrants from sneaking out of the facility and into San Francisco. The remote location also enabled the government to obscure the morally questionable treatment of non-white immigrants at the facility and made it difficult for relatives or supporters to visit anyone held there.

Angel Island opened in 1910 and, from then to 1940, processed some 175,000 Chinese and 60,000 Japanese immigrants. Once they arrived, men and women were separated and shunted into examination areas where they were told to disrobe. Newcomers were tested for disease, and many were deported for relatively minor ailments including diarrhea, hookworm, or the easily treatable eye disease trachoma. Chinese immigrants were measured by stricter standards, including an interrogation by the Board of Special Inquiry. Interrogations lasted for hours or even days and included questions designed to ferret out those lying about their identities as relatives of native-born Chinese. The facility thus became an internment camp for thousands of Chinese caught between immigration and deportation. Inmates were kept in cramped, unsanitary conditions, and were not allowed outdoors except for short exercise periods in fenced-in yards. Chinese inmates rioted in 1919 to protest the quality of the food, resulting in a modest culinary improvement, but one that was only superficial. In 1922, the Assistant Secretary of Labor for the Immigra-

Arriving immigrants being processed at Ellis Island, by Underwood and Underwood, via Wikimedia Commons

tion Department declared the facility unfit for human habitation, though it continued to operate for twenty more years.[97]

The divergent experiences of Europeans and Chinese immigrants arriving in Ellis Island and Angel Island, respectively, demonstrate two very different aspects of the immigrant experience. The use of Angel Island as an unofficial detention facility for so many years raised many difficult concerns, including the human rights implication of such detention and the complete absence of due process in the way that Chinese immigrants were treated in the United States. It is the failure of both the Chinese government, which helped to create the economic stratification that led to Chinese exodus from the mainland, and the United States, which capitulated to the basest fears of the populace, giving in to race-baiting and xenophobia instead of trying to temper the fears of the masses or to engender greater concern for human rights. Had the general American public known what happened at Angel Island or understood the reasons that so many Chinese were willing to brave the racism they would face in the United States for the mere possibility of elevating theirs and their family's status back home, it is possible that there might have been a stronger, or more rapid, public resistance to the 60 years of Chinese exclusion law.

One of the most visible testaments to the plight of Chinese immigrants between 1910 and 1940 can be seen in thousands of poems written, scrawled, or etched into the wooden walls of the holding cells in which Chinese detainees were kept on Angel Island. The poems, many of which were later translated and preserved, demonstrate the conflicting desires of those Chinese who came to America despite the prohibition and prejudice they knew they would face.

_____ *"There are tens of thousands of poems, composed on these walls.*

They are all cries of complaint and sadness.

The day I am rid of this prison and attain success,

I must remember that this chapter once existed.

In my daily needs, I must be frugal.

Needless extravagance leads youth to ruin.

All my compatriots should please be mindful.

Once you have some real gains, return home early."[98]

CONCLUSION

The establishment of Ellis Island had a major impact on American public opinion about immigrants, as Ellis Island became a focal point for the many myths, legends, and amazing true stories of America's immigrants during the Golden Age of Migration. Although resistance to immigrants remained strong, Ellis Island provided positive images of immigrants to counter the rhetoric of anti-immigration activists. Angel Island, by contrast, was largely ignored during much of its history and, as knowledge of the facility has become more widespread, it represented the legacy of America's often prejudicial attitudes about certain types of immigrants. The establishment of federal immigration centers also provided more focus for U.S. immigration policy, by establishing a sole body, the Immigration and Naturalization Service (INS) to oversee the process. In the early twentieth century, these facilities were used to further a new kind of immigration movement designed to restrict the immigration of "undesirable" people to strengthen the moral, mental, and physical fitness of the population.

DISCUSSION QUESTIONS

■ What is the first symbol of American immigration that occurs to you? Give examples of others.

■ Is immigration part of American identity? Is welcoming immigrants part of the nation's collective values? Explain.

■ How does the poem "The New Colossus" relate to Greek mythology? Explain.

■ Was the treatment of detainees at Angel Island the result of racial prejudice? Explain.

Works Used

"Angel Island Immigrant Journeys." *AIISF*. Angel Island Immigration Station Foundation. 2017.

"Ellis Island History," The Statue of *Liberty—Ellis Island Foundation, Inc.*

Ha, Thu-Huong. "The story behind the Statue of Liberty's unexpected transformation into a beacon for refugees and immigrants." *Quartz*. Quartz Media LLC. 1 Feb. 2017.

Lazarus, Emma. "The New Colossus" (2 Nov. 1883), *NPS*. National Park Service. Statue of Liberty. 31 Jan. 2018.

Roberts, Sam. "Story of the First Through Ellis Island Is Rewritten." *New York Times*. New York Times Co. 14 Sept. 2006.

"U.S. Immigration Station, Angel Island." *NPS*. National Park Service. 2018.

Waxman, Olivia B. "Ellis Island's Busiest Day Ever Was 110 Years Ago. Here's Why." *Time*. Time Inc. 17 Apr. 2017.

Wills, Matthew. "The Curious History of Ellis Island." *Jstor Daily*. ITHAKA. 1 Jan. 2017.

Introduction

This chapter explores the American eugenics movement and its effect on immigration policy. Eugenics was, and is, a pseudoscientific movement based on the idea that different races had different biological qualities and that some races were superior to others. Moreover, eugenicists believe that it was possible to make a better type of person, or a better society, by eliminating undesirable races and people with certain types of "defects," similar to how a rancher or farmer might cultivate larger cattle or sheep by choosing the largest healthiest sheep to produce the next generation. Over the first half of the twentieth century, eugenics theory supplemented, emboldened, and replaced traditional racial prejudice with a seemingly intellectual justification.

American eugenicists supported laws to prohibit the immigration of individuals who possessed what they saw as negative qualities or characteristics, including individuals who were mentally unfit or who had physical infirmities. For instance, eugenicists wanted to prohibit the immigration of persons born blind and deaf as a way to remove or restrict inherited vision or hearing problems from the population. Supporters justified these policies by arguing that such individuals would pose a financial drain on society, and so the nation should only accept immigrants who were able to care for themselves. The source document for this chapter is an article by historian Adam Cohen in a 2017 issue of *Smithsonian Magazine* that demonstrates how the restriction of "undesirable" people manifested in policy in the form of an intelligence test given to immigrants arriving at Ellis Island in the early 1900s.

Topics covered in this chapter include:
- Racial prejudice
- Eugenics
- U.S. Supreme Court Cases
- Treatment of the mentally infirm
- Treatment of the disabled
- Evolutionary theory
- Forced sterilization

This Chapter Discusses the Following Source Document:
Cohen, Adam. "This Jigsaw Puzzle Was Given to Ellis Island Immigrants to Test Their Intelligence." *Smithsonian Magazine.* Smithsonian Institution. May 2017.

The Undesirables
Eugenics and Economics in Immigrant Exclusion Policies (1840–1917)

From the late 1800s through the first half of the 1900s, anti-immigrant rhetoric and activism was focused on keeping undesirables out of the country. Laws produced in the states and later mirrored by federal legislation were designed to prohibit or at least limit the migration of individuals who might constitute an economic drain or pose a danger to American culture or society. Although some exclusion laws were aimed at maintaining economic or political stability, the darkest strain of anti-immigrant thought of the era sought to maintain the quality of the American gene pool by prohibiting individuals of inferior races or those who had some genetic infirmity that might degrade the quality of the nation's biological admixture.

Immigration and Morality

America's first immigration law, the Uniform Rule of Naturalization in 1790, held that any person residing in the United States who was of "good moral character," could become a citizen. The designation "good moral character" is, like the language used in many immigration laws, purposefully imprecise. Denying naturalization to those of poor moral character essentially meant that immigration officials had wide discretion in determining who would be denied access. A person of another race might be denied access, therefore, on the basis that he or she cannot prove acceptable moral standards, thus using morality as justification for racial or political exclusion.

Cartoon showing only one group barred, *Frank Leslie's Illustrated Newspaper*, 1882, via Wikimedia Commons

Homosexuals, polygamists, hermaphrodites, and prostitutes were among those frequently targeted for prohibition under statutes that limited immigration to persons of good moral character. Over time, immigration laws became more explicit, including prohibitions against nebulous characterizations like "vagrancy," "lewdness," and "obscenity," which could also be used to prohibit a wide swath of individuals based entirely on the judgments of immigration officials. The generality of these laws enabled police and politicians to use them as a weapon against the poor and otherwise undesirable without angering the rich or upper-class members of society. For instance, there were around 10,000 prostitutes living in New York City in the 1840s, but the police tended to arrest only those who served lower-class communities and stayed well away from brothels and prostitutes catering to the city's elite.

Life was difficult, but potentially profitable for prostitutes of the nineteenth century. In the book *Law and Disorder*, about the birth of the NYPD, historian Bruce Chadwick's research found that a prostitute might earn the equivalent of $100,000 in modern earnings, but was subject to an exploitative and difficult lifestyle. Women might become prostitutes as early as 12 or 13 years old, and it was not uncommon for a prostitute to sleep with over 100 men per week, sometimes serving a mind-boggling 15 to 20 men in a single hour.[99] In San Francisco, hundreds of prostitutes came to service the men working as miners during the gold rush or building the transcontinental railroad. Then, as now, there was a substantial portion of the American white male population willing to have sex outside of their racial and nationalistic persuasion and so immigrant prostitutes from Asia, Mexico, and South America also came to San Francisco in the mid-1800s. In "When Prostitution Wasn't a Crime: The Fascinating History of Sex Work in America," Melissa Gira Grant recalled Journalist Herbert Asbury wrote that "…by the end of 1852, there was no country in the world that was not represented in San Francisco by at least one prostitute."[100]

Objections to the sex trade were most vehement in San Francisco because of the diversity of the prostitute population. Politicians and moral activists working in the area blamed prostitution on the character of the alien women who had come there to work in the sex trade. In 1854, California adopted its first anti-prostitution law, Ordinance No. 546, which gave police the power to target "Houses of Ill-Fame," within the city limits. Police targeted Mexican and Chinese prostitutes exclusively and this speaks to the actual, hidden motivation behind the law. It was actually Chinese prostitutes who the state was interested in prohibiting, as part of the larger anti-Chinese craze that swept across America in the mid-nineteenth century. Eventually, the state dropped the pretense of trying to fight prostitution, and adopted a new statute in 1866, entitled, "An Act for the Suppression of Chinese Houses of Ill-Fame." One of the prime agents of the law was non-Asian prostitutes, who lobbied against their Chinese ilk.[101]

The American Eugenics Movement

The publication of Charles Darwin's *On the Origin of Species* in 1859 brought about a new era in biology and natural history research and a deeper understanding of the Earth's history. The central premise of Darwin's work was the discovery of evolution by natural selection, a process in which the differential survival and reproduction of organisms, which is a function of how well those organisms were able to cope with their environment, led to the birth of new species.

Since most people in the 1800s (as now) believed that humans were fundamentally superior to other animals, and because few were intellectually capable of understanding evolutionary theory, the meaning of evolution mutated in the popular understanding, resulting in the belief that, over time, natural selection creates *superior* species. In actuality, every species that emerges is *adequate* for survival and is *never* perfect. Every species, including humans, have biological flaws that are sufficient, but not ideal, for daily life. For instance, the spinal column, with its s-shape, evolved to support the weight of animals that spent most of their lives in a horizontal position. However, because humans walk on their legs, the s-shaped spine is turned on its end. This is an imperfect arrangement, though the upright stance provides advantages, such as seeing for longer distances, and freeing the hands to do things that hands do. The upright stance was preserved in evolution even though the spine is not perfected for the upright stance and thus the human design is adequate but not perfect, and this is the reason that human backs fail so often and so painfully.[102]

Over time, environmental conditions change, and the traits needed to survive change as well. Some individuals survive and have more offspring, and this leads to the emergence of altered versions of the species that are also just adequate for survival. Evolution doesn't move up or down or from inferior to superior, but rather simply creates species after species that are all simply, and *only*, adequate for survival. The belief that evolution creates perfection or superiority is a misunderstanding fueled

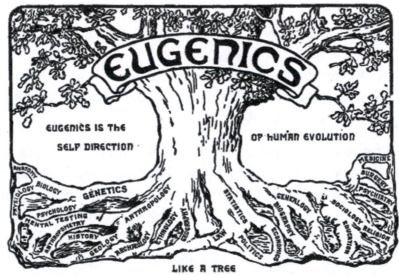

Second International Congress of Eugenics logo, 1921, via Wikimedia Commons

by human's innate desire to see themselves as perfect and superior, and is not based on science. Because humans believed that they were at the top of an evolutionary "ladder," (which is a poor metaphor) it was possible for people to see evolution as a slow march towards biological perfection.

The pseudoscience of "eugenics" was first imagined by English anthropologist and geneticist Francis Galton, who was a cousin to Charles Darwin. Galton wondered, given Darwin's theory of natural selection, if it would be possible for humans to selectively reproduce in such a way as to perfect human talents and capabilities. Would a talented pianist who married and bred with another talented pianist, for instance, produce an offspring whose talent in music was beyond that of either parent? As humans had always found ways of justifying their belief in the superiority of their own race or nationality, eugenics added a frightening scientific dimension to this venerable and prejudicial tradition.

Taking Galton and Darwin's works as their basis, a movement spread across the United States centered on the idea that it was possible to create an ideal human by selectively breeding persons with certain characteristics. Thus, a large number of illegitimate "scientists" emerged publishing papers and books that explained how some races were inferior to others. This type of thinking was then used to "prove" the genetic inferiority of African Americans and Asians and thus to justify segregation, laws against racial miscegenation (inter-racial reproduction), and the exclusion of non-white immigrants from the United States.[103]

California became the center of the American eugenics movement, with groups like the American Eugenics Society and the Galton Society, becoming powerful and respected organizations perceived to be scientific, though they did not practice legitimate scientific research. Groups like these were an enormous force behind the series of immigration laws designed to protect the nation's racial and genetic quality. Eugenicists were crucial to the Chinese Exclusion Act of 1882 and subsequent versions of

Chinese exclusion. They were also a powerful force for racial segregation in the South. Eugenicists were also the primary force behind the laws prohibiting individuals with mental and physical defects from migrating to the United States.

In the 1880s, the U.S. government recognized a variety of mental and behavioral defects and the frequency of these afflictions was measured annually beginning in 1880 and published by the U.S. Census Bureau as the "Defective, Dependent, and Delinquent Classes," or the "3D Schedule." Beginning in 1882, federal law prohibited the immigration of individuals who were blind, deaf, dumb (mute), crippled, bedridden, infirm, insane, or "idiots."

In the 1800s, the term idiot had a different meaning than in the twenty-century; it was used to refer to a certain type of mental health disorder characterized by low intelligence. The idiots fell along a spectrum created through intelligence testing that divided people into one of several categories. Below persons of "normal" intelligence was a class known as "morons," who were above "idiots." The "idiots" were above "imbeciles." Each of these categories also had sub-classifications such that a person could be termed a "middle-grade moron," or a "low-grade idiot."

According to research by Andrea DenHoed, writing in *The New Yorker*,

> *"Morons were considered particularly dangerous: they were smart enough to pass undetected and possibly breed with their superiors."*[104]

The 1882 immigration law specifically prohibited idiots, crippled people, people with diseases and infirmities, and persons who had been diagnosed with insanity. Moderate politicians defended this practice by asserting that such individuals would pose a burden to society, but the eugenics craze of the late 1800s was a major factor, and there were active

lobbyists in the immigration debate pushing for policies that would protect the quality of the American genepool by eliminating defects, disease, and other dysfunctions.

In a 1907 revamp of immigration restrictions, the Federal Government added anyone judged to be "mentally or physically defective" such that they may not be able to earn a living and added the exclusion of "imbeciles" and "feeble-minded persons." Immigration inspectors were thus told to conduct tests to root out any mental abnormality as grounds for exclusion. As more and more undesirable qualities were added to the list, underlying eugenicist influence on immigration policy comes into sharper focus. For instance, a restrictive 1917 iteration of immigration standards listed persons with arthritis, asthma, deafness, deformities, heart disease, poor eyesight, poor physical development, and spinal curvature.

All of this was the product of the American eugenics movement and, in particular, "negative eugenics," a passive eugenics system in which negative qualities were eliminated from the gene pool as a way to improve the entire species. American and European eugenicists went so far as to propose that inferior individuals might not even be subject to the same rights and freedoms as their superior counterparts. For instance, in the 1935 book *Man, the Unknown*, French eugenicist Alexis Carrell wrote:

> *"Indeed, human beings are equal. But individuals are not. The equality of their rights is an illusion. The feeble-minded and the man of genius should not be equal before the law. The stupid, the unintelligent, those who are dispersed, incapable of attention, of effort, have no right to a higher education. It is absurd to give them the same electoral power as the fully developed individuals. Sexes are not equal. To disregard these inequalities is very dangerous. The democratic principle has contributed to the*

collapse of civilization in opposing the development of an elite."[105]

In 1907, the Commissioner General of Immigration described the role of the organization:

_____ *"The exclusion from this country of the morally, mentally, and physically deficient is the principal object to be accomplished by the immigration laws."*[106]

In this article from the May 2017 issue of *Smithsonian Magazine*, journalist Adam Cohen describes immigration practice in the early 1900s and the methods used to detect and exclude the "feeble-minded."

"THIS JIGSAW PUZZLE WAS GIVEN TO ELLIS ISLAND IMMIGRANTS TO TEST THEIR INTELLIGENCE"

by Adam Cohen
Smithsonian Magazine, **May 2017**
Source Document Excerpt

The face puzzle, a box of wooden jigsaw pieces, looks like a child's game, a primitive, flattened-out version of Mr. Potato Head. Start with the biggest piece, a half-inch-thick hunk of wood shaped like a head. Place the others where they belong: the eye-shaped piece, the nose, the mouth and several more that together form an ear. Finish it and you have a profile of a bald man with sharp features smiling a tight little smile.

The wooden puzzle might look like fun, but it was anything but that to the men and women who were once required to solve it. The Feature Profile Test, in the collections of the Smithsonian National Museum of American History, was administered to immigrants at Ellis Island in the early 20th century. Those who failed to assemble it correctly could be labeled "feebleminded" and sent back home.

The Feature Profile Test encapsulates the complex feelings America had toward the immigrants of its time. It was a tool for ushering suitable foreigners into citizenship—

continued

and for turning others away. It constituted an idealistic effort to be fair—while at the same time being cruelly unjust. Yet it represents an almost benign era in American immigration history—because what followed would be far worse.

New York's Ellis Island was, from 1892 to 1954, the nation's main immigration gateway, which some 12 million people passed through. For these new arrivals, who in many cases came from simple rural villages, Ellis Island could be a frightening place—a bedlam of unruly crowds and indecipherable tongues, presided over by grim-faced immigration officers.

Immigrants in the early 1900s were examined for physical and mental illness, questioned about their ability to support themselves financially, and challenged on whether they held radical views. As part of the inquisition, the U.S. Public Health Service administered primitive intelligence tests. "The purpose of our mental measuring scale at Ellis Island," Howard A. Knox explained

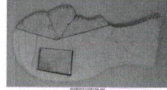

Puzzle intelligence test, Smithsonian Institute

in 1915, "is the sorting out of those immigrants who may, because of their mental make-up, become a burden to the State or who may produce offspring that will require care in prisons, asylums, or other institutions."

It was Knox, a physician, who developed the Feature Profile Test, which he administered from 1912 to 1916. (Knox resigned his post at Ellis Island that year, eventually establishing a practice as a country doctor in New Jersey.) The puzzle represented a progressive reform of sorts. Before it, the public health service measured intelligence with traditional I.Q. tests, whose questions required cultural and linguistic knowledge that many immigrants did not have, causing perfectly intelligent people to test as "imbeciles." The Feature Profile Test relied on more universal knowledge—around the world, noses and ears are in the same places. And it could be "administered with minimal use of language, ideally by use of pantomime alone on the part of both examiner and examinee," notes John T.E.

"This Jigsaw Puzzle Was Given to Ellis Island Immigrants to Test Their Intelligence"
continued

Richardson, author of *Howard Andrew Knox: Pioneer of Intelligence Testing at Ellis Island*.

For all of the democratic impulses behind it, the Feature Profile Test nevertheless could be viewed as an outgrowth of a deplorable ideology. American immigration policy of the time was grounded in eugenics, the pseudoscience of trying to uplift humanity by preventing the "unfit" from having children or, if they lived outside of the country, keep them out.

When Knox administered the Feature Profile Test, the stakes were high, and the conditions far from ideal. Typically, the test-takers had just arrived after a long voyage aboard ship, often in horrific conditions, and they were in a foreign land. They might be sleep-deprived, depressed or ill. And they might never have taken a test before. If they did not complete the puzzle in five minutes, that failure— along with other factors the doctors weighed—could lead to a mother being ripped from her family and shipped back to the Old World. Immigrants were turned back often enough, for a variety of reasons, that Ellis Island earned the nickname "The Island of Tears." Over a fiscal year ending June 30, 1914, nearly one immigrant per 1,000 of the more than one million examined—957 individuals—were deported as mentally defective.

As crude as the puzzle test may seem today, it reflected the belief that healthy immigrants should be admitted. Within a decade, though, anti-immigrant, eugenic and racist forces would persuade Congress to pass the Immigration Act of 1924, which dramatically cut back immigration of Italians, Eastern European Jews and other groups considered undesirable. The immigrants who were shut out of America—including many Jews who would, only a short time later, try to flee the Holocaust—would have gladly taken their chances with Dr. Knox's wooden puzzle.[107]

There are no opinion polls or records that can demonstrate how widespread the belief in eugenics was in the United States in the 1800s and early 1900s. However, that books on eugenics were best-sellers in the American market and hundreds of eugenics articles were published in

magazines and newspapers demonstrates that the idea had significant public support and appeal. Politicians broadened support for this idea by tying their eugenicist theories to economic and class-conflict issues. A politician, therefore, could say that "idiots" and Chinese people should be excluded because they were a burden on society, which was already overburdened and could barely care for its own. This appealed to many people logically and so built support for the eugenics agenda, without having to rely on appeals to racism or xenophobia. Thus, many Americans supported eugenics outright, whereas others unwittingly supported the same policies for different reasons. Jon Saphier, in his book: *High Expectations Teaching: How We Persuade Students to Believe and Act on "Smart Is Something You Can Get"* wrote that in 1995, historian Alan L. Stoskopf summarized the movement this way:

> *"The Eugenics movement was particularly attractive to native-born, white Americans with some education. It addressed many of their anxieties and fears. It also offered them "a rational" way of dealing with those anxieties and fears. Many of these Americans were troubled by the rapid changes that were taking place in the United States in the early 1900s."*[108]

Amazingly, considering how inaccurate and intellectually flawed eugenics theories were later proven as evolutionary science grew more mature, some of the nation's most powerful institutions and intellectuals supported eugenics ideas in the early to mid-1900s. For instance, Harry Laughlin, an American eugenicist working in the early 1900s, testified before Congress regarding immigration in 1924, arguing against the immigration of individuals from parts of Europe supposedly having higher levels of insanity and mental infirmity. In actuality, Laughlin was anti-Semitic, and his arguments were just about prohibiting Jewish immigration, but he was taken seriously at the highest levels of America's political and academic environments.

Laughlin was also instrumental in perhaps the most twisted progeny of the American eugenics movement, the forced sterilization of individuals considered mentally infirm or deficient according to then accepted standards. The first state law regarding mandatory sterilization of the "feeble-minded" was put forward in Michigan in 1897, but was defeated. The first to pass into law was in Indiana in 1907, followed by California and Washington in 1909. Such legislation was still controversial, and there were many who opposed such laws, but belief in eugenics and in the claim that the feeble-minded were a drain on society was so widespread that many of the laws passed. The most famous mandatory sterilization law was adopted in Virginia in 1924, legalizing the forced sterilization of individuals considered intellectually deficient or disabled.

In 1927, the Supreme Court was asked to determine whether the 1924 Virginia law violated the equal protection clause of the Bill of Rights. The controversial case involved Carrie Buck, a Virginia woman labeled "feeble-minded" who challenged the state's efforts to sterilize her. That her challenge alone indicated she was not incapable of intellectual thought might seem obvious to someone living in the twenty-first century, but, even the U.S. Supreme Court did not see it that way in the 1920s. The court ruled that the Virginia law did not violate Buck's constitutional rights, with Chief Justice Oliver Wendell Holmes, Jr., delivering a now infamous majority opinion:

_____ *"We have seen more than once that the public welfare may call upon the best citizens for their lives. It would be strange if it could not call upon those who already sap the strength of the State for these lesser sacrifices, often not felt to be such by those concerned, in order to prevent our being swamped*

with incompetence. It is better for all the world if, instead of waiting to execute degenerate offspring for crime or let them starve for their imbecility, society can prevent those who are manifestly unfit from continuing their kind. The principle that sustains compulsory vaccination is broad enough to cover cutting the Fallopian tubes. Three generations of imbeciles are enough."[109]

Oliver Wendell Holmes, by Harris & Ewing, via Wikimedia Commons

Tragically, between 60 and 70,000 people were subjected to forced sterilization while such laws were in place, with between 7,200 and 8,300 subjected to the practice in Virginia before the law was abolished. For his part in this barbarity, Justice Holmes was resolute in his beliefs. Writing about the issue for Cato Institute in 2011, Trevor Burrus found that Holmes once said to a friend speaking about his career, "One decision that I wrote gave me pleasure, establishing the constitutionality of a law permitting the sterilization of imbeciles."

Historians have since revealed that the sterilization laws were more often used on individuals who were simply seen as delinquent, rather than on individuals who might legitimately have had some form of identifiable mental infirmity. Carrie Buck, who was sterilized by force after Holmes' ruling, was not even mentally disabled. Rather, after having an illegitimate child resulting from being raped by a relative, Buck was labeled as "promiscuous," which was seen as a negative moral quality in Virginia at the time. She was thus labeled "feeble-minded" and sterilized against her will.[110]

In the book *Three Generations, No Imbeciles*, historian Paul Lombardo looks at the history of the sterilization laws, finding that sterilization became a political tool not just for eugenicists, but for others targeting immorality or even misbehavior. In some cases, sterilizations were performed without the person's knowledge and, in other cases, children as young as 10 were sterilized for behavioral issues such as skipping school, or fraternizing with the opposite sex. Sterilization became not simply a tool to root out mental infirmity, but any negative behavioral pattern or rejection of the mainstream Christian morality seen as proper in the community adopting a forced sterilization regime.

World War II, and the atrocities committed by the Nazi Party in their quest to create a perfect racial society, was the beginning of the end for the legitimacy of the American eugenics movement, but not of racially-based immigration policies. Nor did eugenics actually die so much as go into hiding. The forced sterilization laws created by the eugenics movement also refused to go peacefully and the Virginia law that inspired the Supreme Court Case wasn't abolished until 1979. In the late 1800s, as the eugenics movement inspired immigration policies based on preserving a desirable racial and genetic mixture, another anti-Immigration movement was brewing, one that brought the inequities of America's capitalist system and the worker's rights movement to the forefront of the modern stage.

CONCLUSION

Historians have found compelling evidence to suggest that many, if not most, white Americans in the late 1800s and early 1900s believed in eugenics. Prominent eugenicists of the period regularly testified in Congress and had a major impact on legislation, and many legislators and presidential advisors were members of eugenics societies. The eugenics movement was also key in another set of controversial policies that permitted state governments to sterilize individuals seen as feeble-minded or otherwise infirm, though historians have found that sterilization laws were used to punish individuals who violated social rules, such as women seen as "promiscuous." Though eugenics is no longer a prime driver in U.S. policy, the eugenics movement still exists in the United States in 2018 and is now represented through web-based communities like *American Renaissance* and *Storm Front*.

DISCUSSION QUESTIONS

- Was the Supreme Court justified in the case of *Buck v. Virginia*? Why or why not?
- Is it permissible for the government to prohibit the immigration of individuals with physical or mental disabilities? Why or why not?
- Is the term "idiot" used in the same way today that it was in the early 1900s? How is the modern usage different or similar?
- Was eugenics an inherently racist belief system? Explain.

Works Used

Black, Edwin. "Eugenics and the Nazis—the California connection." *SF GATE*. Hearst Communication, Inc. 9 Nov. 2003.

Brignell, Victoria. "When America believed in eugenics." *New Statesman*. Progressive Digital Media. 10 Dec. 2010.

"*Buck v. Bell*." *Cornell Law School*. Legal Information Institute [LII] Supreme Court. 2018.

Burrus, Trevor. "One Generation of Oliver Wendell Holmes, Jr. Is Enough." *Cato At Liberty*. Cato Institute. 23 June 2011.

Carrell, Alexis. *Man, the Unknown*. New York: Harper & Brothers Publishers, 1935.

Chadwick, Bruce. "When New York City was the prostitution capital of the US." *New York Post*. NYP Holdings, Inc. 22 Apr. 2017.

Chan, Sucheng. *Entry Denied: Exclusion and the Chinese Community in America, 1882–1943,* Philadelphia, Temple UP, 1991.

Cohen, Adam. "This Jigsaw Puzzle Was Given to Ellis Island Immigrants to Test Their Intelligence." *Smithsonian Magazine*. Smithsonian Institution. May 2017.

DenHoed, Andrea. "The Forgotten Lessons of the American Eugenics Movement." *New Yorker*. Conde Nast. 27 Apr. 2016.

Dunn, Rob. "The Top Ten Daily Consequences of Having Evolved." *Smithsonian*. Smithsonian Institution. 19 Nov. 2010.

Grant, Melissa Gira. "When Prostitution Wasn't a Crime: The Fascinating History of Sex Work in America." *Alternet*. Alternet. 18 Feb. 2013.

Lee, Jonathan H.X. *Chinese Americans: The History and Culture of a People.* Santa Barbara, CA: ABC–CLIO. 2015.

Saphier, Jon. *High Expectations Teaching: How We Persuade Students to Believe and Act on "Smart Is Something You Can Get".* Thousand Oaks, CA: Corwin, 2017.

Introduction

As the eugenicists were influencing immigration restrictions against other races and members of "undesirable" groups, a new movement emerged in the early 1900s based on the idea of restricting the immigration of people who held "anti-American" ideological views. Like the Alien and Sedition Acts of 1798 discussed in Chapter 3, the Anarchist Exclusion Act of 1903 was an attempt to ban individuals representing dangerous leftist ideologies, and specifically, anarchism, or the belief that societies function better without leaders or traditional governments. This movement was precipitated by the third assassination of an American president, the shooting of William McKinley in 1901, and was the second time in history that national security concerns motivated a broader immigration reform movement.

The source for this chapter is an excerpt of the 1903 immigration act, also known as the Anarchist Exclusion Act, which banned the immigration of a wide range of individuals seen as posing a threat to American culture or society. This not only included anarchists, but also an increasingly broad list of persons with various kinds of illnesses or diseases, or who were poor or economically unstable, and so were considered a potential burden on society. In 1904, the Anarchist Exclusion Act became the subject of a Supreme Court case when British academic John Turner was refused entrance to the United States because of his support for anarchist philosophy.

Topics covered in this chapter include:
- Anarchism
- The Labor and Worker's Rights Movement
- National Security
- Income inequality
- The Haymarket Square Riot
- The Assassination of William McKinley

The War on Anarchy
The Anarchist Exclusion and *Turner v. Williams* (1886–1917)

The assassination of William McKinley in 1901 threw Congress and the American people into the grips of an overblown panic about the dangers of radical immigrants. Two years later, a new immigration law was adopted, focusing on prohibiting anarchists and other groups and classes of individuals seen as posing a potential danger to the United States. This was essentially an early twentieth-century version of the same fears motivating post-9/11 efforts to prohibit the immigration of Muslims out of fear that most of, if not all, Muslims might be potential terrorists.

The Anti-Capitalist Movement

In a 2000 article in *Slate Magazine*, journalist David Greenberg explains that "anarchism," as a political movement, is not, as popular imagination holds, the exaltation of chaos, but rather a political ideology that rejects the need for laws or leaders:

> *"Anarchists don't preach pandemonium. They have a relatively coherent (if fanciful) ideology, which holds that if people in society organize themselves without rulers or laws, natural human instincts for altruism and cooperation will bring about greater freedom, happiness, and equality."*[111]

Anarchism, in the 1800s, was a legitimate strain of left-wing thought in the United States. Representing themselves with black flags (to contrast themselves from the red-flag waving Communists), the anarchists took part in a wave of anti-Capitalist protests that swept through the United States in the late 1800s in response to growing inequity, poverty, joblessness, and homelessness. Acting sometimes together, but more often independently, anarchists, socialists, and communists in this era were the political branches of the nation's labor movement. Each of these strains of political philosophy gave voice, structure, and ideological heft to the long sense of injustice felt by America's working class.

In the monarchies of Europe, people were typically born into a certain caste or class that determined access to the benefits of society. There was little room for movement between the economic classes, and the policies of the monarchy functioned so as to maintain and support the power of the elite class. Those born into lower classes were, therefore, burdened with virtually all the work, without even the possibility of advancing to the next level of the income spectrum. It is, perhaps, not difficult to see why so many monarchies end in revolution, and sometimes with the mass execution of the aristocracy.

Escaping the British monarchy, the founders of the United States sought, in framing the foundational documents and laws of the nation, to prevent the United States from ever becoming an authoritarian system like that they struggled to escape. Fundamental to this effort was the absolute rejection of the kind of centralized power that existed in the monarchies of Europe. Thus, the persistence of the state's rights lobby and the general phobia in U.S. popular thought about centralized authority.

On an economic level, capitalism was the answer to monarchic inequity, a system in which individuals or companies owned the means of production and distribution, funding their own growth and operations with their profits. In capitalist societies, anyone can potentially go all the way from the bottom to the top of society, if they can find a way to manipulate the system. Capitalists, therefore, see themselves as part of a meritocracy where those with merit achieve, and those without merit fail or remain in place.

Of course, capitalist systems don't really work this way. This is because the elite aristocracy and businesses maximize their own profits at the

expense of those at the lowest levels, who perform most of the work and accrue the lowest level of benefit for their work. For instance, according to a 2017 report from the U.S. Federal Reserve, the richest 1 percent of American families control 38.6 percent of the country's wealth, nearly twice as much as the bottom 90 percent. Meanwhile the purchasing power of the bottom levels of American society has either remained unchanged since the 1980s, or has actually fallen during this time.[112]

"COME UNTO ME, YE OPPREST!"

Cartoon showing anarchist attempting to destroy the Statue of Liberty, 1919, via Wikimedia Commons

Though U.S. politicians frequently promise they will address this situation, it does not typically happen because the economic elite has an outsized impact on policy. Therefore, after Donald Trump entered office as president, the predominantly Republican legislature passed a tax bill that will maintain and deepen the current distribution of wealth. A study of the tax bill by the Joint Committee on Taxation, for instance, found that individuals in households earning more than $75,000 per year will be paying $16 billion less than they currently do over the next decade, while the federal government will be taking in $3.4 billion more from households earning less than this.[113] This is how the nation's elite, by protecting themselves and their income, keep the system the same and prevent efforts to redistribute wealth. Thus, even though capitalism provides the *possibility* of rising from "rags to riches," it is still a system in which the poor do most of the work and accrue the least reward.

Socialism is another method of trying to address the inequities of the aristocratic system. In Communist systems, for instance, the people collectively own the means of production and distribution and the govern-

General nativity and race of head of family.	Number of selected families.a	Average family income.	Number of families having a total income—					
			Under $300.b	$300 and under $500.	$500 and under $750.	$750 and under $1,000.	$1,000 and under $1,500.	$1,500 or over.
Native-born of native father:								
White........................	1,070	$865	24	120	339	295	223	69
Negro........................	124	517	5	64	41	11	2	1
Native-born of foreign father, by race of father:								
Bohemian and Moravian.....	24	621	....	8	10	6	....	....
Canadian, French...........	27	892	1	3	10	6	3	4
Canadian, Other............	7	(c)	....	....	1	4	1	1
Cuban......................	1	(c)	....	....	....	....	1	....
Dutch......................	15	698	....	2	8	4	1	....
English....................	42	842	....	10	10	9	10	3
German.....................	213	894	4	21	73	59	34	22
Irish......................	292	926	5	41	76	65	75	30
Lithuanian.................	1	(c)	....	....	....	1	....	....
Norwegian..................	1	(c)	....	....	1	....	....	....
Polish.....................	77	681	1	22	27	16	11	....
Scotch.....................	3	(c)	1	....	1	1	....	....
Slovak.....................	1	(c)	....	1	....	....	....	....
Welsh......................	3	(c)	....	2	....	....	1	....
Total..................	707	866	12	110	217	171	137	60
Total native-born..........	1,901	843	41	294	597	477	362	130
Foreign-born:								
Armenian...................	101	730	9	19	30	27	11	....
Bohemian and Moravian.....	437	773	16	82	165	90	58	26
Brava......................	29	562	....	13	13	2	1	....
Bulgarian..................	7	(c)	1	2	4	....	....	....
Canadian, French...........	477	903	9	43	159	133	90	43
Croatian...................	560	702	58	154	174	85	54	35
Cuban......................	43	881	1	1	8	19	13	1
Danish.....................	19	830	1	1	6	5	6	....
Dutch......................	129	772	2	19	52	30	19	7
English....................	425	956	8	42	111	104	113	47
Finnish....................	137	781	3	6	51	64	7	6
Flemish....................	79	798	6	8	26	25	9	5
French.....................	130	757	5	30	38	31	21	5
German.....................	887	878	21	113	264	231	183	75
Greek......................	49	632	8	17	12	3	6	3
Hebrew.....................	600	655	60	161	237	116	66	20
Irish......................	675	999	14	68	177	153	156	107
Italian, North.............	583	657	53	159	201	104	47	19
Italian, South.............	1,350	569	229	474	394	165	97	21
Japanese...................	1	(c)	....	....	....	....	1	....
Lithuanian.................	763	636	53	200	311	129	52	18
Magyar.....................	880	611	111	235	303	131	63	17
Mexican....................	39	472	3	24	9	2	1	....
Norwegian..................	26	1,015	....	1	2	10	12	1
Polish.....................	2,038	595	215	682	713	252	132	44
Portuguese.................	258	790	6	66	85	49	28	24
Roumanian..................	69	805	7	13	23	10	8	8
Russian....................	76	494	5	39	24	7	1	....
Ruthenian..................	571	569	57	190	222	70	26	6
Scotch.....................	123	1,142	....	12	27	19	37	28
Servian....................	59	465	19	20	12	4	3	1
Slovak.....................	1,243	552	135	410	423	176	85	14
Slovenian..................	163	684	10	51	57	25	12	8
Spanish....................	37	1,099	....	1	4	9	20	3
Swedish....................	460	974	4	25	131	147	103	50
Syrian.....................	142	594	25	42	41	17	13	4
Welsh......................	90	893	6	10	25	13	27	9
Total..................	13,825	704	1,160	3,433	4,534	2,457	1,581	660
Grand total................	15,726	721	1,201	3,727	5,131	2,934	1,943	790

Chart showing income by native and foreign born in the United States at the turn of the 20th century, Internet Archive Book Images, via Wikimedia Commons

ment, which is supposed to represent the people, and control all industry with the stated purpose of distributing the wealth and benefits of citizenship as equally as possible among the people. In practice, the central governments in communist societies tend to be controlled by individuals who use socialist rhetoric to win popular support, but then still place the wealth of society primarily in the hands of an elite with connections to the ruling party or governmental dynasty.

The Communist Party of China, for instance, began as a revolution against the centuries old imperial system that placed the vast majority of Chinese people into a "servant" class. In practice, China's communist party became an authoritarian regime that violently controls public or political dissent to maintain power. The socialist theories upon which China's communism is based are not authoritarian, and the fact that China's government became authoritarian is the result of human flaws and selfishness, with those in power fighting to stay in power at the expense of everyone else.

Anarchists reject both the communist and capitalist systems and see both as fundamentally flawed and exploitative. They argue, instead, that, because power corrupts and governments exploit the people, the best way forward is to abandon leaders and governments entirely. In 2018, anarchism is not a major player in America's left-wing activism. However, in the 1800s, when extreme poverty and unemployment inspired anti-capitalist protests against the government, anarchism was a more influential philosophy.

The Crimes of the Anarchists

In 1867, federal law made the 8-hour workday mandatory. However, few factories or other businesses adhered to the law, and many workers were still working long hours, typically for unsustainable pay. This led to a series of mass protests in the 1870s and 80s. In May of 1886, 40,000-80,000 workers, organized by the Federation of Organized Trades and

Labor Unions, gathered in Chicago for a strike against the factories and to ask the federal government to enforce the 8-hour workday law.

On May 3, police fought with a small group of picketing workers at the McCormick Reaper Plant at Western and Blue Island Avenues, and three of the workers were killed by the officers. In reaction to this incident, labor leaders organized a meeting at Haymarket Square. More than 20,000 laborers were invited, but fears of police violence were high, and only 2,000 showed up. The meeting was peaceful but, just as it was ending, the police showed up and started rousting the last 200 or so who were still there. Fighting broke out and, in the chaos, someone threw a stick of dynamite. One police officer was killed by the explosion, but six others were killed in the fighting that followed, along with at least four workers. Police never discovered who threw the dynamite, or why anyone there had dynamite to throw in the first place, and the incident made national news as the Haymarket Riot.

In the wake of the event, a nationwide state of emergency was called. In Chicago, police rounded up labor leaders, anarchists, socialists, and communists without warrants or due process. Police arrested eight people in connection with the event, but did so using questionable evidence. Four were hanged, one committed suicide, and three were imprisoned for life. Historians now believe that the police investigation was corrupt, aimed at finding individuals to blame for the incident in the absence of legitimate suspects. In 1893, Governor John P. Altgeld pardoned three of the eight individuals arrested who were still imprisoned and called the entire affair a "miscarriage of justice."[114] The Haymarket trial lasted for two months and, by the end, press coverage and political rhetoric painted the entire anarchist movement as a dangerous radical movement intent on overthrowing the government.

Mckinley and His Critics
President William McKinley was in office from 1897 to 1901. McKinley

presided over the Spanish-American War, which led to the U.S. acqui-
sition of Puerto Rico, Guam, and the Philippines and his presidency is
often seen as the beginning of the Progressive Era, which was a political
period in which the nation's progressive political party—at that time the
Republican Party—controlled Congress for nearly 30 years. In later years,
the Republicans would become the nation's conservative party, and the
Democratic Party would become the more progressive of the two parties.

McKinley's election came in the midst of a depression that followed the
Panic of 1893. This was a severe economic depression linked to the
collapse of the nation's two largest employers, the Philadelphia and
Reading Railroad (P&R) and the National Cordage Company, both part of
the railroad industry. It was essentially the result of an overgrown railroad
industry propped up by government financing that had, for years, fueled
massive waves of European immigration and had unwittingly created

an industry too big to support over the
long term. When the companies failed,
unemployment spiked, the panic disrupted the stock market, and banks started
calling their loans. Over fifteen thousand
businesses closed over the course of the
depression, which was blamed largely on
President Grover Cleveland and the Democrats. Thus, McKinley won the election
of 1897, with the largest Republican gains
in history, and this, more than anything,
led to the Progressive Era and the dominance of the Republicans.

When McKinley came into office, widespread unemployment and poverty made
the economy the primary political contro-

President McKinley, back to camera, greeting well-
wishers at a reception in the Temple of Music, Buffalo,
New York, right before the attack that ended his life,
by Johnson Collection, Library of Congress

versy and the primary issue of McKinley's presidency. The depression was the reason for the spread of labor rights protests and strikes that continued throughout McKinley's presidency. Then, on September 7, 1901, an anarchist named Leon Czolgosz shot President William McKinley in the stomach at the World's Fair in Buffalo, New York. McKinley underwent emergency surgery but developed blood poisoning and died eight days later.

Czolgosz was born in Detroit, the son of Polish and German immigrants, and worked in factories and mills for most of his young life. He had become a labor activist in his early twenties and took an interest in socialism. At a labor rights meeting, Czolgosz learned about the theories of well-known American anarchist Emma Goldman, who was one of the organizers of the nation's anarchist movement. Czolgosz was an outsider and was considered something of a radical to others in the anarchist and socialist communities. He had been heard talking about plots and conspiracies and had become increasingly withdrawn from his friends and family. Later investigations found he had been treated for a "mental breakdown" in 1898 and that some friends felt he never really recovered. After shooting McKinley, Czolgosz confessed, saying, "I have done my duty. I did not feel that one man should have so much service, and another man should have none."

According to the *Buffalo Express* article on September 7, the public was enraged and certainly would have killed Czolgosz at the scene if not for the rapid police response.

_____ *"'Murder! Assassin! Lynch him! Hang him!' yelled the thousands, and men, women and children tore at the guards, sprang at the horses and clutched the whirling wheels of the carriage. Nieman (the alias that Czolgosz was using) huddled in the back in the corner concealed by the bodies of two detectives."*[115]

The Anti-Anarchist Movement

The assassination of President McKinley, by a professed anarchist and son of immigrants, was the fuel for a fiery new era of immigration reform. It is typical for citizens of a nation to react to an attack on their nation or one of their leaders with passionate calls for nationalism and isolationism. Research on the period indicates that McKinley was only a mildly popular president entering his second term, but his assassination inspired sympathy and anger from the people, and this anger was stoked by politicians and journalist.

It is, on one hand, easy to see how the public could be led to believe that anarchists were a threat. A political philosophy that rejects the need for *any* government would seem logically to lend itself to trying to *overthrow* or destabilize a government. For certain, anarchism like any other political or philosophical ideology can *become* violent. Christianity is not an inherently violent religion and yet the early colonists of the United States used their faith as justification for the many atrocities enacted on indigenous Americans. Buddhism is also a peaceful faith that was once used as justification for a massive campaign to eradicate Taoists in China. Anarchism rejects government and yet, in the United States, anarchists were workers' rights activ-

FOURTH TIME IS THE CHARM

Despite the fact that William McKinley was the third U.S. president killed in office, the United States government still didn't have a dedicated presidential protection division until after he was assassinated. At the time, the U.S. Secret Service already existed and was in charge of presidential security, but was also in charge of tracking down counterfeiters for the U.S. Treasury Department. After McKinley was killed, Congress decided that the Secret Service should focus solely on protecting the president, the presidential family, and visitors to the White House. President Theodore Roosevelt, who replaced McKinley, was, therefore, the first U.S. President to have a full Secret Service detail.[116]

ists and not violent radicals.

The Haymarket Riot was a fight between labor activists and police, not the result of an anti-government plot. The assassination of McKinley was the action of a lonely, isolated, and most likely mentally-ill man who wanted to make a statement about the very real injustices he observed against those in his social class and likely also wanted to find meaning for himself in a world that left him feeling isolated. He was not part of a group that advocated the violent overthrow of the U.S. government, and his actions were not the product of the ideologies he gravitated to as a struggling young worker coping with poverty.

Records of how the story was covered can be found in *Public Opinion,* a weekly publication that collected op-ed and news articles from national newspapers and journals. Commentary published in the September 12 issue provides an example of how the popular press fanned the flames of anti-immigrant and anti-anarchist anger:

> _____ *"...Whether President McKinley lives or dies, the American people should learn certain lessons at his bedside," says the Boston Transcript, "That anarchy is hating as it is hateful; that it will strike as readily at the freely chosen executive of a republic as at a kind king ruling by 'divine right'; that anarchism must be suppressed here; that liberty of speech is not license to instigate assault; and that finally charity of construction of act and motive in public men is a safeguard against the fierceness of political passion that before now has been known to consume not alone men but governments."* _____

From the *Baltimore Herald*, the publication (*Public Opinion*, Vol. 34) quotes:

"This is a land of freedom, but it is not an asylum for assassins. Those who are banded together for the commission of murder are outlaws, and the most sacred human right—that of self-protection—demands that they be suppressed. Their presence in this country is a cancerous growth upon our republican form of government, and the most drastic measures used to remove them will not be too severe."[117]

Leon Frank Czolgosz, American anarchist who assassinated President McKinley in 1901, via Wikimedia Commons

The anti-anarchist movement was the result of converging factors. First, memories of the Haymarket Riot, ten years earlier, had already created the impression among the public that the anarchists were the most dangerous faction of America's left-wing activists. Second, the growth of labor unions threatened the traditional power structure in America, and a powerful commercial and political lobby emerged to oppose the labor movement. These forces converged after McKinley's death, targeting the anarchists and the labor activists, in general, as enemies of the states.

Fighting an *ideal* proved difficult, however, and the movement resulted in little actual change or significant action. Police arrested known anarchist leaders but were unable to bring charges in most cases because the anarchists were not criminals and not actually plotting to do much besides hold meetings where they lambasted the government for its very real failures. Emma Goldman, the well-known anarchist theorist who had been a hero to Czolgosz, was arrested after McKinley's assassination and accused of taking part. She was, in fact, the most famous figure arrested during the anti-anarchist movement of the early 1900s, and her arrest was widely covered in the popular press. However, police found no evidence that Goldman had known or been involved with the assassin, and so she was released.

The Anarchist Exclusion Act

Essentially, opportunistic politicians and the media drummed McKinley's murder, arguably an isolated event by a lonely, troubled man, into a public panic, reminding the citizenry about the Haymarket Square Riot, and using the two events in concert, though unrelated in reality, to suggest that anarchists, as a group, posed a threat to the United States. Now, because anarchism was more popular in Eastern Europe than in the United States at the time, and there really was no specific domestic target to use as a scapegoat for this controversy, legislators decided on a simple course of action, and added anarchists to the growing list of groups prohibited from immigrating to the United States. The entirety of the Anarchist Exclusion Act comes down to a single new clause in the latest iteration of an otherwise unremarkable immigration bill. This new clause explicitly prohibited the following classes:

ANARCHIST EXCLUSION ACT
Source Document Excerpt

"All idiots, insane persons, epileptics, and persons who have been insane within five years previous; persons who have had two or more attacks of insanity at any time previously; paupers; persons likely to become a public charge; professional beggars; persons afflicted with a loathsome or with a dangerous contagious disease; persons who have been convicted of a felony or other crime or misdemeanor involving moral turpitude; polygamists, anarchists, or persons who believe in or advocate the overthrow by force or violence of the Government of the United States or of all government or of all forms of law…"[118]

The 1903 law was the first time that Congress tried to prohibit the immigration of individuals from a certain ideological group. It would not be the last, however, as there would be a movement to prohibit communist immigration during the Cold War (as well as individuals from Communist countries) and there was a movement to limit or prohibit the immigration of Muslims after the 9/11 terrorist attacks on the United States. President Donald Trump's proposal to suspend immigration from Muslim-majority countries, the controversial "Muslim Ban" of 2017–18, is the most recent policy proposal in that same vein. Then, as in the present, when simple solutions weren't readily apparent for complex national problems, politicians sometimes opted for stoking isolationist or prejudiced impulses towards a similar but ultimately unrelated issue.

The Anarchist Exclusion Act was controversial at the time, as many critics questioned whether prohibiting the immigration of otherwise eligible individuals based solely on their political beliefs violated constitutional protections. The U.S. Constitution does guarantee freedom of thought, association, and religion and guarantees that the benefits of citizenship cannot be taken from an individual because of these characteristics.

In 1904 the Supreme Court heard the case of John Turner, a well-known British philosopher, workers' rights activist, anarchist, and socialist. Turner was the first to be deported under the 1903 act, and was detained on Ellis Island. Turner filed suit and was later released on $5000 bail. While awaiting the Supreme Court trial, Turner traveled and gave speeches to workers' rights and anarchist groups across in several cities. In an article on the incident in the *New York Times*, Turner was quoted describing his experience:

> *"I had a fine time in the pen at Ellis Island. I was stared at as if I was a wild animal in the iron-barred cage nine feet by six. A Government representing 80,000,000 seem[ed] to be actually*

frightened at a small, insignificant man like myself, and I felt complimented."[119]

Though Turner's counsel argued that he was a philosophical anarchist and so not even among the category of people that the law sought to prohibit, the court ruled that the constitutional principles that Turner wished to evoke to, did not apply to him, because he was not a citizen of the United States. Though there were no major speeches or often quoted clauses in the court's opinion, the ultimate result of the *Turner v. Williams* case was that the Supreme Court affirmed that the government had the right to exclude aliens from constitutional protections. The prohibition of anarchists was not unconstitutional as the Constitution applied only to the rights of citizens.[120]

Freedom of thought, religion, and association are often considered core American values and yet, the high-minded principles of American society are a leading priority only so long as Americans feel safe and secure. When the scale tips, and concern for safety and national security gains more momentum, many Americans are willing to set aside principles like due process, equal protection, freedom of speech, freedom of religion, and freedom of association, when politicians tell them that doing so will enable the government to keep them safe.

The Anarchist Exclusion Act of 1903 addressed a problem that didn't actually exist. Although dangerous anarchist movements have existed in history, the U.S. anarchist movement was a social justice movement, not a violent political group. The fact that so many Americans worried over the imagined threat demonstrates how influential fear-based politics and group thinking can be. By contrast, income inequality and the plight of workers, was a far greater threat to the American people (and remains so). The leftist "radicals" targeted at the turn of the century were key players in the workers' rights movement, and the campaign to delegitimize

anarchism became a tool that opponents used to dismiss the workers' rights movement itself, calling it the product of anti-American agitation rather than a reflection of a real phenomenon.

Anarchist Exclusion might have been just another footnote in history were it not for the fact that World War I reignited fears of leftist subversion across the nation. Congress again prohibited, in even stronger language, the immigration of anarchists, with the Alien Act of 1918. In 1919, federal agents conducted a series of raids, known as the Palmer Raids, in which they arrested and ultimately deported 248 anarchists and suspected anarchists, including political activist Emma Goldman. Goldman had the misfortune of being an anarchist at the wrong time and her deportation of Russia, a country that espoused Socialist ideals but created an equally unjust system of part-elite aristocrats, was very much a disappointment to a person with Goldman's revolutionary ideals and intellectual abilities. The Anarchist Exclusion Act falls into the tradition of American immigration policies that grew out of national security concerns, but soon those fears were tangled in with racial prejudice again, leading to the beginning of a new era of immigration based on racial engineering and the increasingly desperate task of trying to maintain the nation's existing political and racial hierarchy.

CONCLUSION

It is not widely known how widespread fear of anarchism was in the early 1900s, but historians have found ample evidence in the popular press to show that the assassination of McKinley was met by fear and outrage among the people. Ten years later, as the United States prepared to enter World War I, concerns about dangerous ideologies and philosophies intensified again and the Anarchist Exclusion Act became the focus of an effort to locate and deport anarchists from the United States. Even this effort was largely symbolic, as the anarchist movement was small, though anarchists of the era did play an important role in the labor rights movement. In many ways, fear of anarchism in the early 1900s was similar to fear of radical Islam in the twenty-first century, with some believing that anarchism was an inherently dangerous belief system and so it was better to remove or restrict anarchism rather than risk anarchist violence.

DISCUSSION QUESTIONS

- Are there any modern legislative acts similar to the Anarchist Exclusion Act of 1903?
- Is the assassination of William McKinley similar or different to the modern mass shootings that have occurred in the United States? Explain.
- Is Communism anti-American? Why or why not?
- How did the Panic of 1893 influence the Anarchist Exclusion Act? Explain your position.

Works Used

Adelman, William J. "The Haymarket Affair." *Illinois Labor History*. Illinois Labor History Society. 2016.

"American Affairs: The Attempt upon the President's Life." *Public Opinion*. Public Opinion Company, Vol. 31, p. 324, 1901.

"An Act To regulate the immigration of aliens into the United States." *Library of Congress*. Fifty-Seventh Congress. Sess. II, Chapter 1012. 3 Mar. 1903.

"Anarchist Turner Tells of His Fight." *New York Times*. New York Times, Co. 14 Mar. 1904.

Bricker, Jesse, et al. "Changes in U.S. Family Finances from 2013 to 2016: Evidence from the Survey of Consumer Finances." *Federal Reserve*. Federal Reserve Bulletin. Vol. 103, No. 3. Sept. 2017.

Bump, Philip. "How the Republican tax bill benefits the rich, according to government analysis." *The Washington Post*. Washington Post Co. 30 Nov. 2017.

Eschner, Kat. "How President William McKinley's Assassination Led to the Modern Secret Service." *Smithsonian*. Smithsonian Institution. 14 Sept. 2017.

Greenberg, David. "Anarchy in the U.S.: A century of fighting the man" *Slate*. Slate Group. 28 Apr. 2000.

"The Trial." *University at Buffalo Libraries*. Pan-American Exposition of 1901. 2018.

"U. S. Rel. Turner v. Williams. (1904)" *FindLaw*. Thompson Reuters. 2018.

Introduction

This chapter explores how World War I impacted the nation's immigration policies. In the lead-up to the war, as military tension spread across Europe, millions of Eastern European immigrants fled to Western Europe and to the United States. Coinciding with this, the Russian Revolution led to a mass exodus of Jews fleeing persecution from Russia's anti-Jewish movement. Americans were reluctant to get involved in the war, and President Woodrow Wilson actively promoted the idea that America should stay neutral. However, as the war began to affect the American economy and threaten the safety of American ships, Wilson changed tactics, starting a massive publicity campaign to promote the idea that the United States should intervene in the conflict.

In 1917 the legislature adopted the most restrictive immigration policy in the nation's history. Eugenicists and more general anti-immigration activists were the main force behind this new immigration reform movement and campaigned for support of the bill by agitating public fears promoting the idea that the influx of Eastern European immigrants would bring disease, crime, and dangerous ideologies. The source for this chapter is a 1906 article in the *Puget Sound American*, "Have We A Dusky Peril?," which describes the public sentiment that led to another major provision of the 1917 bill—an expansion of the Chinese Exclusion act to prohibit the immigration of all Asians and persons from much of the Middle East.

Topics covered in this chapter include:
- Racial prejudice
- Anti-Asian prejudice
- World War I
- Woodrow Wilson Administration

- Eugenics Movement
- Propaganda
- Anti-Semitism

This Chapter Discusses the Following Source Document:
"Have We a Dusky Peril?" *Puget Sound American.* 16 Sept. 1906.

The Immigration Race
World War I and the Immigration Act of 1917

World War I was a time of major changes in the United States. Long-standing tensions over the vast numbers of immigrants coming to the nation each year piqued as the Americans were drawn reluctantly into the first mass European war. From this, a new shared identity began to emerge, though ancient prejudices coupled with new emerging fears also led to the beginning of the most restrictive period in immigration policy in the nation's history.

The Great War

Between 1900 and 1914, an average of 1 million immigrants came to the nation each year. Legislators were caught between opposing forces. On one hand, nativists and anti-immigrant activists objected to the constant influx of immigrants, arguing that the speed with which immigrants were coming was complicating the assimilation process and putting too much of a strain on the economy at the expense of native-born workers. On the other hand, immigrants drove the industrial revolution and the push west that led to the United States becoming the leading global power.

In the lead-up to World War I, there was a surge of immigrants from Bulgaria, Greece, Romania, Serbia, and Turkey, fleeing the Balkan Wars, while Russian immigration also spiked due to the Russian Revolution, and Jewish people persecuted in the anti-Jewish pogroms of Eastern Europe likewise sought sanctuary in the United States. The years just before the war, therefore, brought tensions between nativists and immigrants to a fevered pitch. The war began in 1914, the result of a complex web of factors including the rise of German imperialism and the breakdown of military and trade alliances formed over the previous century. The war developed into a struggle for ownership of Europe between the Central Powers of Germany, Austro-Hungary, and the Ottoman Empire, opposed by Russia, France, and Britain.

Across the Atlantic, American newspapers referred to the conflict as the "European War," reflecting the prevailing attitude that Americans should remain neutral. There were a variety of factors influencing America's hesitancy to get involved in the war, including that as one-third of Americans were immigrants, many still felt ties to one or more of the foreign powers involved. Immigrants who had come from Germany, Austria, or Ireland were generally anti-British and so didn't much want to join the British side in the conflict. Similarly, the many Jewish immigrants who came to America seeking to escape oppression in Russia were not sanguine about joining the Russian cause as part of the allied powers.[121] Furthermore, American business leaders and manufacturers realized early on that neutrality would allow them to profit most by selling products to both sides.[122] Finally, President Woodrow Wilson was against what at the time was called "American intervention," and, instead, tried to broker peace talks. The administration's anti-interventionist stance also helped to shape attitudes about the war among the people.

Until 1917, the predominant attitude among the American people was that the war was a horrible event, but one in which blame could not easily be ascertained, and Americans, therefore, had sympathy for both sides. To give one example of American ambivalence, in 1916 the New York Times featured an article interviewing the captain and crew of a German U-Boat, in which the journalist discussed the captain's fondness for Shakespeare and the minutiae of daily life aboard the ship.[123] Less than a year later, such an article would have been unthinkable as the news media had committed to the interventionist cause that depicted Germany as a ruthless, sub-human empire of savages that needed to be stopped before they took over the world.

The sinking of the British freighter *Lusitania* in May of 2015, which resulted in the death of 128 Americans, was the beginning of the end for American neutrality. Wilson initiated a massive, nationwide propaganda

campaign to drum up support for the war and it worked, with thousands of posters, flyers, and radio advertisements helping to build support for intervention.

More than this, the propaganda effort created a new idea of what it meant to be American, encouraging Americans to leave behind their former nationalistic-identities, and to see themselves as a unified American people independent from, but still indebted to Western and Northern Europe. The message was essentially that Western and Northern Europe were the seed countries for the "real" Americans and that, though Americans were now united and unique, they were members of a global western culture that needed to be defended from the forces of imperialism. By the time America declared war, in April of 1917, most of the public had embraced the need for intervention and many millions were, in fact, enthusiastically patriotic about America's role.

From Chinese Exclusion to Asian Exclusion

Loosely related to the war, in 1917 Congress adopted a new and highly restrictive immigration policy that was largely the product of the American eugenics movement, which built support for its drive to preserve racial purity by highlighting the problems faced by the American working class and claiming that non-white immigrants and immigrants from the "bad" parts of Europe were to blame. The 1917 Immigration Act expanded on Chinese exclusion by barring immigration from what was called the "Asiatic Barred Zone," which included, as stated in the text of the law, "Any country not owned by the U.S. adjacent to the continent of Asia."

Between 1882 and 1917, American anti-Asian racism had deepened. Though Chinese migrants had already been excluded for nearly a quarter century, Americans were increasingly concerned about migrants from other parts of Asia. In fact, the fear had expanded to cover a vast swath of the non-white world and, had it not been for America's history with slavery, African immigration would likewise also have been banned. A

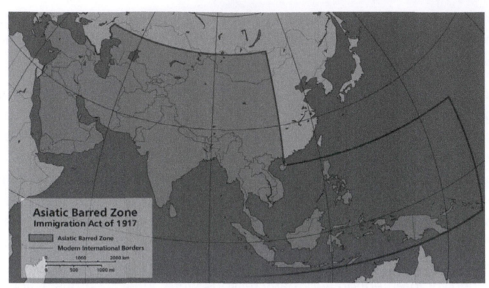

Map of the "Asiatic Barred Zone" as defined in the Immigration Act of 1917, via Wikimedia Commons

lesser known factor in the establishment of the Asiatic Barred Zone came from the shifting demographics of the American Pacific Northwest, which saw an influx of South Asian migrants coming into the United States from Canada, including from India and Malaysia.

The new panic over South Asian invasion reached a peak in the city of Bellingham, Washington, between 1906 and 1908, when an influx of several hundred Indian Sikhs from the Punjab region came to work in Washington's logging industry. According to reports from the local *Bellingham Herald*, some of the lumber mill owners had been having trouble finding a large enough number of laborers from among the local white population. One owner told the newspaper that too many of the white workers were transients interested only in "whiskey money," whereas the Sikhs, who do not consume alcohol, were reliable workers. In very little time, the alarmist presses and nativists in the region depicted the situation as the latest "invasion" of Asians stealing jobs from white workers.[124]

The Sikh men were called "Hindus" by the white residents of Washington and the press and were accused of many different transgressions and personal/professional/racial detriments, a list of reasons for what many of the white residents already wanted to happen for the aliens to be driven out. This happened in September of 1907 when a mob of white workers violently attacked hundreds of Sikhs in the streets, then ran them out of town. According to the *New York Times* coverage:

> *"Racial feeling has played no small part in the affair. Every day whites are being replaced in the mills by the Asiatics. Many instances of women being pushed into the gutters or insulted on street cars by the foreigners were also reported. General uneasiness of the whites is given as a reason for the outbreak."*[125]

It is unlikely that any of the Sikh men attacked or even insulted white women in Bellingham. Students who learn about racial tension may note that this kind of claim is indicative of a population about to engage in "racial cleansing." By claiming that *men* of the target group are preying on *women*, race-baiting instigators play on the primal fears and sexual jealousies of men in the dominant racial group, while also developing an excuse by way of justification for the violence they are contemplating, and insinuating the members of the target race lack the honor and morality to refrain from attacking defenseless or helpless individuals.

This article from the September 16, 1906, issue of the *Puget Sound American* demonstrates how the issue was covered in the local press at the time:

Image of "Have We a Dusky Peril" article from the *Puget Sound American*, digitized by Paul Englesberg, reprinted with permission from South Asia American Digital Archive (SAADA)

HAVE WE A DUSKY PERIL?
HINDU HORDES INVADING THE STATE

Puget Sound American, **September 16, 1906**
Source Document

BELLINGHAM workmen are becoming excited over the arrival of East Indians in numbers across the Canadian border, and fear that the dusky Asiatics with their turbans will prove a worse menace to the working classes than the "Yellow Peril" that has so long threatened the Pacific Coast.

Hordes of Hindus have fastened their eyes on Bellingham and the northwestern part of the United States in general, and the vanguard of an invasion which, in the minds of many discerning people, threatens to overshadow the "yellow peril" has reached this city. Encamped in a weather beaten and patched building, just east of the E.K. Wood Lumber Company's mill, within sight of passing hundreds every day, are more than a dozen swarthy sons of Hindustan. Thousands of worshippers of Brahma, Buddha, and other strange deities of India may soon press the soil of Washington.

It is on a peaceful mission these Asian tribes are bound, but they are counted as the enemies in the industrial warfare of the white man, and their coming is regarded with distrust by the average laboring man, who is carefully studying the cause and effect of the new immigration. It was only a few years ago that these men of Asia began leaving their primeval homes for North America, landing in British Columbia. Now, there are more than 5,000 Hindus in the Canadian province; and they are regarded with such aversion by the industrial classes that the Ottawa government has been petitioned to take drastic measures to turn back this stream of humanity, which is becoming irresistible.

Floods of Hindus Coming

Investigation of Hindu immigration reveals the startling fact that more than 2,000 citizens of India have entered British Columbia in the last two months. This is enough to frighten any community where it is essential that white labor should prevail to insure continuous industrial and commercial advancement, and none realize this more than the British Columbia workman, who has asked his national government to exercise extraordinary power to repress the industrious Oriental.

Principally at the behest of the laboring classes, the federal superintendent of immigration in Canada has been sent to the province to investigate the situation thoroughly. As

"The same act which Excludes Orientals Should Open Wide the Portals of British Columbia to White Immigrations." Cartoon by N.H. Hawkins, Saturday Sunset. (1907)

Cartoon by N.H. Hawkins in the *Saturday Sunset*, 1907, via Wikimedia Commons

Have We a Dusky Peril?
Hindu Hordes Invading the State
continued

a result of these protests it is considered likely that the federal authorities will take advantage of the authority vested in the governor in council, which can, if it chooses, prohibit the entrance of any class of immigrants. Perhaps the chief reason why the Canadian government has proceeded slowly in championing the popular clamor is found in the fact that the Hindus are British citizens.

If the government does use its extraordinary powers, and Hindu immigration is effectually stopped, the United States will have to bear the brunt of the Indian immigration. Prevented from landing in Canada, the East Indians will come direct to America.

At the present time the majority of Hindus reach the Northwest on the Canadian Pacific Steamship Company lines and its pauper passengers have two chances to find a home. If they find nothing in British Columbia they can come to the United States, provided they pass the physical, mental, and contract labor prohibitions. If Canada shuts the Hindus out, Seattle, Portland, and Tacoma will become the chief ports of entry for the easterners in the Northwest.

Steamship Lines Busy

The steamship companies calling at Puget Sound ports can be depended upon to work up a big business in the transportation of Hindus. They are not likely to be outdone by the steamship concerns of the Atlantic, which annually contract with various agents to transport tens of thousands of undesirable Europeans to the United tSates [sic]. Hindus are accorded the same privileges by the immigration laws of the United States as the people of the most favored nations; therefore, in view of Canada's contemplated action, and even without that perspective, nothing, apparently, will prevent or seriously discourage Hindus from coming to this country by thousands.

Hindu immigration to the United States began early in January, 1906. On January 7 Linah Singh and Pola Singh walked over the boundary line at Blaine without previously passing the required examination for admission. Arriving in Bellingham afoot on the Great Northern Railway they were arrested and confined in the city jail. They were found to be unlawfully in the country and were deported via Sumas

continued

While in the local prison the Singhs exhibited several peculiarities of their far off home. They, of course, wore turbans, and threatened to die of starvation rather than eat food cooked by other people. They were finally induced to eat rice, but they devoured it sparingly.

No Unclean Rice

When they were given the opportunity to cook their own rice at the Sumas detention shed they ate big quantities of it. Rice is the principal food of their more fortunate countrymen in Bellingham, and it is said that seventeen men from the land of the cobra and the Bengal tiger surround the pot of rice cooked in the humble Oriental home near the E.K. Wood mill.

Two months after Linah and Pola came to Bellingham five other turbaned beings rode into the city on the Bellingham Bay & British Columbia Railway. They found employment digging ditches, but they did not like the work, and they quit to labor in the E.K. Wood lumber mill. The same liking for timber plants is shown by the majority of Hindus who have settled in the Northwest.

These were soon followed by others who, perhaps, were led to come here through the glowing accounts written by the pioneers. All have been examined by A.J. Ferrandini, the immigration inspector in charge at this port, and he is constantly looking for Hindus who have been rejected at the ports of entry or at the United States immigration headquarters at Vancouver...

NEW MOVEMENT...

Since the Singhs first ate rice in one of Uncle Sam's prisons, more than 100 of their countrymen have entered the United States to the knowledge of the local immigration office and about an equal number has been denied admission. Admissions were refused to all who failed to pass the physical or mental examinations and to such as could not prove that they were not likely to become public charges or contract laborers.

The immigration offices are given the power to reject immigrants even though they find only an implication of contract labor. As an example, of the officers find that a relative or friend has informed the applicant that he can get work at a certain place that can be construed to mean contract labor and the application can be denied. If the applicant has been merely told that there is plenty of work in this country a construction of prohibition cannot be placed on the information. Frequently disease bars the Hindus. Some suffer from trachoma, and fifteen were rejected a week ago on this account. At

Have We a Dusky Peril?
Hindu Hordes Invading the State
continued

Vancouver this year several rejected Indians were bound for Bellingham. Discretionary powers delegated to the officials are often used.

The Hindus who are in Bellingham are, on the whole, remarkably fine-looking men. This is due to the fact that many are ex-soldiers of the Indian army. Their acknowledge handsome appearance does not appeal to the employes [sic] of the mills where they find work and an effort is being made to oust them and this discourage future immigration to Bellingham. Unless the mill owners support the movement against the Orientals and decline to give them work, it will be hard to keep the undesirables out, for the reason that here they receive 50 cents more per day than they do in British Columbia, according to the local mill hands.

Whites Oppose Hindus

Work is plentiful in the mills, in fact, too plentiful, and this is responsible for the ease with which the foreigners have found employment. The scarcity of white men has led mills to accept the service of those whom American workers regard as a common enemy. They feel that wages will be reduced if suppressive measures are not taken in the beginning. They argue, also, that the presence of several scores or hundreds of Hindus in Bellingham will act as a brake on the city's progress. A strong point against them, they say, is that they live cheaply and save their earnings to return to India to spend them.

The Bellingham Hindus are tall and well-formed and they stand erect. They seem to be intelligent and are polite, neat and clean. This is the opinion held by immigration officers, but it must be admitted that the Hindus here are of the lowest class. Of the seventeen said to be in Bellingham eleven have served as soldiers, according to Sanda, whose likeness appears on this page. Inspector Ferrandini says he found them honest and willing to reply to questions of examination. Many Japanese and Chinese who apply for admission are far from being so ready of tongue or so courteous.

The land of the Hindus harbors 300,000,000 souls, and it has been called "an epitome of the whole earth," so varied is its physical characteristics. There the bull, the cow and the monkey are held sacred. In all there are about fifty tribes, which can be traced back to two or three original races. The Hindus form the largest part of the population, and their religion, Brahmanism, is therefore, chief. Of the other principal

continued

religions, Mohammedanism has 60,000,000 followers and Buddhism 8,000,000 believers.

Brahmanism dates back to 1200 B.C., and its sacred books, the Vodas, [sic] are the oldest literary documents known. They consist principally of hymns. Brahmanism was originally a philosophical religion, mingled with the worship of the powers of nature. Brahma was represented by four heads to indicate the four quarters of the globe. In practice, in the course of years, the religion became a system of idolatry, with cruel rites and hideous images.

The caste system, a part of the religion, became a grievous burden, and still is. In the first class are the priests. Warriors are next, followed by traders, and they by the common types.

KEEP THE HINDUS OUT, SAYS WRITER
Bellingham, Sept. 15, 1906
G. Perinet
Editor, American

Having resided in India nine years and closely observed the habits of the Hindus, I consider their advent in this country very undesirable. They are strictly non-progressive and adhere to their old established customs with far more tenacity than either the Japanese or Chinese. Their code of morals is bad (from our point of view), and if allowed the freedom, which they naturally expect in America, they will eventually become troublesome. The most of them have been soldiers under the British government and are well-versed in the use of fire-arms. In conclusion, they have the habit of running amuck, when annoyed, in which case a number of innocent people get butchered. By all means keep them out. [126]

The little-remembered "Dusky Peril" of the early 1900s was the primary reason why Congress, when it came time to decide which races needed to be excluded in 1917, used an odd geographic designation to block out an entire region, which became the "Asiatic Barred Zone." Oddly, Japanese and Philippine people were not included on the list, though the ban included all of China, Myanmar (then Burma), Malaysia, and Central Asia, as well as India. Interestingly, the ban also extended to individuals from the Polynesian Islands and the Arabian Peninsula, thus barring the immigration of people from seven Muslim-majority countries[127], which may sound oddly familiar to Americans in 2018.

Pre-War Fears in the Immigration Debate

Passage of the Immigration Act of 1917, preceded America's official declaration of war by about two months, and wartime concerns were very much on display in the language and overall tone of the law. World War I ended the golden era of mass migration into the United States and the Immigration Act of 1917 signified this change, with harsher, more restrictive immigration policies than ever before. Never in history had America so embodied the immigrant saying popular in the 1800s, "America beckons, but Americans repel."[128]

Also following in the tradition of the 1882 Immigration Act, the 1917 act continued and expanded the list of "undesirable" persons who would not be allowed to immigrate. This list now included a variety of individuals portrayed as posing an economic burden, such as beggars, vagrants, paupers, and persons too poor to pay for their own passage, as well as persons seen as having low moral fiber, including polygamists, prostitutes, and leftist anarchists. The impact of the American eugenicists can be seen in the effort to eliminate defective, deleterious, or undesirable biological characteristics. Persons who fit this bill included individuals of low intelligence, classified officially at the time as "morons, idiots, and imbeciles," as well as persons suffering from a variety of afflictions, such as heart disease, asthma, and arthritis. Also banned were persons with physical defects, including blind, deaf, mute, crippled, or otherwise infirm individuals. To make sure they touched all the bases, the law specifically allowed immigration authorities to deny entrance to persons,

_____ *"...not comprehended within any of the foregoing excluded classes who are found to be and are certified by the examining surgeon as being mentally or physically defective..."*
_____

The 1917 Immigration Act also contained some new provisions that represented the victory of a long-term nativist campaign to mandate literacy. The 1917 Act thus required all immigrants over the age of 16 (excepting some religious refugees) to pass a reading test in their native language. Only those who could read 30 to 40 words were thus allowed entrance. Congress had tried to impose a literacy test for years, but to no avail. Legislation for an immigrant literacy test passed the House of Representatives on five occasions prior to 1917, but failed in the senate, while four different bills made it all the way through the legislature before being vetoed by President Grover Cleveland and President Taft, respectively.[128] Fears about the impending war became a rallying cry for anti-immigration lobbyists who called for a stronger nation through immigration by merit and so the literacy requirements was finally pushed through.

President Wilson was critical of the 1917 law and especially the addition of the literacy test, which he viewed as a major and negative change to the nation's overall approach to immigration. He attempted to veto the bill, but Congress voted to override the veto, thus allowing the bill to become law. Wilson made few comments on immigration as president, though; shortly after his election on November 5, Wilson said, at a speech to the Wilson Cottage, a corrections institution for women in New Jersey:

> *"The men who founded this country had a vision. They said 'Men are brethren'...We have had a vision of brotherhood, of mutual helpfulness, of equal rights; we are going to spread a great polity over this continent which will embody these things and make them real. We are going to keep our doors wide open so that those who seek this thing from the ends of the earth may come and enjoy it."*

From his collective commentary on immigration, it seemed that Wilson envisioned a nation in which the barriers between nationalistic groups would fade away and in which individuals would no longer be Russian-Americans, or Irish-Americans, or Anglo-Americans, but simply Americans. This vision did come about largely because Wilson's administration fostered this view in preparation for the war. In the tradition of the era, however, Wilson could not envision how members of other foreign races might fit into his vision of a unified American people. Speaking about the Chinese Exclusion law in a letter written in 1912, Wilson wrote:

> *"In the matter of Chinese and Japanese coolie immigration I stand for the national policy of exclusion (or restricted immigration). The whole question is one of assimilation of diverse races. We cannot make a homogenous population out of people who do not blend with the Caucasian race...Oriental coolieism will give us another race problem to solve, and surely we have had our lesson."*[129]

President Woodrow Wilson, by Harris & Ewing, via
Wikimedia Commons

CONCLUSION

The 1917 Immigration Act was a major victory for anti-immigration activists and American eugenicists. Capitalizing on the fears that World War I would lead to a massive influx of immigrants from Eastern Europe, anti-immigration activists seized the chance to expand the prohibited classes targeted for exclusion. The congressional record demonstrates that few Americans objected to continuing to prohibit nonwhite immigration, but the prohibition of war refugees and, specifically, Jewish refugees was a major controversy at the time. President Wilson campaigned for a less-restrictive approach to immigration, believing that the United States should welcome eastern and southern European refugees from the war, but a majority of legislators did not support this view and favored isolationism. Ultimately, the fear of refugee migrants, and the restrictive immigration policies that resulted from this fear, brought an end to the period of mass migration from Europe.

DISCUSSION QUESTIONS

- Would the United States ever pass an immigration law like the 1917 Immigration Act again? Why or why not?
- Can you defend the position that only white Europeans can become Americans? Why or why not?
- Why was World War I called the "European War" in the American media?
- Are there current policies or proposals that are similar to the Asiatic Barred Zone? If so, are the modern laws motivated by the same factors that led to the 1917 law?

Works Used

Alvarez, Priscilla. "A Brief History of America's 'Love-Hate Relationship' With Immigration." *Atlantic*. Atlantic Monthly Group. 19 Feb. 2017.

Axelrod, Alan. *Selling the War: The Making of American Propaganda.* New York: Macmillan, 2009 pp. 56–58.

Boissoneault, Lorraine. "Literacy Tests and Asian Exclusion Were the Hallmarks of the 1917 Immigration Act." *Smithsonian*. Smithsonian Institution. 6 Feb. 2017.

"German U-Boat Reaches Baltimore, Having Crossed Atlantic in 16 Days; Has Letter from Kaiser to Wilson." *New York Times*. New York Times, Co. 10 July 1916.

"Have We a Dusky Peril?" *Puget Sound American*. 16 Sept. 1906.

"Immigration Act of 1917." *University of Washington-Bothell Library*. Sixty-Fourth Congress. Sess. II. Chapters 27–29. 1917.

Manseau, Peter. "A forgotten History of Anti-Sikh Violence in the Early-20th-Century Pacific Northwest." *Slate*. Slate Group.

"Mob Drives out Hindus." *New York Times*. New York Times, Co. 6
    Sept. 1907.

Sondhaus, Lawrence. *World War I: The Global Revolution*. New York:
    Cambridge UP, 2011.

Wolfensberger, Don. "Woodrow Wilson, Congress and Anti-Immigrant
    Sentiment in America: An Introductory Essay." *Wilson Center*.
    Woodrow Wilson International Center for Scholars. 12 Mar. 2007.

Introduction

Whereas the previous chapter demonstrates how eugenicists influenced the immigration debate surrounding World War I, this chapter explores American immigration policies in the 1920s, an era that has been called the "tribal twenties" in recognition of how racial prejudice and xenophobia dominated domestic policy. After the war, with many Americans deeply afraid that a new wave of refugees was about to arrive in the United States from war-torn Europe, the anti-immigration movement focused specifically on how best to limit the immigration of undesirable European ethnic groups, while still permitting desirable Europeans to come to the United States. This resulted in the adoption of an emergency immigration law in 1921 created and promoted by the nation's eugenics theorists. Prominent eugenicists like Madison Grant, a personal friend of President Theodore Roosevelt, promoted the idea that there was a scientific hierarchy of quality among the ethnic groups of Europe. The idea espoused that western and northern Europeans were superior, whereas central, southern, and eastern Europeans were inferior, carrying higher levels of disease and being prone to dangerous anti-government ideologies.

The 1921 quota system restricted immigration by placing a quota on immigrants arriving from each nation. The quotas were based on the proportion of persons from that nation living in the United States as per the 1890s Census Report, and so the system was meant to preserve the nation's ethnic and racial proportions. The source for this chapter is a speech given in April of 1924 by Senator Ellison DuRant of South Carolina in which DuRant argues that the emergency quota system should be made a permanent part of the nation's immigration policies. DuRant and supporters were successful with the 1924 Johnson-Reed Act, which made the national quota system the new, permanent basis of America's immigration policies.

Topics covered in this chapter include:
- Eugenics
- Racial prejudice
- Anti-Semitism
- National Quota System
- U.S. Supreme Court Cases
- Calvin Coolidge Administration

This Chapter Discusses the Following Source Document:
"'Shut the Door': A Senator Speaks for Immigration Restriction."
George Mason University. History Matters. 3 Jan. 2017.

The End of Mass Migration
The Beginning of the Quota System (1920–1925)

Until the 1920s, America had an open policy regarding immigration from Europe. World War I changed attitudes as fears of a massive influx of European immigrants fueled an anti-Eastern European and anti-Jewish immigration movement. This was also the result of a new, American identity that had begun to emerge seeing America as part of a Western and Northern European legacy separate from the rest of the world. Thus, the image of Europe had begun to change, with Western and Northern Europe seen as the seeds of American culture, whereas Eastern, Central, and Southern Europe were increasingly portrayed as inferior and less civilized.

The Emergency Quota System (1921)

The Immigration Act of 1917 did not pose any substantial barriers to the immigration of most European migrants, though deportations increased marginally after the law passed. World War I itself had a major impact on immigration. For one thing, many of the ships that transported migrants to the United States were conscripted to serve in the war effort. Further, crossing the Atlantic became exceedingly dangerous in the first era of submarine warfare, and there were instances in which passenger transports were destroyed during the height of the war.[130]

After the war, there was a serious uptick in anti-immigrant sentiment directed towards immigrants from the Central Powers of the Great War, specifically people from Eastern, Central, and Southern Europe. Washington Representative Albert Johnson, who was the Chair of the House Committee on Immigration, was the leader of the nativist anti-immigration movement of the era. He tried to suspend all immigration into the United States in 1919, but the proposal was rejected in Congress. After the war, nativists like Johnson teamed up with eugenicists to promote new policies that met their combined goals.

In general, American eugenicists believed that "Nordic" or "Aryan" white people were the most superior version of humanity that had arisen from the shared human ancestors (some went further by believing that white people and darker people were descended from different ancestor species). Some of the more fervent eugenicists took it a bit further, imagining that there was also a hierarchy of quality between different subsets of the white or European race.

Book by Madison Grant, 1916, that was labeled "scientific racism." via Wikimedia Commons

One book that examined this idea, with a focus specifically on racial balance and tension in America, was the 1916 book *The Passing of the Great Race*, by American lawyer Madison Grant. The book is a classic of what has been called "scientific racism," the effort to justify racial superiority through pseudoscientific theories about racial characteristics and the fitness of different populations. It is important to note that Grant's book still sells to American eugenicists and white nationalists, and reviews of the book on websites like *American Renaissance*, continue to extol the virtues of Grant's racial theories.

Grant was an accomplished environmentalist who helped found the Bronx Zoo and started an important environmental movement to preserve American wildlife and plants. He was a good friend of Theodore Roosevelt, and both men were members of a New York elite descended from aristocratic families and seeing themselves as modern versions of the adventuring explorers of yesteryear.

Grant's interest in wildlife conservation was rooted in the same beliefs that inspired their shared interest in racial purity. This is because eugenics was the scientific equivalent of what in previous eras might have been seen as "manifest destiny" or "spiritual predestination." Grant saw himself, as white Europeans had since the days when Kings and their descendants believed they had been chosen by God to lead, as a representative of a superior ilk, the world's most powerful and perfected race. People like Grant took an interest in nature as one takes an interest in protecting one's own garden, imagining that the point of conservation was to preserve nature for people like him to enjoy and use. All species on the Earth that are not human are described in Christian theology as the property of humanity, and thus people like Grant saw zoological parks, hunting, and conservation as the ways in which God-chosen, or evolutionarily-superior individuals were able to enjoy this shared resource. Inferior persons, from other races or the more degenerate European ethnicities, were much like the wildlife captured and displayed at zoos, interesting scientifically, but not deserving of the same empathy that one afforded others like oneself.[131]

Grant wrote a number of still-published and still-praised texts about what has euphemistically come to be called "human biodiversity." In these texts, Grant's central thesis is to argue that only the Western and Northern European races were responsible for all the positive developments in the United States, having achieved these accomplishments despite the presence of undesirable races and nationalities. He takes this further in *The Passing of the Great Race*, in which Grant suggests a hierarchy of racial superiority among the races of the world, comparing global society to a giant snake, with the Nordic races as the head and the "inferior" races as the tail. The danger, as Grant saw it, was for the inferior races to grow to such a state that the snake's tail would be in charge of the head. By using a metaphor that results in a physical absurdity, Grant thus suggests that nations run by non-white races would be equally illogical and preposterous.

To provide an example of Grant's "wisdom," in *The Passing of the Great Race*, Grant wrote of racial segregation, which he wholeheartedly endorsed as the only logical solution to America's "color problem,":

_____ *"Race feeling may be called prejudice by those whose careers are cramped by it, but it is a natural antipathy which serves to maintain the purity of type. The unfortunate fact that nearly all species of men interbreed freely leaves us no choice in the matter. Either the races must be kept apart by artificial devices of this sort, or else they ultimately amalgamate, and in the offspring the more generalized or lower type prevails."*[132]

In 1919, Washington Representative Albert Johnson appointed Grant to serve as "scientific advisor" to Johnson's House Committee on Immigration. Grant was not a scientist, nor had he any training in genetics or evolutionary biology. However, eugenics was taken so seriously at the time that a lawyer with an interest in pseudoscience like Grant, especially because he was personal friends with Theodore Roosevelt, was seen as an appropriate person to advise the nation regarding scientific issues.

Grant thus testified about his ideas regarding racial segregation, miscegenation, and the hierarchy of race to Congress, and this heavily influenced the congressional debates about immigration in 1919 and 1920. Johnson met resistance with his more extreme calls for a total prohibition of immigration, continually running against those Americans who saw the contributions of immigrants as an important part of American society. Then, in 1920, a surge in European immigration ignited fears that the nation would soon be inundated by immigrants from Europe. Johnson and allied Senator Paul Dillingham thus came up with the idea of a quota system that would drastically restrict immigration and simultaneously preserve the existing balance of races and nationalities.

Political cartoon commenting on America's new immigration quotas that were influenced by popular anti-immigrant and nativist sentiment stemming from WW II, Library of Congress

The Emergency Quota Act of May 9, 1921, also known as the National Origins Act, was the end of the golden age of mass migration. The main objective of the law was to place temporary restrictions on immigration from Southern, Central, and Eastern Europe. Though Congress had already embraced Asian prohibition, prohibitions on European immigration were never going to gain the same level of support. The Emergency Quota Act achieves the same results in a less confrontational way, by allowing immigration from Europe to continue, but in such a way as to preserve the proportions of each group as already present in the nation.[133]

Essentially, the Emergency Quota act limited total immigration each year to 3 percent at most of the total number of foreign-born persons from each country living in the nation at the time of the 1910 U.S. Census. Western and Northern European countries were not included in the quota and so immigration from these countries remained unrestricted.[134] When the bill was drafted, the choice of the 1910 census as the basis for the quota percentages was also controversial. The 1920 Decennial Census was not yet completed, but some members of the committee believed that the bill should be rewritten to reflect the percentages of the 1920 census when they became available. The decision to use the 1910 census was, according to critics, biased to reflect a lower percentage of Eastern European immigrants and, therefore, closer to the goals of the eugenicists.[135]

Johnson and Reed Protect America From Nothing

Just three years later, Congress was again debating a new, more permanent immigration policy. Again, eugenicists lined up to defend and promote the quota system then in place and supporters of the quotas proposed tightening restrictions further as well as adding a consular inspection system such that prospective immigrations could be rejected while still in their native nations, before boarding ships to burden the U.S. immigration authorities. There was surprisingly little resistance to the 1924 iteration of the quota act, but rather, legislators fought over how best to amend the act moving forward. Immigration and diversity advocates tried, therefore, to raise quotas, but the swing of the government was against that course for the time being.

For instance, Senator Ellison D. Smith of South Carolina still felt too many undesirable foreign persons were coming to the United States. Speaking to Congress, he said,

> *"Thank God we have in America perhaps the largest percentage of any country in the world of the pure, unadulterated Anglo-Saxon stock. It is for the preservation for that splendid stock that has characterized us that I would make this not an asylum for the oppressed of all countries, but a country to assimilate and perfect that splendid type of manhood that has made America the foremost Nation in her progress and her power."*[136]

The 1924 Immigration Act, known as the Johnson-Reed Act, based national quotas on the percentage from each nation in 1890, rather than the 1910 census, and the percentage for each country was reduced from 3 to 2 percent. The new law also advanced eugenicist aims in another way as well, by completely prohibiting the immigration of anyone who could not be naturalized.

According to the most recent federal law on naturalization, only free white men and the male descendants of Africans could become naturalized citizens. This had, essentially, been America's policy since the end of the Civil War. Japanese people were caught in limbo by American law. They were permitted to migrate and, at times, to live in the nation for decades, but were never allowed to become citizens. The 1922 case of *Ozawa v. United States* dealt directly with this issue. The case involved a Japanese man, Takao Ozawa, born in Japan, but having resided in the United States for more than 20 years. Ozawa was a graduate of Berkeley, California, High School, and a student at the University of California. He educated his children in American schools, his family attended an American

Christian Church, and he was fluent in English, speaking it in his home.

Chief Justice George Sutherland, delivering the majority opinion for the Supreme Court, said, at the beginning of his statements,

_____ *"That he was well qualified by character and education for citizenship is conceded."*

The case was interesting in that Ozawa had taken an unusual tact, challenging the legal definition of "white," by claiming that he, too, was essentially a free "white" man. The court disagreed, arguing that, even though the framers had not explicitly stated it, the decision to limit naturalization to free white men had to be interpreted in terms of the intention of the law, which was to specify the Anglo-Caucasian race.

_____ *"On behalf of the appellant it is urged that we should give to this phrase the meaning which it had in the minds of its original framers in 1790 and that it was employed by them for the sole purpose of excluding the black or African race and the Indians then inhabiting this country. It may be true that those two races were alone thought of as being excluded, but to say that they were the only ones within the intent of the statute would be to ignore the affirmative form of the legislation. The provision is not that Negroes and Indians shall be excluded, but it is, in effect, that only free white persons shall be included. The intention was to confer the privilege of citizenship upon that class of persons whom the fathers knew as white, and to deny it to all who could not be so classified. It is not enough to say that the framers did not have in mind the brown or yellow races of Asia. It is necessary to go farther and be able to say that*

had these particular races been suggested the language of the act would have been so varied as to include them within its privileges."[137]

The *Ozawa v. United States* case backed the racial basis for immigration law that had already been used for many decades, but did not yet have Supreme Court precedent, a definition of "whiteness" that definitely excluded Japanese people as well as any of the other Asians prohibited in the 1917 Immigration Act.

The year before, the Supreme Court had ruled on another case with the same basis, when an Indian Sikh named Bhagat Singh

Takao Ozawa, via Google Images

Thind argued that he should be eligible for naturalization as a white man because he was descended from "high cast Aryan blood." The Aryan race had been connected with the European white race, or more specifically, the Caucasian racial group by racial "scientists" of the era. Thind thus argued that as a representative of pure Aryan blood, he was Caucasian and thus "white," by a somewhat creative interpretation of contemporary racial science. The court again disagreed, with Justice Sutherland, again, presiding and arguing:

"It may be true that the blond Scandinavian and the brown Hindu have a common ancestor in the dim reaches of antiquity, but the average man knows perfectly well that there are unmistakable and profound differences between them to-day; and

it is not impossible, if that common ancestor could be materialized in the flesh, we should discover that he was himself sufficiently differentiated from both of his descendants to preclude his racial classification with either. The question for determination [261 U.S. 204, 210] is not, therefore, whether by the speculative processes of ethnological reasoning we may present a probability to the scientific mind that they have the same origin, but whether we can satisfy the common understanding that they are now the same or sufficiently the same to justify the interpreters of a statute-written in the words of common speech, for common understanding, by unscientific men-in classifying them together in the statutory category as white persons."[138]

The 1922 and 1923 cases of Ozawa and Thind were challenges to the naturalization system. Indian Sikhs and other South Asians were prohibited explicitly in the Immigration Act of 1917, but Japanese people were still allowed to migrate to the United States as they had been excluded from the 1917 "Asiatic Barred Zone." Motivated in part by these challenges to the nation's racial immigration policies, in 1924 the Johnson-Reed version of the quota system added Japanese people to the list of Asians prohibited from immigration. This brought protests from the Japanese government and increasing tensions between the two nations, but Congress did not bow to these influences and the ban remained. It had become firmly established that the preservation of America's racial composition was more important than foreign relations.[139]

On April 9, 1924, Senator Ellison DuRant Smith spoke before the 68th Congress about racial exclusion. The fiery South Carolina Senator focused on agricultural reform during his time in the legislature, but had

a decidedly traditionalist value structure and had been one of the most stringent opponents of the Women's Suffrage Movement that succeeded despite persons like him. On this issue, DuRant felt that granting women the right to vote would be similar to what he saw as the mistaken act of granting black persons the right to vote with the Fifteenth Amendment. Smith's obviously biased views on race and gender were evident in his commentary to the Congress regarding the 1924 Immigration Act, in which Smith expressed many of the views of America's moderate, racial purists, of the day:

SPEECH BY ELLISON DURANT SMITH
April 9, 1924, Congressional Record, 68th Congress, 1st Session
Source Document Excerpt

It seems to me the point as to this measure—and I have been so impressed for several years—is that the time has arrived when we should shut the door. We have been called the melting pot of the world. We had an experience just a few years ago, during the great World War, when it looked as though we had allowed influences to enter our borders that were about to melt the pot in place of us being the melting pot.

I think that we have sufficient stock in America now for us to shut the door, Americanize what we have, and save the resources of America for the natural increase of our population. We all know that one of the most prolific causes of war is the desire for increased land ownership for the overflow of a congested population. We are increasing at such a rate that in the natural course of things in a comparatively few years the landed resources, the natural resources of the country, shall be taken up by the natural increase of our population. It seems to me the part of wisdom now that we have throughout the length and breadth of continental America a population which is beginning to encroach upon the reserve and virgin resources of the country to keep it in trust for the multiplying population of the country.

I do not believe that political reasons should enter into the discussion of this very vital question. It is of greater concern to us to maintain the institutions of America, to maintain the principles upon which this Government is founded, than to develop and exploit the underdeveloped resources of the country. There are some things that are dearer to us, fraught with more benefit

Speech by Ellison Durant Smtih
continued

to us, than the immediate development of the undeveloped resources of the country. I believe that our particular ideas, social, moral, religious, and political, have demonstrated, by virtue of the progress we have made and the character of people that we are, that we have the highest ideals of any member of the human family or any nation. We have demonstrated the fact that the human family, certainty the predominant breed in America, can govern themselves by a direct government of the people. If this Government shall fail, it shall fail by virtue of the terrible law of inherited tendency. Those who come from the nations which from time immemorial have been under the dictation of a master fall more easily by the law of inheritance and the inertia of habit into a condition of political servitude than the descendants of those who cleared the forests, conquered the savage, stood at arms and won their liberty from their mother country, England.

I think we now have sufficient population in our country for us to shut the door and to breed up a pure, unadulterated American citizenship. I recognize that there is a dangerous lack of distinction between people of a certain nationality and the breed of the dog. Who is an American? Is he an immigrant from Italy? Is he an immigrant from Germany? If you were to go abroad and some one were to meet you and say, "I met a typical American," what would flash into your mind as a typical American, the typical representative of that new Nation? Would it be the son of an Italian immigrant, the son of a German immigrant, the son of any of the breeds from the Orient, the son of the denizens of Africa? We must not get our ethnological distinctions mixed up with out anthropological distinctions. It is the breed of the dog in which I am interested. I would like for the Members of the Senate to read that book just recently published by Madison Grant, *The Passing of the Great Race*. Thank God we have in America perhaps the largest percentage of any country in the world of the pure, unadulterated Anglo-Saxon stock; certainly the greatest of any nation in the Nordic breed. It is for the preservation of that splendid stock that has characterized us that I would make this not an asylum for the oppressed of all countries, but a country to assimilate and perfect that splendid type of manhood that has made America the foremost Nation in her progress and in her power, and yet the youngest of all the nations. I myself believe that the preservation of her institutions depends upon us now taking counsel with our condition and our experience during the last World War.

continued

Without offense, but with regard to the salvation of our own, let us shut the door and assimilate what we have, and let us breed pure American citizens and develop our own American resources. I am more in favor of that than I am of our quota proposition. Of course, it may not meet the approbation of the Senate that we shall shut the door—which I unqualifiedly and unreservedly believe to be our duty—and develop what we have, assimilate and digest what we have into pure Americans, with American aspirations, and thoroughly familiar with the love of American institutions, rather than the importation of any number of men from other countries. If we may not have that, then I am in favor of putting the quota down to the lowest possible point, with every selective element in it that may be.

The great desideratum of modern times has been education not alone book knowledge, but that education which enables men to think right, to think logically, to think truthfully, men equipped with power to appreciate the rapidly developing conditions that are all about us, that have converted the world in the last 50 years into a brand new world and made us masters of forces that are revolutionizing production. We want men not like dumb, driven cattle from those nations where the progressive thought of the times has scarcely made a beginning and where they see men as mere machines; we want men who have an appreciation of the responsibility brought about by the manifestation of the power of that individual. We have not that in this country to-day. We have men here to-day who are selfishly utilizing the enormous forces discovered by genius, and if we are not careful as statesmen, if we are not careful in our legislation, these very masters of the tremendous forces that have been made available to us will bring us under their domination and control by virtue of the power they have in multiplying their wealth.

We are struggling to-day against the organized forces of man's brain multiplied a million times by materialized thought in the form of steam and electricity as applied in the everyday affairs of man. We have enough in this country to engage the brain of every lover of his country in solving the problems of a democratic government in the midst of the imperial power that genius is discovering and placing in the hands of man. We have population enough to-day without throwing wide our doors and jeopardizing the interests of this country by pouring into it men who willingly become the slaves of those who employ them in manipulating these forces of nature, and they few reap the enormous benefits that accrue therefrom.

Speech by Ellison Durant Smith
continued

We ought to Americanize not only our population but our forces. We ought to Americanize our factories and our vast material resources, so that we can make each contribute to the other and have an abundance for us under the form of the government laid down by our fathers.

The Senator from Georgia [Mr. Harris] has introduced an amendment to shut the door. It is not a question of politics. It is a question of maintaining that which has made you and me the beneficiaries of the greatest hope that ever burned in the human breast for the most splendid future that ever stood before mankind, where the boy in the gutter can look with confidence to the seat of the Presidency of the United States; where the boy in the gutter can look forward to the time when, paying the price of a proper citizen, he may fill a seat in this hall; where the boy to-day poverty-stricken, standing in the midst of all the splendid opportunities of America, should have and, please God, if we do our duty, will have an opportunity to enjoy the marvelous wealth that the genius and brain of our country is making possible for us all.

We do not want to tangle the skein of America's progress by those who imperfectly understand the genius of our Government and the opportunities that lie about us. Let up keep what we have, protect what we have, make what we have the realization of the dream of those who wrote the Constitution.

I am more concerned about that than I am about whether a new railroad shall be built or whether there shall be diversified farming next year or whether a certain coal mine shall be mined. I would rather see American citizenship refined to the last degree in all that makes America what we hope it will be than to develop the resources of America at the expense of the citizenship of our country. The time has come when we should shut the door and keep what we have for what we hope our own people to be.[140]

CONCLUSION

In many ways, World War I eroded the barriers between nationality, creating a new and pervasive sense of American unity, but the rapid changes that were sweeping through society exacerbated the fears of nativists and others who feared the mixing of cultures and races for a variety of reasons. Public opinion polls were rare until the late 1930s, and there is a dearth of demographic data that can be used to measure the extent of prejudice in American society at the time. Anecdotal evidence is rich and complex, however, demonstrating that the voices calling for racial equality were still coming from a largely powerless minority.

DISCUSSION QUESTIONS

- How was the 1924 Johnson-Reed Act related to the eugenics movement? Explain.
- What does the statement "Race feeling may be called prejudice by those whose careers are cramped by it…" by eugenicist Madison Grant indicate about the way that eugenicists attempted to discredit their critics? Is this technique still used to discredit political opponents? How?
- Why did the Johnson-Reed proponents want to base the quota system on the 1890 census rather than the 1910 census? Explain.
- Do you agree or disagree with the Supreme Court's decision in *Ozawa v. United States?* Are the arguments provided by Chief Justice Sutherland logical and consistent? Explain.

Works Used

"Emergency Quota Law 1921." *University of Washington-Bothell Library*. Sixty-Seventh Congress; 19 May 1921.

Grant, Madison. *The Passing of the Great Race: Or, the Racial Basis of European History*. New York: Charles Scribner's Sons, 1918, p. 193.

Higham, John. *Strangers in the Land: Patterns of American Nativism, 1860–1925*. New Brunswick, NJ: Rutgers UP, 2002, pp. 505–559.

"Immigration and the Great War." *NPS*. National Park Service. 2017.

O'Leary, Anna Ochoa. *Undocumented Immigrants in the United States: An Encyclopedia of Their Experience*.2014. Santa Barbara, CA: Greenwood P, 2014.

Purdy, Jedediah. "Environmentalism's Racist History." *New Yorker*. Condé Nast. 13 Aug. 2015.

Riley, Jason L. *Let Them In: The Case for Open Borders*. New York: Gotham Books, 2008.

"'Shut the Door': A Senator Speaks for Immigration Restriction."
    George Mason University. History Matters. 3 Jan. 2017.
"Takao Ozawa v. US." (1922) *FindLaw*. Thomson Reuters. US Supreme
    Court. 2016.
"The Immigration Act of 1924." *U.S. Department of State*. Office of the
    Historian. 2017.
"US v. Bhagat Singh Thind." *FindLaw*. Thompson Reuters. US
    Supreme Court. 2016.

Introduction

Whereas refugees were one of the major immigration concerns in the 1920s, as discussed in the previous chapters, the early 1930s saw a period of unprecedented economic instability culminating in the Great Depression. This occurred when there were few pressing international concerns, and so reform movements were focused on domestic issues. Anti-immigrant lobbyists and activists identified a new threat in the form of Mexican migrants and their impact on the labor market in the American west and southwest. In congressional debates, this was referred to as the "Mexican problem" and represents the first time that immigration across the southern border became the nation's main immigration issue.

Between 1929 and 1939, immigration officials, working with local police and vigilante gangs of white residents, captured and deported over one million individuals of Mexican descent from the southwest and as far north as Illinois. A majority of those who were forced or coerced to leave the country were native-born American citizens of Mexican descent, and thus their deportation violated not only federal law but also the Fourteenth Amendment protections guaranteeing due process and equal protection under the law. The source for this chapter is a 2003 article in *The Guardian* newspaper by journalist Gary Younge describing how, in the twenty-first century, some of those citizens expelled were still seeking both recognition and restitution from the American government for the crimes committed against them, their families, and communities during the anti-Mexican purge of the Great Depression.

Topics covered in this chapter include:
- Eugenics
- Racial prejudice

- Undocumented migration
- The Great Depression
- Herbert Hoover Administration
- Franklin Delano Roosevelt Administration
- Anti-Mexican sentiment
- Repatriation

This Chapter Discusses the Following Source Document:
Younge, Gary. "Mexicans expelled in 30s ask for justice." *The Guardian*. Guardian News and Media. 16 July 2003.

Down Mexico Way
Mexican Repatriation and the Great Depression (1929–1939)

The severe economic turbulence of the Great Depression brought about a short-lived anti-Mexican immigration movement that saw the first mass deportations of Mexicans and marked the first time in American history that nativists and anti-immigration ideologues saw immigration through the Southern borders as one of the nation's primary threats. This period led right up to the dawn of World War II, by which time anti-immigration activists saw the European refugee crisis and Jewish immigration as the primary threats and the threat of Mexican immigration, temporarily, fell into the background.

The Docile Mexicans

Prior to the mid-1800s, there was little in the way of Mexican immigration into the United States. The expansion of the Southwest mining and agricultural industries in the late 1800s changed this, as thousands of Mexican migrants came into the Southwest looking for work. The Mexican Revolution (1910–1920) led to a surge in Mexican immigration as the waves of agricultural workers coming to the country were joined by tens of thousands of refugees from the war. While about 20,000 Mexican immigrants came to the country in the 1910s, this number had risen to between 50,000–100,000 per year in the 1920s.

Rising immigration from Mexico had little impact on the immigration debate until the end of the 1920s, which was due to a combination of factors that led to a rise in anti-Mexican nativism and a new focus on the impurity of Hispanic and Latino "types" among the dominant American eugenics movement within the government. Whereas the eugenicists believed that Mexicans and other Latin Americans were inferior, the powerful farm lobby, composed of wealthy white agriculturalists, made fighting Mexican immigration impractical. Furthermore, Mexicans had been portrayed (both by farm-labor advocates and by eugenicists) as an ideal laborer race. Literature about Mexicans in America at the time described them as docile and quiet, but strong enough for the jobs Americans needed done. Further, because they weren't citizens, Mexican laborers could be exploited freely and would provide all the labor a farm owner needed at a fraction of the price that the same owner would have needed to pay whites or even African Americans to do the same jobs.

Thus, a combination of white labor interests and the American focus on other more pressing efforts to protect the country from Jewish and other Eastern European immigrants, led to Mexico being left off the national quotas list in 1921 and 1924. Mexican immigration, therefore, continued largely unimpeded throughout the 1920s, until the Cristero War (1926–1929) brought the Mexican immigration issue to the front of the public debate.

The Cristero War, also known as La Cristiada, was essentially a separation of church-and-state conflict that resulted from the Mexican Constitution of 1917, which placed limits on the political power of the Mexican Catholic Church. Prior to this secularization movement, the Church wielded almost complete authority in Mexican politics, and the effort to limit this influence led to a civil war. Historians estimate that 100,000–200,000 were killed in the violent conflict for power that eventually resulted in a Catholic victory and the preservation of the nation's religious-political elite.[141]

The Cristero War brought Mexico and Mexican immigrants to the attention of the American public, not least because President Calvin Coolidge, and his Ambassador to Mexico Dwight Whitney Morrow, were instrumental in bringing an end to the war by hosting a series of negotiations between newly elected Mexican President Emilio Portes Gil and the Catholic militants. Because America was involved, the issue was major news, and a different view of Mexicans and Mexican Americans began to emerge.

Whereas Mexican laborers had been portrayed using the same adjectives that one used to describe agricultural beasts of burden; as docile, unintelligent, but strong workers, Mexican Catholics living in America joined in protests against the Mexican government during the Cristero War and the American public began to see that Mexicans could become revolutionary and political. This frightened many white people who were comfortable with Mexicans only so long as they seemed an easy population to control. Added to this was the fact that the violence of the Cristero War led to a surge of some 250,000 Mexican migrants crossing the border, exacerbating racial tensions and leading to the first American movement against immigration from America's southern neighbor.

The Great Depression and Mexican Farm Labor

The Great Depression (1929–1941) was the longest and most severe economic depression in the history of the nation. The reasons for the depression are still debated by economists and historians in the twenty-first century, but the result was devastation, especially for the poor and working-class portions of the American population. The nation's GDP fell from $103 to $55 billion between 1929 and 1933, whereas unemployment rose from 8 to 15 percent, constituting nearly one-third of a non-agricultural workforce. By the time Franklin Delano Roosevelt took office in 1933, the state of Mississippi had lost 40 percent of its farms and similar economic ruin was everywhere evident.

Many Americans don't understand that the Great Depression was actually global, though the United States suffered the most severe effects. The poor were disproportionately affected by the depression, and there were few federal or state programs in place to prevent those who lost their jobs, property, and economic stability from declining into abject poverty and homelessness. Interestingly, though the United States was hit hardest by the depression, the effects spread through Europe. The only other nation that suffered massive unemployment like that seen in the United

RACE IN THE GREAT DEPRESSION

For many years, historical accounts of the Great Depression focused on the plight of poor white workers, memorialized by books like *The Grapes of Wrath*, which explored the agricultural migration out of the American "dustbowl." However, African Americans were hit far harder by the depression, losing much of the progress that had been made since the end of slavery. By 1932, about 50 percent of African Americans were out of work. Competition for remaining jobs and resources led to increasing racial violence in the South. For instance, in 1932 there were 8 instances of an African American being lynched, while there were 28 lynchings the following year, as the effects of the depression were spreading through the south. The recovery efforts enacted through Roosevelt's New Deal program also disproportionately benefited white Americans, thus meaning that the effects of the Depression were felt by the African American population for far longer. In Harlem, New York, where African Americans owned or operated 30 percent of businesses in 1932, the depression eroded this progress, and, by 1935, only 5 percent of businesses in the same area were African-American owned.[143]

States was Germany, which was still recovering from World War I. This economic turbulence was a key factor in the militarization of Germany that led to the rise of the Nazi Party, inspired in a large part by the theories of American eugenics, and thus led to the racial cleansing that characterized the Second World War.[142]

By the 1930s, blaming economic turmoil on immigrants or at least on other racial groups was a time-honored American tradition. Thus, it is perhaps unsurprising that, as the Great Depression dawned, white Americans who had largely ignored Mexican immigration to that point began to target Mexicans as the source of America's newest round of economic woes.

The anti-Mexican campaign began just *before* the Depression hit, as the Cristero Revolution, and subsequent influx of Mexican immigrants, coupled with the increasingly political

bent of MexicanAmericans in response to the war, motivated some of the first calls for prohibiting Mexican immigration. The *Saturday Evening Post*, with a readership of nearly three million at the time, pioneered the call for Mexican restriction or exclusion like the Asian restrictions in place since 1882. In 1928 and 1929, the *Saturday Evening Post* ran a series of articles with the titles "The Docile Mexican," "Wet and the Other Mexicans," "The Alien on Relief," and finally, "The Mexican Invasion." In these articles, pundit Kenneth Roberts referred to Mexicans as bringing "countless numbers of American citizens into the world with the reckless prodigality of rabbits," and warning that the mixture of Mexican and white blood or the "mongrelization" of America would create "another mixed race problem." In a 1929 editorial under the title "The Mexican Conquest," the *Saturday Evening Post* said:

African American and white man talking in Muskogee, Oklahoma during the Great Depression, Library of Congress

> *"The very high Mexican birth rate tends to depress still further the low white birth rate. Thus a race problem of the greatest magnitude is being allowed to develop for future generations to regret and in spite of the fact that the Mexican Indian is considered a most undesirable ethnic stock for the melting pot."*[144]

Whereas nativists in the Southwest had long campaigned for Mexicans to be added to the list of undesirable, it wasn't until the Depression hit that Congress was willing to entertain this idea. By 1930, the "Mexican Problem" as it was being called in the press was becoming a federal issue and Congress was entertaining a variety of proposals for how to deal with it, ranging from adding Mexicans to the quota list to the more extreme calls for a complete cessation or deportation.

As quoted in the book *Mexicanos: A History of Mexicans in the United States,* In 1930, Dr. Roy Garis, an economics professor at Vanderbilt University, testified before Congress in regards to the Mexican immigration issue, saying of the Mexican people:

_____ *"Their minds run to nothing higher than animal functions—eat, sleep, and sexual debauchery. In every huddle of Mexican shacks one meets the same idleness, hordes of hungry dogs, and filthy children with faces plastered with flies, disease, lice, human filth, stench, promiscuous fornication, bastardy, lounging, apathetic peons and lazy squaws, beans and dried chili, liquor, general squalor, and envy and hatred of the gringo. These people sleep by day and prowl by night like coyotes, stealing anything they can get their hands on, no matter how useless to them it may be. Nothing left outside is safe unless padlocked or chained down."*[145]

The Repatriation Movement

Cooler heads did not prevail. The campaign against Mexican immigration and to dehumanize the Mexican and Mexican-American people to excuse and legitimize violence or other actions directed towards them, was successful. Beginning around 1930, state governments began forcing or

attempting to coerce Mexicans and Mexican Americans to return to Mexico. This nearly forgotten period in American immigrant history is sometimes called the "Repatriation Movement," which is the label given by representatives of the Herbert Hoover administration in 1930 and 1931, when the movement began. The repatriations would continue for nearly a decade, and represent the first anti-Mexican surge in American history.

Between 1929 and 1939, historians estimate that at least one million Mexicans and Mexican Americans were either deported, forcibly removed, or coerced into leaving the United States for Mexico. An estimated 200,000 left the United States voluntarily, though, in many cases, the threat of detention and deportation or the threat of violence by white authorities in states with large Mexican-American populations were the root cause behind the "voluntary" exodus. The Immigration and Naturalization Service (INS) itself deported 82,000 Mexicans during this period,[146] but also worked with state and local governments (as well as vigilante groups) to force hundreds of thousands more out of the country. In many cases special trains were organized, with fees to the Mexican border pre-paid, and, in other cases, Mexicans were rounded up and placed into truck that drove them into Mexico and dropped them in the desert. Police in towns embracing the movement raided public establishments, herding Mexicans into cars or onto trains or busses driven by social workers and taken to the border.

The most shocking aspect of the Repatriation Movement was the flagrant disregard of constitutional law. Researchers have found that approximately 60 percent of those repatriated were legal U.S. citizens, born in the United States. Professor Cruz Reynoso, a former Justice on

Deportation sign, by Neon Tommy, via Wikimedia Commons

the California Supreme Court was one of the children forcibly deported and remembers, at the time, not even knowing where Mexico was when he was told by his parents that they were leaving Southern California. Hundreds of thousands of Mexicans and Mexican Americans were removed from California, Michigan, Colorado, Texas, Illinois, Ohio, and New York, which were among the states that authorities most aggressively embraced repatriation. This effort violated the legal rights of tens of thousands who were, by virtue of being born in the United States, U.S. citizens and thus supposed to be protected by law, and the actions taken by state police and immigration agencies were thus illegal even at the time.[147]

A 2006 article in *USA Today*, featured an interview with members of a family forcibly removed from Montana during the Repatriation Movement. Ignacio Pina, who was six years old at the time they were deported in 1931, told reporters that men arrived with guns, forcing them from their home, and not allowing them to bring anything with them, even the trunk that held birth certificates proving that Pina and his five siblings were U.S. citizens. The family was placed in jail for ten days, then sent to Mexico by train. After 16 years, Pina was able to obtain a copy of his birth certificate from Utah and was allowed to return to the United States.[148]

In the 2000s, a small group of activists and historians tried to bring the forgotten Repatriation Movement back into the light. This article, from a 2003 issue of *The Guardian* newspaper, discusses the Repatriation Movement and the campaign for recognition and redress in the 2000s.

MEXICANS EXPELLED IN 30S ASK FOR JUSTICE

by Gary Younge

The Guardian, 2003

Source Document

Hundreds of thousands of Hispanics, many of them US citizens, were rounded up in Los Angeles and forcibly deported to Mexico during the Depression to protect white people's jobs, according to a civil case being brought in the city.

The Mexican American Legal Defence and Education Fund and the law firm Kiesel, Boucher and Larson are seeking class-action status for the suit, brought on behalf of an estimated 400,000 people of Mexican descent.

It claims that local officials working with the federal immigration authorities carried out a "coordinated, aggressive campaign to remove people of Mexican ancestry from California in large numbers," in violation of their constitutional rights.

"This lawsuit goes to the essence of who we are as a state and the dignity of a people," Raymond Boucher told the *Los Angeles Times*.

"We have to recognise that in the 1930s we used the Mexican population as a scapegoat. Until we take an honest look in the mirror, none of us is truly safe."

One of the plaintiffs, Emilia Castaneda, said she was nine when she was forced to leave her home in 1935. She was loaded on to a train and sent to Mexico after her father was put out of work by the campaign against foreign labour. "We cried and cried," she said. "I had never been to Mexico. We were leaving everything behind."

They returned to her father's home state, Durango, where they were referred to as repatriadas.

Her Spanish was weak and her family was initially passed between relatives until they found somewhere to stay.

Only when her godmother in Los Angeles obtained a copy of her birth certificate and sent it to her could she return, after presenting it to the US immigration authorities.

"As an American, I didn't deserve to be deported," she said. "All Americans should know this is part of our history so we don't have to experience this again."

Somebody could say: "We were wrong for the injustices committed to

Mexicans Expelled in 30s Ask For Justice
continued

you, and apologise for what was done. Maybe other people who are still in Mexico would hear about this and would come back."

An estimated 60% of those forcibly removed were US citizens.

Mexican immigration became a national issue in the 1920s when the pool of cheap labour Mexicans provided in the west became a source of contention with the rural south, which felt it was being undercut.

By 1930, with unemployment and demands for state welfare growing, President Herbert Hoover began a "repatriation" programme.

The plaintiffs are hoping for the kind of compensation package given by the Reagan administration to Japanese Americans interned during the second world war, settled by the threat of a class-action case.

Joseph Dunn, a Californian state senator who has been building up a case for the Mexicans for the past year, presided over a hearing yesterday to examine the forced removal.

"The deportation programme of the 1930s is not a proud chapter in American history," he said.

"Hopefully, by acknowledging this, we can minimise the likelihood of unjustly treating future immigrants to this great nation."

Mr. Dunn has brought together a number of scholars who have studied the era, who testified in favour of the plaintiffs. Francisco Balderrama, professor of history and Chicano studies at Cal State University Los Angeles, said the forced removals "became a model for the rest of the United States."

Kevin Johnson, an associate dean at the University of California Davis School of Law said: "It's a bedrock principle of US immigration law that US citizens cannot be removed [from the US]. This is why this episode is so troubling to me."

A lawyer for the city, Rocky Delgadillo, said he had not yet seen the case, which was lodged on Tuesday, and so could not comment.[149]

In 2005, Democratic State Senator Joe Dunn of California authored a bill called the Apology Act calling for the State of California to officially apologize for its role in the often-overlooked repatriation movement of the 1930s. Interviewed by *NPR*, Dunn told reporter Melissa Block:

> *"Unfortunately, most of the individuals that were forcibly deported literally were done under armed guard and lock and key. There was a raid in a park in Los Angeles in February of 1931 in which they literally rounded up all the folk in that park who appeared to be of Mexican descent, put them on flatbed trucks under armed guard to Union Station in downtown Los Angeles, on a train that was under lock and key and literally forced them on and—onto the train, and the train took them to the interior of Mexico. Most of the deportations were done by force."*[150]

The California state legislature approved of Dunn's largely symbolic bill, signing the "Apology Act" into law in 2006. Section 8722 of the Act is the one that contains the apology:

> *"The State of California apologizes to those individuals described in Section 8721 for the fundamental violations of their basic civil liberties and constitutional rights committed during the period of illegal deportation and coerced emigration. The State of California regrets the suffering and hardship of those individuals and their families endured as a direct result of the government sponsored Repatriation Program of the 1930s."*[151]

The Mexican Repatriation Movement of the 1930s was, like the effort to exclude Asian Americans from the mid-1800s to the mid-1900s, motivated by protectionism, but fueled by racism. The program as it was eventually carried out by cadres of state police and immigration officials, armed vigilantes, and federal agents, was cruel and unusual in American history, with the prejudice and fear completely overtaking legal considerations of naturalization law to that point. In many ways, the Mexican Repatriation movement was an attempt to legally pursue a policy of ethnic cleansing in an effort to remove members of an allegedly inferior race and to preserve the power and cultural legacy of America's white majority.

CONCLUSION

As in much of history, the loudest voices leave the most lasting mark, and so echoes of anti-Mexican sentiment from Congress remain the most obvious remnant of this era in America's immigration debate. It was not until the 1930s that many Americans outside the southwest were discussing Mexican migration as another "race problem." Historical research shows that anti-Mexican sentiment from this point onward would be more acute, but the fact remained that owners, farmers, and growers in the region still wanted Mexican laborers. Further complicating the debate, these influential business lobbyists promoted the idea that Mexican laborers were not a threat to American society, but rather a boon to productivity, taking jobs that native-born Americans rarely wanted—a sentiment that continues to inform the current debate about Mexican immigration in the twenty-first century.

DISCUSSION QUESTIONS

- Should states and the federal government pay restitution or reparations in cases where the government has violated the rights of individuals because of racial prejudice? Why or why not?
- Are modern opinions about Mexicans and Mexican Americans still affected by racial prejudice? Why or why not?
- In your opinion, why did some Americans fear the "mongrelization" of America in the 1930s? Provide evidence to support your answer.
- Why do you think that anti-Mexican sentiment peaked in the 1930s?

Works Used

"Apology Act for the 1930s Mexican Repatriation Program." *California Legislative Information*. Chapter 8.5 Mexican Repatriation. 1 Jan. 2006.

Bailey, David C. *¡Viva Cristo Rey!: The Cristero Rebellion and the Church-State Conflict in Mexico*. Austin, TX: U of Texas P, 1974.

Gonzales, Manuel G. *Mexicanos: A History of Mexicans in the United States*. Bloomington, IN: Indiana UP, 2009.

Hardman, John. "The Great Depression and the New Deal." *EDGE*. Ethics of Development in a Global Environment. Stanford University. 26 July 1999.

"INS Records for 1930s Mexican Repatriations." *USCIS*. U.S. Citizenship and Immigration Services. Department of Homeland Security. 3 Mar. 2014.

Johnson, Kevin R. "The Forgotten Repatriation of Persons of Mexican Ancestry and Lesson for the War on Terror." *Pace Law Review*. Vol. 26, Iss. 1. Digital Commons. Sept. 2005.

MacMedan, Dan. "U.S. urged to apologize for 1930s deportations." *USA Today*. Gannet Co, Inc. 5 Apr. 2006.

"Remembering California's 'Repatriation Program.'" *NPR*. National Public Radio. 2 Jan. 2006.

Ruiz, Vicki L. *From Out of the Shadows: Mexican Women in Twentieth-Century America*. New York: Oxford UP, 1998.

"The Great Depression (1929–1939)." *George Washington University*. The Eleanor Roosevelt Papers Project. Department of History. 2016.

Younge, Gary. "Mexicans expelled in 30s ask for justice." *The Guardian*. Guardian News and Media. 16 July 2003.

Introduction

At the end of the 1930s, the public debate again turned towards the potential for a coming war as American politicians and the public debated whether the United States should get involved in World War II. This chapter explores how the 1941 attack on Pearl Harbor instigated a movement against Japanese immigrants, and ultimately the imprisonment of America's entire Japanese-American population for the duration of the war, while simultaneously resulting in a government campaign to reduce prejudice against China and the Chinese race.

The document for this chapter is a speech given by President Franklin Roosevelt calling for the end of the nation's long-standing ban on Chinese immigration. This was part of a broad government-sponsored effort to change public perceptions on China, who had become an important ally to the United States in the war against Japanese forces in the Pacific. The effort to end the prohibition against Chinese immigration was controversial as many Americans had come to believe Chinese migrants were a danger to U.S. culture and the economy. Ultimately, the actions taken by Congress were largely symbolic, resulting in little actual change to U.S. immigration policy.

Topics covered in this chapter include:
- World War II
- Japanese internment
- Anti-Japanese sentiment
- National Quota System
- U.S. Supreme Court Cases
- Franklin Roosevelt Administration
- Chinese exclusion

This Chapter Discusses the Following Source Document:
Roosevelt, Franklin D. "Message to Congress on Repeal of the Chinese Exclusion Law." Oct. 11, 1943. *The American Presidency Project*. University of California, Santa Barbara. 2017.

America's Favored Asians
Chinese Exclusion and Japanese Internment (1941-1945)

World War II brought an end to sixty years of Chinese exclusion, enabling, for the first time since 1882, Chinese people to immigrate to the United States, though in limited numbers. However, Congress remained resolute in their decision to continue barring immigration from India, Malaysia, the Arab Peninsula, and other countries within the "Asiatic Barred Zone" established in 1921. The war also brought about a new effort to control dangerous Asian immigrants and their children, in the form of the Japanese internment law that resulted in more than 100,000 Japanese Americans and Japanese-born immigrants being taken prisoner for the duration of the War.

Imprisoning Japanese-Americans

Japanese people were formally excluded from migrating to the United States in 1924, and were the last group of Asians to be excluded. There was, however, already a sizable population of foreign-born Japanese and Japanese-American citizens already living in the United States at the time. As per the 1906 Naturalization Laws, those born in the United States, even if of a race excluded from citizenship, were still citizens and thus, save for an overhaul of naturalization law, the Asian exclusion acts of 1882–1924 did not revoke the citizenship of those Chinese, Japanese, and other Asian-Americans who already had citizenship by virtue of native birth.

On December 7, 1941, the Japanese empire attacked an American military base in Hawaii, at Pearl Harbor. As the first (and only) time the United States suffered a direct attack from a foreign power, the American public reacted with intense fear and panic. The Japanese Empire had joined the Axis Powers, which also included Germany and Italy, in the Second World War. Ultimately, this became an effort to curtail the imperial aims of

Posted sign notifying people of Japanese descent to report for relocation, U.S. National Archives, via Wikimedia Commons

Nazi Germany, which sought to conquer Europe. The Japanese-American conflict was one branch of this broader global war, known as the Pacific Theatre, or the Pacific War.

Beginning the same day that Pearl Harbor was attacked, the FBI began rounding up Japanese resident aliens who had already been added to a list of individuals considered potential subversives as the United States was gearing up for war. Soon Congress was debating what to do about the threat of Japanese people living in the West Coast, with the prevailing fear being that these immigrants, and even native-born Japanese might feel sufficient kinship with their native people to assist the Japanese cause as internal actors. [152]

The fact that the United States had been taken completely by surprise in the attack on Pearl Harbor further stoked fears that there may have been accomplices already in the United States. Congress rapidly convened a commission to study the incident, headed by Chief Supreme Court Justice Owen Roberts, which released a report, known as the Roberts Commission Report, in February of 1942. Though there was no evidence, Roberts' suggestion that there may have been sleeper cells of Japanese people in Hawaii helping to organize the attack, struck a chord with members of Congress and the executive branch. Another important aspect of the debate was that white agriculturalists on the West Coast, having long harbored racial prejudice against the Japanese farmers in their area, used Pearl Harbor as an excuse to actively lobby for the removal of Japanese people from the region.

For instance, Austin Anson, the managing secretary of the California Vegetable Grower-Shipper Association of Salinas testified on the issue in Congress, and told a *Saturday Evening Post* reporter in 1942:

> _____ *"We're charged with wanting to get rid of the Japs for selfish reasons. We might as well be honest.*

We do. It's a question of whether the white man lives on the Pacific Coast or the brown men. They came into this valley to work, and they stayed to take over. They offer higher land prices and higher rents than the white man can pay for land. They undersell the white man in the markets. They can do this because they raise their own labor. They work their women and children while the white farmer has to pay wages for his help. If all the Japs were removed tomorrow, we'd never miss them in two weeks, because the white farmers can take over and produce everything the Jap grows. And we don't want them back when the war ends, either."[153]

It was the report of General John DeWitt, entitled, *Japanese Evacuation from the West Coast,* that sealed the fate of Japanese-Americans more than anything else. In his final report, DeWitt summarized the essence of the fears held by the military, that Japanese-Americans would be caught between allegiances and potentially shift against the United States:[154]

"In the war in which we are now engaged racial affinities are not severed by migration. The Japanese race is an enemy race and while many second and third generation Japanese born on United States soil, possessed of United States citizenship, have become 'Americanized,' the racial strains are undiluted. To conclude otherwise is to expect that children born of white parents on Japanese soil sever all racial affinity and become loyal Japanese subjects, ready to fight and, if necessary to die for Japan in a war against the nation of their parents."

Japanese families leaving Los Angeles, California, during WW II, by Clem Albers,
U.S. National Archives, via Wikimedia Commons

DeWitt's prejudicial arguments were moderate compared to the vigor
and vitriol expressed by other members of Congress unabashed in their
racialized rhetoric. One such comment came from Representative John
Rankin, a Democrat from Mississippi, in a speech to the House of Representatives in 1942:

> *"I'm for catching every Japanese in America,
> Alaska and Hawaii now and putting them in
> concentration camps and shipping them back to
> Asia as soon as possible...This is a race war, as far
> as the Pacific side of the conflict in concerned...
> The White man's civilization has come into conflict
> with Japanese barbarism...One of them must be
> destroyed...Damn them! Let's get rid of them now!"*[155]

The violent racialized rhetoric in Congress was matched in the public and in the press. To provide one example, *Hearst* newspaper columnist Henry McLemore wrote in January of 1942:

> *"I am for immediate removal of every Japanese on the West Coast to a point deep in the interior. I don't mean a nice part of the interior either. Herd 'em up, pack 'em off and give 'em the inside room in the badlands. Let 'em be pinched, hurt, hungry and dead up against it...personally, I hate the Japanese. And that goes for all of them."*[156]

On February 19, President Franklin Roosevelt issued Executive Order 9066, authorizing the U.S. military to designate areas to be used for the temporary detention of Japanese immigrants and native-born Japanese people. More than 120,000 were thus arrested and detained, some until as late as 1946. The interned Japanese were kept under armed guard, behind barbed wire, and were treated like prisoners though none had been tried and convicted. While they were interned, companies seized property owned by Japanese merchants and farmers. When internment ended, Japanese-Americans returned to a highly prejudiced environment in which many were treated as enemy aliens for many years after the end of the war.

As for the American public, they were, in general, very much willing to accept the idea of internment. In December 1942, a year after the attack on Pearl Harbor, Gallup polled Americans about the Japanese situation, asking, "Do you think the Japanese who were moved inland from the Pacific coast should be allowed to return to the Pacific coast when the war is over?" Only 35 percent of respondents answered "yes," while 48 percent believe that they should not be allowed to return to their homes after the war. Gallup then posed a follow-up question, asking "What should be

done with them?" with half of respondents saying that the Japanese prisoners should be sent back to Japan, whereas another 13 percent chose "Put them out of this country," and 10 percent said, "Leave them where they are—under control." The original Gallup report also showed that 7 percent of Americans polled favored killing the Japanese that had been interned.[157]

Overall, polls from across the country found broad support for Japanese internment, with some three-quarters of southern Californians supporting the internment program, compared to 50 percent of Washington residents, 56 percent of Oregonians, and 44 percent of Northern Californians.[158] Even two years later, prejudice was still dominant in opinion polls. A September 1944 National Opinion Research Center survey found, for instance, that 61 percent of Americans thought that whites should be prioritized in hiring decisions over Japanese Americans, with only 21 percent feeling that things should be equal between the two groups.

Fred Korematsu, a Japanese-American citizen living in California, defied the internment order, and stayed in his home. He continued to protest until his case came, in December of 1944, before the Supreme Court. In the case, *Korematsu v. United States*, the court ruled 6 to 3 against Korematsu, with Justice Hugo Black, delivering the majority decision, arguing that the internment program was the result of national security concerns and not racial prejudice. This was, of course, patently untrue. No efforts were made to intern Germans or Italians, even though both countries were also enemies of the United States and despite the fact that intelligence from the era indicated that there were German-American spies in the United States at the time. The actions taken against the Japanese-American citizens were a clear violation of constitutional law and thus, by the 1960s and 70s, Americans were starting to recognize the internment program for what it was, a racially-motivated crime perpetrated by the American government on its own citizens because they were not white. Gerald Ford issued a proclamation in 1976 officially apologizing for the government's actions, whereas another formal governmental apology, and reparations for the families of some 80,000 survivors, were issued under the Reagan administration in 1988.

The Korematsu decision was formally vacated by Judge Marilyn Hall Patel of the Federal District Court of California in 1983, who wrote that the case: "stands as a caution that in times of distress the shield of military necessity and national security must not be used to protect governmental actions from close scrutiny and accountability." Over the years, legal experts have repeatedly voted Korematsu one of the worst decisions in the history of the U.S. Supreme Court.[159]

The Magnuson Act (1943)

Even during another racially-charged panic, World War II also forced Congress and the administration to revisit the nation's oldest and most lasting immigration law, Chinese Exclusion. China was one of the Allied Powers in World War II and, in fact, was the first nation to fight the Japanese Empire in the Pacific. Shared goals and fears made allies of Chinese and American soldiers and, in fact, more than 250,000 Americans served alongside Chinese troops in the China-Burma-India theatre of the war.

The conflict between China and Japan began on July 7, 1937, with a Japanese attack on the Marco Polo bridge outside Beijing. Within a year, Japan had conquered much of the nation, with total control of the eastern cities of Shanghai and Nanjing, and millions of Chinese citizens held as prisoners of war. The war with Japan went global only after the attack on Pearl Harbor, until which time China had no real allies in its fight against Japan's colonial occupation. Further, because the nation had little in the way of resources, they are often discounted in historical discussions of the allies, and yet, their involvement was crucial and the United States military knew it. By keeping at least 600,000 Japanese troops occupied with their resistance to the Japanese occupation, China protected the

other countries in Japan's view while the United States and European allies tackled the European theatre. China suffered dramatically in World War II, with between 3 and 4 million military casualties and as many as 15 to 20 million killed overall, compared to an estimated total of 400,000–420,000 for the United States.[160]

It is unknown whether any of the 250,000 Americans who fought alongside Chinese troops in World War II came home with a more nuanced view of the Chinese people and culture, but, back in the states, most Americans were still very prejudiced against all Asians and this prejudice exploded into vicious bigotry after the Japanese attack on Pearl Harbor. This was a problem for the government, as the U.S. military knew well that China's aid was crucial to an American victory in the Pacific and recognized that a deeper, less antagonistic relationship with China could prove crucial for future efforts to secure global peace. Given the deep-seated racism of the American people, however, it was difficult to convince Americans to set aside these biases and view Chinese people as friends. The American propaganda industry was also, at the time, engaged in a full-blown effort to dehumanize Italian, German, and Japanese people in the eyes of Americans so as to make it easier for Americans to get behind the effort to kill them unencumbered by empathy or humanitarian impulses. The government thus put this propaganda machine to work to promote the perception that, despite 60 years of racism and exclusion, the Chinese people were the benevolent Asian race heroically standing alongside Americans and democracy, in opposition to evil.

Chiang Kai Shek, via Wikimedia Commons

In many ways, the U.S.–China alliance in World War II gave voice to the many Americans who had long appreciated Chinese culture and abhorred the way that Chinese people were treated and maligned by Americans. For instance, *Time* magazine founder Henry Luce, who had grown up in China, was friends with Chinese Republican leader Chiang Kai-Shek, and featured Chiang on the cover of *Time* in 1938. Luce personally wrote many articles informing American readers about the hardships faced by the Chinese under the Japanese occupation and these became part of a government-funded effort to, essentially, "rehumanize" the Chinese race in the eyes of the public. Soong Mei-Ling (Chiang Kai-Shek's wife), who had been educated in America and was fluent in English, traveled to the United States and gave an address before a joint session of Congress, becoming the first Chinese person and the second woman of any nationality, to do so.[161]

At her speech before Congress, Soong Mei-Ling echoed the hopes for multicultural cooperation and friendship that would not become mainstream for some time:

_____ *"We of this generation who are privileged to help make a better world for ourselves and for posterity should remember that, while we must not be visionary, we must have vision so that peace should not be punitive in spirit and should not be provincial or nationalistic or even continental in concept, but universal in scope and humanitarian in action, for modern science has so annihilated distance that what affects one people must of necessity affect all other peoples.*

The term "hands and feet" is often used in China to signify the relationship between brothers. Since international interdependence is now so universally recognized, can we not also say that all nations should become members of one corporate body?"[162]

As United States and Chinese leaders campaigned for the support of white Americans, the United China Relief organization tried to raise funds for war-torn China in the United States. This group also helped with the pro-China propaganda campaign producing posters with slogans like "China Fights On," and "China: First to Fight!" that featured, romantic paintings of Chinese soldiers and their families in the same artistic style as paintings of American and European military heroes. It was a full-blown effort to rehabilitate the Chinese image that involved artistic reimagining of Chinese racial characteristics, political and media exposés on the virtues of Chinese society, and even war-time fiction featuring Chinese characters depicted as heroes.

To imagine how difficult it was to promote positive feelings for one Asian race, whereas actively dehumanizing another, and the efforts to promote empathy and friendship for the Chinese were not free from racialized language and depictions. For instance, a December 22, 1941, article in *Life Magazine*, attempted to teach Americans how to tell Japanese and Chinese people apart, featuring two comparison photographs with notes on their unique features, such as "parchment yellow skin" for Chinese people, as compared to "earthy yellow complexion" for the Japanese. The magazine also described the photo of the Chinese man (who is smiling in the photo) as a "public servant," whereas the frowning Japanese man is described as a "Japanese warrior whose face shows the humorless intensity of ruthless mystics."[163]

Though the U.S. Congress has never been daunted by illogic or hypocrisy when it comes to performing its function, it became increasingly clear that the push for friendly U.S.–Chinese relations was undermined by the fact that, since 1882 Chinese people had been prohibited from migrating to the United States. Furthermore, Japanese propaganda during the war highlighted Chinese exclusion to drive a wedge between the two nations, essentially reminding the Chinese not to trust the Americans, who'd already proven their racism against Asians, in general, and Chinese people, in particular. Congress decided it was time to revisit the law and Warren G. Magnuson, a U.S. Representative from Washington, which was the state that ironically hosted some of the most passionate anti-Chinese lobbyists in the nation, became the chief proponent of the effort. The Magnuson Act also known as the Chinese Exclusion Repeal Act of 1943, officially ended the 61 years of racial exclusion.

Ending Chinese Exclusion wasn't controversial, because it was pretty much meaningless. From 1924 on, the actual Chinese Exclusion Act was merely a symbol of America's enduring belief that Chinese people were uniquely horrible, because a separate provision in the Johnson-Reed Immigration Act of 1924 already denied immigration to every race that could not, in principle, be naturalized. This meant that even without the Chinese Exclusion Act, Chinese people, like all other Asian people, still could not immigrate.

The controversy came when supporters of the repeal suggested that Chinese people should be added to the quota list, allowing them to begin coming to the United States again. Given their population in the 1920 census (which was the basis for the national origin quotas) such an act would have provided 105 visas to immigrants from China each year. Nativists and anti-Asian activists vehemently opposed this, worrying that it would lead to a slow, racial invasion. These fears were complicated by the fact that the quotas had been based on "national origin" and not directly on race or ethnicity, though preserving racial and ethnic balance was undoubtedly the reason for the system. Because Britain is a Western European nation, a large number of visas were set aside each year for British immigration, but few were used because British people had no pressing need to migrate to the United States. However, Britain owned Hong Kong at the time and so immigration critics worried that allowing Chinese immigration could mean that thousands of Chinese people living in Hong Kong would use British visas to come to the United States.

The result was a compromise, one that catered to the xenophobia of the anti-Chinese activists, by creating a quota not based on national representation, but rather, on ethnicity itself. Thus, Chinese coming from any nation, even Canada or Britain, would count against the Chinese quota. The ethnic quota for the Chinese enabled politicians to symbolically prove their claim of friendship with the Chinese without risking a large buildup of Chinese immigrants. The bill did have one controversial effect, however, written in a single clause in section three of the act that, for the first time, officially opened naturalization to Chinese residents. Though given little attention at the time, this was a major milestone, with Chinese immigrants becoming the third racial groups officially allowed not only to migrate, but to become full citizens through the naturalization process.

On October 11, 1943 President Franklin Roosevelt gave a historic statement urging for the repeal in Congress:

SPEECH CALLING FOR THE END OF BAN ON CHINESE IMMIGRATION
President Franklin Roosevelt
October 11, 1943
Source Document Excerpt

"There is now pending before the Congress legislation to permit the immigration of Chinese people into this country and to allow Chinese residents here to become American citizens. I regard this legislation as important in the cause of winning the war and of establishing a secure peace.

China is our ally. For many long years she stood alone in the fight against aggression. Today we fight at her side. She had continued her gallant struggle against very great odds.

China has understood that the strategy of victory in this world war first required the concentration of the greater part of our strength upon the European front. She has understood that the amount of supplies we could make available to her has been limited by difficulties of transportation. She knows that substantial aid will be forthcoming as soon as possible—aid not only in the form of weapons and

Speech Calling for the End of Ban on Chinese Immigration
continued

supplies, but also in carrying out plans already made for offensive, effective action. We and our allies will aim our forces at the heart of Japan—in ever increasing strength until the common enemy is driven from China's soil.

But China's resistance does not depend alone on guns and planes and on attacks on land, on the sea, and from the air. It is based as much in the spirit of her people and her faith in her allies. We owe it to the Chinese to strengthen that faith. One step in this direction is to wipe from the statute books those anachronisms in our law which forbid the immigration of Chinese people into this country and which bar Chinese residents from American citizenship.

Nations, like individuals, make mistakes. We must be big enough to acknowledge our mistakes of the past and to correct them.

By the repeal of the Chinese Exclusion Laws, we can correct a historic mistake and silence the distorted Japanese propaganda. The enactment of legislation now pending before Congress would put Chinese immigrants on a parity with those from other countries. The Chinese quota would, therefore, be only about 100 immigrants a year. There can be no reasonable apprehension that any such number of immigrants will cause unemployment or provide competition in the search for jobs.

The extension of the privileges of citizenship to the relatively few Chinese residents in our country would operate as another meaningful display of friendship. It would be additional proof that we regard China not only as a partner in waging war but that we shall regard her as a partner in days of peace. While it would give Chinese a preferred status over certain other Oriental people, their great contribution to the cause of decency and freedom entitles them to such preference.

If feel confident that the Congress is in full agreement that these measures—long overdue—should be taken to correct an injustice to our friends. Action by the Congress now will be an earnest (expression) of our purpose to apply the policy of the Good Neighbor to our relations with other people...”[164]

CONCLUSION

Public opinion polls from the 1940s indicate that Americans across the country were supportive of Japanese internment and viewed the entire Japanese race as a potential threat to American culture. Some felt that this extraordinary action was necessary to secure the nation from a foreign threat and yet, no similar efforts were taken against German or Italian Americans living in the U. S., despite the fact that Germany and Italy were both enemy nations. Despite claims that the system was motivated by concerns for national security, government actions demonstrated that racism was a primary factor in the Japanese internment. Widespread racial prejudice against members of Asian races deepened during World War II due to a publicly-funded campaign to dehumanize the Japanese, as part of an effort to build support for the war in the Pacific theatre. The American public was thus presented with conflicting messages, being told that some Asian races were friendly and shared similar values, whereas others were enemy aliens whose very nature made them dangerous enemies of American society.

DISCUSSION QUESTIONS

- Was Japanese internment morally or ethically wrong? Explain.
- In what ways is the Japanese internment movement similar and different to the modern effort to ban Muslim migration to the United States?
- What does the final form of the Magnusson Act reveal about Chinese prejudice?
- Roosevelt said, "We must be big enough to acknowledge our mistakes of the past and to correct them." Are there some mistakes that Americans must acknowledge and attempt to correct in the twenty-first century? What are they?

Works Used

Fried, Amy. "Government public opinion research and the Japanese-American internment." *BDN*. Bangor Daily News. Pollways. 29 Dec. 2011.

"How to tell Japs from the Chinese." *Life Magazine*. 22 Dec. 1941, p. 81.

Kang, Jerry. "Denying Prejudice: Internment, Redress, and Denial." *USLA Law Review*. Vol. 51, No 933. 2004.

Loveland, Ian D. *Constitutional Law*. New York: Routledge, 2000.

Mitter, Rana. "Forgotten ally? China's unsung role in World War II." *CNN*. CNN. 31 Aug. 2015.

"Racism & Exclusion." *National Park Service*. Manzanar National Historic Site. 2016.

Roosevelt, Franklin D. "Message to Congress on Repeal of the Chinese Exclusion Law." 11 Oct. 1943. *The American Presidency Project*. University of California, Santa Barbara.

"Soong Mei-Ling, 'Addresses To The House Of Representatives And To The Senate,' February 18, 1943." *USC*. University of Southern California. USC US–China Institute. 1943.

Swift, Art. "Gallup Vault: WWII-Era Support for Japanese Internment." *Gallup News*. Gallup Vault. Aug. 31, 2016.

Taylor, Frank J. "The People Nobody Wants." *Saturday Evening Post*. Saturday Evening Post Society. 9 May 1942.

Tiezzi, Shannon. "When the US and China Were Allies." *The Diplomat*. The Diplomat. 21 Aug. 2015.

Weber, Mark. "The Japanese camps in California." *Journal of Historical Review*. Vol. 2, Iss. 1. p. 50, 1981.

White, Steven. "Many Americans support Trump's immigration order. Many Americans backed Japanese internment camps, too." *The Washington Post*. Washington Post, Co. 2 Feb. 2017.

Introduction

After World War I, fear of an influx of refugees from Eastern, Central, and Southern Europe motivated a powerful anti-immigration movement in the United States, effectively ending the mass migration period. This chapter explores how fear of a new refugee crisis, specifically of Jewish refugees, during and after World War II led to a new anti-immigration movement based on justification used in the past—that an influx of immigrants would pose a danger to American society, values, and economy.

The three sources for this chapter are speeches given by President Harry Truman regarding the immigration of refugees from the war in Europe. Truman campaigned for immigration reform that would enable the nation to become a home for those displaced. The law that was adopted in 1948, the Displaced Persons Act, did not meet with his approval, as the bill was prejudiced against Jewish immigrants and other refugees from Southern, Central, and Eastern Europe. Truman continued to campaign on behalf of these refugees and, in 1950, Congress amended the Displaced Persons Act, removing many of the barriers that prohibited the migration of some groups of refugees from Europe.

Topics covered in this chapter include:
- Racial prejudice
- Anti-Semitism
- Refugee immigration
- Harry S. Truman Administration
- World War II
- Jewish refugees

This Chapter Discusses the Following Source Documents:
Truman, Harry S. "Statement and Directive by the President on Immigration to the United States of Certain Displaced Persons and Refugees in Europe." Dec. 22, 1945. *Truman Library & Museum*. University of Missouri. 2018.
Truman, Harry S. "Statement by the President Upon Signing Bill Amending the Displaced Persons Act." June 16, 1950. *Truman Library and Museum*. University of Missouri. 2018.
Truman, Harry S. "Statement by the President Upon Signing the Displaced Persons Act." June 25, 1948. *The American Presidency Project*. University of California. 2018.

America's Reluctant Humanitarianism
Refugees During and After World War II (1937–1950)

During and after World War II, Congress and the American people were forced to consider whether the United States should do something to help the millions of destitute refugees in Europe and, specifically, the Jewish refugees who had been forcibly removed from their homes and imprisoned in concentration camps, or forced to run from Nazi soldiers, hiding among the other nations of Europe. The refugee crisis was severe, and the European nations were all struggling to adjust and adopt policies to cope with the existence of so many in need. Across the Atlantic, Americans were suspicious and very reluctant to get involved.

Resistance to Refugees

Although there have always been some who believe immigration should be used to help those less fortunate and who celebrate the diversity of America, these attitudes belonged to the liberal minority through much of America's complex history. Thus the "open door" era of immigration so often mentioned in historical texts, was really just an open door to Europe, and not even to all of Europe.

After World War I, Americans were told that there were throngs of Eastern, Central, and Southern European refugees that would soon be trying to gain access to the United States. Eugenicists told the public that these types of Europeans were morally, politically, and socially deficient, less intelligent, had little work ethic, and brought strange diseases that would pose a threat to public welfare. Coupled with nativist fears of job competition, this was sufficient to drum up a strong public resistance, and the nation essentially refused to join with the rest of Europe in coping with the refugee crisis. In fact, the United States went in *entirely* the other direction, closing the open door to Europe and establishing the quota system that limited immigration overall, prohibited immigration of non-whites, and preserved the hierarchy of races and ethnicities.

This leads to World War II. Americans were not sanguine about joining the war effort at all. Many American eugenicists sympathized with Nazi Germany's effort to maintain their nation's racial purity and, in fact, the theories developed by American eugenicists inspired the Nazi ideology. Some Americans favored isolationism, whereas others hoped for a diplomatic solution or felt the war had little to do with the United States, despite several years of coverage describing the atrocities of the Nazi campaign. At the beginning of 1940, about 40 percent of Americans were willing to intervene, according to a collection of polls taken at the time. However, when the Japanese attacked Pearl Harbor, patriotism and nationalism spiked and even eugenicists and white supremacists were willing to get on board, finding it far easier to justify fighting a non-white enemy. Just after the Japanese attack, more than 70 percent of Americans favored intervention.[165]

One of the concerns about getting involved in the war was that there would be another flood of refugees wanting to come into the country, and there were lobbyists in Congress and in the public urging Americans to consider temporarily amending the quota system to accommodate those left homeless and destitute by Nazi Germany's advance across Europe. These voices were, however, coming from a very small minority of Americans.

In July 1938, after a year of media coverage describing how thousands of Germans and Austrians had been forced to flee their homes by the Nazis, *Fortune* magazine took a poll, asking "What is your attitude towards allowing German, Austrian, and other political refugees to come into the United States?" Over 67 percent believed that America should try to keep the refugees out, whereas only 6 percent broadly favored allowing them into the nation. Then, on January 20, 1939, a poll from the American Institute of Public Opinion asked, "It has been proposed to bring to this country 10,000 refugee children from Germany—most of them Jewish—to

be taken care of in American homes. Should the government permit these children to come in?" To this, 30 percent said yes, whereas 61 percent said "no." [166]

These two polls were conducted before and after "Kristallnacht," or the "Night of Broken Glass," on November 9–10, in which the Nazi Party began the first wave of ethnic cleansing, rounding up and killing Jews in Germany, Austria, and Czechoslovakia. The name, derived from the broken glass on the streets after Nazi soldiers smashed in the windows of Jewish homes and businesses, was the event that crystalized the German Nazi plans for the war, making it clear that the party planned to violently exterminate, rather than simply politically controlling, the region's Jewish population.[167]

Harry Truman, Champion of Refugees

In 1945, there were more than 7 million people who had been displaced by the war, and the Allied armies were struggling to return these people to their homes. Ultimately, the refugee crisis led to the creation of Israel from the former British territory of Palestine and to the Israeli-Palestinian crisis that is still one of the world's most controversial humanitarian issues in 2018. Back home, however, Americans were debating what role the United States should play in helping to resettle the more than 800,000 still without homes or communities to return to in Europe. The United States was paying part of the cost of caring for some 617,000 of these persons in Europe, with an estimated expenditure of $130 million per year in the form of contributions to the International Refugees Organization.[168] The question was: should those people be allowed to come to America?

Gallup Polls taken in 1946 and 1947 demonstrate the resistance among the American people. For instance, in 1946, after President Harry Truman gave a speech in which he personally asked Congress and the American people to consider admitting more refugees from Europe, 72 percent of Americans opposed the proposal, as compared to only 16 percent who

President Truman, left, receiving a Menorah from Israel's Prime Minister David Ben-Gurion, center, and Abba Eban, U.S. Ambassador to Israel, Oval Office, 1951, U.S. National Archives, via Wikimedia Commons

approved. Then, in 1947, when Gallup asked about the potential resettlement of just 10,000 of the estimated 800,000 in need of resettlement, 57 percent of Americans said they would disapprove of refugees being moved into their home state, and only 20 percent were willing to entertain the plan.[169]

For his part, President Harry Truman (1945–1953) championed the cause of the refugees in Europe. In speeches he delivered throughout his presidency, he tried desperately to convince the American people that taking in the refugees was the right ethical and moral choice and one that should represent America's commitment to freedom and world peace. Given the resistance in the public, the fight over World War II refugees in Congress was contentious and unproductive. President Truman repeatedly asked Congress to pass a law to admit more refugees, but to little avail.

Truman met such resistance that, in December of 1945, he sidestepped Congress and the American people and issued an executive order, known generally as the "Truman Directive," which was used to admit (quietly), about 23,000 Jewish refugees in 1946. Truman explained this decision to Congress and the public in an impassioned plea delivered on December 22, 1945:

"TRUMAN DIRECTIVE"
December 22, 1945
Source Document

Statement and Directive by the President on Immigration to the United States of Certain Displaced Persons and Refugees in Europe.

THE WAR has brought in its wake an appalling dislocation of populations in Europe. Many humanitarian organizations, including the United Nations Relief and Rehabilitation Administration, are doing their utmost to solve the multitude of problems arising in connection with this dislocation of hundreds of thousands of persons. Every effort is being made to return the displaced persons and refugees in the various countries of Europe to their former homes. The great difficulty is that so many of these persons have no homes to which they may return. The immensity of the problem of displaced persons and refugees is almost beyond comprehension.

A number of countries in Europe, including Switzerland, Sweden, France, and England, are working toward its solution. The United States shares the responsibility to relieve the suffering. To the extent that our present immigration laws permit, everything possible should be done at once to facilitate the entrance of some of these displaced persons and refugees into the United States.

In this way we may do something to relieve human misery and set an example to the other countries of the world which are able to receive some of these war sufferers. I feel that it is essential that we do this ourselves to show our good faith in requesting other nations to open their doors for this purpose.

Most of these persons are natives of Central and Eastern Europe and the Balkans. The immigration quotas for all these countries for one-year total approximately 39,000, two-thirds of which are allotted to Germany. Under the law, in any single month the number of visas issued cannot exceed ten percent of the annual quota. This means that from now on only about 3900 visas can be issued each month to persons who are natives of these countries.

Very few persons from Europe have migrated to the United States during the war years. In the fiscal year 1942, only ten percent of the immigration quotas was used; in 1943, five percent; in 1944, six percent; and in 1945, seven percent. As of November 30, 1945, the

"Truman Directive"
continued

end of the fifth month of the present fiscal year, only about ten percent of the quotas for the European countries has been used. These unused quotas however do not accumulate through the years, and I do not intend to ask the Congress to change this rule.

The factors chiefly responsible for these low immigration figures were restraints imposed by the enemy, transportation difficulties, and the absence of consular facilities. Most of those Europeans who have been admitted to the United States during the last five years were persons who left Europe prior to the war, and thereafter entered here from non-European countries.

I consider that common decency and the fundamental comradeship of all human beings require us to do what lies within our power to see that our established immigration quotas are used to reduce human suffering. I am taking the necessary steps to see that this is done as quickly as possible.

Of the displaced persons and refugees whose entrance into the United States we will permit under this plan, it is hoped that the majority will be orphaned children. The provisions of law prohibiting the entry of persons likely to become public charges will be strictly observed. Responsible welfare organizations now at work in this field will guarantee that these children will not become public charges. Similar guarantees have or will be made on behalf of adult persons. The record of these welfare organizations throughout the past years has been excellent, and I am informed that no persons admitted under their sponsorship have ever become charges on their communities. Moreover, many of the immigrants will have close family ties in the United States and will receive the assistance of their relatives until they are able to provide for themselves.

These relatives or organizations will also advance the necessary visa fees and travel fare. Where the necessary funds for travel fare and visa fees have not been advanced by a welfare organization or relative, the individual applicant must meet these costs. In this way the transportation of these immigrants across the Atlantic will not cost the American taxpayers a single dollar.

To enter the United States, it is necessary to obtain a visa from a consular officer of the Department of State. As everyone knows, a great many of our consular establishments all over the world were disrupted and their operations suspended when the war came. It is physically impossible to reopen and to restaff all of them overnight. Consequently, it is necessary to choose the area in which

continued

to concentrate our immediate efforts. This is a painful necessity because it requires us to make an almost impossible choice among degrees of misery. But if we refrain from making a choice because it will necessarily be arbitrary, no choice will ever be made, and we shall end by helping no one.

The decision has been made, therefore, to concentrate our immediate efforts in the American zones of occupation in Europe. This is not intended however entirely to exclude issuance of visas in other parts of the world.

In our zones in Europe there are citizens of every major European country. Visas issued to displaced persons and refugees will be charged, according to law, to the countries of their origin. They will be distributed fairly among persons of all faiths, creeds and nationality.

It is intended that, as soon as practicable, regular consular facilities will be reestablished in every part of the world, and the usual, orderly methods of registering and reviewing visa applications will be resumed. The pressing need, however, is to act now in a way that will produce immediate and tangible results. I hope that by early spring adequate consular facilities will be in operation in our zones in Europe, so that immigration can begin immediately upon the availability of ships.

I am informed that there are various measures now pending before the Congress which would either prohibit or severely reduce further immigration. I hope that such legislation will not be passed. This period of unspeakable human distress is not the time for us to close or to narrow our gates. I wish to emphasize, however, that any effort to bring relief to these displaced persons and refugees must and will be strictly within the limits of the present quotas as imposed by law.

There is one particular matter involving a relatively small number of aliens. President Roosevelt, in an endeavor to assist in handling displaced persons and refugees during the war and upon the recommendation of the War Refugee Board, directed that a group of about 1000 displaced persons be removed from refugee camps in Italy and settled temporarily in a War Relocation Camp near Oswego, New York. Shortly thereafter, President Roosevelt informed the Congress that these persons would be returned to their homelands after the war.

Upon the basis of a careful survey by the Department of State and the Immigration and Naturalization

"Truman Directive"
continued

Service, it has been determined that if these persons were now applying for admission to the United States most of them would be admissible under the immigration laws. In the circumstances, it would be inhumane and wasteful to require these people to go all the way back to Europe merely for the purpose of applying there for immigration visas and returning to the United States. Many of them have close relatives, including sons and daughters, who are citizens of the United States and who have served and are serving honorably in the armed forces of our country. I am therefore directing the Secretary of State and the Attorney General to adjust the immigration status of the members of this group who may wish to remain here, in strict accordance with existing laws and regulations.

The number of persons at the Oswego camp is, however, comparatively small. Our major task is to facilitate the entry into the United States of displaced persons and refugees still in Europe. To meet this larger problem, I am directing the Secretary of State, the Attorney General, the Secretary of War, the War Shipping Administrator and the Surgeon General of the Public Health Service to proceed at once to take all appropriate steps to expedite the quota immigration of displaced persons and refugees from Europe to the United States. Representatives of these officials will depart for Europe

very soon to prepare detailed plans for the prompt execution of this project.

The attached directive has been issued by me to the responsible government agencies to carry out this policy. I wish to emphasize, above all, that nothing in this directive will deprive a single American soldier or his wife or children of a berth on a vessel homeward bound or delay their return.

This is the opportunity for America to set an example for the rest of the world in cooperation towards alleviating human misery.

DIRECTIVE BY THE PRESIDENT ON IMMIGRATION TO THE UNITED STATES OF CERTAIN DISPLACED PERSONS AND REFUGEES IN EUROPE
Memorandum to: Secretary of State, Secretary of War, Attorney General, War Shipping Administrator, Surgeon General of the Public Health Service, Director General of UNRRA:

The grave dislocation of populations in Europe resulting from the war has produced human suffering that the people of the United States cannot and will not ignore. This Government should take every possible measure to facilitate full immigration to the United States under existing quota laws.

continued

The war has most seriously disrupted our normal facilities for handling immigration matters in many parts of the world. At the same time, the demands upon those facilities have increased many-fold. It is, therefore, necessary that immigration under the quotas be resumed initially in the areas of greatest need. I, therefore, direct the Secretary of State, the Secretary of War, the Attorney General, the Surgeon General of the Public Health Service, the War Shipping Administrator, and other appropriate officials to take the following action:

The Secretary of State is directed to establish with the utmost despatch consular facilities at or near displaced person and refugee assembly center areas in the American zones of occupation. It shall be the responsibility of these consular officers, in conjunction with the Immigrant Inspectors, to determine as quickly as possible the eligibility of the applicants for visas and admission to the United States. For this purpose the Secretary will, if necessary, divert the personnel and funds of his Department from other functions in order to insure the most expeditious handling of this operation. In cooperation with the Attorney General, he shall appoint as temporary vice-consuls, authorized to issue visas, such officers of the Immigration and Naturalization Service as can be made available for this program. Within the limits of administrative discretion, the officers of the Department of State assigned to this program shall make every effort to simplify and to hasten the process of issuing visas. If necessary, blocs of visa numbers may be assigned to each of the emergency consular establishments. Each such bloc may be used to meet the applications filed at the consular establishment to which the bloc is assigned. It is not intended however entirely to exclude the issuance of visas in other parts of the world.

Visas should be distributed fairly among persons of all faiths, creeds and nationalities. I desire that special attention be devoted to orphaned children to whom it is hoped the majority of visas will be issued.

With respect to the requirement of law that visas may not be issued to applicants likely to become public charges after admission to the United States, the Secretary of State shall cooperate with the Immigration and Naturalization Service in perfecting appropriate arrangements with welfare organizations in the United States which may be prepared to guarantee financial support to successful applicants. This may be accomplished

"Truman Directive"
continued

by corporate affidavit or by any means deemed appropriate and practicable.

The Secretary of War, subject to limitations imposed by the Congress on War Department appropriations, will give such help as is practicable in:

a) Furnishing information to appropriate consular officers and Immigrant Inspectors to facilitate in the selection of applicants for visas; and

b) Assisting until other facilities suffice in: (1) transporting immigrants to a European port; (2) feeding, housing and providing medical care to such immigrants until embarked; and

c) Making available office facilities, billets, messes, and transportation for Department of State, Department of Justice, and United Nations Relief and Rehabilitation Administration personnel connected with this work, where practicable and requiring no out-of-pocket expenditure by the War Department and when other suitable facilities are not available.

The Attorney General, through the Immigration and Naturalization Service, will assign personnel to duty in the American zones of occupation to make the immigration inspections, to assist consular officers of the Department of State in connection with the issuance of visas, and to take the necessary steps to settle the cases of those aliens presently interned at Oswego through appropriate statutory and administrative processes.

The Administrator of the War Shipping Administration will make the necessary arrangements for water transportation from the port of embarkation in Europe to the United States subject to the provision that the movement of immigrants will in no way interfere with the scheduled return of service personnel and their spouses and children from the European theater.

The Surgeon General of the Public Health Service will assign to duty in the American zones of occupation the necessary personnel to conduct the mental and physical examinations of prospective immigrants prescribed in the immigration laws.

The Director General of the United Nations Relief and Rehabilitation Administration will be requested to provide all possible aid to the United States authorities in preparing these people for transportation to the United States and to assist in their care, particularly in the cases of children in transit and others needing special attention.

In order to insure the effective execution of this program, the Secretary of State, the Secretary of War,

continued

the Attorney General, War Shipping Administrator and the Surgeon General of the Public Health Service shall appoint representatives to serve as members of an interdepartmental committee under the Chairmanship of the Commissioner of Immigration and Naturalization.[170]

Two things were working against Truman's campaign, ingrained xenophobia and racial prejudice, which many white Americans applied to Jewish people as well as members of other non-white races, and the fear of Communism that was emerging as the threat du jour to American democratic dominance. West Virginia Senator Chapman Revercomb, who was chair of the Immigration Subcommittee of the Senate Judiciary Committee, represented the anti-refugee sentiment that dominated in Congress at the time. Revercomb was most likely also interested in preserving America's racial hierarchy but based his anti-immigration and anti-refugee arguments on the threat of communist subversion. In his December 1946 report to the committee, Revercomb said:

"Many of those who seek entrance into this country have little concept of our form of government. Many of them come from the lands where Communism had its first growth and dominates the political thought and philosophy of the people. Certainly it would be a tragic blunder to bring into our midst those imbued with a communistic line of thought when one of the most important tasks of this government today is to combat and eradicate communism from this country."[171]

Congress refused to deal with the issue, divided between humanitarians and isolationists in their home states. When America finally passed a law permitting the admittance of refugees, it had been so polluted by the fears of American nativists and the machinations of white supremacists that Truman vehemently objected to the bill on its face, but accepted it as a token gesture at least to the suffering of the world. Truman's speech on June 25, 1948 commemorates the signing of Senate Bill 2242, The Displaced Persons Act of 1948[172]:

STATEMENT BY THE PRESIDENT UPON SIGNING THE DISPLACED PERSONS ACT

June 25, 1948
Source Document

It is with very great reluctance that I have signed S. 2242, the Displaced Persons Act of 1948.

If the Congress were still in session, I would return this bill without my approval and urge that a fairer, more humane bill be passed. In its present form this bill is flagrantly discriminatory. It mocks the American tradition of fair play. Unfortunately, it was not passed until the last day of the session. If I refused to sign this bill now, there would be no legislation on behalf of displaced persons until the next session of the Congress.

It is a close question whether this bill is better or worse than no bill at all. After careful consideration I have decided, however, that it would not be right to penalize the beneficiaries of this bill on account of the injustices perpetrated against others who should have been included within its provisions. I have therefore signed the bill in the hope that its injustices will be rectified by the Congress at the first opportunity.

Americans of all religious faiths and political beliefs will find it hard to understand, as I do, why the 80th Congress delayed action on this subject until the end of this session, with the result that most attempts to improve the bill were frustrated.

The 80th Congress certainly had ample time to produce a satisfactory bill. Eighteen months ago, in my State of the Union Message, I stated that I

continued

did not feel that the United States had done its part in the admission of displaced persons. I pointed out that congressional assistance in the form of new legislation was needed.

Six months later, on July 7, 1947, the Congress had not yet acted, I sent a special message on the subject. I reminded the Congress: "We are dealing with a human problem, a world tragedy . . . I urge the Congress to press forward with its consideration of this subject and to pass suitable legislation as speedily as possible." To my regret, the Congress adjourned last summer without passing any displaced persons legislation.

Again, on January 7, 1948, I urged the Congress "to pass suitable legislation at once so that this Nation may do its share in caring for homeless and suffering refugees of all faiths. I believe that the admission of these persons will add to the strength and energy of the Nation."

The Congress did not act "at once." The Senate committee charged with the responsibility of rendering a report on January 10, 1948, asked for, and received, an extension to report on February 10. Instead of reporting on February 10, it reported on March a. The bill which it finally reported, without a single public hearing, was roundly and deservedly criticized by all who were interested in achieving a fair solution of this problem. Through one device or another, debate on the bill by the Senate was postponed from the beginning of March until the end of May. The Senate bill was not passed until June 2. The House of Representatives in the meantime had delayed action and did not pass its bill until June 11. It was not until the last days of the session that the Senate and the House conferees met to put together a compromise.

The compromise resulting from this hasty, last-minute action consisted largely of combining the worst features of both the Senate and House bills.

I have analyzed closely the bill which was sent to me for signature. Its good points can be stated all too briefly: At long last, the principle is recognized that displaced persons should be admitted to the United States. Two hundred thousand displaced persons may be admitted in the next 2 years, as well as 2,000 recent Czech refugees and 3,000 orphans.

The bad points of the bill are numerous. Together they form a pattern of discrimination and intolerance wholly inconsistent with the American sense of justice.

The bill discriminates in callous fashion against displaced persons of the

Statement by the President Upon Signing the Displaced Persons Act, June 25, 1948
continued

Jewish faith. This brutal fact cannot be obscured by the maze of technicalities in the bill or by the protestations of some of its sponsors.

The primary device used to discriminate against Jewish displaced persons is the provision restricting eligibility to those displaced persons who entered Germany, Austria, or Italy on or before December 22, 1945. Most of the Jewish displaced persons who had entered Germany, Austria, or Italy by that time have already left; and most of the Jewish displaced persons now in those areas arrived there after December 22, 1945, and hence are denied a chance to come to the United States under this bill. By this device more than 90 percent of the remaining Jewish displaced persons are definitely excluded. Even the eligible 10 percent are beset by numerous additional restrictions written into the bill.

For all practical purposes, it must be frankly recognized, therefore, that this bill excludes Jewish displaced persons, rather than accepting a fair proportion of them along with other faiths.

The bill also excludes many displaced persons of the Catholic faith who deserve admission. Many anti-Communist refugees of Catholic faith fled into the American zones after December 22, 1945, in order to escape persecution in countries dominated by a Communist form of government. These too are barred by the December 22, 1945, dateline.

It is inexplicable, except upon the abhorrent ground of intolerance, that this date should have been chosen instead of April 21, 1947, the date on which General Clay closed the displaced persons camps to further admissions.

The Jewish and Catholic displaced persons who found asylum in our zones between December 22, 1945, and April 21, 1947, who are wrongly excluded by this bill, fled their native countries for the same basic reasons as Balts who came before December 22, 1945, and Czechs who came after January, 1948, who are rightly included. I sincerely hope that the Congress will remedy this gross discrimination at its earliest opportunity.

There are many other seriously objectionable features in the bill. Some of these are, as follows:

Except for orphans, the bill charges the displaced persons admitted under its provisions to future immigration quotas of their countries of birth, up to

continued

50 percent of the quota per year. Under this system, 50 percent of some quotas will be "mortgaged" for generations. This is a most begrudging method of accepting useful and worthy people and will necessarily deprive many other worthy people of an opportunity to come to the United States in future years. Considering how few permanent immigrants were able to enter this country during the war, it would have been more equitable to admit the displaced persons as nonquota immigrants.

The bill requires that at least 40 percent of the displaced persons allowed to enter this country must come from areas which have been "de facto annexed by a foreign power." This guarantees a disproportionately high percentage of persons from particular areas. It would have been fairer to provide instead for the admission of persons in proportion to the numbers of each group in the displaced persons camps.

The bill reflects a singular lack of confidence by the Congress in the capacity and willingness of the people of the United States to extend a welcoming hand to the prospective immigrants. It contains many restrictive requirements, such as prior assurances of suitable employment and "safe and sanitary housing," unnecessarily complicated investigation of each applicant, and burdensome reports from individual immigrants. I regret that the Congress saw fit to impose such niggardly conditions.

The bill submitted to me also emasculates the salutary provision of the House bill which provided for the granting of permanent residence status to a maximum of 15,000 displaced persons who are already lawfully in this country. The bill now requires a concurrent resolution of the Congress in favor of each individual after his application has been approved by the Attorney General. This requirement has the effect of perpetuating the cumbersome practice of special action by the Congress to adjust the status of individual aliens.

I know what a bitter disappointment this bill is—to the many displaced victims of persecution who looked to the United States for hope; to the millions of our citizens who wanted to help them in the finest American spirit; to the many Members of the Congress who fought hard but unsuccessfully for a decent displaced persons bill. I hope that this bitter disappointment will not turn to despair.

I have signed this bill, in spite of its many defects, in order not to delay further the beginning of a resettlement

Statement by the President Upon Signing the Displaced Persons Act, June 25, 1948
continued

program and in the expectation that the necessary remedial action will follow when the Congress reconvenes.[173]

Deeply dissatisfied with the 1948 bill, Truman continued his campaign to promote refugee resettlement. Congress not only used the language of the 1948 bill to exclude Jewish people, but also Catholics coming from communist countries, who made up about 70 percent of the refugees living in Europe's refugee camps. Ironically, the arguments used to prohibit these individuals, as potential pawns of communism, was patently ridiculous in that many of them refused to return to their homes, precisely because the prevailing administrations after the war were communist, and they objected to communist rule. Quietly, during this same period, the 1948 law was used to seek out and bring over hundreds of Nazi sympathizers and former Nazi soldiers who agreed to work for the government, many serving as agents for the FBI and CIA in the post-war anti-communist panic that took hold in the 40s and 50s.[174]

Fortunately for the Jewish immigrants who did eventually end up gaining admittance to the nation, Truman wasn't alone in his campaign. Continued news coverage of the conditions in Europe and for the displaced population, softened American resistance to Truman's pleas. In 1950, Congress agreed to amend the 1948 Act to admit more of the many Jewish and Catholic refugees awaiting resettlement. The 1950 amendment raised the limit from 200,000 to 415,000 above the quotas as they then existed and, over the next two years, 400,000 had been admitted, primarily from Eastern Europe and the Soviet Union. In June of 1950, Truman released a statement praising Congress and the American people for the amendment:

STATEMENT BY THE PRESIDENT UPON SIGNING THE DISPLACED PERSONS ACT

June 16, 1950
Source Document

IT IS with very great pleasure that I have today signed H.R. 4567, which amends the Displaced Persons Act of 1948.

The improvements embodied in H.R. 4567 now bring the American principles of fair play and generosity to our displaced persons program.

When I reluctantly signed the Displaced Persons Act of 1948, I did so in spite of certain of its provisions which imposed unworkable restrictions and resulted in unfair discriminations. Nevertheless, I felt it was necessary to make a start toward a resettlement program for these victims of totalitarianism who yearned to live as useful citizens in a free country.

I had no doubt then, and I have been confident ever since, that when the will of the American people was truly expressed, these defects in the program would be corrected. This confidence has been fully justified.

H.R. 4567 corrects the discriminations inherent in the previous act. Now, the postwar victims of totalitarianism will be on an equal footing with earlier victims of Nazi aggression.

I am also glad that the new act wisely and generously extends opportunity for immigration to the United States to additional groups of deserving persons who should make fine citizens. Special provisions are made for 10,000 war orphans from the free countries of Europe and for 4,000 European refugees who fled to the Far East to escape one form of totalitarianism and must now flee before a new tyranny. Eighteen thousand honorably discharged veterans of the exiled Polish Army, who were given temporary homes in England after the war, will now have an opportunity to settle permanently in the United States. Ten thousand Greek refugees and 2,000 displaced persons now in Trieste and Italy will also have an opportunity to immigrate to the United States. Provision has been made for the admission into this country of 54,744 refugees and expellees of German origin. In all, the amended law authorizes a total of 400,744 visas, including the 172,230 which have been issued up to May 31, 1950.

It is especially gratifying to me that this expression of American fairness and generosity has been brought about by the combined efforts of both political parties, supported by groups and

Statement by the President Upon Signing the Displaced Persons Act, June 16, 1950
continued

organizations broadly representative of all parts of our country. H.R. 4567 is a splendid example of the way in which joint action can strengthen and unify our country.

The countrymen of these displaced persons have brought to us in the past the best of their labor, their hatred of tyranny, and their love of freedom. They have helped our country grow in strength and moral leadership. I have every confidence that the new Americans who will come to our country under the provisions of the present bill will also make a substantial contribution to our national well-being.

I have today also signed the Executive order required by law, designating the Displaced Persons Commission to carry out the investigations and make the reports required by the statute, regarding the character, history, and eligibility of displaced persons and persons of German ethnic origin seeking admission into the United States. In the discharge of this statutory duty, I am directing the Commission to continue its vigorous and effective protection of the security of the United States.[175]

CONCLUSION

In the post-World War II debate over Jewish and other European immigrants, President Truman campaigned for the United States to embrace displaced persons left in need after the war and to use immigration policy to help those suffering from political violence and oppression. Though Truman stated, in his 1950 speech, that the American people supported him in this, public opinion polls indicated a majority of Americans did not want the United States to take in Jewish or other eastern European immigrants, nor did they want the United States to become a haven for refugees in general. The idea that embracing refugees was a morally and ethically positive way to utilize immigration policies had not yet become main stream, but Truman's campaign was a milestone in the broader shift of public opinion regarding the morality of immigration.

DISCUSSION QUESTIONS

- Do you agree with Truman's attitude about immigration policy and refugees? Why or why not?
- Is the debate over Jewish and European refugees in the 1940s similar or different to the controversy surrounding Syrian refugees in the 2010s? Explain.
- Does America have a duty to use immigration policies as a tool in foreign relations or to address suffering around the world? Why or why not?
- What other reason/s might there be, aside from racial prejudice, to argue against the immigration of Jewish refugees?

Works Used

Berinsky, Adam J., Eleanor Neff Powell, Eric Schickler, and Ian Brett Yohai. "Revisiting Public Opinion in the 1930s and 1940s." *PS*. Political Science & Politics, 44, pp. 515–520 ©Cambridge UP 2011.

Dinnerstein, Leonard. *Uneasy at Home: Antisemitism and the American Jewish Experience*. New York: Columbia UP, 1987.

"Displaced Persons." 14 Apr. 1948.*CQ Researcher*. Sage Publishing. 2018.

"Displaced Persons Act 1948." Public Law 774. 25 June 1948. *University of Washington-Bothell Library*. 2018.

Jones, Jeffrey M. "Americans Again Opposed to Taking In Refugees." *Gallup News*. Gallup Organization. 23 Nov. 2015.

"Kristallnacht." *Holocaust Encyclopedia*. United States Holocaust Memorial Museum. 2018.

Rashke, Richard. "The Horrible Laws that Blocked Jews from the US after World War 2 but Let Nazis in." *History News Network*. George Washington University. 20 Nov. 2016.

Tharoor, Ishaan. "What Americans thought of Jewish refugees on the eve of World War II." *Washington Post*. Washington Post, Co. 17 Nov. 2015.

Truman, Harry S. "Statement and Directive by the President on Immigration to the United states of Certain Displaced Persons and Refugees in Europe." 22 Dec. 1945. *Truman Library & Museum*. University of Missouri. 2018.

Truman, Harry S. "Statement by the President Upon Signing Bill Amending the Displaced Persons Act." 16 June 1950. *Truman Library and Museum*. University of Missouri. 2018.

Truman, Harry S. "Statement by the President Upon Signing the Displaced Persons Act." 25 June 1948. *The American Presidency Project*. University of California. 2018.

Introduction

The controversy over refugees from World War II discussed in the previous chapter gave way to one of the most oppressive periods in American domestic policy in the 1950s, as the nation entered into a long contest for economic/social dominance with China and Russia. This period, called the Cold War, had numerous impacts on immigration policy as the Cold War rhetoric put forward by politicians motivated widespread fear of what they called "dangerous communist ideology." This resulted in the adoption of prohibitions against communist immigration, similar to how the U.S. government prohibited anarchist immigration in the early 1900s.

This chapter discusses the development and debate of the last U.S. immigration law based on the "national quotas" system first put into place in 1921 and made permanent by the 1924 Johnson-Reed Immigration Act (discussed in Chapter 15). The McCarran-Walter Act of 1952 came amidst an intense public and political debate, with an increasing number of politicians and citizens viewing the quota system as outdated and prejudicial, whereas a majority believed that the quotas were necessary and beneficial to protecting and preserving American culture.

The source for this chapter is a speech given by President Harry Truman on his decision to veto the McCarran-Walter Act. Truman had been campaigning for a liberalization of immigration policy since World War II and saw the McCarran-Walter Act as prejudicial and short sighted with regard to the nation's increasing international economic commitments and involvement. Despite his veto, McCarran-Walter became law when Congress voted to override it. The quota debates of the 1950s were different than those of the 1920s—fear of communist subversion and espionage in the 1950s motivated support for the quotas among those concerned that immigrants seeking to attack American society from within posed a threat to national security.

Topics covered in this chapter include:
- Racial prejudice
- Anti-Semitism
- Refugee immigration
- Harry S. Truman Administration
- World War II
- Jewish refugees
- National quotas

This Chapter Discusses the Following Source Document:
Truman, Harry S. "Veto of Bill To Revise the Laws Relating to Immigration, Naturalization, and Nationality." June 25, 1952. *Truman Library & Museum.* University of Missouri. 2018.

The Last Hope of Western Civilization
The Cold War and the McCarran-Walter Act (1950–1958)

From the late 1940s through the late 1980s, America was fighting a "Cold War" against communism. This ideological struggle defined the evolution of American culture and the push and pull between national ideology for decades and was a dominant force in changing immigration patterns and policies. The Korean Conflict (1950–1953) and the Vietnam War (1955–1975) were proxy wars in which the United States supported pro-democracy or pro-capitalist forces against communist or socialist forces supported by China and the Soviet Union. Both conflicts led to new immigration controversies that led to new policies in the United States, as well as refugee crises that brought back the battle between humanitarian and isolationist elements within the U.S. population.

Ideology and the Balance of Power

The ideological battleground of the Cold War disguised the underlying motivations. The communist revolutions that swept across parts of the world in the latter half of the twentieth century were the result of a long-standing imbalance between socio-economic classes, exacerbated by war and cultural tensions. Communists and socialists believe that wealth and production should be collectively owned by the people, and managed by the government such that the benefits of the nation's work and productivity are evenly spread through society. The communist revolutions in China, the Soviet Union, and North Korea (among other places) occurred in nations suffering from severe economic inequality and humanitarian crises, in which a communist movement managed to overthrow the existing government under the promise that this would lead to a new egalitarian age for the long-oppressed and suffering laborers and working class. In practice, China and the Soviet Union's regimes became single-party dictatorships in which a cadre of powerful elites dominated all wealth and property such as to keep the working class frozen in a state of perpetual servitude without even the social freedoms to petition against governmental abuse.

Capitalists believe that wealth should be controlled by whoever creates it and that the competition between individuals and companies spreads that wealth through the system without government intervention. In practice, largely due to the innate selfishness of people, capitalism also results in the creation of a wealth hierarchy in which powerful companies and individuals manipulate politicians and the economic system so as to exploit the labor of the lower classes without providing individuals in those classes with the means to ascend the economic ladder.[176] This kind of drastic wealth inequality is exactly the same type of situation that has led to communist and socialist revolutions, but America is resistant to this primarily because of more than 100 years of campaigning and propaganda depicting communism and socialism as evil or unchristian, and capitalism as egalitarian, uniquely *American*, and virtuous.

In the 1930s and 1940s, America also had communist and socialist movements focused primarily on highlighting and combating income and class inequality. These movements attracted women and minorities who were (and remain in 2018) deeply marginalized in America and thus were (and *are*) the primary victims of socioeconomic inequality. Thus, in the United States, the communist and socialist movements were focused on the rights of labor and minorities, and this made them the enemy of those Americans who wished to maintain the status quo and thus the hierarchy of wealth and power. The conservatives in the United States seeking to maintain their own dominance as a class thus demonized communists, socialists, youth activists, multiculturalists, Eastern Europeans, and Asians whose anti-capitalist activism threatened the existing power structure, and this was the ideological formula that pervaded Cold War America.

The McCarran-Walter Act (1952)

The most important piece of immigration legislation of the early Cold War was the McCarran-Walter act of 1952, a compromise arising from the political debate between those who wished to use immigration policy as a tool in foreign relations, or for humanitarian purposes, and those who wished to maintain the nation's existing system of national quotas, which served to preserve the nation's ethnic and racial composition proportions.

Two new immigration bills were proposed in 1951, one by Congressman Franklin D. Roosevelt, Jr., who was a liberal progressive and saw the broadening of immigration as a way to strengthen foreign relations with increasingly dominant non-European countries. The other was proposed by long-time anti-immigration aficionados Senator Pat McCarran of Nevada and Senator Francis Walter of Pennsylvania. Both men were openly anti-Semitic and had opposed the immigration of Jewish refugees in the 1940s. McCarran and Walter were instrumental in authoring the 1948 Displaced Persons Act that excluded Jewish people from obtaining refugee status, until Truman and supporters of Jewish refugees pushed through an amendment in 1950 that removed these restrictions. McCarran's anti-Semitism was so blatant that, in the 2010s, there still exists an active movement to have his name removed from Nevada landmarks, like McCarran International Airport.[177]

The McCarran-Walter immigration bill had a number of controversial provisions:

First, it preserved the national quota system that was invented and had been used to preserve the nation's ethnic and racial composition. The bill also called for preserving the 1920 Decennial Census as the basis for the quotas. This meant that the number of visas available to people from Finland, for instance, would be based on the percentage of Finnish people living in the nation in 1920. Among opponents to the bill, there was a moderate compromise proposal to base the proportions on the 1930,

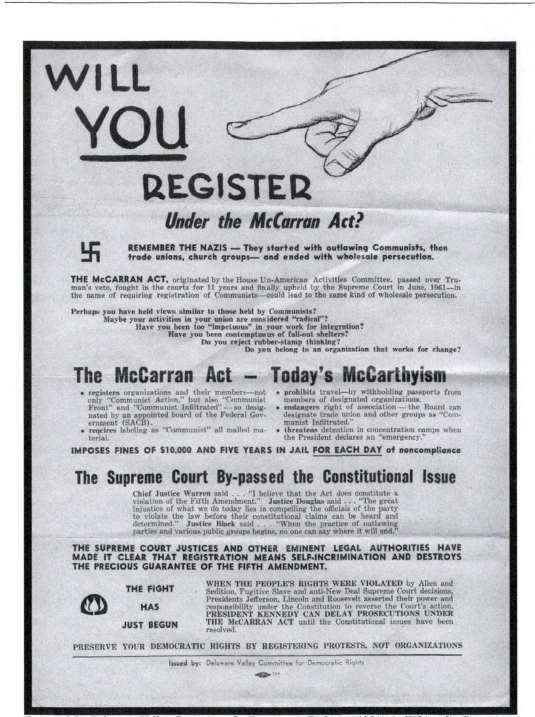

Poster of the Delaware Valley Committee for Democratic Rights, c. 1961, via Wikimedia Commons

1940, or 1950 census instead, but McCarran and supporters stood firm on the 1920 census as the basis for their new law. Further, the proportion was changed such that quotas to each country were based on a rate of one-sixth of one percent of each nationality's population in 1920. This meant that, of the 154,277 visas available for the entire world, 85 percent were only for immigrants from Western and Northern Europe.[178]

To silence critics accusing them of racism and xenophobia, McCarran and Walter agreed to remove the prohibitions on immigrants from the "Asian Barred Zone," which had prohibited Asian immigration from many countries since 1921, and, instead, set immigration for each Asian *race* at between 100–2000. Supporters hailed this part of the bill, claiming that it was a historic end to the racial period of Asian exclusion, but it meant very little. Asian visas were based on race quotas, not national quotas. This meant that a Chinese person and his or her family who migrated into the United State from Canada, for instance, would count against the total allotted to the Chinese race (which was 100–2000 persons per year). Eliminating the Asiatic Barred Zone, therefore, gave proponents of the bill the ability to claim the bill was not racially motivated, while still using the bill to further racial engineering.

Another issue of major concern for critics of the bill, was that there was still a large population of Jewish people living in oppressive regimes in parts of Europe who could not migrate because of the low-quotas applying to their places of origin. Democratic New York congressman Emanuel Celler was one of the primary voices calling for liberalization, arguing that the United States policy to that point was prejudicial and exclusionary, and sent the wrong message to the world in an era that, following the establishment of the United Nations, was seeing the dawn of global government and cooperation.

Another supporter of liberalization was President Harry Truman, who campaigned for an end to national quotas and racially-based immigration as he had for the refugees at the end of World War II. Moreover, the movement towards liberalization was beginning to be reflected in the public. A June 20 memorandum from the White House, for instance, resulting from coverage of the McCarran-Walter debate in the press, revealed that the White House had received 11,000 telegrams, letters, and cards against the bill, many expressing concern for Japanese and Jewish groups, as opposed to 500 letters, cards, and telegrams in support of the legislation.[179]

Conservatives opposed to liberalizing immigration based their stance on many different arguments. Some argued that liberalizing immigration would bring European problems to the United States, whereas others argued that American culture would be threatened by the influx of alien culture or that immigrants would provide material support for communism and could endanger the United States from within. For certain, anti-Semitism was a big factor in the anti-immigration movement of the day and, in fact, McCarran-Walter was interpreted in such a way as to provide extra barriers preventing the immigration of Jewish people. The dilution of the nation's racial balance was thus still a major concern for many in Congress (and in the public). For instance, Representative John Rankin of Mississippi argued during the debate:

> *"Almost every disgruntled element that ever got into trouble in its own country had pleaded for admission into the United States on the ground that they were oppressed at home...Suppose we should...We would be inviting all the Communists in Germany and Italy and all the Fascists and Communists in Spain who are dissatisfied with their present regime...then what about the oppressed of Ethiopia? Would we be expected to invite every Negro in Ethiopia who feels he is oppressed? Should we invite every Chinaman...?"*[180]

In 1952, McCarran famously argued in defense of his stance on immigration:

> *"I believe that this nation is the last hope of Western civilization and if this oasis of the world shall be overrun, perverted, contaminated or destroyed, then the last flickering light of humanity will be extinguished."*[181]

The term "Western civilization" as used by McCarran in 1952 might require explanation for some as, by 1952, the phrase was already a coded expression referring to religion, race, and historical legacy. President Donald Trump used the same term in a 2017 speech to the people of Poland, referring to both Poland and the United States as representatives of "the West" and of "our civilization." Trump's usage reveals how the term Western civilization changed from the era in which it referred to Western Europe and the nations that emerged from western European colonialism. Writing about this issue in 2017, journalist Peter Beinart, writing in *The Atlantic*, explains:

> *"The West is not a geographic term. Poland is further east than Morocco. France is further east than Haiti. Australia is further east than Egypt. Yet Poland, France, and Australia are all considered part of "The West." Morocco, Haiti, and Egypt are not."*[182]

Likewise, "western" does not refer to a purely political designation, or to democratic nations, as reflected in the fact that India and Japan, two of the world's largest democratic nations, are equally excluded from the list of "western nations." Western civilization is a coded term that refers to Christian (preferably Protestant, but to a lesser degree Catholic) nations in which the predominant race is white. McCarran probably wouldn't have included Poland in *his* list of "western" countries, because the eastern European nation was communist and thus not part of what white isolationists like McCarran saw as contributing to their view of "western." For Trump, 80 years later, Poland is definitely "western," in a world rapidly become less white and less Christian and so in which remaining white Christian dominant nations are increasingly seen as part of a unit.

Truman vetoed the bill when it arrived through Congress, and wrote a lengthy response to what he saw as the major defects of the bill, though Congress voted to override the veto, allowing McCarran-Walter to continue the nation's racial engineering program for more than a decade.

PRESIDENT HARRY S. TRUMAN REMARKS ON HIS VETO OF THE MCCARRAN-WALTER IMMIGRATION ACT OF 1952
June 25, 1952
Source Document

To the House of Representatives:
I return herewith, without my approval, H.R. 5678, the proposed Immigration and Nationality Act.

In outlining my objections to this bill, I want to make it clear that it contains certain provisions that meet with my approval. This is a long and complex piece of legislation. It has 164 separate sections, some with more than 40 subdivisions. It presents a difficult problem of weighing the good against the bad, and arriving at a judgment on the whole.

H.R. 5678 is an omnibus bill which would revise and codify all of our laws relating to immigration, naturalization, and nationality.

A general revision and modernization of these laws unquestionably is needed and long overdue, particularly with respect to immigration. But this bill would not provide us with an immigration policy adequate for the present world situation. Indeed, the bill, taking all its provisions together, would be a step backward and not a step forward. In view of the crying need for reform in the field of immigration,

continued

I deeply regret that I am unable to approve H.R. 5678.

In recent years, our immigration policy has become a matter of major national concern. Long dormant questions about the effect of our immigration laws now assume first rate importance. What we do in the field of immigration and naturalization is vital to the continued growth and internal development of the United States—to the economic and social strength of our country—which is the core of the defense of the free world. Our immigration policy is equally, if not more important to the conduct of our foreign relations and to our responsibilities of moral leadership in the struggle for world peace.

In one respect, this bill recognizes the great international significance of our immigration and naturalization policy, and takes a step to improve existing laws. All racial bars to naturalization would be removed, and at least some minimum immigration quota would be afforded to each of the free nations of Asia.

I have long urged that racial or national barriers to naturalization be abolished. This was one of the recommendations in my civil rights message to the Congress on February 2, 1948. On February 19, 1951, the House of Representatives unanimously passed a bill to carry it out.

But now this most desirable provision comes before me embedded in a mass of legislation which would perpetuate injustices of long standing against many other nations of the world, hamper the efforts we are making to rally the men of East and West alike to the cause of freedom, and intensify the repressive and inhumane aspects of our immigration procedures. The price is too high, and in good conscience I cannot agree to pay it.

I want all our residents of Japanese ancestry, and all our friends throughout the far East, to understand this point clearly. I cannot take the step I would like to take, and strike down the bars that prejudice has erected against them, without, at the same time, establishing new discriminations against the peoples of Asia and approving harsh and repressive measures directed at all who seek a new life within our boundaries. I am sure that with a little more time and a little more discussion in this country the public conscience and the good sense of the American people will assert themselves, and we shall be in a position to enact an immigration and naturalization policy that will be fair to all.

In addition to removing racial bars

President Harry S. Truman Remarks on His Veto of the McCarran-Walter Immigration Act of 1952
June 25, 1952
continued

to naturalization, the bill would permit American women citizens to bring their alien husbands to this country as non-quota immigrants, and enable alien husbands of resident women aliens to come in under the quota in a preferred status. These provisions would be a step toward preserving the integrity of the family under our immigration laws, and are clearly desirable.

The bill would also relieve transportation companies of some of the unjustified burdens and penalties now imposed upon them. In particular, it would put an end to the archaic requirement that carriers pay the expenses of aliens detained at the port of entry, even though such aliens have arrived with proper travel documents.

But these few improvements are heavily outweighed by other provisions of the bill which retain existing defects in our laws, and add many undesirable new features.

The bill would continue, practically without change, the national origins quota system, which was enacted, into law in 1924, and put into effect in 1929. This quota system-always based upon assumptions at variance with our American ideals—is long since out of date and more than ever unrealistic in the face of present world conditions.

This system hinders us in dealing with current immigration problems, and is a constant handicap in the conduct of our foreign relations. As I stated in my message to Congress on March 24, 1952, on the need for an emergency program of immigration from Europe, "Our present quota system is not only inadequate to most present emergency needs, it is also an obstacle to the development of an enlightened and satisfactory immigration policy for the long-run future."

The inadequacy of the present quota system has been demonstrated since the end of the war, when we were compelled to resort to emergency legislation to admit displaced persons. If the quota system remains unchanged, we shall be compelled to resort to similar emergency legislation again, in order to admit any substantial portion of the refugees from communism or the victims of overcrowding in Europe.

With the idea of quotas in general there is no quarrel. Some numerical limitation must be set, so that immigration will be within our capacity to absorb. But the overall limitation

continued

of numbers imposed by the national origins quota system is too small for our needs today, and the country by country limitations create a pattern that is insulting to large numbers of our finest citizens, irritating to our allies abroad, and foreign to our purposes and ideals.

The overall quota limitation, under the law of 1924, restricted annual immigration to approximately 150,000. This was about one-seventh of one percent of our total population in 1920. Taking into account the growth in population since 1920, the law now allows us but one-tenth of one percent of our total population. And since the largest national quotas are only partly used, the number actually coming in has been in the neighborhood of one-fifteenth of one percent. This is far less than we must have in the years ahead to keep up with the growing needs of the Nation for manpower to maintain the strength and vigor of our economy.

The greatest vice of the present quota system, however, is that it discriminates, deliberately and intentionally, against many of the peoples of the world. The purpose behind it was to cut down and virtually eliminate immigration to this country from Southern and Eastern Europe. A theory was invented to rationalize this objective. The theory was that in order to be readily assimilable, European immigrants should be admitted in proportion to the numbers of persons of their respective national stocks already here as shown by the census of 1920. Since Americans of English, Irish and German descent were most numerous, immigrants of those three nationalities got the lion's share—more than two-thirds—of the total quota. The remaining third was divided up among all the other nations given quotas.

The desired effect was obtained. Immigration from the newer sources of Southern and Eastern Europe was reduced to a trickle. The quotas allotted to England and Ireland remained largely unused, as was intended. Total quota immigration fell to a half or a third—and sometimes even less—of the annual limit of 154,000. People from such countries as Greece, or Spain, or Latvia were virtually deprived of any opportunity to come here at all, simply because Greeks or Spaniards or Latvians had not come here before 1920 in any substantial numbers.

The idea behind this discriminatory policy was, to put it baldly, that Americans with English or Irish names were better people and better citizens than Americans with Italian or Greek or Polish names. It was thought that people of West European origin made

President Harry S. Truman Remarks on His Veto of the McCarran-Walter Immigration Act of 1952
June 25, 1952
continued

better citizens than Rumanians or Yugoslavs or Ukrainians or Hungarians or Baits or Austrians. Such a concept is utterly unworthy of our traditions and our ideals. It violates the great political doctrine of the Declaration of Independence that "all men are created equal." It denies the humanitarian creed inscribed beneath the Statue of Liberty proclaiming to all nations, "Give me your tired, your poor, your huddled masses yearning to breathe free."

It repudiates our basic religious concepts, our belief in the brotherhood of man, and in the words of St. Paul that "there is neither Jew nor Greek, there is neither bond nor free .... for ye are all one in Christ Jesus."

The basis of this quota system was false and unworthy in 1924. It is even worse now. At the present time, this quota system keeps out the very people we want to bring in. It is incredible to me that, in this year of 1952, we should again be enacting into law such a slur on the patriotism, the capacity, and the decency of a large part of our citizenry.

Today, we have entered into an alliance, the North Atlantic Treaty, with Italy, Greece, and Turkey against one of the most terrible threats mankind has ever faced. We are asking them to join with us in protecting the peace of the world. We are helping them to build their defenses, and train their men, in the common cause. But, through this bill we say to their people: You are less worthy to come to this country than Englishmen or Irishmen; you Italians, who need to find homes abroad in the hundreds of thousands—you shall have a quota of 5,645; you Greeks, struggling to assist the helpless victims of a communist civil war—you shall have a quota of 308; and you Turks, you are brave defenders of the Eastern flank, but you shall have a quota of only 225!

Today, we are "protecting" ourselves, as we were in 1924, against being flooded by immigrants from Eastern Europe. This is fantastic. The countries of Eastern Europe have fallen under the communist yoke— they are silenced, fenced off by barbed wire and minefields—no one passes their borders but at the risk of his life. We do not need to be protected against immigrants from these countries—on the contrary we want to stretch out a helping hand, to save those who have managed to flee into Western Europe, to succor those who are brave enough

continued

to escape from barbarism, to welcome and restore them against the day when their countries will, as we hope, be free again. But this we cannot do, as we would like to do, because the quota for Poland is only 6,500, as against the 138,000 exiled Poles, all over Europe, who are asking to come to these shores; because the quota for the now subjugated Baltic countries is little more than 700—against the 23,000 Baltic refugees imploring us to admit them to a new life here; because the quota for Rumania is only 289, and some 30,000 Rumanians, who have managed to escape the labor camps and the mass deportations of their Soviet masters, have asked our help. These are only a few examples of the absurdity, the cruelty of carrying over into this year of 1952 the isolationist limitations of our 1924 law.

In no other realm of our national life are we so hampered and stultified by the dead hand of the past, as we are in this field of immigration. We do not limit our cities to their 1920 boundaries—we do not hold our corporations to their 1920 capitalizations—we welcome progress and change to meet changing conditions in every sphere of life, except in the field of immigration.

The time to shake off this dead weight of past mistakes is now. The time to develop a decent policy of immigration—a fitting instrument for our foreign policy and a true reflection of the ideals we stand for, at home and abroad—is now. In my earlier message on immigration, I tried to explain to the Congress that the situation we face in immigration is an emergency—that it must be met promptly. I have pointed out that in the last few years, we have blazed a new trail in immigration, through our Displaced Persons Program. Through the combined efforts of the Government and private agencies, working together not to keep people out, but to bring qualified people in, we summoned our resources of good will and human feeling to meet the task. In this program, we have found better techniques to meet the immigration problems of the 1950's.

None of this fruitful experience of the last three years is reflected in this bill before me. None of the crying human needs of this time of trouble is recognized in this bill. But it is not too late. The Congress can remedy these defects, and it can adopt legislation to meet the most critical problems before adjournment.

The only consequential change in the 1924 quota system which the bill would make is to extend a small quota to each of the countries of Asia. But most of the beneficial effects of this gesture are offset by other provisions

President Harry S. Truman Remarks on His Veto of the McCarran-Walter Immigration Act of 1952
June 25, 1952
continued

of the bill. The countries of Asia are told in one breath that they shall have quotas for their nationals, and in the next, that the nationals of the other countries, if their ancestry is as much as 50 percent Asian, shall be charged to these quotas.

It is only with respect to persons of oriental ancestry that this invidious discrimination applies. All other persons are charged to the country of their birth. But persons with Asian ancestry are charged to the countries of Asia, wherever they may have been born, or however long their ancestors have made their homes outside the land of their origin. These provisions are without justification.

I now wish to turn to the other provisions of the bill, those dealing with the qualifications of aliens and immigrants for admission, with the administration of the laws, and with problems of naturalization and nationality. In these provisions too, I find objections that preclude my signing this bill.

The bill would make it even more difficult to enter our country. Our resident aliens would be more easily separated from homes and families under grounds of deportation, both new and old, which would specifically be made retroactive. Admission to our citizenship would be made more difficult; expulsion from our citizenship would be made easier. Certain rights of native born, first generation Americans would be limited. All our citizens returning from abroad would be subjected to serious risk of unreasonable invasions of privacy. Seldom has a bill exhibited the distrust evidenced here for citizens and aliens alike—at a time when we need unity at home, and the confidence of our friends abroad.

We have adequate and fair provisions in our present law to protect us against the entry of criminals. The changes made by the bill in those provisions would result in empowering minor immigration and consular officials to act as prosecutor, judge and jury in determining whether acts constituting a crime have been committed. Worse, we would be compelled to exclude certain people because they have been convicted by "courts" in communist countries that know no justice. Under this provision, no matter how construed, it would not be possible for us to admit many of the men and women who have stood up against

continued

totalitarian repression and have been punished for doing so. I do not approve of substituting totalitarian vengeance for democratic justice. I will not extend full faith and credit to the judgments of the communist secret police.

The realities of a world, only partly free, would again be ignored in the provision flatly barring entry to those who made misrepresentations in securing visas. To save their lives and the lives of loved ones still imprisoned, refugees from tyranny sometimes misstate various details of their lives. We do not want to encourage fraud. But we must recognize that conditions in some parts of the world drive our friends to desperate steps. An exception restricted to cases involving misstatement of country of birth is not sufficient. And to make refugees from oppression forever deportable on such technical grounds is shabby treatment indeed.

Some of the new grounds of deportation which the bill would provide are unnecessarily severe. Defects and mistakes in admission would serve to deport at any time because of the bill's elimination, retroactively as well as prospectively, of the present humane provision barring deportations on such grounds five years after entry. Narcotic drug addicts would be deportable at any time, whether or not the addiction

was culpable, and whether or not cured. The threat of deportation would drive the addict into hiding beyond the reach of cure, and the danger to the country from drug addiction would be increased.

I am asked to approve the reenactment of highly objectionable provisions now contained in the Internal Security Act of 1950—a measure passed over my veto shortly after the invasion of South Korea. Some of these provisions would empower the Attorney General to deport any alien who has engaged or has had a purpose to engage in activities "prejudicial to the public interest" or "subversive to the national security." No standards or definitions are provided to guide discretion in the exercise of powers so sweeping. To punish undefined "activities" departs from traditional American insistence on established standards of guilt. To punish an undefined "purpose" is thought control.

These provisions are worse than the infamous Alien Act of 1798, passed in a time of national fear and distrust of foreigners, which gave the President power to deport any alien deemed "dangerous to the peace and safety of the United States." Alien residents were thoroughly frightened and citizens much disturbed by that threat to liberty.

President Harry S. Truman Remarks on His Veto of the McCarran-Walter Immigration Act of 1952
June 25, 1952
continued

Such powers are inconsistent with our democratic ideals. Conferring powers like that upon the Attorney General is unfair to him as well as to our alien residents. Once fully informed of such vast discretionary powers vested in the Attorney General, Americans now would and should be just as alarmed as Americans were in 1798 over less drastic powers vested in the President.

Heretofore, for the most part, deportation and exclusion have rested upon findings of fact made upon evidence. Under this bill, they would rest in many instances upon the "opinion" or "satisfaction" of immigration or consular employees. The change from objective findings to subjective feelings is not compatible with our system of justice. The result would be to restrict or eliminate judicial review of unlawful administrative action.

The bill would sharply restrict the present opportunity of citizens and alien residents to save family members from deportation. Under the procedures of present law, the Attorney General can exercise his discretion to suspend deportation in meritorious cases. In each such case, at the present time, the exercise of administrative discretion is subject to the scrutiny and approval of the Congress. Nevertheless, the bill would prevent this discretion from being used in many cases where it is now available, and would narrow the circle of those who can obtain relief from the letter of the law. This is most unfortunate, because the bill, in its other provisions, would impose harsher restrictions and greatly increase the number of cases deserving equitable relief.

Native-born American citizens who are dual nationals would be subjected to loss of citizenship on grounds not applicable to other native-born American citizens. This distinction is a slap at millions of Americans whose fathers were of alien birth.

Children would be subjected to additional risk of loss of citizenship. Naturalized citizens would be subjected to the risk of denaturalization by any procedure that can be found to be permitted under any State law or practice pertaining to minor civil law suits. Judicial review of administrative denials of citizenship would be severely limited and impeded in many cases, and completely eliminated in others. I believe these provisions raise serious constitutional questions.

continued

Constitutionality aside, I see no justification in national policy for their adoption.

Section 401 of this bill would establish a Joint Congressional Committee on Immigration and Nationality Policy. This committee would have the customary powers to hold hearings and to subpoena witnesses, books, papers and documents. But the Committee would also be given powers over the Executive branch which are unusual and of a highly questionable nature. Specifically, section 401 would provide that "The Secretary of State and the Attorney General shall without delay submit to the Committee all regulations, instructions, and all other information as requested by the Committee relative to the administration of this Act."

This section appears to be another attempt to require the Executive branch to make available to the Congress administrative documents, communications between the President and his subordinates, confidential files, and other records of that character. It also seems to imply that the Committee would undertake to supervise or approve regulations. Such proposals are not consistent with the Constitutional doctrine of the separation of powers.

In these and many other respects, the bill raises basic questions as to our fundamental immigration and naturalization policy, and the laws and practices for putting that policy into effect.

Many of the aspects of the bill which have been most widely criticized in the public debate are reaffirmations or elaborations of existing statutes or administrative procedures. Time and again, examination discloses that the revisions of existing law that would be made by the bill are intended to solidify some restrictive practice of our immigration authorities, or to overrule or modify some ameliorative decision of the Supreme Court or other Federal courts. By and large, the changes that would be made by the bill do not depart from the basically restrictive spirit of our existing laws—but intensify and reinforce it.

These conclusions point to an underlying condition which deserves the most careful study. Should we not undertake a reassessment of our immigration policies and practices in the light of the conditions that face us in the second half of the twentieth century? The great popular interest which this bill has created, and the criticism which it has stirred up, demand an affirmative answer. I hope the Congress will agree to a careful reexamination of this entire matter.

President Harry S. Truman Remarks on His Veto of the Mccarran-Walter Immigration Act of 1952
June 25, 1952
continued

To assist in this complex task, I suggest the creation of a representative commission of outstanding Americans to examine the basic assumptions of our immigration policy, the quota system and all that goes with it, the effect of our present immigration and nationality laws, their administration, and the ways in which they can be brought in line with our national ideals and our foreign policy.

Such a commission should, I believe, be established by the Congress. Its membership should be bi-partisan and divided equally among persons from private life and persons from public life. I suggest that four members be appointed by the President, four by the President of the Senate, and four by the Speaker of the House of Representatives. The commission should be given sufficient funds to employ a staff and it should have adequate powers to hold hearings, take testimony, and obtain information. It should make a report to the President and to the Congress within a year from the time of its creation.

Pending the completion of studies by such a commission, and the consideration of its recommendations by the Congress, there are certain steps which I believe it is most important for the Congress to take this year.

First, I urge the Congress to enact legislation removing racial barriers against Asians from our laws. Failure to take this step profits us nothing and can only have serious consequences for our relations with the peoples of the far East. A major contribution to this end would be the prompt enactment by the Senate of H.R. 403. That bill, already passed by the House of Representatives, would remove the racial bars to the naturalization of Asians.

Second, I strongly urge the Congress to enact the temporary, emergency immigration legislation which I recommended three months ago. In my message of March 24, 1952, I advised the Congress that one of the gravest problems arising from the present world crisis is created by the overpopulation in parts of Western Europe. That condition is aggravated by the flight and expulsion of people from behind the iron curtain. In view of these serious problems, I asked the Congress to authorize the admission of 300,000 additional immigrants to the United States over a three year period. These immigrants would include Greek nationals, Dutch nationals, Italians

continued

from Italy and Trieste, Germans and persons of German ethnic origin, and religious and political refugees from communism in Eastern Europe. This temporary program is urgently needed. It is very important that the Congress act upon it this year. I urge the Congress to give prompt and favorable consideration to the bills introduced by Senator Hendrickson and Representative Celler (S. 3109 and H.R. 7376), which will implement the recommendations contained in my message of March 24.

I very much hope that the Congress will take early action on these recommendations. Legislation to carry them out will correct some of the unjust provisions of our laws, will strengthen us at home and abroad, and will serve to relieve a great deal of the suffering and tension existing in the world today.[183]

CONCLUSION

The debate over McCarran-Walter was widely covered in the media and public opinion polls showed that a majority of Americans, especially white Americans, favored retaining the quota system overall. Demographers and social scientists did not determine to what degree public support for the quotas was based on national security, economic stability, or racial prejudice, but all three areas of concern were demonstrated among the public and in Congress. What is interesting about the debates from this era is how campaigns from Truman and others favoring a more liberal approach to immigration affected the youth in the 1950s, who would go on to become voters and legislators who helped shape America's most liberal immigration reform era in the 1960s.

DISCUSSION QUESTIONS

- In your opinion, what is the meaning of the term "Western Civilization?"
- Should immigration policy be used to further foreign relations and humanitarian concerns? Why or why not?
- Do you agree or disagree with Truman's belief that the McCarran-Walter Act violated the principles of the Declaration of Independence? Explain.
- Does communism pose a threat to American culture or identity? Why or why not?

Works Used

Beinart, Peter. "The Racial and Religious Paranoia of Trump's Warsaw Speech." *The Atlantic*. Atlantic Monthly Group. 6 July 2017.

Ingraham, Christopher. "The riches 1 percent now owns more of the country's wealth than at any time in the past 50 years." *The Washington Post*. Washington Post Co. 6 Dec. 2017.

"The Immigration and Nationality Act of 1952 (The McCarran-Walter Act)." *U.S. Department of State*. Office of the Historian. Milestones. 2017.

"Memorandum from William J. Hopkins, 20 June 1952." *Truman Library and Museum*. University of Missouri. 2018.

Montero, David. "There is a renewed push to remove the McCarran name in Nevada." *Los Angeles Times*. Tronc Publishing. 27 Mar. 2017.

Shanks, Cheryl Lynne. *Immigration and the Politics of American Sovereignty, 1890–1990*. Ann Arbor, MI: U of Michigan P, 2009.

Truman, Harry S. "Veto of Bill To Revise the Laws Relating to
Immigration, Naturalization, and Nationality." 25 June 1952.
Truman Library & Museum. University of Missouri. 2018.

Zahra, Tara. *The Great Departure: Mass Migration from Eastern
Europe and the Making of the Free World.* New York: W.W. Norton &
Company, 2016.

Introduction

This chapter discusses the controversy surrounding temporary Mexican migrants and illegal migration from Mexico. Mexican migration and immigration first became a leading immigration concern in the 1930s, resulting in a decade long anti-Mexican movement. However, in the 1940s and 1950s, growers and farm owners lobbied the federal government to enable a more widespread temporary worker program that would allow the use of affordable migratory labor. This resulted in a series of bilateral agreements between the U.S. and Mexican governments permitting hundreds of thousands of temporary laborers, known as Braceros, to migrate into the United States for seasonal work.

The Mexican migrant laborer programs continued from the 1920s to the 1960s in various forms. However, demand for laborers was far higher than the supply of legal migrants through the Bracero Programs, which ultimately led to a vast increase in unauthorized migration. Business owners enabled this situation by hiring undocumented migrants (who worked for wages lower than legal workers) rather than only hiring legal temporary migrants or native workers. This angered nativists, white labor activists, and supporters of legal migrant work programs. The document for this chapter is a speech given in 1952 by Juanita Garcia, a legal migrant worker bemoaning the lack of regulation that led to competition between legal migrants and unauthorized migrants. Concern about illegal migration led to "Operation Wetback," a military-style effort to purge the nation of illegal migrants. Though widely promoted as a success, the program failed in many regards; specifically, it did not significantly reduce illegal migration because Congress and the states were reluctant to punish business owners who hired undocumented migrants. As federal immigration agents focused on border control instead of on those who hired illegal workers, the flow of undocumented migrants not only continued, but increased.

Topics covered in this chapter include:
- Racial prejudice
- Anti-Mexican sentiment
- Deportation programs
- Migrant worker programs
- Border Patrol and protection
- Unauthorized Mexican migration

This Chapter Discusses the Following Source Document:
Garcia, Juanita. "Migratory Labor. Hearings before Subcommittee on Labor and Labor-Management Relations." 82nd Congress, 2nd Session. 1952. *Digital History*. University of Houston. 2016.

Opportunity and Exploitation
The Bracero Program (1917–1964)

The United States is the wealthiest nation in the world. In 2017, the United States accounted for nearly 25 percent of the world's wealth, but this was a significant reduction from the mid-twentieth century, when the United States accounted for a full 40 percent of the global GDP. Many of the biggest immigration controversies in U.S. history were and are a factor of the economic disparity between the United States and the rest of the world's nations. For instance, when Chinese immigrants were coming to the United States in large numbers to work on the railroads and in mining camps, potential earnings in the United States were so much higher (in terms of absolute purchasing power) that Chinese laborers earning even desperately low wages in America could still use that money to make a major difference for the lives of their families back home. The same situation drove and continues to drive legal and illegal migration from Mexico.

The Migrant Labor Lobby

The Bracero Program (named for the Spanish word for manual labor) began with a bilateral agreement between the United States and Mexico in 1917 that brought over thousands of Mexican laborers on short-term migrant agreements to work in the U.S. agriculture and railroad industries. Similar agreements were adopted on a semi-annual basis from 1917 to 1921, fueling the growth of the western agricultural industry. The disparity between the United States and Mexican economies during this period meant that a migrant worker from Mexico could accept extremely low wages working in the United States and still have enough income, comparatively, to improve his or her situation markedly when returning home. Some, however, after arriving, sought better wages further North, and thus escaped the farm labor contracts to live illegally in many of America's cities, and this was the very beginning of the illegal Mexican migration controversy that became the primary focus of immigration reform from the late twentieth century through the present.[184]

Mexican labor filled an important niche during the period after the United States banned Chinese labor (in 1882) and especially after the 1921 law that also drastically restricted European migration. In towns and communities where migrant Mexican laborers were common, the temporary worker programs were often controversial. Nativists were concerned for American jobs, whereas eugenicists and white supremacists saw Mexicans as a threat to the nation's cultural melting pot. The first round of bilateral Bracero Programs ended in 1921, as American immigration policy shifted further towards isolationism. Farm organizations in the southwest petitioned the government to bring the programs back, leaving legislators caught between the two sides of the debate. In addition, the Mexican government was not satisfied with how the 1917–1921 programs had been managed as many of the participating workers suffered from strong discrimination in the United States and accrued little in benefit due to unpaid contracts and exploitation by U.S. merchants, who often charged Mexican migrants more for food, clothing, and other necessities.

Numerous historians have reported that there was a prevailing belief that some ethnic quality of Mexicans made them especially suited for migrant labor, willing to forego economic stability in favor of short-term profit. It was common for Mexicans to be described as "homing pigeons" who would always, dutifully return to Mexico at the end of their contracts, and so would not become a long-term drain on the American economy, nor pollute the nation's racial mixture. There was a campaign, among farm associations eager to continue the flow of Mexican migrants, to depict Mexicans as having racial qualities that made them suitable for labor, including a general docility of temperament and a lack of interest in political activism.[185]

The U.S. farm owners who lobbied for migrant worker programs were not immune to racial prejudice, but argued that they had little choice. A representative of the California Farm Bureau said of the situation in 1926:

"We, gentlemen, are just as anxious as you are not to build the civilization of California or any other western district upon a Mexican foundation. We take him because there is nothing else available. We have gone east, west, north, and south and he is the only man-power available to us."[186]

Farm lobbyists managed to keep Mexican migrant programs going throughout the 1920s, though the programs were halted entirely during the Great Depression, which inspired the nation's first anti-Mexican movement that resulted in the forced expulsion of thousands of Mexican immigrants and Mexican-American citizens. This anti-Mexican surge gradually diminished towards the end of the 1930s, as America shifted its attention away from domestic issues and towards the national threat of World War II.

During World War II, when another labor shortage threatened the farm industry, especially in the southwest, farm and labor unions petitioned the government to return to migrant labor programs. The Mexican government was reluctant to return to a system that had been discriminatory and prejudicial to their people, but, when the U.S. government agreed to guarantee the contracts provided to laborers, the two nations reached an agreement, with the first 500 Braceros brought into California in September of 1942.

The Bracero Program of 1942 was authorized by Executive Order 8802, which contained provisions prohibiting discrimination and guaranteeing transportation, paid for by the government, between Mexico and the United States. To address nativist fears, the EO also prohibited farm owners from displacing native-born workers in preference of migrants. Further, the EO held that laborers must be paid a minimum of $0.30 per hour in U.S. currency, whether working full-time or part-time. At the time, the minimum wage in California was $0.45 per hour, meaning that hiring migrant workers was a major benefit to the farm owners who participated in the program.[187] The wartime Bracero Program peaked in 1944, with around 62,000 admissions that year.

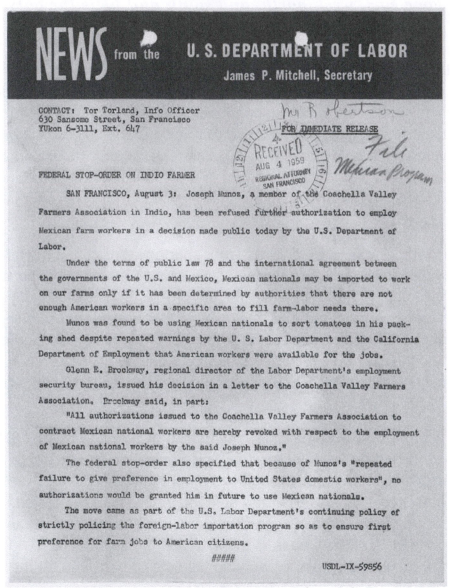

News from the U.S. Department of Labor, "Federal Stop-Order on Indio Farmer," 1959, U.S. National Archives, via Wikimedia Commons

From Braceros to Wetbacks

Though the wartime program ended officially in 1947, there were still channels in place to allow farmers to recruit Braceros each year. In the late 1940s, the Mexican labor market began to change. Whereas at one-time growers and farm owners seeking cheap laborers had to participate in the Bracero program, after years of migrant labor contracts, large number of illegal Mexican migrants were beginning to come to the United States and a large number of farm owners and growers began shifting from contract migrants to illegal migrants. Increasing profits is the only reason this occurred. By hiring unauthorized migrants, growers and farm owners saved even more on labor and did not have to pay their share of transportation costs and other costs associated with the official temporary worker programs.

In the 1940s, there were no penalties in place for farmers who were found to be employing illegal migrants and, in fact, the immigration authorities had a relatively simple process in place for dealing with the situation, called "drying out the wetbacks," in which an illegal migrant was taken back to the Mexican border, given papers allowing them to legally work, and then returned, as a legal Bracero, to the farm where they were found. The term "wetback" was the most common racial epithet used for Mexicans at the time, and referred to illegal Mexican workers entering the country by swimming across the Rio Grande River. By the end of the 1940s, the number of illegal migrants had outpaced the number of contract laborers coming from Mexico. For instance, in 1949, around 20,000 migrants came to the United States on temporary worker permits, whereas there were some 87,000 illegal migrants who were later legalized through the "drying out the wetbacks" system.

Illegal migration was a major controversy in the early 1950s as Congress debated overhauls to the nation's immigration system. The President's Commission on Migratory Labor released a study in 1951 recommending

Seen here are the first Mexican Braceros (manual laborers) to arrive in California in 1917, via Wikimedia Commons

that the only way to stem the tide was to levy fines on employers found using illegal migrants.[188] These studies were influential and the anti-illegal immigration lobby was powerful and thus, the 1952 McCarran-Walter Act also contained provisions based, in part, on these findings, making harboring illegal aliens a felony punishable by a fine of $2000 and a possible five-year prison term. However, the southern, southwestern, and western farm associations were also powerful, and their lobbying and political donations resulted in a loophole, known as the "Texas proviso," saying that "employing" an illegal immigrant is not the same as "harboring," and thus exempted the growers and farm owners from any penalty for their continued use of unauthorized labor.[189]

After several years of resistance to Mexican migration in Congress, the Korean War created a new alleged labor shortage that farm groups used to petition the federal government for a new Bracero Program. Supporters of the program hoped that legalizing the flow of immigrants would reduce the impetus for unauthorized migration, whereas others argued that the expansion of the legal program might also help mitigate exploitation of illegal migrants. The lobby was successful and the U.S. government formalized the Bracero Program with a 1951 amendment to the Agricultural Act of 1949. This officially made the Bracero Program part of the federal government's agricultural assistance system.[7]

At the time, migratory workers coming to the United States legally also protested the growth of the illegal migrant population competing with them for jobs. Although the Border Patrol would later target the illegal migrants themselves, it was understood by those familiar with the way the system worked at the time, that the primary agents of this inequity were the growers, ranchers, and farm owners. In 1952, migrant farm worker Juanita Garcia testified for the Subcommittee on Labor and Labor-Management Relations in the 2nd session of the 82nd Congress:

TESTIMONY TO THE SUBCOMMITTEE ON LABOR AND LABOR-MANAGEMENT RELATIONS BY JUANITA GARCIA
1952
Source Document

I work in the field and in the packing sheds. I lost my job in a packing shed about two weeks ago. I was fired because I belonged to the National Farm Labor Union. Every summer our family goes north to work. We pick figs and cotton. My father, my brothers and sisters also work on farms. For poor people like us who are field laborers, making a living has always been hard. Why? Because the ranchers and companies have always taken over.

When I was a small kid my dad had a small farm but he lost it. All of us used to help him. But dad got older and worn out with worries every day. Lots of us kids could not go to school much. Our parents could not afford the expenses. This happened to all kids like us. Difficulties appear here and there every day. Taxes, food, clothing, and everything go up. We all have to eat. Sometimes we sleep under a leaky roof. We have to cover up and keep warm the best way we can in the cold weather.

In the Imperial Valley we have a hard time. It so happens that the local people who are American citizens cannot get work. Many days we don't work. Some days we work 1 hour. The wetbacks and nationals from Mexico have the whole Imperial Valley. They have invaded not only the Imperial Valley but all the United States. The nationals and wetbacks take any wages the ranchers offer to pay them. The wages get worse every year. Last year most local people got little work. Sometimes they make only $5 a week.

Testimony to the Subcommittee on Labor and Labor-Management Relations by Juanita Garcia
1952
continued

That is not enough to live on, so many people cannot send their children to school.

Many people have lost their homes since 1942 when the nationals and wetbacks started coming. Local people work better but wetbacks and nationals are hired anyway.

Last year they fired some people from the shed because they had nationals to take their jobs. There was a strike. We got all the strikers out at 4:30 in the morning. The cops were on the streets escorting the nationals and wetbacks to the fields. The cops had guns. The ranchers had guns, too. They took the wetbacks in their brand-new cars through our picket line. They took the nationals from the camps to break our strike. They had 5,000 scabs that were nationals. We told the Mexican consul about this. We told the Labor Department. They were supposed to take the nationals out of the strike. They never did take them away.

It looks like the big companies in agriculture are running the United States. All of us local people went on strike. The whole valley was hungry because nobody worked at all. The melons rotted in the fields. We went out and arrested the wetbacks who were living in caves and on the ditches and we took them to the border patrol. But the national scabs kept working. Isn't the Government supposed to help us poor people? Can't it act fast in cases like this?[191]

President Harry Truman signed the Bracero bill into law on July 13, 1951, but expressed serious concerns about the program, primarily in that the program as formulated by Congress ignored much of what the President's Commission on Migratory Labor had uncovered about the state of the program to that point. Under pressure from southwestern legislators and lobbyists, however, Truman agreed to pass the law through rather than vetoing the bill and sending it back to Congress for revision.[192]

Getting Tough on Immigration (Kind of)

As the Bracero Program proceeded, illegal migration increased as well. Between 1942 and 1964 (the entire duration of the Bracero Program), there were some 4.6 million legal Braceros admitted, and at least 4.9 million illegal Mexican migrants apprehended by border patrols and immigration officers. In August of 1953, then Attorney General Herbert Brownell toured the southwest to investigate the migrant situation, describing what he found as among the nation's "gravest law-enforcement problems." Brownell then worked to create solutions for the illegal migrant problem that included a military-style campaign to locate and forcibly remove undocumented migrants from the southwest. This was the program that the federal government ultimately accepted, initiated in 1954 under the name "Operation Wetback."

During the 2016 Presidential Campaign, conservative Donald Trump revived the mindset of 1950s conservative legislators who, faced with an illegal immigration controversy, adopted the 1954 military-style deportation program then known as Operation Wetback. Trump claimed, in interviews, that he would eject the nation's 11 million undocumented workers, then review cases and allow some of them back on a provisional basis. Beyond the glaring impracticality of the solution, there was a homespun logic that appealed to those with little understanding of what such an effort would entail. Trump based his argument, in part, on what he saw as the success of Operation Wetback in the 1950s. In a debate in November, Trump said:

> *"Dwight Eisenhower, good president, great president, people liked him. I like Ike, right? The expression. I like Ike. Moved a million 1/2 illegal immigrants out of this country, moved them just*

*beyond the border. They came back. Moved them
again, beyond the border, they came back. Didn't like
it. Moved them way south. They never came back."*[193]

Donald Trump's knowledge of Operation Wetback likely comes from those who defended the expensive and largely ineffective program in the 1950s and, in so doing, greatly exaggerated the effectiveness of the operation itself. For one thing, the 1.3 million people that the Border Patrol, and the leaders of Operation Wetback claimed were apprehended during the operation, is, at best, an exaggeration and, at worst, a political fabrication meant to cover for the broad failure of their program. Anger over illegal immigration prompted the "get tough" on illegal immigrant approach embodied by Operation Wetback, and it was, at the time, a test of the hard-nosed, police approach to patrolling the borders.

There were, to be certain, thousands of immigrants deported during the first few months of Operation Wetback and, as Trump asserted, one of the strategies *was* to remove migrants to far away locations to make it impractical for them to return. For the thousands rounded up onto trucks and boats and forcibly taken into the Mexican desert, there were many deaths and widespread documented instances of physical abuse. In her book *Impossible Subjects*, historian Mae Ngai writes about some of the controversial events associated with the program, including one instance in which immigration authorities dumped hundreds of thousands of Braceros (who were legally working in the country) in the desert where 88 died of sun stroke before the Red Cross intervened. Aggressive deportations ended altogether in 1956 after seven workers drowned in an incident aboard the ship *Mercurio* during the process of relocating 500 apprehended Mexicans across the river. The deaths brought a formal protest from Mexico, and the program was quietly put to bed.[194]

Historian Kelly Lytle Hernandez, author of the book *Migra! A History of the U.S. Border Patrol*, found in her research that the entire Border Patrol at the time, consisting of just 1,079 officers, wasn't even remotely capable of deporting 1.3 million migrants, but, instead, inflated their numbers by apprehending the same people again and again, sometimes multiple times in one day. Interviews with individuals present during the program reveal that border agents were often just counting individuals they saw crossing back into Mexico on their own, who may have been illegals or Braceros, who were then added to the list of "voluntary departures." Far more effective, Hernandez argues in her book, was the strategy employed by Border Patrol agents before, during, and after Operation Wetback, in which the agents spent most of their time making deals with farm owners and growers, convincing them to voluntarily switch from illegal migrants to legal Braceros.[195]

Attorney General Brownell, like Donald Trump in 2017, was not a specialist in immigration, nor had he any specific experience with the Border Patrol. Operation Wetback was a political theatre, more symbolic than anything else, but appealed to the simplistic logic of those who saw illegal immigration as a crime and the enforcement of border security as a black-and-white issue without any margins or grey areas. The limited actual success of Operation Wetback was not due to strength, the rule of law, or a more aggressive strategy, but to slow, gradual negotiation, backroom deals, and, most importantly, international cooperation. In a 2006 study published in the *Western Historical Quarterly*, historian Kelly Hernandez demonstrates that the Mexican government and the U.S. government worked together to control the borders at the time and that this was far more effective than a unilateral strategy from either nation could have been. Mexico, also needing laborers for its agricultural and manufacturing industries, thus worked closely with the United States to promote Braceros and limit illegal migration.[196]

The true nature of the Operation Wetback program was not evident in the way that the operation was marketed and sold to the American people. It is, therefore, not surprising that those without a detailed knowledge of history, like Donald Trump and many other anti-Mexican immigration advocates, would have absorbed the propaganda presented by government PR officials without understanding how the program worked.

The Exploitation Machine

Historical economists have found that growers and farming associations greatly exaggerated the need for migrant laborers. Rather than having little choice but to petition for migrants, these farm owners and agricultural companies seized on the opportunity for cheaper labor, increasing profits, even when other sources of citizen labor were available. Mexican-American labor activist Ernesto Galarza led a movement against the Bracero Program while it was in place, seeing it as exploitative. His 1956 report, *Strangers in Our Fields* documented some of the ways in which the regime of farm owners and labor leaders had taken advantage of the migrant workers participating in the program.

Among other things, Galarza's research found that housing provided to Braceros was substandard, that the workers endured prejudicial treatment by white owners and laborers, and that the workers were required to work longer-than-average hours in inhospitable, potentially dangerous conditions. One specific issue noticed by Galarza was that the workers were typically forced to use "short-handled" hoes, which growers felt forced the workers to be more careful and reduced damage to crops. The workers disliked the short-handled hoes because they forced them to stoop over while working and so caused back and muscular problems. The use of short-handled hoes was eventually made illegal by a 1975 Supreme Court decision, though they remained in use illegally into the 1980s. In addition, Galarza found that growers deducted the cost of food, housing, and other expenses from the pay given to Braceros, which

would have been illegal had the workers been U.S. citizens, but was not prohibited explicitly in the 1951 Bracero Program and so continued unencumbered by legal issues.[197]

The Mexican migration debate is often obscured by misinformation. The Republic of Mexico is not a developing nation because of the inherent inferiority of the Mexican governmental system, or because of corruption (though that does exist), or a lack of effort and intelligence on the part of the Mexican people, but rather, is the result of historic and political patterns that create and maintain a hierarchy of power between nations in the same way that those same forces create hierarchies of power between classes within a nation. Illegal migration was the product of an industry controlled by American business owners, supported by politicians, who exploited Mexican labor to increase their profits. By opting for illegal labor rather than participating in regulated programs, these companies did right for themselves and their investors, but also facilitated a pattern that developed into one of the nation's greatest humanitarian crises in later decades. The unregulated freedom of companies and entrepreneurs to pursue profit at the expense of human rights and national interest is thus the key to understanding how the exploitation of poor people and poor nations support a product of the hierarchies of wealth characteristic of the world's leading powers.

CONCLUSION

There were no public opinion polls measuring sentiment on Operation Wetback directly, but the congressional record indicates strong resistance from within United States and Mexico. Some U.S. and Mexican politicians argued that migrant laborers were essential to the economies of both nations, while others objected, based on humanitarian concerns against the military-style methods being used to eject Mexican migrants from the country. Although prejudice against Mexican people was still prevalent, attitudes about race were beginning to change, inspired, in part, by the dawn of a widespread progressive movement that swept across the country, fueling the youth, anti-war, and Civil Rights movements. Policies like Operation Wetback deepened the gulf between the conservative establishment and America's youth, who, in the next generation, began playing a more dominant role in the evolution of America's domestic and foreign policies.

DISCUSSION QUESTIONS

■ What does the Operation Wetback program indicate about modern proposals to deport illegal migrants in the United States?

■ Should the United States return to temporary worker programs as a way to lessen demand for unauthorized migration? Explain your answer.

■ Does prejudice against Mexicans and Mexican-Americans play an important role in American culture? Why or why not?

■ What are some of the moral and/or ethical issues involved in the Mexican immigration debate in the 1950s? Are any of these issues relevant in the modern debate?

Works Used

"An ACT to amend the Agricultural Act of 1949." *UWB*. University of Washington-Bothell Library. Public Law 78. 12 July 1951.

"Freedom Day." *New York Times*. New York Time, Co. 19 Oct. 1986.

Galarza, Ernesto. "Strangers in our Fields." Washington, DC: U.S. Section Joint United States–Mexico Trade Union Committee. 1956.

Garcia, Juanita. "Migratory Labor. Hearings before Subcommittee on Labor and Labor-Management Relations." 82nd Congress, 2nd Session. *Digital History*. University of Houston. 2016.

Hernandez, Kelly Lytle. "The Crimes and Consequences of Illegal Immigration: A Cross-Border Examination of Operation Wetback, 1943 to 1954." *The Western Historical Quarterly*. Vol. 37, No. 4 (Winter, 2006).

Kang, S. Deborah. *The INS on the Line: Making Immigration Law on the US–Mexico Border, 1917–1954*. New York: Oxford UP, 2017 pp. 140–142.

Lind, Dara. "Operation Wetback, the 1950s immigration policy Donald Trump loves, explained." *VOX*. Vox Media. 11 Nov. 2015.

Martin, Philip. "Braceros: History, Compensation." *Rural Migration News*. University of California–Davis. Vol. 12, No. 2. Apr. 2006.

Martin, Philip L., Michael Fix, and Edward J. Taylor. *The New Rural Poverty: Agriculture & Immigration in California*. Washington, DC: The Urban Institute P, 2006 p. 12.

Peralta, Eyder. "It Came Up In The Debate: Here Are 3 Things To Know About 'Operation Wetback.'" *NPR*. National Public Radio. 11 Nov. 2015.

Reston, Maeve, and Gabe Ramirez. "How Trump's deportation plan failed 62 years ago." *CNN*. CNN. 19 Jan. 2016.

Sanchez, George J. *Becoming Mexican American: Ethnicity, Culture, and Identity in Chicanos Los Angeles, 1900–1945*. New York: Oxford UP, 1993.

"The Emergency Farm Labor Supply Program 1943–1947 (The Bracero Program) Agreement." *OPB*. Oregon Public Broadcasting. The Oregon Experience Archive. 2018.

"The Recommendations of the President's Commission on Migratory Labor." U.S. Department of Labor. Apr. 1952. *UC-Berkeley Library*. Digital Collection. 2018.

Introduction

This chapter looks at the end of national quotas and how this fundamental shift in immigration policy ushered in a new era of diversity in American society. During the 40 years that the quota system was in place, it limited immigration rates overall while also preserving the balance of racial and ethnic groups in American society. The last of the quota laws, the 1952 McCarran-Walter Act (as discussed in Chapter 19), met with strong resistance in the 1950s, but the conservative establishment retained control of Congress and was able to forestall efforts to liberalize immigration policies. Between the 1950s and the mid-1960s, however, massive changes were taking place in American society. Sweeping social justice movements were gaining traction, highlighting injustices inherent in the nation's traditional hierarchies of power. A new generation in leadership positions resulted in a series of the most progressive laws in American history.

The source for this chapter is a speech given by Lyndon B. Johnson upon the signing the Hart-Celler Act that ended the national quota system. Johnson and the legislators who championed the bill were unaware of how the law would actually change American society, viewing it more as a symbolic end to an inherently prejudicial approach to immigration. Over the ensuing decades, American immigrants increasingly came from Asia and Africa, thus diversifying American society to a greater degree than even the progressive politicians of the 1960s imagined.

Historians have noted that the progressivism of the 1960s might not have been nearly as successful without the violent resistance of conservatives who viewed these changes as a threat to their identity and power. The assassination of progressive public figures like John F. Kennedy, Martin Luther King, Jr., and Malcolm X, and the violent televised police crackdowns on Civil Rights protestors, therefore, guaranteed the success of the progressive movement as moderates distanced themselves from those within the nation's conservative population willing to use violence to maintain their power.

Topics covered in this chapter include:
- Racial prejudice
- Civil Rights Movement
- Progressive immigration policies
- National quotas system
- Lyndon B. Johnson Administration

This Chapter Discusses the Following Source Document:
Johnson, Lyndon B. "Immigration and Nationality Act of 1965." Full Remarks. Oct. 2, 1965. *LBJ Library*. Immigration and Nationality Act Media Kit. 2018.

Liberty and Progress
Hart-Celler and the End of America's Racial Engineering
(1960–1965)

In many ways, the 1960s was the first and only time that the U.S. immigration debate was dominated by progressive voices. That decade saw the end of the national quotas program and the beginning of a long and (largely unintentional) flood of immigration from non-white countries. For the conservatives who dominated the immigration debate for nearly all the nation's history, the 1960s marked the end of a golden age of white American hegemony, leading to the diversification of America's towns and cities. More than anything else, it was this era that created the angst and anger of modern white conservatives who now feel they must look back to before the 1960s when identifying America's "greatest" age.

Reversing the Status Quo

Breaking the conservative hold on immigration policy was the result of many converging factors.

First, by 1965, America was beginning to emerge from the eugenics fog that, for decades, fostered a widespread belief in a pseudoscientific hierarchy of superiority among the races and nationalities of the world. Historian John Higham called this period the "Tribal Twenties," in his book *Strangers in the Land*, arguing that racial-thinking and racial prejudice had become so widespread as to constitute an essential baseline for American people, rather than an outlier.

_____ *"Public opinion echoed the perturbations of the nativist intelligentsia as never before. The general magazines teemed with race-thinking, phrased nearly always in terms of an attack on the new immigration...the national news magazine* **Current Opinion** *wrote about keeping America white*

> *with as much gusto as the Imperial Wizard of the Ku Klux Klan discussed the lessons of eugenics.*"[198]

It took many years for Americans to begin reexamining their underlying racial prejudices and preconceptions in more than a superficial way. World War II helped to bring eugenics and white supremacy into disfavor by demonstrating dramatically how dangerous the ideologies could be in the hands of a group powerful enough to turn ethnic cleansing from theory to practice. For nearly 100 years, all the immigration policies passed by Congress sought to preserve the nation's racial balance, either by explicitly prohibiting non-white immigrants or by using the quota system (1921–1967) to maintain the *proportions* between races.

The advances of the Youth Activist Movement, the Civil Rights Movement, the Women's Rights Movement, and the Worker's Rights Movement gave voices to the long voiceless in American society and thus the 1960s were the first time that these long-marginalized classes of Americans began to exert real power over the direction of the nation's evolution. White men were still running the show in the 1960s but were also starting to realize that they needed to at least *appear* to be supportive of the values emerging from America's sidelined classes, if they were going to keep their power and identity in American society.

The Civil Rights Debate in Immigration Reform

In 1965, Representative Emanuel Celler of New York and Philip A. Heart of Michigan wrote a landmark immigration reform bill that, among other things, called for the immediate abolishment of the "national quota" system.[199] In the lead up to the historic 1965 debate, Emanuel Celler had long argued that the quota system was racist, prejudicial, and did not represent the fundamental American values of equality and fair play intended by the founding fathers. Celler and former President Truman were, in fact,

President Johnson visits Liberty Island to sign the Immigration Act of 1965, by Yoichi Okamoto, via Wikimedia Commons

the most outspoken critics of the 1952 McCarran-Walter Act that preserved the quota system (and further discriminated against Jewish and Italian immigrants) throughout the 1950s. By the time the congressional debate over the Hart-Celler Bill was taking place in 1964 and 1965, things had changed. Celler was a senior member of the House of Representatives, and the progressive approaches he had championed were gradually becoming more mainstream.

Another progressive politician who helped create the momentum against the quota system and, in fact, the entire history of American immigration policy, was John F. Kennedy. Kennedy's 1958 book, *A Nation of Immigrants*, written while he was still senator, was a passionate argument in favor of liberalizing the immigration system and celebrating the ways in which immigrants had contributed to American culture. As the nation's first Catholic president, whose family had endured anti-Catholic and anti-Irish prejudice, Kennedy's thesis was that it was the diversity and variety of America that made the nation great, and unique, and that had produced the nation's characteristic identity and values. This idea may not seem revolutionary in 2018, but, for most of American history, historians, history books, and politicians had highlighted the contributions and culture of America's white Anglo-Saxons, ignoring or at least downplaying the contributions of individuals from any other group.[200]

Although the Hart-Celler Act *was* controversial, the bill came between two wide-reaching, highly contentious laws that drew far more attention at the time. First was the Civil Rights Act of 1964. This law outlawed discrimination based on race, color, religion, sex, or national origin, and required equal access to employment, public property, and schools. In many ways, slavery did not really end until the Civil Rights Act was passed and, even then, it was just the beginning of a long-term struggle to undo the ingrained systematic manifestations of the nation's racist legacy that still determine access to the benefits of citizenship in 2018.[201] As the Hart-Celler debate continued in the press and in Congress, another piece of legislation was garnering the lion's share of attention, the 1965 Voting Rights Act, which, when passed, gave the federal government the power to end the discriminatory practices used in the states for years to disenfranchise African American voters.[202]

Coming in between the 1964 Civil Rights Act and the 1965 Voting Rights Act, the Hart-Celler immigration act received comparatively little attention. There were, however, many objections raised in the congressional hearings. Some, like Democrat Sam Ervin of North Carolina tried to make the argument that the Hart-Celler Bill discriminated against the people of Britain, arguing:

_____ *"They gave us our language and our common law, they gave a large part of our political philosophy... [this bill] puts them on exactly the same plane as the people of Ethiopia are put, where the people of Ethiopia have the same right to come to the United States under this bill as the people from England, the people of France, the people of Germany, the people of Holland and...with all due respect to Ethiopia, I don't know of any contributions that Ethiopia has made to the making of America."*[203]

Most of the arguments during the 1965 hearings were about non-white immigrants from Asia and Africa and what effect they might have on the country. Though many felt that the United States should remain at least *predominantly* white and western/northern European, arguments in this vein were based not on outward expressions of racial isolation or prejudice, but rather, on alleged fairness to cultures that had contributed to the formation of American society. For instance, Democrat Spessard Holland from Florida argued:

_____ *"Why, for the first time, are the emerging nations of Africa to be placed on the same basis as are our mother countries—Britain, Germany, the Scandinavian nations, France, and the other nations from which most Americans have come?"*[204]

This comment is blatantly prejudicial, ignoring that nearly 11 percent of the nation, or some 20 million citizens of the United States in 1960 were of African descent.

The final push towards the passage of the bill hinged on lobbying by President Lyndon B. Johnson who became president only because of the assassination of John F. Kennedy. Johnson's successes moving progressive legislation through Congress, was, in part, due to Kennedy's passing and the feelings that this tragic event engendered in the population. Not only was Kennedy's death a tragedy to many who lived through it but it represented an American culture with which they could not identify. Supporting the progressive legislation that followed—legislation that was filled with calls for liberty, equality, and the righting of historic injustice—spoke to this tragedy in the American people's minds and hearts.

In the end, Hart-Celler passed by a large margin and did not cause a major outrage at the time. Critics of the bill shifted their opposition to the still-pending voting rights act. For their part, Johnson and supporters of the Hart-Celler Act weren't entirely aware of the kind of changes the immigration bill would bring about. Many genuinely believed that America's immigrants would still primarily come from the white population's "mother countries," and didn't really expect the major influx of Latin American, African, and Asian immigrants that resulted from the bill's passage.

Over the coming decades, American culture changed, becoming far more diverse. The bill exacerbated the controversy over unauthorized Mexican migration that began to develop after the Bracero Program of the 1950s. The influx of so many immigrants from different cultures made the process of assimilating the immigrant population more complex, though this is not demonstrably a problem, even if many feel that it is. It is unlikely that Johnson and the other Democrats had any concept that much of this would happen, and, in fact, in his speech upon signing the bill, standing in front of the Statue of Liberty, Johnson described it as a symbolically meaningful, but functionally prosaic piece of legislation.

REMARKS OF PRESIDENT LYNDON B. JOHNSON UPON THE SIGNING OF THE IMMIGRATION AND NATIONALITY ACT

Source Document

Mr. Vice President, Mr. Speaker, Mr. Ambassador Goldberg, distinguished Members of the leadership of the Congress, distinguished Governors and mayors, my fellow countrymen:

We have called the Congress here this afternoon not only to mark a very historic occasion, but to settle a very old issue that is in dispute. That issue is, to what congressional district does Liberty Island really belong—Congressman Farbstein or Congressman Gallagher? It will be settled by whoever of the two can walk first to the top of the Statue of Liberty.

This bill that we will sign today is not a revolutionary bill. It does not affect the lives of millions. It will not reshape the structure of our daily lives, or really add importantly to either our wealth or our power.

Yet it is still one of the most important acts of this Congress and of this administration.

For it does repair a very deep and painful flaw in the fabric of American justice. It corrects a cruel and enduring wrong in the conduct of the American nation.

Speaker McCormack and Congressman Celler almost 40 years ago first pointed that out in their maiden speeches in the Congress. And this measure that we will sign today will really make us truer to ourselves both as a country and as a people. It will strengthen us in a hundred unseen ways.

I have come here to thank personally each Member of the Congress who labored so long and so valiantly to make this occasion come true today, and to make this bill a reality. I cannot mention all their names, for it would take much too long, but my gratitude—and that of this Nation—belongs to the 89th Congress.

We are indebted, too, to the vision of the late beloved President John Fitzgerald Kennedy, and to the support given to this measure by the then Attorney General and now Senator, Robert F. Kennedy.

In the final days of consideration, this bill had no more able champion than the present Attorney General, Nicholas Katzenbach, who, with New York's own "Manny" Celler, and Senator Ted Kennedy of Massachusetts,

Remarks of President Lyndon B. Johnson Upon the Signing of the Immigration and Nationality Act
continued

and Congressman Feighan of Ohio, and Senator Mansfield and Senator Dirksen constituting the leadership of the Senate, and Senator Javits, helped to guide this bill to passage, along with the help of the Members sitting in front of me today.

This bill says simply that from this day forth those wishing to immigrate to America shall be admitted on the basis of their skills and their close relationship to those already here.

This is a simple test, and it is a fair test. Those who can contribute most to this country—to its growth, to its strength, to its spirit—will be the first that are admitted to this land.

The fairness of this standard is so self-evident that we may well wonder that it has not always been applied. Yet the fact is that for over four decades the immigration policy of the United States has been twisted and has been distorted by the harsh injustice of the national origins quota system.

Under that system the ability of new immigrants to come to America depended upon the country of their birth. Only 3 countries were allowed to supply 70 percent of all the immigrants.

Families were kept apart because a husband or a wife or a child had been born in the wrong place.

Men of needed skill and talent were denied entrance because they came from southern or eastern Europe or from one of the developing continents.

This system violated the basic principle of American democracy—the principle that values and rewards each man on the basis of his merit as a man.

It has been un-American in the highest sense, because it has been untrue to the faith that brought thousands to these shores even before we were a country.

Today, with my signature, this system is abolished.

We can now believe that it will never again shadow the gate to the American nation with the twin barriers of prejudice and privilege.

Our beautiful America was built by a nation of strangers. From a hundred different places or more they have poured forth into an empty land, joining and blending in one mighty and irresistible tide.

continued

The land flourished because it was fed from so many sources—because it was nourished by so many cultures and traditions and peoples.

And from this experience, almost unique in the history of nations, has come America's attitude toward the rest of the world. We, because of what we are, feel safer and stronger in a world as varied as the people who make it up—a world where no country rules another and all countries can deal with the basic problems of human dignity and deal with those problems in their own way.

Now, under the monument which has welcomed so many to our shores, the American Nation returns to the finest of its traditions today.

The days of unlimited immigration are past.

But those who do come will come because of what they are, and not because of the land from which they sprung.

When the earliest settlers poured into a wild continent there was no one to ask them where they came from. The only question was: Were they sturdy enough to make the journey, were they strong enough to clear the land, were they enduring enough to make a home for freedom, and were they brave enough to die for liberty if it became necessary to do so?

And so it has been through all the great and testing moments of American history. Our history this year we see in Viet-Nam. Men there are dying—men named Fernandez and Zajac and Zelinko and Mariano and McCormick.

Neither the enemy who killed them nor the people whose independence they have fought to save ever asked them where they or their parents came from. They were all Americans. It was for free men and for America that they gave their all, they gave their lives and selves.

By eliminating that same question as a test for immigration the Congress proves ourselves worthy of those men and worthy of our own traditions as a Nation.

ASYLUM FOR CUBAN REFUGEES

So it is in that spirit that I declare this afternoon to the people of Cuba that those who seek refuge here in America will find it. The dedication of America to our traditions as an asylum for the oppressed is going to be upheld.

I have directed the Departments of State and Justice and Health, Education, and Welfare to immediately make all the necessary arrangements

Remarks of President Lyndon B. Johnson Upon the Signing of the Immigration and Nationality Act
continued

to permit those in Cuba who seek freedom to make an orderly entry into the United States of America.

Our first concern will be with those Cubans who have been separated from their children and their parents and their husbands and their wives and that are now in this country. Our next concern is with those who are imprisoned for political reasons.

And I will send to the Congress tomorrow a request for supplementary funds of $12,600,000 to carry forth the commitment that I am making today.

I am asking the Department of State to seek through the Swiss Government immediately the agreement of the Cuban Government in a request to the President of the International Red Cross Committee. The request is for the assistance of the committee in processing the movement of refugees from Cuba to Miami. Miami will serve as a port of entry and a temporary stopping place for refugees as they settle in other parts of this country.

And to all the voluntary agencies in the United States, I appeal for their continuation and expansion of their magnificent work. Their help is needed in the reception and the settlement of those who choose to leave Cuba. The Federal Government will work closely with these agencies in their tasks of charity and brotherhood.

I want all the people of this great land of ours to know of the really enormous contribution which the compassionate citizens of Florida have made to humanity and to decency. And all States in this Union can join with Florida now in extending the hand of helpfulness and humanity to our Cuban brothers.

The lesson of our times is sharp and clear in this movement of people from one land to another. Once again, it stamps the mark of failure on a regime when many of its citizens voluntarily choose to leave the land of their birth for a more hopeful home in America. The future holds little hope for any government where the present holds no hope for the people.

And so we Americans will welcome these Cuban people. For the tides of history run strong, and in another day they can return to their homeland to find it cleansed of terror and free from fear.

Over my shoulders here you can see Ellis Island, whose vacant corridors echo today the joyous sound of long ago voices.

continued

And today we can all believe that the lamp of this grand old lady is brighter today—and the golden door that she guards gleams more brilliantly in the light of an increased liberty for the people from all the countries of the globe.

Thank you very much.[205]

Cuban refugees being picked up in Camarioca, Cuba, 1965, National Park Service

Many critics have since argued that the Hart-Celler Act (and 1960s progressivism, in general) were bad for America. This is largely a matter of opinion and not demonstrable through any quantitative measure. Whether one appreciates or regrets the impact of the 1960s depends largely on whether one believes that racial diversity strengthens or weakens the nation. The United States in 2018 was the most diverse in the history of the nation and, in fact, stood one generation away from the permanent end to America's long-standing status as a white-majority country. In the 1960s, there was still a chance, however remote, that immigration legislation might have prevented the end of America's long program of racial engineering, but this possibility ended with Hart-Celler and the diversification of the nation that followed. Because of constitutional law, the many non-white Americans that came to the United States after the Hart-Celler Act passed were eligible to become American citizens, as were their children, and their children's children. Thus, America in 2018 was a nation owned by many races and ethnicities and no longer by a Western or Northern European majority. It is likely that American diversity in the twenty-first century is not the image that many early Americans had in mind when they saw the nation as a haven for European political and religious refugees. Nonetheless, the modern state of American diversity has come to represent, for billions of Americans, a different manifestation of the well-worn "nation of immigrants" ideal, embracing the needy of the *world*, and not just of Europe, and struggling together to create a melting pot from a far more disparate list of ingredients.

CONCLUSION

A Harris poll in 1965 indicated that 70 percent of Americans believed that immigration to the United States should be based on skills or merit and not on nationality. Polls also found, however, that Americans were more willing to accept white, western European immigrants over nonwhite, Jewish, or Eastern European immigrants. Resistance to the Hart-Celler Act might have been more pronounced, therefore, had Americans been aware of how the bill would actually impact American society, which translated into an influx of nonwhite immigrants and the broader diversification of American culture. Even as Americans embraced liberalization, the 1965 Harris Poll showed that more than 30 percent (the largest group measured) still felt that immigration rates should be decreased, with only 7 percent wanting immigration rates to increase. Resistance to the liberalization of immigration was also limited because few Americans at the time considered immigration to be a top priority, with many focused on the seemingly more impactful social issues of the era, including the 1964 Civil Rights Act and 1965 Voting Rights Act, which ended segregation and the state laws that had been long used to marginalize the nation's minority citizens.

DISCUSSION QUESTIONS

- In your opinion, should immigration preference be based on skills and merit, or on place of origin or ethnicity? Explain your answer.
- How did the Civil Rights movement impact the debate over immigration reform?
- Was the diversification of America that occurred after the Hart-Celler Act good or bad for the country overall? Explain your position.
- Was the Hart-Celler Act discriminatory against some groups of Europeans? Explain.

Works Used

"Civil Rights Act of 1964." *NPS*. National Park Service. 2018.

Eckerson, Helen F. "Immigration and National Origins." *The Annals of the American Academy of Political and Social Science*. Vol. 367, The New Immigration (1966), pp. 4–14.

Gjelten, Tom. *A Nation of Nations: A Great American Immigration Story*. New York: Simon & Schuster, 2015 pp. 119–121.

Higham, John. *Strangers in the Land: Patterns of American Nativism, 1860–1925*. New Brunswick, NJ: Rutgers UP, 1955.

Johnson, Lyndon B. "Immigration and Nationality Act of 1965." Full Remarks. 2 Oct. 1965. *LBJ Library*.

Kammer, Jerry. "The Hart-Celler Immigration Act of 1965." *CIS*. Center for Immigration Studies. 30 Sept. 2015.

Orchowski, Margaret Sands. *The Law that Changed the Face of America: The Immigration and Nationality Act of 1965*. New York: Rowman & Littlefield, 2015.

"Public Trust in Government: 1958–2017." *Pew Research*. Pew Research Center. 3 May 2017.

"The 1965 Enactment." *DOJ*. U.S. Department of Justice. 2017.

Introduction

This chapter explores the evolution of American immigration policy with regard to admitting refugees. During the Cold War, the United States was involved in a contest for economic and military dominance with the communist nations of the Soviet Union and China. Unable to enter into direct conflict, the United States and its communist rivals instead engaged in proxy wars, fueling independence and revolutionary struggles in developing nations in an effort to sway the evolution of those nations either towards capitalism or communism. These proxy struggles included violent conflicts in Korea, Vietnam, and Central America, among others. In each case, these actions led to refugee crises, with hundreds of thousands fleeing wars and oppression; in each case, the U.S. government debated whether or not to adjust immigration policies to admit some or all of the refugees fleeing these conflicts.

This chapter looks at three Cold War refugee crises specifically: the 1956 Hungarian refugee crisis; the 1970s Vietnam refugee crisis; and the 1980 Mariel Boatlift. In each case, most Americans were opposed to admitting refugees, sometimes citing nativist economic concerns, and other times viewing refugees as a threat to national security or American culture. The source for this chapter is a 1977 article from *The Guardian*, in which journalist Martin Woollacott describes the refugee situation in Vietnam and makes a case for international aid.

Topics covered in this chapter include:
- Refugee immigration
- The Cold War
- The Vietnam Conflict
- The Hungarian Revolution
- The Mariel Boatlift Controversy

- Nativism
- Racial prejudice

This Chapter Discusses the Following Source Document:
Woollacott, Martin. "The Boat People." *The Guardian*. Guardian News and Media. 3 Dec. 1977.

Cold War Refugees
The South Asian and Cuban Refugee Crises (1975–1980)

The racially-charged term "Mexican standoff," has no clear origin, though historians and linguists have found that the phrase seems to have entered the American lexicon in the late 1800s. In the common parlance, it refers to a standoff or stalemate between two or three parties in which each party has equal power and thus in which no one can ultimately win without initiating his or her own destruction. Though most likely derived, in the vein of phrases like "Indian giver," from some prejudicial assessment about Mexican morality or ethics, the phrase was commonly bandied about by scholars, politicians, and popular writers throughout the Cold War as a metaphor for the nuclear stalemate between the Cold War powers.[206]

With open warfare impossible, the struggle to become the world's leading military and economic power proceeded through a series of vicious proxy conflicts in which the lives of those living in developing nations were often forfeit to the machinations of the world's dominant powers. The Korean Conflict and the Vietnam Conflict are the two primary examples. In both cases, the United States, China, and the Soviet Union funded opposite sides to direct the evolution of those Asian nations towards either democracy or communism.

In both cases, the ensuing conflicts resulted in humanitarian crises that became controversies in American politics. One of the controversial issues throughout the Cold War, was whether the United States should welcome refugees from communist nations. This issue existed at the confluence of opposing messages and impulses. On one hand, politicians had been busily campaigning since the early 1950s to convince Americans that communism was a threat and that communists might subversively work to bring down the government from within. On the other hand, the 1960s brought about a new era in terms of American views on foreign cultures that included a focus on immigration as a tool for foreign policy and the furtherance of global human rights.

The Hungarian Revolution

Historians have noted that Americans rarely approve of bringing refugees into the United States. For instance, in 1939, when the Gallup Poll asked Americans whether the United States should take in several thousand German children orphaned and displaced in World War II, 67 percent opposed the idea. In 1946, when Gallup asked about a proposal to bring in Jewish and other European refugees displaced by the war and then living in makeshift shelters set up by allied forces, 72 percent disapproved of the idea.[207]

That America eventually welcomed World War II refugees was the result of years of campaigning on the part of President Truman and allies and, even when the refugees were finally accepted, the public was still wary and suspicious. America's reluctance to use the wealth of the nation to help the less fortunate from other nations is a factor of a centuries old "America First" movement within American society, part of an ancient conservative ideal that seeks to reserve the material and social wealth of the nation for members of a target group typically depicted as "real" Americans, or "original" Americans, or "native" Americans (though this does not mean indigenous American natives).

By the time the first Cold War refugee crisis hit the media, Americans had already been conditioned to view communists and communism as a pervasive, clandestine threat to the very core of American values and ideals. The anti-communist witch hunts of the McCarthy Era in the early 1950s brought this fear to such sharp focus that Americans turned against themselves, with many willing to believe that the American youth and Civil Rights movements, as well as American academia and the entertainment industry, were rife with communists looking to quietly and insidiously subvert democracy.

In 1956, a student demonstration in the Hungarian city of Budapest sparked a revolt against the communist regime in the Soviet Union. Four days later, Russian military suppressed the revolution and 10,000 Hungarians fled to Austria to escape death or persecution by the Russian military. This was the *first* refugee crisis covered on American television and was widely covered in the print media and in reels shown before films. Scenes of refugees in snow-covered Austria circulated through America for two years as the crisis kept growing. By the time the exodus of refugees stopped, some 200,000 had fled the country for Austria or Yugoslavia.

Hungarians boarding a plane for America, 1956, Getty Images

The Austrian government and people, working with the government of Yugoslavia and its people, engaged in one of the most efficient humanitarian efforts in the history of the world. After Austria's interior minister Oskar Helmer announced that every Hungarian refugee would be granted political asylum, the populace took this message to heart. Thousands of citizens arrived on the border, bringing blankets and supplies, and helping to set up camps for the hungry, suffering migrants.[208] The emergency response of the Austrian nation still suffering after World War II was unprecedented, and author James Michener wrote in his book *The Bridge at Andau*, "It would require another book to describe in detail Austria's contribution to freedom…if I am ever required to be a refugee, I hope I make it to Austria."[209]

Over the first ten weeks of the crisis, over 100,000 of the eventual 200,000 had been resettled to one of 37 countries that agreed to take in some portion of the displaced population.[210] The United States took in 5,000 refugees in 1956, and it is uncertain how the American people felt about this first influx of Hungarians. Widespread news coverage had depicted the suffering Hungarians in very positive terms, highlighting their youthfulness, health, pro-democratic leanings, capabilities, work ethic, and opposition to communism and tyranny—all ideals that Americans had come to see as symbolically representative of Americanism.

The first Gallup poll about the Hungarian refugees asked whether Americans (providing they had space) would be willing to host one or more refugees temporarily from the original 5,000 accepted. To this question, 50 percent said they would be willing, with 35 percent saying they were not willing. In September of 1957, Gallup asked whether the 5,000 already brought to the country should be allowed permanent residence, and, to this, 44 percent said no, as compared to 41 percent who said yes.

On the issue of what to do with the refugees already in the country, Americans demonstrated a willingness to help, but only to a point. However, on the issue of whether to take in *more* refugees, Americans were far less accepting. In 1958 Gallup polled American opinions about a proposal to take in a further 60,000 Hungarian refugees and, it is worth noting, since the phrasing of poll questions has a major impact, that the question specifically referred to the Hungarians as people "fleeing communism." Even when phrased in this way, 55 percent did not approve, with only 33 percent willing to allow the refugees entrance.[211]

The Boat People

After the collapse of South Vietnam in 1975, U.S. forces evacuated 130,000 Vietnamese, Laotian, and Cambodian refugees to temporary camps. News of this vast refugee population became a controversy in the United States as news columnists and television reporters covered

the issue. Some politicians believed it was America's duty to allow some of the displaced refugees to settle in the United States, whereas others disagreed. The Harris Poll organization was the first to measure public opinion on the status of the refugees, asking whether the 130,000 political refugees should be allowed to settle in the United States. In May of 1975, just over 50 percent disapproved of a plan for Indochinese resettlement, and only 26 percent believed they should be allowed to come to America. Despite this, the 130,000 were resettled in the United States.[212]

The federal government initiated a series of programs to integrate the first wave of Indochinese refugees, and the assimilation program did not engender any serious controversy in the United States. In the end, 130,000 was not an extreme challenge for the United States in terms of integration, though some local issues made the news regarding the pro-

Vietnamese boat people, by Phil Eggman, via Wikimedia Commons

gram. The crisis intensified at the end of the decade as word started to circulate about thousands of refugees attempting to flee the region in boats, many caught nationless and destitute, on overcrowded boats that were trapped at sea. In this article from a 1977 issue of Britain's *Guardian* newspaper, columnist Martin Woollacott describes the "boat people" refugee crisis and the urgent need for humanitarian aid:

THE BOAT PEOPLE
by Martin Woollacott
The Guardian, December 3, 1977
Source Document

Refugee officials and diplomats call them "the boat people". Some are indeed fishermen, but most are city folk who, before they slipped away from their homes in Saigon and other towns with hearts knocking, and gold and dollars sewn into their clothes, they knew nothing of the ocean or its dangers.

Nobody knows how many have drowned or been murdered by pirates. But more than two years after the fall of Saigon, they are still coming, and in increasing numbers. They run the gauntlet of the pirates to the Thai cost where the Thais, their camps already full of Cambodians and Laotians, are beginning to turn them away. They arrive hopefully off Singapore which, until recently, they have wrongly seen as a haven, to be ordered out—at gunpoint if necessary. A few blunder down into Indonesian waters, and some head for the Philippines or Hong Kong. But for those who go south, there is now one preferred final destination—Australia, where the arrival earlier this week of a modern trawler with 180 people aboard, including seven Vietnamese soldiers who were overpowered and locked up, has caused political consternation and a diplomatic incident.

The lush little island of Tengah, eight miles off the Malaysian coast, could have been the setting for South Pacific and, indeed, a neighbouring island was the location for that film. Now its palm trees and white sand beaches are the scene of a genuine drama, for the Malaysian government has set it aside as a concentration point for Vietnamese refugees.

For anyone who worked in Vietnam, nostalgia is unavoidable. There is the quacking sound of the language. There is the little girl in the pink dress washing her knickers in the sea who giggles, and then hides the giggle with her hand in a gesture that could only be Vietnamese. There is the very Vietnamese fact that refugees are cutting down timber on this Malaysian island and selling it as firewood to Malaysians, and most of all, there is the familiar impact of the Vietnamese ego—sharp, strong, selfish and shrewd, but rarely unmixed with charm and usually compelling respect.

The refugees' stories have a sameness that can be summed up in the word "incompatibility", although they also reflect badly on the Communists' failure to find some role for the old South Vietnamese middle class other

continued

than agricultural labour. The elected camp chief, Nguyen Hoang Cuong, is a case in point. A businessman and university lecturer, he was given a job in a firm of which he had been a part owner before the liberation. Then the police took him away. He spent nearly a month in detention on the charge of having assisted a former associate of Air Marshal Ky to leave the country. The charge was true, but it had happened before the fall of Saigon, so he was released. "But it was enough for me", he says in his fluent English. "I realised that people like myself would not have any place, any job, and any future with the regime. Sooner or later I would be taken to a re-education camp. So I was determined to escape." After four attempts, he succeeded.

Malaysia is looking after nearly 5,000 of these "boat people"; Thailand probably has a similar number and there are smaller groups in Hong Kong, the Philippines, and Singapore. None of the South-East Asian countries is prepared to let more than a handful stay permanently, and some, like Singapore, won't even let them stay on a temporary basis. The current American quota of 15,000 for Indo-Chinese refugees falls far short of the total of 80,000, most of them not sea refugees, in camps mainly in Thailand. Thus Australia has become "the last hope", according to Nguyen Hoang Cuong. The Malaysians have not taken away the refugees' boats and, if they want to go on, they are not stopped. On Tengah, refugees are working now to refurbish four for the long trip to Australia. They are capable of carrying 120 people. They delayed sailing after promises from Australian immigration officials, under urgent instructions from the harried Fraser government in Canberra, that they will be considered as normal migrants. But if the promises are not kept, they vow they will set off.

As the Australian immigration minister said recently: "The potential is there for large numbers of people to reach Australia in small boats now that the trail has been blazed." Nearly 800 refugees, including the latest batch aboard the big trawler, have already reached northern Australia. Given the care with which Vietnamese apparently continue to listen to the BBC, the Voice of America, and Radio Australia, the new "trail" to Australia will already be general knowledge back in Vietnam.

"When will it end?" a Malaysian diplomat asked plaintively, back in Singapore. The answer is almost certainly that it will get worse, and that diplomatic difficulties with Vietnam, largely avoided till now, are going to become a dimension of the problem. The Vietnamese have already demanded the return of the refugees abroad the

The Boat People
continued

trawler as "pirates". The Australians have refused. Vietnam has made a similar demand that the Philippines return a cargo vessel they say was hijacked in June. The Philippines government intends instead to try the alleged offenders in Manila.

The almost certain result of the increasing number of sea escapes is that the Vietnamese will intensify security measures. There will be more guards on shore and on the boats and future escapes will inevitably involve more violence and even killing. Where there is violence the question of hijacking arises. Already several governments, including that of Malaysia, have announced that escapees from Vietnam will henceforth be treated as illegal aliens rather than refuges.

One can sense the growing irritation of South-East Asian governments. Why don't these people accept their fate instead of, however heroically, crossing the sea to park themselves in countries that don't want them and can't cope with them? Australia, partly replacing the United States and France was the end of a painful transmission belt, is equally annoyed.

But the refusal of the Vietnamese to accept the inevitable is the characteristic which, on both sides, prolonged their civil war beyond all expectation. And there are reckoned to be some 100,000 boats up and down South Vietnam's long coastline, so this is one problem that is not going to go away.[213]

The "Boat People" crisis was all over the news in the United States and some politicians were actively promoting government action. In June of 1979 President Jimmy Carter authorized doubling the number of Indochinese refugees being brought into the nation, to 14,000 per month, saying in a speech at the Tokyo Economic Summit on June 29:

"The plight of refugees from Vietnam, Laos and Cambodia poses a humanitarian problem of historic proportions and constitutes a threat to the peace and stability of Southeast Asia. Given the tragedy and suffering which are taking place, the problem calls for an immediate and major response."[214]

In July of 1979, a CBS/*New York Times* poll found that a majority of Americans, despite continued coverage of the suffering of the refugees, were opposed to allowing refugees to settle in the United States. A full 62 percent disapproved of Carter's decision to increase the number of refugees coming to America, with only 34 percent in support.[215] A Gallup Poll on the same issue, taken also in 1979, found 57 percent opposed allowing the "boat people" to enter the country, with 32 percent approving.[216] Opposition to Vietnamese refugees was more pronounced than opposition to Hungarian refugees in 1958, reflecting both a different situation and political climate and also the fact that Hungarian refugees were typically seen as white Europeans who could more easily integrate, whereas fewer Americans believed that Southeast Asian refugees would be able to integrate as easily into national culture.

The Cuban Refugee Crisis

On April 1, 1980, as the then communist nation of Cuba was in the midst of a severe housing crisis and suffering from rising unemployment levels, Hector Sanyustiz and four other Cubans drove a bus through the fence of Cuba's Peruvian embassy. Castro wanted the escapees returned, but the Peruvian government refused and, by April 6, 10,000 Cubans crowded the embassy seeking asylum and, ultimately, to emigrate out of Cuba. The Spanish and Costa Rican embassies agreed to take a small number of the hopeful emigres, but the status of most of them was uncertain. Then, unexpectedly, Fidel Castro announced that the port of Mariel would be opened to any Cubans who wished to leave the country, so long as they could arrange passage off the island. Cuban exiles already living in the United States organized a fleet of boats to pick up the thousands of Cubans waiting on the Mariel port for extraction, but the issue of whether they could legally come to the United States had not been decided.[217]

Over the course of a couple of months, 125,000 Cubans fled to the United States in an armada of 1,700 boats, overwhelming the Coast guard.

Cuban refugees arrive in Key West, Florida during Mariel Boatlift in 1980, U.S. Coast Guard, via Wikimedia Commons

The boats had been overfilled, with little thought for safety. One boat capsized on May 17, resulting in fourteen deaths. In all, twenty-seven migrants are believed to have died trying to migrate. At first, Jimmy Carter and allies supported bringing the Cubans to the United States but rumors that some of those on the boats had been released from Cuban prisons or mental hospitals inspired a strong resistance.

These rumors were, in part, inspired by Castro himself, who, in state press releases, claimed that those leaving the country were among the nation's least desirable. This was a strategy to limit further exodus and to insult the United States, insinuating that only degenerates would want to go emigrate to the nation. This propaganda campaign reduced support for the "Marielitos" in the United States, where many criticized Carter for agreeing to take them in. The rumors that the Marielitos were criminal was not correct. More than 80 percent of them had no criminal record, 1500 were mentally and physically disabled, and a significant number were queer and transgender people deeply persecuted in Cuba. These types of people, however, were also not wanted by most Americans and the rescue effort became a major controversy.[218] In June of 1980, a CBS/*New York Times* poll asked respondents, "Many refugees from Cuba have come to the U.S. recently. Do you approve or disapprove of allowing most of these Cuban refugees to settle in the U.S.?" In total, 71 percent disapproved of allowing the Cubans to stay, with only 25 percent in support of allowing them to remain.[219]

In 2017, Donald Trump used the example of the Mariel Boatlift as evidence for the misguided nature of Democratic immigration policies, with Trump spokesman Stephen Miller citing a widely discredited study saying that the arrival of the 125,000 Cubans depressed wages in Florida. The argument thus implied is that the Democrats had been too liberal about immigration, leading to an influx of Cubans who competed with local laborers for jobs. Firstly, more well-respected studies demonstrate that the depression on the local economy was significant, but not unexpected given the size of the population arriving in the city, and that the economy recovered and grew stronger after the arrival of the Marielitos.[220]

The assertion that the Mariel Boatlift symbolizes the problems with the "Democratic" approach to immigration is an ill-informed view. The Mariel Boatlift was only peripherally about immigration, and was, more than anything, about how the nation responded to humanitarian crises at its borders. Alleviating local economic strain might have been a matter of federal management and, to the degree that those efforts failed, the Carter administration may then be, in part, responsible for that aspect of the crisis. Nativist sentiment was high in Florida after the initial settlement of the refugees, and it might've been wise to try and spread some of the refugees across a larger area, but, ultimately, the Florida economy rebounded, and the Cuban immigrants built a now thriving Cuban-American community that, in later years, Republicans and Conservatives saw as an ally in their political aims.

CONCLUSION

Debates over the fate of refugees during the Cold War revealed that the American people had never been widely supportive of admitting refugees. When asked, in 2015, whether the nation should admit some of the millions of displaced Syrians who fled the nation's violent civil war, most Americans were against admitting Syrian refugees overall. Resistance to refugees is complicated by the fact that refugees are typically impoverished and come from regions undergoing violent conflict, and some of the resistance against refugees reflect fear that refugee populations will bring these same problems to America, burdening American society. Because a majority of Americans are skeptical of admitting refugees, each refugee crisis typically resulted in a surge of conservative anti-immigration activism. Overall, however, successful integration of refugees also diversified American culture and led to more liberal views of immigration and diversity overall.

DISCUSSION QUESTIONS

- What are some of the pros and cons of admitting refugees as immigrants?
- Does the fact that the U.S. military is involved in the conflict that produces refugees affect the U.S. responsibility to take in immigrants? Why or why not?
- Should the United States accept Syrian refugees? Why or why not?
- Are American attitudes about refugees affected by racial or ethnic prejudice? Explain.

Works Used

Axelrod, Alan. *The Real History of the Cold War: A New Look at the Past*. New York: Sterling, 2009 p. 170.

Bardach, Ann Louise. "Marielitos and the changing of Miami." *Los Angeles Times*. Tronc Media. 24 Apr. 2005.

Coaston, Jane. "The scary ideology behind Trump's immigration instincts." *Vox*. Vox Media. 18 Jan. 2018.

Capó, Julio Jr. "The White House Used This Moment as Proof the U.S. Should Cut Immigration. Its Real History Is More Complicated." *Time*. Time, Inc. 4 Aug. 2017.

Card, David. "The Impact of the Mariel Boatlift on the Miami Labor Market." *Industrial and Labor Relations Review*. Vol. 43, No. 2. (Jan. 1990), pp. 245–257.

Carter, Jimmy. "Tokyo Economic Summit Conference Remarks to Reporters at the Conclusion of the Conference." June 29, 1979. *The American Presidency Project*. University of Southern California. 2018.

Colville, Rupert. "Fiftieth Anniversary of the Hungarian uprising and refugee crisis." *UNHCR*. The United Nations Refugee Agency. 23 Oct. 2006.

Desilver, Drew. "U.S. public seldom has welcomed refugees into country." *Pew Research*. Pew Fact Tank. 19 Nov. 2015.

Jones, Jeffrey M. "Americans Again Opposed to Taking in Refugees." *Gallup*. Gallup News. 23 Nov. 2015.

Lister, Tim. "Today's refugees follow path of Hungarians who fled Soviets in 1956." *CNN*. CNN World. 7 Sept. 2015.

Michener, James A. *The Bridge at Andau*. New York: Random House, 2014.

Newport, Frank. "Historical Review: Americans' Views on Refugees Coming to U.S." *Gallup*. Gallup News. 19 Nov. 2015.

Woollacott, Martin. "The Boat People." *The Guardian*. Guardian News and Media. 3 Dec. 1977.

Wu, Jean Yu-Wen Shen, and Thomas Chen. *Asian American Studies Now*. New Brunswick, NJ: Rutgers UP, 2010 p. 605.

Madden, Mary, and Lee Rainie. "Americans' Attitudes About Privacy, Security and Surveillance." *Pew Research*. Pew Research Center. Internet and Technology. May 20, 2015. Web. 3 Nov. 2017.

Menn, Joseph. "Distrustful U.S. allies force spy agency to back down in encryption fight." *Reuters*. Thomson Reuters. Sept. 21, 2017. Web. 3 Nov. 2017.

Olmstead, Kenneth and Aaron Smith. "Americans and Cybersecurity." *Pew Research*. Pew Research Center. Jan. 26, 2017. Web. 4 Nov. 2017.

Perlroth, Nicole, Larson, Jeff, and Scott Shane. "N.S.A. Able to Foil Basic Safeguards of Privacy on Web." *New York Times*. New York Times Company. Sept. 5, 2013. Web. 29 Oct. 2017.

Introduction

The refugee crises of the Cold War discussed in the previous chapter led to a new conservative movement under President Ronald Reagan in the 1980s. Reagan was a moderate conservative whose immigration policies were a compromise between progressive and conservative concerns. This resulted in the Simpson-Mazzoli Act of 1986, which was bipartisan legislation designed to appeal to moderates on both sides of the political aisle. The most controversial provision of the bill was a proposal to provide a path to legal citizenship for nearly 3 million Mexican migrants living illegally in the United States.

The source for this chapter is a speech on immigration policy delivered by Ronald Reagan in 1981. Like the 1986 policy proposal that followed, this speech demonstrates the Reagan administration's attempts to craft a policy that might appeal to both sides of the immigration debate. The basis of the policy was threefold: increasing border security, penalizing American businesses that hired undocumented laborers, and creating a path to legalization for undocumented migrants living illegally in the U.S. Conservatives have since viewed Reagan's immigration policies as one of the greatest failures of his administration, though the limited success of the bill in controlling immigration was largely the fault of far-right conservatives who prevented laws that would punish American businesses hiring undocumented workers from becoming part of the Simpson-Mazzoli Act.

Topics covered in this chapter include:
- Refugee immigration
- Jimmy Carter Administration
- Ronald Reagan Administration
- Cold War

- Unauthorized migration
- Temporary worker programs
- Legalization of illegal migrants

This Chapter Discusses the Following Source Document:
Reagan, Ronald. "Statement on United States Immigration and
    Refugee Policy." July 30, 1981. *The American Presidency Project*.
University of California. 2017.

Aliens Are Out There
Changing Attitudes on Immigration

In the 1970s and 1980s, illegal immigration developed from a relatively minor concern to one of the top controversies in American politics. During the Jimmy Carter and Ronald Reagan administrations, congressional debates and executive orders were more frequently targeted at addressing this problem than at any time in the past. In part, this was because the movement to embrace level immigration had been so successful, overall, that critics of immigration shifted much of their attention from legal to illegal migrants.

The First Illegal Immigration Debate

The first illegal immigrant controversy to become a national issue occurred after the 1882 Chinese Exclusion Act banned Chinese immigrants from coming to the United States. The problem was that before the passage of the act U.S. law meant that Chinese people born in the United States to legal residents became U.S. citizens by birth and thus were protected by law. Furthermore, laws to that point allowed any native-born citizens to bring his or her blood relatives to join them in the United States. Nativists fought against this law but were overruled by the proportion of Americans who favored keeping the law to promote family reunification, which was part of a broad "family values" ideal in immigration law.

Thus, after the prohibition on Chinese immigration, but with U.S. companies in the west still eager for more laborers, tens of thousands of Chinese migrants, known as the "paper sons and daughters" migrated into the United States using forged identity documents to claim to be children or blood relatives of native-born Chinese-Americans. Immigration authorities passed numerous laws and provisions to prevent this, but many were admitted and remained in the United States, building many of the nation's Chinatown neighborhoods and communities across the United States.[221]

Had there been no work available, it is unlikely that illegal Chinese migration would have continued at such high levels. However, because Chinese laborers were still typically willing to work for less than white workers, and because as non-citizens without federal protections, they could more readily be exploited, the demand for cheap Chinese labor endured, and Chinese migrants continued trying to slip through immigration authorities.

The Origins of Illegal Mexican Migration

America's next illegal immigration controversy focused on the Mexican immigrants who first began coming to the United States in much the same way as the Chinese migrants of the early 1800s, as temporary laborers or as indentured servants working in the farms, ranches, and factories of the west and southwest. Until the mid-1940s, there was little opposition to Mexican immigration. Many of the nativists and racial engineers who opposed Asian migration believed that Mexican migrants weren't dangerous because few wanted to actually stay in the United States, but rather would migrate back and forth seasonally.

Lobbying by farm owners, growers, and factory owners in the west and southwest fueled a long series of temporary worker programs that brought hundreds of thousands of Mexican laborers through the nation on temporary worker contracts. This led to an increase in illegal migration as well; and this concerned nativists, white labor activists, and white supremacists. These disparate, but united groups, then fueled two major anti-Mexican movements, one in the 1930s that resulted in the forced deportation of thousands of Mexicans living in the United States (most of whom were actually native-born Mexican-Americans) and then the "Operation Wetback" program of 1954, which has often been hailed by nativists as proving the effectiveness of the "law and order" approach, but actually demonstrated how difficult and limited such an approach is when dealing with complex problems. Despite surges of opposition, lobbying by American business owners seeking to profit from Mexican migrants kept tem-

porary worker programs going until 1975, when pressure from nativists and the growth of the illegal population resulted in the cancellation of the last of the temporary worker programs.

Interestingly, the focus on Mexican migration peaked even as the proportion of Mexican migrants in the U.S. workforce fell . The proportion of Mexican workers in states across the country, from Kansas, to Arizona and New Mexico, was higher in the 1920s than in the 1990s and yet, it was during the 1980s and 1990s that illegal Mexican workers became the primary symbol of America's alleged immigration problems and were typically cited as the primary reason for various immigration reform efforts.[222]

Republicans Become the Anti-Immigration Party

In 1955, public opinion polls indicated that most Americans (76 percent) either wanted to reduce immigration (39 percent) or, at least, keep it at current levels (37 percent), with only a small percentage of Americans (13 percent) believing that the United States should increase immigration. This general breakdown in opinion remained relatively unchanged throughout the entirety of the 1960s and 1970s, with minor changes surrounding immigration controversies, like the debate over whether to admit Southeast Asian refuges (the so-called "boat people") in the 1970s. Opposition to illegal immigrants peaked in the 1980s, following a massive conservative campaign to portray illegal migration as an economic burden to the United States and a threat to U.S. workers. In 1982, 89 percent of Americans overall believed that the nation should decrease (66 percent) or keep immigration at current levels (23 percent), with only 4 percent supporting increased immigration.[223]

The Republican Party's anti-immigration push in the late 1970s was strategic in that it was the Democratic Party that had first liberalized the nation's immigration policies. The influx of non-white immigrants into the nation between the 1960s and 1980s intensified racial tension and the perception of racial competition for employment, and the Republican Party thus portrayed itself as the party that would protect both American jobs and white American identity against the economic drain and racial strain created by what they portrayed as misguided Democratic liberalization. This remained the official Republican Party stance into the twenty-first century and, in fact, the political mobilization of racial prejudice and nativism were the fundaments of Donald Trump's immigration policy proposals in 2017 and 2018. The essential message to voters in the lead-up to the Reagan-Carter presidential campaign, was that the Democrats had failed on immigration reform because they weren't prepared to get tough on immigrants and to aggressively control the borders.

The Reagan Legacy

Ronald Reagan has been touted by Republicans as the father of modern conservatism. He was the last Republican President to garner support from the nation's moderates and the last Republican who might've been

able to win the presidency even without the most extreme elements of the far right. In a 2011 Gallup Poll, Reagan was rated as the nation's best president of all time, garnering 19 percent of the votes by Gallup, and, therefore, right above Abraham Lincoln with 14 percent, and Bill Clinton with 13 percent. No other modern conservative in the poll reached higher than 2 percent of the vote.[224] Reagan's ranking on the list demonstrates that Reagan had bipartisan appeal, with policies that appealed broadly to moderates of both parties and, therefore, though often exalted with pride by modern conservatives,

President Ronald Reagan, via Wikimedia Commons

Reagan's approach was fundamentally different than the standard GOP policies of the modern era.

By the time Donald Trump became the leader of the Republican Party, things had changed. With little to no moderate support, Trump managed only a narrow electoral victory, lost the popular vote by the lowest margin in history, and managed, at his most popular appeal during his first year in office, only 41 percent approval. Reagan, by contrast, recorded a peak of 68 percent approval during his first year.[225] The difference between Reagan and modern GOP candidates like Trump, comes down to popular appeal and the ability to engender respect from one's opponents. Reagan had this ability and moderates were willing to trust him, whereas Republicans like Trump and George W. Bush were too indebted to far-right interests to reach out to moderates and so failed to garner any serious degree of bipartisan respect or support.

On immigration, Reagan appealed to hardline conservatives by promising to crack down on illegal immigration. Immigration was a prime talking point of the 1980 elections and preceding debates, with Reagan promising a comprehensive immigration reform policy unlike anything ever attempted that would constitute the first legitimate effort to control the nation's borders. Nativists and anti-immigration lobbyists were lulled into thinking that Reagan thought like they did, but they were wrong and failed to consider Ronald Reagan's background.

Reagan was from California and had spent much of his life around Mexicans and Mexican-Americans and his familiarity fostered a more nuanced view. Social scientists have long understood that racial prejudice is quickly eroded by close contact, and that the most overtly racist or prejudiced attitudes are characteristic of individuals who have little to no direct familiarity with the target group of their prejudices. A white person living outside a predominantly black community and watching the behavior of black neighbors from a removed position, is, therefore, far more susceptible to racialized and biased thinking about that group than an individual who lives inside that community and so whose day-to-day interactions illuminate the failings inherent in racial generalities. Reagan knew Mexican people, both legal and illegal immigrants, and both groups were a familiar part of his environment. Although he agreed with the conservative line that the borders needed to be protected, he also believed that the migrants (both legal and illegal) were human beings deserving of consideration, empathy, and understanding.

After winning the election, Reagan continued to make immigration a focus of his presidency, though the reform policy he promised didn't actually arrive until 1986. However, the nuance and humanitarian tendencies of the immigration policies that came through Reagan's administration were reflected in how he spoke about the issue.

STATEMENT ON UNITED STATES IMMIGRATION AND REFUGEE POLICY
July 30, 1981
Source Document

Our nation is a nation of immigrants. More than any other country, our strength comes from our own immigrant heritage and our capacity to welcome those from other lands. No free and prosperous nation can by itself accommodate all those who seek a better life or flee persecution. We must share this responsibility with other countries.

The bipartisan select commission which reported this spring concluded that the Cuban influx to Florida made the United States sharply aware of the need for more effective immigration policies and the need for legislation to support those policies.

For these reasons, I asked the Attorney General last March to chair a Task Force on Immigration and Refugee Policy. We discussed the matter when President Lopez Portillo visited me last month, and we have carefully considered the views of our Mexican friends. In addition, the Attorney General has consulted with those concerned in Congress and in affected States and localities and with interested members of the public.

continued

The Attorney General is undertaking administrative actions and submitting to Congress, on behalf of the administration, a legislative package, based on eight principles. These principles are designed to preserve our tradition of accepting foreigners to our shores, but to accept them in a controlled and orderly fashion:

- We shall continue America's tradition as a land that welcomes peoples from other countries. We shall also, with other countries, continue to share in the responsibility of welcoming and resettling those who flee oppression.

- At the same time, we must ensure adequate legal authority to establish control over immigration: to enable us, when sudden influxes of foreigners occur, to decide to whom we grant the status of refugee or asylee; to improve our border control; to expedite (consistent with fair procedures and our Constitution) return of those coming here illegally; to strengthen enforcement of our fair labor standards and laws; and to penalize those who would knowingly encourage violation of our laws. The steps we take to further these objectives, however, must also be consistent with our values of individual privacy and freedom.

- We have a special relationship with our closest neighbors, Canada and Mexico. Our immigration policy should reflect this relationship.

- We must also recognize that both the United States and Mexico have historically benefited from Mexicans obtaining employment in the United States. A number of our States have special labor needs, and we should take these into account.

- Illegal immigrants in considerable numbers have become productive members of our society and are a basic part of our work force. Those who have established equities in the United States should be recognized and accorded legal status. At the same time, in so doing, we must not encourage illegal immigration.

- We shall strive to distribute fairly, among the various localities of this country, the impacts of our national immigration and refugee policy, and we shall improve the capability of those agencies of the Federal Government which deal with these matters.

Statement on United States Immigration and Refugee Policy
July 30, 1981
continued

- We shall seek new ways to integrate refugees into our society without nurturing their dependence on welfare.

- Finally, we recognize that immigration and refugee problems require international solutions. We will seek greater international cooperation in the resettlement of refugees and, in the Caribbean Basin, international cooperation to assist accelerated economic development to reduce motivations for illegal immigration.

Immigration and refugee policy is an important part of our past and fundamental to our national interest. With the help of the Congress and the American people, we will work towards a new and realistic immigration policy, a policy that will be fair to our own citizens while it opens the door of opportunity for those who seek a new life in America.[226]

The Simpson-Mazzoli Act of 1986

Reagan's immigration reform bill was authored by Wyoming Senator Alan K. Simpson and Kentucky Senator Romano Mazzoli. In its original form it contained funding for increased border patrol measures and laws that would prohibit hiring illegal immigrants, thus for the first time breaking with the tradition of prohibiting immigration without targeting those who hired illegal immigrants. The act also contained another, unexpected provision drastically at odds with all conservative immigration policies—a measure that would offer amnesty to all illegal migrants living in the United States since 1982. This ground-breaking provision provided temporary legal status to illegal migrants who came forward, paid a $185 fee, and agreed to an interview to determine if the person had "good moral character." The legalized immigrant would then, after 18 months, become eligible for a green card, provided they learned to speak English.[227]

Immigration counseling at the National Amnesty Consultants help illegal immigrants get help with new immigration laws, by Bruce Berman, LIFE Images Collection, Getty Images

Speaking to National Public Radio (NPR), former Wyoming Senator Alan K. Simpson explains that the amnesty provision was gently put forward in a law that was touted as being primarily about border control and protecting American jobs.

"We used the word 'legalization,' and everybody fell asleep lightly for a while, and we were able to do legalization."

The controversial provision granted amnesty to 2.9 million illegal migrants and, though the bill was considered a failure by many Republicans at the time, Reagan and Simpson, two of the bill's primary architects, were pleased with the amnesty portion of the law and its effect.

As Simpson explained to NPR,

> _____ *"[Reagan] knew that it was not right for people to be abused. Anybody who's here illegally is going to be abused in some way, either financially [or] physically. They have no rights."*

He added later in the interview.

> _____ *"It's not perfect, but 2.9 million people came forward. If you can bring one person out of an exploited relationship, that's good enough for me."*[228]

The Simpson-Mazzoli bill has since been seen, especially by conservatives, as a major failure. Rather than reducing immigration, the bill actually led to an increase in illegal immigration over subsequent years, with the unauthorized population growing from 3–5 million to more than 11 million in 2018. However, the failure of the bill was guaranteed before Reagan ever signed it because labor interests and unwillingness to allocate sufficient funds made the enforcement provisions of the bill superficial at best.

First, the planned prohibitions and penalties for individuals or companies hiring illegal immigrants raised concern from pro-business lobbyists and politicians who needed their support and campaign contributions. Thus, when the bill was released, all employers had to do to avoid penalties was to demonstrate that the workers had papers in their possession that could "reasonably" be believed to be genuine, which meant that any decent fake document exempted the employer from penalties. Second, employers skirted the issue by hiring workers through contractors and subcontractors, and so weren't directly responsible for making sure their workers were legal as that responsibility fell on the contractors. In total, nearly 80 percent of western agricultural work was handled through contractor staffing and, therefore, this loophole allowed employers to continue hiring illegal migrants (who were still cheaper) with impunity.

Finally, the effort to decrease immigration by providing a stronger Border Patrol was disastrous. Whereas illegal migrants had typically arrived in the United States through one of a few entry points, increased Border Patrol at those areas simply spread the illegal migrant population across more of the southwest. This made enforcement largely impractical and led, eventually, to the border fence and border wall proposals of subsequent Republican administrations. As immigrants spread across the border, finding new entry points to subvert border crossing patrols, even the possibility of controlling the border began to seem impractical if not entirely impossible. Subsequent studies have demonstrated that it would require military-grade deployment and billions in investment to create a program that will likely be only moderately effective.[229]

Lessons That Were Never Learned

In 2018, some politicians still refer to "amnesty" as the failure of the Simpson-Mazzoli Act of 1986, but this assessment is incorrect. The failure of the Simpson-Mazzoli Act was, like the failure to control illegal immigration from the 1880s through the 1980s, a product of the power of the pro-business lobby and American phobia regarding regulation. Whereas there may always be some who wish to migrate to the United States, illegal immigration is an "industry" in the United States—the result of the fact that there are individuals and businesses willing to hire illegal migrants to increase their profits and decrease their business costs. Simpson-Mazzoli was meant to cut off the demand, which they hoped would lead to a reduction in supply. Instead, the bill did not reduce demand, and in fact, the framers of the bill had not correctly assessed the level of demand that existed. Demand continued to increase, so immigration increased, and the symbolic efforts to control the borders (the favored Republican policy from Reagan to Trump) did little to stem this flow.

Reagan's immigration legacy is complex, because the administration on one hand proffered and attempted a far stronger prevention policy than ever in the past, but also considered the human rights aspects of the immigration situation to that point. In the future, Republicans would more closely mirror the attitudes of the far-right anti-immigration opponents who had little concerns for the impact of their policies on the immigrants and saw this portion of the American population as criminals whose criminal behavior (as well as non-citizen status) negated the need to consider their welfare.

CONCLUSION

Reagan has remained one of the most popular Republican presidents in history, in part because he was able to garner significant support from moderates on both sides of the political divide. As a result, there was little controversy in terms of public backlash, when Reagan and allies outlined the policy ideas that became the Simpson-Mazzoli Act. The administration was addressing both fears of nativists, by promising to get serious about border control and enforcement, and concerns of liberals who felt the illegal migration situation was also a human rights issue. Although public opinion polls continued to demonstrate resistance to immigration overall and staunch support for a broadly restrictive immigration policy, the human rights dimension of immigration had become a more important part of the public debate and Reagan was the first conservative president who attempted to address this issue in his immigration policies.

DISCUSSION QUESTIONS

- Was the amnesty program developed under the Reagan administration good or bad for America? Explain your position on the issue.
- Should politicians of either party promote policies that represent a compromise between conservatives and progressives in the United States or should politicians represent the majority political view in their area? Explain.
- Is unauthorized migration a major problem in the United States? Why or why not? How important a problem is immigration in the United States? Explain.
- Would you support an amnesty or legalization program for migrants already living in the United States? Why or why not?

Works Used

"A Reagan Legacy: Amnesty For Illegal Immigrants." *NPR*. National Public Radio. 4 July 2010.

Fussell, Elizabeth. "Warmth of the Welcome: Attitudes towards Immigrants and Immigration Policy." *Annual Review of Sociology*. July 2014, Vol. 40, pp. 479–498. PDF.

Koslowski, Rey. "The Evolution of Border Controls as a Mechanism to Prevent Illegal Immigration." *MPI*. Migration Policy Institute. Reports. Feb. 2011.

Newport, Frank. "American Say Reagan Is the Greatest U.S. President." *Gallup*. Gallup News. 18 Feb. 2011.

Peters, Gerhard. "Presidential Job Approval Ratings Following the First 100 Days." *The American Presidency Project*. U of California. 2017.

Plumer, Brad. "Congress tried to fix immigration back in 1986. Why did it fail?" *Washington Post*. Washington Post, Co. 30 Jan. 2013.

Reagan, Ronald. "Statement on United States Immigration and Refugee Policy." 30 July 1981. *The American Presidency Project*. U of California. 2018.

Robert Siegel and Selena Simmons-Duffin. "How Did We Get To 11 Million Unauthorized Immigrants?" *NPR*. National Public Radio. 7 Mar. 2017.

Wang, Hansi Lo. "Chinese-American Descendants Uncover Forged Family Histories." *NPR*. National Public Radio. 17 Dec. 2013.

Introduction

This chapter explores the human rights dimension to immigration policy and the growing concern for the rights of immigrants among the American people in the 1980s and 1990s. The ethical and moral dimensions of immigration explored in the 1980s became a primary focus in the debate in the twenty-first century. In the 1980s, the Reagan administration partially funded three civil wars—in El Salvador, Guatemala, and Nicaragua. The wars devastated each of the three countries, leading to a mass exodus of refugees. The Reagan administration refused to recognize the refugees as victims of war crimes because doing so would have admitted U.S. culpability. This led to the birth of the Sanctuary Movement, in which a collection of churches and religious leaders took in and assisted Central American refugees in defiance of immigration policy and federal law.

Simultaneously, a series of court cases in Texas brought the issue of undocumented immigrant rights to the forefront of the public debate when the state attempted to pass a law that would ban undocumented children from attending the state's public schools. The source for this chapter includes excerpts from the Supreme Court case of *Plyler v. Doe* addressing whether the states could penalize or otherwise reject the children of undocumented migrants.

Topics covered in this chapter include:
- Immigrant welfare
- Immigrant rights
- U.S. Supreme Court cases on immigration
- Sanctuary Movement
- Ronald Reagan Administration
- Refugee policy
- Cold War

This Chapter Discusses the Following Source Document:
"Plyler v. Doe." 1982. *Cornell Law School*. LII. Supreme Court.
   2017.

Immigrant Rights and Welfare
Immigrant Children and the Sanctuary Movement (1980–1990)

As the now familiar modern conservative approach to immigration reform was taking shape, there was another movement developing in the United States focused on the welfare and human rights of immigrants and their children. The rights of immigrants, which before the 1980s was a concept rarely considered, became a prime issue in the immigration debates of the 2000s and 2010s, centering on whether to grant amnesty or at least a path to citizenship for immigrant children and adults brought to the nation as children by undocumented parents.

The Refugee Act (1980) and the Sanctuary Movement

In a 1988 article in the *New York Times*, Professor Edwin Guthman of the University of Southern California asked,

> *"When people believe their Government is applying the law unfairly and violating human rights, is it their moral duty to engage in civil disobedience if their protests have no effect?"*[230]

The issue that Guthman was speaking about was the beginning of the "sanctuary movement," in which citizens, groups, and cities, concerned for the plight of migrant workers, violated immigration law to provide safety and aid to immigrants. In the 2010s, sanctuary cities emerged, refusing to participate in federal deportation programs or efforts to round up illegal immigrants. This municipal rebellion had its roots in a religious movement from the 1980s.

President Jimmy Carter fundamentally changed American policy on refugees with the passage of the Refugee Act of 1980. The Vietnamese refugee crisis resulting from the Vietnam War was the primary motivation for the law, as the effort to help the thousands of refugees who were stranded on boats after fleeing violence in Vietnam made it clear that existing policy on refugees was woefully inadequate for the modern world. The act raised the annual limit on refugees from 17,400 to 50,000 and brought American policies on refugees in sync with international standards established by the 1951 UN Convention on Human Rights and the 1967 Protocol on Refugees.

Before the 1980 law, American law only recognized refugees from Eastern and Central Europe who were persecuted by Communism, a holdover from the nation's first refugee crisis after World War II and from the prevailing "Red Menace" period in American domestic and foreign policy. With the 1980 law, the United States adopted a definition of a refugee as someone from any nation or culture with a "well-founded fear of persecution," or violence because of race, religion, nationality, or membership in a specific group. In addition, the Refugee Act of 1980 also created a new government office, the Office of Refugee Resettlement, to manage all future refugee crises.[231]

The bill became law at the very end of Carter's presidency, at a time when immigration and refugees were a hot and controversial topic. Public opinion polls from the era indicated that most of the American people were opposed to taking in Vietnamese refugees and the fact that the government accepted tens of thousands of Southeast Asians fleeing Vietnam caused a backlash against Carter and immigrants in general. This came also at a time when civil wars spread through parts of Central America, initiating a mass exodus of Salvadorans, Nicaraguans, and Guatemalans who came through Mexico and to the United States seeking shelter.

The civil wars in El Salvador, Guatemala, and Nicaragua were all populist, socialist uprisings against authoritarian governments that had long repressed and subjugated the populations in each of the three nations. The fact that the civil wars involved socialist uprisings affected the way that the United States reacted to the wars, because the United States was still

very much dedicated to the Cold War fight against communism. As a result, American administrations used foreign policy to further American interests regarding "beating Communism" in the race for global dominance. For those reasons, the Reagan Administration's response to the crisis was to give military and financial aid to the authoritarian governments of Guatemala and El Salvador, because the populist resistance movements were socialist. In Nicaragua, the socialist revolution had already resulted in the ouster of dictator Anastasio Somoza in 1979, with a new revolutionary government established under Frente Sandinista and so the Reagan administration funded a rebel group known as the Contras, to fight against the Sandanista government.

In El Salvador the authoritarian government, now bolstered by U.S. financial and military aid, used a system of "death squads" that conducted mass executions and illegal arrests of union leaders, activists, and individuals seen as "sympathizers" of the attempted socialist uprising, including many priests and nuns who had not participated in the uprising but gave support to the injured refugees. In Guatemala, U.S. support funded a regime that conducted hundreds of murders and arrests, without due process, of dissidents and alleged communist sympathizers. In both cases, the U.S. government funded tyranny because that tyranny was directed at socialism and socialism was seen as anathema to the U.S. government's foreign policy agenda.[232]

Beginning in 1981, thousands of Salvadorans, Nicaraguans, and Guatemalans fled through Mexico and into the United States. The U.S. government was in a bind, because the refugees coming into the country were fleeing their government and claiming persecution and yet, the United States was helping those same governments commit those same atrocities and so could not accept the claims that the refugees were being persecuted unjustly without also admitting complicity in those actions. Refugees from El Salvador and Guatemala were thus categorized as "economic migrants," which allowed the administration to deny that they were victims of governmental human rights violations.

Without status as refugees of violence and persecution, admission rates were low. About one-fourth to one-third of asylum seekers from Iran, Eastern Europe, and Asia were approved for asylum, because they were fleeing communist dictatorships, whereas by 1984 only 3 percent of Salvadorans and Guatemalans had been accepted into the United States as economic refugees and none had been classified as asylum seekers.

To make matters worse, the Justice Department and the INS worked together to keep the crisis quiet and to dispose of the refugees without causing additional controversy. They did this by gathering migrants into detention centers where they were not given access to legal counsel and where INS agents pressured the prisoners into agreeing to "voluntarily" return to their countries of origin. Thousands who refused to voluntarily leave were forcibly deported back to the war-torn nations they were seeking to escape, in blatant violation of U.S. commitments to human rights and welfare. More than 75,000 were eventually killed in El Salvador's civil war and as many as 200,000 in the Guatemalan civil war. What's worse, in the wake of the wars, the same weapons sent by the United States to fund their anti-socialist campaigns in Central American armed the criminal gangs that terrorized the populations of all three countries, and neighboring Honduras, leaving the entire region known as the "Northern Triangle" as one of the world's most violent places in 2018.[233]

The Sanctuary Movement began in Arizona where Reverend John Fife of the Southside Presbyterian Church in Tucson began taking in Salvadoran and Guatemalan refugees and helping them to apply for refugee status. Fife was later joined in this mission by James Corbett, leader of a Quaker community occupying a ranch outside Tucson. After two years, when none of the refugees they assisted had been granted asylum, the situation began to become clear. Reverend Fife then announced that his church, in

defiance of INS policy, would become a "sanctuary" for the refugees coming to the United States.

Fife's movement spread and, within months there was a network of churches in California, Texas, and Chicago who were actively taking in refugees, providing them with food and other needs, and helping them migrate illegally into the United States. By the mid-1980s, more than 150 congregations across the nation were openly defying the government to participate in the movement, and the sanctuary system they created was being endorsed by churches and religious organizations around the country and throughout Mexico. Among other services, the sanctuary churches provided food, legal representation, medical care, jobs, and assistance bringing family members from their native countries.

Sanctuary defendant Reverend John Fife and his wife Marianne, Tucson, Arizona, received a suspended sentence for smuggling aliens from Central America into the U.S., Getty Images

The Department of Justice sent spies to infiltrate the Sanctuary Movement, and these spies helped to identify 16 United States and Mexican activists who were arrested and charged with smuggling aliens, including three nuns, two priests, and a minister. The entire affair came to a head in a well-publicized 1985 trial in Texas.

The Texas trials were a landmark moment in judicial history in several ways. Activists and lawyers, who donated their time to defend them, used the Nuremberg principles that emerged from post-World War II trials of Nazi war tribunals to accuse the U.S. government, even Reagan himself, of war crimes. It was also the first time that United Nations conventions on refugees and human rights were used in a domestic trial to defend violating U.S. law when U.S. law, in the opinion of the defendants, violated the Nuremberg principles and the U.S. commitment to *international* law. During the trial, the Sanctuary Movement was compared to the abolitionist movement and the "Underground Railroad" that smuggled hundreds of thousands of escaped slaves to freedom. At the trial, some of the activists involved argued that their actions were not fundamentally or morally different than in that historic struggle, subverting law in pursuit of higher human rights principles. Ultimately, eight of those who participated were found guilty, but most received suspended sentences or house arrest as prosecutors were unwilling to push for more severe penalties.[234] Ultimately, Congress took up the cause and in 1990 passed an emergency provision to grant refugee status to the remaining refugees.

The Sanctuary Movement of the 1980s was the direct predecessor of the Sanctuary Movement of the 2010s in which, again, religious communities began taking a stance against the deportation of individuals who, if returned to their home countries, might face violence and persecution, whether political or economic. The movement intensified over the question of whether the adult children of illegal immigrants should be treated the same as immigrants who knowingly and willingly flouted U.S. law, or whether, as individuals who grew up in the United States and whose unauthorized presence is through no fault of their own, they should be subject to different treatment. The morality of these questions became part of a broadening of human rights awareness that spread through the United States in the 1980s. The key issue at that time was education, initiating a legal controversy still relevant in the modern immigration debate.

The Right to an Education

In 1975, the State of Texas enacted section 21.031 of the Texas Education Code. The controversial provision allowed the state's public schools to charge tuition to undocumented children who wished to attend public schools. There is no public record regarding how the legislature arrived at the decision to enact the law, and there was no legislative debate preceding its passage. The law also allowed the state to withhold funds from schools that continued to educate undocumented students after the passage of the law. Some school districts simply kicked out all undocumented children whereas others charged tuition of up to $1000 per year or simply ignored the decision and continued to admit undocumented students undeterred. When several poor students were ejected from their classrooms and schools, the Mexican-American Legal Defense and Educational Fund (MALDEF) filed a legal suit that was later consolidated with a similar suit filed in Houston.[235]

When the case came before the district court, the defense argued that the law was intended to limit illegal migration, and, further that a massive increase in illegal enrollment was causing a strain on the schools, and so that barring undocumented migrants would increase the quality of education for native-born students. The district court found that none of these claims were convincing in that, the law would not impact illegal migration, that the increase in enrollment was due to legal resident children, not undocumented children, and that, whereas expelling undocumented migrants might save the district money, it would not increase the quality of education. The state then appealed, though the Court of Appeals concurred with the District Court and, thus, the Supreme Court agreed to hear the case.[236]

In 1982, the Supreme Court ruled 5–4 that the law passed by the State of Texas violated the constitutional rights of the children under the Fourteenth Amendment guarantee of equal protection under the law. All five justices of the court rejected unanimously the state of Texas's claim that illegal immigrants were not covered by the equal protection clause, but were split on the deeper issue, which is whether the alien children's right to equal protection meant that they had the right to the same education as other children. On this point, a majority agreed that undocumented children did have this right.[237]

Justice Brennan delivered the majority opinion before the court:

SUPREME COURT JUSTICE BRENNAN'S MAJORITY OPINION ON *PLYLER V. DOE*
June 1982
Source Document

The Fourteenth Amendment to the Constitution is not confined to the protection of citizens. It says:

Nor shall any state deprive any person of life, liberty, or property without due process of law; nor deny to any person within its jurisdiction the equal protection of the laws.

These provisions are universal in their application, to all persons within the territorial jurisdiction, without regard to any differences of race, of color, or of nationality, and the protection of the laws is a pledge of the protection of equal laws.

In concluding that "all persons within the territory of the United States," including aliens unlawfully present, may invoke the Fifth and Sixth Amendments to challenge actions of the Federal Government, we reasoned from the understanding that the Fourteenth Amendment was designed to afford its protection to all within the boundaries of a State.

Later in his opinion, Brennan's commentary struck to the heart of the immigration debate and to the unforeseen consequences of the unintended creation of an "underclass" of undocumented migrants.

Supreme Court Justice Brennan's Majority Opinion
continued

Sheer incapability or lax enforcement of the laws barring entry into this country, coupled with the failure to establish an effective bar to the employment of undocumented aliens, has resulted in the creation of a substantial "shadow population" of illegal migrants—numbering in the millions—within our borders. This situation raises the specter of a permanent caste of undocumented resident aliens, encouraged by some to remain here as a source of cheap labor, but nevertheless denied the benefits that our society makes available to citizens and lawful residents. The existence of such an underclass presents most difficult problems for a Nation that prides itself on adherence to principles of equality under law.

The children who are plaintiffs in these cases are special members of this underclass. Persuasive arguments support the view that a State may withhold its beneficence from those whose very presence within the United States is the product of their own unlawful conduct. These arguments do not apply with the same force to classifications imposing disabilities on the minor children of such illegal entrants. At the least, those who elect to enter our territory by stealth and in violation of our law should be prepared to bear the consequences, including, but not limited to, deportation. But the children of those illegal entrants are not comparably situated. Their "parents have the ability to conform their conduct to societal norms," and presumably the ability to remove themselves from the State's jurisdiction; but the children who are plaintiffs in these cases "can affect neither their parents' conduct nor their own status."

In concurrence, Justice Harry Blackmun wrote:

Supreme Court Justice Brennan's Majority Opinion
continued

In my view, when the State provides an education to some and denies it to others, it immediately and inevitably creates class distinctions of a type fundamentally inconsistent with those purposes, mentioned above, of the Equal Protection Clause. Children denied an education are placed at a permanent and insurmountable competitive disadvantage, for an uneducated child is denied even the opportunity to achieve. And when those children are

Supreme Court Justice Brennan's Majority Opinion
continued

members of an identifiable group, that group—through the State's action—will have been converted into a discrete underclass. Other benefits provided by the State, such as housing and public assistance, are, of course, important; to an individual in immediate need, they may be more desirable than the right to be educated. But classifications involving the complete denial of education are, in a sense, unique, for they strike at the heart of equal protection values by involving the State in the creation of permanent class distinctions. In a sense, then, denial of an education is the analogue of denial of the right to vote: the former relegates the individual to second-class social status; the latter places him at a permanent political disadvantage.

Delivering another concurring opinion, Justice Lewis Powell, wrote:

Supreme Court Justice Brennan's Majority Opinion
continued

The classification in question severely disadvantages children who are the victims of a combination of circumstances. Access from Mexico into this country, across our 2,000-mile border, is readily available and virtually uncontrollable. Illegal aliens are attracted by our employment opportunities, and perhaps by other benefits as well. This is a problem of serious national proportions, as the Attorney General recently has recognized. See ante at 218–219, n. 17. Perhaps because of the intractability of the problem, Congress—vested by the Constitution with the responsibility of protecting our borders and legislating with respect to aliens—has not provided effective leadership in dealing with this problem.[n1] It therefore is certain that illegal aliens will continue to enter the United States and, as the record makes clear, an unknown percentage of them will remain here. I agree with the Court that their children should not be left on the streets uneducated.

Although the analogy is not perfect, our holding today does find support in decisions of this Court with respect to the status of illegitimates. In Weber v. Aetna Casualty & Surety Co., 406 U.S.), we said: Visiting . . . condemnation on the head of an infant for the misdeeds of the parents is illogical, unjust, and contrary to the basic concept of our system that legal burdens should bear some relationship to individual responsibility or wrongdoing.

Dissenting with most of the court, Justice Warren E. Burger argued that the court's ruling was an overreach, with the justices of the court substituting for the legislature and executive branches.

Supreme Court Justice Brennan's Majority Opinion continued

The failure of enforcement of the immigration laws over more than a decade and the inherent difficulty and expense of sealing our vast borders have combined to create a grave socioeconomic dilemma. It is a dilemma that has not yet even been fully assessed, let alone addressed. However, it is not the function of the Judiciary to provide "effective leadership" simply because the political branches of government fail to do so.

The Court's holding today manifests the justly criticized judicial tendency to attempt speedy and wholesale formulation of "remedies" for the failures—or simply the laggard pace—of the political processes of our system of government. The Court employs, and, in my view, abuses, the Fourteenth Amendment in an effort to become an omnipotent and omniscient problem solver. That the motives for doing so are noble and compassionate does not alter the fact that the Court distorts our constitutional function to make amends for the defaults of others.[238]

The *Plyler v. Doe* case and the Sanctuary Movement of the 1980s are ancestor moments that lead directly to the immigration debate in 2018. Donald Trump's decision to discontinue an amnesty and citizenship program for the undocumented migrants brought to the United States as children sparked hundreds of nationwide protests against Trump's administration and motivated a sanctuary movement more passionate than any since the 1980s. In this new sanctuary movement, whole cities declared themselves "sanctuary cities" that would not participate in federal efforts to locate and deport illegal immigrants.

Trump has been widely critical of the sanctuary city movement and has suggested that the federal government might cut funding to cities providing a harbor for illegal migrants. Some of the Trump administration spokespeople stated in interviews that 80 percent of Americans disapproved of the entire sanctuary city idea, but this figure was taken out of context and referred only to a general question from unregulated Web panel that city police should, in principle, work with immigration authorities. More recent polls, based on more specific questions found the following:

A February 2017 McClatchy-Marist poll first *described* "Sanctuary Cities" to those taking the poll as cities that do not enforce immigration laws and, in some cases, allow immigrants to live there and access services. The poll then asked whether participants believed such cities should exist. In total, 50 percent or respondents said that such cities were needed, whereas 41 percent said there was no reason for Sanctuary Cities to exist. The poll then asked whether the federal government should cut funding to Sanctuary Cities, to which 42 percent supported cutting funding and 53 percent were opposed. Even a Fox News poll in February 2018, which tend to skew towards the conservative viewpoint, found 53 percent opposed taking federal funds from Sanctuary Cities, versus 41 percent in support of such an action.[239]

Throughout most of American history, the majority of Americans have been highly critical of undocumented immigrants and immigration. The recent softening of public opinion concerning Sanctuary Cities may reflect the broad disapproval of the Trump administration overall, with Trump's approval ratings having ranged between 30 and 40 percent during his presidency but might also reflect the broadening consciousness of the American people regarding the many human rights issues that complicate the immigration question.

In the past, conservative presidents and politicians who chose immigration as one of their pet issues, were better able to inspire widespread nativism, but it might be that this is no longer possible. One of the perva-

sive effects of the multiculturalist push of the 1960s–1980s was a broadening of American consciousness regarding a number of issues involving race, culture, and social justice. It is possible that the typical audience for conservative anti-immigration rhetoric has simply dwindled over time. In the future, conservative politicians might, therefore, need to adopt a more Reagan-esque approach, attempting to develop policies that address conservative concerns, while offering compromises to moderates and liberals who now make up a larger share of the American public and will more than likely increase their share in the future.

CONCLUSION

In *Plyler v. Doe*, the Supreme Court ruled that the potential damage done by preventing a child from accessing the educational system posed more of a danger to human rights and welfare than the cost of providing free education to that same child regardless of legal status. Although admitting that undocumented migrant children were in the country illegally, the court chose to view child welfare as the more important concern. The issue of whether undocumented migrants should ever have a right to access services funded by public taxation has remained contentious since the case and is an underlying issue in the modern immigration debate. Public opinion polls from the era did not directly record public reaction to the *Plyler v. Doe* case, but historians researching the period have found a deeply conflicted public, critical of illegal migration on one hand but increasingly concerned about the civil rights and welfare implications of the nation's immigration policies on the other.

DISCUSSION QUESTIONS

■ Were those who participated in the Sanctuary Movement of the 1980s justified in breaking the law? Why or why not?

■ Was the Supreme Court's ruling in *Plyler v. Doe* justified or not? Explain.

■ Should the United States have accepted the Central American refugees from civil wars in El Salvador, Guatemala, and Nicaragua? Why or why not?

■ Do you agree or disagree with government policies regarding the Cold War-era civil wars in Central America? Did the threat of communist takeovers in those countries necessitate U.S. military involvement?

Works Used

Garcia, Maria Cristina. *Seeking Refuge: Central American Migration to Mexico, the United States, and Canada*. U of California P, 2006.

Guthman, Edwin. "Underground Railroad, 1980's Style." *New York Times*. New York Times, Co. 25 Sept. 1988.

Gzesh, Susan. "Central Americans and Asylum Policy in the Reagan Era." *MPI*. Migration Policy Institute. 1 Apr. 2006.

Labrador, Rocio Cara, and Danielle Renwick. "Central America's Violent Northern Triangle." *CFR*. Council on Foreign Relations. 18 Jan. 2018.

Olivas, Michael A. "The Story of *Plyler v. Doe*." *UH*. University of Houston Law Center. 2004.

"Plyler v. Doe." *Cornell Law School*. LII. Supreme Court. 2017.

"Plyler v. Doe." *US Courts*. Administrative Office of the US Courts. 2017.

"Refugee Act of 1980." *National Archives Foundation*. National Archives Foundation. 2018.

Romero, Anthony D. "School Is For Everyone: Celebrating *Plyler v. Doe*." *ACLU*. American Civil Liberties Union. 11 July 2012.

Ye Hee Lee, Michelle. "Do 80 percent of Americans oppose sanctuary cities?" *The Washington Post*. Washington Post, Co. 28 Mar. 2017.

Introduction

This chapter looks at immigration policies in the 1990s, during which time concern about unauthorized immigration peaked among the public, though immigration was not one of the nation's leading concerns. The 1990s saw two major changes regarding immigrant preference in the United States, reflecting economic and political concerns of the era. The first was the H-1B visa program created to provide a relatively rapid path to citizenship or temporary legal status for individuals possessing certain skills seen as valuable in the United States, especially advanced technical and medical skills. The second was the beginning of the now-controversial diversity lottery system that allows a certain number of visas to be used by prospective immigrants from nation's underrepresented in the American population.

The document for this chapter is a 2003 article from *The Guardian*, in which Rob Evans and David Hencke discuss the ideological ban on communist, socialist, and anarchist immigrants that remained in place until the 1990s. The effort to repeal the ideological prohibitions in immigration law was largely symbolic, as amendments to immigration had already largely ended the practice of rejecting immigrants because of political beliefs. However, as discussed in the article, over the years, the ideological ban had been used to prohibit visits to the United States from prominent foreign individuals based on, among other things, perceived connections to perceived dangerous ideologies. The issue of an ideological ban on immigration would again become prominent in the twenty-first century after the 9/11 terrorist attacks inspired a movement to ban the immigration of Muslims.

Topics covered in this chapter include:
- Ideological immigration restrictions
- Skill-based preference in immigration
- High-skilled labor
- Diversity Visa program
- The Bill Clinton Administration
- Cold War

This Chapter Discusses the Following Source Document:
Evans, Rob, and David Hencke. "US felt ban on Graham Greene 'tarnished its image.'" *The Guardian*. Guardian News and Media. 21 Sept. 2003.

The End of the Cold War
Immigration Law and Diversity

There were two major pieces of immigration legislation during the 1990s, one in 1990 and the next in 1996. Both were heavily based on conservative lobbying, but also embracing some degree of liberalization, such as with the 1990 long-overdue abandonment of prohibitions against communist immigration. Concern about immigration remained high throughout the decade with most Americans wanting to reduce the number of immigrants coming into the nation, and this was, in part, the result of a conservative campaign that used illegal Mexican migrants to account for economic woes more realistically the result of the failure of the government to assist the working class in adjusting to broader economic patterns. In all, immigration law in the 1990s was influenced heavily by the end of the Cold War and a renewed focus on domestic, rather than international, threats.

A Peak in Anti-Immigration Attitudes

The 1960s was a time of liberalization in all sectors of American society and saw the lowest levels of resistance to immigration ever recorded in the United States. In part, this was the result of a long-term immigration reduction strategy based on national quotas and designed, ultimately, to preserve the nation's racial/ethnic proportions. This policy officially ended in 1965, resulting in major changes in immigration patterns. Whereas immigration from Europe decreased, or remained steady, the relaxation of national limits led to increasing immigration from Africa, Mexico, Central America, South America, and Asia. This led to a push back against immigration, with more Americans believing that immigration levels needed to be reduced through the 1970s and 1980s, and peaking in the 1990s, which saw the highest level of resistance to immigration recorded during the twentieth century. This peak was the result of many converging factors, including broad resistance to non-white immigration and a long-term campaign by conservatives linking illegal immigration to loosely-connected job losses in the working class.

In 1965 the CBS/*New York Times* poll found that roughly 33 percent of Americans wanted immigration rates to be reduced. This was while federal legislation ended the national quota system that had kept immigration rates low for more than 40 years. In 1965, the largest share of those polled (39 percent), believed that immigration rates should be kept at their current levels. The liberalization of immigration and the end of national quotas, although creating a more egalitarian system, did not match with the desires of most Americans. By 1977, after more than a decade of increasing immigration rates, the percentage who believed immigration rates should be reduced had increased to 42 percent and, by 1986, that percentage had increased to 49 percent.

This led into the 1990s, when immigration tension reached an all time high. In June 1993 and July 1995, the CBS/*New York Times* poll found that 65 percent of Americans wanted immigration reduced. It was, therefore, in the mid-1990s that the full pushback against the liberalization of immigration and subsequent diversification of the United States reached its peak. By 1999, only 44 percent said they wanted to reduce immigration, which then dropped to 38 percent in 2000. Even immediately after the September 11, 2001 terrorist attacks, anti-immigration sentiment never returned to mid-1990s levels. In October 2001 there was an understandable surge in those who wanted immigration reduced to 58 percent, but the percentage fell quickly and never returned to 1995 levels.[240]

The anti-immigration surge reached such elevated levels in 1990 was, in part, because the 1990s saw a low level of international tensions; and so, Americans were focused on domestic concerns, including immigration and the job market. Though the 9/11 terrorist attacks did result in a short-term surge of isolationism, this was not a lasting trend. In the 2000s, as the United States engaged in national building efforts in the Middle East,

the share of Americans who wanted immigration levels increased rose markedly, though this was still firmly a minority view.

High Tech Migrants

One of the major changes in immigration that occurred in the 1990s was the creation of the H-1B visa system that allowed American companies to recruit skilled overseas workers. H-1B visas were meant to attract immigrants who had advanced training in STEM (science, technology, engineering, mathematics) fields, and this fueled the rapid growth of the U.S. tech and biotechnology industries. Hospitals, research organizations, and engineering companies used the program readily, casting a wider eye towards overseas candidates when trying to keep up with the massive tech boom sweeping through the American economy.

The H-1B visa program was, to the American economy of the 1990s and 2000s, what the Bracero Program was to the economy of the 1940s and 1950s. Like the Bracero Program, which was initiated to fill gaps in the manual labor and agriculture industries, the H-1B visa program was essentially a temporary worker program for STEM fields. The H-1B program was not controversial when it was created, but, over time, critics alleged

that companies were misusing the program to exploit skilled immigrants in much the same way that the Bracero Program exploited Mexican laborers. A 2015 report from the Economic

High-tech immigrant worker, iStock

Policy Institute (EPI) indicated, for instance, that H-1B employees in the tech industry earned between $60,000–$70,000 for jobs that typically paid more than $90,000 to American workers. This exploitation of foreign workers also encouraged outsourcing for high-skilled labor, sometimes to the detriment of native-born students in STEM fields.[241]

Though proponents of the system argued that there was still a shortage of STEM workers in the American workforce, some analysts believe the need for foreign workers has been exaggerated by companies looking to increase their profits by decreasing labor costs. For instance, Rutgers University analyst Hal Salzman found in one study that only 50 percent of U.S. STEM graduates obtain a job in their field, which is partially the result of relatively stagnant wages. Salzman argues that, if there really was a pressing need for IT skills, wages in the field should increase to reflect this. However, a more comprehensive review of the problem by Yi Xue and Richard Larson of MIT found that both assertions were true. In some STEM fields, there was a measurable shortage of qualified American candidates, thus justifying the need for H-1B applicants; but in other STEM fields, there were more American candidates than the job market could support.[242] In 2016, a review of the tech market in *The Economist* found evidence of a significant shortage in STEM-qualified candidates for a number of important fields, and reviewed labor experts who suggested that, by 2020, there might be as many as 1 million unfilled STEM jobs in the United States.[243]

The Diversity Program

Another major change to America's immigration system that occurred in the 1990s was the adoption of the Diversity Immigrant Visa program, also called the "DV," "Diversity Visa Lottery," or "Green Card Lottery." This system established a program in which, each year, the Department of State was able to make up to 50,000 visas available to individuals from countries underrepresented in the United States. The Diversity Lottery section

of the 1990 immigration act was one of the bill's most progressive provisions and was initially proposed by New York Democrat Chuck Schumer, but the history of the bill reveals a more complex political situation.

Dzhokhar Tsarnaev in 2013 on a Federal courthouse security camera, is a Kyrgystani-American terrorist convicted of planting bombs at the 2015 Boston Marathon, via Wikimedia Commons

The 1964 Immigration Reform act abolished the 1920–1965 immigration quota system that essentially allowed nearly unlimited immigration from western and northern Europe. Immigrants from this part of the world have always been a favorite for Americans, many of whom see their own lineages traced back to the first generations of immigrants from Britain, France, Germany, Ireland, Italy, and Scandinavia. The end of national quotas resulted in widespread concern about the numbers of immigrants coming into the country; and so, in 1976, the government placed a 20,000 per year total on visas for every country, regardless of population size. From 1976 on, therefore, immigration from every country was on an equal plane, with preference for immigrants in the United States tilted towards family unification and skill-based merit. Thus, immigrants with immediate family willing to sponsor their immigration were more likely to be accepted, as were those whose education or job training made them eligible for certain categories of jobs.

A downturn in the Irish economy in the 1970s led to a surge in Irish immigrants wanting to come to the United States. However, few had immediate family to sponsor them, nor the skills and education needed to qualify for skill-based visas. The result was that thousands of Irish immigrants came to the United States on tourist visas and overstayed, becoming illegal migrants. Italian immigrants faced a similar problem, with a larger number seeking entrance every year; many were sponsored by immediate family, but unable to come because of the 20,000-per-year limit. Had this problem involved Ethiopian, Tanzanian, or Paraguayan immigrants, it is unlikely that Congress would have done anything to address the situation at all, but, because there is a large, influential Irish-American and Italian-American population in the United States, the situation for Irish and Italian immigrants motivated action in the legislature. A group of Irish-American legislators, including Brian Donnelley, Edward Kennedy, and Thomas "Tip" O'Neal thus helped create a system to award 10,000 special "diversity" visas to "adversely affected countries," which became part of the Immigration Reform and Control Act of 1986. The word diversity was used to sell the bill to those who felt immigration should help to make the nation more multicultural and thus increased Irish and Italian immigration in the 1980s.[244]

The diversity lottery (with a new limit of 50,000 visas) was made permanent in the 1990 Immigration Act. By the mid-1990s, Irish and Italian immigrants were no longer using the program, which was largely the result of the formation of the European Union, which made it far easier and more lucrative for EU country citizens to migrate within the union rather than coping with the laborious process of immigrating to the United States. As a result, Diversity Visas were available for a diverse array of immigrants from Africa, Asia, and the Middle East. There have been some efforts to remove the DV program from the immigration system, including by one of the bill's original sponsor's, Chuck Schumer. In 2013, while Congress was debating an immigration reform bill that ultimately failed when the Republican-led legislature refused to work with President Obama, Schumer supported removing the Diversity Lottery program. However, as the reform bill failed, the DV system remained in place.

In 2017, an Uzbek immigrant admitted through the diversity program drove a vehicle onto a bike and jogging path in New York City, killing 8 and injuring 11, almost all of whom were foreign tourists visiting the city. The assailant, Sayfullo Saipov, was a Muslim who had been living in the United States since 2010, when he received a visa through the program. According to friends and co-workers, Saipov was not a particularly religious man when he arrived, but, for reasons that remain unclear, about a year before his attack he began showing an interest in radical politics, withdrawing from friends and family, and spending much of his time isolated and alone.[245]

President Trump used the opportunity to blame Democratic politician Chuck Schumer, one of his strongest opponents in the Democratic congressional minority, and thus to gain political leverage. He did this by claiming that the diversity lottery Schumer had sponsored in 1990 was the cause of the problem and was letting terrorists into the country.

First, Trump tweeted:

> *"The terrorist came into our country through what is called the 'Diversity Visa Lottery Program,' a Chuck Schumer beauty. I want merit based."*[246]

In further tweets and interviews, Trump claimed that his administration was working to end "Democrat Lottery Systems" that he characterized as dangerous and claimed was only based on a desire to be "politically correct." This echoes Trump's mythopoetic narrative of himself as a person who doesn't let political correctness get in the way of what's best for the American people. Trump's portrayal of himself as an "outsider" willing to make "tough choices," was the marketing strategy of his campaign, though his policy proposals have demonstrated that, far from being a radical, Trump's policies on immigration and many other issues are reiterations of traditionalist conservatism as old as the nation itself.

Immediately after Trump began using the New York attack to gain political leverage, reporters, politicians, immigration experts, and citizens pointed out the fundamental flaws in Trump's statements.

1. The diversity program in the 1990s was a bi-partisan effort.
2. Chuck Schumer favored ending the program in 2013 for different reasons in a bill rejected by the Republican-led legislature.
3. Saipov was not an Islamic radical at the time he was admitted and was subjected to the same examinations and questions as any other immigrant, including persons admitted on "merit-based" programs.
4. Police found that Saipov had become radicalized *after* living in the United States for six years, before which time he displayed (to friends and co-workers) seemingly no interest in radical Islamic philosophy.
5. Whereas the diversity lottery did allow Saipov into the country, in 1997 another person admitted through a diversity program, an Egyptian Muslim named Abdel Rahman Mosabbah reported evidence of terrorist activity to police that resulted in the prevention of a New York City subway bombing that might otherwise have killed hundreds.[247]

President Trump's handling of the 2017 vehicle attack is a perfect illustration of how politicians sometimes use tragedy or crisis to benefit themselves. With his tweets, Trump is able to make it appear that he is concerned about the issue, but, without risking his political capital by actually dealing with the issue. By galvanizing supporters against his enemies in Congress with the allegation that Democratic politicians favor "political correctness" over preventing terrorism, Trump distracts, rather than addresses, the actual issues raised by Saipov's attack. Namely, how should the United States combat *internal* radicalization, which has affected both native-born and foreign-born residents and citizens of the United States? Furthermore, what, if anything, can be done to prevent the growth of religious radicalism and conservative fundamentalism around the world, and can this be done without engendering further racial and religious prejudice against Muslims who are not radical and do not support the violence committed by a radicalized minority?

Political Protectionism

The Cold War craze of the 1940–1980s had many effects, but one of the most lingering was the American fear of communism and communist subversion. With the fall of the Berlin Wall in 1989, the Cold War symbolically ended, though the real impetus for the ideological struggle had long since disappeared. With the end of the Cold War, Congress was faced with numerous unnecessary laws that reflected the simplistic ideological goals of the nation's conservative lobby at the beginning of the Cold War, one of which was the long-time prohibition on the immigration of individuals holding undesirable political or philosophical beliefs.

The McCarran-Walter Act of 1952 was controversial at the time and passed only by overriding a veto by President Harry Truman. The McCarran-Walter bill was an isolationist, nativist, and racially prejudicial law that used the threat of the Communism to maintain the nation's national quotas that had been created to ensure that white western Europeans remained the largest ethnic group in the United States. The conservatives of the era promoted McCarran-Walter as a way to prevent subversion, though this was largely a fabrication.

Through the 1960s to 1980s, the McCarran-Walter bill's prohibition on communist or socialist immigration seemed increasingly ridiculous, but the real problem was in how the law had been enforced. Over the years, the prohibition on communism was used to deny access to a host of internationally-famous figures, including British author Graham Greene, who was turned away in 1956 when trying to visit New York while one of his plays was being performed in the city. He was rejected for having been a member of the Communist Party of England in his youth. Others included famed naturalist Farley Mowat, on the basis that he promoted subversive views. In 1954, the law was used to exclude Canadian Pierre Elliott Trudeau because Trudeau had attended an economic conference in

Moscow in 1952. Trudeau went on to become Prime Minister of Canada from 1968 to 1984.

Sponsoring the repeal of the 1952 ideological provision, Senator Daniel Patrick Moynihan of New York famously said.

> _____ **"For a generation and more these miserable provisions made the United States present itself to other nations as a nation of fearful, muddled, intimidated citizens. We are not that; we are not that, and now at least our statutes accord with the facts."**[248]

Speaking to the *Washington Post* about his effort to repeal the provision, Moynihan said,

> _____ **"I don't think we have appreciated the hurt this legislation has done to the United States over the years. It presents us as a fearful and subliterate and oppressive society."**

The repeal of the ideological exclusion provision from the original McCarran-Walter Act was largely symbolic, as a 1977 measure by Senator George McGovern of South Dakota already prevented immigration from turning an individual away unless it could be shown that the person posed a threat to national security. The process of turning away communists was thus already largely over by the time Moynihan's repeal became law in 1990.

Newspapers covering the repeal of the McCarran-Walter ideological exclusion often mentioned the high-profile exclusion of British author Graham Greene, but an article published in 2003 in *The Guardian* provides interesting historic detail to Greene's exclusion and the paranoia that characterized the Cold War panic in the United States:

US FELT BAN ON GRAHAM GREENE 'TARNISHED ITS IMAGE'

by Rob Evans and David Hencke
The Guardian, September 21, 2003
Source Document

US officials admitted that the entry ban on Graham Greene because of his sometime Communist party membership tarnished the country's image, newly released documents show.

They conceded that he had been a member of the British Communist party for only four weeks when a 19-year-old student, "as a joke." They admitted his writing clearly showed that he was anti-communist, according to the documents obtained by *The Guardian* under the US Freedom of Information Act.

Greene, a fierce critic of US foreign policy for decades, appeared to enjoy ridiculing Washington for denying him a visa "because the Americans have me down as a Commie." The ban on communists arose from the anti-Soviet paranoia of the Cold War. Applicants for visas had to answer the question: "Are you or have you ever been a member of the Communist party"?

The ban was criticised for excluding other literary figures: Gabriel Garcia Marquez, Dario Fo, Pablo Neruda and Carlos Fuentes were all reported to have been kept out.

FBI files show that in 1952 Greene was classified as "inadmissible to US because of membership in the Communist party of England," placed under guard and put on a plane out of America. His telegrams were opened and read by the government.

Greene told officials that he was going to write a book about the experience and that "he would make a lot of publicity over his being detained." In December 1956 Greene wanted to stay in New York for six months because one of his plays was being performed.

In a memo a senior immigration official noted that the state department believed that while an Oxford student Greene had joined the Communist party in 1923 for a joke.

"Membership continued for a period of approximately four weeks, during which time he contributed two shillings to the Communist party of Great Britain."

The state department recommended a waiver "based on the applicant's prominence," adding: "He is internationally known as a writer and

US Felt Ban on Graham Greene 'Tarnished Its Image'
continued

from the philosophies expressed in his writings it is evident that he is anti-communist."

"The department of state is of the opinion that to refuse a visa to this applicant would result in widespread publicity adverse to the interest of the United States."

The immigration department files show that after this visit Greene was allowed into the US on several occasions, as "there was no evidence that he has violated the terms of his prior admissions."

In 1961, for instance, when he wanted to spend three weeks discussing the Broadway production of his play The Complaisant Lover, the immigration department wrote : "[His] affiliation with the Communist party terminated almost 40 years ago and the purpose of his trip may benefit American theatre interests."

Nevertheless Greene never hid his criticism of America in his writings, particularly America's involvement in Latin America. He set many of his books in the area, including *Our Man in Havana*, *The Power and the Glory*, and the *Honorary Consul* and often met government leaders hostile to American interests including Fidel Castro and Daniel Ortega, who headed the Sandinista government in Nicaragua during the 1980s.

It was revealed last year that the FBI kept close tabs on the novelist, at times opening his mail and recording his conversations. As late as 1984 American diplomats in London cabled Washington, saying: "Unsurprisingly, Greene's views on the United States government policies and actions are not flattering."

Under McCarran-Walter, the government was free to exclude people based on a wide-variety of beliefs and affiliations. The provision thus appealed to those fearful of communism, but allowed for the exclusion of many other classes of individuals. There were, in fact, 33 classes of persons excluded in the law, including anarchists, communists, communist sympathizers, people who wrote about communism, polygamists, and, notably, homosexuals. In 1952, Senator Pat McCarran apparently believed that these individuals were a serious danger and claimed, "…

criminals, Communists, and subversives of all descriptions are even now gaining admission into this country like water through a sieve."[249]

However, although the 1990 repeal got a lot of coverage in the press and the proponents described the historic measure with ideological rhetoric, critics immediately noted that the law still gave wide discretion for ideological exclusion under new provisions added to prevent the immigration of terrorists. For instance, the law still allowed immigration officials to ask whether a person was or had ever been a member of the Communist Party and barred representatives and officials of the Palestinian Liberation Organization (PLO), enshrining United States pro-Jewish and anti-Palestinian bias into law for the first time. In addition, the 1990 law had a new "foreign policy" provision that allowed authorities to reject individuals whose admission might cause "potentially serious adverse foreign policy consequences." Critics argued that the law thus might have been used to justify the exclusion of Salvadoran and Guatemalan refugees who tried to come to the United States in the 1980s but were denied because the U.S. government was supporting the same governments that had been persecuting and murdering those refugees.[250]

The provisions on terrorists and terrorism folded into the Immigration Act of 1990 connect directly with post-9/11 immigration policy, demonstrating that the United States never has had any era in which there wasn't at least one broad ideological threat that the government sought to highlight as the foreign danger du jour. For many, the terrorist fears of the 1990s were borne out by the terrorist attacks of 2001, justifying the fear that legislators were responding to even in 1990. Indeed, some analysts saw the wind changing even then. In an article entitled, *The Muslims Are Coming! The Muslims Are Coming!,* published in a 1990 issue of the conservative magazine *National Review*, right-wing columnist Daniel Pipes said:

_____ *"Fears of a Muslim influx have more substance than the worry about jihad. West European societies*

> *are unprepared for the massive immigration of brown-skinned peoples cooking strange foods and not exactly maintaining Germanic standards of hygiene. Muslim immigrants bring with them chauvinism that augurs badly for their integration into the mainstream."*[251]

Pipes and those who think in similar ways no doubt feel that history, from 1990 to 2018, gave credence to the issues they raised a decade or more before. Pipes has been called "Islamophobic" by critics and, in fact, expresses thinking that could demonstrably be called prejudicial, but his assessment that the integration of Islamic immigrants into the United States would be fraught with difficulties is, to many, an accurate assessment.

When faced with the integration of a very different culture, there are always those who call for prohibition, expulsion, or resistance. This is the same attitude that gave rise to the nativist movement to keep America white against an influx of Chinese immigrants in the 1880s. For individuals of both cultures preparing to integrate with one another, there is a perceived danger that the process will threaten one's familiar cultural identity or that the qualities of the "other" are too strange to be embraced into one's own culture. As Pipes notes, some aspects of a culture *cannot* be integrated into another culture. Thus, individuals from cultures where women are subjugated and without rights cannot be allowed to practice those aspects of their culture in the United States, lest the United States abandon its commitment to equal rights between genders, however poorly that has been realized thus far. It is important to note that immigration, for all the dangers and tensions it may create, is also one avenue to erase and ease cultural tensions, giving individuals from different cultures experience with one another to replace the assumptions and biases that otherwise pervade.

CONCLUSION

The diversity visa became controversial in 2017 when an individual admitted through the program committed a mass vehicular attack in New York City. This led to calls for merit-based, rather than diversity-based, immigration during the 2018 immigration reform debate. Overall, none of the various provisions adopted to reform the immigration system in the 1990s were particularly controversial. The leading issue in the immigration debate of that era was illegal migration, but there were no effective measures proposed or adopted to address it and, in general, the public was far more concerned about other national issues. In 1995, for instance, about 49 percent of Americans listed restoring the ban on gays serving in the military as the most visible political issue of the year. In 1997, top issues included combating China's global economic growth, dismantling the nuclear arsenal of Russia, and Arab-Israeli Peace. There was, however, a small group of far-right conservatives in the 1990s who listed unauthorized migration as a primary concern, a group that would come to prominence after the contentious 2000 election of George W. Bush gave the conservative movement another opportunity to address immigration policy.

DISCUSSION QUESTIONS

- Should the United States continue to recruit immigrants with certain kinds of skills through the H-1B or a similar program? Why or why not?
- Is promoting diversity a legitimate reason to allow immigrants into the United States? Why or why not?
- How does the U.S. immigration policy portray the country to other nations? Explain.
- Should the United States base immigration preference on skills or family unification? Explain your position.

Works Used

Alvarez, Priscilla. "The Diversity Visa Program Was Created to Help Irish Immigrants." *The Atlantic*. Atlantic Monthly Group. 1 Nov. 2017.

"A blueprint for getting more women into information technology." *The Economist*. Economist Newspaper, Inc. 12 Dec. 2016.

Cole, David. "Mccarran-Walter Act Reborn?" *Washington Post*. Washington Post, Co. 18 Nov. 1990.

Dickey, Christopher. "The Diversity Visa Winner Who Saved New York From a Terror Attack." *Daily Beast*. The Daily Beast LLC. 2 Nov. 2017.

Evans, Rob, and David Hencke. "US felt ban on Graham Greene 'tarnished its image.'" *The Guardian*. Guardian News and Media. 21 Sept. 2003.

Hira, Ron. "New Data Show How Firms Like Infosys and Tata Abuse the H-1B Program." *EPI*. Economic Policy Institute. Working Economics Blog. 19 Feb. 2015.

Holmes, Steven A. "Legislation Eases Limits on Aliens." *New York Times*. New York Times, Co. 2 Feb. 1990.

"Immigration." *Gallup*. Gallup News. 2017.

Kilgannon, Corey, and Joseph Goldstein. "Sayfullo Saipov, the Suspect in the New York Terror Attack, and His Past." *New York Times*. New York Times, Co. 31 Oct. 2017.

Kirby, Jen. "Trump blasts 'Diversity Visa Lottery Program,' after NYC terror attack." *VOX*. Vox Media. 1 Nov. 2017.

Pipes, Daniel. "The Muslims are Coming! The Muslims are Coming!" *National Review*. 19 Nov. 1990.

Tichenor, Daniel J. *Dividing Lines: The Politics of Immigration Control in America*. Princeton, NJ: Princeton UP, 2002.

Torres, Nicole. "The H-1B Visa Debate, Explained." *HBR*. Harvard Business Review. 4 May 2017.

Introduction

Emerging from eight years of moderate progressive leadership under the popular Clinton administration, a contentious 2000 election resulted in electing George W. Bush as president. Bush did not win the popular vote and entered the presidency without a popular mandate and with some level of resistance from the nation's progressives and liberals. This chapter explores the George W. Bush administration's immigration policies before and after the terrorist attacks of 9/11 and examines how the ensuing "War on Terror" and focus on national security affected attitudes about immigration. Like the immigration policies developed under President Reagan, prior to the 9/11 attacks, the Bush administration was pursuing a moderate reform policy that included a focus on border control, a temporary worker program, and a path to citizenship for at least some of the then 11 million undocumented migrants living in the nation.

The document for this chapter is a speech given by President George W. Bush in 2004, when he was still promoting the idea of a temporary worker program not unlike the Bracero Program of the 1950s. Bush commanded significant support from conservative Latinos during his first presidential campaign, in part because he supported policies outside the increasingly punitive approach favored by the far right. Ultimately, Bush's immigration proposal and the possibility of a bilateral agreement failed to gain sufficient support from the far right, and as this group was gaining power in the Republican party, diplomatic solutions were abandoned in favor of a focus on border security.

Topics covered in this chapter include:
- Border control
- 9/11 terrorist attacks

- George W. Bush Administration
- Unauthorized migration
- Temporary worker programs
- Latino conservatism

The second Twin Tower collapses after the terrorist attack on September 11, 2001, by Robert Miller, National Institute of Standards & Technology, via Wikimedia Commons

This Chapter Discusses the Following Source Document:
Bush, George W. "President Bush Proposes New Temporary Worker Program." *Georgewbush-white house*. The White House. Jan. 7, 2004.

Terrorism Gets in the Way
Immigration and the Latino Conservative Movement

On September 11, 2001, nineteen militants hijacked four U.S. commercial airplanes, which they used to attack buildings and landmarks symbolic of American culture and government. A total of 2997 people were killed, including firefighters, port authority officers, and police attempting to rescue victims of the initial attacks. Among the most famous and impactful tragedies in the history of the United States, the 9/11 terrorist attacks, as they came to be called, left an enduring mark on every part of U.S. culture, to such an extent that, in their wake, people regularly spoke of pre- and post-9/11 America itself.

The 9/11 attacks also fundamentally changed American policies regarding immigration and foreign relations. This led to an immigration system based more on national security and less on human rights and welfare. However, these changes came during a time when immigration was becoming less of a priority for the American people, who were increasingly concerned about income inequality and the overall state of the working and middle class. In the immediate aftermath of the attacks, immigration and terrorism were briefly top issues, though the economy again dominated public opinion soon after.

The Immigration Reform That Never Was

The type of immigration policy developed within each presidential regime depends, in part, on how the sitting president views immigrants. When Ronald Reagan was in office, Reagan's familiarity with legal and illegal immigration, as a resident and governor of California, led to policies that tried to address the concerns of anti-immigration advocates, although recognizing that the situation is complex and not simply a matter of law enforcement, but also of human rights and welfare. George W. Bush, having been governor of Texas, also had a nuanced view of immigrants and immigration. Unlike many conservatives more detached from the realities of immigration, Bush knew that most of the Mexican migrants coming to the United States were not bad people, but simply people in need whose work clearly benefitted American business as much as it had the migrants who legally and illegally entered the nation. Prior to 9/11, therefore, Bush's strategy, as he touted in his 1999 campaign, was to work closely with then Mexican President Vincente Fox to create what Bush called a "special relationship" with Mexico, comparing it to the relationship between the United States and Britain.[252]

In February of 2001, Bush met with Fox at Fox's ranch in Monterrey, Mexico. In joint press releases, both men highlighted their shared commitment to combating the drug trade, illegal border crossing, environmental degradation, immigration, and the shared interest in the Mexican oil industry. From the beginning, Bush suggested that part of his immigration reform policy would be to institute a guest worker program, essentially a revival of the Bracero Programs of 1942–1965, and to provide a path to legal permanent residency and eventually citizenship for the estimated 3–5 million Mexicans living and working in the United States. Bush was careful not to use the terms "legalization" or "amnesty" that had become controversial after the conservative backlash against Reagan-era policies, but the essentials of the plan were similar, converting illegal migrants to guest workers, then to permanent residents, and, eventually, to citizens. Bush and Fox then met again on September 4 and 5 of 2001 in a summit in Washington that again resulted in much of the same rhetoric and diplomatic photo opportunities, though they were still some distance from any concrete policy proposals.

It was essentially the very beginning of what looked to be a diplomatic, bilateral phase in the immigration debate; and yet, it never came to be.[253] Just days later, Bush's administration threw aside the "special relationship" strategy in favor of addressing the terrorist threat through an aggressive focus on national security.

When the initial phase of the GOP's efforts to calm Americans down after 9/11 was finished, and Bush was seeking election to a second term, the administration returned to the bilateral immigration program briefly. Further meetings between Bush and Fox were held, as well as policy meetings where experts in the field discussed possible options. In early 2004, Bush again proposed a temporary worker program that would gradually transition many of the nation's undocumented migrants to citizenship, while maintaining the benefits of existing illegal migration to both Latino and U.S. business owners and workers.

In this speech, given by Bush in 2004, the president outlined some of the broad strokes of his guest worker program, positioned by the president within the history of U.S. immigration policy:

PRESIDENT BUSH PROPOSES NEW TEMPORARY WORKER PROGRAM
Remarks by the President on Immigration Policy
January 7, 2004
Source Document

THE PRESIDENT: Thanks for coming, thanks for the warm welcome, thanks for joining me as I make this important announcement—an announcement that I believe will make America a more compassionate and more humane and stronger country.

I appreciate members of my Cabinet who have joined me today, starting with our Secretary of State, Colin Powell. (Applause.) I'm honored that our Attorney General, John Ashcroft, has joined us. (Applause.) Secretary of Commerce, Don Evans. (Applause.) Secretary Tom Ridge, of the Department of Homeland Security. (Applause.) El Embajador of Mexico, Tony Garza. (Applause.) I thank all the other members of my administration who have joined us today.

I appreciate the members of Congress who have taken time to come: Senator Larry Craig, Congressman Chris Cannon, and Congressman Jeff Flake. I'm honored you all have joined us, thank you for coming.

I appreciate the members of citizen groups who have joined us today. Chairman of the Hispanic Alliance

President Bush Proposes New Temporary Worker Program
continued

for Progress, Manny Lujan. Gil Moreno, the President and CEO of the Association for the Advancement of Mexican Americans. Roberto De Posada, the President of the Latino Coalition. And Hector Flores, the President of LULAC.

Thank you all for joining us. (Applause.)

Many of you here today are Americans by choice, and you have followed in the path of millions. And over the generations we have received energetic, ambitious, optimistic people from every part of the world. By tradition and conviction, our country is a welcoming society. America is a stronger and better nation because of the hard work and the faith and entrepreneurial spirit of immigrants.

Every generation of immigrants has reaffirmed the wisdom of remaining open to the talents and dreams of the world. And every generation of immigrants has reaffirmed our ability to assimilate newcomers—which is one of the defining strengths of our country.

During one great period of immigration—between 1891 and 1920—our nation received some 18 million men, women and children from other nations. The hard work of these immigrants helped make our economy the largest in the world. The children of immigrants put on the uniform and helped to liberate the lands of their ancestors. One of the primary reasons America became a great power in the 20th century is because we welcomed the talent and the character and the patriotism of immigrant families.

The contributions of immigrants to America continue. About 14 percent of our nation's civilian workforce is foreign-born. Most begin their working lives in America by taking hard jobs and clocking long hours in important industries. Many immigrants also start businesses, taking the familiar path from hired labor to ownership.

President G.W. Bush and Mexican president Vicente Fox, 2005, by Krisanne Johnson, White House, via Wikimedia Commons

continued

As a Texan, I have known many immigrant families, mainly from Mexico, and I have seen what they add to our country. They bring to America the values of faith in God, love of family, hard work and self reliance—the values that made us a great nation to begin with. We've all seen those values in action, through the service and sacrifice of more than 35,000 foreign-born men and women currently on active duty in the United States military. One of them is Master Gunnery Sergeant Guadalupe Denogean, an immigrant from Mexico who has served in the Marine Corps for 25 years and counting. Last year, I was honored and proud to witness Sergeant Denogean take the oath of citizenship in a hospital where he was recovering from wounds he received in Iraq. I'm honored to be his Commander-in-Chief, I'm proud to call him a fellow American. (Applause.)

As a nation that values immigration, and depends on immigration, we should have immigration laws that work and make us proud. Yet today we do not. Instead, we see many employers turning to the illegal labor market. We see millions of hard-working men and women condemned to fear and insecurity in a massive, undocumented economy. Illegal entry across our borders makes more difficult the urgent task of securing the homeland.

The system is not working. Our nation needs an immigration system that serves the American economy, and reflects the American Dream.

Reform must begin by confronting a basic fact of life and economics: some of the jobs being generated in America's growing economy are jobs American citizens are not filling. Yet these jobs represent a tremendous opportunity for workers from abroad who want to work and fulfill their duties as a husband or a wife, a son or a daughter.

Their search for a better life is one of the most basic desires of human beings. Many undocumented workers have walked mile after mile, through the heat of the day and the cold of the night. Some have risked their lives in dangerous desert border crossings, or entrusted their lives to the brutal rings of heartless human smugglers. Workers who seek only to earn a living end up in the shadows of American life—fearful, often abused and exploited. When they are victimized by crime, they are afraid to call the police, or seek recourse in the legal system. They are cut off from their families far away, fearing if they leave our country to visit relatives back home, they might never be able to return to their jobs.

The situation I described is wrong. It is not the American way. Out of common sense and fairness, our

President Bush Proposes New Temporary Worker Program
continued

laws should allow willing workers to enter our country and fill jobs that Americans have are not filling. (Applause.) We must make our immigration laws more rational, and more humane. And I believe we can do so without jeopardizing the livelihoods of American citizens.

Our reforms should be guided by a few basic principles. First, America must control its borders. Following the attacks of September the 11th, 2001, this duty of the federal government has become even more urgent. And we're fulfilling that duty.

For the first time in our history, we have consolidated all border agencies under one roof to make sure they share information and the work is more effective. We're matching all visa applicants against an expanded screening list to identify terrorists and criminals and immigration violators. This month, we have begun using advanced technology to better record and track aliens who enter our country—and to make sure they leave as scheduled. We have deployed new gamma and x-ray systems to scan cargo and containers and shipments at ports of entry to America. We have significantly expanded the Border Patrol—with more than a thousand new agents on the borders, and 40 percent greater

funding over the last two years. We're working closely with the Canadian and Mexican governments to increase border security. America is acting on a basic belief: our borders should be open to legal travel and honest trade; our borders should be shut and barred tight to criminals, to drug traders, to drug traffickers and to criminals, and to terrorists.

Second, new immigration laws should serve the economic needs of our country. If an American employer is offering a job that American citizens are not willing to take, we ought to welcome into our country a person who will fill that job.

Third, we should not give unfair rewards to illegal immigrants in the citizenship process or disadvantage those who came here lawfully, or hope to do so.

Fourth, new laws should provide incentives for temporary, foreign workers to return permanently to their home countries after their period of work in the United States has expired.

Today, I ask the Congress to join me in passing new immigration laws that reflect these principles, that meet America's economic needs, and live up to our highest ideals. (Applause.)

continued

I propose a new temporary worker program that will match willing foreign workers with willing American employers, when no Americans can be found to fill the jobs. This program will offer legal status, as temporary workers, to the millions of undocumented men and women now employed in the United States, and to those in foreign countries who seek to participate in the program and have been offered employment here. This new system should be clear and efficient, so employers are able to find workers quickly and simply.

All who participate in the temporary worker program must have a job, or, if not living in the United States, a job offer. The legal status granted by this program will last three years and will be renewable—but it will have an end. Participants who do not remain employed, who do not follow the rules of the program, or who break the law will not be eligible for continued participation and will be required to return to their home.

Under my proposal, employers have key responsibilities. Employers who extend job offers must first make every reasonable effort to find an American worker for the job at hand. Our government will develop a quick and simple system for employers to search for American workers. Employers must not hire undocumented aliens or temporary workers whose legal status has expired. They must report to the government the temporary workers they hire, and who leave their employ, so that we can keep track of people in the program, and better enforce immigration laws. There must be strong workplace enforcement with tough penalties for anyone, for any employer violating these laws.

Undocumented workers now here will be required to pay a one-time fee to register for the temporary worker program. Those who seek to join the program from abroad, and have complied with our immigration laws, will not have to pay any fee. All participants will be issued a temporary worker card that will allow them to travel back and forth between their home and the United States without fear of being denied re-entry into our country. (Applause.)

This program expects temporary workers to return permanently to their home countries after their period of work in the United States has expired. And there should be financial incentives for them to do so. I will work with foreign governments on a plan to give temporary workers credit, when they enter their own nation's retirement system, for the time they have worked in America. I also support

President Bush Proposes New Temporary Worker Program
continued

making it easier for temporary workers to contribute a portion of their earnings to tax-preferred savings accounts, money they can collect as they return to their native countries. After all, in many of those countries, a small nest egg is what is necessary to start their own business, or buy some land for their family.

Some temporary workers will make the decision to pursue American citizenship. Those who make this choice will be allowed to apply in the normal way. They will not be given unfair advantage over people who have followed legal procedures from the start. I oppose amnesty, placing undocumented workers on the automatic path to citizenship. Granting amnesty encourages the violation of our laws, and perpetuates illegal immigration. America is a welcoming country, but citizenship must not be the automatic reward for violating the laws of America. (Applause.)

The citizenship line, however, is too long, and our current limits on legal immigration are too low. My administration will work with the Congress to increase the annual number of green cards that can lead to citizenship. Those willing to take the difficult path of citizenship—the path of work, and patience, and assimilation—should be welcome in America, like

generations of immigrants before them. (Applause.)

In the process of immigration reform, we must also set high expectations for what new citizens should know. An understanding of what it means to be an American is not a formality in the naturalization process, it is essential to full participation in our democracy. My administration will examine the standard of knowledge in the current citizenship test. We must ensure that new citizens know not only the facts of our history, but the ideals that have shaped our history. Every citizen of America has an obligation to learn the values that make us one nation: liberty and civic responsibility, equality under God, and tolerance for others.

This new temporary worker program will bring more than economic benefits to America. Our homeland will be more secure when we can better account for those who enter our country, instead of the current situation in which millions of people are unknown, unknown to the law. Law enforcement will face fewer problems with undocumented workers, and will be better able to focus on the true threats to our nation from criminals and terrorists. And when temporary workers can travel legally and freely, there will be more efficient management of our borders and more effective enforcement against

continued

those who pose a danger to our country. (Applause.)

This new system will be more compassionate. Decent, hard-working people will now be protected by labor laws, with the right to change jobs, earn fair wages, and enjoy the same working conditions that the law requires for American workers. Temporary workers will be able to establish their identities by obtaining the legal documents we all take for granted. And they will be able to talk openly to authorities, to report crimes when they are harmed, without the fear of being deported. (Applause.)

The best way, in the long run, to reduce the pressures that create illegal immigration in the first place is to expand economic opportunity among the countries in our neighborhood. In a few days I will go to Mexico for the Special Summit of the Americas, where we will discuss ways to advance free trade, and to fight corruption, and encourage the reforms that lead to prosperity. Real growth and real hope in the nations of our hemisphere will lessen the flow of new immigrants to America when more citizens of other countries are able to achieve their dreams at their own home. (Applause.)

Yet our country has always benefited from the dreams that others have brought here. By working hard for a better life, immigrants contribute to the life of our nation. The temporary worker program I am proposing today represents the best tradition of our society, a society that honors the law, and welcomes the newcomer. This plan will help return order and fairness to our immigration system, and in so doing we will honor our values, by showing our respect for those who work hard and share in the ideals of America.

May God bless you all. (Applause.)[254]

That Bush never returned to the pre-9/11 immigration strategy is also likely a result of the fact that his Reagan-esque proposals in 2001 were met with criticism by powerful factions of the GOP that did not approve of compromise with regard to illegal immigration but saw the issue as a battleground in the fight to secure the racial demographics of America.

The End of Latino Conservatism

Bush was the last Republican president of an older-style of American conservatism and one of the last Republicans who successfully tried to deepen the party's appeal with American minorities. Like Reagan in the 1980s, George W. Bush saw Latinos as the future of American conservatism. This was based on the idea that conservative Latinos, many of whom were traditionalist Catholics, were broadly focused on family values and opposed things like abortion, thus overlapping with GOP priorities. According to Lionel Sosa, who managed Latino outreach for Ronald Reagan in 1980, Reagan famously stated:

_____ *"Latinos are Republican. They just don't know it yet."*
_____

By coupling traditional values with a willingness to forego a punitive approach to Latino migration in favor of a more nuanced embrace of Latinos (legal and illegal) as important players in American culture, Reagan received 32 percent of the Latino vote in 1980, the highest percentage of Latino voters ever commanded by a Republican to that point. George W. Bush, by promising many of the same types of policies, made an even bigger stride, receiving nearly 44 percent of the Latino vote in 2000.[255] Local and legislative politicians had similar results by focusing on the overlaps between Latino and white conservatism and downplaying the punitiveapproach to illegal migration.

The need to curry the Latino vote was also demographically pragmatic, emerging from the recognition that the Hispanic/Latino community was America's fastest growing ethnic and economic group. A *Pew Research* study in 2016 indicated that the Latino population had reached 58 million in 2016 and accounted for half of all population growth since 2000.[256] Bush and other GOP politicians saw this trend coming, as Reagan had in the 1980s, and were eager to secure Latino support to build a stronger GOP. However, in reflection, the effort to curry Latino support was doomed from its inception because the Republican Party was too closely linked to the more extreme xenophobic brand of conservatism embod-

ied by white nationalists and supremacists like the Alt-Right movement of the 2010s that became a key to Donald Trump's presidential victory. Like Trump, conservatives in this vein prefer a far less-intellectually taxing absolutist approach to immigration, seeing border control as a simplistic matter of law enforcement and criminality and viewing the growth of the Latino population as a threat to their vision of American culture. These two sides of the Republican agenda are not compatible and so, as the GOP gravitated further towards white nationalism, Latino support drifted further away.

One of the biggest blows that preceded the end of the Latino GOP movement was Proposition 187, passed in 1994 by governor Pete Wilson of California, which denied illegal aliens the right to access state services. Whereas the bill was typically nativist, seeking to preserve the benefits of state residency for legal residents, and so appealed to the absolutist law-and-order contingent of the GOP base, the nation's largest conservative Latino group, the Republican National Hispanic Assembly (RNHA), opposed the bill. The RHNA, founded by conservative Latino and Hispanic business leaders like Benjamin Fernandez, who became the first Latino to run for president, in 1980, supported some of the same strict enforcement measures favored by GOP politicians, but could not support Proposition 187, knowing full well that such a bill would drive Latino voters away from the Republican party in the state. Conservative Latinos like Fernandez, who was the son of unauthorized migrants, thus found themselves at odds with the party he'd supported through the 1980s and into the 1990s.

Speaking about the Proposition 187 schism between white and Latino conservatives in the 1990s, Northwestern University Professor Geraldo Cadava wrote in a 2016 article for *Medium*,

_____ *"It wasn't always easy for Hispanic conservatives to support the Republican Party.*

> *They recognized the tendencies of nativists to lump them together with undocumented Mexicans as part of a generalized threat to American identity. At a fundraiser for then-Governor Reagan in 1972, prominent Hispanic businessmen 'winced' when a marching band at the event played, 'To the Halls of the Montezumas,' a U.S.-Mexico War era song American troops played as they conquered Mexico City.*"[257]

The Power of the Far Right

It is unclear how successful Bush-era immigration policy might have been if not for the 9/11 terrorist attacks. It is possible that Bush's plans to work closely with Fox and the Mexican government might have been more successful than the mish-mash of policies that were eventually put into place, catering to the long-standing desires of nativists that were peripherally connected, at best, to the desire to prevent terrorism.

The Bush presidency, lasting two terms, pushed the GOP further towards the right as moderate and minority voters gravitated away from the party's increasingly nativist and isolationist bent. In part this was because the anti-immigrant views of the far right were no longer majority American views. Opposition to immigration overall had been declining since the 1990s, when America saw the largest peak of concern about immigration in the modern era. Domestic concerns were at the forefront during the George H.W. Bush and Bill Clinton presidencies; and so, immigration and border protection were more popular, but still not leading issues for most Americans. The influence of the anti-immigration hard-liners on the George W. Bush presidency hurt the GOP because it drove away moderate and minority support.

Analyzing statistics collected by *Pew Research*, a Migration Policy Institute study in 2009 showed, that the percentage of Americans listing

immigration as the most important problem in the United States was only about 1 percent in 2003. The backlash against Bush's proposals for a temporary worker program, which angered nativists and hardliners, resulted in a surge, but only to 3 percent calling immigration the top problem. In 2006, the Bush Administration, now largely controlled by far-right views, supported a border fence proposal against the recommendations of all legitimate experts in the field, but to the adulation of anti-immigrant and anti-Mexican absolutists.However, the goals of this group were not within the current general sway of public opinion and, in fact, the view that immigration was "bad for America," was at an all-time low of 30 percent, whereas there was a surge in the number of Americans, nearly 70 percent, feeling that immigration was good for America.[258]

The Bush administration's need to balance nativists and white nationalists against moderates and the general sway of public opinion was not beneficial to the GOP. Subsequent GOP candidates did poorly against Barack Obama and even the next GOP candidate to win the presidency, Donald Trump, did so only thanks to the electoral college system, losing the popular vote by the biggest margin in history.Unwilling to accept this embarrassing statistic, President-elect Trump publicly alleged illegal immigrants had voted against him in the election in spite of all evidence to the contrary. The surprise GOP victory in the 2016 presidential election heralded a new era of divergence from moderate or minority views within the party and ushered in deepening ties with far-right factions.

CONCLUSION

Immigration reform was not a top priority for most Americans after the 9/11 terrorist attacks. Pew research found that more than 80 percent of Americans between 2001 and 2003 considered terrorism the nation's top concern, followed by the economy, jobs, and improving education. Of all the possible issues presented to the public, border control and illegal immigration did not rank in the top 15–20 issues for most Americans. Researchers focusing specifically on immigration have found that American opinions on the issue were softening. A majority of Americans still felt immigration should be reduced or should stay the same, and a majority still felt unauthorized migration was a problem, but Americans, on average, were becoming more likely to see immigration as a nuanced issue with complex subjects involving national security as well as human rights concerns.

DISCUSSION QUESTIONS

■ Do you approve of a temporary worker program like that proposed by George W. Bush? Why or why not?

■ Is it important for politicians to appeal to supporters across ideological lines? Why or why not?

■ Are politicians who are directly familiar with Mexican-American and undocumented migrant culture better equipped to develop policies regarding immigration? Why or why not?

■ Do the Bush-era immigration proposals presented in this chapter demonstrate broader changes in American attitudes about immigration?

Works Used

Bush, George W. "President Bush Proposes New Temporary Worker Program." *Georgewbush-whitehouse*. The White House. 7 Jan. 2004.

Cadava, Geraldo. "Long before Trump's Mexico wall, Prop. 187 killed Hispanic conservatism." *Timeline*. Medium. 1 July 2016.

Flores, Antonio. "How the U.S. Hispanic population is changing." *Pew Research Center*. Pew Research. 18 Sept. 2017.

Frej, Willa. "How U.S. Immigration Policy Has Changed Since 9/11." *Huff Post*. Huffington Post. 9 Sept. 2016.

Gutiérrez, Ramón. "George W. Bush and Mexican Immigration Policy." Cairn. *Revue Française D'Études Américaines*. Vol. 113, No. 3 (2007), pp. 70–76.

Mehlman, Ken. "Hispanic outreach crucial to GOP." *Politico*. Political Inc. 1 May 2007.

Suro, Roberto. "America's Views of Immigration: The Evidence from Public Opinion Surveys." *Migration Policy Institute*. Transatlantic Council on Migration. May 2009.

Introduction

Whereas the previous chapter looked at how the Bush administration attempted to build moderate support through an immigration policy that addressed the concerns of both the right and left, this chapter looks at how national security concerns after the 9/11 terrorist attacks directly influenced immigration reform. The 9/11 attacks led to several years of intensive governmental reform intended to advance and enhance national security. This included the establishment of new governmental agencies, a massive expansion of the nation's domestic security and intelligence facilities, and a controversial military invasion of Iraq. In terms of immigration, the predominance of national security concerns motivated major changes in this arena as well. First and foremost, immigration enforcement was placed under a new organization, Immigration and Customs Enforcement (ICE), which was part of the newly-created Department of Homeland Security (DHS).

The changes made to immigration policies resulting from the 9/11 period can generally be seen as falling into two broad categories. The first are the policies adopted by the Bush administration that controversially targeted intense scrutiny of Muslims and individuals from Muslim-majority countries. Some of these policies faced legal challenges and were eventually abandoned when the administration was unable to justify targeting Muslims for reasons that were not prejudicial. The second category of immigration policy changes resulting from the 9/11 period became permanent. The document for this chapter is an article by Jake Flanagin in a 2015 issue of *Quartz Magazine* that reflects on how 9/11 permanently changed the nature of America's immigration policies and governmental attitude about immigrants overall.

Topics covered in this chapter include:
- 9/11 terrorist attacks
- National security
- Ideological prohibitions
- George W. Bush Administration
- Anti-Muslim sentiment

This Chapter Discusses the Following Source Document:
Flanagin, Jake. "9/11 Forever Changed the Concept of Immigration in the US." *Quartz*. Atlantic Media. 11 Sept. 2015.

Immigration in the Age of Fear
From ICE to NSEERS to Islamophobia (2001–2008)

The fight to end terrorism became the battle-cry for people with a wide variety of agendas, and thus policies in the Bush-era tended to be broadly national-security minded even when data and experts in various fields argued (frequently) that the policies the Bush administration pursued would not effectively address terrorism. The fact that so much of Bush-era policy failed to gain the support of experts who study the underlying issues, like immigration, national security, terrorism, and foreign policy, damaged the image of the GOP. It was not until the election of Barack Obama, the nation's first African-American president, that the GOP regained momentum by aligning more closely with white nationalists and nativists.

Bush-era immigration policy can be described as having two phases. The first was a set of policies designed to target potential Islamic radicals that involved many aggressive, prejudicial, and highly controversial policies and practices. The second was the development of more long-term policies to capture and deport illegal migrants and to strengthen the nation's border security. The effectiveness of either phase is debatable and difficult to analyze because there are few clear measures that separate post-9/11 policies and systems from pre-9/11 policies and systems, in terms of prevention. Overall, the effort to reduce radical violence in the world or in the United States was unsuccessful as terrorism, both from Islamic radicals and from domestic radical groups, increased markedly since the beginning of the "War on Terror."

Consolidation of Immigration and National Security

One of the key federal responses to the 9/11 terrorist attacks was the creation of a cabinet-level domestic security organization, the Department of Homeland Security (DHS) in 2003. In terms of immigration, the 9/11 attacks gave justification for a wide-reaching consolidation of immigration powers by the federal government, one part of which involved combining the U.S. Customs Service, the Immigration and Naturalization Service, the Federal Protective Service, and the Federal Air Marshals Service into a single investigative bureau called Immigration and Customs Enforcement (ICE). This was supposed to facilitate information sharing and cooperation between individuals involved in various parts of customs and immigration enforcement and investigation.[259]

At the time the Homeland Security Act became law (2002), it was unclear how the law would affect immigration other than providing immigration authorities with a far catchier acronym. Over subsequent months, a variety of new and often controversial policies were put into place that gradually expanded the role of Homeland Security.

During the first phase of post-9/11 policies, immigration authorities conducted a large number of highly-controversial detentions and interrogations of immigrants and foreign-born residents. More than 8,000 nonimmigrants and several thousand immigrants from Muslim countries were selected for interrogation and possible detention. Under the NSEERS program (National Security Entry-Exit Registration System), adult males from 25 Muslim-majority countries were required to be fingerprinted, photographed, and registered with the FBI. The NSEERS program was used to conduct more than 80,000 interviews and to deport 13,000 individuals from countries with potential links to the Islamic radical group Al-Qaeda. Much of this was done without due process and in secret proceedings and so generated protest from civil libertarians. Details on the people who were deported and targeted were never made available to the public and, therefore, it was difficult to determine whether the aggressive anti-Islamic phase of the Bush-era immigration period was justified. Certainly, much of what was done would not have met judicial or constitutional scrutiny, though the courts, in general, decided that the administration had the au-

thority to conduct these controversial operations because of the national emergency posed by the terrorist threat.

Though concern over Muslim terrorism was high, the broad targeting of Muslims, whether one feels it was necessary, was prejudicial by design. Many of those who supported the administration's most egregiously prejudicial policies were influenced by misinformation and propaganda. There was a movement, immediately after the terror attacks and still ongoing, to promote the idea that terrorism is the result of an ideological war between Islam and "Western" culture.

Prejudicial misinformation is a common tactic used by people who feel that their culture and identity is threatened by alien or foreign influence. During the paranoia of the anti-Communist movement in the 1940s and 1950s, for instance, right-wing pundits often depicted the situation as an ideological struggle, though the contest between China, the Soviet Union, and the United States is more realistically depicted as a contest for global economic and military dominance. In his infamous, propagandistic speech in Wheeling, Virginia, anti-communism pariah Joseph McCarthy described the Cold War as "...a final, all-out battle between communistic atheism and Christianity." Of course, most people in the Soviet Union are Christian, and so...less than reliable information from McCarthy on many different levels.[260]

Fear of an Islamic threat to American society is, in part, the result of the fact that Islam is the world's fastest growing religion, with more Muslims in the world than Christians. Thus, as with all ideological debates, Americans fearing a threat to their cultural identity have reacted with militant attitudes, calls for isolationism, and rhetorical attacks on Islam itself. Desperate to draw others into what they see as a dire ideological war, ideologues and activists exaggerate, propagandize, and misrepresent the state of affairs to draw those vulnerable to manipulation to their cause. For instance, Brigitte Gabriel, founder of the anti-Muslim group ACT! For

America, claimed in 2015 that:

> _____ **"The radicals are estimated to be between 15 to 25 percent, according to all intelligence services around the world. You're looking at 180 million to 300 million people dedicated to the destruction of Western Civilization."**[261]
>
> _____

In 2014, conservative columnist Ben Shapiro claimed in a YouTube video,

> _____ **"We're above 800 million Muslims radicalized, more than half the Muslims on Earth. That's not a minority. That's now a majority."**[262]
>
> _____

Shapiro and Gabriel create their misinformation campaigns by selectively manipulating statistics generated by legitimate intellectuals who study the world's population. Such claims are then popularized by a system of interlinked fake news sites that are operated by white nationalists who view the growth of Islam as a threat to white, Christian dominance of the United States and the world. Legitimate estimates of the number of radical Muslims in the world suggest that the number is closer to 0.01 percent of the total global population. This is nothing even close to the figures quoted by Shapiro and Gabriel, but their goal is not to inform, but rather, to heighten fear and thus build support for their alternate view of America's future.

For Muslim-Americans, Muslim immigrants, and those Muslims then hoping or planning to migrate to the United States for jobs, education, or any other purpose, post-9/11 America was a far less welcoming and far more dangerous place. In 2001, there were 93 reported hate crimes against Muslims in the United States, whereas there were 12 such attacks in 2000. Paranoia and suspicion of Muslim-Americans and, especially, foreign-born persons of Arab descent, never returned to pre-9/11 levels

and, in fact, worsened over time. From 2002 to 2014 there were between 34 and 56 hate crimes directed at Muslims each year.

Republicans in the 2010s have done little to dissuade the support of white nationalists and supremacists, but also frequently claim they have done nothing to actively support these groups and that the party, as a whole, rejects racism. However, the ways in which conservatives attempted to discredit Barack Obama during his presidency are telling. There was an unprecedented effort to question Obama's citizenship and whether he was "really American," as well as an effort to portray him as a secret Muslim involved in a nonwhite, Islamic agenda. These weren't only fringe claims, but were echoed, in fact, by future President Donald Trump, then a reality-television celebrity. Trump thus demonstrated his allegiance to white nationalists and nativists by echoing these same false claims and these same facets of American culture were largely responsible for Trump's presidential victory over a internally-divided progressive majority.

Further evidence that the surge in racism, white nationalism, and nativism were key to Trump's conservative resurgence can be seen in the fact that crimes against Muslims climbed to the highest levels in history during Trump's presidential campaign, as Trump validated and appeared to share the anti-Islamic sentiments of America's white nationalists. Therefore, whereas there were 91 hate-crime attacks against Muslims in 2015, this number increased to 127 in 2016 alone.[263]

Permanent Changes?

Most of the more controversial policies adopted in the immediate wake of the 9/11 attacks were altered or abandoned over the next couple of years. Much of this was due to the concerns from civil libertarians and challenges in the courts. As the Bush administration gave way to the historic Obama administration, it gradually became clear that, even though the initial fear of terrorism had waned considerably, some aspects of the nation's immigration system had perhaps permanently shifted towards national security concerns. In this article from *Quartz* in 2015, journalist Jake Flanagin reflects on the changes wrought in U.S. immigration policy by 9/11 and its aftermath:

9/11 FOREVER CHANGED THE CONCEPT OF IMMIGRATION IN THE US

by Jake Flanagin
Quartz, September 11, 2015

Following the Sept. 11, 2001 terrorist attacks, the United States government implemented a series of policy changes that would forever change the country's immigration landscape. Because all 19 of the men who carried out attacks on the World Trade Center and Pentagon that day were foreign nationals—terrorists, it must be noted, who had all entered the country legally—detecting and preventing the entry of would-be terrorists became the central motivation for post-9/11 immigration policy.

As such, the Immigration and Naturalization Service (INS), which had overseen all immigration and permanent residency attainment from within the US Department of Justice (DOJ) since 1993, was dissolved in 2003. It was replaced by the broader infrastructure of the Department of Homeland Security (DHS), which was signed into existence by president George W. Bush directly following the 9/11 attacks in November of 2001.

Specifically, the functions previously carried out by INS were replaced by three subagencies of DHS:

1. US Customs and Border Protection, which oversees customs and border security, under the auspices of which the US Border Patrol operates.
2. US Citizenship and Immigration Services, which oversees naturalization and the attainment of legal residency.

US Immigration and Customs Enforcement (ICE), which oversees enforcement of immigration laws in the US, as well as immigrant detention and deportations. ICE is also responsible for enforcing the notorious Secure Communities and 287(g) programs.

While intended to increase coordination and efficiency between agencies, the absorption of all immigration policy execution and enforcement within a single body like the DHS is troubling for a number of reasons. Perhaps most

continued

importantly, it fundamentally alters the core American philosophy toward immigration, moving it away from one that is primarily welcoming to one that is largely deflective.

It also renders the average immigrant as guilty until proven innocent in many ways. Take the biometric tracking of foreign nationals on US soil, for example. Carried out through subagencies like the Office of Biometric Identity Management (OBIM)—the most recent iteration of the hugely problematic National Security Entry-Exist Registration System (NSEERS)—biometric tracking required men from 25 predominantly Muslim countries to register their fingerprints and biometric data upon arrival in the US.

There is also the establishment of the Transportation Security Administration (TSA) to contend with. Though probably a necessary addition to the national-security arsenal, it has become a breeding ground for rampant discrimination and racial profiling.

It's not hard to see how this re-situating of immigration policymaking has reflected a cultural shift in broader American society. Since 9/11, the visibility of anti-immigrant sentiments has exploded to the extent that it is now a chief campaign platform for Republican presidential hopefuls. This is a major departure from conservative standard-bearers of pre-9/11 America; president Ronald Reagan was identifiably pro-immigration and pro-amnesty, after all.

Obviously, security agencies and law enforcement need to be kept abreast of the country's in- and outflow of people. And perhaps the zealotry with which agencies like ICE operates (ICE deports more non-criminals than criminals) has helped prevent another domestic act of terror on the scale of 9/11 in the 14 years since. But to keep immigration oversight solely within the confines of a government department specifically engineered to combat terrorism is supreme overkill. And as with most cases of supreme overkill, in the process of rooting out a dangerous minority, it punishes scores of innocent people who could have otherwise had a positive impact on American society. It's also fantastically expensive to deport people who don't need to be deported—people who otherwise pay *into* flailing federal entitlement programs.

Going forward, it would be better to revive the INS in some capacity, perhaps reinstating it under the DOJ (as immigration is, above all else, an issue of *legality*). Or perhaps, given the importance of immigration processing, it should have its own federal executive department. Canada, for instance, has

9/11 Forever Changed the Concept of Immigration in the US
continued

a separate Department of Citizenship and Immigration Canada (CIC), with its own minister in the Canadian cabinet. The Canadian Border Services Agency handles border-crossing from a security standpoint, and effectively pulls personnel from CIC and the Canadian Food Inspection Agency (CFIA), with general border enforcement. The United States could implement a similar body, utilizing the resources of the State Department, DOJ, and DHS to ensure a fair-minded, non-discriminatory, but still security-conscious immigration system.

Maintaining immigration as first and foremost an area of national security both squanders precious resources and dangerously subverts one of this country's foundational messages: "Give me your tired, your poor, your huddled masses yearning to breathe free." Instead, the post 9/11 message has been: "Who are you? What do you want? How did you get here? Yeah, actually, *get out*."[264]

The consolidation of immigration and national security functions described by Flanagin refers to a variety of new systems and regimes designed to help law enforcement agencies to cooperate and share information. Among the host of new measures adopted after 2001 were a series of automated databases for information management, including:

- The Visa Security Program (VSP): a new program for screening visa applications at consular posts around the world, which screens applicants. By 2010, the VSP had screened 950,000 applications and denied visas to at least 1,000.

- The US–VISIT (U.S. Visitor and Immigration Status Indicator Technology) Program: Collects biometric data, fingerprints and photographs on individuals visiting through U.S. land, sea, and airports. Information collected is added to IDENT (Automatic Biometric Identification System), a federal database storing over 108 million fingerprint records.

Vice President Cheney (center) Senator Saxby Chambliss (second from right) and DHS Secretary Michael Chertoff (right) listen to U.S. border agent discuss technology used to train law enforcement personnel, 2005, by David Bohrer, White House, via Wikimedia Commons

- SEVIS (Student Exchange Visitor Information System): Collects biometric data from foreign students that can be checked against criminal and terrorist databases. SEVIS-participating schools notify the federal government when students change class schedules or majors.

In addition, new organizations were created to target illegal immigration. This includes the National Fugitive Operation Program that pursues and deports noncitizens who failed to leave the country after being ordered to leave, and the Secure Communities program that gives deportation agents access to local arrest records to help immigration agents locate and deport immigrants and noncitizens arrested and booked into local jails and holding facilities.

Flanagin is clearly a critic of the overall direction that immigration has taken since 2001, and it can be argued that the general tenor of the immigration system became far less welcoming. However, millions still travel and immigrate to the United States, attending U.S. schools, working in U.S. companies, and, in general, participating in and ultimately adding to American society and culture. The fear of terrorism did not stop immigration, nor did it end positive immigrant outcomes, but it led to a period of fear, suspicion, and anger in which many were hurt and abused.

But it is worth noting that the fear still motivating U.S. immigration policy has retained its potency because, even after 17 years of effort, the United States has not found a legitimate way to combat the rise of radicalism. If anything, violence and terrorism only intensified in the wake of the U.S. War on Terror. From 2008 to 2016, for instance, there were 63 attempted terrorist attacks in the United States committed by Islamic radicals. Thankfully, police, security, and vigilant citizens helped to stop 76 percent of these attacks before they occurred. Though Islamic terrorism gets by far the most media and political attention, it is not America's biggest radical threat in the 2010s. Between 2008 and 2016, there were 115 terrorist attacks in the United States committed by native right-wing radicals, most of whom were white nationalists or white supremacists. Unfortunately, police and citizens were only able to prevent about 35 percent of native right-wing attacks, which is largely because the systems in place to detect and stop radicalism has been designed to target Islamic terrorism specifically. [265]

Whether the United States will develop an effective strategy for combating terrorism remains unclear. Though the United States has become highly skilled in combating individual terrorists and groups, this has not reduced radicalism on the broader sphere. The CIA has used drones to conduct hundreds of strikes against radical leaders, individuals, and bases in a number of nations with active radical groups. There were, for instance, 128 drone strikes in Pakistan in 2010, killing between 700 and 1000 suspected terrorist targets. The United States has, in fact, gotten better at finding and killing terrorists and yet radicalism has not waned, and new groups have emerged to replace those that have been eliminated. Even if all current radicals were killed or imprisoned, it is unlikely that radicalism would disappear, because the underlying motivations remain.

As of 2018, none of the nations currently combating "terror" have developed strategies for eliminating the underlying factors that lead to radicalization; and, in fact, domestic radicalization remains the greatest threat to those living in the United States and other economically-dominant nations.

CONCLUSION

Although Americans in the 1990s were more likely to say that immigrants were a burden to the country, public opinion polls from the 2000s showed that most Americans had begun to view immigrants as a benefit rather than a burden to the country, adding positively to American society. Overall, the economy and national security were the nation's top concerns, and immigration fell into the background throughout the 2000s. This gradual shift in public opinion continued, unabated, despite a passionate campaign from the far right warning that immigration needed to be curtailed to prevent terrorism. This concern, though distinctly a minority issue, became more prominent as the far-right elements of the Republican party gained power in the resistance to the Obama Administration's eight years of moderate progressive policies.

DISCUSSION QUESTIONS

- Were the policies developed by the government that targeted Muslim-Americans and Muslim immigrants prejudicial? Why or why not?
- Has America become a less welcoming country after the 9/11 terrorist attacks? Explain.
- What are some reasons why people might exaggerate claims about the number of terrorists in the world?
- Were the anti-terrorism policies enacted under the Bush administration effective in combating terrorism? Explain.

Works Used

Flanagin, Jake. "9/11 forever changed the concept of immigration in the US." *Quartz*. Quartz Media LLC [US]11 Sept. 2015.

Greenberg, Jon. "Ben Shapiro says a majority of Muslims are radicals." *Politifact*. Punditfact. 5 Nov. 2014.

"Judging the Impact: A Post 9/11 America." *NPR*. National Public Radio. 16 July 2004.

Kishi, Katayoun. "Assaults against Muslims in U.S. surpass 2001 level." *Pew Research*. Pew Research Center. FACTTANK. 15 Nov. 2017.

LaCasse, Alexander. "How many Muslim extremists are there? Just the facts, please." *CSMonitor*. The Christian Science Monitor. 13 Jan. 2015.

McCarthy, Joseph. "'Enemies from Within' Speech Delivered in Wheeling, West Virginia (1950)." *Digital History Project*. University of Houston.

Neiwert, David. "Home Is Where the Hate Is." *The Investigative Fund*. The Nation Institute. 22 June 2017.

Introduction

This chapter looks at one of the many perennial proposals favored by a portion of America's conservative population regarding border control—building a wall or fence along the U.S.–Mexico, or U.S.–Canadian borders. In the 2000s, when George W. Bush made border control a focus of his immigration reform platform, the dominance of the far right in the immigration debate effectively stalled the Bush-era reform efforts except for the border wall proposal. The Bush administration's Secure Fence Act of 2006 funded the construction of fences and walls along high-traffic portions of the U.S.–Mexico border, which were unsuccessful at reducing illegal migration. The policy also met with criticism because it was more expensive and took longer to complete than the Bush administration first claimed.

The source for this chapter is a speech by George W. Bush presenting the Secure Fence Act of 2006. In this speech, Bush continued to campaign in support of a fast-track for the legalization of some unauthorized migrants and for a new temporary worker program, though neither of these programs gained sufficient support among the far right to become law. Donald Trump, noting the failures of the Bush-era border fence, proposed building a larger wall across the entire border during his 2016 campaign. Once he became president, Trump amended this idea, proposing an $18 billion wall covering half the border, which would be constructed over the next decade. The Trump border wall proposal did not gain majority support among the public, with critics citing the cost of the program, the question of potential effectiveness, and concern that construction of the wall poses a serious environmental threat.

Topics covered in this chapter include:
- Racial prejudice
- George W. Bush Administration
- Donald Trump Administration
- Border wall
- Unauthorized migration
- National security

This Chapter Discusses the Following Source Document:
"Fact Sheet: The Secure Fence Act of 2006." *Georgebush-White House*. White House. Oct. 26, 2006.

The Great Wall of America
The Border Wall Debate

If there is one major link between the conservatism expressed by Donald Trump and that embraced by George W. Bush, it is a preference for simple, proximate solutions to America's immigration and national security problems. Faced with the potential threat of Islamic terrorism, the conservatives of the George W. Bush era favored policies that essentially amounted to suspecting all Muslims, and sorting the "good ones" from the "bad ones" later, whereas Trump has called for a prohibition on immigration from predominantly Muslim countries, a different, yet similarly-molded policy. On illegal immigration from Mexico, both conservative movements favored another simplistic solution, building a wall between the two countries. Noting that the Bush-era wall was not successful, Trump-era conservatives have proposed a much bigger wall.

Whether a Trump-style border wall will be successful depends on how one defines success and on how one envisions the goals of the United States regarding immigration and foreign relations. Recent examples of fences used to control immigration indicate that a wall, *only* if coupled with significant continued investment, maintenance, and other measures, can greatly reduce the flow of illegal migration. The question is, whether this is the future that Americans want. Using border walls to enhance security is, in fact, an ancient, venerable tradition, though history shows that such efforts are not likely to be remembered for their success, but rather for the symbolic victory won by those who manage to tear those same walls down.

From Wall to Shining Wall

Conservatives and nativists have been proposing border walls and fences between the United States and Mexico since at least the 1950s, but the idea didn't gain any actual traction until the 1990s. Then, a number of states took the matter on directly, building small sections of fencing blocking off areas frequently used for illegal migration. The first federal effort to solve illegal migration using a wall came with the Bush administration's Secure Fence Act of 2006.

How the Fence Act of 2006 came about is an interesting twist of history in that, prior to 9/11, Bush was in favor of a far different solution to illegal migration that involved creating a legal guest worker program and a bilateral treaty with Mexico. This approach never materialized due to strong conservative opposition within the GOP controlled legislature and because the 9/11 terrorist attacks thrust the United States into a period dominated by fear and national security policy. At the time, some conservatives felt very strongly that the U.S.—Mexican border was a major security concern, in that terrorists might use the border to cross into the United States.

President G.W. Bush signs the Secure Fence Act of 2006, by Kimberlee Hewitt, via Wikimedia Commons

In 2002, veteran political analyst and expert in U.S.—Mexican relations Robert S. Leiken wrote in an op-ed for the Brookings Institution:

> *"...Mexico is now more critical to the United States. If our back door is not to remain open to terrorists, we need Mexico's cooperation. Building the rule of law in Mexico has become a U.S. security concern. And a Mexican immigration accord would be a first step towards closing our back door, but gently."*[266]

Had Bush's early ideas about immigration reform come to fruition, the future that Leiken promoted might have been realized. Such a solution appealed to people like George W. Bush, a former governor who knew how to reach across diplomatic lines, and to Leiken, a man who spent years in Mexico and Central America and was sympathetic to the Mexican and Central American side of the immigration debate. The two men saw cooperation and diplomacy as perhaps the best and most lasting solution, because it addressed needs on both sides of the border, and had the potential to create solutions based on mutual benefit, rather than unilateral domination.

Politicians in the 2000s, especially right after the 9/11 attacks, weren't eager to embrace such complex and politically-fraught solutions. They wanted to appear as fighters and not intellectuals, as doing something, rather than thinking about things, and wanted to portray themselves and the country they were helping to build as strong and independent, not as needing the rest of the world to get things done. This attitude was evident in Bush's promise that the United States would invade Iraq unilaterally after the international community largely condemned the proposed military policy. Wounded by the insult of an attack on U.S. soil, politicians gravitated away from debate and towards absolutism and political dichotomizing. It was this attitude that resulted in the United States moving away from a cooperative agreement with Mexico and towards an altogether more simplistic idea, building a giant fence between the two countries to keep terrorists (and Mexican immigrants) out.

The Secure Fence Act of 2006 was a largely symbolic gesture that catered to the desires of both nativists and those concerned about potential terrorism through the Southern Border and was part of a broader effort to enhance border security. This involved an increase in funding for border control operations and information sharing measures to allow immigration control agents on the border to easily access terrorist lists and other federal data. The act was marketed to the American people as the first immigration act that would finally achieve the long-term fever dream of nativists and the national-security minded alike: control of the nation's borders.

In marketing the Secure Fence Act to the public, the White House produced a fact sheet, outlying some of the basic features of the act and discussing its application to the effort to control immigration:

> _____ *"This bill will help protect the American people. This bill will make our borders more secure. It is an important step toward immigration reform."* _____

FACT SHEET: THE SECURE FENCE ACT OF 2006

George W. Bush
October 26, 2006
Source Document

Today, President Bush Signed The Secure Fence Act—An Important Step Forward In Our Nation's Efforts To Control Our Borders And Reform Our Immigration System. Earlier this year, the President laid out a strategy for comprehensive immigration reform. The Secure Fence Act is one part of this reform, and the President will work with Congress to finish the job and pass the remaining elements of this strategy.

The Secure Fence Act Builds On Progress Securing The Border By Making Wise Use Of Physical Barriers And Deploying 21st Century Technology, We Can Help Our Border Patrol Agents Do Their Job And Make Our Border More Secure. The Secure Fence Act: Authorizes the construction of hundreds of miles of additional fencing along our Southern border;

Authorizes more vehicle barriers, checkpoints, and lighting to help prevent people from entering our country illegally;

Authorizes the Department of Homeland Security to increase the use of advanced technology like cameras, satellites, and unmanned aerial vehicles to reinforce our infrastructure at the border.

Comprehensive Immigration Reform Begins With Securing The Border. Since President Bush took office, we have:

More than doubled funding for border security—from $4.6 billion in 2001 to $10.4 billion this year;

Increased the number of Border Patrol agents from about 9,000 to more than 12,000—and by the end of 2008, we will have doubled the number of Border Patrol agents since the President took office;

Deployed thousands of National Guard members to assist the Border Patrol;

Upgraded technology at our borders and added infrastructure, including new fencing and vehicle barriers;

Apprehended and sent home more than 6 million people entering America illegally; and

We are adding thousands of new beds in our detention facilities, so we can continue working to end "catch and release" at our Southern border.

This Act Is One Part Of Our Effort To Reform Our Immigration System, And We Have More Work To Do

The Secure Fence Act of 2006
continued

Comprehensive Immigration Reform Requires That We Enforce Our Immigration Laws Inside America. It is against the law to knowingly hire illegal workers, so the Administration has stepped up worksite enforcement. Many businesses want to obey the law, but cannot verify the legal status of their employees because of the widespread problem of document fraud, so the President has also called on Congress to create a better system for verifying documents and work eligibility.

Comprehensive Immigration Reform Requires That We Reduce The Pressure On Our Border By Creating A Lawful Path For Foreign Workers To Enter Our Country On A Temporary Basis. A temporary worker program would meet the needs of our economy, reduce the appeal of human smugglers, make it less likely that people would risk their lives to cross the border, and ease the financial burden on State and local governments by replacing illegal workers with lawful taxpayers. Above all, a temporary worker program would add to our security by making certain we know who is in our country and why

they are here.

Comprehensive Immigration Reform Requires That We Face The Reality That Millions Of Illegal Immigrants Are Here Already. The President opposes amnesty but believes there is a rational middle ground between granting an automatic path to citizenship for every illegal immigrant and a program of mass deportation. Illegal immigrants who have roots in our country and want to stay should have to pay a meaningful penalty for breaking the law, pay their taxes, learn English, work in a job for a number of years, and wait in line behind those who played by the rules and followed the law.

Comprehensive Immigration Reform Requires That We Honor The Great American Tradition Of The Melting Pot. Americans are bound together by our shared ideals, an appreciation of our history, respect for the flag we fly, and an ability to speak and write the English language. When immigrants assimilate and advance in our society, they realize their dreams, renew our spirit, and add to the unity of America.[267]

Only part of the Bush-era immigration reform package became law. In all of the speeches Bush gave about immigration reform, he highlighted two features that never came to pass, a pathway to citizenship for illegal

immigrants, and the guest worker program. Bush was attempting to find something of a middle ground, but the hardline conservatives rejected these aspects of the plan. In the end, the bill that passed retained the features that appealed most to hardline conservatives, but without those that appealed to moderates and liberals. The fact that it failed, therefore, reflects poorly not on the overall strategy, but on the fact that the parts of the bill that were passed were insufficient to accomplish real reform. What the Secure Fence Act did achieve was to set aside funding for a fence to cover about one-third of the 2000-mile Mexican—U.S. border, but the completion of that project proved to be immensely expensive and complicated.

The wall project was never completely finished. Legal and geographic obstacles stood in the way in addition to monetary hurdles and an overall lack of public interest or faith in the project. As the wall passed from Bush to the Obama administration, therefore, though the still Republican-controlled legislature tried to force the Obama administration to complete Bush's promises, the project drew little support from the public and failed to meet the expectations or hopes of Republicans. More than anything else, during the Obama years, the fence was a tactic used by Republicans to accuse Obama of not being serious about border protection.

The border wall then fell into the background until Donald Trump announced that he would build a bigger wall that would cover the entire border, suggesting that the failure of the Bush-era fence program was largely a matter of not doing the job right. The Trump wall controversy started on June 16, 2015, when Trump said,

> *"I will build a great wall—and nobody builds walls better than me, believe me—and I'll build them very inexpensively. I will build a great, great wall on our southern border, and I will make Mexico pay for that wall. Mark my words."*[268]

This simple 2015 statement contains three separate claims:
1. That Trump was going to build a wall.
2. That the wall will not be expensive
3. That Mexico will pay for a border wall between the United States and Mexico

Journalists and analysts thus examined each of these statements, with articles discussing whether Trump might be able to get a wall built and how much it might cost and whether Mexico could, somehow, be forced into paying for the wall.

The "Mexico will pay for the wall" claim became a sub-controversy within the larger controversy and Trump quickly moved away from this part of his initial statement. President Enrique Peña Nieto stated publicly that Mexico did not believe in the need or desire for a border wall and would not pay for the wall, which led to a leaked call between Trump and President Nieto in which Nieto told Trump that Mexico would not pay for the wall, to which Trump essentially asked Nieto to please not make that fact public.[269] In 2017, Pew Research found that only 16 percent of Americans believed Trump's claim that Mexico would pay for the wall.[270]

Legislators, immigration experts, architects, environmentalists, human rights advocates, constitutional scholars, Indigenous rights activists, and millions of passionate American citizens have raised serious concerns about the wall and have called for Trump to abandon the idea. The wall proposal did not, in fact, draw majority support from the public, though Trump soldiered on, ignoring critics while continuing to claim that the wall would be built.

Trump later announced that his administration was going to cancel the DACA program started by President Barack Obama, which was intended to provide a legal path to citizenship for about 3.6 million people who were brought to the United States illegally as children, and had

since spent their lives living as U.S. citizens, though without legal status. Trump's decision brought criticism from both Republicans and Democrats as more than 80 percent of the public disapproved of his decision to cancel the program. Trump revealed that he was planning on using the fate of those 3.6 million people as leverage in an attempt to force Democrats and Republican opponents to support his border wall. This did not immediately work and the issue remained highly contentious into 2018.

By October of 2017, the Trump-era wall program was gaining steam. Though Trump had yet to win majority support in the public or the legislature, the Republican-led Congress agreed to pay for proposals and six U.S. companies were eventually chosen to build prototype walls for consideration.[271]

Good Fences and Good Neighbors

Supporters of the border wall have made several claims about how the wall might approve the United States, including that the wall will:

1. Protect the nation from terrorists.
2. Reduce the flow of illegal drugs.
3. Prevent illegal immigration.

Preventing Terrorism

When Americans express fear about terrorism in the twenty-first century, they mean primarily radical Islamic terrorism. One of the main justifications for the wall or fence is that Islamic terrorists might use the Mexican border to sneak into the country. There was little support among experts in the 2000s for this belief but, in the intervening years, there have been instances in which persons of interest have been found using the Mexican border to try to enter the United States.

In 2013 and 2014, Texas officials apprehended 143 "special interest aliens" attempting to cross the southern border. None of the individual apprehended were found to be terrorists, but they were from countries

President Trump (center) reviewing U.S. Custom and Border Protection's wall prototypes in Otay Mesa, California at the Mexican border, via Wikimedia Commons

known to harbor state terrorism and so the incidents provided what conservatives saw as proof that the unsecure southern border was a legitimate terrorist threat.[272] In an interview with the *New York Times* in 2017, Deputy Director of George Washington University's program on extremism Seamus Hughes explained that the southern border has actually been one of the ways that American radicals leave the country to join terrorist organizations overseas, but that there are far easier ways for foreign terrorists to enter the United States than by smuggling themselves through the Mexican border.[273]

Preventing Drugs and Drug Cartels

In general, experts believe that the wall is unlikely to put a major dent in the drug trade. For instance, the 2016 Drug Enforcement Administration Report says that the primary way that illegal narcotics enter the United State is through smuggling narcotics in hidden compartments within vehicles passing legally through U.S. ports of entry. This has long been known and many efforts are in place to combat these methods and so the wall should make little difference to this effort. Smugglers have also used tunnels, boats, drones, and even catapults to get drugs into the United States. In 2016, for instance, the DEA found 225 such tunnels being used to smuggle drugs into the country.

Rosalie Pacula, of the RAND Drug Policy Research Center, told *Politico*:

> *"Traffickers have been very innovative in finding strategies to circumvent existing walls and border control thus far, and more of the same strategy (i.e. more of a wall) doesn't offer much promise as a successful strategy."*[274]

Combating the drug trade is difficult because there is an illegal drug industry in the United States and so many U.S. citizens participate in helping smugglers to beat methods in place to prevent the flow of narcotics. Few drugs coming into the United States come through with illegal migrants crossing over the border and so, the border wall and the drug trade are peripherally related at best.

Preventing Illegal Immigration

Depending on how the border wall comes to fruition, the plan may indeed have a major impact on immigration. There are several examples from other countries demonstrating how border walls can be effective in reducing illegal migration while also demonstrating some of the challenges involved in such programs.

Israel is the global leader in border walls, having constructed two, with another under construction in 2018.[275] These include:

- West Bank Wall—Constructed in 2002 to protect Israel from Palestinian terrorism, the barrier includes a 26-foot concrete wall and electrified fence, reaching for 435 miles.
- Israel-Egypt Wall—Covers the western border of Egypt, stretching for 140 miles, and between 15–12 feet high, topped with barbed wire. The project cost $400 million.
- Israel-Gaza Wall—a blockade, extending underground to prevent tunneling, between Israel and the Gaza Strip.

Prime Minister Benjamin Netanyahu has stated that the walls have completely stopped illegal immigration, and, while this claim is not considered completely accurate, the walls, along with other provisions in Israel's broader anti-immigration efforts, have collectively reduced illegal immigration dramatically. The Sinai wall is Israel's most effective. Although about 60,000 Africans passed through Egypt to Israel between 2005 to 2012, only about 12 were reported to have crossed illegally in 2016. Israel's wall along the West Bank is less effective, with roughly 50–60,000 Palestinians still crossing into Israel every year. To make the walls effective, Israel needs continued investment. The West Bank wall, for instance, costs $250 million per year to maintain.[276]

How these examples compare to a possible U.S.–Mexico border wall is unclear. The U.S.–Mexico border is far longer and more geographically complex than any of the walls constructed by Israel. Further, the Palestinian threat is so ingrained into the fabric of Israeli culture that there is broad support for the amount of continued investment needed to make the fences and walls effective.[277]

Something There Is That Doesn't Love a Wall

The primary problems associated with the border wall/fence proposal, fall into one of several categories:

1. Cost;
2. Environmental Concerns;
3. Public Support; and
4. Ethical and Moral Issues.

Cost

In January of 2018, the *Wall Street Journal* released the first breakdown of the costs associated with Trump's wall proposal. According to the report, the entire project, which included new walls, replacing old fences, hiring new personnel, and installing a high-tech monitoring system, is expected to cost $18 billion. In all, this will add 316 miles of additional wall and fence to that which already exists, bringing the total coverage to 970 miles, or a little under half of the border.[278] This cost was a feature in

Trump's 2018 budget, which revealed that American taxpayers, and not the Mexican government, will be asked to fund the project.

It is unlikely that the border wall will cost only $18 billion by the time the project is completed. Government projects have a well-known tendency to cost far more than the initial estimates and even the buildup process to the wall has been expensive. Trump and Congress set aside $20 million, for instance, for six companies to build prototypes of the wall. The first financial controversy surrounding such a large program came in January, when media outlets announced that the city of San Diego had incurred between $1–2.6 million in taxpayer costs just for protecting the eight wall prototypes commissioned. The city's primary complaint was that none of the money invested to protect the prototypes from activists and vandals was going to be reimbursed back to the city from the government.[279] Writing in *the Guardian*, Journalist Julia Carrie Wong said of the controversy:

_____ *"Included in that outlay is $118,092.66 on a chain-link fence to protect the towering hunks of concrete and steel that are supposed to protect American citizens from American citizens who object to their presence."*[280]

_____

Environmental Concerns

Trump is on record a climate change skeptic, against the weight of the world's scientific consensus. The Trump administration removed all information about climate change from the White House website and Trump's appointee to lead the EPA, Scott Pruitt, suggested in an interview that global warming could be good for people.[281]

In January, the Homeland Security Secretary Kristjen Neilson gave a notice through the Federal Register that the administration was waiving dozens of environmental regulations to speed up construction of the wall, essentially ignoring rules from the National Environment Policy Act, the Endangered Species Act, the Clean Water Act, the National Historic Preservation Act, and the Antiquities Act to expedite the wall's construction.[282]

According to a January 26, 2017, article in *Scientific American*, Trump's border wall is almost universally seen by environmental activists and scientists as an impending environmental disaster. The construction of the wall will increase carbon emissions, the wall itself will divert the flow of rain water and thus cause both drought and flooding, and the many species that live in the border areas will have their migratory routes and search for resources blocked. Environmental scientists familiar with the region said that the Bush-era and Obama-era walls had already led to erosion and flooding and that the disruption to the flow of wildlife will be crucial to many species' survival. Ocelots, jaguars, and wolves are among just a few of the endangered animals that live along the border region and that absolutely require free migration for survival.

Dan Millis, of the Sierra Club's Borderlands project said:

> *"In terms of climate adaptation, building a border wall is an act of self-sabotage. And the reason I say that is we're already seeing wildlife migrations blocked with the current walls and fences that have already been built. We have hundreds of these walls that were built without dozens of environmental protections."*[283]

Public Opinion

The American people are divided on the issue of the border wall, and were also divided when the Bush Administration pushed through its border wall proposal in 2006.

The first efforts to measure public support for a border wall/fence came in the 1990s when state governments were enacting their own state-funded

border wall and fence programs. In 1993, a poll from Gallup found that 27 percent of people favored the border wall idea, compared to 71 percent who did not. By 1995, Gallup found 35 percent for the idea, versus 62 percent opposed.

Polling organizations only began measuring opinion on *federal* wall proposals in 2006, and this came after a full-tilt, multimillion-dollar marketing campaign to build public support for the idea. In 2006, Fox news recorded the highest level of support ever, with 50 percent support for a U.S.–Mexico wall, and, oddly, *56* percent support for a wall along the Canadian border. However, A CBS poll from that same year provides better results, because CBS first informed survey takers by providing pro and con arguments before they were asked to answer questions. Only 29 percent supported Bush's wall when the various arguments were presented to them. Even at this time, when concern over border security was peaking, the proposal only managed minority support. However, 62 percent supported the far less controversial idea of increasing the number of border patrol agents.

When Trump's border wall proposal first hit the news in 2015, Bloomberg reported 41 percent in favor, and 55 percent opposed to the idea. About the same percentages also supported a wall along the Canadian border. In general, support for border walls of any kind range from 33–45 percent across all polling organizations. Differing ways of asking the question affect responses, but, in general, opposition to the wall has maintained at least a 10-percentage point lead from the beginning of Trump's first mention of idea.[284] The most recent polling, from Pew Research indicates that support is waning, with Pew finding 62 percent opposing the proposal as opposed to 35 percent who support the idea.[285]

The Moral and Ethical Angle
On a philosophical level, walls don't often work because they don't address the *demand* for access to the resources on one or the other side.

Walls are the most primitive, simplistic way to protect resources or to prevent contamination. They reduce the immediate presence of a problem, but fail over the long-term because they do not address underlying causes or motivations. This is not only true of the border walls approach, but of any approach that prioritizes prohibition over deeper and more complex efforts to address underlying causes. Another example can be found in America's failed drug wars.

In the prohibition era, politicians in the United States tried to address alcoholism by prohibiting alcohol, but this effort reduced only the *supply*, and not the *demand*. What resulted was a sharp rise in organized crime and violence and people switching from commercial alcohol to home-made alcohol and other more dangerous alternatives. The result was an increase in alcohol-related deaths and a deepening of the problems that prohibition was intended to address.

That Border walls continue to be popular reflects the fact that many of the problems facing human societies are highly complex and difficult to solve. The opioid addiction problem in the United States for instance, has brought about a host of policies based on cutting off the supply of opioids, but many critics have pointed out that this is not really the problem. As Dean of Health Sciences at West Virginia University wrote in *Huffington Post* in 2016:

> *"The opioid epidemic is merely a symptom of a much larger crisis, one we as Americans must learn to solve: the crisis of isolation, despair and hopelessness."*[286]

Over the years, both conservatives and liberals have observed that the relationship between the United States and Mexico is exploitative and morally flawed. American businesses have long exploited Mexican labor-

ers and the Mexican drug cartels that have ravaged their society were created and are still fueled by American demand for narcotics. Illegal immigration itself could *not* exist if it weren't for the willingness of U.S. businesses to maximize their own profit by exploiting migrants rather than hiring native workers. The life of an illegal immigrant is difficult and often exploitative and those who choose this life do it because they see no better option to try and care for themselves and their families. The same is true of the African and Palestinian migrants who illegally try to flock into Israel. These are people whose societies are impoverished and who are seeking better lives for themselves and those they care about.

As climate change continues, and the environmental conditions in Mexico worsen, the need for migration will grow more severe. Donald Trump has used Israel as the example of how his border wall proposal can succeed and yet Israel is a nation that has not even begun to solve its problems. The Palestinians expelled from their ancestral lands and now living stateless in impoverished territories on Israel's borders constitute one of the world's biggest human rights crises. Even if one believes that Palestinian terrorism condemns the Palestinian population to permanent internment, it is unlikely that many could believe Palestinian children born into that society deserve the fate to which they have been left and in the creation of which they had no hand. Though the appeal of the border wall is simplistic and naïve, its effects will be severe and wide ranging. It is, therefore, relevant not only to consider one's feelings on illegal migration in the present, but also, what kind of world one hopes to create for the future.

CONCLUSION

Politicians and most of the public were skeptical of the border wall proposal when it was first debated during Trump's 2016 campaign and over the first year of his presidency. Broadly speaking, the Trump administration's immigration policies catered towards far-right interests and failed to gain moderate or progressive support. Polls from a variety of sources demonstrated that immigration during this time ranked near the bottom of the leading priorities for Americans, lower than terrorism, the economy, the cost of health care, social security, Medicare, or the environment. Immigration has, however, remained a focus for the Trump administration.

DISCUSSION QUESTIONS

- Should immigration reform be a top issue for the government? Why or why not?
- What are some reasons to support Donald Trump's border wall proposal? Explain each reason in terms of opinion or priority.
- What are some reasons to reject Donald Trump's border wall proposal? Explain each reason in terms of opinion or priority.
- Should the United States work with Mexico on the border security issue? Why or why not?

Works Used

Beard, Jacob. "Top Ten Origins: History's Greatest Walls, Good Neighbors or Bad Policy?" *Origins*. Ohio State University. Department of History. 2018.

Bolstad, Erika. "Trump's Wall Could Cause Serious Environmental Damage." *Scientific American*. Nature America, Inc. 26 Jan. 2017.

Embury-Dennis, Tom. "Trump's environment chief Scott Pruitt suggests climate change could be good for humanity." *Independent*. Independent News and Media. 8 Feb. 2018.

"Fact Sheet: The Secure Fence Act of 2006." *Georgewbush-White House*. White House. Oct. 26, 2006.

Flores, Esteban. "Walls of Separation." *HIR*. Harvard International Review. 27 July 2017.

"Good Fences, Good Neighbors: Public Opinion on Border Security." *Roper Center*. Cornell University. 2015.

James, Mike. "Trump seeks $18 billion to extend border wall over 10 years." *USA Today*. USA Today. 6 Jan. 2018.

Joshi, Anu. "Donald Trump's Border Wall—An Annotated Timeline." *Huffington Post*. Huffington Post. 1 Mar. 2017.

Kershner, Isabel. "Trump Cites Israel's 'Wall' as Model. The Analogy Is Iffy." *New York Times*. New York Times co. 27 Jan. 2017.

Leiken, Robert S. "War On Terror: Mexico More Critical Than Ever for U.S." *Brookings*. Brookings Institution. 24 Mar. 2002.

Marsh, Clay. "Opioid Addiction Isn't The Disease; It's The Symptom." Well-Being. *Thrive Global*. Huffington Post.9 Aug. 2017.

Miller, Greg, Vitkovskaya, Julie, and Reuben Fischer-Baum. "'This deal will make me look terrible': Full transcripts of Trump's calls with Mexico and Australia." *The Washington Post*. Washington Post Co. 3 Aug. 2017.

O'Keefe, Ed, David Weigel, and Paul Kane. "Nancy Pelosi's filibuster-style speech tops eight hours in bid to force immigration votes." *Washington Post*. Washington Post Co. 7 Feb. 2018.

Rodriguez, Nicole. "Trump's Border Wall Was a $2.6 Million Hit on San Diego Taxpayers." *Newsweek*. Newsweek, LLC.19 Jan. 2018.

Schmitt, Eric, and Linda Qiu. "Fact Check: The Trump Administration's Arguments for a Border Wall." *New York Times*. New York Times co. 27 Apr. 2017.

Steckelberg, Aaron, Chris Alcantara, and Tracy Jan. "A look at Trump's border wall prototypes." *The Washington Post*. Washington Post Company. 31 Oct. 2017.

Suls, Rob. "Most Americans continue to oppose U.S. border wall, doubt Mexico would pay for it." *Pew Research*. Pew Research Center. 24 Feb. 2017.

Tomsen, Jaqueline. "Trump waives dozens of environmental rules to speed up construction of border wall." *The Hill*. Capitol Hill Publishing Group. 22 Jan. 2018.

Valverde, Miriam. "Will a border wall stop drugs from coming into the United States?" *Politifact*. Politifact. 26 Oct. 2017.

Westcott, Lucy. "What History Tells Us About Building A Wall To Solve A Problem." *Newsweek*. Newsweek, LLC. 14 Oct. 2015.

Wilson, Reid. "Texas officials warn of immigrants with terrorist ties crossing southern border." *Washington Post*. Washington Post, Co. 26 Feb. 2015.

Wong, Julia Carrie. "Trump's border wall: prototypes loom large, but where are the protesters?" *The Guardian*. Guardian News and Media. 29 Jan. 2018.

Introduction

This chapter explores the debate over the DREAMers, undocumented individuals brought to the United States as children, who grew up within the United States without citizenship status. The bipartisan effort to create legislation that would provide a path to citizenship for the dreamers began in the 2000s and resulted in the Obama administration creating a temporary residency program, known as DACA (Deferred Action for Childhood Arrivals) when the legislature failed to reach a compromise on the issue. President Trump cancelled Obama's DACA program in 2018, in an effort to garner support for his other, more controversial, immigration policies.

A substantial majority of Americans, including a majority of legislators, agree that the DREAMers should be saved from deportation and given a path to legal residency. Efforts to accomplish this have failed, primarily, because a minority of legislators exploited the political consensus on the issue to build support for other political goals that do not have cross-ideological support. The primary document for this chapter is a speech given by President Barack Obama upon the establishment of the DACA program in which he explains the moral and ethical justification behind his decision to issue the Executive Order.

Topics covered in this chapter include:
- Racial prejudice
- Humanitarian issues in immigration
- Children of undocumented migrants
- Undocumented migration

The American Dreamers
The Dreamers and DACA (2012–2018)

Illegal migration created an unforeseen problem that became one of the biggest immigration debates of the 2010s, involving millions of individuals now living in the United States who were brought to the nation as children by undocumented parents. The parents violated U.S. law by migrating into the United States, but these children, sometimes called the DREAMers (a name taken from the legislative effort to determine their status) did not make this same choice. Furthermore, these individuals have since spent their formative years living as Americans, though without legal status. Many speak only English and have only ever known U.S. culture, having attended U.S. schools, and worked in U.S. companies. Politicians have long recognized that this group of undocumented migrants were different, morally and ethically, from those who, as adults, chose to migrate illegally; and so there has been a long debate over how American law and policy should deal with this facet of the undocumented population.

Humanitarianism or Political Leverage?

The debate over the DREAMers has been ongoing for more than 17 years. During that entire time, the status of DREAMers has been a unique issue within the broader immigration debate in that a majority of people, including most legislators, agree on the fundamental proposal that these individuals should be allowed to both remain in the United States and to become citizens. Both Republican and Democratic senators and representatives have attempted to craft legislation giving the DREAMers a path to citizenship but, in each case, politicians have failed to achieve this by attempting to use widespread support for the DREAMers as leverage to pass more controversial immigration laws. This is happening in 2018 again.

The debate over the DREAMers, the name they have been given in popular culture, comes from the DREAM (Development, Relief, Education for Alien Minors) Act of 2001, a bipartisan piece of legislation that developed out of a proposal first created by Democratic Illinois Representative Luis Gutiérrez. Gutiérrez wanted to provide a path to citizenship for these individuals who, it was argued in congressional debates, were American in spirit and culture, but not status. Utah Republican Orrin Hatch created a more moderate version of Gutiérrez' original bill for the senate, under the title DREAM Act. Utah Republican Chris Cannon then produced a complimentary House Bill known as the Student Adjustment Act of 2001, which was meant to work alongside the DREAM Act to facilitate the process of enrolling the DREAMers in a higher education program. Despite bipartisan support, neither act became law because deeper disagreements over immigration reform resulted in filibusters and legislative deadlock.

The DREAM Act, and other versions of the Student Adjustment Act, were brought back for consideration in 2003–04, 2005–06, 2007–08, 2009–10, 2011–12, 2013–14, and 2017–18. The 2007–08 version of the bill was revised and sponsored by Democratic Illinois Senator Richard Durbin, who then remained one of the primary congressional proponents of this idea into 2017. The 2007–08 version of the DREAM Act became part of the Comprehensive Immigration Reform Act of 2007, which not only called for a path to citizenship for the DREAMers, but also contained far more controversial proposals.[287]

President George W. Bush, took a more moderate stance regarding illegal Mexican immigration, which is arguably, in part, inspired by his familiarity with Mexican people, the industries that employ illegal migrants, and as a resident and former Governor of Texas. Bush not only supported the effort to provide a path to citizenship for the DREAMers, but had also hoped to create a guest worker program that would serve as a platform for legalizing the migrant worker industry for many of the 11 million un-

documented migrants living in the nation. This effort did not meet with the approval of some conservative senators and representatives who saw illegal migrants as criminals and potentially as a threat to national security. Meanwhile, more liberal politicians disapproved of sections of the 2007 immigration reform bill involving border security and deportation. The bill thus fell victim to a congressional filibuster and was eventually abandoned.

The 2007 debate over the DREAM Act demonstrates how this debate played out, in general, over subsequent years. In 2010, the DREAM Act was part of a bill that included a repeal of the military "Don't Ask, Don't Tell" policy, which was controversial and thus failed again to pass through Congress. In 2011, Texas Senator John Cornyn, and Senator John McCain of Arizona, as well as a number of other Republicans refused to consider the bill unless Congress agreed to provide further funding for border control. Frustrated by the partisan deadlock, states began taking the matter into their own hands. In 2011, both California[288] and Illinois[289] passed their own versions of the DREAM Act, garnering bipartisan support in state legislatures and thus began to offer some of the protections and services featured in federal bills.

In 2013, President Barack Obama decided to deal with the subject by issuing an Executive Order, known as the Deferred Action for Childhood Arrivals or DACA. Essentially, DACA was intended to be temporary, as reflected in the fact that the order called for "deferred" action. The following is President Barack Obama's speech on the need and justification for the DACA Program:

REMARKS BY THE PRESIDENT ON IMMIGRATION

Barack Obama
June 15, 2012
Source Document

Rose Garden
2:09 P.M. EDT
THE PRESIDENT: Good afternoon, everybody. This morning, Secretary Napolitano announced new actions my administration will take to mend our nation's immigration policy, to make it more fair, more efficient, and more just—specifically for certain young people sometimes called "Dreamers."

These are young people who study in our schools, they play in our neighborhoods, they're friends with our kids, they pledge allegiance to our flag. They are Americans in their heart, in their minds, in every single way but one: on paper. They were brought to this country by their parents—sometimes even as infants—and often have no idea that they're undocumented until they apply for a job or a driver's license, or a college scholarship.

Put yourself in their shoes. Imagine you've done everything right your entire life—studied hard, worked hard, maybe even graduated at the top of your class—only to suddenly face the threat of deportation to a country that you know nothing about, with a language that you may not even speak.

That's what gave rise to the DREAM Act. It says that if your parents brought you here as a child, if you've been here for five years, and you're willing to go to college or serve in our military, you can one day earn your citizenship. And I have said time and time and time again to Congress that, send me the DREAM Act, put it on my desk, and I will sign it right away.

Now, both parties wrote this legislation. And a year and a half ago, Democrats passed the DREAM Act in the House, but Republicans walked away from it. It got 55 votes in the Senate, but Republicans blocked it. The bill hasn't really changed. The need hasn't changed. It's still the right thing to do. The only thing that has changed, apparently, was the politics.

As I said in my speech on the economy yesterday, it makes no sense to expel talented young people, who, for all intents and purposes, are Americans—they've been raised as Americans; understand themselves to be part of this country—to expel these young people who want to staff our labs, or start new businesses, or defend our

continued

country simply because of the actions of their parents—or because of the inaction of politicians.

In the absence of any immigration action from Congress to fix our broken immigration system, what we've tried to do is focus our immigration enforcement resources in the right places. So we prioritized border security, putting more boots on the southern border than at any time in our history—today, there are fewer illegal crossings than at any time in the past 40 years. We focused and used discretion about whom to prosecute, focusing on criminals who endanger our communities rather than students who are earning their education. And today, deportation of criminals is up 80 percent. We've improved on that discretion carefully and thoughtfully. Well, today, we're improving it again.

Effective immediately, the Department of Homeland Security is taking steps to lift the shadow of deportation from these young people. Over the next few months, eligible individuals who do not present a risk to national security or public safety will be able to request temporary relief from deportation proceedings and apply for work authorization.

Now, let's be clear—this is not amnesty, this is not immunity. This is not a path to citizenship. It's not a permanent fix. This is a temporary stopgap measure that lets us focus our resources wisely while giving a degree of relief and hope to talented, driven, patriotic young people. It is—

Q   (Inaudible.)

THE PRESIDENT: —the right thing to do.

Q   —foreigners over American workers.

THE PRESIDENT: Excuse me, sir. It's not time for questions, sir.

Q   No, you have to take questions.

THE PRESIDENT: Not while I'm speaking.

Precisely because this is temporary, Congress needs to act. There is still time for Congress to pass the DREAM Act this year, because these kids deserve to plan their lives in more than two-year increments. And we still need to pass comprehensive immigration reform that addresses our 21st century economic and security needs—reform that gives our farmers and ranchers certainty about the workers that they'll have. Reform that gives our science

Remarks by the President on Immigration
continued

and technology sectors certainty that the young people who come here to earn their PhDs won't be forced to leave and start new businesses in other countries. Reform that continues to improve our border security, and lives up to our heritage as a nation of laws and a nation of immigrants.

Just six years ago, the unlikely trio of John McCain, Ted Kennedy and President Bush came together to champion this kind of reform. And I was proud to join 23 Republicans in voting for it. So there's no reason that we can't come together and get this done.

And as long as I'm President, I will not give up on this issue, not only because it's the right thing to do for our economy—and CEOs agree with me— not just because it's the right thing to do for our security, but because it's the right thing to do, period. And I believe that, eventually, enough Republicans in Congress will come around to that view as well.

And I believe that it's the right thing to do because I've been with groups of young people who work so hard and speak with so much heart about what's best in America, even though I knew some of them must have lived under the fear of deportation. I know some have come forward, at great risks to themselves and their futures, in hopes

it would spur the rest of us to live up to our own most cherished values. And I've seen the stories of Americans in schools and churches and communities across the country who stood up for them and rallied behind them, and pushed us to give them a better path and freedom from fear—because we are a better nation than one that expels innocent young kids.

And the answer to your question, sir— and the next time I'd prefer you let me finish my statements before you ask that question—is this is the right thing to do for the American people—

Q   (Inaudible.)

THE PRESIDENT: I didn't ask for an argument. I'm answering your question.

Q   I'd like to—

THE PRESIDENT: It is the right thing to do—

Q   (Inaudible.)

THE PRESIDENT: —for the American people. And here's why—

Q   —unemployment—

THE PRESIDENT: Here's the reason: because these young people are going to make extraordinary contributions,

continued

and are already making contributions to our society.

I've got a young person who is serving in our military, protecting us and our freedom. The notion that in some ways we would treat them as expendable makes no sense. If there is a young person here who has grown up here and wants to contribute to this society, wants to maybe start a business that will create jobs for other folks who are looking for work, that's the right thing to do. Giving certainty to our farmers and our ranchers; making sure that in addition to border security, we're creating a comprehensive framework for legal immigration —these are all the right things to do.

We have always drawn strength from being a nation of immigrants, as well as a nation of laws, and that's going to continue. And my hope is that Congress recognizes that and gets behind this effort.

All right. Thank you very much.

Q   What about American workers who are unemployed while you import foreigners?[290]

The unidentified individual(s) heckling President Obama's speech on the DACA order echoed long-standing nativist fears and beliefs about immigration. Some Americans at the time that Obama enacted DACA were unable to see the difference between the DACA situation and wider immigration concerns. For instance, the concern that the DACA program was a factor in furthering unemployment is simply a misunderstanding, because the program is not about "importing immigrants," as the critic claims, but refers only to those who have *already* been living *and* in most cases working in the United States. These concerns are more relevant to the question of whether to prohibit *further* illegal immigration, but not directly to the fate of the DREAMers, who were, as President Obama explained, already part of American society.

The DACA Program

According to the 2012 Executive Order, the DACA program provided a temporary deferment of deportation action against individuals meeting a certain list of criteria. A person could apply for enrollment in the program, which provided a two-year temporary legal residency permit, to all applicants who:

1. were under the age of 31 as of June 15, 2012;
2. came to the United States before reaching their sixteenth birthday;
3. have continuously resided in the United States since June 15, 2007, up to the present time;
4. were physically present in the United States on June 15, 2012, and at the time of making your request for consideration of deferred action with USCIS;
5. had no lawful status on June 15, 2012;
6. are currently in school, have graduated or obtained a certificate of completion from high school, have obtained a general education development (GED) certificate, or are an honorably discharged veteran of the Coast Guard or Armed Forces of the United States; and
7. have not been convicted of a felony, significant misdemeanor, or three or more other misdemeanors, and do not otherwise pose a threat to national security or public safety.

Individuals who agreed to enroll in the program were required to obtain the necessary documents to prove that they met the criteria for the program, to complete USCIS form 1-821D, I-765, and I-765WS, to pay $465 dollars in fees, and to submit biometric information (fingerprints, identification records, etc.) to the state.[291]

Essentially, the DACA program asked those choosing to enroll to take a risk. By identifying themselves to the government, they then risked deportation or other legal action. As of 2017, when the program was officially cancelled, 690,000 DREAMers had applied for the program.[292] This is only, however, a small portion of the DREAMers population in total. In January of 2018, *USA Today* published an article citing statistics from the Migration Policy Institute (MPI) a non-profit think tank dedicated to studying migration, suggesting that the actual DREAMer population might be as large

President Barack Obama speaks about immigration with a group of DREAMers who are part of the Deferred Action for Childhood Arrivals (DACA), the Oval Office, 2015, by Saul Loeb/AFP/Getty Images

as 3.6 million.[293] This figure had been obscured by media reports speaking about the number of people who may have applied for DACA, which was estimated at between 500,000 and 800,000, until statistics became available, which didn't occur until after the program was cancelled.

Using DREAMers For Political Leverage

During his 2016 presidential campaign, Trump hinted at a new comprehensive immigration policy that included ending the DACA program.

> *"We will immediately terminate President Obama's two illegal executive amnesties in which he defied federal law and the Constitution to give amnesty to approximately five million illegal immigrants, five million."*

Just before the election, Trump displayed a change of heart on the

DREAMers issue, saying in November of 2016:

_____ *"They got brought here at a very young age, they've worked here, they've gone to school here. Some were good students. Some have wonderful jobs. And they're in never-never land because they don't know what's going to happen."*[294]

In January, Richard Durbin reported that Trump personally told him, "We're going to take care of those kids." That spring, Durbin and other supporters of the DREAM Act met with Trump surrogates for weeks of meetings, though the talks were unproductive. Then on September 5, 2017, the Trump administration announced, in a speech by Attorney General Jeff Sessions, that the administration was going to cancel the DACA program. Sessions claimed that economics and the rule of law were the primary concerns, stating that the DACA Executive Orders were illegal and unconstitutional and that the program had resulted in Americans losing jobs that went to illegal migrants.

Throughout the subsequent weeks, it became clear that, once again, the DREAM Act, or a newer modern iteration of it, was again being used as leverage in an effort by the Trump Administration to force agreement with Trump's other immigration proposals, including the proposal for an $18 billion wall on the southern border and a proposal to withdraw funds for cities that harbor illegal migrants. This put both Republican and Democratic legislators in a difficult situation, many of the administration's goals for immigration reform, such as the border wall, or the withdrawal of support for Sanctuary Cities, does not have majority support among the public. These ideas are popular primarily with the far-right, and to a lesser degree, with moderate conservatives. Thus, if legislators agree to the administration's demands, those same legislators risk losing support in their own states. Months of debate resulted in several prospective "deals"

in which Republicans and Democrats announced they were close to an agreement, but ultimately none of the negotiations resulted in an agreement. As of February of 2018, the status of the DREAMers remains uncertain as the issue has been, again, tied to broader and much more controversial ideas about how to reform the immigration system overall.[295]

Perceptions and Divisions

The website *American Renaissance*, which caters to those interested in eugenics, intellectual racism, and white nationalism, reposted the *USA Today* article stating that the DREAMers population was as large as 3.6 million. The commentary that ensued echoes many of the oldest ideas about nationality, ownership, race, and citizenship, including:

Missy

How did they forget what a country is? It is not made up of people who sneak in for free benefits. It is not made up of people who came here only for a job. It is not made up of former slaves. It is not made up of people who hate each other, have nothing in common, and speak different languages. They let people in who are not, and never will be, part of the country.

Journey

You are correct. The biggest challenge in the survival of this country is to only let in the ones who understand what this country was founded on. The Founders, founding population, and consequent generations risk their limbs and lives for the survival of this country. Additionally, countless others worked hard and sacrificed to build a nation from scratch. Now, because of greed and corruption, this country's future is unsecure.[296]

The conservative website *Breitbart*, whose CEO Steven Bannon was formerly Trump's chief strategist, then published a blog post by content creator Neil Munro who described the revelation as an example of a liberal plot to conceal the actual nature of the issue from the people. This has become part of the far-right narrative about immigration, that the Democratic Party politicians are attempting to make the United States more diverse because minorities vote for Democrats and so that this is part of an agenda to win political currency.

President Trump has been associated with the far-right to a greater degree than any past Republican president has been well documented. Although opinions on Trump are mixed, it would be far more damaging to the Trump administration to lose far-right support than it would have been for previous Republican Presidents like George W. Bush or Ronald Reagan, both of whom favored moderate policies in many cases in an effort to draw bipartisan support.

Websites like *Breitbart*, and the *Drudge Report* have gotten a major boost in apparent relevancy because of Trump's interest in this kind of media. The claims of far-right anti-immigration enthusiasts have thus become part of the larger debate, but they do not accurately reflect the attitudes of the public as a whole.

On January 18, 2018, CBS News released one of the most recent polls about the DACA program and the DREAMers, the results of which showed a rare degree of bipartisan agreement. In total, the poll found 87 percent support for allowing DREAMers to stay so long as they attended school, served in the military, and did not have a criminal record, as opposed to only 11 percent favoring deporting the DREAMers. This support was across all political groups, with 79 percent of Republicans, 92 percent of Democrats, and 87 percent of Independents in agreement on the issue.[297] The CBS Poll demonstrated the most extreme level of support for the DREAMers and DACA, but other polls have also demonstrated a clear majority. For instance, a January 2018 Harvard University/Harris Poll found 77 percent support for allowing the DREAMers to remain in the United States, including 66 percent of Republicans.[298]

Considering that the Trump Administration has made the proposed border wall a contingency for agreeing to pass legislation that would prevent DREAMers from being deported, the discussion about the DACA issue also now involves the border wall itself. The same January 2018 poll indicates that Americans, in general, do not want a border wall. In total, only 35 percent supported the wall, as opposed to 60 percent who opposed the idea. On this issue, Americans were more divided, with a majority of Republicans and Independents supportive of the idea, but not to a large enough percentage to shift the balance to an overall majority.[299]

The public perception of the DREAMers is not reflected in the way the issue has progressed in American politics. Legislators have failed to reach bipartisan agreements, and this is primarily the result of the fact that a portion of the legislature has refused to deal with the issue directly, but continually tether the DREAMers to more controversial issues. Trump has taken a more extreme tact than many politicians in the past by tying the DREAMers to other immigration proposals that are also not widely popular. The border wall, for instance, lacks support not only because Democrats are broadly supportive of immigrants or immigration, but also because there are many people across partisan lines who disapprove of the idea for a variety of reasons, including the cost, logistical issues, and the environmental consequences that will result from such a project.

The DACA issue, therefore, provides an excellent example of how political inaction occurs. In many cases, issues for which there is broad agreement are left unaddressed because politicians use this bipartisan support as leverage for other more controversial political goals. When Trump announced he was cancelling the DACA program, former President Obama issued a statement criticizing the action:

"To target these young people is wrong— because they have done nothing wrong. It is self-defeating—because they want to start new businesses,

staff our labs, serve in our military, and otherwise contribute to the country we love. And it is cruel. What if our kid's science teacher, or our friendly neighbor turns out to be a Dreamer? Where are we supposed to send her? To a country she doesn't know or remember, with a language she may not even speak?

Let's be clear: the action taken today isn't required legally. It's a political decision, and a moral question. Whatever concerns or complaints Americans may have about immigration in general, we shouldn't threaten the future of this group of young people who are here through no fault of their own, who pose no threat, who are not taking away anything from the rest of us. They are that pitcher on our kid's softball team, that first responder who helps out his community after a disaster, that cadet in ROTC who wants nothing more than to wear the uniform of the country that gave him a chance. Kicking them out won't lower the unemployment rate, or lighten anyone's taxes, or raise anybody's wages...

Ultimately, this is about basic decency. This is about whether we are a people who kick hopeful young strivers out of America, or whether we treat them the way we'd want our own kids to be treated. It's about who we are as a people—and who we want to be.

What makes us American is not a question of what we look like, or where our names come from, or the way we pray. What makes us American is our fidelity to a set of ideals—that all of us are created equal;

that all of us deserve the chance to make of our lives what we will; that all of us share an obligation to stand up, speak out, and secure our most cherished values for the next generation. That's how America has traveled this far. That's how, if we keep at it, we will ultimately reach that more perfect union."[300]

CONCLUSION

Public opinion polls from the 2000s through 2018 show that a significant majority of Americans agree with the moral and ethical arguments that have been put forth as justification for allowing the DREAMers to remain in the United States and to become citizens. The broad support and concern for the DREAMers has been vividly demonstrated in 2017 and 2018 by hundreds of protests of the Trump administration's decision to cancel the DACA program, which also demonstrate how human rights has become an increasingly important aspect of the nation's immigration debate.

DISCUSSION QUESTIONS

■ Should the federal government allow the DREAMers to remain in the United States? Why or why not?

■ Is the status of the DREAMers being used as political leverage to broker support for other immigration issues? Why or why not?

■ How does the fact that DREAMers did not decide to violate immigration laws affect your opinion of the situation?

■ Is the DREAMers debate important in comparison with other current issues? Explain.

Works Used

"Consideration of Deferred Action for Childhood Arrivals (DACA)." *USCIS*. U.S. Citizenship and Immigration Services. 4 Feb. 2018.

De Pinto, Jennifer, Fred Backus, Kabir Khanna, and Anthony Salvanto. "Most Americans support DACA, but oppose border wall—CBS News poll." *CBS News*. 20 Jan. 2018.

"DREAM Act Congressional Legislative History," *University of Houston*. University of Houston Law School. 2017.

Gomez, Alan. "There are 3.6M 'DREAMers'—a number far greater than commonly known." *USA Today*. USA Today. 18 Jan. 2018.

"Illinois DREAM Act Signed by Governor Quinn." *HuffPost*. Huffington Post. 2 Oct. 2011.

Lind, Dara. "How many immigrants have DACA, really? We finally have one answer—just as they start to lose it." Vox. 6 Oct 2017.

McGreevy, Patrick, and Anthony York. "Brown signs California Dream Act." *Los Angeles Times*. Los Angeles Times. 9 Oct. 2011.

"Monthly Harvard-Harris Poll: January 2018 Re-Field." *Harvardharris Poll*. Harvard University Center for American Political Studies. Jan. 2018.

"Remarks by the President on Immigration." *Obama White House*. Office of the Press Secretary. 15 June 2012.

Shear, Michael D. "How Washington Reached the Brink of a Shutdown." *New York Times*. New York Times, Co. 19 Jan. 2018.

"There Are 3.6M 'Dreamers'—A Number Far Greater Than Commonly Known." *AMREN*. American Renaissance. 19 Jan. 2018.

"'This Is About Basic Decency.' Obama Rips Trump Over DACA Decision," *Time*. Time Inc. 5 Sept. 2017.

Valverde, Miriam. "Timeline: DACA, the Trump administration and a government shutdown." *Politifact*. Politifact. 22 Jan. 2018.

Introduction

This chapter explores President Trump's effort to ban migration or visitation from several countries, most of which are Muslim-majority with connections to radical Islamic movements. The effort to prohibit the immigration of Muslims has been proposed within far-right groups since the 9/11 terrorist attacks, though Trump is the first president to attempt turning such efforts into law. The travel ban proposals were rejected by a series of federal courts and appeals courts because they determined that the administration's intention was to prohibit Muslim migration, not immigration from dangerous countries as was later claimed in his Executive Orders on the topic.

The Trump travel ban debate is a modern version of an old immigration debate. The Alien and Sedition Acts (discussed in Chapter 3) and the Anarchist Exclusion Act (discussed in Chapter 13) were the earliest examples of this debate—whether America should prohibit the immigration of individuals who harbor dangerous ideologies or who come from "enemy" nations or cultures. The same arguments used to support the travel ban have been used to argue against Japanese, Catholic, Anarchist, Communist, and Socialist immigrants and foreign visitors. The source for this chapter is a 2012 article in *Smithsonian Magazine* that looks at the history of religious tolerance in the United States, demonstrating that Americans have not often embraced freedom of religion to the same degree that such freedom is enshrined in the U.S. Constitution.

Topics covered in this chapter include:
- Ideological prejudice
- Anti-Muslim sentiment
- Donald Trump
- National security

- Radical violence
- Islamism

This Chapter Discusses the Following Source Document:
Davis, Kenneth C. "America's True History of Religious Tolerance."
Smithsonian. Smithsonian Institution. Oct. 2010.

The Fight for American Ideology
The Travel Ban and American Religious Identity (2016–2018)

One of the controversial proposals of the Trump administration's first year was the effort to ban immigration from Muslim-majority countries known to have far-right radical groups. Various Muslim immigration bans or restrictions have been considered since the 9/11 terrorist attacks, reflecting the fear that Islamic radicals will sneak into the country and conduct terrorist attacks. This fear is not without precedent as it was discovered that the terrorists who hijacked the planes on 9/11 had all emigrated from majority Muslim nations, had entered the country on student visas, and overstayed their welcome. Donald Trump is the first politician to attempt an actual ban on Muslim immigration, though his efforts to do so failed to meet with judicial scrutiny on constitutional grounds.

America Is a Nation Of Diversity

The men sometimes called the "founding fathers" of the United States believed the freedom of religion was so important to a free society that they enshrined this principal into the "Supreme Law of the Land," the United States Constitution. Freedom of religion was included in the very First Amendment to the U.S. Constitution adopted in 1791 and thus became part of those very special ten amendments that make up the U.S. Bill of Rights. As per the original language of the First Amendment:

"Congress shall make no law respecting an establishment of religion, or prohibiting the free exercise thereof; or abridging the freedom of speech, or the press; or the right of the people peaceably to assemble, and to petition the government for a redress of grievances."[301]

The First Amendment contains two separate clauses that guarantee two *different* freedoms of religion:

The Exercise Clause: "Congress shall make no law respecting an establishment of religion…"

The Free Exercise Clause: "…or prohibiting the free exercise thereof."

These two clauses have been the subject of numerous debates over the years and the exact meaning of each clause has been subject to judicial tests in the Supreme Court. The Exercise Clause has been interpreted as meaning that the United States government is prohibited from establishing a state religion, or any law that favors one religion over any other. The Free Exercise clause then prohibits the government from establishing a law that restricts the ways in which people practice any legitimate religion.[302]

As of 2018, the First Amendment is still part of the Bill of Rights and the U.S. Constitution. This means that the U.S. government, and the state governments, are constitutionally prohibited from:
1. passing a law making *any* religion illegal;
2. ordering any churches to be closed based on of religion;
3. passing any law that favors one religion over another;
4. passing any law that restricts rights based on religion;
5. passing any law that discriminates based on religion; and
6. officially supporting any religion.

What this means is that America is (legally and constitutionally speaking) as much a Muslim, or Jewish nation as it is a Christian nation. There are 3.3–3.4 million Muslims living in the United States, comprising approximately 2.1 percent of the nation's population. By contrast, only 1.4 percent of the population in 2018 are Jewish.[303] The United States recognizes many brands of organized religion. Further, as freedom of religion is enshrined in American law and respects all religions, even those practiced

by a small minority of Americans, America has become a land of many religions and great diversity.

Any American is free to believe that America is only properly Christian, or Protestant, or Catholic, or anything they choose. This is a matter of belief. A person may justify this argument by pointing out that Christianity is the most important religion in U.S. history, or that the clear majority of Americans are Christian. These statements may be true, but, for as long as they have been true, America has also been a nation dedicated to the idea that true freedom requires absolute freedom of religion. Any person in the United States is free to believe or not believe, or to practice or not practice as he or she sees fit. Therefore, all religions are American religions and none of them are. This is not an activist statement, nor a statement about what America *should* be, but rather, an explanation of how constitutional law defines American religious identity.

The Muslim Problem

Islam, Christianity, and Judaism are all sister religions that share numerous characteristics and are all considered branches of the Abrahamic Faiths, a group of religions that all developed from the same roots. All three religions utilize the Old Testament to some degree and some of the same figures appear in all three faiths, such as the biblical, Judaic, and Koranic figure Abraham.

In 2018, approximately one quarter of all people (1.8 billion) were Muslim. Islam is the world's second largest religion and the world's fastest-growing faith. The Southeast Asian nation of Indonesia houses the world's largest Muslim population, followed by India, followed by the nations of the Asia-Pacific region. With a population of 1.8 billion spanning the globe, it is not surprising that Islam has become very diverse.[304] For instance, many Americans may not be aware that Islam has been part of the culture of China for 1,400 years, having been brought to China along the Silk Road. There, the Chinese Hui Muslims of Henan Province created a respected branch of Chinese martial arts that produced famous styles like Xinyi Liuhe Quan (literally—Fist of Mind, Intention, and Six Harmonies) and Qi Shi Quan (Boxing of Seven Postures).

In the United States, Islam is not well known or understood. A Pew Research study found that 25 percent of Americans say they know nothing at all about the religion, whereas an additional 30 percent say they know "little" about Islam.[305] Despite a general lack of familiarity, ever since the 9/11 terrorist attacks and subsequent U.S. efforts to eliminate terrorism around the world, fear of Muslims has spread through the United States population. As of 2017, 41 percent of Americans believe that Islam encourages violence. A slight majority of Americans (52 percent) disagree and believe that Islam does not encourage violence to a greater degree than any other religion.[306]

Since 9/11, there has been an active lobby in the United States to portray Islam itself as the cause of terrorism and to suggest that the United States is involved in an ideological war between Islam and Christianity, or between Islamism and Democracy. This has led to many different reactionary proposals, such as closing mosques in the United States, prohibiting Muslim immigration, deporting all Muslims from the United States, etc. This general attitude is reflected in a variety of ways, including the rise of anti-Islam groups like "Stop the Islamization of America" and in hate crimes against Muslims in the United States. A 2017 Pew Research report found that 2016 had the highest number of attacks against Muslims since 2001 (right after the 9/11 terrorist attacks), with 127 attacks on Muslims reported in 2016 (versus 93 in 2001). By contrast, in 2000 there were only 12 recorded attacks.[307]

Social scientists believe that perhaps 0.01 to 0.1 percent of the world's Muslims might be involved or sympathetic to radical right-wing militant action or violence. The remaining 99.9 to 99.99 percent of the world's Muslims are, therefore, not radicals and research indicates, in general,

that Muslims tend to be at least as critical if not more critical of attacks against civilians for any purpose. For instance, Gallup Polls in 2010 and 2011 found that 89 percent of Muslims in America believe it is never justified for an individual or group to target civilians, whereas only 71 percent of Protestants and 71 percent of Catholics shared this same view. Similarly, the report found that 78 percent of American Muslims believed it was never justified for the military to target civilians, whereas many of both Protestants (58 percent) and Catholics (58 percent) believed that it was sometimes justified for the military to target civilians.[308]

Radicalism is the result of a perceived threat against one's culture or identity and, in the twenty-first century, many radical groups around the world can be described as having adopted far-right ideologies. This is reflected, in the United States, in the recent spike in white nationalist and neo-Nazi violence. Americans, however, have been led to believe that most terrorism is Islamic in nature and therefore connected to immigration. For instance, on February 28, 2017, Donald Trump made this statement in his first congressional address:

> *"Our obligation is to serve, protect, and defend the citizens of the United States. We are also taking strong measures to protect our nation from radical Islamic terrorism. (Applause.) According to data provided by the Department of Justice, the vast majority of individuals convicted of terrorism and terrorism-related offenses since 9/11 came here from outside of our country."*[309]

Researchers have found, however, that between 2001 and 2016, 74 percent of all terrorist attacks in the United States were committed by white, far-right extremists. Even of the Islamic radical attacks in the United States, 85 percent of the attacks recorded in this time were committed by

U.S. citizens. Far-right radicalism, and domestic radicalism are, therefore, the primary U.S. terrorist threat in 2018, rather than foreign Islamic radicalism.[310]

Dylann Roof, the white nationalist who killed nine African American people in a Charleston, South Carolina Church in 2015, was not targeting those he believed had personally aggrieved him but was making a political statement about the perceived threat to white culture or identity through the diversification of America. Roof is, thus, a terrorist using violence against civilians to send a political message. Like Roof, many of those who take part in Islamic terrorist cells see their culture and identities under threat. That this has become more common in the twenty-first century is because traditionalist, fundamentalist, and far-right ideologies are becoming less common. At one time in history, white, Christian men felt that they were the dominant group in the United States, just as for much of history, Muslim fundamentalists occupied a privileged place in the cultures of some predominantly Muslim nations. Progressive political movements around the world, and the increasing cultural exchange between nations, have threatened the dominance of these groups; and these groups, having no legitimate method to fight back against this threat, resort to attacks on civilians in the effort to make a political statement.

This cycle of violence has not been one-sided. The United States military and its allies have killed thousands of noncombatant Muslim civilians in their effort to defeat terrorist cells. Whether this is justified is a matter of debate, but it means that there are many Muslims living around the world whose relatives, friends, and families have been killed by American military and CIA drone strikes. Researchers have found evidence that drone strikes used to target radicals in Syria, Pakistan, Iraq, and Afghanistan often occur outside of war zones in residential areas. Researcher Bill Roggio, who has made an extensive study of U.S. drone strikes believes

that civilian casualties could make up between 5 and 20 percent of those killed by the strikes, which is primarily because there is no clear way to differentiate between civilians and radical targets when conducting a strike.[311]

The essential point is there are many different types of violent radical ideology and that any religious or ideological belief, be it Islam, Christianity, white nationalism, black nationalism, or left-wing extremism, can become violent and used as justification for terrorism. The clear majority of Islamic terrorist attacks have targeted other Muslims and the fight to defeat these groups has been primarily Muslim-against-Muslim, with the United States playing only a minor role. For instance, the fight against the military group known as the Islamic State in Iraq (ISIL) has been led by Iraqi Muslims who support the secular government and by Muslim Kurdish Peshmerga fighters. These are Muslims who object to the violence of Islamic extremists and are fighting to remove these groups from their countries and communities. By contrast, the several thousand troops that the United States has dedicated to these struggles constitute a vanishingly small contribution to the global conflict.

Travel Ban or Muslim Ban

Donald Trump's statements have indicated that he believes Islam and Muslims (in general) are a threat to U.S. culture. This was first evident in his criticisms of President Barack Obama and in Trump's insinuations that Obama is secretly Muslim.

On March 30, 2011, in a radio interview, Donald Trump said about the President Barack Obama:

> *"He doesn't have a birth certificate, or if he does, there's something on that certificate that is very bad for him. Now, somebody told me—and I have no idea if this is bad for him or not, but perhaps it*

would be—that where it says 'religion,' it might have 'Muslim.' And if you're a Muslim, you don't change your religion, by the way."

On December 7, 2015, Trump's campaign issued this statement:

_____ "Donald J. Trump is calling for a total and complete shutdown of Muslims entering the United States until our country's representatives can figure out what is going on."

On March 22, 2016, Trump said to Fox Business:

_____ "We're having problems with the Muslims, and we're having problems with Muslims coming into the country. You have to deal with the mosques, whether we like it or not, I mean, you know, these attacks aren't coming out of—they're not done by Swedish people."[312]

Many Americans feel that these statements reveal the genesis and purpose of Donald Trump's travel ban proposals. Shortly after winning the election, Donald Trump asked former New York Mayor Rudy Giuliani to help create a Muslim ban that would meet legal scrutiny. Giuliani, realizing that U.S. law would prohibit a ban based entirely on religion, suggested that the administration should target countries where active radical violence has occurred, thus promoting the ban as a matter of national security, rather than an ideological prohibition.

On January 27, 2017, shortly after assuming the presidency, Trump issued an Executive Order (EO) banning foreign nationals from seven predominantly Muslim countries from visiting the country. The EO also completely suspended the entry of all Syrian refugees and prohibited all

refugee immigration for 120 days. The EO was met with nationwide protests, and the American Civil Liberties Union (ACLU) took the issue to the courts, seeking an injunction to prevent immigration officials from deporting Muslims trapped by the ban. On January 29, a New York Federal Court granted the first of these injunctions. Four additional injunctions were granted in subsequent days by other courts. Washington Attorney General Bob Ferguson filed a lawsuit on January 30 seeking to have several provisions of the EO declared unconstitutional. On March 3, the issue came before Federal Judge James Robart in Seattle, who agreed with Attorney General Bob Ferguson that the EO was unconstitutional because it targeted persons based on their religious beliefs. The Department of Justice appealed the ruling, but an appeals court concurred with Robart, and the first phase of the Muslim ban was defeated.

On March 6, the Trump administration tried again with a revised EO that removed Iraq from the list of banned countries along with several other changes. On March 15, District Judge Derrick Watson of Hawaii blocked the Executive Order before it could take effect. Though there were many considerations in Justice Watson's opinion on the case, he cited the Establishment Clause as the primary constitutional block to the proposed ban.

_____ *"The clearest command of the Establishment Clause is that one religious denomination cannot be officially preferred over another...To determine whether the executive order runs afoul of that command, the Court is guided by the three-part test for Establishment Clause claims set forth in* Lemon v. Kurtzman, *403 U.S., 602, 612-13 (1971). According to* Lemon, *government action (1) must have a primary secular purpose, (2) may not have the principal effect of advancing or inhibiting religion, and (3) may not foster excessive entanglement with religion...Because the Executive Order at issue here cannot survive the secular purpose prong, the Court does not reach the balance of the criteria."*[313]

The administration initially called for appeal but failed to find a judicial authority who would support the ban. The Supreme Court agreed to hear the case, but the administration later withdrew the second version of the EO from consideration, and the Supreme Court, therefore, did not hear arguments on the merit of the order. The Muslim Ban was then retooled again, creating what was called "Muslim Ban 3.0," released on September 24, 2017. This time more non-Muslim countries, like Venezuela and North Korea, were added to the list, though the Executive Order still targeted Muslim majority countries primarily. The ACLU again appeared in Maryland arguing against the ban. On October 17, 2017 the third version of the ban was rejected in a Hawaii District Court ruling, blocking enforcement of the order. In February of 2018, the U.S. Court of Appeals for Virginia similarly determined that the third travel ban was unconstitutional.[314] As of February 2018, the case was awaiting Supreme Court review.

Ironically, had Trump not openly espoused his belief that Muslims should be prohibited from entering the United States, the travel bans since proposed may have met judicial scrutiny.

Prior to Trump's first Muslim ban EO, some polling organizations had found a slight majority in support of the ban. After the first order was issued, polls showed a small majority opposed to the ban, with a CNN/ORC Poll finding 53 percent of Americans opposed the ban, whereas a Gallup Poll found a more significant shift, with 55 percent opposed and 42 percent approving. However, by July, opinion had shifted again, with a small majority again supporting the EO according to some polls. In general, Republicans were broadly supportive, whereas Democrats were broadly opposed across all polls.[315]

Though public support may influence governmental action, it is not the key issue in the Muslim ban case. The key issue is whether the Executive Order is constitutional and whether the Trump Administration can convince the courts that the reasons for the ban are secular and not based on religion. So far, no court has found that the administration is able to prove secular motives for the ban and, thus, it has failed to win legal support. Even if the Supreme Court rules to allow the travel ban to go into effect, such a ruling will be highly controversial and will meet with, at most, the approval of a minority of the American public. America has, in the past, restricted immigration based on ideology, and there is precedent for this kind of immigration reform. However, over time, the legal opinion on this type of immigration order has changed. Jurists and legal experts now more often see these types of policies as discriminatory and ineffective in the effort to protect national security.

Religious Tolerance

Many historians have helped to elucidate the history of racial tolerance and violence in the United States. At one point, when there were virtually no Muslims or Jews living in the United States, religious zealots targeted Catholics as the undesirable religious radicals of the era. Discrimination against Catholics lasted for centuries, with prohibitions on Catholics running for office, attempts to ban the immigration of Catholics, and violent riots targeting Catholic churches and citizens.

Anti-Catholic prejudice in the 1800s was very similar to Muslim prejudice in the 2018. For instance, the 1834 book *The Awful Disclosures of Maria Monk*, a fake memoir supposedly written by a Canadian Catholic, claimed that Catholics killed babies and had secret sexual slavery rings. Lyman Beecher, co-founder of the American Temperance Society conducted a mass campaign against the Catholics in the 1840s, warning that they would take American jobs and spread disease and commit crimes. In the 1900s, the Ku Klux Klan targeted Catholics, Jews, immigrants, and black Americans, all of whom were seen as a threat to the hegemony of the ruling class, then defined not just as white Americans, but as white Protestant Americans of Western and Northern European descent.[316] One of the common complaints against Catholics, from the 1700s to the 1960s, was that they were radicals. The fact that Catholics had been behind revolutionary movements in Ireland (against Britain) and in Germany, and in Mexico, bolstered the claim that Catholicism was an inherently dangerous and antiestablishment branch of Christianity.

This article from a 2010 issue of *Smithsonian Magazine* explores religion among the colonists and later revolutionaries who founded the United States, as well as the many historic conflicts that prove even within a nation enshrining freedom of religion, that the issue was always contentious:

AMERICA'S TRUE HISTORY OF RELIGIOUS TOLERANCE
by Kenneth C. Davis
Smithsonian Magazine, October 2010
Source Document

Wading into the controversy surrounding an Islamic center planned for a site near New York City's Ground Zero memorial this past August, President Obama declared: "This is America. And our commitment to religious freedom must be unshakeable. The principle that people of all faiths are welcome in this country and that they will not be treated differently by their government is essential to who we are." In doing so, he paid homage to a vision that politicians and preachers have extolled for more than two centuries—that America historically has been a place of religious tolerance. It was a sentiment George Washington voiced shortly after taking the oath of office just a few blocks from Ground Zero.

But is it so?

In the storybook version most of us learned in school, the Pilgrims came to America aboard the *Mayflower* in search of religious freedom in 1620. The Puritans soon followed, for the same reason. Ever since these religious dissidents arrived at their shining "city upon a hill," as their governor John Winthrop called it, millions from around the world have done the same, coming to an America where they found a welcome melting pot in which everyone was free to practice his or her own faith.

continued

The problem is that this tidy narrative is an American myth. The real story of religion in America's past is an often awkward, frequently embarrassing and occasionally bloody tale that most civics books and high-school texts either paper over or shunt to the side. And much of the recent conversation about America's ideal of religious freedom has paid lip service to this comforting tableau.

From the earliest arrival of Europeans on America's shores, religion has often been a cudgel, used to discriminate, suppress and even kill the foreign, the "heretic" and the "unbeliever"—including the "heathen" natives already here. Moreover, while it is true that the clear majority of early-generation Americans were Christian, the pitched battles between various Protestant sects and, more explosively, between Protestants and Catholics, present an unavoidable contradiction to the widely held notion that America is a "Christian nation."

First, a little overlooked history: the initial encounter between Europeans in the future United States came with the establishment of a Huguenot (French Protestant) colony in 1564 at Fort Caroline (near modern Jacksonville, Florida). More than half a century before the *Mayflower* set sail, French pilgrims had come to America in search of religious freedom.

The Spanish had other ideas. In 1565, they established a forward operating base at St. Augustine and proceeded to wipe out the Fort Caroline colony. The Spanish commander, Pedro Menéndez de Avilés, wrote to the Spanish King Philip II that he had "hanged all those we had found in [Fort Caroline] because...they were scattering the odious Lutheran doctrine in these Provinces." When hundreds of survivors of a shipwrecked French fleet washed up on the beaches of Florida, they were put to the sword, beside a river the Spanish called Matanzas ("slaughters"). In other words, the first encounter between European Christians in America ended in a blood bath.

The much-ballyhooed arrival of the Pilgrims and Puritans in New England in the early 1600s was indeed a response to persecution that these religious dissenters had experienced in England. But the Puritan fathers of the Massachusetts Bay Colony did not countenance tolerance of opposing religious views. Their "city upon a hill" was a theocracy that brooked no dissent, religious or political.

The most famous dissidents within the Puritan community, Roger Williams and Anne Hutchinson, were banished following disagreements over theology and policy. From Puritan Boston's earliest days, Catholics ("Papists")

America's True History of Religious Tolerance
continued

were anathema and were banned from the colonies, along with other non-Puritans. Four Quakers were hanged in Boston between 1659 and 1661 for persistently returning to the city to stand up for their beliefs.

Throughout the colonial era, Anglo-American antipathy toward Catholics—especially French and Spanish Catholics—was pronounced and often reflected in the sermons of such famous clerics as Cotton Mather and in statutes that discriminated against Catholics in matters of property and voting. Anti-Catholic feelings even contributed to the revolutionary mood in America after King George III extended an olive branch to French Catholics in Canada with the Quebec Act of 1774, which recognized their religion.

When George Washington dispatched Benedict Arnold on a mission to court French Canadians' support for the American Revolution in 1775, he cautioned Arnold not to let their religion get in the way. "Prudence, policy and a true Christian Spirit," Washington advised, "will lead us to look with compassion upon their errors, without insulting them." (After Arnold betrayed the American cause, he publicly cited America's alliance with Catholic France as one of his reasons for doing so.)

In newly independent America, there was a crazy quilt of state laws regarding religion. In Massachusetts, only Christians were allowed to hold public office, and Catholics were allowed to do so only after renouncing papal authority. In 1777, New York State's constitution banned Catholics from public office (and would do so until 1806). In Maryland, Catholics had full civil rights, but Jews did not. Delaware required an oath affirming belief in the Trinity. Several states, including Massachusetts and South Carolina, had official, state-supported churches.

In 1779, as Virginia's governor, Thomas Jefferson had drafted a bill that guaranteed legal equality for citizens of all religions—including those of no religion—in the state. It was around then that Jefferson famously wrote, "But it does me no injury for my neighbor to say there are twenty gods or no God. It neither picks my pocket nor breaks my leg." But Jefferson's plan did not advance—until after Patrick ("Give Me Liberty or Give Me Death") Henry introduced a bill in 1784 calling for state support for "teachers of the Christian religion."

Future President James Madison stepped into the breach. In a carefully argued essay titled "Memorial and Remonstrance Against Religious Assessments," the soon-to-be father of

continued

the Constitution eloquently laid out reasons why the state had no business supporting Christian instruction. Signed by some 2,000 Virginians, Madison's argument became a fundamental piece of American political philosophy, a ringing endorsement of the secular state that "should be as familiar to students of American history as the Declaration of Independence and the Constitution," as Susan Jacoby has written in *Freethinkers*, her excellent history of American secularism.

Among Madison's 15 points was his declaration that "the Religion then of every man must be left to the conviction and conscience of every... man to exercise it as these may dictate. This right is in its nature an inalienable right."

Madison also made a point that any believer of any religion should understand: that the government sanction of a religion was, in essence, a threat to religion. "Who does not see," he wrote, "that the same authority which can establish Christianity, in exclusion of all other Religions, may establish with the same ease any particular sect of Christians, in exclusion of all other Sects?" Madison was writing from his memory of Baptist ministers being arrested in his native Virginia.

As a Christian, Madison also noted that Christianity had spread in the face of persecution from worldly powers, not with their help. Christianity, he contended, "disavows a dependence on the powers of this world...for it is known that this Religion both existed and flourished, not only without the support of human laws, but in spite of every opposition from them."

Recognizing the idea of America as a refuge for the protester or rebel, Madison also argued that Henry's proposal was "a departure from that generous policy, which offering an Asylum to the persecuted and oppressed of every Nation and Religion, promised a lustre to our country."

After long debate, Patrick Henry's bill was defeated, with the opposition outnumbering supporters 12 to 1. Instead, the Virginia legislature took up Jefferson's plan for the separation of church and state. In 1786, the Virginia Act for Establishing Religious Freedom, modified somewhat from Jefferson's original draft, became law. The act is one of three accomplishments Jefferson included on his tombstone, along with writing the Declaration and founding the University of Virginia. (He omitted his presidency of the United States.) After the bill was passed, Jefferson proudly wrote that the law "meant to comprehend, within the mantle of its protection, the Jew, the Gentile, the Christian and the

America's True History of Religious Tolerance
continued

Mahometan, the Hindoo and Infidel of every denomination."

Madison wanted Jefferson's view to become the law of the land when he went to the Constitutional Convention in Philadelphia in 1787. And as framed in Philadelphia that year, the U.S. Constitution clearly stated in Article VI that federal elective and appointed officials "shall be bound by Oath or Affirmation, to support this Constitution, but no religious Test shall ever be required as a Qualification to any Office or public Trust under the United States."

This passage—along with the facts that the Constitution does not mention God or a deity (except for a pro forma "year of our Lord" date) and that its very first amendment forbids Congress from making laws that would infringe of the free exercise of religion—attests to the founders' resolve that America be a secular republic. The men who fought the Revolution may have thanked Providence and attended church regularly—or not. But they also fought a war against a country in which the head of state was the head of the church. Knowing well the history of religious warfare that led to America's settlement, they clearly understood both the dangers of that system and of sectarian conflict.

It was the recognition of that divisive past by the founders—notably Washington, Jefferson, Adams and Madison—that secured America as a secular republic. As president, Washington wrote in 1790: "All possess alike liberty of conscience and immunity of citizenship. ...For happily the Government of the United States, which gives to bigotry no sanction, to persecution no assistance requires only that they who live under its protection should demean themselves as good citizens."

He was addressing the members of America's oldest synagogue, the Touro Synagogue in Newport, Rhode Island (where his letter is read aloud every August). In closing, he wrote specifically to the Jews a phrase that applies to Muslims as well: "May the children of the Stock of Abraham, who dwell in this land, continue to merit and enjoy the good will of the other inhabitants, while every one shall sit in safety under his own vine and figtree, and there shall be none to make him afraid."

As for Adams and Jefferson, they would disagree vehemently over policy, but on the question of religious freedom they were united. "In their seventies," Jacoby writes, "with a friendship that had survived serious political

continued

conflicts, Adams and Jefferson could look back with satisfaction on what they both considered their greatest achievement—their role in establishing a secular government whose legislators would never be required, or permitted, to rule on the legality of theological views."

Late in his life, James Madison wrote a letter summarizing his views: "And I have no doubt that every new example, will succeed, as every past one has done, in shewing that religion & Govt. will both exist in greater purity, the less they are mixed together."

While some of America's early leaders were models of virtuous tolerance, American attitudes were slow to change. The anti-Catholicism of America's Calvinist past found new voice in the 19th century. The belief widely held and preached by some of the most prominent ministers in America was that Catholics would, if permitted, turn America over to the pope. Anti-Catholic venom was part of the typical American school day, along with Bible readings. In Massachusetts, a convent—coincidentally near the site of the Bunker Hill Monument—was burned to the ground in 1834 by an anti-Catholic mob incited by reports that young women were being abused in the convent school. In Philadelphia, the City of Brotherly Love, anti-Catholic sentiment, combined with the country's anti-immigrant mood, fueled the Bible Riots of 1844, in which houses were torched, two Catholic churches were destroyed and at least 20 people were killed.

At about the same time, Joseph Smith founded a new American religion—and soon met with the wrath of the mainstream Protestant majority. In 1832, a mob tarred and feathered him, marking the beginning of a long battle between Christian America and Smith's Mormonism. In October 1838, after a series of conflicts over land and religious tension, Missouri Governor Lilburn Boggs ordered that all Mormons be expelled from his state. Three days later, rogue militiamen massacred 17 church members, including children, at the Mormon settlement of Haun's Mill. In 1844, a mob murdered Joseph Smith and his brother Hyrum while they were jailed in Carthage, Illinois. No one was ever convicted of the crime.

Even as late as 1960, Catholic presidential candidate John F. Kennedy felt compelled to make a major speech declaring that his loyalty was to America, not the pope. (And as recently as the 2008 Republican primary campaign, Mormon candidate Mitt Romney felt compelled to address the suspicions still directed toward the Church of Jesus Christ of Latter-

America's True History of Religious Tolerance
continued

day Saints.) Of course, America's anti-Semitism was practiced institutionally as well as socially for decades. With the great threat of "godless" Communism looming in the 1950s, the country's fear of atheism also reached new heights.

America can still be, as Madison perceived the nation in 1785, "an Asylum to the persecuted and oppressed of every Nation and Religion." But recognizing that deep religious discord has been part of America's social DNA is a healthy and necessary step. When we acknowledge that dark past, perhaps the nation will return to that "promised...lustre" of which Madison so grandiloquently wrote.[317]

Freedom of religion has always been difficult for some Americans to accept and the attempts to prohibit or persecute Catholics, Jews, and Muslims demonstrate that this is still an ongoing undercurrent of American thought. It is important to understand that all religious groups in the United States tend to develop unique approaches to their faiths that reflect broader American philosophy and ideals. On issues of freedom and equality, American Muslims are similar if not more liberal in some cases than other religious groups. For instance, more Muslims (52 percent) believe that homosexuality should be accepted in American society than Evangelical Christians (36 percent), which is the largest religious group in the United States, comprising 25.4 percent of all religious adherents.[318] In terms of patriotism, members of all faiths are similar, with a *Pew Research* study in 2017 finding that 92 percent of American Muslims agreed that they were "proud to be American."

Unless Americans plan to change the Constitution to either abolish freedom of religion or to prohibit the Islamic faiths, or plan to conduct religious cleansing to remove the nation's 3.4 million Muslims, then Islam will remain a part of the United States and a contributor to U.S. culture. That some object to this is well documented, but the capability to change this fact is not within the power of those groups currently.

In an interview, Trump said.

> *"I think Islam hates us. There's a tremendous hatred there. They want to change your religion."*

Contrary to the Trump administration's stated fears of lax immigration policy leading to Islamic radicalism on American soil, Bernard Haykel, Princeton University expert on terrorism and religious radicalism, argues that American Muslims are better integrated than in much of Europe, and that this accounts for the fact that there have been fewer Islamic terrorist attacks in the United States than in France or Britain. Former FBI Director James Comey told the *Los Angeles Times* that the FBI efforts to stop extremist violence has been successful largely because Muslim Americans provide information to the FBI on possible extremist plots and activities. According to Comey:

> *"They do not want people committing violence, either in their community or in the name of their faith."*[319]

If experts like Haykel and Comey are correct, the best way to prevent extremism is to try and integrate members of the Muslim faith into the United States and to stand behind the principal that any one, of any faith, creed, or culture, can become American so long as they are willing to embrace the nation and its laws.

President Trump presides over a bi-partisan meeting about immigration, Cabinet Room, 2018, by Chip Somodevilla/Getty Images

CONCLUSION

The Trump administration's travel ban, if approved by the U.S. Supreme Court, will likely not receive support from a majority of Americans. Resistance to the ban demonstrates that fewer Americans in 2018 are comfortable with this kind of immigration policy than in the past, when bans on ideologies like communism and socialism met with widespread approval. The travel ban debate is evidence of the increasingly progressive American attitudes about immigration overall. The Trump administration's immigration agenda faces constitutional challenges, a lack of majority support, and widespread protests.

DISCUSSION QUESTIONS

- Are Muslims a threat to national security? Explain.
- How does communication from politicians over social media affect public opinion on immigration?
- Should the United States welcome Syrian refugees from the Syrian Civil War? Why or why not? Does the fact that most of the Syrian refugees are Muslim influence your opinion on this issue? Explain.
- Are the travel ban proposals based on prejudice? Why or why not?

Works Used

"Bill of Rights of the United States of America (1791)." *Bill of Rights Institute*. Bill of Rights Institute. 2018.

Carroll, Rory. "America's dark and not-very-distant history of hating Catholics." *Guardian*. Guardian News and Media. 12 Sept. 2015.

Chapin, Laura. "Bigots Will Be Bigots." *U.S. News*. U.S. News and World Report. 6 Feb. 2017.

Davis, Kenneth C. "America's True History of Religious Tolerance." *Smithsonian*. Smithsonian Institution. Oct. 2010.

Friedersdorf, Conor. "The Obama Administration's Drone-Strike Dissembling." *The Atlantic*. Atlantic Monthly Group. 14 Mar. 2016.

Johnson, Jenna and Abigail Hauslohner. "'I think Islam hates us': A timeline of Trump's comments about Islam and Muslims." *The Washington Post*. Washington Post Co. 20 May 2017.

Kishi, Katayoun. "Assaults against Muslims in U.S. surpass 2001 level." *Pew Research*. Pew Research Center. 15 Nov. 2017.

Lipka, Michael. "Muslims and Islam: Key findings in the U.S. and around the world." *Pew Research Center*. Pew Research. Facttank. 9 Aug. 2017.

Liptak, Adam. "Trump's Latest Travel Ban Suffers Blow From a Second Appeals Court." *New York Times*. New York Times Co. 15 Feb. 2018.

McElroy, John Harmon. "Understanding the First Amendment's Religion Clauses." *ISI*. Intercollegiate Review. Intercollegiate Studies Institute. Spring 2011.

McManus, Doyle. "To avoid a Manchester-type bombing on American soil, integrate Muslims." *Los Angeles Times*. Los Angeles Times. 24 May 2017.

Mohamed, Besheer. "A new estimate of the U.S. Muslim population." *Pew Research*. Pew Research Center.6 Jan. 2016.

Naurath, Nicole. "Most Muslim Americans See No Justification for Violence." *Gallup News*. Gallup. 2 Aug. 2011.

"Public Remains Conflicted Over Islam." *Pew Research*. Pew Research Center. 24 Aug. 2010.

"Religious Landscape Study." *Pew Research*. Pew Research Center. 2018.

"State of Hawai'i and Ismael Elshickh Vs. Donald J. Trump, Et Al— Order." *ACLU*. American Civil Liberties Union. 2018.

Trump, Donald. "Remarks by President Trump in Joint Address to Congress." *White House*. Trump White House. 28 Feb. 2017.

Valverde, Miriam. "A look at the data on domestic terrorism and who's behind it." *Politifact*. Politifact, LLC. 16 Aug. 2017.

"Voters Say Islamic Leaders Should Do More to Promote Peace," *Rasmussen Reports*. Rasmussen Reports, LLC. 30 May 2017.

Wang, Amy B. "'Brave and selfless' Oregon stabbing victims hailed as heroes for standing up to racist rants." *The Washington Post*. Washington Post, Co. 28 May 2017.

Ideas about immigration run the gamut from those who believe the United States should be isolated from the nations of the world to radically liberal theories calling for a universal right to migrate. This diversity in attitudes and views complicates efforts to reach consensus and ultimately results in a situation wherein whatever policy a nation adopts, there is likely to be at least a large minority who disagree with the basic values and ideals that such a policy represents.

Are Immigrants Bad?

In the 1800s, anti-Chinese posters and publications warned that Chinese laborers were being shipped in to break strikes and were replacing black and Irish laborers on the railroads. It was said they were inherently criminal, feeling no moral compunction in thieving wages needed by native-born laborers, and that they were culturally degenerate, willing to sleep in cramped conditions and to eat rats and mice. These stereotypes were part of a propaganda campaign against not only Chinese immigrants, but the Chinese race and culture itself. By portraying Chinese people as morally deficient opportunists, pundits hoped to engender hatred of Chinese people and culture among laborers and the poor. By depicting them as culturally immoral and alien, pundits engendered the belief that Chinese culture and American culture were incompatible. By depicting Chinese people as inherently unethical and as potentially disease ridden, pundits engendered hatred of Chinese people among those concerned about crime and public safety.

The "Chinese problem," as it is often described, was thus portrayed in such a way as to make the Chinese the enemy of the nation, of morality, of American ideals, of the labor movement, and, in general, of America itself. The August 1869 poem "John Chinaman" demonstrates how the various threats posed by Chinese immigrants were used to create a broader perception of Chinese people as a unique threat to American identity:

> _____ *You sturdy tillers of the soil,*
> *Prepare to leave full soon;*
> *For when John Chinaman comes in*
> *You'll find there is not room.*
> *Like an Egyptian locust plague,*
> *Or like an eastern blight,*
> *He'll swarm you out of all your fields,*
> *And seize them as his right.*
> *Let the mechanics pack his traps,*
> *And ready make to flit;*
> *He cannot live on rats and mice,*
> *And so he needs must quit.*
> *At the full cost of a blood war,*
> *We've garnered in a race;*
> *One set of serfs of late we've freed,*
> *Another takes its place.*
> *Come friends, we'll have to leave this land*
> *To nobles and to slaves;*
> *For, if John Chinaman come in,*
> *For us—there's only graves.*[320]

Racial prejudice aside, these claims are:
1. Immigrants take jobs from Americans and drain the economy;
2. Immigrants cannot assimilate into American culture; and
3. Immigrants are criminal or morally bereft.

These are essentially the same arguments used against immigrants in 2018. Historians have found that the arrival of Chinese migrants in 1800s California did not result in anything resembling the economic

depression or job shortages that anti-immigration activists feared and claimed was already happening. Are these claims any truer now than they were in 1882?

Immigrants in the Workforce

Of the 465 occupations listed by the Bureau of Labor, immigrants constitute a majority of the workforce in only four fields, and those four, collectively, account for only 1 percent of the U.S. labor market. Even in these majority-immigrant fields, native-born workers still constitute nearly half (47 percent) of the workforce.

Jobs stereotypically thought to be "immigrant jobs" are actually more fully-staffed by native-born workers:

- Maids and housekeepers: 55 percent native-born;
- Taxi drivers and chauffeurs: 58 percent native-born;
- Grounds maintenance workers and gardeners: 65 percent native-born;
- Porters, bellhops, and concierges: 71 percent native born; and
- Janitors: 75 percent native born.[321]

Trump advisor Stephen Miller told reporters in 2017:

"We've seen significant reductions in wages for blue-collar workers, massive displacement of African-American and Hispanic workers, as well as the displacement of immigrant workers from previous years who oftentimes compete directly against new arrivals who are being paid even less."

Miller was asked to provide evidence, and cited a paper by Harvard economist George Borjas, who produced a study of the 1980 Mariel Boatlift. Borjas focused specifically on the effect of the influx of Cuban immigrants on the job market and wages for teenage high-school drop-outs and found that wages for these workers fell by 10–30 percent on the short term. Princeton economist David Card found evidence of this same trend in his 1990 study of the Mariel Boatlift, but studied the entire labor market, rather than focusing on a more narrow group of workers. Card found that the economic impact of the Boatlift was minimal and temporary, after which the influx of immigrants stimulated significant growth in the local economy, ultimately creating jobs and diversifying the market.

The use of the Mariel Boatlift as evidence that immigrants harm the economy is not ideal. Between April and October of 1980, 125,000 Cubans migrated to Florida. It was a major humanitarian crisis, and not simply a matter of migration. With such a large number settling in a small area, over such a short period of time, the effects of the influx were exacerbated and yet, even in this extreme situation, the Boatlift had an overall positive effect on the economy. That some groups experienced a negative impact has been demonstrated, but does not speak to the overall impact of immigration itself, but rather, to the unintended consequences of extreme surges of immigration into limited geographic markets.[322]

A study released in 2016 by the National Academies of Sciences, from a team headed by Cornell University economist Francine D. Blau, found that, overall, immigrants cause little to no negative effect for wages and employment of native-born workers. Blau and colleagues found that immigration can depress the wages for some groups over the short term but argue that these temporary negative effects are more than compensated by long-term economic growth and market diversification.

It has been suggested that immigrants drain federal resources, putting a strain on the welfare system. The same 2016 Cornell study found two things: first, that legal immigrants, who are eligible for some federal aid benefits, access such services at a far lower rate than

native-born citizens. Second, undocumented migrants, who cannot legally access welfare benefits, still contribute to the system through taxes, but do not take a significant amount out of the system. Two research organizations examining undocumented migrants in 2010 found that they pay between $12 and $17.6 billion in taxes *into* the social security system without being able to access the benefits of the system themselves. [323] This means that removing all undocumented migrants from the nation would essentially mean $12–17 billion less for social security each year, with the same number of persons eligible for benefits.

In April of 2017, a group of 1,470 economists wrote an open letter to Donald Trump, Paul Ryan, and other GOP leaders who'd voiced support for Trump's nativist, 1800s-style immigration reform proposals, stating that immigration does far more good for the economy than it does harm. Four specific points were made explicit in the letter:

- Immigration brings entrepreneurs who start new businesses that hire American workers.
- Immigration brings young workers who help offset the large-scale retirement of baby boomers.
- Immigration brings diverse skill sets that keep our workforce flexible, help companies grow, and increase the productivity of American workers.
- Immigrants are far more likely to work in innovative, job-creating fields such as science, technology, engineering, and math that create life-improving products and drive economic growth.[324]

Although it is documented that immigration can, in some circumstances and situations, depress wages or remove jobs that might otherwise go to American-born workers, the consensus among most of American economists is that immigrants provide far more benefit than detriment to the American economy.

Immigrants and Crime

The claim that immigrants are more prone to crime is often based on the idea that some races and nationalities are inherently criminal. Immigration critics argue that persons who come from poverty, or areas rife with crime, haven't learned how to behave in a lawful society.

The most recent comprehensive research on the subject comes from a 2015 study, "The Integration of Immigrants into American Society," by a group of researchers at the National Academy of Sciences (NAS). The study concluded that the perception that immigrants increase crime rates has been perpetuated by individuals referred to in the study as "issue entrepreneurs" who promote the idea specifically to drive support for restrictive immigration policies. The study acknowledged that more data and research was needed but argued that the statistical relationship between immigration and crime was conclusive. As per the report's conclusion:

> *"Far from immigration increasing crime rates, studies demonstrate that immigrants and immigration are associated inversely with crime. Immigrants are less likely than the native-born to commit crimes, and neighborhoods with greater concentrations of immigrants have much lower rates of crime and violence than comparable nonimmigrant neighborhoods. However, crime rates rise among the second and later generations, perhaps a negative consequence of adaptation to American society."*[325]

Another organization, the American Immigration Council, produced a research report in 2015 that demonstrated a negative correlation between immigration and crime at the national level. The researchers

found that between 1990 and 2013, the immigrant population was growing at a faster rate than at any time since the 1800s (from 7.9 percent to 13.1 percent of the overall population). During that same time, crime rates around the country declined by 48 percent.[326]

Immigrants and Assimilation

There is no general agreement how assimilation should be measured, or to what degree assimilation is important. Some studies indicate that immigrants assimilate into U.S. culture better than in some European nations, where immigrant populations remain more isolated and sometimes face more intense prejudice. Researchers have noted that the high degree to which American Muslims have assimilated into U.S. culture has been one of the most important factors in helping the FBI and police to combat terrorist attacks by radicalized Muslims.

Some sociologists have attempted to study assimilation by measuring the degree to which immigrants learn and use English. A 2013 study looked at German immigrants in the early 1900s and found that, even in the second generation, only 35 percent spoke English. By sharp contrast, more first-generation immigrants and new arrivals (50 percent) speak at least some English than even second-generation immigrants in 1900. By the second generation, more than 92 percent of Latino immigrants were fluent or near-fluent in English and most of the remaining 8 percent spoke at least some English in addition to their native language.[327]

Others have suggested that assimilation is about embracing American values. President Trump suggested that immigrants take an "ideological test" to determine if they would fit in with American culture. It would be difficult to distill American values in any more than a superficial way, given how little agreement there often is regarding what constitutes *American* values. For instance, is diversity a value? Many native-born Americans would not agree that it is. Is environmentalism a value? What about opposition to racism? What about gun rights?[328]

The Merit-Based System

President Trump has stated a desire to shift to a "merit-based" immigration system, offering the success of the Canadian and Australian merit-based immigration systems as proof of how well such a system works.

The following compares the three systems (U.S., Canada and Australia):

- Levels of immigration per capita: Each year, Canada admits a number of immigrants equal to 0.74 percent of its population, whereas Australia admits immigrants equaling 1.1 percent of its population. By contrast, under the current system, the United States admits 0.31 percent of the population each year.
- Levels of family-based immigration: In Canada, approximately 0.23 percent of all immigrants are admitted on a family-based basis, whereas 0.26 percent of Australian immigrants are also admitted based on family preference. In the United States, 0.23 percent of U.S. immigrants are admitted on the same basis.
- Number of workers: In Australia, 24 percent of immigrants admitted each year are workers, whereas 25 percent of immigrants to Canada are workers. By contrast, 0.04 percent of American immigrants migrate for work in the United States, despite claims of green-card workers taking a large share of American jobs.[329]
- Low-skilled and high-skilled workers: Canada and Australia do not focus only on high-skilled workers when determining who can migrate into the nation in their merit-based systems, but rather look for skills at every level of the economic spectrum. Each year, Canada also has a far higher percentage of visas given to untrained and agricultural workers than in the United States.[330]

The idea of merit-based immigration has bipartisan support and appeals to many Americans on an economic level, whereas others see the system as more egalitarian both to migrants and to native-born citizens. However, in both Canada and Australia, the merit-based systems work because both nations cast a wide net, looking for individuals with skills that might be needed at every level of their workforce. This is the way to utilize immigration to fuel growth; in general such policies do not reduce immigration, but encourage it.

The World Without Borders

Although there is rarely any agreement about how to reform immigration, it is generally agreed that every nation must carefully monitor and control its borders. But what if controlling the nation's borders *is* the problem?

The Universal Declaration of Human Rights (UDHR) was adopted at the United Nations General Assembly in Paris in 1948. Having emerged through World War II, the participating nations believed it was necessary to codify the universal rights that should be afforded to all humans. One of the rights included in the 1948 UDHR was the right to leave one's country. Consider a situation in which a person, living in a certain community, cannot find sustainable work, or is under threat of war, famine, or lawlessness. All people, according to the UDHR, should be free to leave this area to escape such a situation, but there is no corresponding right for such a person to go anywhere else.

Although politicians argue about merit-based, family-based, or skill-based immigration systems, all begin with the belief that it is necessary for a nation to restrict movement and then to filter and control the flow of people *in*, though not necessarily *out* of each nation. The need to control the borders is not the irrefutable result of a cost/benefit analysis, but merely an artifact of the prehistoric battle for control that tethered sovereignty to the physical control of one's population. Many believe that without border controls nations would be flooded by crime and their economies in shambles, but this belief is not often tested.

George Mason University economist Bryan Caplan believes that human beings should have a fundamental right to migrate. Caplan is the author of numerous research papers exploring the economics of global migration and has come to believe that "open borders," a proposal that would eliminate all restrictions to migration, could essentially end global poverty. Caplan's controversial theory is based on a simple idea that each market has shortages and surpluses of labor and that by allowing free movement each nation can fill shortages and alleviate surpluses. Caplan acknowledges that such a system would face many challenges. For instance, American workers who find work in Mexico might be unwilling to migrate for work because of political instability and violence and addressing these problems should be the focus, in Caplan's view. For example, American workers who agreed to fill Mexican labor shortages might be protected by a bilateral agreement that provided safety and security measures, supported by both nations agreeing to facilitate an exchange of laborers on a temporary or permanent basis.

Economist Michael Clemens is not a supporter of absolute "open borders," like Caplan, but his economic research on global labor patterns has led him to believe that immigration control does far more harm than good. Clemens believes in the potential of regional networks with open borders and economies between two or more nations, enabling far more liberal and unregulated movement of labor to better distribute labor skills among more societies and thus increase the potential for economic stability for a variety of those in need. Clemens believes that eliminating most or all immigration borders in the world

might increase the global domestic product by a conservative 67 to 147 percent. In a *Washington Post* article in 2016, Clemens said that if only 5 percent of those living in poor countries were allowed to work temporarily or permanently in richer countries, it would add trillions to the global economy and would be more effective at stimulating growth than removing every other barrier to trade and international investment.[331]

Some are concerned that open borders would increase crime or would leave the nation open to a terrorist attack. Others worry that open borders would be disastrous for native-born workers. These concerns might be justified, but not necessarily. Open borders supporters have generated numerous plans for how an open border society might cope with such issues. For one thing, an open borders policy does not mean open citizenship. The benefits of citizenship would be offered to those who make a deeper commitment to permanent residency beyond the need for work. Taxes might be higher on non-citizen workers so as to provide temporary or even long-term assistance to citizens suffering from fluctuations in the labor market. The extra revenue created by the overall growth in the economy, coupled with reduced investment in border protection, provides resources that might be used to strengthen national security and public safety. Given that immigrants typically contribute little to overall crime rates, open borders supporters argue that such a society would not result in lawlessness.[332]

The Morality of Immigration

Every economist and sociologist who supports the open borders idea also cites morality as among their chief reasons for being drawn to the concept. Researchers like Clemens and Caplan believe that the U.S. immigration system, currently, is an immoral institution.

To summarize a thought experiment presented in a blog post by University of Colorado Philosophy Professor Michael Huemer:

_____ *Imagine a situation in which a person, named Marvin, is attempting to reach a market to trade services for food. There are people in the market who have food to trade and want or need Martin's skills. However, Marvin's road to the market is blocked by Sam (who has many nieces and nephews). Sam has a weapon and threatens violence if Marvin doesn't leave. Marvin cannot access the marketplace and so starves and dies. Is Sam responsible for Marvin's death? By actively refusing to allow Marvin access to the market, has Sam killed Marvin?*

This thought experiment is a metaphor for the U.S. immigration system. The United States, the world's wealthiest nation by a wide degree, shares its southern border with a developing country in which millions are in need, are willing to work, and cannot access a market robust enough to trade sustainable wages for their labor. That the United States, by force, prevents those willing migrants from crossing the border where work is available, makes the nation a direct actor in the perpetuation of poverty in Mexico. Is the United States guilty of violating their human rights? Is the nation guilty of murder when one of those same migrants starves to death?[333]

Alex Tabarrok of George Mason University highlights the moral aspect of this debate, arguing that the closed borders of the world are one of

the humankind's greatest moral failings, consigning millions to poverty based on the chance of where and when they were born. Opening borders, Tabarrok argues, would be akin to eliminating slavery or granting women the right to vote, an expansion of humanity's fundamental moral commitment to one another.

In 2018, few politicians are actually considering anything as radical as open borders, but the idea raises interesting questions. For most of history, humans have defined their moral commitments by a certain set of borders. Those borders may extend to the bounds of one's body, one's house, one's neighborhood, one's state, one's nation, one's ideology, or one's race. One who believes that their allegiance should be to America first, before another country, or to Christians first, instead of Islam or Judaism, is choosing to define his or her moral commitment by a specific identity or ideology. Although this decision is not necessarily wrong or flawed, it is not the only way that people define the morality of their participation in the world. For some, the unity of humanity transcends one's national identity.

Apollo 14 Astronaut Edgar Mitchell told *Quartz Magazine* in 2015:

> *"Something happens to you out there. You develop an instant global consciousness, a people orientation, an intense dissatisfaction with the state of the world, and a compulsion to do something about it."*[334]

This has since been named the "Overview Effect," a psychological reaction to the sight of Earth from space that engenders a visceral sense of the fragility of the planet, the interconnectedness of people, and the illusory nature of the boundaries that alienate us. Similar revelations of global connectedness have been found to occur in those who engage in transcendental meditation or who have experienced spiritual visions. That all humans are kin, and that there is more that unites than divides one human from another, is a realization so ancient and profound that it is the basis for many the world's dominant religions. It is this view, the broader view, that fuels altruism and inspires the physician braving a foreign war zone, or the missionaries who open orphanages in at-risk communities, or the thousands who travel to help victims of natural disasters each year abroad.

Social scientists and historians have found that attitudes about immigration have become more progressive. Americans are now more likely than at any time in the past, to believe that immigrants are good for America and the world, rather than a detriment. It is no accident that this change has occurred alongside America's digital diversification and the globalization of culture. Increasingly, Americans are presented with the option to see themselves as more than just Americans, but as part of a global whole that transcends the traditional barriers between tribes. Ultimately it is that same ideal, the desire to build a new unity from disparate parts, that motivated the unification of America's colonies into a nation. Now, nations are increasingly becoming a world.

All of the fears that people have about immigration—that immigrants will steal jobs, commit crimes, or erode cultural values and American identity—are valid. So are the views of those who see immigration as a factor of America's global identity and morality and who wish to use immigration to create progressive change in the world. As always, the move to progress, tempered by the wisdom to conserve at each stage, will determine how the nation evolves in each new chapter. Whether America adopts restrictive or liberal immigration policies, the nation's existing diversity means that America will continue to become more diverse from within, and this also means that American values will continue to evolve.

Immigration reflects and shapes American identity and, ultimately, becomes a bridge between American culture and the cultures of the world. It is arguable that many of America's proudest achievements have been fueled by immigration. Nowhere is this more evident than in American art and popular culture, where the influences of America's interracial and intercultural mélange are pervasive and undeniable. It is arguable that the diversity of the American experience is what makes American art and culture so broadly appealing on the global sphere, imparting a unique character and emotional poignancy that reflects the triumphs and tribulations of the push and pull of cultural integration and isolation.

Works Used

"An Open Letter from 1,470 Economists on Immigration." *New American Economy*. New American Economy. 12 Apr. 2017.

Branson-Potts, Hailey. "Trump wants immigrants to 'share our values.' They say assimilation is much more complex." *LA Times*. Los Angeles Times. 11 Apr. 2017.

Camarota, Steven A., and Karen Zeigler. "Jobs Americans Won't Do? A Detailed Look at Immigrant Employment by Occupation." *CIS*. Center for Immigration Studies. 17 Aug. 2009.

Dolan, Eric W. "Studies find the need to feel unique is linked to belief in conspiracy theories." *PsyPost*. PsyPost. 8 Aug. 2017.

Ewing, Walter A., and Daniel E. Martínez. "The Criminalization of Immigration in the United States." *American Immigration Council*. Special Report. July 2015.

Goldhill, Olivia. "Astronauts report an 'overview effect' from the awe of space travel—and you can replicate it here on Earth." *Quartz*. Quartz Media. 6 Sept. 2015.

Heumer, Michael. "Is There a Right to Immigrate." *Social Theory and Practice*. Vol. 36, No. 3 (2010), pp. 429–61.

Kelly, Amita. "FACT CHECK: Have Immigrants Lowered Wages For Blue-Collar American Workers?" *NPR*. National Public Radio. 4 Aug. 2017.

"Low-Skilled Immigrants." *IGM Chicago*. IGM Forum. 10 Dec. 2013.

Nowrastex, Alex. "More Family-Based Immigrants in Australia & Canada than in the United States." *CATO*. Cato at Liberty. 11 Apr. 2017.

"Orrenius, Pia M., and Madeline Zavodny. "A Comparison of the U.S. and Canadian Immigration Systems." *NAS*. National Academies of Science. 22 Sept. 2014.

Preston, Julia. "Immigrants Aren't Taking Americans' Jobs, New Study Finds." *New York Times*. New York Times, Co. 21 Sept. 2016.

Raviv, Shaun. "If People Could Immigrate Anywhere, Would Poverty Be Eliminated?" *The Atlantic*. Atlantic Monthly Group. 26 Apr. 2013.

Swanson, Ana. "Opening up borders: An idea economists tend to love and politicians detest." *Washington Post*. Washington Post, Co. 14 Oct. 2016

Tchen, John Kuo Wei. *New York before Chinatown: Orientalism and the Shaping of American Culture: 1776–1882*. Baltimore, MD: The John Hopkins UP, 1999.

Waters, Mary C., and Marisa Gerstein Pineau (Eds.). "The Integration of Immigrants into American Society." *NAP*. National Academies Press. 2015.

Wilkerson, Miranda E., and Salmons, Joseph. "Linguistic Marginalities: Becoming American without Learning English." *Journal of Transnational American Studies*. 2012.

NOTES

1. Rosenbaum, "The Shocking Savagery of America's Early History."
2. Grizzard and Smith, *Jamestown Colony: A Political, Social, and Cultural History*.
3. Kimmel, "Does the Dakota Access Pipeline Violate Treaty Law?"
4. "Historical Record: 1614 Treaty," *Charles City County*.
5. "Conference between Governor Burnet and the Indians," *University of Nebraska*.
6. "Treaty With the Delawares: 1778," *Yale Law School*.
7. Capriccioso, "Illuminating the Treaties That Have Governed U.S.-Indian Relationships."
8. Schilling, "The True Story of Pocahontas."
9. "Statements from the Debate on Indian Removal," *Columbia University*. 2016.
10. Wang, "Broken Promises On Display At Native American Treaties Exhibit."
11. "What is Genocide?" *USHMM*. United States Holocaust Memorial Museum. Holocaust Encyclopedia. 2017.
12. Brauer and Caruso, "For Being Aboriginal," in Anderton, C.H. and Jurgen Brauer, eds. *Economic Aspects of Genocides, Other Mass Atrocities, and their Prevention*.
13. "H. Con. Res.331," *Senate.gov*.
14. Smith, "The Demographic History of Colonial New England."
15. Weissman, "U.S. Income Inequality: It's Worse Today Than It Was in 1774."
16. "Declaration of Independence: A Transcription," *National Archives*.
17. Calloway, "American Indians and the American Revolution."
18. "A Century of Lawmaking for a New Nation," *Library of Congress*, pp. 103–104.

19.   Mirrer, "As American as the Haitian Revolution."

20.   Paine, "Thoughts on the Present State of American Affairs."

21.   "Immigration Timeline," *Liberty Ellis Foundation.*

22.   Frank and Kramnick, "What 'Hamilton' Forgets About Hamilton."

23.   Magness, "Alexander Hamilton as Immigrant."

24.   "The XYZ Affair and the Quasi-War with France," *Office of the Historian.*

25.   Boyd, "American Federalism, 1776 to 1997."

26.   "A Century of Lawmaking for a New Nation," *Library of Congress*, pp. 597–598.

27.   "1798 Naturalization Act," University of Washington-Bothell Library.

28.   "1798 Alien Enemies Act," University of Washington-Bothell Library.

29.   Anderson, "When Criticizing The President Was Against The Law."

30.   Rollo, "Gerald of Wales' 'Topographia Hibernica': Sex and the Irish Nation."

31.   Friedman, "What Is a Nativist?"

32.   Bulik, "1854: No Irish Need Apply."

33.   O'Toole, *The Faithful*, p. 89.

34.   Donnelly, "The Irish Famine."

35.   Boissoneault, "How the 19th-Century Know-Nothing Party Reshaped American Politics."

36.   Hingston, "Bullets and Bigots: Remembering Philadelphia's 1844 Anti-Catholic Riots."

37.   O'Neil, "A look back-Irish immigrants fight back in 1854 nativist riots."

38.   Moses, "Irish-Americans: Remember from whence you came."

39.   Lind, "Why historians are fighting about "No Irish Need Apply" signs—and why it matters."

40.   LeMay and Barkan, *U.S. Immigration and Naturalization Laws and Issues,* p. 19.

41.   Blakemore, "Five Things to Know About the Declaration of Sentiments."

42.   "Declaration of Sentiments," *ECSSBA*.

43.   "Married Women's Property Laws," *Library of Congress*.

44.   Barkhorn, "Vote No on Women's Suffrage."

45.   "An Act to Secure the Right of Citizenship," *Library of Congress*.

46.   Flanagin, "For the last time, the American Civil War was not about states' rights."

47.   "Constitution of the Confederate States; March 11, 1861," *Yale Law School*.

48.   "Confederate States of America," *Yale Law School*.

49.   "A Brief History," *Civil War Trust*.

50.   Arrington, "Industry and Economy during the Civil War."

51.   Lincoln, "Speech to Germans at Cincinnati, Ohio."

52.   "Lincoln on the Know-Nothing Party," *National Park Service*.

53.   Hing, *Defining America: Through Immigration Policy,* p. 21.

54.   "An Act to Encourage Immigration," *New York Times.*

55.   Gugliotta, "New Estimate Raises Civil War Death Toll."

56.   Doyle, Don H. "The Civil War Was Won by Immigrant Soldiers."

57.   "Amendment XIV," *Cornell Law School*.

58.   "An Act to amend the Naturalization Laws," *Library of Congress*.

59.   Dudden, *Fighting Chance*, pp. 77–80.

60.   Kelly, Bold, & Raymond, *The Oxford History of Popular Print Culture, Vol 6*, pp. 254–256.

61.   "Amendment XV," *Cornell Law School*.

62.   "Minor v. Happersett," *Cornell Law School*.

63.   Gandhi, "A History of Indentured Labor Gives 'Coolie' It's Sting."

64.   Fuchs, "150 Years Ago, Chinese Railroad Workers Staged the Era's Largest Labor Strike."

65.   Singh, "A Chinaman's chance."

66.   Hollender, "The Harms of Regulation Phobia."

67.   Roosevelt, *A Square Deal*, p. 161

68.   Ambrose, *Nothing Like it in the World*, pp. 230–242.

69.   Goyette, "How Racism Created America's Chinatowns."

70.   Lynch, "Chinese Laborers Built Sonoma's Wineries. Racist Neighbors Drove Them Out."

71.   Bolenese, "3 Reasons Why Chinese Were the MVPs on the Railroad."

72.   Cottle, "Hoekstra Ad Revives Anti-Asian Strain in American Politics."

73.   Harte, "Plain Language from Truthful James."

74.   Weiner, "Pete Hoekstra's China ad provokes accusations of racism."

75.   Arnesen, *Encyclopedia of U.S. Labor and Working-class History, Vol 1*."

76.   Pfaelzer, *Driven Out*, pp. 36-37.

77.   "California's Anti-Coolie Act of 1862," *San Diego State University*.

78.   "An Act to Prohibit the 'Coolie Trade' by American Citizens," *Library of Congress*.

79.   Jue, "Anson Burlingame, an American Diplomat."

80.   "The Burlingame-Seward Treaty, 1868," *Department of State*.

81.   "Transcript of the Chinese Exclusion Act," *Our Documents*.

82.   "Chinese Immigration and the Chinese Exclusion Acts," *Department of State*.

83.   "The Strange Case of the Chinese Laundry," *Thirteen*.

84.   Goldin, Cameron, and Balarajan, *Exceptional People*, p. 58.

85.   *Laws of the State of New-York*, pp. 567–68.

86.   "Henderson v. Mayor of City of New York," *FindLaw*.

87.   Kramer, "The Case of the 22 Lewd Chinese Women."

88.   "Chy Lung v. Freeman," *FindLaw*.

89.   "1882 Immigration Act," *University of Washington-Bothell Library*.

90.   "Origins of the Federal Immigration Service," *USCIS*.

91.   Wills, "The Curious History of Ellis Island."

92.   Roberts, "Story of the First Through Ellis Island Is Rewritten."

93.   "Ellis Island History," *Liberty Ellis Foundation*.

94.   Waxman, "Ellis Island's Busiest Day Ever Was 110 Years Ago. Here's Why."

95.   Ha, Thu-Huong. "The story behind the Statue of Liberty's unexpected transformation into a beacon for refugees and immigrants."

96.   "The New Colossus—full text." *NPS*.

97.   "U.S. Immigration Station, Angel Island," *National Park Service*.

98.   "Angel Island Immigrant Journeys," *AIISF*.

99.   Chadwick, "When New York City was the prostitution capital of the US."

100. Grant, "When Prostitution Wasn't a Crime."

101. Chan, *Entry Denied*, pp. 94–98.

102. Dunn, "The Top Ten Daily Consequences of having Evolved."

103. Black, "Eugenics and the Nazis–the California connection."

104. DenHoed, "The Forgotten Lessons of the American Eugenics Movement."

105. Carrell, *Man, The Unknown*, p. 271.

106. Brignell, "When America believed in eugenics."

107. Cohen, "This Jigsaw Puzzle Was Given to Ellis Island Immigrants to Test Their Intelligence."

108. Saphier, "High Expectations Teaching," p. 20.

109. "Buck v. Bell," *Cornell Law School*.

110. Burrus, "One Generation of Oliver Wendell Holmes, Jr. Is Enough."

111. Greenberg, "Anarchy in the U.S."

112. Bricker, et al., "Changes in U.S. Family Finances from 2013 to 2016."

113. Bump, "How the Republican tax bill benefits the rich, according to government analysis."

114. Adelman, "The Haymarket Affair."

115. "Leon Czolgosz and the Trial," *University of Buffalo Libraries*.

116. Eschner, "How President William McKinley's Assassination Led to the Modern Secret Service."

117. "American Affairs: The Attempt Upon the President's Life," *Public Affairs*, p. 324.

118. "An Act to Regulate the immigration of aliens into the United States," *Library of Congress*.

119. "Anarchist Turner Tells of His Fight," *New York Times*.

120. "Turner v. Williams," FindLaw.

121. Sondhaus, *World War I: The Global Revolution*, pp. 306–308.

122. Axelrod, *Selling the War*, pp. 56–58.

123. "German U-Boat Reches Baltimore," *New York Times*, p. 1.

124. Manseau, "A Forgotten History of Anti-Sikh Violence in the Early-20th–Century Pacific Northwest."

125. "Mob Drives out Hindus." *New York Times*. New York Times, Co. 6 Sept. 1907.

126. Alvarez, "A Brief History of America's 'Love-Hate Relationship' With Immigration."

127. "Immigration Act of 1917." *University of Washington-Bothell Library*. Sixty-Fourth Congress. Sess. II. Chapters 27–29. 1917.

128. Boissoneault, "Literacy Tests and Asian Exclusion Were the Hallmarks of the 1917 Immigration Act."

129. Wolfensberger, "Woodrow Wilson, Congress and Anti-Immigrant Sentiment in America."

130. "Immigration and the Great War," *NPS*.

131. Purdy, "Environmentalism's Racist History."

132. Grant, *The Passing of the Great Race*, p. 193.

133. O'Leary, *Undocumented Immigrants in the United States*, 2013.

134. Emergency Quota Law, *University of Washington-Bothell Library*.

135. Higham, *Strangers in the Land*, pp. 505–559.

136. Riley, *Let Them In*.

137. "Takao Ozawa v. US," *FindLaw*.

138. "US v. Bhagat Singh Thing," *FindLaw*.

139. "The Immigration Act of 1924," *U.S. Department of State*.

140. "'Shut the Door': A Senator Speaks for Immigration Restriction," *George Mason University*.

141. Bailey, *¡Viva Cristo Rey!*

142. "The Great Depression (1929–1939), *George Washington University*.

143. Hardman, "The Great Depression and the New Deal."

144. Ruiz, *From Out of the Shadows*, p. 28.

145. Gonzales, *Mexicanos*, p. 148.

146. "NS Records for 1930s Mexican Repatriations," *USCIS*.

147. Johnson, "The Forgotten Repatriation of Persons of Mexican Ancestry and Lessons for the War on Terror."

148. MacMedan, "U.S. urged to apologize for 1930s deportations."

149. Younge, "Mexicans expelled in 30s ask for justice."

150. "Remembering California's 'Repatriation Program'," *NPR*.

151. "Apology Act for the 1930s Mexican Repatriation Program," *California Legislative Information*.

152. Kang, "Denying Prejudice: Internment, Regress, and Denial."

153. Taylor, "The People Nobody Wants."

154. Loveland, *Constitutional Law*.

155. Weber, "The Japanese Camps in California," p. 50.

156. "Racism and Exclusion," *National Park Service*.

157. Swift, "Gallup Vault: WWII-Era Support for Japanese Internment."

158. Fried, "Government public opinion research and the Japanese-American internment."

159. White, "Many Americans support Trump's immigration order."

160. Mitter, "Forgotten ally?"

161. Tiezzi, "When the US and China Were Allies."

162. "Soong Mei-Ling," *USC US-China Institute*.

163. "How to tell Japs from the Chinese," *Life Magazine*, p. 81.

164. Roosevelt, "Message to Congress on Repeal of the Chinese Exclusion Laws."

165. Berinsky, et al., "Revisiting Public Opinion in the 1930s and 1940s," pp. 517–520.

166. Tharoor, "What Americans thought of Jewish refugees on the eve of World War II."

167. "Kristallnacht," *Holocaust Encyclopedia*.

168. "Displaced Persons," *CQ Researcher*.

169. Jones, "Americans Again Opposed to Taking in Refugees."
170. Truman, "Statement and Directive by the President on Immigration."
171. Dinnerstein, *Uneasy at Home*, p. 205.
172. "Displaced Persons Act of 1948," *University of Washington-Bothell*.
173. Truman, "Statement by the President Upon Signing the Displaced Persons Act."
174. Rashke, "The Horrible Laws that Blocked Jews from the US after World War 2 but let Nazis in."
175. Truman, "Statement by the President Upon Signing Bill Amending the Displaced Persons Act."
176. Ingraham, "The riches 1 percent now owns more of the country's wealth than at any time in the past 50 years."
177. Montero, "There is a renewed push to remove the McCarran name in Nevada."
178. "The Immigration and Nationality Act of 1952," *U.S. Department of State*.
179. "Memorandum from William J. Hopkins, June 20, 1952," *Truman Library and Museum*.
180. Shanks, *Immigration and the Politics of American Sovereignty*, pp. 104–105.
181. Zahra, *The Great Departure*.
182. Beinart, "The Racial and Religious Paranoia of Trump's Warsaw Speech."
183. Truman, "Veto of Bill to Revise the Laws Relating to Immigration, Naturalization, and Nationality."
184. Martin, "Braceros: History, Compensation."
185. Sanchez, *Becoming Mexican American*, p. 200.
186. Martin, Fix & Taylor, *The New Rural Poverty*, p. 12.
187. "The Emergency Farm Labor Supply Program Agreement."
188. "The Recommendations of the President's Commission on Migratory Labor," *UC-Berkeley Library*.

189. "Freedom Day," *New York Times*.
190. "An ACT to amend the Agricultural Act of 1949," *University of Washington-Bothell Library*.
191. Garcia, "Migratory Labor."
192. Kang, *The INS on the Line*, p. 140–142.
193. Lind, "Operation Wetback, the 1950s immigration policy that Donald Trump loves, explained."
194. Peralta, "It Came Up in The Debate: Here Are 3 Things To Know About 'Operation Wetback.'"
195. Reston and Ramirez, "How Trump's deportation plan failed 62 years ago."
196. Hernandez, "The Crimes and Consequences of Illegal Immigration: A Cross-Border Examination of Operation Wetback, 1943 to 1954."
197. Galarza, "Strangers in our Fields."
198. Higham, *Strangers in the Land*, 277.
199. Eckerson, "Immigration and National Origins."
200. Kammer, "The Hart-Celler Immigration Act of 1965."
201. "Civil Rights Act of 1964," *National Park Service*.
202. "The 1965 Enactment," *Department of Justice*.
203. Gjelten, *A Nation of Nations*, pp. 119–121.
204. Orchowski, *The Law that Changed the Face of America*, p. 75.
205. Johnson, "Immigration and Nationality Act of 1965."
206. Axelrod, *The Real History of the Cold War*, p. 170.
207. Jones, "Americans Again Opposed to Taking in Refugees."
208. Lister, "Today's refugees follow path of Hungarians who fled Soviets in 1956."
209. Michener, *The Bridge at Andau*.
210. Colville, "Fiftieth Anniversary of the Hungarian uprising and refugee crisis."
211. Newport, "Historical Review: Americans' Views on Refugees Coming to U.S."

212. Wu and Chen, *Asian American Studies Now*, p. 605.

213. Woollacott, "The Boat People."

214. Carter, "Tokyo Economic Summit Conference Remarks to Reporters at the Conclusion of the Conference."

215. Desilver, "U.S. public seldom has welcomed refugees into country."

216. Jones, "Americans Again Opposed to Taking in Refugees."

217. Bardach, "Marieltos and the Changing of Miami."

218. Capó, "The White House Used This Moment as Proof the U.S. Should Cut Immigration."

219. Desilver, "U.S. public seldom has welcomed refugees into country."

220. Card, "The Impact of the Mariel Boatlift on the Miami Labor Market."

221. Wang, "Chinese-American Descendants Uncover Forged Family Histories."

222. Siegel and Simmons-Duffin, "How Did We Get To 11 Million Unauthorized Immigrants?"

223. Fussell, "Warmth of the Welcome."

224. Newport, "American Say Reagan Is the Greatest U.S. President."

225. Peters, "Presidential Job Approval Ratings Following the First 100 Days."

226. Reagan, "Statement on United States Immigration and Refugee Policy."

227. Plumer, "Congress tried to fix immigration back in 1986. Why did it fail?"

228. "A Reagan Legacy: Amnesty for Illegal Immigrants," *NPR*.

229. Koslowski, "The Evolution of Border Controls as a Mechanism to Prevent Illegal Immigration."

230. Guthman, "Undergrond Railroad, 1980's Style."

231. "Refugee Act of 1980," *National Archives Foundation*.

232. Garcia, *Seeking Refuge*.

233. Labrador and Renwick, "Central America's Violent Northern Triangle."

234. Gzesh, "Central Americans and Asylum Policy in the Reagan Era."

235. Romero, "School Is For Everyone: Celebrating Plyler v. Doe."

236. "Plyler v. Doe," *US Courts*.
237. Olivas, "The Story of *Plyler v. Doe*."
238. "Plyler v. Doe," *Cornell Law School*.
239. Ye Hee Lee, "Do 80 percent of Americans oppose sanctuary cities?"
240. "Immigration," *Gallup Poll*.
241. Hira, "New Data Show How Firms Like Infosys and Tata Abuse the H-1B Program."
242. Torres, "The H-1B Visa Debate, Explained."
243. "A blueprint for getting more women into information technology," *The Economist*.
244. Alvarez, "The Diversity Visa Program Was Created to Help Irish Immigrants."
245. Kilgannon and Goldstein, "Sayfullo Saipov, the Suspect in the New York Terror Attack, and His Past."
246. Kirby, "Trump blasts 'Diversity Visa Lottery Program,' after NYC terror attack."
247. Dickey, "The Diversity Visa Winner Who Saved New York From a Terror Attack."
248. Holmes, "Legislation Eases Limits on Aliens."
249. Tichenor, *Dividing Lines*, p. 192.
250. Cole, "Mccarran-Walter Act Reborn?"
251. Pipes, "The Muslims are Coming! The Muslims are Coming!"
252. Frej, "How U.S. Immigration Policy Has Changed Since 9/11."
253. Gutiérrez, "George W. Bush and Mexican Immigration Policy."
254. Bush, "President Bush Proposes New Temporary Worker Program."
255. Mehlman, "Hispanic outreach crucial to GOP.".
256. Flores, "How the U.S. Hispanic population is changing."
257. Cadava, "Long before Trump's Mexico wall, Prop. 187 killed Hispanic conservatism."
258. Suro, "Americans Views of Immigration."
259. "Judging the Impact: A Post 9/11 America," *NPR*.

260. McCarthy, "Enemies from Within."

261. LaCasse, "How many Muslim extremists are there? Just the facts, please."

262. Greenberg, "Ben Shapiro says a majority of Muslims are radicals."

263. Kishi, "Assaults against Muslims in U.S. surpass 2001 level."

264. Flanagin, "9/11 forever changed the concept of immigration in the US."

265. Neiwert, "Home Is Where the Hate Is."

266. Leikin, "War On Terror: Mexico More Critical Than Ever for U.S."

267. "Fact Sheet: The Secure Fence Act of 2006," *Georgewbush-White House.*

268. Joshi, "Donald Trump's Border Wall—An Annotated Timeline."

269. Miller, Vitkovskaya, and Fischer-Baum, "'This deal will make me look terrible': Full transcripts of Trump's calls with Mexico and Australia."

270. Suls, "Most Americans continue to oppose U.S. border wall, doubt Mexico would pay for it."

271. Steckelberg, Alcantara, and Jan, "A look at Trump's border wall prototypes."

272. Wilson, "Texas officials wan of immigrants with terrorist ties crossing southern border."

273. Schmitt and Qiu, "Fact Check: The Trump Administration's Argument for a Border Wall."

274. Valverde, "Will a border wall stop drugs from coming into the United States?"

275. Westcott, "What History Tells Us About Building a Wall To Solve a Problem."

276. Kershner, "Trump Cites Israel's 'Wall' as Model. The Analogy Is Iffy."

277. Flores, "Walls of Separation."

278. James, "Trump seeks $18 billion to extend border wall over 10 years."

279. Rodriguez, "Trump's Border Wall Was a $2.6 Million Hit on San Diego Taxpayers."

280. Wong, "Trump's border wall: prototypes loom large, but where are the protesters?"

281. Embury-Dennis, "Trump's environment chief Scott Pruitt suggests climate change could be good for humanity."
282. Thomsen, "Trump waives dozens of environmental rules to speed up construction of border wall."
283. Bolstad, "Trump's Wall Could Cause Serious Environmental Damage."
284. "Good Fences, Good Neighbors: Public Opinion on Border Security," *Roper Center*.
285. Suls, "Most Americans Continue to oppose U.S. border wall, doubt Mexico will pay for it."
286. Marsh, "Opioid Addiction Isn't The Disease; It's the Symptom."
287. "DREAM Act Congressional Legislative History," *University of Houston*.
288. McGreevy and York, "Brown signs California Dream Act."
289. "Illinois DREAM Act Signed by Governor Quinn," *Huffington Post*.
290. "Remarks by the President on Immigration," *Obama White House*.
291. "Consideration of Deferred Action for Childhood Arrivals (DACA)," *USCIS*.
292. Lind, "How many immigrants have DACA, really? We finally have one answer—just as they start to lose it."
293. Gomez, "There are 3.6M 'DREAMers'—a number far greater than commonly known."
294. Valverde, "Timeline: DACA, the Trump administration and a government shutdown."
295. Shear, "How Washington Reached the Brink of a Shutdown."
296. "There Are 3.6M 'Dreamers'—A Number Far Greater Than Commonly Known," *AMREN*.
297. De Pinto, Backus, Khanna, and Salvanto, "Most Americans Support DACA, but oppose border wall—CBS News poll."
298. "Monthly Harvard-Harris Poll: January 2018 Re-Field," *Harvardharris Poll*.
299. De Pinto, Backus, Khanna, and Salvanto, "Most Americans Support DACA, but oppose border wall—CBS News poll."

300. "'This Is About Basic Decency'. Obama Rips Trump Over DACA Decision," *Time*.

301. "Bill of Rights of the United States of America (1791)," *Bill of Rights Institute*.

302. McElroy, "Understanding the First Amendment's Religion Clauses."

303. Mohamed, "A new estimate of the U.S. Muslim population."

304. Lipka, "Muslims and Islam: Key findings in the U.S. and around the world."

305. "Public Remains Conflicted Over Islam," *Pew Research*.

306. "Voters Say Islamic Leaders Should do More to Promote Peace," *Rasmussen Reports*.

307. Kishi, "Assaults against Muslims in U.S. surpass 2001 level."

308. Naurath, "Most Muslim Americans See No Justification for Violence."

309. Trump, "Remarks by President Trump in Joint Address to Congress."

310. Valverde, "A look at the data on domestic terrorism and who's behind it."

311. Fridersdorf, "The Obama Administration's Drone-Strike Dissembling."

312. Johnson and Hauslohner, "'I think Islam hates us': A timeline of Trump's comments about Islam and Muslims."

313. "State of Hawai'i and Ismael Elshikh vs. Trump, Et AL-Order," *ACLU*.

314. Liptak, "Trump's Latest Travel Ban Suffers Blow From a Second Appeals Court."

315. Chapin, "Bigots Will Be Bigots."

316. Carroll, "America's dark and not-very-distant history of hating Catholics."

317. Davis, "America's Trust History of Religious Tolerance."

318. "Religious Landscape Study," *Pew Research*.

319. McManus, "To avoid a Manchester-type bombing on American soil, integrate Muslims."

320. Tchen, *New York before Chinatown*, p. 174.

321. Camarota and Zeigler, "Jobs Americans Won't Do?"

322. Kelly, "FACT CHECK: Have Immigrants Lowered Wages For Blue-Collar American Workers?"

323. Preston, "Immigrants Aren't Taking Americans' Jobs, New Study Finds."

324. "An Open Letter from 1,470 Economists on Immigration," *New American Economy*.

325. Waters and Pineau, "The Integration of Immigrants into American Society."

326. Ewing and Martínez, "The Criminalization of Immigration in the United States."

327. Wilkerson and Salmons, "Linguistic Marginalities: Becoming American without Learning English."

328. Branson-Potts, "Trump wants immigrants to 'share our values.' They say assimilation is much more complex."

329. Nowrasteh, "More Family-Based Immigrants in Australia & Canada than in the United States."

330. Orrenius and Zavodny, "A Comparison of the U.S. and Canadian Immigration Systems."

331. Swanson, "Opening up borders: An idea economists tend to love and politicians detest."

332. Raviv, "If People Could Immigrate Anywhere, Would Poverty Be Eliminated?"

333. Heumer, "Is There a Right to Immigrate?"

334. Goldhill, "Astronauts report an 'overview effect' from the awe of space travel—and you can replicate it here on earth."

Primary & Secondary Sources

"1798 Alien Enemies Act." *UWB*. University of Washington-Bothell Library. US Immigration Legislation Online. Session II, Chap. 66, Statute 570. 5th Congress; 6 July 1798.

"1798 Naturalization Act." *UWB*. University of Washington-Bothell Library. US Immigration Legislation Online. Session II, Chap. 54, Statute 566. 5th Congress, 17 June 1798.

"An Act to Amend the Naturalization Laws and to punish Crimes against the same, and for other Purposes." *LOC*. Library of Congress. Forty-First Congress, Sess. II. 2018.

"An Act to Encourage Immigration." *New York Times*. New York Times, Co. 3 Aug. 1864.

"An Act to regulate the immigration of aliens into the United States." *LOC*. Library of Congress. Federal Reserve Bulletin. Vol. 103, No. 3. Sept. 2017.

"An Act to Secure the Right of Citizenship to Children of Citizens of the United States born out of the Limits Thereof." *LOC*. Library of Congress. Thirty-Third Congress. Sess. II. 1855. 2018.

Bolognese, Jeffrey. "3 Reasons Why Chinese Workers Were the MVP's on the Transcontinental Railroad." *Medium*. SASEprints. Society of Asian Scientists and Engineers. May 20, 2016.

Bush, George W. "President Bush Proposes New Temporary Worker Program." *Georgewbush-white house*. The White House. Jan. 7, 2004.

Cohen, Adam. "This Jigsaw Puzzle Was Given to Ellis Island Immigrants to Test Their Intelligence." *Smithsonian Magazine*. Smithsonian Institution. May 2017.

Davis, Kenneth C. "America's True History of Religious Tolerance." *Smithsonian*. Smithsonian Institution. Oct. 2010.

Evans, Rob, and David Hencke. "US felt ban on Graham Greene 'tarnished its image.'" *The Guardian*. Guardian News and Media. 21 Sept. 2003.

"Fact Sheet: The Secure Fence Act of 2006." *Georgebush-White House*. White House. Oct. 26, 2006.

Flanagin, Jake. "9/11 Forever Changed the Concept of Immigration in the US." *Quartz*. Atlantic Media. 11 Sept. 2015.

Garcia, Juanita. "Migratory Labor. Hearings before Subcommittee on Labor and Labor-Management Relations." 82nd Congress, 2nd Session. 1952. *Digital History*. University of Houston. 2016.

"Have We a Dusky Peril?" *Puget Sound American*. 16 Sept. 1906.

Johnson, Lyndon B. "Immigration and Nationality Act of 1965." Full Remarks. Oct. 2, 1965. *LBJ Library*. Immigration and Nationality Act Media Kit. 2018.

Kramer, Paul A. "The Case of the 22 Lewd Chinese Women." *Slate*. The Slate Group. 23 Apr. 2012.

Lind, Dara. "Why Historians are Fighting About 'No Irish Need Apply' Signs—and Why it Matters." *VOX*. Vox Media. 4 Aug. 2015.

"Plyler v. Doe." 1982. *Cornell Law School*. LII. Supreme Court. 2017.

Reagan, Ronald. "Statement on United States Immigration and Refugee Policy." July 30, 1981. *The American Presidency Project*. University of California. 2017.

"Remarks by the President on Immigration." *Obama White House*. White House. Office of the Press Secretary. June 15, 2012.

Roosevelt, Franklin D. "Message to Congress on Repeal of the Chinese Exclusion Law." Oct. 11, 1943. *The American Presidency Project*. University of California, Santa Barbara. 2017.

"'Shut the Door': A Senator Speaks for Immigration Restriction." *George Mason University*. History Matters. 3 Jan. 2017.

"The New Colossus—full text." *NPS*. National Park Service. Statue of Liberty. 3 Aug. 2017.

"Transcript of the Chinese Exclusion Act (1882)." *Our Documents*. The U.S. National Archives. 2018.

"Treaty With the Delawares: 1778." *Yale University*. Avalon Project. Lillian Goldman Law Library. 2008.

Truman, Harry S. "Statement and Directive by the President on Immigration to the United States of Certain Displaced Persons and Refugees in Europe." Dec. 22, 1945. *Truman Library & Museum*. University of Missouri. 2018.

Truman, Harry S. "Statement by the President Upon Signing Bill Amending the Displaced Persons Act." June 16, 1950. *Truman Library and Museum*. University of Missouri. 2018.

Truman, Harry S. "Statement by the President Upon Signing the Displaced Persons Act." June 25, 1948. *The American Presidency Project*. University of California. 2018.

Truman, Harry S. "Veto of Bill To Revise the Laws Relating to Immigration, Naturalization, and Nationality." June 25, 1952. *Truman Library & Museum*. University of Missouri. 2018.

"Uniform Rule of Naturalization." *LOC*. Library of Congress, 2016.

Woollacott, Martin. "The Boat People." *The Guardian*. Guardian News and Media. 3 Dec. 1977.

Younge, Gary. "Mexicans expelled in 30s ask for justice." *The Guardian*. Guardian News and Media. 16 July 2003.

Glossary

A

Alien Foreign-born person who is not a citizen (by birth or naturalization) of the country in which he or she resides

Anti-modernism Broadly-defined philosophical position that views the progress of a society or culture as undesirable and so seeks to supplant one incarnation of society with a past incarnation of society usually seen as more "pure" or "beneficial"

Assimilation Process of adjusting to a culture; method used to assist individuals in adjusting or to force individuals to adjust to a certain set of cultural characteristics

C

Conservatism Political view based on trying to preserve perceptively valuable aspects of culture and that opposes change that is seen as a threat to core values or cultural beliefs/ideals

E

Emigration Act of leaving one country to settle permanently in another country

I

Immigration Act of entering a foreign country to live

L

Legal Permanent Resident or Resident Alien Person who legally resides in a country on a permanent basis but is not a naturalized or native-born citizen

Left-Wing (Leftist) Political term that refers to the more liberal, socialist, or radical factions in a political system

Liberalism Political view that places emphasis on change and personal liberty and less emphasis on traditional values

M

Migration Permanent or temporary movement from one region, or country, to another

N

Nationalism Philosophical/political view that places emphasis on patriotism and the belief in the superiority of one's society in comparison to one or more other societies, as well as the need to preserve a set of characteristics seen as fundamental or beneficial in one's society

Nativism Term used in the United States to refer to a philosophy that seeks to protect the interests of native-born U.S. citizens over those of residents or immigrants

Naturalization Legal process of becoming a United States citizen

P

Progressivism Political view based on the process of trying to identify undesirable characteristics within a society and to create changes that push cultural evolution in one way or another

R

Racism Belief that members of any or every racial group possess characteristics specific to that group; the belief that the characteristics that differentiate one race from another also make one race superior or inferior to another race

Right-Wing Political term referring to the more conservative branches of a nation's political system

T

Traditionalism Political view that places emphasis on traditions or long-established cultural patterns/values

Tribalism Behavior pattern that involves strong loyalty to one's own social or cultural group and often suspicion or hostility to persons outside of that group

U

Undocumented Migrant or Illegal Migrant/Immigrant Individuals who reside permanently or temporarily in a country without legal permission

X

Xenophilia Love or affinity for foreign groups or individuals

Xenophobia Dislike or fear of people from other cultures or countries, especially when based on subjective or irrational reasons

Historical Snapshots

1793

- France declared war on England
- The "Reign of Terror," a purge of those suspected of treason against the French Republic, began in France
- Louis XVI was executed by guillotine
- Jean Pierre Blanchard made the first balloon flight in North America, in Philadelphia
- The German Reformed Church was established in the U.S. by Calvinist Puritans
- China's emperor turned away the British fleet and declared that China possessed all things in abundance and had no need of British goods
- Christian Sprengel published detailed descriptions of the manner in which different flowers are pollinated
- Claude Chappe established the first long-distance semaphore telegraph line
- Eli Whitney invented the cotton gin and applied for a patent
- French troops conquered Geertruidenberg in the Netherlands
- Noah Webster established New York's first daily newspaper, *American Minerva*
- Tennis was first mentioned in an English sporting magazine
- The Republican calendar replaced the Gregorian calendar in France
- The first American fugitive slave law passed which required the return of escaped slaves
- President George Washington's second inauguration speech was only 133 words long
- The Humane Society of Philadelphia was organized
- Benjamin Rush successfully treated an epidemic of yellow fever
- The Louvre in Paris opened as a museum

- The first U.S. state road was authorized, running from Frankfort, Kentucky to Cincinnati, Ohio

1798

- Congress agreed to pay a yearly tribute to Tripoli to protect U.S. shipping
- Russia appointed the first Jewish censor to review Hebrew books
- Representative Matthew Lyon of Vermont spat in the face of Representative Roger Griswold of Connecticut in the U.S. House of Representatives after an argument
- The Federal Street Theater in Boston was destroyed by a fire
- The Republic of Switzerland was formed
- The United States Department of the Navy was established by an Act of Congress
- Judith Sargent Murray wrote *The Gleaner,* essays on women's education and alternatives to marriage
- The Mission San Luis Rey de Francia was founded in California
- U.S. passed the Alien Act which allowed the president to deport dangerous aliens
- The Sedition Act prohibited "false, scandalous and malicious" writing against the president and U.S. government
- The U.S. Public Health Service was formed and the U.S. Marine Hospital was authorized
- Napoleon Bonaparte's army annexed Egypt, seized Malta and captured Naples
- The Eleventh Amendment regarding judicial powers was ratified
- Twenty-two sea captains founded the East India Marine Society, which later became the Peabody Essex Museum, in Salem, Massachusetts, to preserve exotic treasures brought back from oversea voyages
- The concept of manufacturing interchangeable parts was incorporated by Eli Whitney in the production of firearms for the U.S. government
- A patent for a screw threading machine was awarded to David

Wilkinson of Rhode Island
- Samuel Taylor Coleridge and William Wordsworth published *Lyrical Ballads*

1799

- George Washington died at age 67 at his Mount Vernon, Virginia home
- The *USS Constellation* captured the French frigate *Insurgente*
- Napoleon Bonaparte participated in a coup and declared himself first consul, or dictator, of France; five nations united against France
- Western agriculturalists first described the qualities of sweet corn, which was being grown by the Iroquois
- Pennsylvania pioneered the printed ballot
- The Rosetta Stone was discovered in Egypt by an officer in Napoleon's army
- Edward Jenner's smallpox vaccination was introduced
- The Bank of Manhattan opened in New York City
- The metric system was established in France
- An American patent for a seeding machine was granted to Eliakim Spooner of Vermont
- The last known blaauwboch, or blue antelope, was shot in Africa
- The Russian government granted the Russian-American Company a trade monopoly in Alaska
- Jacques-Louis David painted *The Rape of the Sabine Women*
- Eli Whitney received a government contract for 10,000 muskets
- The first American law regulating insurance was passed in Massachusetts
- The Dutch East India Company fell bankrupt

1800

- The Library of Congress in Washington, DC, was created with a $5,000 allocation
- The French regained the territory of Louisiana from Spain by secret

treaty
- John Adams became the first president to live in the White House
- William Herschel discovered infrared radiation from the sun
- The population of New York topped 60,000
- World population was believed to be 800 million people, double the population in 1500
- Rev. Mason Locke Weems authored *A History of the Life and Death, Virtues and Exploits of General George Washington*
- Martha Washington set all her slaves free
- Robert Fulton tested a 20-foot model of his torpedo-armed submarine
- In presidential voting, Thomas Jefferson and Aaron Burr tied, forcing the decision into the House of Representatives, which selected Jefferson on the thirty-sixth round
- A letter mailed from Savannah, Georgia, to Portland, Maine, required 20 days
- Congress convened for the first time in Washington, DC
- John Chapman, known as Johnny Appleseed, began planting tree orchards across western Pennsylvania, Ohio and Indiana
- Alessandro Volta demonstrated an early battery known as an electricity pile
- Belgium's textile industry dramatically expanded after a working spinning machine was smuggled from Britain and then widely copied
- The free black community of Philadelphia petitioned Congress to abolish slavery
- The first commercial Valentine greeting card appeared

1805

- The Michigan Territory was created and separated from the Indiana Territory and the city of Detroit was designated as its capital
- U.S. Marines attacked pirates on the Barbary Coast of North Africa on the shores of Tripoli
- Charles Wilson Peale founded the Pennsylvania Academy of Fine Arts

- Napoleon Bonaparte was crowned king of Italy
- The Lewis and Clark expedition crossed the Rocky Mountains and reached the Pacific Ocean
- American boxer Bill Richmond knocked out Jack Holmes in Kilburn Wells, England
- The Treaty of Pressburg ended hostilities between France and Austria
- Admiral Nelson defeated the French and Spanish fleet at the Battle of Trafalgar
- The *Times* of London published its first illustration January 10, showing the funeral of Lord Nelson
- The first American covered bridge spanned the Schuylkill River in New York
- The Female Charitable Society, the first women's club, was organized in America
- William H. Wollaston discovered rhodium
- Tangerines reached Europe for the first time, coming directly from China
- Chief Justice Samuel Chase was acquitted by the Senate impeachment trial, ending the Republican campaign against the Federalist bench
- The first California orange grove was planted at San Gabriel Mission near Los Angeles
- Virginia required all freed slaves to leave the state or risk imprisonment or deportation
- The French Revolutionary calendar law was abolished

1808

- The importation of slaves into the United States was banned as of January 1 by an act of Congress
- Napoleon invaded Spain with an army of 150,000, routing the Spanish
- Henry Crabb Robinson became the world's first war correspondent when the *Times* of London sent him to report on the Peninsular War in Spain

- Thomas Jefferson rejected petitions that he run for a third term, citing the example set by George Washington
- Anthracite coal was first burned as an experimental fuel by Wilkes-Barre in Pennsylvania
- Bavaria produced a written constitution that abolished serfdom and proclaimed the principle of equality of citizens before the law
- John Jacob Astor incorporated the American Fur Company with himself as sole stockholder
- The S.S. *Phoenix* was launched by New Jersey engineer John Stevens, the first steamboat with an American-built engine
- Inventor Richard Trevithick demonstrated his steam locomotive *Catch-me-who-can* on a circular track near London's Euston Road
- Parliament repealed an Elizabethan statute declaring theft from a person a capital offense
- French confectioner Nicolas Appert developed a method of vacuum-packing food in jars
- The first Parisian restaurant with fixed prices opened in the Palais Royal
- The first college orchestra in the United States was founded at Harvard
- The first U.S. land-grant university was founded at Ohio University in Athens, Ohio
- The Medical Society of the State of New York was founded
- Alexis Bouvard accurately predicted the orbital locations of Jupiter and Saturn
- The first volume of *American Ornithology* by Alexander Wilson was published

1810

- The U.S. Census recorded the United States population of 7,239,881, 19 percent of whom were black
- The Maryland legislature authorized a lottery to build a memorial to George Washington

- The first United States fire insurance joint-stock company was organized in Philadelphia
- Spanish artist Francisco Goya began his series of etchings *The Disasters of War* depicting the Peninsular War
- Illinois passed the first state vaccination legislation in the U.S.
- Goats were introduced to St. Helena Island and began the devastation that caused extinction of 22 of 33 endemic plants
- An electrochemical telegraph was constructed in Germany
- The French Catholic Church annulled the marriage of Napoleon I and Josephine
- The first Irish magazine in America, *The Shamrock*, was published
- The British Bullion Committee condemned the practice of governments printing too much money and causing inflation
- King Kamehameha conquered and united all the Hawaiian Islands
- The first billiard rooms were established in London, England
- The sale of tobacco in France was made a government monopoly
- The Cumberland Presbyterian Church of Kentucky was excluded from the Presbyterian Church
- Napoleon ordered the sale of seized U.S. ships
- Tom Cribb of Great Britain defeated American African American boxer Tom Molineaus in 40 rounds in the first interracial boxing championship
- Simon Bolivar joined the group of patriots that seized Caracas in Venezuela and proclaimed independence from Spain
- Australian Frederick Hasselborough discovered Macquarie Island while searching for new sealing grounds

1813

- American forces captured Fort George, Canada
- Congress chartered the Second Bank of the United States
- American forces under General Zebulon Pike captured York, now Toronto

- The first pineapples were planted in Hawaii
- The *Demologos*, the first steam-powered warship, was launched in New York City
- The U.S. Congress authorized steamboats to carry mail
- The British announced a blockade of Long Island Sound, leaving only the New England coast to shipping
- The first mass production factory began making pistols
- A Swiss traveler discovered the Great and Small temples of Ramses II in Egypt
- David Melville of Newport, Rhode Island, patented an apparatus for making coal gas
- Jane Austen published *Pride and Prejudice*
- Simon Bolivar returned to Venezuela and took command of a patriot army, recapturing Caracas from the Spaniards
- Rubber was patented
- The first raw cotton-to-cloth mill was founded in Waltham, Massachusetts
- The U.S. invasion of Canada was halted at Stoney Creek
- Commander Oliver Perry defeated the British in the Battle of Lake Erie
- The Society for Preventing Accidents in Coal Mines in Sunderland was founded under the auspices of the Duke of Northumberland

1815

- Andrew Jackson defeated the British at the Battle of New Orleans after the War of 1812 was officially over
- Napoleon and 1,200 men left Elba to start the 100-day re-conquest of France but were defeated by British forces under Wellington at the Battle of Waterloo
- Humphry Davy invented the miner's safety lamp for use in coal mines, which allowed miners to mine deep coal seams despite the presence of methane

- The world's first commercial cheese factory was established in Switzerland
- Congress appropriated funds for the restoration of the White House and hired James Hoban, the original designer and builder, to do the work
- John Roulstone of Massachusetts penned the first three lines of "Mary Had a Little Lamb" after a classmate named Mary was followed to school by her pet lamb
- The first New England missionaries arrived in Hawaii
- William Prout postulated that atomic weights of elements were multiples of that for hydrogen
- Three thousand post offices had been opened in the United States
- Austrian composer Franz Schubert produced two symphonies, two masses, 20 waltzes and 145 songs
- The Library of Congress, which was burned during the War of 1812, was reestablished with Thomas Jefferson's personal library of 6,500 volumes
- Sunday observance in the Netherlands was regulated by law
- A United States flotilla ended the decades-old piracy of Algiers, Tunis and Tripoli when the U.S. declared war on Algiers for taking U.S. prisoners and demanding tribute

1823

- Georgia passed the first state birth registration law
- The streets of Boston were lit by gas lamps
- President Monroe proclaimed the Monroe Doctrine, stating "that the American continents . . . are henceforth not to be considered as subjects for future colonization by European powers"
- James Fenimore Cooper published *The Pioneers*
- The Reverend Hiram Bingham, leader of a group of New England Calvinist missionaries, began translating the Bible into Hawaiian
- The poem "A Visit from St. Nicholas" by Clement C. Moore, often called "'Twas the Night Before Christmas," was published in the *Troy Sentinel*

(New York)
- The death penalty for more than 100 crimes was abolished in England
- The growing popularity of sending Christmas cards drew complaints from the Superintendent of Mail who said the high volume of the cards was becoming a burden on the United States Postal System
- The Mission San Francisco de Solano de Sonoma was established to convert the Native Americans and develop local resources
- Charles Macintosh of Scotland invented a waterproof fabric useful in the creation of raincoats
- Franz Schubert composed his song cycle *Die Schone Mullerin*
- Former slave Thomas James helped found the African Methodist Episcopal Zion Society, the forerunner of the Underground Railroad
- Rugby football originated in Rugby School, England
- The British medical journal *The Lancet* began publication

1826

- The American Temperance Society was formed in Boston
- Beethoven's String Quartet #13 in B flat major (Opus 130) premiered in Vienna
- Samuel Mory patented the internal combustion engine
- Weber's opera *Oberon* premiered in London
- The USS *Vincennes* left New York to become the first warship to circumnavigate the globe
- Russia and Norway established a border that superseded the arrangement made 500 years earlier in the Treaty of Novgorod
- Simón Bolívar helped the new South American republic of Bolivia gain independence and recognition from Peru
- Former U.S. presidents Thomas Jefferson and John Adams both died on July 4, the fiftieth anniversary of the signing of the Declaration of Independence
- A Pennsylvania law made kidnapping a felony, effectively nullifying the Fugitive Slave Act of 1793

- Explorer Gordon Laing became the first European to reach Timbuktu
- Lord & Taylor department store opened in New York at 47 Catherine Street
- Connecticut's six-mile Windsor Locks Canal opened to provide safe passage around the Enfield Falls and rapids in the Connecticut River 12 miles upstream from Hartford
- The first horse-powered railroad in America opened in Quincy, Massachusetts, at a granite quarry with three miles of track
- Gideon B. Smith planted the first of the new quick-growing Chinese mulberry trees in the United States and spurred development of the silk industry
- French chemist Antoine-Jérôme Balard discovered the element bromine
- After Pope Leo XII ordered that Rome's Jews be confined to the city's ghetto, thousands of Jews fled Rome and the Papal States
- Sing Sing Prison opened its first cell block some 30 miles north of New York City on the Hudson River
- The Zoological Gardens in Regent's Park were founded by the Zoological Society of London

1829
- French mathematician Evarise Galois introduced the theory of groups
- The New England Asylum for the Blind, the first in the U.S., was incorporated in Boston
- Scottish explorer John Ross discovered the magnetic North Pole
- Jons Berzelius discovered element 90, thorium
- Andrew Jackson was inaugurated as the seventh United States president
- The original Siamese twins, Chang and Eng Bunker, arrived in Boston for an exhibition to the Western world
- Giachinno Rossini's opera William Tell was produced in Paris
- Mormon Joseph Smith was ordained by John the Baptist-- according to

Joseph Smith
- Niépce and Louis Jacques Mandé Daguerre formed a partnership to develop photography
- William Austin Burt of Michigan received a patent for the typographer, a forerunner of the typewriter
- Stiff collars became part of a man's dress
- Slavery was abolished in Mexico
- The American Bible Society published Scripture in the Seneca Indian language
- Forty million buffalo inhabited the American West
- The Chesapeake Bay Canal was formally opened
- The length of a yard was standardized at 36 inches
- The British Parliament passed the Catholic Emancipation Act, which granted freedom of religion to Catholics and permitted Catholics to hold almost any public office
- The Indian custom of immolating a widow along with her dead husband was abolished in British India
- David Walker published *Walker's Appeal*, an American pamphlet that opposed slavery
- American annual per-capita alcohol consumption reached 7.1 gallons
- The cornerstone was laid for the United States Mint

1834

- Poker emerged as a Mississippi riverboat game
- Thirty-five thousand slaves were freed in South Africa as slavery was abolished throughout the British Empire
- New York and New Jersey made a compact over ownership of Ellis Island
- "Turkey in the Straw" became a popular American tune
- Sardines were canned in Europe for the first time
- One of New York City's finest restaurants, Delmonico's, sold a meal of soup, steak, coffee and half a pie for $0.12

- Louis Braille invented a system of raised dot writing to enable the blind to read
- Carl Jacobi discovered "uniformly rotating self-gravitating ellipsoids"
- Cyrus Hall McCormick patented a reaping machine
- Sandpaper was patented by Isaac Fischer Jr. of Springfield, Vermont
- The first railroad tunnel in the United States was completed in Pennsylvania
- The U.S. Senate censured President Andrew Jackson for taking federal deposits from the Bank of the United States
- The Spanish Inquisition was abolished
- Federal troops were used to control a labor dispute near Williamsport, Maryland, among Irish laborers constructing the Chesapeake and Ohio Canal

1836

- The Whig Party held its first national convention in Albany, New York
- The Alamo, defended by 182 Texans for 13 days, was besieged by 3,000 Mexicans led by Santa Anna
- Samuel Colt patented the first revolving barrel multishot firearm
- Charles Darwin returned to England after five years aboard the HMS *Beagle*
- The Republic of Texas declared its independence from Mexico and elected Samuel Houston as its president
- Martin Van Buren was elected to the U.S. presidency
- Reconstruction began on Synagogue of Rabbi Judah Hasid in Jerusalem
- Arkansas entered the Union as the twenty-fifth state
- California gained virtual freedom from Mexico following a revolt led by Juan Bautista Alvarado
- Spain relinquished its territorial claims in Central America after years of fighting with the British
- Chile's dictator Diego Portales initiated a war with a Peruvian-Bolivian

coalition over trade issues

- Abolitionist Angelina E. Grimké issued a pamphlet titled, "Appeal to Christian Women of the Southern States"
- Twenty-three of New York's 26 fire insurance companies declared bankruptcy as claims mounted for losses sustained in the 1835 Manhattan fire
- The Long Island Rail Road ran its first train between New York and Boston
- The S.S. *Beaver,* tested under steam at Vancouver, became the first steamboat to be seen on the Pacific Coast
- The hot-air balloon *Royal Vauxhall* lifted from London's Vauxhall Gardens and landed 18 hours later in the German duchy of Nassau.
- The first English-language newspaper, *Sandwich Island Gazette and Journal of Commerce*, was published in Hawaii
- The University of Wisconsin was founded at Madison
- Philadelphia's first penny daily, The *Philadelphia Public Ledger,* began publication
- The Prix du Jockey Club horse race had its first running outside Paris
- A phosphorus match was patented by Alonzo D. Phillips
- New York City's Park Hotel opened on the northwest corner of Broadway and Vesey Streets

1838

- The first telegraph message was sent using dots and dashes
- J. M. W. Turner painted *The Fighting Temeraire*
- The steamship the *Great Western*, built by British engineer Isambard Kingdom Brunel, sailed from Bristol to New York in a record 15 days
- New York passed the Free Banking Act, which popularized the idea of state-chartered banks
- The First Afghan War began; the British garrison at Kabul was wiped out
- Procter & Gamble Company was formed

- Charles M. Hovey introduced a strawberry grown from seed produced by hybridization, the first fruit variety that originated through breeding on the North American continent
- John Wright Boott received the first recorded shipment of tropical orchids to the United States
- Matthias Schleiden discovered that all living plant tissue was composed of cells
- The U.S. Mint in New Orleans began operation, producing dimes
- Thomas Henderson, Friedrich Struve and Friedrich Bessel made the first measurements of the distance to stars using the parallax method
- Samuel F. B. Morse made first public demonstration of the telegraph
- Mammoth Cave in Kentucky was purchased by Franklin Gorin as a tourist attraction
- Mexico declared war on France
- Frederick Douglass, American abolitionist, escaped slavery disguised as a sailor
- Tennessee became the first state to prohibit alcohol
- The Territory of Iowa was organized
- The first Braille Bible was published by the American Bible Society

1846

- The Mexican-American War started with a battle between the Mexican and U.S. armies at Palo Alto in Texas
- The Oregon Treaty settled the boundary line between the U.S. and British possessions in Canada at the forty-ninth parallel
- Using the temperature of the Earth, Irish physicist William Thomson estimated that the planet was 100 million years old
- German chemist Christian Schonbein discovered that a mixture of sulfuric acid and saltpeter was explosive when it dried
- The double cylinder rotary press was introduced, capable of producing 8,000 sheets an hour
- Congress chartered the Smithsonian Institution

- Ether anesthesia was used for the first time by dentist William Thomas Green Morton in surgery at Massachusetts General Hospital in Boston
- The movement of the Mormons to settle in the west began
- Robert Thomson obtained an English patent on a rubber tire
- Iowa became the twenty-ninth state
- Elias Howe patented the sewing machine
- The saxophone was patented by Antoine Joseph Sax
- Michigan ended the death penalty within its borders
- The *Oregon Spectator* became the first newspaper to be published on the West Coast

1848

- Britain suspended the Habeas Corpus Act in Ireland following the potato famine and protests
- The Treaty of Guadalupe Hidalgo ended the Mexican War with the United States
- Wisconsin entered the Union as the thirtieth state
- The first Woman's Rights Convention opened in Seneca Falls, New York, under the leadership of Elizabeth Cady Stanton
- German missionary-explorer Johannes Rebmann, became the first European to observe the snow-covered Mount Kilimanjaro, Africa's highest peak
- John Jacob Astor died, leaving a fortune of $20 million acquired in the fur trade and New York real estate
- The Pacific Mail Steamship Company contracted with engineers to build a rail link across the Isthmus of Panama to facilitate transportation between Atlantic Coast ports and San Francisco
- State of Maine Pure Spruce Gum was introduced, the world's first commercial chewing gum
- Britain took the Mosquito Coast from Nicaragua
- James Marshall found gold in Sutter's Mill in Coloma, California
- The ballet *Faust* premiered in Milan, Italy

- James K. Polk became the first U.S. president photographed in office
- French King Louis-Philippe abdicated the throne, resulting in the development of the Second French Republic
- Karl Marx and Frederick Engels published *The Communist Manifesto* in London, England
- Hungary became the constitutional monarchy under King Ferdinand of Austria
- The Territory of Oregon was organized by an act of Congress out of the U.S. portion of the Oregon Country below the forty-ninth parallel
- Waldo Hanchett patented the dental chair
- The first shipload of Chinese laborers arrived in San Francisco
- The Shaker song *Simple Gifts* was written by Joseph Brackett in Alfred, Maine
- American born Joseph Jenkins Roberts was sworn in as the first president of the independent African Republic of Liberia

1849

- The photographic slide was invented
- French officer Claude-Etienne Minie invented a bullet known as the Minie ball
- Abraham Lincoln patented a lifting and buoying device for vessels; he was the only U.S. president to apply for a patent
- Elizabeth Blackwell became the first woman in the United States to receive a medical degree
- Colonel John W. Geary became the first postmaster of San Francisco
- Harriet Tubman escaped from slavery in Maryland
- M. Jolly-Bellin discovered the process of dry cleaning by accident when he upset a lamp containing turpentine and oil onto his clothing and observed the cleaning effect
- The safety pin was patented by Walter Hunt of New York City
- The U.S. Gold Coinage Act authorized the coining of the $20 Double Eagle gold coin

- The Pfizer drug company was founded in Brooklyn
- The U.S. Territory of Minnesota was organized
- A patent was granted for an envelope-making machine
- Joseph Couch patented a steam-powered percussion rock drill
- Zachary Taylor was sworn in as the twelfth American president
- California petitioned to be admitted into the Union as a free state
- The gas mask was patented by L.P. Haslett

1852

- Ohio made it illegal for women and children under 18 to work more than 10 hours a day
- Gun manufacturer Smith & Wesson was founded in Springfield, Massachusetts
- Louis Napoleon established the Second French Empire and called himself Emperor Napoleon III
- In Ireland, Edward Sabine showed a link between sunspot activity and changes in Earth's magnetic field
- The commercial value of Concord grapes in humid eastern states was discovered
- James Joule and Lord Kelvin demonstrated that a rapidly expanding gas cools
- Emma Snodgrass was arrested in Boston for wearing pants
- The first Holstein cow was transported to North America on a Dutch ship on which sailors had requested milk
- Massachusetts ruled that all school-age children must attend school
- Harriet Beecher Stowe's *Uncle Tom's Cabin* was published in Boston
- Wells, Fargo & Company was established in San Francisco
- The first British public toilet was opened in London
- Miami Medical College in Cincinnati was founded
- Anti-Jewish riots broke out in Stockholm
- The first Chinese immigrants arrived in Hawaii
- The *Uncle Sam* cartoon figure made its debut in the *New York Lantern*

weekly
- The first edition of Peter Mark Roget's Thesaurus was published
- Antonius Mathijsen developed plaster of Paris casts for setting fractures

1854

- The Crimean War began with Britain and France declaring war on Russia
- The Republican Party was organized at Ripon, Wisconsin, by former Whigs and disaffected Democrats opposed to the extension of slavery
- Mexico's *La Reforma* period began with the issuance of the Plan de Ayutla, which called for the ouster of the dictator Antonio López de Santa Anna
- *New York Tribune* journalist James Redpath traveled through the slave states urging slaves to run away
- Arctic explorer Elisha Kent Kane passed 80 degrees north, the farthest point reached by any expedition
- The U.S. Mint opened a San Francisco branch and paid miners the official rate of $16 per ounce for gold
- The Kansas and Nebraska territories were created
- The Chicago & Rock Island Railroad reached Rock Island in the Mississippi, giving Chicago its first rail link to America's key waterway
- U.S. railroads used telegraph messages for the first time to send information ahead about the location of trains and thus alert engineers to possible safety problems
- A Vatican ruling made the Immaculate Conception of the Virgin an article of faith and established papal infallibility in all matters of faith and morals
- Abraham Lincoln made his first political speech at the Illinois State Fair
- English chemist Alexander William Williamson explained for the first time the function of a catalyst in a chemical reaction

- A cholera epidemic in Chicago killed 5 percent of the city's population
- The Young Men's Hebrew Association was founded in Baltimore, Maryland
- U.S. Roman Catholics came under attack by the new American Party which opposed immigration and compared the Roman Catholic Church to Southern slave owners
- A paper mill at Roger's Ford in Chester County, Pennsylvania, produced paper from wood pulp at low cost
- *Walden, or Life in the Woods* by Henry David Thoreau was published
- The first street-cleaning machine in the U.S. was used in Philadelphia
- "The Charge of the Light Brigade" by Alfred Tennyson was written, glorifying Lord Cardigan's actions at the Battle of Balaclava
- "Jeanie with the Light Brown Hair" was a poplar song written by Stephen C. Foster
- The Otis safety elevator impressed visitors to the World's Fair in New York City

1858

- RH Macy & Company opened its first store at 6th Avenue and 34th Street in NYC
- Italian chemist Stanislao Cannizzaro differentiated between atomic and molecular weights
- The Butterfield Overland Mail Company began delivering mail from St. Louis to San Francisco
- Charles R. Darwin and Alfred Wallace independently proposed natural selection theories of evolution
- The invention of the Mason jar stimulated use of large quantities of white sugar for preserves
- U.S. Senate candidate Abraham Lincoln first used the phrase "A house divided against itself cannot stand"
- Minnesota became the thirty-second state
- A pencil with an eraser attached to one end was patented by Hyman L.

Lipman of Philadelphia

- Admission of $0.50 was charged at the All Star baseball game between New York and Brooklyn
- Hamilton Smith patented a rotary washing machine
- The New York Symphony Orchestra held its first performance
- The first edition of Gray's *Anatomy of the Human Body* was published
- Mary Ann Evans published her first collection of tales, *Scenes of Clerical Life*, under the pseudonym George Eliot
- The first transatlantic cable was completed but failed in less than one month in operation
- Mendelssohn's *Wedding March* was first played at the wedding of Queen Victoria's daughter Princess Victoria to the crown prince of Prussia

1862

- Paper money was introduced into the United States
- Richard J Gatling patented and manufactured the machine gun, which was used against Native Americans
- Victor Hugo's novel *Les Miserables* dramatically highlighted social problems in France
- Charles Darwin published the first thorough study of orchid pollination
- The U.S. Department of Agriculture was created
- Louis Pasteur convincingly disproved the theory concerning spontaneous generation of cellular life
- General Robert E. Lee took command of the Confederate armies of Virginia and North Carolina
- Jean Joseph Etienne Lenoir built the first gasoline-engine automobile
- The Homestead Act was passed, providing cheap land for settlement of the Nebraska Territory
- Congress established a Commissioner of Internal Revenue to deal with Civil War debt and collect tax on whiskey
- Slavery was abolished in Washington, DC

- The Sioux uprising erupted in Minnesota
- Union forces were defeated by Confederates at the second battle of Bull Run in Manassas, Virginia
- "The Battle Hymn of the Republic" by Julia Ward Howe was published in *The Atlantic Monthly* as an anonymous poem
- The Battle of Shiloh in Tennessee resulted in the deaths of 9,000 soldiers
- The United States population--north and south--was 31 million

1863

- The Emancipation Proclamation, issued by President Lincoln, took effect January 1, technically freeing nearly four million U.S. slaves
- The first homestead under the Homestead Act was claimed near Beatrice, Nebraska
- Union forces suffered defeat at Chancellorsville, Virginia, with casualties totaling over 16,700
- West Virginia entered the Union as the thirty-fifth state
- Union forces defeated Robert E. Lee's forces in Gettysburg, Pennsylvania
- The National Banking Act was signed into law by President Lincoln to raise money to finance the Union war effort, establish a uniform national currency and provide a dependable market for government bonds
- The first black regiment, the 54th Massachusetts, left Boston to fight in the Civil War
- The International Machinists and Blacksmiths Union adopted a resolution at Boston demanding an eight hour work day instead of a 12-hour one
- The Central Pacific Railroad construction began with ground-breaking ceremonies at Sacramento, California
- Former Mississippi riverboat pilot Samuel Langhorne Clemens adopted the pen name "Mark Twain" in a published letter printed in Carson

City's Territorial Enterprise
- *Tales of a Wayside Inn* by Henry Wadsworth Longfellow was published which included the poem "Paul Revere's Ride"
- Edouard Manet's painting, *Le déjeuner sur l'herbe,* was exhibited at the Salon des Refuses in Paris, depicting a nude woman picnicking with two clothed men
- A new Football Association established in England drew up definitive rules for "soccer"
- The first major U.S. racetrack for flat racing opened at Saratoga Springs, New York
- The first four-wheeled roller skates were patented by New York inventor James L. Plimpton
- The Capitol dome at Washington, DC, was capped to complete the structure's construction
- Disruption of sugar plantations in the South sent U.S. sugar prices soaring and brought an increase in sugar planting in the Hawaiian Islands
- President Lincoln proclaimed national Thanksgiving Day to commemorate the feast given by the Pilgrims in 1621

1864
- Abraham Lincoln was re-elected president with Andrew Johnson as his vice president
- Both the Union and Confederate armies suffered significant losses in the Battle of Spotsylvania, Virginia
- Union Major General William T. Sherman's troops set fires that destroyed much of Atlanta during their march through the South
- Congress first authorized the use of the phrase "In God We Trust" on a coin
- Secretary of War Edwin Stanton signed an order establishing a military burial ground at Confederate General Robert E. Lee's home estate in Arlington, Virginia

- Maryland voters adopted a new constitution that included the abolition of slavery
- Nevada became the thirty-sixth state
- The first salmon cannery in the United States was established at Washington, California
- Inflation devalued Confederate currency to $4.60 per $100 note
- Both the University of Kansas and the University of Denver were formed
- The Geneva Convention established the neutrality of battlefield facilities
- The Knights of Pythias was founded in Washington, DC
- George Pullman and Ben Feld patented the railroad sleeping car
- U.S. wheat prices reached $4.00 per bushel
- Confederate agents set Barnum Museum on fire in an attempt to burn New York City
- European immigrants poured into America to take advantage of the Homestead Act free land
- Louis Pasteur invented pasteurization for wine

1880–1881

- The U.S. population was 50 million; 65 percent of the people lived in the country
- 539,000 Singer sewing machines were sold, up from 250,000 in 1875
- The United States boasted 100 millionaires
- A&P operated 95 grocery stores from Boston to Milwaukee
- The plush Del Monte Hotel in Monterey, California, opened
- The country claimed 93,000 miles of railroad
- Halftone photographic illustrations appeared in newspapers for the first time
- Midwest farmers burned their corn for fuel; prices were too low to warrant shipping
- President James A. Garfield was assassinated

- The Diamond Match Company was created
- Marquette University was founded in Milwaukee
- Barnum & Bailey's Circus was created through the merger of two companies
- Chicago meatpacker Gustavus F. Swift perfected the refrigeration car to take Chicago dressed meat to the East Coast markets
- Josephine Cockrane of Illinois invented the first mechanical dishwasher
- A U.S. Constitutional amendment to grant full suffrage to women was introduced in Congress; it was introduced every year until its passage in 1920
- Economic unrest swept California, including its Chinese laborers, who numbered 75,000 and represented nine percent of the population
- Thanks to high tariffs, the U.S. Treasury was running an annual surplus of $145 million
- The U.S. had 2,400 magazines and daily newspapers, plus 7,500 weekly newspapers
- The typewriter and the telephone were both novelties at the 1876 Centennial in Philadelphia; by 1880, approximately 50,000 telephones existed nationwide, a number that would triple to 1.5 million by the turn of the twentieth century
- The camera was increasing in importance as an instrument of communications among all people; George Eastman's famous slogan was "You Push the Button, We Do the Rest" helped make Kodak a part of many American homes
- Most magazines carried little advertising in 1880; *Harper's Monthly* refused all advertising but those of its publisher until 1882
- Only 367 hospitals had been founded nationwide in 1880

1882–1883

- An internal combustion engine powered by gasoline was invented by German engineer Gottlieb Daimler

- Electric cable cars were installed in Chicago, travelling 20 blocks and averaging a speed of less than two miles per hour
- Only two percent of New York homes had running water
- The Andrew Jergens Company was founded to produce soaps, cosmetics and lotions
- Canadian Club whiskey was introduced by the Hiram Walker Distillery
- Van Camp Packing Company produced six million cans of pork and beans for shipment to Europe and U.S. markets
- Brooklyn Bridge opened
- *Ladies' Home Journal* began publication, with Cyrus H. K. Curtis as its publisher
- Thomas Edison invented the radio tube
- The first malted milk was produced in Racine, Wisconsin
- The first pea-podder machine was installed in Owasco, New York, replacing 600 cannery workers
- The American Baseball Association was established
- The United States banned Chinese immigration for 10 years
- A three-mile limit for territorial waters was agreed upon at the Hague Convention
- Robert Lewis Stevenson's *Treasure Island* was first published
- Boxer John L. Sullivan defeated Paddy Ryan to win the heavyweight boxing crown
- The first skyscraper was built in Chicago, topping out at 10 stories
- Robert Koch described a method of preventative inoculation against anthrax

1884

- Theodore Roosevelt's wife died two days after giving birth to Alice Lee Roosevelt; his mother, Martha, had died just a few hours earlier
- Over 100 suffragists, led by Susan B. Anthony, demanded that President Chester A. Arthur support female suffrage
- Mississippi established the first state college for women in America

- Standard Time was adopted throughout the United States
- The first long-distance telephone call was made, between Boston and New York City
- The Institute for Electrical & Electronics Engineers (IEEE) was founded
- Civil War hero General William T. Sherman refused the Republican presidential nomination, saying, "I will not accept if nominated and will not serve if elected."
- A Chinese army defeated the French at Bacle, Indochina
- Congress declared Labor Day a legal holiday
- The Statue of Liberty was presented to the United States in ceremonies in Paris, France, to commemorate 100 years of American independence
- The first documented photograph of a tornado was taken near Howard, South Dakota
- The Equal Rights Party, formed during a convention of suffragists in San Francisco, nominated Belva Ann Bennett Lockwood of Washington, D.C., for president and Marietta Snow as her running mate
- The U.S. Naval War College was established in Newport, Rhode Island
- Greenwich was established as the universal time meridian of longitude
- Transparent paper-strip photographic film was patented by George Eastman
- Democrat Grover Cleveland was elected to his first term as president, defeating Republican James G. Blaine
- John B. Meyenberg of St. Louis patented evaporated milk
- Army engineers completed construction of the Washington monument

1885

- A coup d'état in Eastern Rumelia led directly to a war between Serbia and Bulgaria
- John Ward and several teammates secretly formed the Brotherhood of Professional Base Ball Players, the first baseball union
- Johann Strauss' operetta, *The Gypsy Baron,* premiered in Vienna;

Johannes Brahms's *4th Symphony in E* was first performed
- Tacoma, Washington vigilantes drove out Chinese residents and burned their homes and businesses
- The Canadian Pacific Railroad reached the Pacific Ocean
- Baseball set all players' salaries at $1,000-$2,000 for the 1885 season
- Pope Leo XIII published the encyclical *Immortale Dei*
- Paul Daimler, son of Gottlieb Daimler, became the first motorcyclist when he rode his father's new invention on a round trip of six miles
- The first photograph of a meteor was taken
- Dr. William W. Grant of Davenport, Iowa, performed the first appendectomy
- Bachelor Grover Cleveland entered the White House as president
- Mark Twain's *Adventures of Huckleberry Finn* was published
- The Washington Monument was dedicated
- The U.S. Post Office began offering special delivery for first-class mail
- The Eastman Film Co. of Rochester, New York, manufactured the first commercial motion picture film
- The Salvation Army was officially organized in the U.S.
- Texas was the last Confederate state readmitted to the Union
- The Congo Free State was established by King Leopold II of Belgium
- The first mass production of shoes occurred in Lynn, Massachusetts
- French scientist Louis Pasteur successfully tested an anti-rabies vaccine on a boy bitten by an infected dog
- Ulysses S. Grant, commander of the Union forces at the end of the Civil War and the eighteenth president of the United States, died in Mount McGregor, New York, at age 63
- Leo Daft opened America's first commercially operated electric streetcar in Baltimore
- In Rock Springs, Wyoming Territory, 28 Chinese laborers were killed and hundreds more chased out of town by striking coal miners
- The first gasoline pump was delivered to a gasoline dealer in Ft.

Wayne, Indiana

1886

- A general strike that escalated into the Haymarket Riot built momentum toward the eight-hour workday in the U.S.
- Emil Berliner began his work that resulted in the invention of the gramophone
- Pharmacist Dr. John Stith Pemberton invented a carbonated beverage that would be named Coca-Cola and began advertising his product in the *Atlanta Journal*
- In the case of *Santa Clara County v. Southern Pacific Railroad,* the U.S. Supreme Court ruled that corporations have the same rights as living persons
- *The Strange Case of Dr Jekyll and Mr. Hyde* was first published
- Karl Benz patented the first successful gasoline-driven automobile, the Benz Patent Motorwagen, which was built in 1885
- The first trainload of oranges was shipped from Los Angeles to the East over the transcontinental railroad
- President Grover Cleveland married Frances Folsom in the White House, becoming the only president to wed in the executive mansion
- The American Federation of Labor (AFL) was formed by 26 craft unions led by Samuel Gompers
- The first U.S.-based nurses' magazine, *The Nightingale*, was published in New York City
- Charles Hall filed a patent for his process of turning aluminum oxide into molten aluminum
- After almost 30 years of conflict, Apache leader Geronimo surrendered with his last band of warriors to General Nelson Miles at Skeleton Canyon in Arizona
- William Stanley, Jr. created the first practical alternating current transformer device, known as the induction coil
- President Grover Cleveland dedicated the Statue of Liberty in New

York Harbor
- Heinrich Hertz verified the existence of electromagnetic waves
- Scotch whisky distiller William Grant & Sons was founded

1888–1889
- The gramophone was invented
- Benjamin Harrison was elected president of the United States
- The alternating-current electric motor was developed
- Anti-Chinese riots erupted in Seattle
- *National Geographic Magazine* began publication
- The first typewriter stencil was introduced
- Parker Pen Company was started in Janesville, Wisconsin
- Tobacco merchant Washington B. Duke produced 744 million cigarettes
- The Ponce de Leon Hotel was opened in St. Augustine, Florida
- The Oklahoma Territory lands, formerly reserved for Indians, were opened to white settlers
- Safety Bicycle was introduced; more than one million would be sold in the next four years
- Electric lights were installed in the White House
- Aunt Jemima pancake flour was invented in St. Joseph, Missouri
- Calumet baking powder was created in Chicago
- "Jack the Ripper" murdered six women in London
- George Eastman perfected the "Kodak" box camera
- J.P. Dunlop invented the pneumatic tire
- Heinrich Hertz and Oliver Lodge independently identified radio waves as belonging to the same family as light waves

1890–1891
- Massive immigration that was transforming the nation left the rural South largely unaffected
- Two-thirds of the nation's 62.9 million people still lived in rural areas;

32.7 percent were immigrants or the children of at least one immigrant parent

- New Irish women immigrants to America, in demand as servants, outnumbered the men in 1890
- The census showed that 53.5 percent of the farms in the US were fewer than 100 acres
- The first commercial dry cell battery was invented
- Three percent of Americans, age 18 to 21, attended college
- *Literary Digest* began publication
- Population of Los Angeles reached 50,000, up 40,000 in 10 years
- Restrictive anti-black "Jim Crow" laws were enacted throughout the South
- The first full-service advertising agency was established in New York City
- Thousands of Kansas farmers were bankrupted by the tight money conditions
- The $3 million Tampa Bay Hotel was completed in Florida
- American Express Traveler's Cheque was copyrighted
- Ceresota flour was introduced by the Northwest Consolidated Milling Company
- George A. Hormel & Co. introduced the packaged food Spam
- Painter Paul Gauguin arrived in Papeete, Tahiti
- The penalty kick was introduced into soccer
- The International Brotherhood of Electrical Workers was organized
- New Scotland Yard became the headquarters of the London Metropolitan Police
- Eugène Dubois discovered *Homo erectus* fossils in the Dutch colony of Java
- Bicycle designer Charles Duryea, 29, and his toolmaker brother James designed a gasoline engine capable of powering a road vehicle
- Edouard Michelin obtained a patent for a "removable" bicycle tire that

could be repaired quickly in the event of puncture
- The Jarvis winch, patented by Glasgow-born Scottish shipmaster John C. B. Jarvis, enabled ships to be manned by fewer men and helped develop the windjammer
- Rice University and Stanford were chartered
- John T. Smith patented corkboard using a process of heat and pressure to combine waste cork together for insulation
- American Express issued the first traveler's checks
- Commercial bromine was produced electrolytically by Herbert H. Dow's Midland Chemical Company in Michigan
- Bacteriologist Anna Williams obtained her M.D. from the Women's Medical College of New York and worked in the diagnostic laboratory of the city's Health Department, the first such lab in America
- Chicago's Provident Hospital became the first interracial hospital in America
- The lapidary encyclical "Of New Things" by Pope Leo XIII declared that employers have the moral duty as members of the possessing class to improve the "terrible conditions of the new and often violent process of industrialization"
- Educator William Rainey Harper became president of the new University of Chicago with funding from merchant Marshall Field and oilman John D. Rockefeller
- Irene Coit became the first woman admitted to Yale University
- The electric self-starter for automobiles was patented
- The Automatic Electric Company was founded to promote a dial telephone patented by Kansas City undertaker Almon B. Strowger, who suspected that "central" was diverting his incoming calls to a rival embalmer
- Important books included *Tess of the d'Urbervilles* by Thomas Hardy; *The Light That Failed* by Rudyard Kipling; *The Picture of Dorian Gray* by Oscar Wilde, and *Tales of Soldiers and Civilians* by Ambrose Bierce

1892–1893

- American industry was benefiting from the 1890 decision by Congress to increase tariffs on foreign goods from 38 to 50 percent, making U.S. manufactured items less expensive
- New York City boss Richard Croker's fortune was estimated to be $8 million, not including his own railway car and a $2.5 million stud farm
- An improved carburetor for automobiles was invented
- The first successful gasoline tractor was produced by a farmer in Waterloo, Iowa
- Chicago's first elevated railway went into operation, forming the famous Loop
- The $1 Ingersoll pocket watch was introduced, bringing affordable timepieces to the masses
- The General Electric Company was created through a merger
- Violence erupted at the steelworkers' strike of the Carnegie-Phipps Mill at Homestead, Pennsylvania
- President Benjamin Harrison extended for 10 years the Chinese Exclusion Act, which suspended Chinese immigration to the United States
- The United States population included 4,000 millionaires
- The name Sears, Roebuck & Company came into use
- Pineapples were canned for the first time
- Diesel patented his internal combustion engine
- The Census Bureau announced that a frontier line was no longer discernible; all unsettled areas had been invaded
- The first automatic telephone switchboard was activated
- Cream of Wheat was introduced by Diamond Mill of Grand Forks, North Dakota
- New York's 13-story Waldorf Hotel was opened
- The first Ford motorcar was road tested
- The Philadelphia and Reading Railroad went into receivership

- Wrigley's Spearmint and Juicy Fruit chewing gum were introduced by William Wrigley, Jr.

1894

- Approximately 12,000 New York City tailors struck to protest sweatshops
- The first Sunday newspaper color comic section was published in the *New York World*
- Antique-collecting became popular, supported by numerous genealogy-minded societies
- A well-meaning group of anglophiles called the America Acclimatization Society began importing English birds mentioned in Shakespeare, including nightingales, thrushes and starlings, for release in America
- Overproduction forced farm prices to fall; wheat dropped from $1.05 a bushel in 1870 to $0.49 a bushel
- The first Greek newspaper in America was published as the *New York Atlantis*
- New York Governor Roswell P. Flower signed the nation's first dog-licensing law, with a $2.00 license fee
- Hockey's first Stanley Cup championship game was played between the Montreal Amateur Athletic Association and the Ottawa Capitals
- Thomas Edison publicly demonstrated the kinetoscope, a peephole viewer in which developed film moved continuously under a magnifying glass
- Workers at the Pullman Palace Car Company in Illinois went on strike to protest a wage reduction; President Cleveland ordered federal troops onto the trains to insure mail delivery
- Labor Day was established as a holiday for federal employees
- Congress established the Bureau of Immigration
- Congress passed a bill imposing a 2 percent tax on incomes over $4,000, which was ruled unconstitutional by the U.S. Supreme Court
- The United States Government began keeping records on the weather

- Astronomer Percival Lowell built a private observatory in Flagstaff, Arizona, and began his observations of Mars
- The Regents of the University of Michigan declared that "Henceforth in the selection of professors and instructors and other assistants in instruction in the University, no discrimination will be made in selection between men and women"
- French Baron Pierre de Coubertin proposed an international Olympics competition to be held every four years in a different nation to encourage international peace and cooperation
- The *Edison Kinetoscopic Record of a Sneeze* was released in movie theaters

1895

- Mintonette, later known as volleyball, was created by William G. Morgan in Holyoke, Massachusetts
- Oscar Wilde's last play, *The Importance of Being Earnest*, was first shown at St. James's Theatre in London
- The Treaty of Shimonoseki was signed between China and Japan, marking the end of the first Sino-Japanese War
- The U.S. Supreme Court ruled that the federal government had the right to regulate interstate commerce, legalizing the military suppression of the Pullman Strike
- The first professional American football game was played in Latrobe, Pennsylvania, between the Latrobe YMCA and the Jeannette Athletic Club
- Rudyard Kipling published the story "Mowgli Leaves the Jungle Forever" in *Cosmopolitan* illustrated magazine
- George B. Selden was granted the first U.S. patent for an automobile
- Wilhelm Röntgen discovered a type of radiation later known as x-rays
- Oscar Hammerstein opened the Olympia Theatre, the first to be built in New York City's Times Square district
- Alfred Nobel signed his last will and testament, setting aside his estate

to establish the Nobel Prize after his death
- Two hundred African-Americans left from Savannah, Georgia, headed for Liberia
- George Brownell patented a machine to make paper twine
- The Anti-Saloon League of America was formed in Washington D.C.
- Frederick Blaisdell patented the pencil
- George Washington Vanderbilt II officially opened his "Biltmore House" on Christmas in Asheville, North Carolina
- Auguste and Louis Lumière displayed their first moving picture film in Paris
- The London School of Economics and Political Science was founded in England
- W. E. B. Du Bois became the first African-American to receive a Ph.D. from Harvard University
- The gold reserve of the U.S. Treasury was saved when J. P. Morgan and the Rothschilds loaned $65 million worth of gold to the U.S. Government

1896–1897

- The bicycle industry reported sales of $60 million; the average bike sold for $100
- The earliest trading stamps, issued by S&H Green Stamps, were distributed
- Michelob beer was introduced
- The Klondike gold rush in Bonanza Creek, Canada, began
- The *Boston Cooking School Cook Book* was published, advocating the use of precise measurements to produce identical results
- Radioactivity was discovered in uranium
- William Ramsay discovered helium
- Five annual Nobel Prizes were established in the fields of physics, physiology and medicine, chemistry, literature, and peace
- Bituminous coal miners staged a 12-week walkout

- Continental Casualty Company was founded
- Dow Chemical Company was incorporated
- Radio transmission over long distances was achieved by Gugielmo Marconi
- Winton Motor Carriage Company was organized
- The NYC Health Board began enforcing a law regulating women in mercantile establishments
- Mail Pouch tobacco was introduced
- Ronald Ross discovered the malaria bacillus
- Wheat prices rose to $1.09 per bushel
- Jell-O was introduced by Pearl B. Wait
- Boston's H.P. Hill used glass bottles to distribute milk

1897

- Thorstein Veblen developed the concepts for his book, *Theory of the Leisure Class*, which stated, "conspicuous consumption of valuable goods is a means of reputability to the gentlemen of leisure"
- Continental Casualty Company was founded
- Radical Emma Goldman, advocate of free love, birth control, homosexual rights and "freedom for both sexes," was arrested
- The Royal Automobile Club was founded in London
- John Davison Rockefeller, worth nearly $200 million, stopped going to his office at Standard Oil and began playing golf and giving away his wealth
- The Presbyterian Assembly condemned the growing bicycling fad for enticing parishioners away from church
- Motorcar production reached nearly 1,000 vehicles
- Nearly 150 Yiddish periodicals were being published, many of which advocated radical labor reform, Zionism, and even anarchism, to obtain reform
- Republican William McKinley was sworn into office as America's 25th president, helped by $7 million raised by manager businessman Mark

Hanna, compared with $300,000 raised by opponent William Jennings Bryan

- Prospectors streamed to the Klondike in search of gold
- The Winton Motor Carriage Company was organized

1898

- "Happy Birthday to You," composed by sisters Mildred and Patty Hill in 1893 as "Good Morning to All," was becoming popular
- The "grandfather clause" marched across the South, ushering in widespread use of Jim Crow laws and restricting most blacks from voting
- Pepsi-Cola was introduced in North Carolina, by pharmacist Caleb Bradham
- J.P. Stevens & Company was founded in New York
- Toothpaste in collapsible metal tubes was available due to the work of Connecticut dentist Lucius Sheffield
- The trolley replaced horsedrawn cars in Boston
- Wesson Oil was introduced
- The boll weevil began spreading across cotton-growing areas of the South
- *The New York Times* dropped its price from $0.03 to $0.01, tripling circulation
- The Union Carbide Company was formed
- Uneeda Biscuit was created
- Bricklayers made $3.41 per day and worked a 48-hour week, while marble cutters made $4.22 per day
- America boasted more than 300 bicycle manufacturing companies
- Cellophane was invented by Charles F. Cross and Edward J. Bevan

1900

- President William McKinley used the telephone as part of his re-election campaign; he was the last Union soldier to be elected president

- Nationwide, 13,824 motorcars were on the road
- Hamburgers were introduced by Louis Lassen in New Haven, Connecticut
- The number of advertising agencies in New York City increased from 44 in 1870 to more than 400
- Firestone Tire and Rubber Company was founded based on a patent for attaching tires to rims
- John Davison Rockefeller's wealth was estimated to be $200 million
- A dinner party in New York attracted publicity when cigarettes rolled in $100 bills were given to guests before dinner
- The cost of telephone service fell dramatically as more companies offered a 10-party line, allowing that many customers to share one line
- The U.S. led the world in productivity, based on gross national product, producing $116 billion compared with $62.2 billion in Great Britain, $42.8 billion in France and $42 billion in Germany
- 30,000 trolley cars operated on 15,000 miles of track across America
- Cities like New York and San Francisco had one saloon for every 200 people
- Louis Comfort Tiffany opened his first glass studio in New York
- America's economic boom entered its fourth year with 0.1 percent inflation
- Cigarette smoking was extremely popular and widely advertised, particularly by American Tobacco
- Excavation had begun on the New York subway system
- U.S. railroads were charging an average of $0.75 per ton-mile, down from $1.22 in 1883
- Automobile manufacturer Ransom Olds sold 425 cars during the year
- The U.S. College Entrance Examination Board was formed to screen college applicants using a Scholastic Aptitude Test
- The Junior League of the New York Settlement House attracted young débutantes to serve the less fortunate

- Puerto Rico, obtained in the Spanish-American War in 1898, was declared a U.S. territory
- A tidal wave in Galveston, Texas, killed 4,000 people
- The U.S. Navy bought its first submarine

1901

- Major movies included *The Philippines and Our New Possessions, The Conquest of the Air, Drama at the Bottom of the Sea* and *Execution of Czolgosz,* the man who shot President William McKinley
- Pogroms in Russia forced many Jews to America
- The U.S. constructed a 16-inch, 130-pound breech-loading rifle that was the most powerful in the world
- Popular songs included "Ain't Dat a Shame?," "The Night We Did Not Care," "When You Loved Me in the Sweet Old Days" and "Maiden with the Dreamy Eyes"
- The first U.S. Open golf tournament under USGA rules was held at the Myopia Hunt Club in Hamilton, Massachusetts
- The U.S. granted citizenship to the five civilized tribes: the Cherokee, Creek, Choctaw, Chicasaw and Seminole
- West Point officially abolished the practice of hazing cadets
- The Boston Museum of Fine Arts was given funds to purchase Velásquez's portrait, *Don Baltazar and His Dwarf*
- Books included *Up from Slavery* by Booker T. Washington, *To a Person Sitting in Darkness* by Mark Twain, *The Psychopathology of Everyday Life* by Sigmund Freud, *The Octopus* by Frank Norris and *Springtime and Harvest* by Upton Sinclair
- North Carolina proposed a literacy amendment for voting
- *The Settlement Cookbook,* published by a Milwaukee settlement worker to help immigrant women, carried the phrase, "The way to a man's heart is through his stomach"
- Peter Cooper Hewitt created the first mercury-vapor electric lamp
- Four widows of Revolutionary War soldiers remained on pensions; one

veteran of the war of 1812 still lived
- Researchers discovered a connection between obesity and heart disease
- Of the 120,000 U.S. military troops on active duty, 70,000 were stationed in the Philippines fighting the insurgency
- South Dakota passed legislation making school attendance mandatory for children eight to 14 years of age
- The first vacuum cleaner was invented to compete with the Bissell Carpet Sweeper
- The military began placing greater emphasis on the science of nutrition after England had to reject three out of five men in its recruiting for the Boer War in 1899
- Vice President Teddy Roosevelt was made an honorary member of the Hebrew Veterans of the War with Spain; many of its members had fought as Roosevelt's Rough Riders during the Spanish-American War
- Christy Mathewson of New York pitched professional baseball's first no-hitter, defeating St. Louis 5-0
- The length of time required to cross the Atlantic Ocean was one week, compared to one month in 1800
- The median age of men for their first marriage was 25.9 years, and 21.9 for women

1902–1903
- The Brownie Box camera was introduced by Eastman Kodak Company, costing $1.00
- Firestone Tire and Rubber Company began operations based on a patent for attaching tires to rims
- The first modern submarine, the *Holland,* was purchased by the navy
- Uneeda Biscuits achieved sales of more than 10 million packages per month
- Life expectancy nationwide in 1900 was estimated to be 47 years
- The U.S. census reported the U.S. population at 76 million and projected that it would grow to 106 million over the next 20 years,

pushed by a steady influx of immigrants

- Membership in the American Federation of Labor reached the million-person mark
- The National Association of Manufacturers launched an anti-union campaign that promoted the right of Americans to work when and where they pleased, depicting labor organizers as agitators and socialists
- The price of coal in New York went from $5.00 to $30.00 a ton during a five-month strike of anthracite coal workers
- Rayon was patented by U.S. Chemist A. D. Little
- Russian American Morris Michtom and his wife introduced the teddy bear with movable arms, legs, and head
- Philip Morris Corporation was founded
- Charles Lewis Tiffany, founder of Tiffany and Co., died, leaving an estate of $35 million
- The automat restaurant was opened by Horn & Hardart Baking company in Philadelphia
- The Wright Brothers made the first sustained manned flights in a controlled gasoline-powered aircraft
- The 24-horsepower Chadwick motorcar cost $4,000, capable of going 60 mph
- Massachusetts created the first automobile license plate
- Bottle-blowing machines cut the cost of manufacturing electric light bulbs
- The Harley-Davidson motorcycle was introduced
- An automatic machine to clean a salmon and remove its head and tail was devised by A.K. Smith, speeding processing and cutting costs
- Sanka Coffee was introduced by German coffee importer Ludwig Roselius

1904

- Marie Louise Van Vorst infiltrated factories to expose the problems of

child labor
- Post Toasties were introduced by the Postum Company
- The St. Louis Fair spawned iced tea and the ice cream cone
- *Ladies' Home Journal* published an exposé of the U.S. patent medicine business
- Montgomery Ward mailed three million free catalogues, while Sears, Roebuck distributed a million copies of its spring catalogue
- Typhoid fever in NYC was traced to "Typhoid Mary" Mallon, a carrier of the disease who took jobs handling food, often under an assumed name
- The National Women's Trade Union League was formed by middle-class and working women to foster women's education and help women organize unions
- The New York Society for the Suppression of Vice targeted playing cards, roulette, lotto, watches with obscene pictures, and articles of rubber for immoral use
- Florida gained the title to the Everglades swamp and immediately made plans for drainage
- Louis Sherry's on NYC's 5th Avenue opened the New York Riding Club, where members could eat in the saddle
- A Packard Model F went from San Francisco to New York City in 51 days, the first authenticated transcontinental auto trip
- Women's groups led by the wealthy, who were fighting for better conditions for working women, were branded "the mink brigade"
- Horace Fletcher's book *ABC of Nutrition* advocated chewing your food 32 times a bite, sparking a special trend for mastication
- Malaria and yellow fever disappeared from the Panama Canal after army surgeons discovered the link to mosquitoes and developed successful disease control
- The sixth moon of Jupiter was sighted
- Marie Curie discovered two new radioactive elements in uranium ore—

radium and polonium

- *The Shame of the Cities* by Lincoln Steffens, *History of the Standard Oil Company* by Ida Tarbell, and *In Reckless Ecstasy* by Carl Sandburg were published

- Laura Ziegler held a grand opening for her brothel in Fort Smith, Arkansas, hosted by the mayor and other dignitaries; her cost of $3 was higher than the $1 charged at most establishments

- President Teddy Roosevelt ruled that Civil War veterans over 62 years were eligible to receive a pension

- Central heating, the ultraviolet lamp, Dr. Scholl arch supports, E. F. Hutton, the Caterpillar Tractor Company and offset printing all made their first appearance

- Thorstein Veblen coined the phrase "conspicuous consumption" to describe the useless spending habits of the rich in his book, *Theory of Business Enterprise*

- The counterweight elevator was designed by the Otis Company, replacing the hydraulic elevator and allowing buildings to rise more than 20 stories

- The U.S. paid $40 million to purchase French property in the Panama Canal region

- The New York subway opened, with more than 100,000 people riding on the first day

- Popular songs included "Give My Regards to Broadway," "Meet Me in St. Louis, Louis" and "Come Take a Trip in My Air-Ship"

- A massive fire in Baltimore destroyed 26,000 buildings

- The Olympics were held in St. Louis as part of the St. Louis Exposition, and basketball was presented as a demonstration sport

- Novocain, the crash helmet, snow chains and the vacuum tube were invented

1905–1906

- Industrial Workers of the World (IWW) attacked the American

Federation of Labor for accepting the capitalist system
- A New York law limiting hours of work in the baking industry to 60 per week was ruled unconstitutional by the Supreme Court
- U.S. auto production reached 15,000 cars per year, up from 2,500 in 1899
- William Randolph Hearst acquired *Cosmopolitan* magazine for $400,000
- Royal Typewriter Company was founded by New York financier Thomas Fortune Ryan
- Sales of Jell-O reached $1 million
- Oklahoma was admitted to the Union
- Planters Nut and Chocolate Company was created
- A-1 Sauce was introduced in the U.S. by Hartford's G.F. Heublein & Brothers
- Samuel Hopkins Adams' *The Great American Fraud* exposed the fraudulent claims of many patent medicines
- Anti-liquor campaigners received powerful support from the Woman's Christian Temperance Union, lead by Frances E. Willard, who often fell to her knees and prayed on saloon floors
- Former President Grover Cleveland wrote in *The Ladies' Home Journal* that women of sense did not wish to vote: "The relative positions to be assumed by men and women in the working out of our civilizations were assigned long ago by a higher intelligence than ours."
- President Theodore Roosevelt admonished well-born white women who were using birth control for participating in willful sterilization, a practice known as racial suicide

1907–1908
- *The New York Times* inaugurated the custom of dropping an illuminated ball to greet the new year in what everyone now calls Times Square
- Cadillac was advertised at $800.00, a Ford Model K at $2,800.00

- Horses were sold for $150.00 to $300.00
- The first self-contained electric clothes washer was developed in Chicago
- The American Society for Keeping Woman in Her Proper Sphere was formed
- The first Christmas "stamps" were sold to raise money for tuberculosis research
- Mother's Day is celebrated, unofficially, in Philadelphia, Pennsylvania
- New York City passed the Sullivan Ordinance prohibiting women from smoking in public places
- Publication of the *Christian Science Monitor* began
- Wealthy American Reformer Maud Younger founded the Waitresses' Union in San Francisco after waitressing herself in order to learn about the life of working women
- The first canned tuna fish was packed in California
- Westinghouse Electric went bankrupt
- Two subway tunnels were opened to traffic in New York City
- The "Rich Man's Panic" resulted in financial reforms that increased the flexibility of the money supply and eventually led to the Federal Reserve Act of 1913
- The U.S. Supreme Court issued a unanimous ruling holding that laws limiting the maximum number of hours that women can work to 10 hours a day are constitutional
- Many U.S. banks closed as economic depression deepened
- President Theodore Roosevelt called a White House Conference on conservation
- Cornelius Vanderbilt's yacht, the *North Star,* was reported to cost $250,000 with a yearly maintenance bill of $20,000
- The 47-story Singer Building in New York became the world's tallest skyscraper
- Both the Muir Woods in California and the Grand Canyon were named

national monuments worthy of preservation

- The first transatlantic wireless telegraph stations connected Canada to Ireland, and messages could be sent for $0.15 a word
- The AC spark plug, Luger pistol, and oscillating fan all came on the market
- Alpha Kappa Alpha, the first sorority for black women, was founded in Washington, D.C.
- Nancy Hale became the *New York Times'* first female reporter
- The U.S. Army bought its first aircraft, a dirigible, but because no one could fly it except its owner, it was never used
- The Olympic Games were played in London with the U.S. the unofficial winner with 23 gold medals
- Thomas Edison's Amberol cylinders, with more grooves per inch, extended the length of time a single recording would play from two to four minute
- More than 80 percent of all immigrants since 1900 came from Central Europe, Italy, and Russia

1909

- D.W. Griffith featured 16-year-old Mary Pickford in his films and she made $40.00 a week starring in silent movies
- 20,000 members of Ladies Waist Maker's Union staged a three-month strike and won most of their demands
- A tobacconist convention protested the automobile, concerned that it would lure people away from homes and clubs and smoking would be diminished
- The Sixteenth Amendment to the Constitution, authorizing income taxes, was passed by Congress
- More than 25 miners were killed in an explosion at the Saint Paul Mine in Cherry, Illinois
- Chicago's Jane Addams, founder of Hull House, ended her term as appointed member of the Chicago Board of Education, where she had

lobbied for compulsory education and laws to end child labor

- Milton Hershey, the father of the modern candy industry, had sales of $5 million a year making almond bars, kisses, and chocolate cigars
- The National Association for the Advancement of Colored People was founded by W.E.B. DuBois, Chicago reformer Jane Addams, Mary W. Ovington, and others
- The International Ladies' Garment Worker's Union called a strike to protest poor working conditions and low wages
- The Kansas attorney general ruled that women may wear trousers
- Western women began to wear V-neck shirts, which some condemned as immoral
- The U.S. Congress passed the Mann White Slave Traffic Act to prohibit interstate and foreign transport of females for immoral purposes
- The U.S. Senate heard a resolution to abolish sex discrimination in the Constitution

1910–1911

- Nationwide only 43 percent of 16-year-olds were still in school
- Western Union abolished the $0.40 to $0.50 charge for placing telegraph messages by telephone
- *Women's Wear Daily* began publication in New York
- U.S. cigarette sales reached 8.6 billion cigarettes, with 62 percent controlled by the American Tobacco Trust
- Florida orange shipments rebounded to their 1894 level
- 70 percent of bread was baked at home, down from 80 percent in 1890
- *The Flexner Report* showed most North American medical schools were inferior to those in Europe
- Halley's Comet stirred fear and excitement, as many hid in shelters or took 'comet' pills for protection
- The average man made $15.00 for a 58-hour work week and 42 percent was spent on food
- A movement began to restrict the sale of morphine except by

prescription
- More than 10,000 nickelodeons were now operating nationwide
- Father's Day and the Boy Scouts of America made their first appearances
- The concept of the "weekend" as a time of rest gained popularity
- New York's Ellis Island had a record one-day influx of 11,745 immigrants in 1911
- 2,200 communities nationwide had between 2,500 and 50,000 people; in 1860 the number was 400 communities
- Actress Blanche Sweet was one of D.W. Griffith's regulars in the one- and two-reelers that dominated the movie industry
- David Horsley moved his study from Bayonne, New Jersey, to the Los Angeles suburb of Hollywood to establish a movie studio on Sunset Boulevard
- The Underwood Company attempted to create a noiseless typewriter
- The Triangle Shirtwaist factory fire in New York City aroused nationwide demands for better work conditions, a fire made deadly because the single exit door was locked to prevent the workers from stealing thread
- A record 12,000 European immigrants arrived at Ellis Island on a single day
- During a discussion concerning trade with Canada, a congressional group proposed to annex the neighboring country
- The Self-Mastery Colony in New Jersey and Parting of the Ways home in Chicago were created to help the deserving poor
- California women gained suffrage by constitutional amendment
- F.W. Woolworth was incorporated
- The electric self-starter for the motorcar was perfected and adopted by Cadillac
- Marmon Wasp won the first Indianapolis 500-mile race, averaging 75 miles per hour

- Direct telephone links were opened between New York and Denver
- The use of fingerprinting in crime detection became widespread
- On the fiftieth anniversary of the Battle of Bull Run, Civil War veterans from both the North and South mingled at the battlefield site
- Marie Curie won an unprecedented second Nobel Prize, but was refused admission to the French Academy of Science
- 60,000 Bibles were placed in hotel bedrooms by the Gideon Organization of Christian Commercial Travelers
- The socialist-backed magazine, *The Masses,* was founded in Greenwich Village, printing articles concerning "what is too naked for the money-making press."
- A climbing divorce rate of one in 12 marriages, from one in 85 in 1905, caused concerns

1912–1913

- Congress extended the eight-hour day to all federal employees
- Women composed a quarter of all workers employed in nonagricultural jobs
- L.L. Bean was founded by merchant Leon Leonwood Bean
- Medical schools opened their doors to women in the 1890s, but admission was restricted to five percent of the class
- One-third of American households employed servants, who worked 11 to 12 hours a day
- Domestic service was the largest single category of female employment nationwide, often filled by immigrants
- Nationwide approximately 57 percent of 16- and 17-year-olds no longer attended school
- Ford produced more than 22 percent of all U.S. motorcars
- Oreo biscuits were introduced by National Biscuit Company to compete with biscuit bon-bons
- A merger of U.S. film producers created Universal Pictures Corporation
- A&P began rapid expansion featuring stores that operated on a cash-

and-carry basis
- Brillo Manufacturing Corporation was founded
- Congress strengthened the Pure Food and Drug Law of 1906
- The 60-story Woolworth building opened in New York
- Peppermint Life Savers were introduced as a summer seller when chocolate sales traditionally declined
- 5,000 suffragists marched down Pennsylvania Avenue in Washington, D.C., where they were heckled and slapped
- Congress strengthened the Pure Food and Drug Law of 1906
- The "Armory Show" introduced Post-Impressionism and Cubism to New York
- Vitamin A was isolated at Yale University
- Zippers, in use since 1891, became popular
- Grand Central Station in New York City was completed
- Henry Ford pioneered new assembly-line techniques in his car factory
- A Chicago company produced the first refrigerator for domestic use
- The first jury of women was drawn in California
- The first federal income tax was imposed on incomes over $3,000, affecting 62,000
- U.S. industrial output rose to 40 percent of the world's total production, up from 20 percent in 1860
- Camel, the first modern, blended cigarette, was produced, with a package design inspired by "Old Joe," a dromedary in the Barnum & Bailey circus
- A sheriff in Spartanburg, South Carolina, was tried for preventing a lynching, then acquitted
- Teacher Bridget Peixico was fired after 19 years by the New York Board of Education when she became a mother, but reinstated by the courts, which ruled that "illness...caused by maternity (cannot be) construed as neglect of duty."
- The Schaeffer pen, Quaker Puffed Rice, Chesterfield cigarettes, a

dental hygienist's course, and the erector set were all introduced for the first time

1914

- The Federal League, baseball's third major league after the American and National Leagues, expanded to eight teams
- Rookie baseball pitcher George "Babe" Ruth debuted with the Boston Red Sox
- Movie premieres included *The Perils of Pauline, The Exploits of Elaine, Home Sweet Home,* and *Kid Auto Races at Venice*
- Theodore W. Richards won the Nobel Prize in chemistry for his work in the determination of atomic weights
- Thyroxin, the major thyroid hormone, was isolated by Edward Kendall at the Mayo Clinic
- Yale University opened its Coliseum-sized "Bowl" large enough to seat 60,000
- *The New Republic* magazine, passport photo requirements, non-skid tires, international figure skating tournaments, Kelvinator and The American Society of Composers, Authors and Publishers (ASCAP) all made their first appearance
- Pope Pius X condemned the tango as "new paganism"
- Former President Theodore Roosevelt returned from South America with 1,500 bird and 500 mammal specimens and a claim that he had discovered a new river
- The writings of Margaret Sanger sparked renewed controversy about birth control and contraception
- Chicago established the Censorship Board to remove movie scenes depicting beatings or dead bodies
- Tuition, room and board at Harvard University cost $700 per year
- Ford Motor Company produced 240,700 cars, nearly as many as all other companies combined
- The outbreak of war in Europe spurred U.S. production of pasta, which

had previously been imported

- Popular songs included "St. Louis Blues," "The Missouri Waltz," "Play a Simple Melody," "Fido Is a Hot Dog Now," and "If You Don't Want My Peaches, You'd Better Stop Shaking My Tree"
- In college football, five first team All Americans were from Harvard
- New York was the nation's largest city with population of 5.3 million, Chicago boasted 2.4 million, Philadelphia 1.7 million and Los Angeles 500,000 President Woodrow Wilson declared Mother's Day an official holiday

1915–1916

- The United States population passed 100 million
- Boston had constructed 26 playgrounds in the city
- An attempt by Congress to exclude illiterates from immigrating, a bill promoted by the unions to protect jobs, was vetoed by President Howard Taft in 1913, reasoning that illiteracy, which was often due to lack of opportunity, was no test of character
- U.S. Pullman-car porters pay reached $27.50 per month, prompting U.S. Commission on Industrial Relations to ask if wages were too high
- Kraft processed cheese was introduced by Chicago-based J.L. Kraft and Brothers
- Pyrex glass was developed by Corning Glass researchers
- IWW organizer Joe Hill was executed by firing squad
- The Woman's Peace Party was founded with social worker Jane Addams, the founder of Hull House in Chicago, as its first president
- The Victor Talking Machine Company introduced a phonograph called the Victrola
- An easy divorce law requiring only six months of residence was passed in Nevada
- D.W. Griffith's controversial three-hour film epic, *The Birth of a Nation*, opened in New York, with a ticket cost of an astronomical $2.00
- A Chicago law restricted liquor sales on Sunday

- American Tobacco Company selected salesmen by psychological tests
- After Mexico requested that the United States remove its troops during the Mexican Civil War, 17 Americans and 38 Mexicans died in a clash
- The U.S. bought the Virgin Islands from Denmark for $25 million
- Railway workers gained the right to an eight-hour day, preventing a nationwide strike
- Ring Lardner published *You Know Me Al: A Busher's Letters*, John Dewey wrote *Democracy and Education* and Carl Sandburg's *Chicago Poems* was released
- The Federal Land Bank System was created to aid farmers in acquiring loans
- Popular songs included "Ireland Must Be Heaven for My Mother Came from There" and "There's a Little Bit of Bad in Every Good Little Girl"
- Orange Crush, Nathan's hotdogs, Lincoln Logs and mechanical windshield wipers all made their first appearance
- Margaret Sanger opened the first birth control clinic in the country, distributing information in English, Italian and Yiddish
- The Mercury dime and Liberty fifty-cent piece went into circulation
- High school dropout Norman Rockwell published his first illustration in *The Saturday Evening Post*
- Actor Charlie Chaplin signed with Mutual for a record $675,000 salary
- Multimillionaire businessman Rodman Wanamaker organized the Professional Golfers Association of America
- South Carolina raised the minimum working age of children from 12 to 14
- Lucky Strike Cigarettes were introduced, costing $0.10 for a pack of 20
- Stanford Terman introduced the first test for measuring intelligence, coining the term "IQ" for intelligence quotient

1917

- Oregon defeated the University of Pennsylvania 14–0 in college football's 3rd Annual Rose Bowl

- German saboteurs set off the Kingsland Explosion at Kingsland, New Jersey, leading to U.S. involvement in World War I
- President Woodrow Wilson called for "peace without victory" in Europe before America entered World War I
- An anti-prostitution rally in San Francisco attracted 27,000 people after which 200 houses of prostitution were closed
- WW I Allies intercepted the Zimmermann Telegram, in which Germany offered to give the American Southwest back to Mexico if Mexico declared war on the United States; America responded by declaring war on Germany
- The Original Dixieland Jazz Band recorded their first commercial record, which included the "Dixie Jazz Band One Step"
- The Jones Act granted Puerto Ricans United States citizenship
- The first Pulitzer Prizes were awarded to: Laura E. Richards, Maud Howe Elliott, and Florence Hall for their biography, *Julia Ward Howe;* Jean Jules Jusserand for *With Americans of Past and Present Days*; and Herbert Bayard Swope for *New York World*
- The Silent Protest was organized by the NAACP in New York to protest the East St. Louis Riot as well as lynchings in Texas and Tennessee
- An uprising by several hundred farmers against the newly created WWI draft erupted in central Oklahoma and came to be known as the Green Corn Rebellion
- Dutch dancer Mata Hari was falsely accused by the French of spying for Germany and executed by firing squad
- President Woodrow Wilson used the Federal Possession and Control Act to place most U.S. railroads under the United States Railroad Administration, hoping to more efficiently transport troops and materiel for the war effort

1918

- As an energy-saving measure, the nation adopted daylight saving time during the war, 150 years after it was first recommended by Benjamin

Franklin
- Girls Scouts collected peach stones which, when heated, turned into charcoal for use in gas mask filters
- Women assembled bombs in defense plants, learned to repair cars, carried the mail, directed traffic and worked as trolley car conductors
- The Committee on Public Information turned out patriotic press releases and pamphlets by the millions and drew upon a roster of 75,000 speakers to provide speeches for every occasion
- Civilians abstained from wheat on Mondays and Wednesdays, meat on Tuesdays, and pork on Thursdays and Saturdays
- Some Americans swore off any beer that had a German name, sauerkraut became "liberty cabbage," hamburger was "Salisbury steak," and dachshunds were called "liberty pups"
- Labor unrest was at its most turbulent since 1890, as inflation triggered 2,665 strikes involving over four million workers
- Inflation reached 8.9 percent, dramatically increasing prices
- *The Economic Consequences of the Peace* by J. M. Keynes, *Ten Days That Shook the World* by John Reed and *Winesburg, Ohio* by Sherwood Anderson were all published
- Seventy lynchings occurred in the South as membership in the Ku Klux Klan increased to 100,000 across 27 states
- Herbert Hoover was named director of a relief organization for liberated countries, both neutral and enemy
- Peter Paul's Konobar, the Drake Hotel in Chicago and a state gas tax (in Oregon) all made their first appearance
- Hockey's Stanley Cup was cancelled after one player died and many others were stricken with the deadly flu

1919–1920
- Boston police struck against pay scales of $0.21 to $0.23 per hour for 83- to 98-hour weeks.
- The cost of living in New York City was up 79 percent from 1914

- The dial telephone was introduced in Norfolk, Virginia
- Wheat prices soared to $3.50 per bushel as famine swept Europe
- Kellogg's All-Bran was introduced by the Battle Creek Toasted Corn Flakes Company
- U.S. ice cream sales reached 150 million gallons, up from 30 million in 1909
- *The New York Daily News* became the first tabloid (small picture-oriented) newspaper
- Boston Red Sox pitcher and outfielder Babe Ruth hit 29 home runs for the year and the New York Yankees purchased his contract for $125,000
- More than four million American workers struck for the right to belong to unions
- The Bureau of Labor Statistics reported that 1.4 million women had joined the American work force since 1911
- Following the 1918 strike by the Union Streetcar Conductors protesting the employment of female conductors, the War Labor Board ruled in favor of the continued employment of women
- Southern leaders of the National Association of Colored Women protested the conditions of domestic service workers, including the expectation of white male employers of the right to take sexual liberties with their servants

1921

- The first religious radio broadcast was heard over station KDKA AM in Pittsburgh, Pennsylvania
- Henry E. Huntington bought Gainsborough's *The Blue Boy* and Reynolds' *Portrait of Mrs. Siddons* for $1 million
- Books included John Dos Passos' *Three Soldiers*; *Symptoms of Being Thirty-Five* by Ring Lardner; *The Outline of History* by H.G. Wells, and *Dream Psychology* by Sigmund Freud
- The DeYoung Museum opened in Golden Gate Park, San Francisco

- The Mounds candy bar, Eskimo Pie, Betty Crocker, Wise potato chips, Band-Aids, table tennis, and Drano all made their first appearance
- The Allies of World War I Reparations Commission decided that Germany was obligated to pay 132 billion gold marks ($33 trillion) in annual installments of 2.5 billion
- The Emergency Quota Act was passed by Congress, establishing national quotas on immigration
- Cigarette consumption rose to 43 billion annually despite its illegality in 14 states
- The first vaccination against tuberculosis was administered
- Researchers at the University of Toronto led by biochemist Frederick Banting announced the discovery of the hormone insulin
- Adolf Hitler became Führer of the Nazi Party
- Harold Arlin announced the Pirates-Phillies game from Forbes Field over Westinghouse KDKA in Pittsburgh in the first radio broadcast of a baseball game
- Sixteen-year-old Margaret Gorman won the Atlantic City Pageant's Golden Mermaid trophy to become the first Miss America
- Literature dealing with contraception was banned and a New York physician was convicted of selling *Married Love*
- Centre College's football team, led by quarterback Bo McMillin, defeated Harvard University 6-0 to break Harvard's five-year winning streak
- Albert Einstein was awarded the Nobel Prize in Physics for his work with the photoelectric effect
- During an Armistice Day ceremony at Arlington National Cemetery, the Tomb of the Unknowns was dedicated by President Warren G. Harding
- Hyperinflation was rampant in Germany after the Great War, where 263 marks were needed to buy a single American dollar

1922

- Seventeen-year-old Clara Bow won a magazine contest for "The Most Beautiful Girl in the World," while Charles Atlas won for "World's Most Perfectly Developed Man"
- During his third trial, movie star Roscoe "Fatty" Arbuckle was exonerated of starlet Virginia Rappe's murder, but not before a highly publicized sex trial
- The self-winding wristwatch, Checker Cab, Canada Dry ginger ale, and State Farm Mutual auto insurance all made their first appearance
- California became a year-round source of oranges
- Automobile magnate Henry Ford, who earned $264,000 a day, was declared a "billionaire" by the Associated Press
- Radio station WEAF objected to airing a toothpaste commercial, deciding that care of the teeth was too delicate a subject for broadcast
- The first commercially prepared baby food was marketed
- The U.S. Post Office burned 500 copies of James Joyce's *Ulysses*
- The mah-jongg craze swept the nation, outselling radios
- Protestant Episcopal bishops voted to erase the word obey from the marriage ceremony
- Thom McAn introduced mass-produced shoes through chain stores for $3.99 a pair
- Hollywood's black list of "unsafe" persons stood at 117
- Radio became a national obsession, listened to for concerts, sermons and sports
- Syracuse University banned dancing
- A cargo ship was converted into the first U.S. aircraft carrier
- Publications for the year included T.S. Eliot's *The Waste Land*, F. Scott Fitzgerald's *The Beautiful and the Damned* and H.G. Wells's *The Outline of History*; Willa Cather won the Pulitzer Prize for *One of Ours*
- The tomb of King Tutankhamen, in the Valley of the Kings, Egypt, was discovered

- New York's Delmonico's Restaurant closed
- The first mechanical telephone switchboard was installed in New York
- Broadway producer Florenz Ziegfeld forbade his stars to perform on radio because it "cheapens them"
- *Vanity Fair* reported that the flapper "will never . . . knit you a necktie, but she'll go skiing with you. . . . She may quote poetry to you, not Indian love lyrics but something about the peace conference or theology"

1923–1924

- The Popsicle was patented under the name Epsicle
- Butterfinger candy was marketed by dropping parachuted bars from an airplane
- Commercially canned tomato juice was marketed by Libby McNeill & Libby
- The electric shaver was patented by Schick
- A.C. Nielson Company was founded
- Zenith Radio Corporation was founded
- 10 auto makers accounted for 90 percent of sales; a total of 108 different companies were now producing cars
- Hertz Drive Ur Self System was founded, creating the world's first auto rental concern
- 30 percent of all bread was baked in the home, down from 70 in 1910
- The first effective chemical pesticides were introduced
- *American Mercury* magazine began publication
- Radio set ownership reached three million
- Ford produced two million Model T motorcars, with the price of the touring car falling to $290.00
- Dean Witter and Company was founded
- Microbiologists isolated the cause of scarlet fever
- Emily Post published *Etiquette,* which made her the arbiter of American manners

1925-1926

- James Buchanan "Buck" Duke donated $47 million to Trinity College at Durham, North Carolina and the college changed its name to Duke
- College football surpassed boxing as a national pastime, largely because of the popularity of "Galloping Ghost" Red Grange
- With prohibition the law of the land, party-goers hid liquor in shoe heels, flasks form-fitted to women's thighs, and perfume bottles
- The Charleston, a dance that originated in Charleston, South Carolina, was carried north and incorporated into the all-black show *Shuffle Along*; white dancers immediately adopted the lively dance
- The U.S. Supreme Court declared unconstitutional an Oregon law that required all grammar school-aged children to attend school
- When Henry Ford paid $2.4 million in income tax, 500,000 people wrote to him begging for money
- The Methodist Episcopal General Conference lifted its ban on theatre attendance and dancing
- Walt Disney began creating cartoons, featuring "Alice's Wonderland"
- Currently, 56 different companies were selling home refrigerators, with an average price of $450
- The permanent wave, contact lenses, IBM, deadbolt locks, and the college-bound notebook all made their first appearance
- Florida land prices collapsed as investors learned that their purchased lots were under water
- The $10 million Boca Raton Hotel in Florida was completed
- Al Capone took control of Chicago bootlegging
- Chesterfield cigarettes were marketed to women for the first time
- Aunt Jemima Mills was acquired by Quaker Oats Company for $4 million
- Machine-made ice production topped 56 million pounds, up 1.5 million from 1894
- The first ham in a can was introduced by Hormel

- The first blue jeans with slide fasteners were introduced by J.D. Lee Company
- Synthetic rubber was pioneered by B.F. Goodrich Rubber Company chemist Waldo Lonsburg Serman
- Cars appeared for the first time in such colors as "Florentine Cream" and "Versailles Violet"
- 40 percent of Americans earned at least $2,000 a year
- "Yellow-Drive-It-Yourself-Systems" became popular, costing $0.12 a mile for a Ford and $0.22 a mile for a 6-cylinder car
- Earl Wise's potato chips were so successful he moved his business from a remodeled garage to a concrete plant
- Wesson Oil, National Spelling Bees, and the *New Yorker* magazine all made their first appearances
- Congress reduced the taxes on incomes of more than $1 million, from 66 to 20 percent
- The Book-of-the-Month Club was founded
- To fight the depression in the automobile industry, Henry Ford introduced the eight-hour day and five-day work week
- With prohibition under way, the Supreme Court upheld a law limiting the medical prescription of whiskey to one pint every 10 days
- 2,000 people died of poisoned liquor
- *The illegal liquor trade netted $3.5 billion a year, with bootleg Scotch at $48 a case
- The movies became America's favorite entertainment, with more than 14,500 movie houses showing 400 movies a year
- The United States sesquicentennial was celebrated
- *True Story Magazine* reached a circulation of two million with stories such as "The Diamond Bracelet She Thought Her Husband Didn't Know About"
- Flues with slide fasteners were introduced by H.D. Lee Company
- Philadelphia's Warwick Hotel and the Hotel Carlyle in New York were

opened

- 40 percent of all first-generation immigrants owned their own homes, while 29 percent of all second-generation immigrants were homeowners
- Kodak introduced 16 mm film
- Sinclair Lewis refused to accept the Pulitzer Prize because it "makes the writer safe, polite, obedient, and sterile"
- Martha Graham debuted in New York as a choreographer and dancer in *Three Gopi Maidens*
- *The Jazz Singer,* the first talking film, made its debut
- Women's skirts, the shortest of the decade, now stopped just below the knee with flounces, pleats, and circular gores that extended from the hip
- Ethel Lackie of the Illinois Athletic Club broke the world's record for the 40-yard freestyle swim with a time of 21.4 seconds

1927–1928

- 20 million cars were on the road, up from 13,824 in 1900
- Transatlantic telephone service between London and New York began at a cost of $75.00 for three minutes
- J.C. Penney opened its 500th store, and sold stock to the public
- Wonder Bread was introduced
- Broccoli became more widely marketed in the United States
- Rice Krispies were introduced by W.K. Kellogg
- Peanut butter cracker sandwiches, sold under the name NAB, which stands for National Biscuit Company, were sold for $0.05 each
- U.S. per capita consumption of crude oil reached 7.62 barrels
- Presidential candidate Herbert Hoover called for "a chicken in every pot and two cars in every garage"
- The Ford Model A appeared in four colors including "Arabian Sand"
- The Hayes list of dos and don'ts for Hollywood films included licentious or suggestive nudity, ridicule of clergy, and inference of sexual perversion

- The Al Capone gang netted $100 million in the illegal liquor trade as Prohibition continued
- President Calvin Coolidge urged the nation to pray more
- The post-war education obsession included a variety of "how-to" courses and books
- A phonograph with an automatic record changer was introduced
- Volvo, Lender Bagels, and Movietone News all made their first appearances
- The German dirigible *Graf Zeppelin* landed in Lakehurst, New Jersey, on its first commercial flight across the Atlantic
- Future President Herbert Hoover promoted the concept of the "American system of rugged individualism" in a speech at New York's Madison Square Garden
- Three car mergers took place: Chrysler and Dodge; Studebaker and Pierce-Arrow; and Chandler and Cleveland
- The Boston Garden officially opened
- The first successful sound-synchronized animated cartoon, Walt Disney's *Steamboat Willie* starring Mickey Mouse, premiered
- The first issue of *Time* magazine was published, featuring Japanese Emperor Hirohito on its cover
- North Carolina Governor O. Max Gardner blamed women's diet fads for the drop in farm prices
- *Bolero* by Maurice Ravel made its debut in Paris
- George Gershwin's musical *An American in Paris* premiered at Carnegie Hall in NYC
- The clip-on tie was created
- Real wages, adjusted for inflation, had increased 33 percent since 1914
- Nationalist Chiang Kai-shek captured Peking, China, from the communists and gained U.S. recognition
- Aviator Amelia Earhart became the first woman to fly across the Atlantic Ocean from Newfoundland to Wales in about 21 hours

- The first all-talking movie feature, *The Lights of New York,* was released
- Fifteen nations signed the Kellogg-Briand Peace Pact, developed by French Foreign Minister Aristide Briand and U.S. Secretary of State Frank Kellogg
- Actress Katharine Hepburn made her stage debut in *The Czarina*
- Scottish bacteriologist Alexander Fleming discovered curative properties of penicillin
- *My Weekly Reader* magazine made its debut
- Ruth Snyder became the first woman to die in the electric chair
- Bell Labs created a way to end the fluttering of the television image
- President Calvin Coolidge gave the Congressional Medal of Honor to aviator Charles Lindbergh

1929

- A Baltimore survey discovered rickets in 30 percent of the children
- The U.S. Presidential inauguration was carried worldwide by radio
- German Kurt Barthel set up the first American nudist colony in New Jersey, which began with three married couples
- Of the 20,500 movie theaters nationwide, 9,000 installed sound during the year to adapt to "talkies"
- Calvin Coolidge was elected director of the New York Life Insurance Company
- The "Age of the Car" was apparent everywhere, as one-way streets, traffic lights, stop signs, and parking regulations were hot topics
- At least 32,000 speakeasies thrived in NYC, while the Midwest called similar institutions "beer flats," "Blind Pigs," and "shock houses"
- On September 3, the stock market peaked and on November 13, it reached bottom, with U.S. securities losing $26 billion in value
- Within a few weeks of the stock market crash (Black Tuesday), unemployment rose from 700,000 to 3.1 million nationwide
- Following the stock market crash, New York Mayor Jimmy Walker

urged movie houses to show cheerful movies

- Coast-to-coast commercial travel required 48 hours using both airplanes and overnight trains
- Lt. James Doolight piloted an airplane using instruments alone
- Commander Richard E. Byrd planted a U.S. flag on the South Pole
- W.A. Morrison introduced quartz-crystal clocks for precise timekeeping
- Ford introduced a station wagon with boxed wood panels
- Radio program *Amos 'n' Andy* was so popular that Atlantic City resorts broadcast the show over loudspeakers
- Admission to New York theaters ranged from $0.35 to $2.50
- On St. Valentine's Day, six notorious Chicago gangsters were machine-gunned to death by a rival gang
- American manufacturers began to make aluminum furniture, especially chairs
- The cartoon *Popeye*, the Oscar Meyer wiener trademark, 7-Up, front-wheel-drive cars, and *Business Week* magazine all made their first appearances

1930–1931

- Unemployment passed four million
- More than 1,352 banks closed in 1930, and 2,294 closed in 1931
- The first analog computer was placed in operation by Vannevar Bush
- The U.S. car boom collapsed in the wake of the Depression and one million auto workers were laid off
- Gasoline consumption rose to nearly 16 billion gallons
- Trousers became acceptable attire for women who played golf and rode horses
- Radio set sales increased to 13.5 million
- Advertisers spent $60 million on radio commercials
- Boeing hired eight nurses to act as flight attendants
- *Fortune Magazine* was launched by Henry R. Luce at $1.00 per issue
- The University of Southern California polo team refused to play

against the University of California at Los Angeles until its one female member was replaced by a male

- Laurette Schimmoler of Ohio became the first woman airport manager, earning a salary of $510 a year
- The fledgling movie industry now employed 100,000 people
- Alka-Seltzer was introduced by Miles Laboratories
- Clairol hair products were introduced by U.S. chemists
- Bird's Eye Frosted Foods were sold nationally for the first time
- Unemployment reached eight million, or 15.9 percent, inflation was at -4.4 percent, and the gross national product at -16 percent
- For the first time, emigration exceeded immigration
- As the sale of glass jars for canning increased, sales of canned goods declined
- Admissions to state mental hospitals tripled in 1930-1931 over the previous eight years
- More than 75 percent of all cities banned the employment of wives
- The National Forty-Hour Work Week League formed, calling for an eight-hour workday in an effort to produce more jobs
- Major James Doolittle flew from Ottawa to Mexico City in a record 11 hours and 45 minutes
- Pope Pius XI posed for the first telephoto picture to be transmitted from the Vatican, a picture that took 10 minutes to transmit
- To generate income, Nevada legalized both gambling and the six-month divorce
- Nearly 6,000 cases of infantile paralysis struck New York and many cities experienced partial quarantines
- Farmers attempted to stop an invasion of grasshoppers with electrified fences; 160,000 miles of America's finest farmlands were destroyed by the insect
- Alka-Seltzer was introduced by Miles Laboratories
- Chicago gangster Al Capone was convicted of evading $231,000 in

federal taxes
- New York's Waldorf-Astoria Hotel was opened
- Silent film extra Clark Gable appeared in the movie *A Free Soul*, gaining instant stardom, while Universal studios recruited Bette Davis

1932

- *Forbes* magazine predicted that the number of television sets would reach 100,000, up from 15,000 in 1931
- As the depression worsened, wages dropped 60 percent in only three years
- Wages for picking figs were $0.10 per 50-pound box, $1.50 a day for 15 boxes; for picking peas the pay was $0.14 cents a pound
- New York's Radio City Music Hall, with 6,200 seats, opened as the world's largest movie theater
- The Winter Olympics in Lake Placid, New York created an interest in snow skiing
- The Zippo lighter, Mounds candy bar, Fritos corn chips, Johnson Glo-Coat wax, and tax on gasoline all made their first appearance
- Reacting to the depression, President Herbert Hoover reduced his own salary by 20 percent
- The FBI created a list of "public enemies"
- *Light in August* by William Faulkner, *The Good Earth* by Pearl S. Buck, *Death in the Afternoon* by Ernest Hemingway and *Sweeney Agonistes* by T. S. Eliot were all published
- James Chadwick discovered the neutron
- Radio premieres included "The George Burns and Gracie Allen Show," "National Barn Dance," "The Jack Benny Program" and "Tom Mix"
- Unemployment was officially recorded at 23.6 percent
- Across America, 31 percent of homes had telephones
- Amelia Earhart became the first woman to make a solo transatlantic flight
- Movie openings included *Mata Hari, Scarface, Dr. Jekyll and Mr. Hyde* and *Tarzan, the Ape Man*

- President Hoover declared: "Grass will grow in the streets of 100 cities" if Franklin Roosevelt was elected
- The "Great I Am" Movement, promising wealth to its followers, gained popularity
- The Federal Reserve Board's index of production was down 55 percent from 1929
- Baseball cards began to appear in packages of bubble gum, accompanied by tips on how to improve one's game

1933

- Construction of the Golden Gate Bridge began in San Francisco Bay
- Congress voted for independence for the Philippines, against President Hoover
- The Twentieth Amendment to the United States Constitution was ratified, changing Inauguration Day from March 4 to January 20, starting in 1937
- *The Lone Ranger* debuted on the radio
- The New York City-based Postal Telegraph Company introduced the singing telegram
- In Miami, Florida, Giuseppe Zangara attempted to assassinate President-elect Franklin D. Roosevelt
- *Newsweek* was published for the first time
- *King Kong*, starring Fay Wray, premiered at Radio City Music Hall in NYC
- Mount Rushmore National Memorial was dedicated
- President Franklin Roosevelt proclaimed, "The only thing we have to fear, is fear itself."
- Frances Perkins became U.S. Secretary of Labor and the first female Cabinet member
- Dachau, the first Nazi concentration camp, was opened
- The Civilian Conservation Corps was established to relieve unemployment

- Karl Jansky detected radio waves from the Milky Way Galaxy, leading to radio astronomy
- The Tennessee Valley Authority was created
- The Century of Progress World's Fair opened in Chicago
- Walt Disney's *Silly Symphony* cartoon *The Three Little Pigs* was released
- The first drive-in theater opened in Camden, New Jersey
- The electronic pari-mutuel betting machine was unveiled at the Arlington Park race track near Chicago
- The first Major League Baseball All-Star Game was played at Comiskey Park in Chicago
- Army Barracks on Alcatraz was acquired by the Department of Justice for a federal penitentiary
- Albert Einstein arrived in the United States as a refugee from Nazi Germany
- The Dust Bowl in South Dakota stripped topsoil from desiccated farmlands
- The Twenty-first Amendment officially went into effect, legalizing alcohol in the U.S.
- The first Krispy Kreme doughnut shop opened in Nashville, Tennessee

1934

- Leni Riefenstahl directed *Triumph of the Will*, documenting the rise of the Third Reich in Germany
- Donald Duck, Walgreen's drugstores, Flash Gordon, Seagram's Seven Royal Crown and the term "hi-fi" all made their first appearance
- Ernest and Julio Gallo invested $5,900 in a wine company
- The birth of the Dionne quintuplets in Ontario stirred international interest
- The ongoing drought reduced the national corn crop by nearly one billion bushels
- Edna St. Vincent Millay published *Wine from These Grapes*; F. Scott

Fitzgerald completed *Tender Is the Night*
- Dicumarol, an anticoagulant, was developed from clover
- "Tumbling Tumbleweeds," "I Only Have Eyes for You" and "Honeysuckle Rose" were all popular songs
- The Securities and Exchange Commission was created
- *It Happened One Night* won Best Picture, Best Director (Frank Capra), Best Actress (Claudette Colbert) and Best Actor (Clark Gable)
- The U.S. Gold Reserve Act authorized the president to devalue the dollar
- Enrico Fermi suggested that neutrons and protons were the same fundamental particles in two different quantum states
- The FBI shot John Dillinger, Public Enemy No. I, generating a hail of publicity
- Greyhound bus lines cut its business fares in half to $8 between New York and Chicago to encourage more traffic

1935–1936
- The Social Security Act passed Congress
- The Emergency Relief Appropriation Act gave $5 billion to create jobs
- Fort Knox became the United States Repository of gold bullion
- One-tenth of one percent of U.S. corporations made 50 percent of earnings
- Sulfa-drug chemotherapy was introduced to relieve veneral disease sufferers
- Nylon was developed by Du Pont
- Beer cans were introduced
- One-third of farmers received U.S. treasury allotment checks for not growing crops
- New York State law allowed women to serve as jurors
- Polystyrene became commercially available in the United States for use in products such as kitchen utensils and toys
- An eight-hour work day became law in Illinois

- Margaret Mitchell's *Gone with the Wind* sold a record one million copies in six months
- A *Fortune* poll indicated that 67 percent favored birth control
- Trailer sales peaked; tourist camps for vacationing motorists gained popularity
- Approximately 38 percent of American families had an annual income of less than $1,000
- Ford unveiled the V-8 engine
- Recent advances in photography, including the 35 mm camera and easy-to-use exposure meters, fueled a photography boom
- The population of America reached 127 million
- *Life* magazine began publication, with an early claim that one in 10 Americans had a tattoo
- New York's Triborough Bridge opened, with a toll of $0.25
- The National Park Service created numerous federal parks and fish and game preserves, adding a total of 600,000 additional acres to state preserves
- Mercedes-Benz created the first diesel-fueled passenger car
- The WPA Federal Art Project employed 3,500 artists who produced 4,500 murals, 189,000 sculptures and 450,000 paintings
- Dust storms destroyed large portions of farmland in Kansas, Oklahoma, Colorado, Nebraska and the Dakotas
- A sleeper berth from Newark to Los Angeles cost $150
- New York's Fifth Avenue double-decker bus fare was between $0.05 and $0.10
- Margaret Mitchell's book, *Gone with the Wind*, sold a record one million copies in six months
- The photo-finish camera, bicycle traffic court, screw-cap bottle with pour lip, the Presbyterian Church of America and Tampax all made their first appearance
- Congress passed the Neutrality Acts designed to keep America out of

foreign wars

- A revolt against progressive education was led by Robert M. Hutchins, president of the University of Chicago
- Molly Dewson of the National Consumers' League led a fight to gain the appointment of more female postmasters
- The first successful helicopter flight was made
- The "Chase and Sanborn Hour," with Edgar Bergen and Charlie McCarthy, and "The Shadow," starring Robert Hardy Andrews, both premiered on radio

1937–1938

- The United Automobile Workers were recognized by General Motors as sole bargaining agent for employees
- Minimum wage policy for women was upheld by the Supreme Court
- Packard Motor Car Company sold a record 109,000 cars
- General Motors introduced automatic transmission
- Icemen made regular deliveries to more than 50 percent of middle class households
- Spam was introduced by George A. Hormel & Company
- *Popular Photography* magazine began publication
- Congress's wage-and-hour law limited the work week to 44 hours
- Recovery stumbled, *Wall Street's Dow Jones Industrial Average* fell
- Eastern Airlines was created
- Owens-Corning Fiberglass Corporation was incorporated to produce products utilizing newly developed fiberglass
- High-definition color television was demonstrated
- The ballpoint pen was patented
- Consumption of beef and dairy products increased by three percent
- Nylon stockings went on sale
- From September 1, 1936, to June 1, 1937, 484,711 workers were involved in sit down strikes
- A study showed that people spent 4.5 hours daily listening to the radio

- Spinach growers erected a statue to cartoon character Popeye in Wisconsin
- Seeing-eye dogs came into use for aiding the blind
- The Fair Labor Standards Act established the Minimum Hourly Rate at 25 cents
- The Federal National Mortgage Association known as Fannie Mae was established
- Aviator Howard Hughes set a new record, flying around the world in three days, 19 hours
- The March of Dimes' Polio Foundation was created by Franklin Roosevelt
- A Gallup poll indicated that 58 percent of Americans believed that the U.S would be drawn into war, and 65 percent favored boycotting German goods
- Race horse *Seabiscuit* defeated *War Admiral*, earning the title best horse in America
- Action comics issued the *Superman* comic
- New York staged a World's Fair called "The World of Tomorrow" which was visited by 25 million people
- Fifty percent of Americans polled selected radio as the most reliable news medium, while 17 percent chose newspapers
- Orson Welles's radio adaptation of *The War of the Worlds* was broadcast, causing mass panic by listeners who thought that his story of aliens landing in the eastern U.S. was real
- Adolf Hitler was named *Time* magazine's "Man of the Year"
- Kate Smith sang Irvin Berlin's "God Bless America" on an Armistice Day radio broadcast
- Disney Studios released *Snow White and the Seven Dwarfs*
- Thornton Wilder's play *Our Town* was performed
- A toothbrush became the first commercial product made with nylon yarn as the bristles

- Oil was discovered in Saudi Arabia
- Heavyweight boxing champion Joe Louis knocked out Max Schmeling in round one of their rematch at Yankee Stadium in New York City
- In the prior five years, 60,000 German immigrants had arrived in America
- Movie box office receipts reached an all-time high and averaged an annual $25 per family

1939

- World War II began in Europe with the Germans invading Poland in September and the Russians invading Finland in November
- The Birth Control Federation of America began its "Negro Project" designed to control the population of people it deemed less fit to rear children
- The Social Security Act was amended, allowing extended benefits to seniors, widows, minors, and parents of a deceased person
- After the Daughters of the American Revolution (DAR) denied her the chance to sing at Constitution Hall because of her race, Marian Anderson sang at the Lincoln Memorial in Washington, D.C., before a crowd of 75,000
- *Reader's Digest* reached a circulation of eight million, up from 250,000 10 years earlier
- Despite the depression, the sale of radios continued to rise so that 27.5 million families owned 45 million radio sets
- The Federal Theatre Project was disbanded after accusations of communist influence
- Hollywood production code restrictions were lifted, allowing Clark Gable in *Gone with the Wind* to say, "Frankly, my dear, I don't give a damn."
- Enrico Fermi and John R. Dunning of Columbia University used the cyclotron to split uranium and obtain a massive energy release, suggesting a "chain reaction"

- Paul Miller developed the insecticide DDT
- Due to the war, Finland stopped shipping cheese to the U.S., and Swiss production took its place
- Gangster Louis Lepke surrendered to popular newspaper and radio columnist Walter Winchell, who handed him over to J. Edgar Hoover
- The U.S. Supreme Court ruled that sit-down strikes were illegal
- The first baseball game was televised
- General Motors controlled 42 percent of the U.S. market in cars and trucks, and the company's 220,000 employees made an average of $1,500 annually
- Transatlantic airmail service, the marketing of nylon stockings, the use of fluorescent lighting, and Packard's air-conditioned automobile were all introduced
- The Sears, Roebuck catalogue still featured horse-drawn farm wagons, washing machines run by gasoline, and refrigerators designed to cool with a block of ice
- Zippers on men's trousers became standard equipment

1940

- RKO released Walt Disney's second full-length animated film, *Pinocchio,* and Tom and Jerry make their debut in *Puss Gets the Boot*
- Martin Kamen and Sam Ruben discovered Carbon-14, the basis of the radiocarbon dating method used to determine the age of archaeological and geological finds
- *Truth or Consequences* debuted on NBC Radio
- Booker T. Washington became the first African-American to be depicted on a U.S. postage stamp
- Following the resignation of Neville Chamberlain, Winston Churchill became prime minister of the Great Britain
- McDonald's restaurant opened in San Bernardino, California
- In WWII action, the Dutch and Norway armies surrendered to German forces as France fell

- President Franklin D. Roosevelt asked Congress for approximately $900 million to construct 50,000 airplanes per year
- The Auschwitz-Birkenau concentration and death camp opened in Poland
- WW I General John J. Pershing, in a nationwide radio broadcast, urged all-out aid to Britain in order to defend America, while national hero Charles Lindbergh led an isolationist rally at Soldier Field in Chicago
- The U.S. transferred 50 U.S. destroyers to Great Britain in return for 99-year leases on British bases in the North Atlantic, West Indies, and Bermuda
- Nazi Germany rained bombs on London for 57 consecutive nights
- In Lascaux, France, 17,000-year-old cave paintings were discovered by a group of young Frenchmen hiking through Southern France
- The Selective Training and Service Act of 1940 created the first peacetime draft in U.S. history
- The U.S. imposed a total embargo on all scrap metal shipments to Japan
- Franklin D. Roosevelt defeated Republican challenger Wendell Willkie to become the first and only third-term president
- Agatha Christie's mystery novel *And Then There Were None* was published

1942–1943

- Unemployment nationwide fell to 4.7 percent from its 1933 high of 25.2 percent
- Office of Price Administration was formed to control prices
- A tire-rationing plan and gas rationing began
- Paine, Webber, Jackson, & Curtis was created
- Zinc-coated pennies were issued by the U.S. Mint
- Florida surpassed California as the leading U.S. producer of oranges
- Kellogg introduced Raisin Bran cereal
- Sunbeam bread was introduced

- Maxwell House instant coffee was included in military K rations
- Dannon yogurt was introduced
- U.S. automobile production was halted until 1945
- Congress approved income-tax withholding from paychecks
- Zenith Radio Corporation introduced a $40.00 hearing aid
- Shoes were rationed to three pairs per year, per person
- The sale of sliced bread was banned
- Sale of Bibles increased 25 percent as religious books grew in popularity
- Women's trousers sold 10 times more than the previous year
- Vegetables consumed in the U.S. came from victory gardens (40 percent) and gardens developed by Japanese-Americans detained in camps
- The motion picture industry produced 80 war movies
- Enrico Fermi secretly accomplished a controlled nuclear fission reaction at the University of Chicago; he sent a coded message to President Franklin D. Roosevelt: "The Italian navigator has entered the new world."
- Reports of the deportation of Jews from Occupied Western Europe reached the U.S.

1944

- President Roosevelt's $109 billion federal budget earmarked $100 billion for the war effort
- Rent controls were imposed nationwide
- American Broadcasting Company (ABC) was created by Lifesavers millionaire Edward Noble
- Russell Marker pioneered the oral contraceptive, Syntex S.A.
- An automatic, general purpose digital computer was completed at Harvard University
- The Federal Highway Act established the interstate highway system
- War was costing the U.S. $250 million per day

- The GI Bill of Rights was enacted to finance college education for veterans
- U.S. soybean production rose as new uses were found for beans
- U.S. grocers tested self-service meat markets
- Gasoline averaged $0.21 per gallon
- American Jewish Congress reported that over three million Jews were killed by the Nazis
- Paper shortages limited Christmas cards, causing recycling of brown grocery bags and publishers to experiment with soft-cover books
- *Amos 'n' Andy* was canceled after 15 years and 4,000 consecutive radio shows
- Uncle Ben's converted rice appeared
- On D-Day (June 6) the Normandy invasion was mounted by 6,939 naval vessels, 15,040 aircraft, and 156,000 troops; 16,434 were killed, 76,535 were wounded, and 19,704 went missing
- Nearly half the steel, tin, and paper needed for the war was provided by salvaged goods
- Jell-O became a popular dessert substitute for canned fruit, and baking powder sales fell as women continued to join the work force
- Horse racing was banned because of the war
- A New York judge found the book *Lady Chatterley's Lover* obscene and ordered publisher Dial Press to trial
- Bill Mauldin's cartoon *Willie & Joe,* originally in *Yank* and *Stars and Stripes,* was picked up by the domestic press and achieved great acclaim
- More than 81,000 GIs were killed, wounded, or captured in the Battle of the Bulge, Germany's last big offensive of the war
- Because of a shortage of cheese and tomato sauce, the sale of pasta fell dramatically
- Gen. Douglas MacArthur returned to the Philippines; his American army annihilated the troops commanded by Gen. Tomoyuki Yamashita,

the Tiger of Malaya; 50,000 Japanese were killed, and fewer than 400 were captured

- Nationwide, 372,000 German POWs were being held in the United States
- The Dow Jones reached a high of 152, a low of 135, and unemployment was 1.2 percent
- Victory bonds became an obsession, with actress Hedy Lamarr offering to kiss any man who bought $25,000 worth; Jack Benny auctioned his $75 violin—*Old Love in Bloom*— for a million dollars' worth of bonds
- "Kilroy was here" became the graffiti symbol of valor for GIs everywhere
- Herr Adolf Hitler was among the citizens of enemy nations whose assets were frozen during the war; $22,666 from the sale of *Mein Kampf* was later used to pay Americans' claims against enemy nationals
- Chiquita brand bananas were introduced
- $80 million was spent on spectator sports in the U.S. who had 409 golf courses
- Seven laboratories refined and improved DDT, of which 350,000 pounds monthly was used by the military to spray in an effort to reduce typhus and malaria

1945
- President Franklin Delano Roosevelt died in office and Harry Truman became president
- WW II ended
- Penicillin was introduced commercially
- Approximately 98 million Americans went to the movies each week
- The Beechcraft Bonanza two-engine private plane was introduced
- The U.S. Gross National Product was $211 billion, double the GNP of 1928
- Ballpoint pens, costing $12.50 each, went on sale
- About one million Americans suffered from malaria

- Tupperware Corporation was formed
- Strikes idled 4.6 million workers, the worst stoppage since 1919
- The Dow Jones Industrial Average peaked at a post-1929 high of 212.50
- Wage and price controls ended in all areas except rents, sugar, and rice
- U.S. college enrollments reached an all-time high of more than 2 million
- Ektachrome color film was introduced by Kodak Company
- Tide Detergent was introduced
- Timex watches were introduced with at starting price of $6.95
- Hunt Foods established "price at time of shipment" contracts with customers
- The U.S. birth rate soared to 3.4 million, up from 2.9 million in the previous year
- Super glue and coats for lapdogs were introduced
- New York State forbade discrimination by employers, employment agencies and labor unions on the basis of race, the first time in American history a legislative body enacted a bill outlawing discrimination based on race, creed, or color
- The Boy Scouts collected 10 million pounds of rubber and more than 370 million pounds of scrap metal during the war, while Chicago children collected 18,000 tons of newspapers in just five months
- Ernie Pyle's *Brave Men,* a celebration of military heroism, sold more than a million copies; Richard Wright's *Black Boy,* a memoir of black life, sold 540,000 copies
- An RCA 10-inch television set sold for $374.00

1946

- United Airlines announced it had ordered jet planes for commercial purposes
- Dr. Benjamin Spock's *The Common Sense Book of Baby and Child Care* was published, written while he was in the Navy Medical Corps in charge of severe disciplinary cases

- FDR's stamp collection brought $211,000 at auction
- Automobile innovation included wide windows on the Studebaker and combined the wood station wagon and passenger car with the Chrysler Town and Country
- With more men returning from war, the birth rate increased 20 percent over 1945
- Albert Einstein and other distinguished nuclear scientists from the Emergency Committee of Atomic Science promoted the peaceful use of atomic energy
- A year after the end of WW II, the military went from 11 million to one million soldiers
- As wages and prices increased, the cost of living went up 33 percent over 1941
- With sugar rationing over, ice cream consumption soared
- The National Broadcasting Company and Philco Corporation established a two-way television relay service between New York and Philadelphia
- Blacks voted for the first time in the Mississippi Democratic primary
- Oklahoma City offered the first rapid public treatment of venereal diseases
- Former Secretary of State Henry Wallace became editor of the *New Republic*
- *The New Yorker* published John Hersey's *Hiroshima*
- John D. Rockefeller, Jr., donated $8.5 million for the construction of the United Nations building along the East River in New York City
- *Family Circle, Scientific American,* and *Holiday* all began publication

1947

- A Gallup poll reported that 94 percent of Americans believed in God
- Gerber Products Company sold two million jars of baby food weekly
- *A Streetcar Named Desire* by Tennessee Williams opened on Broadway
- The Freedom Train, with 100 of America's greatest documents, toured

- the United States
- The American Meat Institute reported that Americans abandoned wartime casseroles for meat five nights a week
- Seventy-five percent of all corn production was now hybrid
- *Esquire* magazine promoted the "bold look" for the man of "self-confidence and good taste," featuring wide tie clasps, heavy gold key chains, bold striped ties, big buttons and coordinating hair color and clothing
- Bikini bathing suits arrived on American beaches
- The American Friends Service Committee won the Nobel Peace Prize
- One million homes had television sets
- Gillette and Ford paid $65,000 to sponsor the first televised baseball World Series, during which an estimated 3.7 million people watched the Brooklyn Dodgers fall to the New York Yankees
- New York began a fluoridation program for 50,000 children
- Drive-up windows at banks were gaining popularity
- House prices doubled, and the price of clothing increased 93 percent from 1939
- Minute Maid Corp., Ajax, Everglades National Park, the Cannes Film Festival and the Tony Awards all made their first appearance
- American Association of Scientific Workers urged the U.S. to study bacteriological warfare

1948

- Nationwide, 50 cities banned comic books dealing with crime or sex, as psychiatrist Fredric Wertham charged that heavy comic-book reading contributed to juvenile delinquency
- President Harry Truman ordered racial equality in the armed forces
- Jack Benny sold his NBC radio program to CBS for $2 to $3 million, and the IRS took 75 percent for personal income taxes
- A transistor developed by Bell Telephone Laboratories permitted miniaturization of electronic devices such as computers, radios and

television
- Gerber Products Company sold two million cans and jars of baby food weekly
- Dial soap was introduced as the first deodorant soap
- Garbage disposals, heat-conducting windshields, Nestlé's Quick, Michelin radial tires and Scrabble all made their first appearance
- The Nikon camera was introduced to compete with the Leica
- 360,000 soft-coal workers went on strike, demanding $100 per month in retirement benefits at age 62
- Dwight D. Eisenhower requested that the Democratic Party draft him as a candidate for president of the United States
- Peter Goldmark of CBS invented a high-fidelity, long-playing record containing up to 45 minutes of music
- Ben Hogan won the U.S. Open and was the top PGA money winner with $36,000
- A new liquid hydrogen fuel was created that was touted as having the potential to send men to the moon
- The Dow-Jones Industrial Average hit a high of 193
- The United Nations passed the Palestine Partition Plan, creating the State of Israel
- Mahatma Gandhi was assassinated by a Hindu extremist

1949
- Visas were no longer necessary for travel to many countries outside the Iron Curtain
- The FCC ended an eight-year ban on radio editorializing, and stations were warned to present all sides of controversial questions
- Harry Truman, surprising the pollsters, won a second term, inviting blacks, for the first time, to the Presidential Inaugural, which was telecast
- The postwar baby boom leveled off with 3.58 million live births
- The minimum wage rose from $0.40 to $0.75 an hour

- Congress increased the president's salary to $100,000 per year, with an additional $50,000 for expenses
- The Polaroid Land camera, which produced a picture in 60 seconds, sold for $89.75
- Following the communist takeover of China, and Russia's development of the A-bomb, many feared an impending war with Russia
- The United Nations Headquarters in New York was dedicated
- Despite inflation fears, prices began to fall
- The Dow Jones hit a high of 200, while unemployment averaged 5.9 percent
- More than 500,000 steelworkers went on strike, which ended when companies agreed to workers' pension demands
- Hank Williams joined the country music program, the *Grand Ole Opry*.
- *Life* magazine asked, "Jackson Pollock: Is He the Greatest Living Painter in the U.S.?"
- The Hollywood Ten were fired for refusing to tell the House Un-American Activities Committee if they were communists, filed suit against Hollywood producers
- A poll indicated that women believed three children constituted the ideal family and wanted no babies until the second year of marriage, while 70 percent of families believed in spanking, and less than 30 percent said grace at meals
- Baby-boom children reached kindergarten age and educators estimated that school enrollment would increase 39 percent the following year
- Postwar demand for automobiles fueled a record-breaking buying spree
- Gov. James E. Folsom of Alabama signed a bill forbidding the wearing of masks, attempting to stop raids by hooded men who whipped people, particularly minorities
- 90 percent of boys and 74 percent of girls questioned in a national poll of HS students believed it was "all right for young people to pet or 'neck' when they were out on dates"

- Lawyer Frieda Hennock was the first woman member of the Federal Communications Commission

1950–1951

- The Korean War began
- Congress increased personal and corporate income taxes
- Auto registrations showed one car for every 3.7 Americans
- Blue Cross insurance programs covered 3.7 million Americans
- Five million homes had television sets, compared to 45 million with radios
- President Harry Truman ordered the Atomic Energy Committee to develop the hydrogen bomb
- Boston Red Sox Ted Williams became baseball's highest paid player with a $125,000 contract
- Senator Joseph McCarthy announced that he had the names of 205 known Communists working in the State Department
- Otis Elevator installed the first passenger elevator with self-opening doors
- Coca-Cola's share of the U.S. cola market was 69 percent compared to Pepsi-Cola's share at 15 percent
- The FBI issued its first list of the Ten Most Wanted Criminals
- The first kidney transplant was performed on a 49-year old woman at a Chicago hospital
- Charles M. Schultz's comic strip, *Peanuts,* debuted in eight newspapers
- Smokey the Bear, an orphaned cub found after a forest fire in New Mexico, became the living symbol of the U.S. Forestry Service
- *Betty Crocker's Picture Cookbook* was published
- Miss Clairol hair coloring and Minute Rice was marketed
- M&M candy, created in 1940, was now stamped with an "M" to assure customers they were getting the real thing
- The first Xerox copy machine was introduced
- The average cost of a four-year college was $1,800, up 400 percent since

1900

- The 22nd Amendment to the Constitution, limiting the term of the president to two terms, was adopted
- Univak, the first general-purpose electronic computer, was dedicated in Philadelphia
- CBS introduced color television in a program hosted by Ed Sullivan and Arthur Godfrey
- Lacoste tennis shirts with an alligator symbol were introduced in the U.S. by French manufacturer Izod
- Earl Tupper created the home sale party to market his plastic storage containers directly to householders
- *Jet* news magazine was launched
- Chrysler Corporation introduced power steering in cars
- More than 75 percent of all U.S. farms were now electrified
- Harvard Law School admitted women
- Nationwide 3.8 million people played golf on approximately 5,000 courses, comprising 1.5 million acres of land
- North Korean forces crossed the thirty-eighth parallel, took Seoul, and rejected American truce offers
- H&R Block, formed in 1946 in Kansas City, began offering tax preparation services when the IRS stopped preparing people's taxes
- Margaret Sanger urged the development of an oral contraceptive
- The Metropolitan Life Insurance Company reported a link between 15 pounds of excess weight and dying younger than the average life span
- Massive flooding covered more than a million acres of land in Oklahoma, Kansas, Missouri and Illinois
- The latest census reported that eight percent of the population was more than 65 years old, up from four percent in 1900
- For the first time in history, women outnumbered men in the U.S.
- Julius and Ethel Rosenberg were sentenced to death for espionage against the U.S.

- President Truman dispatched an air force plane when Sioux City Memorial Park in Iowa refused to bury John Rice, a Native American who had died in combat; his remains were interred in Arlington National Cemetery
- Sugarless chewing gum, dacron suits, pushbutton-controlled garage doors, telephone company answering service, college credit courses on TV, and power steering all made their first appearance
- Charles F. Blair flew solo over the North Pole
- Entertainer Milton Berle signed a 30-year, million-dollar-plus contract with NBC
- New York and other major cities increased the cost of a phone call from $0.05 to $0.10

1952

- The Federal Reserve Board voted to dissolve the A.P. Giannini banking empire, headed by Transamerica Corporation, which controlled the nation's largest bank, Bank of America
- Popular movies included *High Noon, The Greatest Show on Earth,* and *The African Queen*
- The Metropolitan Opera in New York charged $8.00 for an evening performance and $30 per seat on opening night
- Books published included *Invisible Man, East of Eden, The Natural, The Old Man and the Sea,* and *Charlotte's Web*
- Vice presidential candidate Richard M. Nixon declared he was not a quitter in his famous "Checkers" speech
- Jonah Salk at the University of Pennsylvania began testing a vaccine against polio
- W. F. Libby of the University of Chicago dated Stonehenge in England to 1842 BC
- Reports circulated that the U.S. had exploded a hydrogen bomb
- Sony introduced the transistor radio
- Songs included "Walking My Baby Back Home," "Wheel of Fortune,"

and "Glow Worm"
- Nationwide, 55,000 people were stricken with polio, an all-time high
- The New Revised Standard Version of the Holy Bible was published
- The U.S. Air Force reported 60 UFO sightings in two weeks
- President Harry Truman ordered seizure of the nation's $7 billion steel industry to prevent a walkout of 650,000 workers, but the Supreme Court ruled the move unconstitutional
- *The Today Show* premiered on NBC-TV
- Edward Mills Purcell and Felix Bloch won the Nobel Prize in physics for work in the measurement of magnetic fields in atomic nuclei
- *Mad Magazine* was introduced, with a circulation of 195,000; 55 percent of college students and 43 percent of high school students voted it their favorite periodical
- Products making their first appearance included the 16 mm home movie projector, two-way car radios, adjustable showerheads, bowling alleys with automatic pin boys and Kellogg's Sugar Frosted Flakes
- Fifty-two million automobiles were on the highways, up from 25 million in 1945
- Thirty-seven-year-old Jersey Joe Walcott knocked out Ezzard Charles to become the oldest heavyweight boxing champion at 37
- An all-white jury in North Carolina convicted a black man for leering at a white woman 75 feet away, deemed assualt

1953
- The Screen Actors Guild adopted by-laws banning communists from membership
- A link was made between coronary heart disease and diets high in animal fats
- New York subway fares rose from $0.05 to $0.15
- Nationwide, 30 million attended performances of classical music, 15 million attended major league baseball, and 7.2 million children took music lessons

- The Dow Jones Industrial Average showed a high of 293 and a low of 255
- Per capita state taxes averaged $68.04
- An airmail stamp cost $0.07 per ounce and a postcard stamp cost $0.02
- All-black military units had largely disappeared, with 90 percent integrated into white military units
- Leland Kirdel wrote in *Coronet* magazine, "The smart woman will keep herself desirable. It is her duty to be feminine and desirable at all times in the eyes of the opposite sex."
- In the McCarthyism age, libraries were ordered to remove books by "communists, fellow travelers, and the like"
- Lucille Ball and Desi Arnaz signed an $8 million contract to continue "I Love Lucy" for 30 months
- Optimistic about peace with Korea, president Dwight D. Eisenhower restored the traditional Easter egg roll for children on the White House lawn
- *TV Guide* and *Playboy* both began publication
- The number of comic books exploded, comprising 650 titles
- Nationwide, 25 percent of young Americans were now attending college, thanks to the GI Bill—an increase of 65 percent from before the Second World War
- President Eisenhower pledged rigid economy in government, a lifting of controls, and an effort toward a more balanced budget
- During his inaugural address, Eisenhower called on Americans to make whatever sacrifices necessary to meet the threat of Soviet aggression, defining the contest as a matter of freedom against slavery
- Charlie Chaplin said it was "virtually impossible" to continue work in the United States because of "vicious propaganda" by powerful reactionary groups
- General Motors introduced the Chevrolet Corvette, the first plastic-laminated, fiberglass sports car, at a cost of $3,250

- Elvis Presley paid $4.00 to cut "My Happiness" in Memphis for his mother's birthday
- Russia's Joseph Stalin died in May and the coronation of England's Queen Elizabeth occurred in June
- New York's Seeman Brothers introduced the instant ice tea
- Nearly half of U.S. farms now had tractors
- 17 million homes had television sets
- Four out of five men's shirts sold in America were white
- The DC-7 propeller plane, Sugar Smacks, 3-D cartoons and movies, and Irish Coffee all made their first appearance

1954–1955

- The Supreme Court declared racial segregation in public schools illegal
- The first nuclear-powered submarine, *Nautilus,* was launched
- Gasoline averaged $0.29 per gallon
- Texas Instruments introduced the first practical silicon transistor
- Taxpayers with incomes of more than $100,000 paid more than $67,000 each in taxes
- Sales of Viceroy cigarettes leaped as smokers shifted to filter-tipped cigarettes
- Open-heart surgery was introduced by Minneapolis physician C. Walton Lillehe
- RCA introduced the first color television set
- The $13 million, 900-room Fontainebleau Hotel opened at Miami Beach
- *Sports Illustrated Magazine* was introduced
- Swanson & Sons introduced frozen TV dinners
- Dr. Jonas E. Salk, U.S. developer of anti-polio serum, started inoculating school children in Pittsburgh, Pennsylvania
- The U.S. boasted 1,768 million newspapers, publishing 59 million copies daily
- The U.S. population contained six percent of the world's population, 60 percent of all cars, 58 percent of all telephones, 45 percent of all radio

sets, and 34 percent of all railroads

- Marian Anderson, the first black soloist of the Metropolitan Opera, appeared as Ulrica in *Un Ballo* in Maschera
- Blacks in Montgomery, Alabama, boycotted segregated city bus lines, and Rosa Parks was arrested for refusing to give up the only seat available, which was in the front of the bus
- The first Chevrolet V-8 engine motorcar was introduced
- The federal minimum wage rose from $0.75 to $1.00 per hour
- Whirlpool Corporation was created by the merger of three companies
- *National Review* and *Village Voice* began publication
- Crest was introduced by Proctor and Gamble
- Special K breakfast food was introduced by Kellogg Company
- The nation now had 1,800 suburban shopping centers
- The number of millionaires in the United States was reported to be 154
- New television shows introduced that year included *The Adventures of Rin Tin Tin, Father Knows Best, Lassie,* and *Tonight* with Steve Allen.
- HEW Secretary Oveta Culp Hobby opposed the free distribution of the Salk vaccine to poor children as "socialized medicine by the back door"
- Disneyland in Anaheim, California, opened
- The first television press conference featured President Dwight Eisenhower
- Smog and poisoned air became a public concern
- *Confidential Magazine* had a circulation of 4.5 million readers
- President Eisenhower suffered a heart attack, and the stock market plunged $14 billion
- The population explosion created a shortage of 120,000 teachers and 300,000 schoolrooms
- Weekly church attendance comprised 49 million adults—half the total adult population
- Jacqueline Cochran became the first woman to fly faster than the speed of sound

- Nationwide, the U.S. had 214,000 physicians, 95,000 dentists, and 1,604,000 hospital beds
- The Chase Manhattan Bank, Sperry Rand, H&R Block, and the Dreyfus Fund all made their first appearance
- Racial segregation on interstate buses and trains was ordered to end
- President Eisenhower submitted a 10-year, $101 billion highway construction program to Congress
- The AFL and CIO merged, with George Meany as president
- The Dow Jones Industrial Average hit a high of 488, and a low of 391
- The Ford Foundation gave $500 million to colleges and universities nationwide
- Whirlpool Corporation merged with Seeger Refrigerator Company and began producing refrigerators, air conditioners, and cooking ranges

1956

- The nation boasted 7,000 drive-in theaters
- The DNA molecule was photographed for the first time
- Teen fashions for boys included crew cut haircuts known as "flattops"
- Procter and Gamble created disposable diapers called Pampers
- Ford Motor Company went public and issued over 10 million shares which were sold to 250,000 investors
- A survey showed 77 percent of college-educated women were married, 41 percent worked part-time, and 17 percent worked full-time
- Boston religious leaders urged the banning of rock 'n' roll
- Eleven percent of all cars sold were station wagons
- Airlines carried as many passengers as trains
- Broadway openings included *Waiting for Godot, Long Day's Journey into Night, My Fair Lady, Bells Are Ringing and Separate Tables*
- After vowing never to allow Elvis Presley's vulgarity on his TV show, Ed Sullivan paid Presley $50,000 for three appearances
- Midas Muffler Shops, Comet, Raid, Salem cigarettes, La Leche League, Imperial margarine and women ordained as ministers in the

Presbyterian Church all made their first appearance

- Don Larsen of the New York Yankees pitched the first perfect game in the World Series
- John F. Kennedy won the Pulitzer Prize for *Profiles in Courage* and *Russia Leaves the War* by George F. Kennan won in the U.S. History category
- An art canvas purchased in Chicago for $450 was discovered to be a Leonardo valued at $1 million
- Television premieres included *As the World Turns, The Edge of Night, The Huntley-Brinkley Report, The Price Is Right* and *The Steve Allen Show*
- Soviet Premier Nikita Khrushchev assailed past President Joseph Stalin as a terrorist, egotist and murderer
- American colleges began actively recruiting students from the middle classes
- Martin Luther King, Jr. said, "Nonviolence is the most potent technique for oppressed people. Unearned suffering is redemptive."
- Hit songs included "Blue Suede Shoes," "Hound Dog," "Mack the Knife," "The Party's Over" and "Friendly Persuasion"
- European autos gained in popularity, including Volkswagens, Jaguars, Ferraris, Saabs and Fiats
- Ngo Diem was elected president of South Vietnam

1957–1958

- President Eisenhower sent paratroopers to Little Rock, Arkansas, to protect nine black students seeking to attend all-white Central High School
- "Beat" and "beatnik" took hold as words to describe the "Beat Generation"
- Unemployment in the U.S. reached 5.2 million, a post-war high
- Martin Luther King, Jr., helped organize the Southern Christian Leadership Conference (SCLC) and became its first president

- Evangelist Billy Graham held a five-month-long revival at Madison Square Garden in New York that attracted more than 500,000 people
- After 38 years, *Collier's Magazine* published its final issue
- Tennis player Althea Gibson became the first black athlete to win at Wimbledon
- *Sputnik I,* the first manmade satellite, was sent into orbit around the earth by the Soviets
- Painkiller Darvon was introduced by Eli Lilly
- A University of Wisconsin study showed that 20 percent of Americans lived in poverty
- New York's first trolley car was retired
- Frisbee was introduced by Wham-O Manufacturing
- Per capita margarine consumption exceeded butter
- A record 4.3 million babies were born
- The cost of 100,000 computerized multiplication computations fell from $1.26 in 1952 to $0.26.
- Volkswagen sold 200,000 Beetles and Ford introduced the Edsel
- An intensive study of birth control with pills was begun in Puerto Rico
- *Fortune* named Paul Getty America's richest man, with his wealth estimated at $1 billion
- Average wages for a factory production worker were $2.08 an hour, or $82.00 a week
- BankAmericard credit card was introduced
- First-class postal rates climbed to $0.04 per ounce
- The VD rate increased from 122,000 cases to 126,000, the first increase since 1948
- Sweet'n' Low sugarless sweetener was introduced
- The Everly Brothers' song "Wake Up Little Susie" was banned in Boston
- One in three women went regularly to the beauty shop, many for apricot or silver-colored hair

1958

- *Life Magazine*'s series, "Crisis in Education," focused on major U.S. educational problems, including poor curricula, overcrowding, and poorly paid teachers
- The Pizza Hut chain began in Kansas City
- Paul Robeson, denied a passport for eight years because of his Leftist comments, was allowed to tour overseas
- The cost of college doubled from 1940 to 1958 to $1,300 a year
- The construction of a nuclear power plant at Bodega Head, California, was stopped by a court action of environmental groups
- Gasoline cost 30.4 cents per gallon
- Paperback edition of *Lolita* sold a million copies
- Elvis Presley was inducted into the army as No. 53310761
- Eleanor Roosevelt was first on the "Most Admired Women" list for the 11th time, and Queen Elizabeth was second
- SANE (Scientists Against Nuclear Energy) was formed with 25,000 members
- Several television quiz shows were exposed for providing contestants with answers beforehand
- Ford Motor Company introduced the Edsel
- Unemployment reached a postwar high of 6.8 percent
- The United States' standing army included 2.6 million men and women
- Kansas and Colorado were invaded by grasshoppers
- John Kenneth Galbraith's book *The Affluent Society* contended that materialism and conformity characterized the U.S. and argued for redistribution of income to end poverty
- The sale of television sets topped 41 million
- First-class postal rates climbed to $0.04 per ounce
- Sixty-four percent of American households now had incomes above $4,000 a year
- More than 250,000 people attended the Jehovah's Witness Convention

at Yankee Stadium
- The Grammy award, John Birch Society, Chevrolet Impala, Sweet 'n' Low, Cocoa Krispies, American Express, and Green Giant canned beans all made their first appearance

1959

- To offset the rising cost of tinplate, Coors beer started using an aluminum can
- Movie premieres included *Ben-Hur* starring Charlton Heston; *Some Like It Hot* with Tony Curtis, Marilyn Monroe and Jack Lemmon; and *Pillow Talk* featuring Doris Day, Rock Hudson and Tony Randall
- Mary Leakey discovered the skull of the 1.78 million-year-old *Australopithecus* in the Olduvai Gorge, Tanganyika
- Television's top-10 shows were *Gunsmoke*; *Wagon Train*; *Have Gun, Will Travel*; *The Danny Thomas Show*; *The Red Skelton Show*; *Father Knows Best*; *77 Sunset Strip*; *The Price Is Right*; *Wanted: Dead or Alive* and *Perry Mason*
- The Soviet *Lunik II* became the first manmade object to strike the moon
- Rock 'n' roll stars Buddy Holly, Ritchie Valens and the Big Bopper were killed in an airplane crash
- Modern art was declared duty-free
- The U.S. Navy successfully orbited a Vanguard satellite, the forerunner of the first weather station in space
- "A Raisin in the Sun," "The Miracle Worker," "The Tenth Man," "Five Finger Exercise," "Sweet Bird of Youth" and "Mark Twain Tonight" all premiered on Broadway
- Fiction bestsellers included *Exodus* by Leon Uris, *Doctor Zhivago* by Boris Pasternak, *Hawaii* by James Michener, *Lady Chatterley's Lover* by D. H. Lawrence, *The Ugly American* by William J. Lederer and Eugene L. Burdick, *Poor No More* by Robert Ruark and *Dear and Glorious Physician* by Taylor Caldwell

- NASA selected the *Mercury* Seven astronauts: John Glenn, Scott Carpenter, Virgil Grissom, Gordon Cooper, Walter Schirra, Donald Slayton and Alan Shepard
- Perry Como signed a $25 million contract with Kraft Foods

1960

- The National Association of Broadcasters reacted to a payola scandal by threatening fines for any disc jockeys who accepted money for playing particular records
- Four students from North Carolina Agricultural and Technical State University in Greensboro, North Carolina, began a sit-in at a segregated Woolworth's lunch counter, which triggered similar nonviolent protests throughout the southern U.S.
- Joanne Woodward received the first star on the Hollywood Walk of Fame
- Adolph Coors III, chairman of the board of the Coors Brewing Company, was kidnapped for $500,000 and later found dead
- The U.S. announced that 3,500 American soldiers would be sent to Vietnam
- Arthur Leonard Schawlow and Charles Hard Townes received the first patent for a laser
- The U.S. launched the first weather satellite, TIROS-1
- *Ben Hur* won the Oscar for Best Picture
- A Soviet missile shot down an American spy plane; pilot Francis Gary Powers was captured, tried, and released 21 months later in a spy swap with the U.S.
- President Dwight D. Eisenhower signed the Civil Rights Act of 1960 into law
- The U.S. FDA approved birth control as an additional indication for the drug Searle's Enovid, making it the world's first approved oral contraceptive pill
- Nuclear submarine *USS Triton* completed the underwater

circumnavigation of Earth

- The Soviet Union beat Yugoslavia 2-1 to win the first European Football Championship
- Harper Lee released her critically acclaimed novel *To Kill a Mockingbird*
- Presidential candidates Richard M. Nixon and John F. Kennedy participated in the first televised presidential debate
- Nikita Khrushchev pounded his shoe on a table at a United Nations General Assembly meeting to protest the discussion of Soviet Union policy toward Eastern Europe
- Black entertainer Sammy Davis, Jr. married Swedish actress May Britt, causing a stir
- Basketball player Wilt Chamberlain grabbed 55 rebounds in a single game
- Production of the DeSoto automobile brand ceased
- President Eisenhower authorized the use of $1 million toward the resettlement of Cuban refugees, who were arriving in Florida at the rate of 1,000 a week
- The U.S. Supreme Court declared in *Boynton v. Virginia* that segregation on public transit was illegal
- The U.S. Census listed all people from Latin America as white, including blacks from the Dominican Republic, European whites from Argentina, and Mexicans who resembled Native Americans
- The world population was 3,021,475,000

1961–1962

- President Kennedy established the Peace Corps two months after his inauguration
- DNA genetic code was broken
- New York's First National Bank offered fixed-term certificates of deposit
- IBM's Selectric typewriter was introduced

- Harper and Row was created through a merger
- Right wing activities of the John Birch Society stirred concerns in Congress
- Black and white "Freedom Riders" tested integration in the South, and were attacked and beaten in Alabama
- Cigarette makers spent $115 million on television advertising
- R.J. Reynolds acquired Pacific Hawaiian Products Company in an attempt to diversify away from tobacco products
- Sprite was introduced by Coca-Cola Company
- A Gallup poll recorded that 74 percent of teens interviewed believed in God, 58 percent planned to go to college, most of the 16- to 21-year-old girls interviewed expected to be married by age 22, and most wanted four children
- 4,000 servicemen were sent to Vietnam as advisers
- Minimum wage rose from $1.00 to $1.25 per hour
- Canned pet foods were among the top three selling categories in grocery stores
- The Cuban missile crisis pitted the United States against the Soviet Union
- President Kennedy reduced tariff duties to stimulate foreign trade
- Electronic Data Systems was founded by H. Ross Perot
- 90 percent of American households had at least one television set
- The American Broadcasting Company (ABC) began color telecasts 3.5 hours per week
- Diet-Rite Cola was introduced as the first sugar-free soft drink
- Tab-opening aluminum drink cans were introduced
- In May, 1962, the stock market plunged 34.95 points, the sharpest drop since the 1929 crash
- Late-night television show, *The Tonight Show*, with Johnny Carson, began
- Demonstrations against school segregation occurred throughout the

South
- President John F. Kennedy contributed his salary to charity
- The Dow Jones Industrial Average reached a high of 767
- Movie premieres included *To Kill a Mockingbird*, *Long Day's Journey into Night*, *The Manchurian Candidate*, *The Longest Day* and *Lawrence of Arabia*
- The Students' Nonviolent Coordinating Committee (SNCC) organized the freedom ballot in the South, aggressively registering blacks to vote in Mississippi, Alabama and Georgia
- Astronaut John Glenn orbited the earth three times, saying, "It was quite a day. I don't know what you can say about a day when you see four beautiful sunsets."
- Popular songs included "Go Away, Little Girl," "What Kind of Fool Am I?," "I Left My Heart in San Francisco" and "The Sweetest Sounds"
- Nine New York daily newspaper unions staged a strike that lasted five months
- Walter Cronkite replaced Douglas Edwards on the *CBS Evening News*
- Jackie Robinson was inducted as the first African-American into the Baseball Hall of Fame
- *One Flew over the Cuckoo's Nest* by Ken Kesey, *Happiness Is a Warm Puppy* by Charles M. Schulz, *Sex and the Single Girl* by Helen Gurley Brown, and *Pigeon Feathers* by John Updike were all published
- *Mariner II* became the first successful interplanetary probe, confirming that the high temperatures of Venus were inhospitable to life
- Rachel Carson's book *Silent Spring* stated that more than 500 new chemicals were entering our bodies because of widespread insecticide use
- *Who's Afraid of Virginia Woolf?* opened on Broadway
- Inflation was at 0.4 percent, unemployment at 5.5 percent
- Eighty percent of households had a telephone

1964

- The first meeting between leaders of the Roman Catholic and Orthodox churches since the fifteenth century took place between Pope Paul VI and Patriarch Athenagoras I in Jerusalem
- In his first State of the Union Address, President Lyndon Johnson declared a "War on Poverty"
- Surgeon General Luther Leonidas Terry reported that smoking may be hazardous to one's health (the first such statement from the U.S. Government)
- Thirteen years after its proposal and nearly two years after its passage by the Senate, the 24th Amendment, prohibiting the use of poll taxes in national elections, was ratified
- General Motors introduced the Oldsmobile Vista Cruiser and the Buick Sport Wagon
- The Beatles vaulted to the #1 spot on the U.S. singles charts with "I Want to Hold Your Hand," and launched the "British Invasion" with an appearance on *The Ed Sullivan Show*
- The Supreme Court ruled that congressional districts must be approximately equal in population
- Muhammad Ali beat Sonny Liston in Miami Beach, Florida, and was crowned the Heavyweight Champion of the World
- Teamsters President Jimmy Hoffa was convicted by a federal jury of tampering with a federal jury in 1962
- In *New York Times Co. v Sullivan*, the Supreme Court ruled that, under the First Amendment, speech criticizing political figures cannot be censored
- The first Ford Mustang rolled off the assembly line at Ford Motor Company
- A Dallas, Texas, jury found Jack Ruby guilty of killing John F. Kennedy assassin Lee Harvey Oswald
- Merv Griffin's game show *Jeopardy!* debuted on NBC

- The Beatles dominated the top five positions in the Billboard Top 40 singles in America: "Can't Buy Me Love," "Twist and Shout," "She Loves You," "I Want to Hold Your Hand," and "Please Please Me"
- Three high school friends in Hoboken, NJ, opened the first BLIMPIE restaurant
- The Rolling Stones released their debut album, *The Rolling Stones*
- The New York World's Fair opened to celebrate the 300th anniversary of New Amsterdam being taken over by British forces and renamed New York in 1664
- John George Kemeny and Thomas Eugene Kurtz ran the first computer program written in BASIC (Beginners' All-purpose Symbolic Instruction Code), an easy-to-learn, high-level programming language
- College students marched through Times Square and San Francisco in the first major student demonstration against the Vietnam War
- Three civil rights workers were murdered near Philadelphia, Mississippi, by local Klansmen, cops, and a sheriff
- President Johnson signed the Civil Rights Act of 1964 into law, legally abolishing racial segregation in the United States
- At the Republican National Convention in San Francisco, presidential nominee Barry Goldwater declared that "extremism in the defense of liberty is no vice," and "moderation in the pursuit of justice is no virtue"
- The Supreme Court ruled that, in accordance with the Civil Rights Act of 1964, establishments providing public accommodations must refrain from racial discrimination
- Cosmic microwave background radiation was discovered
- Dr. Farrington Daniels's book, *Direct Use of the Sun's Energy*, was published by Yale University Press
- The first Moog synthesizer was designed by Robert Moog

1965

- Americans purchased $60 million worth of prescription weight-loss drugs, twice the dollar amount spent just five years earlier

- "Flower Power" was coined by Allen Ginsburg at a Berkeley antiwar rally
- Unemployment, at 4.2 percent, was at its lowest point in eight years
- The 1,250-room Washington Hilton opened in Washington, DC
- The U.S. Immigration Bill abolished national origin quotas
- Avis Rent-A-Car was acquired by International Telephone and Telegraph
- The Voting Rights Act, which eliminated literacy tests and provided federal oversight in elections, stimulated a dramatic increase in voting by African-Americans
- America's place in harvesting seafood fell from first in 1945 to fifth as the country became a major fish importer
- The U.S. Supreme Court struck down a Connecticut statute forbidding the use of contraceptives and eliminated state and local film censorship
- Pope Paul VI visited the United Nations headquarters and delivered a message of peace
- After extended hearings on cigarette smoking, Congress required that cigarette packages warn: "Caution: Cigarette smoking may be hazardous to your health"
- Americans paid $7.5 million more than in 1940 for prepackaged food
- The birth rate fell to 19 per 1,000 people, the lowest since 1940
- Cereal packaged with fruits preserved through freeze-drying was introduced
- Miniskirts, Cranapple, Diet Pepsi, the Sony home videotape recorder and all-news radio stations made their first appearance
- A 150-mile commuter rail system in San Francisco and Oakland began construction
- Kraft foods sponsored the first commercial television program transmitted between the U.S. and Switzerland via the *Early Bird* communications satellite

- Production of soft-top convertible automobiles reached a record 507,000
- For the first time since 1962, the administration did not ask Congress for a fallout shelter construction program
- The U.S. Public Health Service announced an ambitious program to eradicate syphilis in the U.S. by 1972

1966–1967

- Student protests against the Vietnam War began
- Student deferments from the draft were abolished, and draft calls reached 50,000 young men a month
- The National Organization for Women (NOW) was founded
- The largest year-to-year rise in the cost of living since 1958 was announced—2.8 percent
- The term "Black Power" was introduced into the Civil Rights movement, signifying the rift between the pacifist followers of Martin Luther King, Jr.'s SCLC and the militants following Stokely Carmichael, SNCC and CORE
- Taster's Choice freeze-dried instant coffee was introduced
- 41 percent of non-white families made less than $3,000 annually
- *New York World Journal & Tribune* closed; *Rolling Stone* magazine was founded
- 2.7 million Americans received food stamp assistance
- Nearly 10,000 farmers received more than $20,000 each in subsidies
- Annual per capita beef consumption reached 105.6 pounds
- Burger King Corporation was acquired by Pillsbury Corporation
- New style dance halls, like the Fillmore in San Francisco, introduced strobe lights, liquid color blobs, glow paint, and psychedelic posters
- The Clean Waters Restoration Act allocated funds for preventing river and air pollution
- The National Association of Broadcasters instructed all disc jockeys to screen all records for hidden references to drugs or obscene meanings
- The U.S. population passed 200 million

- The Rare and Endangered Species list was introduced by the Department of the Interior
- The phrase "Third World" for underdeveloped countries gained currency of usage
- Connection between a low-cholesterol diet and a reduced incidence of heart disease was shown in a five-year study
- Both CBS and NBC televised the Super Bowl
- The first rock festival was held at Monterey, California, featuring the Grateful Dead and Big Brother and the Holding Company starring Janis Joplin
- Heavyweight boxer Muhammad Ali was denied conscientious objector status after refusing induction in the Army
- The United States revealed that it had developed an anti-ballistic missile defense plan against Chinese attack
- Hit songs included *Natural Woman, Soul Man, I Never Loved a Man, Penny Lane, By The Time I Get to Phoenix,* and *Can't Take My Eyes Off You*
- Army physician Captain Harold Levy refused to train Green Berets heading to Vietnam in the treatment of skin disease, and was court-martialed and sent to prison
- Coed dorms opened at numerous colleges across the country
- *Sgt Pepper's Lonely Hearts Club Band* by the Beatles won a Grammy for best album
- Jogging, Mickey Mouse watches, protest buttons and psychedelic art were popular fads
- U.S. troop levels in Vietnam reached 225,000 and the U.S. death toll reached 15,997
- Thurgood Marshall became the first African American appointed to the U.S. Supreme Court
- Television premieres included *The Flying Nun, The Carol Burnett Show, Ironsides* and *The Phil Donahue Show*

- Annual beef consumption, per capita, reached 105.6 pounds, up from 99 pounds in 1960
- Black leader Rap Brown said of the ghetto riots, "Violence is as American as apple pie"

1968–1969

- The U.S. gross national product reached $861 billion
- Vietnam War protests intensified across the nation
- Richard Nixon was elected president
- BankAmericard holders numbered 14 million, up 12 million in two years
- Civil Rights leader Rev. Martin Luther King, Jr., was assassinated in Memphis, Tennessee and riots occurred in over 199 cities nationwide
- Senator Robert F. Kennedy was assassinated in Los Angeles shortly after winning the California Democratic primary
- Responding to the King and Kennedy assassinations, Sears & Roebuck removed toy guns from its Christmas catalog
- Automobile production reached 8.8 million
- Volkswagen captured 57 percent of the U.S. automobile import market
- Television advertising revenues hit $2 billion, twice that of radio
- First-class postage climbed to $0.06
- Yale College admitted women
- Uniform Monday Holiday Law was enacted by Congress, creating 3-day holiday weekends
- Nationwide 78 million television sets existed
- Neil Armstrong walked on the moon
- Pantyhose production reached 624 million pairs in 1969, up from 200 million in 1968
- The average U.S. farm produced enough food for 47 people, and the average farm government subsidy was $1,000
- Blue Cross health insurance covered 68 million Americans
- *Penthouse* magazine began publication, and *Saturday Evening Post*

folded

- The National Association of Broadcasters began phasing out cigarette advertising
- The U.S. began the first troop withdrawals from Vietnam, and Vietnam casualties exceeded the total for the Korean War
- Richard Nixon's 43.3 percent victory was the lowest presidential margin since 1912
- Pope Paul VI's ban on contraception was challenged by 800 U.S. theologians
- 20,000 people were added monthly to NYC's welfare rolls, as one-fourth of the city's budget went to welfare
- The Vietnam War became the longest war in U.S. history and approximately 484,000 U.S. soldiers were fighting in it
- President Nixon announced the withdrawal of 25,000 U.S. troops from South Vietnam
- Music concerts drew millions as artists such as the Rolling Stones, the Who, Joan Baez, Jimi Hendrix and the Jefferson Airplane launched tours
- A copy of the first printing of the Declaration of Independence sold for $404,000
- "The Johnny Cash Show," "Hee Haw," and "The Bill Cosby Show" all premiered
- Following student protests, universities nationwide either made ROTC voluntary or abolished the program
- After weeks of debate, U.S. and Vietnam delegates agreed only on the shape of the table used when South Vietnam and the National Liberation Front joined the talks
- Black militant defendant Bobby Seale was ordered bound and gagged by Judge Julius Hoffmann when Seale repeatedly disrupted the Chicago Eight trial
- The popularity of paperback novels detailing life in "today's easy-living,

easy-loving playground called suburbia" skyrocketed
- Actor Richard Burton bought Elizabeth Taylor a 69.42-carat diamond from Cartier
- John Lennon and Yoko Ono married
- 448 universities experienced strikes or were forced to close as student demands included revisions of admissions policies and the reorganization of academic programs
- *Penthouse* magazine, vasectomy outpatient service and automated teller machines all made their first appearance
- The underdog New York Jets, led by quarterback Joe Namath, upset the Baltimore Colts to become the first AFL Super Bowl winner
- Robert Lehman bequeathed 3,000 works valued at more than $100 million to the Metropolitan Museum of Art
- Bestsellers included Philip Roth's *Portnoy's Complaint*, Jacqueline Susann's *The Love Machine*, Mario Puzo's *The Godfather*, and Penelope Ashe's *Naked Came the Stranger*
- To protest the Miss America contest, feminists dropped girdles and bras in the trash
- Hippie cult leader Charles Manson was charged with the Hollywood murders of pregnant Sharon Tate and three others
- The first draft lottery was held

1970

- Pan American Airways offered the first commercially scheduled 747 service from John F. Kennedy International Airport to London's Heathrow Airport
- Black Sabbath's debut album, regarded as the first heavy metal album, was released
- The Chicago Seven defendants were found not guilty of conspiring to incite a riot, in charges stemming from violence at the 1968 Democratic National Convention, while five were found guilty on the lesser charge of crossing state lines to incite a riot

- The Nuclear Non-Proliferation Treaty went into effect, after ratification by 56 nations
- The United States Army charged 14 officers with suppressing information related to the My Lai massacre in Vietnam
- Postal workers in a dozen cities went on strike for two weeks and President Nixon assigned military units to New York City post offices
- Earth Day was proclaimed by San Francisco Mayor Joseph Alioto
- Paul McCartney announced the disbanding of the Beatles, as their twelfth album, *Let It Be*, was released
- An oxygen tank in the *Apollo 13* spacecraft exploded, forcing the crew to abort the mission and return in four days
- Four students at Kent State University in Ohio were killed and nine wounded by Ohio National Guardsmen during a protest against the U.S. incursion into Cambodia
- The U.S. promoted its first female generals: Anna Mae Hays and Elizabeth P. Hoisington
- *Venera 7* was launched and became the first spacecraft to successfully transmit data from the surface of another planet
- The Women's Strike for Equality took place down Fifth Avenue in New York City
- Elvis Presley began his first concert tour since 1958 at the Veterans Memorial Coliseum in Phoenix, Arizona
- The first New York City Marathon took place
- Guitarist Jimi Hendrix died in London of drug-related complications
- *Monday Night Football* debuted on ABC
- In Paris, a Communist delegation rejected President Nixon's October 7 peace proposal for the Vietnam War as "a maneuver to deceive world opinion"
- Garry Trudeau's comic strip *Doonesbury* debuted in dozens of U.S. newspapers
- Southern Airlines Flight 932 crashed, killing all 75 on board, including

37 players and five coaches from the Marshall University football team

- The Soviet Union landed *Lunokhod 1* on the moon—the first roving remote-controlled robot to land on a natural satellite
- The North Tower of the World Trade Center was the tallest building in the world at 1,368 feet
- Alvin Toffler published his book *Future Shock*

1971

- President Richard Nixon ordered a 90-day freeze on wages and prices
- First-class postal rates rose to $0.08 per ounce
- *New York Times* published the first installment of the "Pentagon Papers," a classified history of American involvement in the Vietnam War, and 75 percent of those polled opposed publication of the secret papers
- Tennis player Billie Jean King became the first woman athlete to earn $100,000 in one year
- The Supreme Court mandated busing as a means of achieving school desegregation
- A poll showed that 34 percent of Americans found marriage obsolete, up from 24 percent in 1969
- *Look* magazine ceased publication
- Beef consumption per capita rose from 113 pounds to 128.5 pounds
- Cigarette advertising was banned by Congress from television
- Three fourths of all moviegoers were under age 30
- *Gourmet* magazine circulation doubled to 550,000 in just four years as the fancy food industry continued to grow
- Phrases "think tank," "body language," "gross out," and "workaholic" all entered the language
- The National Cancer Act was passed, providing $1.5 billion a year for research, as the president urged an all-out attempt to find a cure
- The Supreme Court ruled that qualification for conscientious-objector status necessitated opposing all wars, not just the Vietnam War

- The Metropolitan Museum of Art paid a record $5.5 million for a Velásquez portrait
- The diamond-bladed scalpel was developed for eye microsurgery
- Young women were appointed U.S. Senate pages for the first time
- The U.S. Supreme Court ruled that companies may not refuse to hire women with small children if the same policy is not applied to men
- The United States Public Health Service no longer advised children to be vaccinated against smallpox
- Direct dialing began between New York and London
- Snowmobiles, dune buggies, auto trains, and a law banning sex discrimination all made their first appearance

1972–1973

- Nearly 30 percent of U.S. petroleum was imported
- Dow Jones closed at 1,003.15 on November 14, above 1,000 for the first time
- San Francisco Bay Area Rapid Transit System opened
- *Ms. Magazine* began publication and *Life* magazine suspended publication
- The Polaroid SX-70 system produced color prints
- NYC's 110-story World Trade Center opened
- America's birth rate fell to 15.8 per 1,000, the lowest since 1917
- The average farmer produced enough food for 50 people and farm labor represented five percent of the work force
- The median sales price of an existing single-family house reached $28,900
- Vodka outsold whiskey for the first time
- The Law Enforcement Assistance Administration's budget rose to $700 million
- By a five-to-four vote, the Supreme Court ruled that capital punishment was "cruel and unusual punishment" pending further legislation from the states

- The number of fast-food establishments increased to 6,784, up from 1,120 in 1958
- The Massachusetts Supreme Court ruled unconstitutional a law prohibiting the sale of contraceptives to single persons
- Congress passed Title IX, which entitled women to participate equally in all sports
- The Nobel Peace Prize was awarded to Henry Kissinger and North Vietnamese Le Duc Tho, who refused the honor
- Television premieres included *Barnaby Jones*, *Police Story*, *The Young and the Restless* and *The Six-Million-Dollar Man*
- Space-exploring *Pioneer X* produced significant detail of Jupiter and its great red spot
- *The Sting* with Paul Newman and Robert Redford captured the Academy Award for Best Picture
- Popular movies included *The Paper Chase*, *Scenes from a Marriage*, *The Last Detail*, *The Exorcist* and *American Graffiti*
- A computerized brain scanner known as CAT was marketed
- Hit songs for the year were "Tie a Yellow Ribbon," "Delta Dawn," "Let's Get It On," "Me and Mrs. Jones," "Rocky Mountain High," "Could It Be I'm Falling in Love?" and Roberta Flack earned the Best Record Grammy for "Killing Me Softly with His Song"
- Richard Nixon resigned the presidency of the United States and vice president Gerald Ford became president
- The OPEC oil embargo raised the price of crude oil by 300 percent, causing shortages and long lines at the nation's gasoline pumps
- Bestsellers included *Jonathan Livingston Seagull* by Richard Bach, *Once Is Not Enough* by Jacqueline Susann, *Breakfast of Champions* by Kurt Vonnegut, Jr. and *I'm O.K., You're O.K.* by Thomas Harris
- Words and phrases entering popular usage were Skylab, juggernaut, biofeedback, ego trip, let it all hang out, and nouvelle cuisine
- The "pet rock" fad captured the imagination of America

1974–1975

- The pocket calculator was marketed
- 110,000 clothing workers staged a nationwide strike
- Unemployment reached 6.5 percent, the highest since 1961
- The universal product code was designed for the supermarket industry
- Year-long daylight savings time was adopted to save fuel
- 3M developed Post-it stock to stick paper to paper
- ITT's Harold Green was the nation's highest paid executive at $791,000 per year
- Time, Inc., issued *People Magazine* devoted to celebrity journalism
- Walgreen's drug chain exceeded $1 billion in sales for the first time
- The first desktop microcomputer became available
- The Equal Opportunity Act forbade discrimination based on sex or marital status
- Minnesota became the first state to require businesses, restaurants, and institutions to establish no-smoking areas
- New York City averted bankruptcy with a $2.3 billion federal loan
- The biggest money-making films of the year were *Towering Inferno, Earthquake*, and *The Exorcist*
- Beef consumption fell nine percent, while chicken consumption rose nearly 35 percent
- Car sales fell 35 percent from 1973, and home construction was down 40 percent
- McDonald's opened its first drive-through restaurants
- AT&T, the world's largest private employer, banned discrimination against homosexuals
- Time-sharing of vacation real estate was introduced in the United States
- A record 120,000 Americans declared personal bankruptcy
- The "typical" nuclear family—working father, housewife, and two children—represented only seven percent of the population; average

family size was 3.4, down from 4.3 in 1920
- Harvard changed its five-to-two male to female admissions policy to equal admissions
- Unemployment reached 9.2 percent
- The Atomic Energy Commission was dissolved
- The Supreme Court ruled that the mentally ill cannot be hospitalized against their will unless they are dangerous to themselves or to others
- Chrysler, and other auto companies, offered rebates to counter record low sales
- The Brewers' Society reported that Americans consumed an average of 151 pints of beer per year, 11.5 pints of wine, and 9.1 pints of spirits
- *Penthouse* sales surpassed those of *Playboy*
- The Rolling Stones tour grossed $13 million, and singer Stevie Wonder signed a record contract for $13 million
- A Massachusetts physician was convicted of manslaughter by a Boston jury for aborting a fetus and was sentenced to a year's probation
- Rape laws were changed in nine states, lessening the amount of corroborative evidence necessary for conviction and restricting trial questions regarding the victim's past sex life
- An endangered whooping crane was born in captivity
- TV advertisements for tampons appeared for the first time

1976–1977
- The Dow Jones Industrial Average peaked at 1,004, inflation hit 8.7 percent, and unemployment hit 8.3 percent
- Jimmy Carter was elected president
- Bicentennial festivities swept the nation, highlighted by 'Operation Sail' in NYC in which 16 of the world's tallest and oldest windjammers along with thousands of other ships began a tour of the world's major ports
- Congress passed a law to admit women to military academies
- The Supreme Court ruled that employers were not required to give

paid maternity leave

- Renowned lawyer F. Lee Bailey defended Patty Hearst, daughter of publisher William Randolph Hearst, against changes of bank robbery claiming she was 'brainwashed'
- President Gerald Ford ordered a major inoculation campaign against a projected swine flu epidemic
- The repeal of the Fair Trade law prevented manufacturers from fixing retail prices
- Colossus Cave, the first computer game, was designed at Princeton
- The arrest rate for women since 1964 rose three times faster than the rate for men
- Sales of bran cereals and high fiber bread increased dramatically, as consumers responded to widely published medical reports of health benefits of high-fiber diets
- California legalized the concept of "living wills," giving the terminally ill the right to decree their own deaths
- The Apple computer was developed in a California garage
- Average SAT scores dipped to 472 (math) and 435 (English) from 501 and 480 in 1968
- One of five children lived in a one-parent home, as three out of five marriages ended in divorce
- ABC offered the industry's first $1 million per year contract to Barbara Walters of NBC
- Clothier Abercrombie & Fitch declared bankruptcy
- Mobil Petroleum bought Montgomery Ward for $1 billion
- Balloon angioplasty was developed for reopening diseased arteries of the heart
- 20,000 shopping malls generated 50 percent of total retail sales nationwide
- American Express became the first service company to top $1 billion in sales

- *Li'l Abner* cartoon ceased publication
- Three major networks controlled 91 percent of prime-time audiences
- Cheryl Tiegs, the world's highest-paid model, earned $1,000 a day
- 1.9 million women operated businesses
- The U.S. and Canada signed a pact to build a gas pipeline from Alaska to the Midwest
- Consumers boycotted coffee due to soaring prices
- Sales of imported cars broke all records, passing 1.5 million
- The Supreme Court reversed a New York law that prohibited the distribution of contraceptives to minors
- The FDA banned the use of the additive Red Dye # 2 in foods, drugs, and cosmetics
- Widespread looting occurred during a blackout in NYC and Westchester county that affected nine million people
- Pepsi topped Coca-Cola in sales for the first time
- 45 million people watched the highest-rated TV interview in history, featuring former President Richard Nixon on the *David Frost* program, for which he was paid $600,000, plus 10 percent of the show's profits
- The Supreme Court ruled that the spanking of schoolchildren by teachers was constitutional
- CBS anchor Walter Cronkite helped arrange a meeting in Israel between Egyptian president Anwar Sadat and Israeli Prime Minister Menachem Begin
- Elvis Presley died, and within a day of his death, two million of his records sold
- Men's fashion became more conservative, marked by narrow, small-patterned silk ties and Oxford and broadcloth shirts
- More than 400,000 teenage abortions were performed, a third of the U.S. total
- The CB radio fad resulted in record sales
- Generic products, pocket TVs, and public automatic blood pressure

machines all made their first appearance

1978

- Television's late-night host, Johnny Carson, made $4 million, while *Happy Days'* star Henry Winkler made $990,000
- Alex Haley's book *Roots* sparked an interest in genealogy, particularly among African- Americans
- Fifty percent of all shoe sales were sneakers, topping 200 million pairs
- Airline deregulation eliminated federal controls on fares and routes, as eight airlines controlled 81 percent of the domestic market
- Legal retirement age was raised to 70
- Gold sold for $245 per ounce
- California voters adopted Proposition 13 to control property taxes
- The tax code permitted 401(k) savings plans for the first time
- Legalized gambling in Atlantic City, NJ; microchip technology in washing machines; *Garfield* cartoons; pocket math calculators; and 45-rpm picture disc records all made their first appearance
- Morris the Cat, the advertising symbol for Nine Lives cat food, died at the age of 17
- The number of unmarried couples living together more than doubled from 523,000 in 1970 to 1,137,000
- Attracted by jobs and housing, more than 1,000 families were moving to Dallas, Texas, each month
- Pepsico acquired Mexican fast-food chain, Taco Bell
- The cost of a first-class postage stamp rose to $0.15 per ounce
- The USDA warned of the dangers of nitrites in processed and cured meat products, reporting that sodium nitrite may cause cancer
- Edith Bunker, a character on the television show *All in the Family*, said, "With credit, you can buy everything you can't afford"
- The King Tutankhamen show touring America produced $5 million for the Cairo Museum
- Attendance for the North American Soccer League rose 50 percent to

5.3 million fans
- *If Life Is a Bowl of Cherries—What Am I Doing in the Pits?* by Erma Bombeck, *The World According to Garp* by John Irving and *The Complete Book of Running* by James Fixx were all on the bestseller list

1979
- The divorce rate increased 68 percent since 1968 and the median duration of marriage was 6.6 years
- The Sony Walkman, a portable cassette player with headphones, was introduced
- U.S. Trust reported that 520,000 Americans—one in every 424—were millionaires
- Sales of health foods zoomed from $140 million in 1940 to $1.6 billion
- Jiffy Lube fast oil-change automotive service center opened
- Inflation was at its worst in 33 years, and prices increased more than 13.3 percent
- The Supreme Court ruled that "husbands only" alimony laws were unconstitutional
- Ford Motor Company acquired 25 percent of Japan's Mazda Motor Company
- The near-meltdown of a nuclear power plant at Three Mile Island ignited anti-nuclear fears nationwide
- California became the first state to initiate gas rationing, creating alternate-day purchasing
- Avon Products acquired Tiffany and Company
- The prime lending rate at banks hit 14.5 percent
- Massachusetts became the seventh state to increase the legal drinking age from 18 to 20
- Jane Fonda and Tom Hayden toured 50 cities to speak out against nuclear power
- Electronic blackboards, nitrite-free hot dogs, Cracker Jack ice cream bars and the video digital sound disc all made their first appearance

- The play *Grease* passed *Fiddler on the Roof* as the longest-running Broadway show
- More than 315,000 microcomputers were sold

1980

- Yellow ribbons became a symbol of American concern for the hostages in Iran
- The divorce rate had grown from one in three marriages in 1970 to one in two
- The World Health Organization announced that smallpox had been eradicated
- A 10-year study correlated fatal heart disease to the saturated-unsaturated fat ratio in the diet
- The combination of First Lady Nancy Reagan's elegance and the wedding of Lady Diana to Prince Charles stimulated a return to opulent styles
- Cordless telephones, front-wheel-drive subcompact cars, 24-hour-a-day news coverage and *Discover* magazine made their first appearance
- The prime rate hit 21 percent, and gold was $880 per ounce
- Supply-side economics proposed that government increase incentives, such as tax reform, to stimulate production
- The 1980 U.S. Census reported the smallest population growth since the Great Depression
- *Dallas, M*A*S*H, The Dukes of Hazzard, 60 Minutes, Three's Company, Private Benjamin, Diff'rent Strokes, House Calls, The Jeffersons* and *Too Close for Comfort* were top-rated television shows
- An eight-year Veteran's Administration study showed Vietnam vets suffered more emotional, social, educational and job-related problems than did veterans of other wars
- Top albums of the year included Pink Floyd's *The Wall,* Blondie's *Eat to the Beat, Off the Wall* by Michael Jackson and *Glass Houses* by Billy Joel

- Researchers at the University of California, San Diego, reported that "passive smoking" can lead to lung cancer
- The "Stop Handguns Before They Stop You" Committee ran an advertisement reading, "Last year handguns killed 48 people in Japan, 8 in Great Britain, 34 in Switzerland, 52 in Canada, 58 in Israel, 21 in Sweden, 42 in West Germany, 10,720 in U.S. God Bless America"

1981–1982

- The IBM Personal Computer was marketed for the first time
- 12,000 striking air-traffic controllers were fired by President Ronald Reagan
- Public debt hit $1 trillion
- New York and Miami increased transit fares from $0.60 to $0.75 per ride
- Kellogg's introduced Nutri-Grain wheat cereal
- U.S. first-class postal rates went to $0.18, then $0.20
- Sears & Roebuck bought real estate broker Coldwell Banker & Co., and a securities concern, Dean Witter Reynolds
- The U.S. population hit 228 million
- National unemployment rose to eight percent, including 16.8 percent for blacks and 40 percent for black teenagers
- A court order broke up the A&T U.S. monopoly into AT&T long-distance and regional telephone companies
- The Japanese marketed a wristwatch-sized television with a 1.2-inch screen
- *USA Today,* the first national general interest daily newspaper, was introduced
- 2.9 million women operated businesses
- Braniff International Airline declared bankruptcy
- United Auto Workers agreed to wage concessions with Ford Motor Company
- U.S. Steel acquired Marathon Oil

- The computer "mouse" was introduced by Apple
- The first successful embryo transfer was performed
- NutraSweet was introduced as a synthetic sugar substitute
- 35.3 million lived below the poverty line
- Cellular telephones ("carphones") became available to motorists, costing $3,000 plus $150.00 per month for service
- VCR sales increased 72 percent from the previous year; the U.S. now boasted 3.4 million units in use
- The Rubik's Cube tested the patience of Americans
- Dr. Ruth began her radio talk show, emphasizing sexual issues

1983

- Prices for computers plummeted—Timex sold a personal computer for $99.95, while the Commodore VIC 20 sold for $199—and they were used in 1.5 million homes—five times the number in 1980
- The first artificial heart transplant recipient was Barney Clark, age 61
- The Vietnam Veterans' Memorial, inscribed with the 57,939 names of American soldiers killed or missing in Vietnam, was dedicated in Washington, DC
- Dun and Bradstreet reported a total of 20,365 bankruptcies by October, the highest figure since the Great Depression
- The United Auto Workers agreed to wage concessions with Ford Motor Company
- Efforts at library censorship tripled, and books under fire included *The Adventures of Huckleberry Finn*, *The Grapes of Wrath*, and *The Catcher in the Rye*
- The computer "mouse" was introduced by Apple
- The first successful embryo transfer was performed
- Columbia, the last all-male college in the Ivy League, began accepting women
- President Ronald Reagan proclaimed May 6 "National Day of Prayer" and endorsed a constitutional amendment to permit school prayer,

which was defeated

- A professional football strike cut the regular season to nine games
- The proposed equal rights amendment (ERA) ran out of time for passage, receiving 35 of the 38 state ratifications required
- Ocean Spray was introduced in paper bottles
- The compact disk, polyurethane car bumpers, the Honda Accord, and the NCAA major college basketball championship for women all made their first appearances
- Ameritech received the FCC's first cellular phone license
- Bestselling books included *In Search of Excellence* by Thomas J. Peters and Robert H. Waterman, *Megatrends* by John Naisbitt, *Jane Fonda's Workout Book* by Jane Fonda and *On the Wings of Eagles* by Ken Follet
- Over-the-counter drug packaging became more "tamper-proof" in response to the 1982 cyanide tampering of Tylenol bottles in Chicago
- Hit songs featured "Billie Jean," "Every Breath You Take," "Maniac," "Total Eclipse of the Heart," "Say, Say, Say," and "Islands in the Stream"
- Average tuition for four-year private colleges was $7,475, while Harvard cost $8,195
- Martin Luther King, Jr. became the first person since Abraham Lincoln whose birthday was declared a national holiday
- Worldwide AIDS cases totaled 2,678, with 1,102 deaths since it appeared in 1978
- MTV was received in 17.5 million homes
- *A Chorus Line* became the longest-running show in Broadway history
- Following the terrorist truck bombing in Beirut that killed 239 Marines, South Carolina Senator Ernest Hollings said, "If they've been put there to fight, then there are far too few. If they've been put there to be killed, there are far too many."
- The per-capita personal income in New York was $12,314; in Alaska, $16,257; and in Mississippi, $7,778

- Magazines with the highest circulation were *Reader's Digest, TV Guide, National Geographic, Modern Maturity, Better Homes and Gardens,* and *AARP News Bulletin*

1984

- Dow and six other chemical companies settled with Agent Orange victims for $180 million
- The California Wilderness Act passed, designating 23 new areas in 20 states
- The Supreme Court modified the Miranda ruling to say that illegally obtained evidence was admissible in court if otherwise obtainable
- Vanessa Williams, the first black Miss America, resigned after sexually explicit photographs of her surfaced in a national magazine
- Major movie openings included *Amadeus, The Killing Fields, Places in the Heart, Beverly Hills Cop, Ghostbusters, The Gods Must Be Crazy, The Karate Kid* and *Terminator*
- The American Cancer Society made specific dietary food recommendations endorsing whole grains and fruits and vegetables high in vitamin A and C
- Bruce Merrifield won the Nobel Prize in chemistry for developing an automated method to make proteins
- *The Bill Cosby Show* premiered on television featuring for the first time a professional upper middle class black family
- The Olympics produced a record $150 million surplus after being run as a private enterprise for the first time
- After four-year closure and a cost of $55 million, the Museum of Modern Art in NYC reopened at twice its original size
- Androgynous rock singers such as Michael Jackson, Boy George, Prince, Duran Duran and Grace Jones captured national attention
- President Reagan proclaimed in his State of the Union speech, "America is back standing tall, looking to the eighties with courage, confidence and hope"

- The unemployment rate reached 7.5 percent, and stock market reached a high of 1,287
- Television premieres included *Miami Vice, The Bill Cosby Show, Murder, She Wrote,* and *Highway to Heaven*
- Ages of the U.S. Supreme Court justices became an issue in the national election with five of the nine justices over the age of 75
- Sheep cloning, a woman walking in space, the Apple Macintosh, required seatbelts use, male bunnies at the Playboy Club and PG-13 ratings all made their first appearance
- The Reagan administration threatened to withdraw aid from nations that advocated abortion

1985

- The AMA reported that medical malpractice suits had tripled since 1975, and the average award increased from $95,000 to $333,000
- The U.S. Army ruled that male officers were forbidden to carry umbrellas
- Videocassette movie-rental income equaled movie theater receipts
- "Live Aid" concerts in Philadelphia and London were viewed on television by 1.6 billion people and grossed $70 million for famine-stricken Africa
- Highly addictive, inexpensive cocaine derivative "crack" became popular, selling for $5 to $10 per vial
- Parents and school boards fought over keeping AIDS-afflicted children in public schools
- General Westmoreland dropped his $120 million 1982 libel suit against CBS for its documentary alleging that he deceived the public concerning Vietcong strength
- A single optic fiber carried 300,000 simultaneous phone calls in Bell Laboratory tests
- Capital Cities Communications bought television network ABC for $3.5 billion

- The Nobel Peace Prize went to the International Physicians for the Prevention of Nuclear War, founded by two cardiologists, one at Harvard, the other in Moscow
- The Supreme Court upheld affirmative-action hiring quotas
- World oil prices collapsed, bottoming out at $7.20 per barrel
- The U.S. national debt topped $1.8 trillion
- NYC transit fares rose from $0.75 to $1.00
- Coca-Cola introduced new-formula Coke but public outcry forced Coke to bring back the "Classic Coke" one year later
- Rock Hudson became one of the first public figures to acknowledge his battle with AIDS, raising public awareness of the disease
- The words golden parachute, leveraged buyout, and poison pill all entered the corporate language

1986–1987

- U.S. Protestants numbered 53 million in more than 23,000 churches
- The Supreme Court upheld Affirmative Action hiring quotas
- The U.S. national debt topped $2 billion
- The Dow Jones Industrial Average hit 1,955 and the prime rate dropped to seven percent
- Retailer Sears & Robuck celebrated its 100th anniversary
- Office Depot, one of the first office supply warehouse-type stores, opened in Lauderdale Lakes, Florida
- A supercomputer capable of 1,720 billion computations per second went online
- The first bio-insecticides, designed to eliminate insects without harming the environment, were announced
- Elementary and secondary schoolteachers earned an average salary of $26,700
- Approximately 35 percent of high school graduates entered college
- The Hands Across America chain, stretching from New York City to Long Beach, California, raised $100 million for the poor and homeless

- Eight airlines controlled 90 percent of the domestic market
- The Clean Water Bill passed to address pollution of estuaries and rainwater
- A New York Stock Exchange seat sold for $1.5 million
- The trade deficit hit a record $16.5 billion
- Harvard University celebrated its 350th birthday
- Fitness foods (high in fiber and low in sodium, fat, cholesterol, calories, caffeine) accounted for 10 percent of the $300 billion retail food market
- The first open-air use of a genetically engineered bacteria, a frost retardant, was attempted on strawberry plants
- Under a new law, three Americans became the first foreign lawyers permitted to practice in Japan
- The stock market peaked at 2,722 in August, then fell a record 508 points in a single day in October
- When sports coverage of the U.S. Tennis Open intruded into traditional news time, journalist Dan Rather stormed off the set and TV screens were blank for six minutes
- The federal budget exceeded $1 trillion for the first time
- *The Last Emperor*, *Fatal Attraction*, *Three Men and a Baby* and *Radio Days* all held their movie premieres
- Fifty thousand people gathered at Graceland in Memphis, Tennessee, on the tenth anniversary of Elvis Presley's death
- Sixty percent of American kitchens had microwave ovens
- Forty states restricted smoking in public buildings, restaurants and schools, following the Surgeon General's warnings on the negative impact of secondhand smoke
- Toni Morrison's *Beloved* won the Pulitzer Prize for fiction; David Herbert Donald won the biography prize for *Look Homeward: The Life of Thomas Wolfe*
- The last known dusky seaside sparrow died of old age, marking the extinction of the species

- Congress overrode the president's veto of the $20 billion Clean Water Bill
- The phrase "couch potato" came into popular usage
- Allan Bloom's book, *The Closing of the American Mind*, criticized the U.S. educational system and called for a return to "great books" in its attack on cultural relativism
- Fifty-eight-year-old artist Andy Warhol died of a heart attack after routine gallbladder surgery
- Ansell America became the first condom manufacturer to advertise on television
- Professional baseball player Mark McGwire set a rookie home run record at 49
- The Supreme Court ruled that states may require all-male private clubs to admit women

1988

- Black teenager Tawana Brawley gained national publicity when she claimed she was raped by a group of white men; a grand jury found no evidence of the charges and called her advisors, including Al Sharpton, "unethical"
- Ninety percent of major corporations reported sexual harassment complaints
- Former chief aid Donald Regan claimed that Nancy Reagan used astrology to plan her husband's activities
- Women accounted for nearly half of all graduating accountants, one third of MBAs and one quarter of lawyers
- American lawyers' salary averaged $914 a week, nurses $516, and secretaries $299
- Robots were used for picking fruit
- Fundamentalists picketed *The Last Temptation of Christ*, but the film was an unexpected financial success
- Professional heavyweight boxer Mike Tyson's fight with Michael Spinks

produced a $40 million gate, and Spinks was knocked out in one round
- U.S. auto makers produced 13 million cars and trucks
- Harvard scientists obtained the first animal patent for a genetically engineered mouse with immune properties
- *The Eight-Week Cholesterol Cure*, *The Bonfire of the Vanities*, *Trump: The Art of the Deal* and *Swim with the Sharks without Being Eaten Alive* were all bestsellers
- Philip Morris bought Kraft for $12.9 billion
- Scientific experiments on the Shroud of Turin indicated that it dated from the Middle Ages, not from the time of Christ's death
- Pulitzer Prize for history was awarded to Taylor Branch's *Parting the Waters: America in the King Years 1954-1963*

1989

- Television's top programs included *Roseanne*, *The Cosby Show*, *Cheers*, *A Different World*, *Dear John*, *The Wonder Years* and *Golden Girls*
- Congress passed $166 billion legislation to bail out the savings and loan industry
- Cocaine and crack cocaine use was up 35 percent over 1985
- Sony of Japan purchased Columbia Pictures, sparking comments of Japan invading Hollywood
- Demonstrators at Tiananmen Square carried a Styrofoam Statue of Liberty as part of the protest against the Chinese government
- Scientists speculated that the New World Peruvian architecture could be as old as the Egyptian pyramids
- The movie *Batman* grossed $250 million, the fifth-highest in movie history
- *Field of Dreams*; *When Harry Met Sally*; *Glory*; *Driving Miss Daisy*; *Sex, Lies and Videotape*; and *Roger and Me* premiered at movie theaters
- Calvin Klein's lean and refined look, with soft fabrics and little or no jewelry predominated women's fashion

- *The Heidi Chronicles* by Wendy Wasserstein won both the Tony Award and the Pulitzer Prize
- Baseball Commissioner Bart Giamatti banned ballplayer Pete Rose from playing baseball for life for allegedly betting on games
- *The Joy Luck Club* by Amy Tan, *The Satanic Verses* by Salman Rushdie, *The Temple of My Familiar* by Alice Walker, *The Oldest Living Confederate Widow Tells All* by Allan Gurganus and *A Brief History of Time* by Stephen Hawking were bestsellers
- In Chicago, U.S. veterans protested at the Art Institute where the American flag was draped on the floor
- "Wind Beneath My Wings" by Bette Midler won a Grammy Award for best song
- Top singles for the year included "Every Rose Has Its Thorn" by Poison, "Miss You Much" by Janet Jackson, "Girl, You Know Its True" by Milli Vanilli and "Love Shack" by the B-52's

1990

- The Food and Drug Administration approved a low-calorie fat substitute
- Gross national product fell after eight years of growth, while housing values plummeted and consumer confidence shrank
- The *Hubble* space telescope was launched into orbit
- First appearances included McDonald's in Moscow; car models Infiniti, Saturn, and Lexus; gender-specific disposable diapers; caller ID systems; and the contraceptive implant Norplant
- Census data showed that 25 percent of the population were members of a minority group, with Asians and Pacific Islanders the fastest-growing minorities
- Dieting became a $33 billion industry
- John J. Audubon's book, *Birds of America,* sold for $3.96 million at auction
- Television premieres included *The Simpsons, Law and Order, Twin*

Peaks and *Seinfeld*
- Women constituted 11 percent of U.S. military troops, up from three percent in 1973
- An EPA report claimed that 3,800 people died annually from second-hand smoke
- The timber industry of the Pacific Northwest was outraged when the northwest spotted owl was declared an endangered species
- *Dances with Wolves* was named the Academy Awards' best picture; *Pretty Woman, Total Recall, Goodfellas* and *Home Alone* were also released
- The stock market hit a high of 2,999.75, inflation was at 5.4 percent and unemployment at 6.1 percent
- Both President Bush and Premier Gorbachev called for Iraqi withdrawal following its invasion of Kuwait

1991

- Allied forces attacked Iraq with 2,232 tons of explosives the first day, the largest strike in history, at the beginning of the Gulf War
- The economy officially went into a recession for the first time since 1982
- A record 23,300 homicides were reported nationwide
- Arlette Schweitzer, 42, acted as surrogate mother for her daughter who was born without a uterus, giving birth to her own grandchildren—twins
- Single parents rose 41 percent from 1980, while the number of unmarried couples living together was up 80 percent
- One quarter of all newborns were born to single women
- Michael Jackson signed a $1.1 billion multi-year contract with Sony
- First-class postage increased from $0.25 to $0.29
- The U.S. trade deficit hit an eight-year low
- First marriage median age was 26.3 years for men and 24.1 years for women

- Cartoon character Blondie, wife of Dagwood Bumstead, announced her need for a career
- The U.S. Supreme Court ended forced busing, originally ordered to end racial segregation
- Congress approved family leave, allowing up to 12 weeks for family emergencies
- Airlines Eastern and Pan Am went into bankruptcy, with Delta taking over most Pan Am routes and becomming the leading carrier
- The Federal Reserve slashed interest rates to spur the economy
- A single sheet of the first printing of the Declaration of Independence, bought at a flea market in the backing of a $4.00 painting, was sold for $2,420,000
- School violence escalated, and 25 percent of whites and 20 percent of blacks said they feared being attacked in school
- Walter H. Annenberg bequeathed his $1 billion art collection to the Metropolitan Museum of Art
- *Scarlett*, Alexandra Ripley's sequel to *Gone with the Wind*, sold a record 250,000 copies in one day
- Simon LeVay's study showed anatomical hypothalamic differences in gay and heterosexual men, lending credibility to the biological origin of sexual orientation
- General Motors announced plans to close more than 20 plants over several years, eliminating more than 70,000 jobs
- Motorola introduced the 7.7-ounce cellular telephone

1992

- Unemployment topped 7.1 percent, the highest in five years
- U.S. bombed Iraq for its failure to comply with United Nations-sponsored inspections
- The 10 most popular television shows were *60 Minutes*; *Roseanne*; *Murphy Brown*; *Cheers*; *Home Improvement*; *Designing Women*; *Coach*; *Full House*; *Murder, She Wrote*; and *Unsolved Mysteries*

- David Letterman was paid $16 million to move to CBS, opposite late-night host Jay Leno; Johnny Carson's last night as host of *The Tonight Show* drew a record 55 million viewers
- Bestsellers included Rush Limbaugh's *The Way Things Ought to Be*, H. Norman Schwarzkopf's *It Doesn't Take a Hero*, John Grisham's *The Pelican Brief* and Anne Rice's *The Tale of the Body Thief*
- The Supreme Court ruled that cross-burning is protected under the First Amendment, and that prayer at public school graduations is unconstitutional
- Royalties for Barbara and George Bush's dog's autobiography, *Millie's Book*, earned them $890,000
- In Kenya, Meave Leakey discovered the oldest hominid fossil to date, estimated to be 25 million years old and believed to be from the period of the ape-human divergence
- Movie openings included *Unforgiven*, *The Crying Game*, *Scent of a Woman*, *Malcolm X*, *Aladdin*, *Sister Act*, *Basic Instinct*, *The Last of the Mohicans*, *A River Runs Through It* and *White Men Can't Jump*
- Rudolph Marcus won the Nobel Prize in chemistry for his theory of electron-transfer reactions
- Eric Clapton won a Grammy award for his record "Tears in Heaven" and his album, "Unplugged"
- Poverty rose to 14.2 percent, the highest level since 1983
- At the Olympic Summer Games in Barcelona, the U.S. basketball team included Larry Bird, Magic Johnson and Michael Jordan
- More than 20,000 people in California bought guns after the Los Angeles riots, which erupted when the men accused of beating Rodney King were acquitted
- In Washington, DC, more than 500,000 people marched for abortion rights
- New-age clear beverages, mega CD video games, The Mall of America and the Intel 486 chip made their first appearance

- Research indicated that the level of HDL, or good cholesterol, may be more important than the overall blood cholesterol score
- The FDA restricted the use of silicone-gel breast implants for reconstructive purposes

1993

- A bomb blast injured hundreds in the World Trade Center bombing in New York City, and Mohammed A. Salameh was arrested for the bombing when he attempted to reclaim his $400 car rental deposit
- Major League baseball owners announced new initiatives on minority hiring
- Law enforcement agents raided a religious cult in Waco, Texas, igniting a storm of protests
- U.S. pledged $1.6 billion in aid to assist in Russian reforms
- An Oregon law permitted physician-assisted suicide
- Michigan's Dr. Jack Kevorkian was jailed twice for assisting patients' suicides
- President Bill Clinton promised "universal health coverage" comparable to that of *Fortune 500* companies, designed to help the 64 million who lacked adequate coverage
- Women received combat roles in aerial and naval warfare
- Civil rights advocate Ruth Bader Ginsburg was named to the U.S. Supreme Court
- *Jurassic Park* became the highest-grossing movie of all time
- IBM announced an $8.9 billion restructuring, and eliminated 60,000 jobs
- President Clinton supported easing a ban on homosexuals in the military
- Statistics showed that one of three American workers were in their job less than a year, and almost two out of three less than five years
- The brown Brownie uniform changed after 66 years to include pastel tops, culotte jumpers, and floral print vests

- The inflation rate remained at 2.7 percent, the lowest in seven years
- The U.S. began testing of the French abortion pill RU-486
- Cosmologists discovered that stars and other observable matter occupied less than 10 percent of the universe
- Sears & Robuck ended its mail-order catalog business
- Thirty-year mortgages dropped to 6.7 percent, the lowest in 25 years
- The Ford Taurus topped the Honda Accord in total car sales
- The Pentium processor, one-pound personal digital assistant, and Mighty Max Toby Terrier all made their first appearances

1994

- The North American Free Trade Agreement (NAFTA) was established
- Olympic skater Nancy Kerrigan was clubbed on the right leg by an assailant, under orders from figure skating rival Tonya Harding's ex-husband
- The Superhighway Summit was held at UCLA, the first conference to discuss the growing information superhighway
- President Bill Clinton and Russian President Boris Yeltsin signed the Kremlin Accords, stopping preprogrammed aiming of nuclear missiles toward each country's targets, and also provided for the dismantling of the nuclear arsenal in Ukraine
- In South Carolina, Shannon Faulkner became the first female cadet to attend The Citadel, although soon dropped out
- Byron De La Beckwith was convicted of the 1963 murder of Civil Rights leader Medgar Evers
- Edvard Munch's painting *The Scream* was stolen in Oslo
- Aldrich Ames and his wife were charged with spying for the Soviet Union by the U.S. Department of Justice
- In *Campbell v. Acuff-Rose Music, Inc.*, the Supreme Court ruled that parodies of an original work are generally covered by the doctrine of fair use
- *Schindler's List* won seven Oscars including Best Picture and Best

Director at the 66th Academy Awards, hosted by Whoopi Goldberg
- The journal *Nature* reported the finding in Ethiopia of the first complete *Australopithecus afarensis* skull
- Kurt Cobain, songwriter and front man for the band Nirvana, was found dead, apparently of a single, self-inflicted gunshot wound
- The Red Cross estimated that hundreds of thousands of Tutsis had been killed in the Rwanda massacre
- Nelson Mandela was inaugurated as South Africa's first black president
- Nicole Brown Simpson and Ronald Goldman were murdered outside the Simpson home in Los Angeles, California and football great O.J. Simpson was charged in the killings
- President Clinton signed the Assault Weapons Ban, which banned the manufacture of new weapons with certain features for a period of 10 years
- The first version of Web browser Netscape Navigator was released

1995–1996
- The Supreme Court ruled that only a constitutional amendment can enforce term limits on Congress
- 25 percent of Americans continued to smoke cigarettes despite health warnings
- The Dow Jones Industrial Average peaked at 5,216 and unemployment was at 5.6 percent
- Casual Fridays were introduced at the workplace
- After 130 years, Mississippi lawmakers ratified the 13th Amendment abolishing slavery
- The FBI reported another sharp decline in crime rates
- President Bill Clinton's approval rating surpassed 50 percent for the first time
- About 55 percent of women provided half or more of household income
- The Centers for Disease Control reported a leveling-off of teen sexual activity, and that 52.8 percent used condoms

- New York became the 38th state to reinstate capital punishment
- Ford sold more trucks than cars, as demand for light trucks, minivans and sports utility vehicles, increased in urban and rural areas
- Mars released a blue M&M candy for the first time
- The 25th anniversary of Earth Day was celebrated
- Dow Corning declared bankruptcy after failure of its silicone breast device
- The U.S. banned the manufacture of freon because of its effect on the ozone layer
- Iraqi leader Saddam Hussein decreed economic austerity measures to cope with soaring inflation and widespread shortages caused by U.N. sanctions
- President Bill Clinton and Monica Lewinsky, a White House intern, engaged in sexual encounters at the White House
- The U.S. Army disclosed that it had 30,000 tons of chemical weapons stored in Utah, Alabama, Maryland, Kentucky, Indiana, Arkansas, Colorado and Oregon
- Sheik Omar Abdel-Rahman and nine followers were handed long prison sentences for plotting to blow up New York-area landmarks
- France detonated its sixth and most powerful nuclear bomb
- New protease-blocking drugs were shown to be effective in combating AIDS
- Congress voted overwhelmingly to rewrite the 61-year-old Communications Act, freeing the television, telephone and home computer industries to jump into each other's fields
- World chess champion Garry Kasparov beat IBM supercomputer "Deep Blue," winning a six-game match in Philadelphia
- The Space Telescope Science Institute announced that photographs from the *Hubble Space Telescope* confirmed the existence of a "black hole" equal to the mass of two billion suns
- Alanis Morissette's *Jagged Little Pill* won best rock album and album

of the year at the Grammy Awards

- Dr. Jack Kevorkian was acquitted of assisted suicide for helping two suffering patients kill themselves
- Liggett became the first tobacco company to acknowledge that cigarettes are addictive and cause cancer
- The first of the Nixon White House tapes concerning Watergate were released
- Nevada's governor designated a 98-mile stretch of Route 375 the Extraterrestrial Highway
- The Senate passed an immigration bill to tighten border controls, make it tougher for illegal immigrants to get U.S. jobs, and curtail legal immigrants' access to social services
- Guatemala's leftist guerrillas and the government signed an accord to end 35 years of civil war
- The federal government set aside 3.9 million acres in California, Oregon and Washington state for the endangered marbled murrelet

1997

- Despite a one-day plunge of 554 points, the stock market soared, up 20 percent for the third straight year, and job creation continued
- Princess Diana's death generated more press coverage than any event in the century as millions watched her televised funeral
- Controversy erupted over allegations that large contributors were invited by President Bill Clinton to stay overnight in the White House Lincoln Bedroom
- Oprah Winfrey launched a highly successful book club on her television program to encourage reading
- The price of personal computers (Compaq, Hewlett Packard, IBM) fell below $1,000
- Jerry Seinfeld announced the last season for his television show, *Seinfeld*, despite a $5 million-per-episode offer to continue
- Violent crime in NYC dropped by 38 percent; the 981 homicides was

the lowest since 1968

- Microsoft came under antitrust scrutiny for insisting that its Internet browser was intrinsic to its Windows 95 product
- The newest Barbie doll featured a larger waistline, smaller breasts, more modest clothing, and a friend in a wheelchair
- The leading tobacco companies made a $368 billion settlement with the states to settle smoking death claims
- Scottish researchers announced the cloning of an adult mammal, a sheep named Dolly
- Severe asthma, common in poor urban areas, was linked to cockroaches
- President Clinton gained line-item veto power for the first time
- Affirmative Action programs, designed to aid minorities, came under attack
- Digital cameras, DVD players, voice recognition software, and prosthetic knee joints all made their first appearances

1998

- The Dow Jones reached 9,374, and inflation was at 1.6 percent
- The undergraduate tuition at Harvard reached $22,802
- President Bill Clinton was impeached
- *Gotham: A History of New York to 1898* by Edwin G. Burrows won the Pulitzer Prize for U.S. History
- Welfare recipients dropped below four percent, the lowest in 25 years, and unemployment, interest rates, murders, juvenile arrests, births to unwed mothers, infant mortality, and gas prices also fell to 25 to 35 year lows
- Government-measured rates of obesity targeted 50 percent of the population
- Biotechnological stocks showed long anticipated potential, increasing 44 percent
- Major efforts were begun to avert the potential catastrophic "Y2K" blackout when computers may misread the year 2000 as 1900

- The South Carolina legislature approved a constitutional amendment to remove 103-year-old language that made marriages between blacks and whites illegal
- The IRS Reform Bill shifted the burden of proof from the taxpayer to the IRS
- 17 major newspapers called for President Bill Clinton's resignation after he admitted a sexual relationship with a White House intern
- *Titanic* was the highest grossing film in history at $850 million
- Tobacco companies made a $260 billion settlement with states for smoking-related illnesses

1999

- The U.S. claimed 274 of the world's 590 billionaires worldwide
- Of the original 30 companies in the 1896 Dow Jones Industrial Index, only General Electric survived the Great Depression, two world wars and the terms of 20 U.S. presidents
- *Worth* magazine declared Jupiter Island, Florida, the most expensive town in the country, whose median home price was $3.9 million
- The average American woman was 5'4", weighed 142 pounds and was a size 12
- The top one percent of earners in America had an average net worth of $5.5 million
- The annual reunion of Thomas Jefferson's descendents included the descendents of those who claimed their parents were Jefferson and his slave Sally Hemings
- NATO's mistaken bombing of the Chinese embassy in Belgrade caused further deterioration of U.S. and Chinese relations
- A series of fatal shootings at high schools across the country revived the gun-control debate and prompted many to call for mandatory background checks for gun purchases
- AIDS-related deaths fell nearly 50 percent
- The Modern Library's "100 Best Novels of the Century" list included

Ulysses, The Great Gatsby, A Portrait of the Artist as a Young Man, Lolita, Brave New World, The Sound and the Fury and *Catch-22*
- Viagra, for male erectile dysfunction, sold at a record rate of $10 a pill
- China announced that it had developed on its own the ability to make neutron bombs and miniature atomic weapons

2000
- Millennium celebrations were held throughout the world despite fears of major computer failures from the "Y2K" bug, fears that proved largely unwarranted
- America Online was bought out by Time Warner for $162 billion in the largest-ever corporate merger
- Charles Schulz, creator of the comic strip *Peanuts*, died at the age of 77
- President Bill Clinton proposed a $2 billion program to bring Internet access to low-income houses
- The Russian submarine K-141 Kursk sank in the Barents Sea, killing the 118 sailors on board
- The U.S. Supreme Court gave police broad authority to stop and question people who run from a police officer
- The International Whaling Commission turned down requests from Japan and Norway to allow expanded whaling
- The Millennium Summit among world leaders was held at the United Nations
- President Bill Clinton created the Giant Sequoia National Monument to protect 328,000 California acres of trees from timber harvesting
- Judge Thomas Penfield Jackson ruled that Microsoft violated the Sherman Antitrust Act by tying its Internet browser to its operating system
- George W. Bush was declared the winner of the presidential race in a highly controversial election against Al Gore
- The female-oriented television cable channel Oxygen made its debut
- Carlos Santana won eight Grammy awards, including Album of the

Year for *Supernatural*

2001

- U.S. golf courses increased from 13,353 in 1986 to 17,701
- Unmarried couples heading U.S. households increased from 3.2 million in 1990 to 5.5 million in 2000
- Typical set of childhood vaccinations cost $385, up from $10 in 1971
- Education reform was approved, requiring annual standardized tests in grades three through eight by 2005-6
- Former President Jimmy Carter was honored with the Nobel Peace Prize
- The War Against Terrorism legislation, authorizing the president to use force against those who perpetrated or assisted in the September 11 attacks, passed the House and Senate without objection
- A letter containing the dangerous infection anthrax was mailed to Senator Tom Daschle's office, after which the Senate Office Building was closed for three months
- Unemployment stood at nearly six percent, up from 3.9 percent a year earlier
- The USA PATRIOT Act expanded the powers of the police to wiretap telephones, monitor Internet and e-mail use, and search the homes of suspected terrorists
- President George W. Bush said during his 2002 State of the Union address: "States like those (Iraq, Iran and North Korea) and their terrorist allies, constitute an axis of evil, aiming to threaten the peace of the world"
- Enron, a $50 billion energy-trading company, became the largest U.S. company to file for bankruptcy
- The Dow-Jones Industrial Average reached a high of 11,337, and a low of 8,235
- The much-anticipated movie version of the book *Harry Potter and the Sorcerer's Stone* grossed $150 million in five days

- China was formally granted permanent normal trade status, reversing a 20-year policy of requiring an annual review for the country to expand its human rights activities
- U.S. forces continued to search for terrorist mastermind Osama bin Laden
- The United States withdrew from the 1972 Antiballistic Missile Treaty, thereby allowing the military to test and deploy missile-defense systems without restraints

2003

- Surveys indicated that 80 percent of Americans were unwilling to sacrifice taste for more healthy foods
- Iraq's oil ministry, which produced 3.5 million barrels of oil a day only five years ago, produced only five percent of that number
- School districts dominated by blacks and Hispanics spent $902 less per student on average than mostly white school districts
- *Harry Potter and the Order of the Phoenix* sold 5 million copies in the first week of publication
- Surveys showed that 40 percent of all U.S. e-mail was spam
- Thanks in part to file swapping, the sale of CDs was down 20 percent from the year 2000
- Surveys indicated that 83 percent of children believed they would go to college, 68 percent thought they would get married, and 12 percent thought they would join the armed forces
- Space Shuttle *Columbia* disintegrated during re-entry over Texas, killing all seven astronauts on board
- More than 10 million people in over 600 cities worldwide protested the planned invasion of Iraq by the United States
- An American businessman was admitted to the Vietnam France Hospital in Hanoi, Vietnam, with the first identified case of the SARS epidemic, and both patient and doctor died of the disease
- The journal *Nature* reported that 350,000-year-old upright-walking

human footprints had been found in Italy
- The Iraq War began with the invasion of Iraq by the U.S. and U.S. forces quickly seized control of Baghdad, ending the regime of Saddam Hussein
- Syracuse (New York) won the college basketball National Championship
- The Human Genome Project was completed, with 99 percent of the human genome sequenced to 99.99 percent accuracy
- Pen Hadow became the first person to walk alone, without outside help, from Canada to the North Pole
- Eric Rudolph, the suspect in the Centennial Olympic Park bombing in 1996, was captured in Murphy, North Carolina
- Martha Stewart and her broker were indicted for using privileged investment information and then obstructing a federal investigation, causing Stewart to resign as chairperson and chief executive officer of Martha Stewart Living
- The Spirit of Butts Farm completed the first flight across the Atlantic by a computer-controlled model aircraft; the flight set two world records for a model aircraft-for duration (38 hours, 53 minutes) and for non-stop distance (1,883 statute miles)
- The Concorde made its last scheduled commercial flight
- The U.S. Supreme Court upheld Affirmative Action in university admissions and declared sodomy laws unconstitutional
- Cherokee Nation of Oklahoma approved a new constitution re-designating the tribe "Cherokee Nation" without "of Oklahoma" and specifically disenfranchising the Cherokee Freedmen
- The Florida Marlins defeated the New York Yankees to win their second World Series title

2004
- Pakistani scientists admitted giving Libya, Iran and North Korea the technology to build nuclear weapons

- The U.S. required international travelers to be fingerprinted and photographed before entering the country
- President George W. Bush proposed a plan the would allow illegal immigrants working in the United States to apply for temporary guest worker status and increase the number of green cards granted each year
- Paul O'Neill, former treasury secretary, told TV news program *60 Minutes* that the Bush administration had been planning an attack against Iraq since the first days of Bush's presidency
- Two NASA Rovers landed on Mars and sent back spectacular images of the planet
- The Salvation Army reported that Joan Kroc, heir to the McDonald's fortune, had left the nonprofit entity $1.5 billion
- A computer worm, called MyDoom or Novarg, spread through Internet servers, infecting one in 12 e-mail messages
- Terrorists exploded at least 10 bombs on four commuter trains in Madrid, Spain, during rush hour, killing 202 people and wounding 1,400
- The California Supreme Court ordered San Francisco to stop issuing marriage licenses to same-sex couples
- NASA reported the discovery of a distant object in our solar system that closely resembled a planet
- The Bush administration admitted that it failed to give the commission investigating the September 11, 2001 terrorist attacks thousands of pages of national security papers
- President Bush said in a national broadcast that to abandon Iraq would fuel anti-American sentiment around the world
- Several hundred thousand demonstrators gathered in Washington, DC, to protest the Bush administration's policy on reproductive rights
- The popular search engine Google went public
- A federal judge in San Francisco said the Partial Birth Abortion Ban

Act was unconstitutional because it lacked a medical exception to save a woman's life, and placed an unnecessary burden on women who sought abortions

- United Nations Secretary General Kofi Annan said the war in Iraq was illegal and violated the U.N. charter
- The International Committee of the Red Cross found that military personnel used physical and psychological abuse at the Guantanamo prison in Cuba that was "tantamount to torture"

2005

- *Deep Impact* was launched from Cape Canaveral by a Delta 2 rocket
- The *Huygens* probe landed on Titan, the largest moon of Saturn
- George W. Bush was inaugurated in Washington, DC, for his second term as the forty-third president of the United States
- The Kyoto Protocol went into effect, without the support of the U.S. and Australia
- The People's Republic of China ratified an anti-secession law, aimed at preventing Taiwan from declaring independence
- Pope John Paul II died, prompting over four million mourners to travel to the Vatican
- The first thirteenth root calculation of a 200-digit number was computed mentally by Frenchman Alexis Lemaire
- Demonstrators marched through Baghdad denouncing the U.S. occupation of Iraq, two years after the fall of Saddam Hussein, and rallied in the square where his statue had been toppled in 2003
- Pope Benedict XVI succeeded Pope John Paul II, becoming the 265th pope
- The Superjumbo jet aircraft Airbus A380 made its first flight from Toulouse
- The Provisional IRA issued a statement formally ordering an end to the armed campaign it had pursued since 1969, and ordering all its units to dump their arms

- The largest UN World Summit in history was held in New York City
- Cartoons that included depictions of Muhammad printed in the Danish newspaper Jyllands-Posten triggered Islamic protests and death threats
- The second Chinese spacecraft, *Shenzhou 6,* was launched, carrying Fei Junlong and Nie Haisheng for five days in orbit
- Scientists announced that they had created mice with small amounts of human brain cells in an effort to make realistic models of neurological disorders
- Another second was added, 23:59:60, called a leap second, to end the year 2005; the last time this occurred was on June 30, 1998

2006-2007

- NASA's Stardust mission successfully returned dust from a comet
- United Airlines emerged from bankruptcy after 4 years, the longest such filing in history
- In Super Bowl XL, the Pittsburgh Steelers defeated the Seattle Seahawks 21-10
- The Blu-ray Disc format was released in the United States
- Massive antiwar demonstrations, including a march down NYC's Broadway marked the third year of war in Iraq
- Warren Buffett donated more than $30 billion to the Bill & Melinda Gates Foundation
- The Military Commissions Act of 2006 was passed, suspending habeas corpus for "enemy combatants"
- A Pew Research Center survey revealed that 81 percent of Americans believed it was "common behavior" for lobbyists to bribe members of Congress
- More than a million immigrants, primarily Hispanic, staged marches in over 100 cities, calling for immigration reform
- Liquids and gels were banned from checked and carry-on airplane baggage after London Police made 21 arrests in connection with an

apparent terrorist plot to blow up planes traveling from the United Kingdom to the United States

- The International Astronomical Union defined "planet," demoting Pluto to the status of "dwarf planet" more than 70 years after its discovery
- Two stolen Edvard Munch paintings, *The Scream* and *Madonna*, were recovered in a police raid in Oslo, Norway
- President George W. Bush used the fifth anniversary of the September 11, 2001, attacks to emphasize the link between Iraq and winning the broader war on terrorism, asserting that "if we give up the fight in the streets of Baghdad, we will face the terrorists in the streets of our own cities"
- Google bought YouTube for $1.65 billion
- *Pirates of the Caribbean: Dead Man's Chest* became the fastest film in Hollywood history to reach the billion-dollar mark worldwide in box office receipts
- Former Iraqi leader Saddam Hussein was sentenced to death by hanging after an Iraqi
- court found him guilty of crimes against humanity
- Massachusetts enacted Universal Health Coverage, requiring all residents to have either public or private insurance
- PlayStation 3 and Wii were released in North America
- •Smoking was banned in all Ohio bars, restaurants, workplaces and other public places
- The Ronettes, Patti Smith, and Van Halen were all inducted into Rock and Roll Hall of Fame
- Elton John played Madison Square Garden for the sixtieth time to celebrate his sixtieth birthday, joined by Whoopi Goldberg, Robin Williams, and former President Bill Clinton
- Live Earth, a worldwide series of concerts to initiate action against global warming, took place
- Led Zeppelin reunited for their first show in 25 years

- Celine Dion made the final performance of her five-year engagement at Caesars Palace in Las Vegas
- The International Red Cross and Red Crescent Movement adopted the Red Crystal as a non-religious emblem for use in its overseas operations
- A 2,100-year-old melon was discovered by archaeologists in western Japan
- The final book of the Harry Potter series, *Harry Potter and the Deathly Hallows*, was released and sold over 11 million copies in the first 24 hours, becoming the fastest-selling book in history
- Track and field star Marion Jones surrendered the five Olympic medals she won in the 2000 Sydney Games after admitting to doping
- Beyoncé launched The Beyoncé Experience in Tokyo, Japan
- Russian President Vladimir Putin was named *Time* magazine's 2007 Person of the Year
- The Picasso painting *Portrait of Suzanne Bloch,* and *Candido Portinari's O Lavrador de Café* were stolen from the São Paulo Museum of Art

2008

- Americans elected Barack Obama as the first African American U.S. President
- An economic recession —known as the Great Recession—began that rivaled the Great Depression of the 1930s, caused in large part by banks pushing securities backed by high-interest loans to homebuyers
- President George W. Bush signed a $700 billion bill on October 3 to bail out banks and stem the financial crisis
- Television shows winning an Emmy award included NBC's *30 Rock, Comedy Central's The Daily Show with Jon Stewart,* and the first season of AMC's drama, *Mad Men*
- Seth MacFarlane signed a $100 million deal with the Fox television network to keep *Family Guy* and *American Dad* on the air until 2012,

making MacFarlane the world's highest paid television writer

- *Good Masters! Sweet Ladies! Voices from a Medieval Village* won the 2008 Newbery Medal for children's literature
- Bernard Madoff was arrested and charged with securities fraud in a $50 billion Ponzi scheme
- California became the second state to legalize same-sex marriage after the state's own Supreme Court ruled a previous ban unconstitutional; the first state was Massachusetts, in 2004
- *Slumdog Millionaire*, a movie about a young man from the slums of Mumbai, India, won the Academy Award for best film, and a total of eight Oscars
- Australian actor and director Heath Ledger died from an accidental overdose at age 28, a few months after finishing filming for *The Dark Knight* for which he was posthumously awarded the Oscar for Best Supporting Actor
- The British alternative rock band *Coldplay* won the Grammy award for Song of the Year for "Viva la Vida," Spanish for either "long live life" or "live the life"
- Pope Benedict XVI visited the United States
- Bill Gates stepped down as chairman of Microsoft Corporation to work full-time for the nonprofit Bill & Melinda Gates Foundation
- Toshiba recalled its HD DVD video formatting, ending its format war with Sony's Blu-Ray Disc
- Gold prices on the New York Mercantile Exchange hit $1,000 an ounce
- Greg Maddux pitched his 5,000th career inning against the San Francisco Giants on September 19
- The New York Yankees played their final home game at Yankee Stadium against the Baltimore Orioles; they started the next season in a new stadium built across the street
- The Detroit Lions finished the football season 0-16, the first time in National Football League history that a team went winless in a 16-

game season

2009

- Barack Obama was inaugurated as the 44th president of the United States in front of a crowd of over one million
- Michael Jackson died of a physician administered drug overdose, which brought a worldwide outpouring of grief
- US Airways Flight 1549 lost power in both engines shortly after takeoff from La Guardia, forcing the pilot to land in New York's Hudson River; all 155 passengers and crew were rescued with no casualties
- President Obama signed executive orders to close the Guantanamo Bay detention camp within one year and to prohibit torture in terrorism interrogations
- President Obama ordered the deployment of 17,000 additional US troops to Afghanistan
- When insurance giant AIG reported nearly $62 billion in losses during the fourth quarter, the government gave it $30 billion more in aid; AIG later announced $450 million in executive bonuses, despite its central role in the global financial meltdown and receiving billions in government bailouts
- NASA launched *Kepler Mission*, a space photometer which searches for planets in the MilkyWay that could be similar to Earth and habitable by humans
- President Obama overturned a Bush-era policy that limited federal funding for embryonic stem cell research
- Governor John Lynch signed a bill allowing same-sex marriage in New Hampshire, the sixth state in the union to do so
- President Obama announced vehicle emissions and mileage requirements under which vehicles would use 30 percent less fuel and emit one-third less carbon dioxide by 2016
- The Senate passed a bill to impose new regulations on the credit card industry, curbing fees and interest hikes and requiring more

transparent disclosure of account terms
- Physician George Tiller, known for giving late-term abortions, was murdered during a Sunday service at his church in Wichita, Kansas
- The Great Recession officially ended
- Analog television broadcasts ended in the United States as the Federal Communications Commission required all full-power stations to send their signals digitally
- After an eight-month recount battle, former comedian Al Franken was sworn in as the junior senator of Minnesota, giving Democrats a majority of 60 seats
- Microsoft released Windows 7
- North Korean leader Kim Jong-il pardoned two American journalists, who were imprisoned for illegal entry, after former President Clinton met with Kim in North Korea
- Sonia Sotomayor became the third woman and the first Latina to serve on the U.S. Supreme Court
- The Justice Department announced the largest health care fraud settlement in history, $2.3 billion, involving Pfizer
- An 8.3-magnitude earthquake triggered a tsunami near the Samoan Islands, destroying many communities and harbors in Samoa and American Samoa, and killing at least 189
- President Obama won the Nobel Peace Prize
- President Obama signed the Matthew Shepard and James Byrd Jr. Hate Crimes Prevention Act, extending federal hate crime law to include crimes motivated by a victim's gender, sexual orientation, gender identity, or disability
- The New York Yankees defeated the Philadelphia Phillies to win their 27th World Championship

2010
- The Eureka earthquake shook the north coast of California, causing $43 million in losses and 35 injuries

- Google announced it was the target of a cyberattack from China
- A special election was held in Massachusetts in which Republican Scott Brown replaced the late US Senator Ted Kennedy
- The Air Force Academy in Colorado Springs opened a worshiping site for earth-centered religions on its campus promoting religious tolerance
- The Tea Party movement hosted its first convention in Nashville, Tennessee
- In Super Bowl XLIV the New Orleans Saints beat the Indianapolis Colts 31-17
- President Obama established the National Commission on Fiscal Responsibility and Reform
- The US Navy officially announced that it would end its ban on women in submarines
- A SeaWorld employee in Orlando, Florida, was killed by a killer whale during a live performance
- The District of Columbia's same-sex marriage law went into effect
- At the 82nd Academy Awards, *The Hurt Locker* won six Oscars including the first Best Director award for a woman, Kathryn Bigelow
- NASA announced that 2010 would likely become the warmest year on record due to global warming
- President Obama signed the Patient Protection and Affordable Care Act into law aiming to insure 95 percent of Americans
- An explosion at the Deepwater Horizon oil rig killed 11 workers and sank the rig, initiating a massive offshore oil spill in the Gulf of Mexico, considered the largest environmental disaster in US history
- The Dodd-Frank Wall Street Reform and Consumer Protection Act was signed into law by President Obama
- Former US Solicitor General Elena Kagan was sworn in as Justice of the Supreme Court
- The last US combat troops left Iraq
- President Obama confirmed that two packages sent to the U.S. from

Yemen were filled with explosives
- The San Francisco Giants defeated the Texas Rangers to win their first World Series in 56 years
- The Federal Reserve announced it would buy $600 billion in bonds to encourage economic growth
- The San Francisco Board of Supervisors banned McDonald's Happy Meal toys, citing obesity concerns
- WikiLeaks founder Julian Assange began releasing confidential U.S. diplomatic documents
- General Motors introduced the first Chevrolet Volt plug-in hybrid electric vehicle
- President Obama signed the Don't Ask, Don't Tell repeal into law
- The Federal Communications Commission passed new net neutrality laws

2011

- Southern Sudan held a referendum on independence, paving the way for the creation of the new state
- An estimated two billion people watched the wedding of Prince William, Duke of Cambridge, and Catherine Middleton at Westminster Abbey in London
- Osama bin Laden, the founder and leader of the militant group Al-Qaeda, was killed during an American military operation in Pakistan
- The Green Bay Packers' 31-25 defeat of the Pittsburgh Steelers in Super Bowl XLV attracted 111 million viewers, making the Fox broadcast the most watched program in American TV history
- Sony, IMAX, and Discovery Communications launched 3net, a new 3D TV channel
- The world's first artificial organ transplant was completed, using an artificial windpipe coated with stem cells
- Space Shuttle *Atlantis* landed successfully at Kennedy Space Center, concluding NASA's space shuttle program

- NASA announced that its Mars Reconnaissance Orbiter captured photographic evidence of possible liquid water on Mars during warm seasons
- *Pirates of the Caribbean: On Stranger Tides* grossed $1,043,871,802 to become the eighth film to have surpassed the billion dollar mark
- ABC cancelled of two of its long-running daytime dramas—*All My Children*, after 41 years, and *One Life to Live*, after 43 years
- Cellular phone company Verizon Wireless announced it would phase out its famous "Can You Hear Me Now?" campaign, which began in 2002
- The global population reached seven billion people

2012

- Utah banned discounts/specials on alcoholic drinks, essentially outlawing Happy Hour
- San Francisco raised the minimum wage to over $10 per hour, making it the highest in the country
- Photography pioneer Kodak filed for bankruptcy protection, no longer able to compete in the digital age
- Approximately 111.3 million viewers (one-third of the U.S. population) watched the Super Bowl
- The Kellogg Company purchased snack maker Pringles from Procter & Gamble for $2 .7 billion
- The 84th Academy Awards saw *The Artist* win Best Picture—the first silent film to win that award since *Wings* in 1927
- The shooting of Trayvon Martin, an unarmed, black 17-yearold, by George Zimmerman in Florida, ignited nationwide discussion of the role of race in America.
- *Encyclopædia Britannica* announced the end of its print editions, continuing online only
- The United States, Japan, and the European Union filed a case against China at the WTO regarding export restrictions on rare earth metals

- American golfer Bubba Watson won the U.S. Masters, defeating Louis Oosthuizen of South Africa in a playoff
- The Guggenheim Partners purchased the Los Angeles Dodgers for $2.1 billion, the most ever paid for a professional sports franchise
- Licenses for autonomous cars in the U.S. were granted in Nevada to Google
- Goldman Sachs director Rajat Gupta was convicted of three counts of securities fraud and one count of conspiracy related to insider trading in 2011
- Connecticut repealed the death penalty
- Moody's downgraded the credit rating of 15 major world banks
- NBCUniversal bought full control of the U.S. news website MSNBC.com and rebranded it as NBCNews.com
- U.S. swimmer Michael Phelps won his 19th career Olympic gold metal, with a win in the 4 x 200-meter freestyle relay
- American scientists Robert Lefkowitz and Brian Kobilka won the Nobel Prize in Chemistry for their discoveries of the inner workings of G protein-coupled receptors
- Felix Baumgartner broke the world human ascent by balloon record, AIG announced it would pay $450 million in bonuses to top executives, despite its central role in the global financial meltdown and receiving a $173 billion government bailout; a massive public outcry followed before space diving out of the Red Bull Stratos helium-filled balloon over Roswell, New Mexico
- The Walt Disney Company purchased Lucasfilm Ltd. from George Lucas for $4.05 billion, a deal that included rights to the Star Wars and Indiana Jones franchises
- Washington became the first state to legalize marijuana
- Hostess, which includes such brands as Twinkies, announced it would file for bankruptcy, liquidate its assets, and lay off 18,500 workers

2014

- The Ebola virus epidemic in West Africa infected over 21,000 people and killed at least 8,000
- Malaysia Airlines Flight 370 disappeared over the Gulf of Thailand with 239 people on board, presumably crashing into the Indian Ocean
- Malala Yousafzai, a 17-year-old Muslim from Pakistan, became the youngest person to win the Nobel Peace Prize, sharing the prize with Kailash Satyarthi, a Hindu from India, for their struggle against the repression of girls and women
- The Disney movie soundtrack *Frozen* was the most popular U.S. album for 13 weeks
- Colorado allowed the sale of recreational marijuana from legally licensed businesses.
- *12 Years a Slave* won the Oscar for Best Picture, grossing just under $188 million
- *Transformers: Age of Extinction* was the top grossing movie, drawing more than $1 billion in box office receipts
- The XXII Olympic Winter Games were held in Sochi, Russia
- Belgium became the first country in the world to make euthanasia legal for terminally ill patients of any age
- Russia annexed the Ukrainian territory of Crimea and began a covert military offensive against the Ukraine
- American science educator "Bill Nye, the Science Guy" defended evolution in the classroom in a debate with creationist Ken Ham
- "Happy" by Pharrell Williams was the No. 1 song on the pop charts for 10 consecutive weeks
- President Obama announced the resumption of normal relations between the United States and Cuba
- "Black Jeopardy!" became one of *Saturday Night Live's* most popular skits with cast member Kenan Thompson as game show host "Alex Treblack"

- Sony Pictures canceled its planned release of *The Interview* after threats from North Korea against the Seth Rogen-Evan Goldberg comedy that depicts the assassination of North Korea's dictator; criticism against Sony led the studio to release the film on video on demand

2015

- The Federal Communications Commission published its rule on net neutrality regulations
- NASA's *Messenger* spacecraft concluded its four-year orbital mission over Mercury
- Maryland Governor Larry Hogan declared a state of emergency in Baltimore when protests against the death of Freddie Gray in police custody turned violent
- Dzhokhar Tsarnaev was sentenced to death for the 2013 Boston Marathon bombing
- Cuba was officially removed from the US State Sponsors of Terrorism list
- Former Olympian Bruce Jenner became the first transgender person to appear on the cover of *Vanity Fair* magazine
- Rachel Dolezal resigned as president of the NAACP Spokane, Washington amid allegations that she claimed to be black but was actually white
- In a 6-3 decision, the Supreme Court upheld subsidies for the Patient Protection and Affordable Care Act (also known as Obamacare) nationwide
- The Supreme Court ruled that the Constitution guarantees a right to same-sex marriage
- BP (British Petroleum) agreed to pay the Department of Justice an $18.7 billion settlement in reparation for the 2010 oil spill that dumped over 125 million gallons of oil into the Gulf of Mexico
- The South Carolina State House removed the Confederate battle flag

from its grounds after weeks of protest, and placed it in a museum
- *Birdman* won four Oscars including Best Picture and Best Director
- Iran and a coalition including the U.S. came to an agreement in which UN sanctions against Iran would be lifted in exchange for reduction of Iran's stockpile of enriched uranium
- President Obama announced the Clean Power Plan which included the first-ever Environmental Protection Agency standards on carbon pollution from U.S. power plants
- Kim Davis, a clerk for Rowan County, Kentucky, was found in contempt of court and jailed for five days for refusing to issue marriage licenses to same-sex couples
- NASA announced strong evidence that liquid water flows on Mars during the summer months, increasing the chance of sustainable life on the planet
- President Obama ordered up to 50 U.S. special operations ground troops to be deployed in Syria to fight Islamic State militants
- Defense Secretary Ashton Carter announced that all combat roles in the military must be opened to women
- An arrest warrant was issued for comedian Bill Cosby for the alleged drugging and sexual assault of an employee at Temple University in 2004, following dozens of similar allegations

2017

- Donald J. Trump became the 45th president of the United States
- The Women's March in Washington DC comprised nearly three million, in response to the inauguration of Donald Trump, making it the biggest protest in U.S. history
- President Trump signed an executive order withdrawing the US from the controversial trade pact, the Trans-Pacific Partnership (TPP)
- The Trump administration froze all new research grants and contracts for the Environmental Protection Agency and temporarily barred its employees from posting press releases or updates to the agency's social

media accounts
- The Dow Jones Industrial Average reached an all-time high of 20,000 points
- President Trump signed an executive order banning the entry of refugees of the Syrian civil war into the United States indefinitely, and all nationals of Iran, Iraq, Syria, Libya, Somalia, Sudan, and Yemen to the US for 90 days
- Neil Gorsuch filled the vacant seat on the Supreme Court left by the sudden death of Antonin Scalia
- President Trump signed an executive order to review and eventually scale back the Dodd-Frank Wall Street Reform and Consumer Protection Act put in place after the Great Recession
- In Super Bowl LI, the New England Patriots defeated the Atlanta Falcons 34-28
- Police forcibly evicted all remaining Dakota Access Pipeline protesters, arresting 33
- *Moonlight* won Best Picture at the 89th Academy Awards
- Rock and roll pioneer Chuck Berry died at the age of 90
- President Trump signed the Energy Independence Executive Order, intended to boost coal and other fossil fuel production
- The U.S. Justice Department named former FBI chief Robert Mueller as special counsel to investigate alleged Russian interference in the 2016 U.S. election and possible collusion between President Trump's campaign and Moscow
- The first gene editing of human embryos in the U.S. took place using CRISPR
- A third attempt to repeal Obamacare failed after it was voted down by 51 votes to 49
- Violent clashes broke out at a Unite the Right rally, where 32-year-old Heather Heyer was killed and many others injured when a neo-Nazi intentionally ploughed his car into a group of people

- The first total solar eclipse of the 21st century took place in the U.S.
- Hurricane Harvey, a category 4 tropical cyclone, made landfall in Texas
- A directive was signed by President Trump banning transgender military recruits
- North Korea fired a ballistic missile over northern Japan
- The Trump administration announced that the Deferred Action for Childhood Arrivals (DACA) immigration policy, set by the Obama administration, would end
- Millions of homes were left without power as the center of Hurricane Irma hit mainland Florida
- Hurricane Maria struck the U.S. territory of Puerto Rico, leaving the island devastated

2018

- A total lunar eclipse occurred while the moon was at perigee and during a blue moon, being known as the super blue blood moon
- SpaceX successfully launched the maiden flight of Falcon Heavy, its most powerful rocket
- The Winter Olympics were held in Pyeongchang, South Korea, followed by the Paralympics
- A shooting at Marjory Stoneman Douglas High School in Parkland, Florida left 17 dead and 15 injured – the sixth school shooting in two months
- In Superbowl LII, the Philadelphia Eagles defeated the New England Patriots 41-33
- The Shape of Water won the Academy Award for Best Picture
- Michael Wolff published *Fire and Fury: Inside the Trump White House*, with descriptions of chaotic interactions among White House staff, and derogatory descriptions of the Trump family by former WH Chief Strategist Steve Bannon
- Oprah Winfrey won the Cecil B. DeMille Award at the Golden Globes, giving a rousing speech that had social media calling for her presidential run in 2020

- Time's Up, a movement against sexual harassment, was founded by Hollywood celebrities in response to continuous allegations of sexual misconduct against Hollywood big-wigs. The movement raised $20 million in two months for its legal defense fund
- Jordan Peele became the first African American to win the Academy Award for Best Original Screenplay for his film *Get Out*
- Special Counsel Robert S. Meuller III continued his investigations into Russian interference in the 2016 U.S. presidential election
- The *Wall Street Journal* reported that President Trump paid off pornographic actress Stormy Daniels to keep their affair quiet
- Famed fashion designer Hubert de Givenchy died at his home in Paris
- Businessman, hedge fund manager, and "pharma-bro" Martin Shkreli was sentenced to seven years in federal prison and $7.4 million in fines for securities fraud
- Former USA Gymnastics national team doctor Larry Nassar was sentenced to 40 to 175 years in prison after pleading guilty to several counts of sexual assault of minors
- The Cleveland Indians baseball team retired the use of their logo and mascot "Chief Wahoo" after deeming it racially inappropriate

Bibliography

"1798 Alien Enemies Act." *UWB*. University of Washington-Bothell Library. US Immigration Legislation Online. Session II, Chap. 66, Statute 570. 5th Congress; 6 July 1798.

"1798 Naturalization Act." *UWB*. University of Washington-Bothell Library. US Immigration Legislation Online. Session II, Chap. 54, Statute 566. 5th Congress, 17 June 1798.

"1882 Immigration Act." *Library UWB*. University of Washington-Bothell Library. PDF. 2018.

"The 1965 Enactment." *DOJ*. U.S. Department of Justice. 2017.

Adelman, William J. "The Haymarket Affair." *Illinois Labor History*. Illinois Labor History Society. 2016.

Alvarez, Priscilla. "A Brief History of America's 'Love-Hate Relationship' With Immigration." *Atlantic*. Atlantic Monthly Group. 19 Feb. 2017.

Alvarez, Priscilla. "The Diversity Visa Program Was Created to Help Irish Immigrants." *The Atlantic*. Atlantic Monthly Group. 1 Nov. 2017.

Ambrose, Stephen E. *Nothing Like It in the World: The Men Who Built the Transcontinental Railroad*. New York: Touchstone Books, 2000, pp. 230–242.

"Amendment XIV." *Cornell*. Cornell Law School. U.S. Constitution. LII. 2018.

"Amendment XV." *Cornell*. Cornell Law School. U.S. Constitution. LII. 2018.

"American Affairs: The Attempt upon the President's Life." *Public Opinion*. Public Opinion Company, Vol. 31, p. 324, 1901.

"An ACT to amend the Agricultural Act of 1949." *UWB*. University of Washington-Bothell Library. Public Law 78. 12 July 1951.

"An Act to amend the Naturalization Laws and to punish Crimes against the same, and for other Purposes." *LOC*. Library of Congress. Forty-First Congress, Session II. PDF. 2018.

"An Act to Encourage Immigration." *New York Times*. New York Times Co. 3 Aug. 1864.

"An Act To regulate the immigration of aliens into the United States." *Library of Congress*. Fifty-Seventh Congress. Sess. II, Chapter 1012. 3 Mar. 1903.

"An Act to Secure the Right of Citizenship to Children of Citizens of the United States born out of the Limits Thereof." *Library of Congress*. Thirty-Third Congress. Sess. II. 1855. PDF. 2018.

"Anarchist Turner Tells of His Fight." *New York Times*. New York Times, Co. 14 Mar. 1904.

Anderson, Stuart. "When Criticizing The President Was Against The Law." *Forbes*. Forbes, Inc. 17 Dec. 2016.

"Angel Island Immigrant Journeys." *AIISF*. Angel Island Immigration Station Foundation. 2017.

"An Open Letter from 1,470 Economists on Immigration." *New American Economy*. New American Economy. 12 Apr. 2017.

"Apology Act for the 1930s Mexican Repatriation Program." *California Legislative Information*. Chapter 8.5 Mexican Repatriation. 1 Jan. 2006.

"A Reagan Legacy: Amnesty For Illegal Immigrants." *NPR*. National Public Radio. 4 July 2010.

Arnesen, Eric. *Encyclopedia of U.S. Labor and Working-Class History, Volume 1*. New York: Routledge P, 2007.

Arrington, Benjamin T. "Industry and Economy during the Civil War." *NPS*. National Park Service. 2017.

Axelrod, Alan. *Selling the War: The Making of American Propaganda*. New York: Macmillan, 2009 pp. 56–58.

Axelrod, Alan. *The Real History of the Cold War: A New Look at the*

Past. New York: Sterling, 2009 p. 170.

Bailey, David C. *¡Viva Cristo Rey!: The Cristero Rebellion and the Church-State Conflict in Mexico*. Austin, TX: U of Texas P, 1974.

Bardach, Ann Louise. "Marielitos and the changing of Miami." *Los Angeles Times*. Tronc Media. 24 Apr. 2005.

Barkhorn, Eleanor. "Sarah Palin Misinterprets Robert Frost." *The Atlantic*. Atlantic Monthly Group. 25 May 2010.

Barkhorn, Eleanor. "'Vote No on Women's Suffrage': Bizarre Reasons For Not Letting Women Vote." *The Atlantic*. Atlantic Monthly Group. 6 Nov. 2012.

Beard, Jacob. "Top Ten Origins: History's Greatest Walls, Good Neighbors or Bad Policy?" *Origins*. Ohio State University. Department of History. 2018.

Beinart, Peter. "The Racial and Religious Paranoia of Trump's Warsaw Speech." *The Atlantic*. Atlantic Monthly Group. 6 July 2017.

Berinsky, Adam J., Eleanor Neff Powell, Eric Schickler, and Ian Brett Yohai. "Revisiting Public Opinion in the 1930s and 1940s." *PS*. Political Science & Politics, 44, pp. 515–520 ©Cambridge UP 2011.

"Bill of Rights of the United States of America (1791)." *Bill of Rights Institute*. Bill of Rights Institute. 2018.

Black, Edwin. "Eugenics and the Nazis—the California connection." *SF GATE*. Hearst Communication, Inc. 9 Nov. 2003.

Blakemore, Erin. "Five Things to Know About the Declaration of Sentiments." *Smithsonian*. Smithsonian Institution. 8 June 2016.

"A Blueprint for getting more women into information technology." *The Economist*. Economist Newspaper, Inc. 12 Dec. 2016.

Boissoneault, Lorraine. "How the 19th-Century Know-Nothing Party Reshaped American Politics." *Smithsonian*. Smithsonian Institution. 26 Jan. 2017.

Boissoneault, Lorraine. "Literacy Tests and Asian Exclusion Were the Hallmarks of the 1917 Immigration Act." *Smithsonian*. Smithsonian Institution. 6 Feb. 2017.

Bolognese, Jeff. "3 Reasons Why Chinese Were the MVPs on the Transcontinental Railroad." *Medium*. SASEprints. Society of Asian Scientists and Engineers, 20 May 2016.

Bolstad, Erika. "Trump's Wall Could Cause Serious Environmental Damage." *Scientific American*. Nature America, Inc. 26 Jan. 2017.

Boyd, Eugene. "American Federalism, 1776 to 1997: Significant Events." Library of Congress. Congressional Research Service. 1997.

Branson-Potts, Hailey. "Trump wants immigrants to 'share our values.' They say assimilation is much more complex." *LA Times*. Los Angeles Times. 11 Apr. 2017.

Brauer and Caruso, "For Being Aboriginal," in Anderton, C.H. and Jurgen Brauer, eds. *Economic Aspects of Genocides, Other Mass Atrocities, and their Prevention*. New York: Oxford UP, 2016. p. 293.

Bricker, Jesse, et al. "Changes in U.S. Family Finances from 2013 to 2016: Evidence from the Survey of Consumer Finances." *Federal Reserve*. Federal Reserve Bulletin. Vol. 103, No. 3. Sept. 2017.

"A Brief History." Overview of Slavery in the United States. Civil War Trust. 2018, www.civilwar.org/learn/articles/slavery-united-states.

Brignell, Victoria. "When America believed in eugenics." *New Statesman*. Progressive Digital Media. 10 Dec. 2010.

"*Buck v. Bell*." *Cornell Law School*. Legal Information Institute [LII] Supreme Court. 2018.

Bulik, Mark. "1854: No Irish Need Apply." *Times Insider*. New York Times, Co. 8 Sept. 2015.

Bump, Philip. "How the Republican tax bill benefits the rich, according to government analysis." *The Washington Post*. Washington Post Co. 30 Nov. 2017.

"The Burlingame-Seward Treaty, 1868." *U.S. Department of State*. Office of the Historian. Milestones. 2016.

Burrus, Trevor. "One Generation of Oliver Wendell Holmes, Jr. Is Enough." *Cato At Liberty*. Cato Institute. 23 June 2011.

Bush, George W. "President Bush Proposes New Temporary Worker Program." *Georgewbush-whitehouse*. The White House. 7 Jan. 2004.

Cadava, Geraldo. "Long before Trump's Mexico wall, Prop. 187 killed Hispanic conservatism." *Timeline*. Medium. 1 July 2016.

"California's Anti-Coolie Act of 1862." *SDSU*. San Diego State University. Department of Political Science. 2016.

Calloway, Collin G. "American Indians and the American Revolution." *National Park Service*. U.S. Department of the Interior. Dec. 2008.

Camarota, Steven A., and Karen Zeigler. "Jobs Americans Won't Do? A Detailed Look at Immigrant Employment by Occupation." *CIS*. Center for Immigration Studies. 17 Aug. 2009.

Capó, Julio Jr. "The White House Used This Moment as Proof the U.S. Should Cut Immigration. Its Real History Is More Complicated." *Time*. Time, Inc. 4 Aug. 2017.

Capriccioso, Rob. "Illuminating the Treaties That Have Governed U.S.-Indian Relationships." *Smithsonian*. Smithsonian Institution. 21 Sept. 2014.

Card, David. "The Impact of the Mariel Boatlift on the Miami Labor Market." *Industrial and Labor Relations Review*. Vol. 43, No. 2. (Jan. 1990), pp. 245–257.

Carrell, Alexis. *Man, the Unknown*. New York: Harper & Brothers Publishers, 1935.

Carroll, Rory. "America's dark and not-very-distant history of hating Catholics." *Guardian*. Guardian News and Media. 12 Sept. 2015.

Carter, Jimmy. "Tokyo Economic Summit Conference Remarks to Reporters at the Conclusion of the Conference." June 29, 1979. *The American Presidency Project*. University of Southern California. 2018.

"A Century of Lawmaking for a New Nation: U.S. Congressional Documents and Debates, 1774–1875." *Library of Congress*. 2016.

Chadwick, Bruce. "When New York City was the prostitution capital of the US." *New York Post*. NYP Holdings, Inc. 22 Apr. 2017.

Chang, Gordon H. and Shelley Fisher Fishkin. "'The Chinese Helped Build America'." *Forbes*. Forbes Inc. 12 May 2014.

Chan, Sucheng. *Entry Denied: Exclusion and the Chinese Community in America, 1882–1943,* Philadelphia, Temple UP, 1991.

Chapin, Laura. "Bigots Will Be Bigots." *U.S. News*. U.S. News and World Report. 6 Feb. 2017.

"Chinese Immigration and the Chinese Exclusion Acts." *Department of State*. Office of the Historian.

"Chy Lung v. Freeman." *FindLaw*. Thomson Reuters. 2018.

"Civil Rights Act of 1964." *NPS*. National Park Service. 2018.

Clement, Scott and David Nakamura. "Survey finds strong support for 'dreamers'." *The Washington Post*. Washington Post, Co. 25 Sept. 2017.

Coaston, Jane. "The scary ideology behind Trump's immigration instincts." *Vox*. Vox Media. 18 Jan. 2018.

Cohen, Adam. "This Jigsaw Puzzle Was Given to Ellis Island Immigrants to Test Their Intelligence." *Smithsonian Magazine*. Smithsonian Institution. May 2017.

Cole, David. "Mccarran-Walter Act Reborn?" *Washington Post*. Washington Post, Co. 18 Nov. 1990.

Colville, Rupert. "Fiftieth Anniversary of the Hungarian uprising and refugee crisis." *UNHCR*. The United Nations Refugee Agency. 23 Oct. 2006.

"Confederate States of America—A Declaration of the Causes Which Impel the State of Texas to Secede from the Federal Union." *Yale Law School*. Lillian Goldman Law Library. The Avalon Project. Documents in Law, History, and Diplomacy. 2008.

"Conference between Governor Burnet and the Indians." *University of Nebraska, Lincoln*. Early Recognized Treaties with American Indian Nations.

"Consideration of Deferred Action for Childhood Arrivals (DACA)." *USCIS*. U.S. Citizenship and Immigration Services. 4 Feb. 2018.

"Constitution of the Confederate States; March 11, 1861." *Yale Law School*. Lillian Goldman Law Library. The Avalon Project. Documents in Law, History, and Diplomacy. 2008.

Cottle, Michelle. "Hoekstra Ad Revives Anti-Asian Strain in American Politics." *Newsweek*. Newsweek, LLC. 13 Feb. 2012.

Davis, Kenneth C. "America's True History of Religious Tolerance." *Smithsonian*. Smithsonian Institution. Oct. 2010.

"Declaration of Independence: A Transcription," *National Archives*. U.S. National Archives. 26 June 2017.

"Declaration of Sentiments and Resolutions: Woman's Rights Convention, Held at Seneca Falls, 19–20 July 1848." *ECSSBA*. Elizabeth Cady Stanton & Susan B. Anthony Papers Project. Rutgers University. 2010.

DenHoed, Andrea. "The Forgotten Lessons of the American Eugenics Movement." *New Yorker*. Conde Nast. 27 Apr. 2016.

De Pinto, Jennifer, Fred Backus, Kabir Khanna, and Anthony Salvanto. "Most Americans support DACA, but oppose border wall—CBS News poll." *CBS News*. 20 Jan. 2018.

Desilver, Drew. "U.S. public seldom has welcomed refugees into country." *Pew Research*. Pew Fact Tank. 19 Nov. 2015.

Dickey, Christopher. "The Diversity Visa Winner Who Saved New York From a Terror Attack." *Daily Beast*. The Daily Beast LLC. 2 Nov. 2017.

Dinnerstein, Leonard. *Uneasy at Home: Antisemitism and the American Jewish Experience*. New York: Columbia UP, 1987.

"Displaced Persons." 14 Apr. 1948.*CQ Researcher*. Sage Publishing. 2018.

"Displaced Persons Act 1948." Public Law 774. 25 June 1948. *University of Washington-Bothell Library*. 2018.

Dolan, Eric W. "Studies find the need to feel unique is linked to belief in conspiracy theories." *PsyPost*. PsyPost. 8 Aug. 2017.

Donnelly, Jim. "The Irish Famine." *BBC*. BBC History. 17 Feb. 2011.

Doyle, Don H. "The Civil War Was Won by Immigrant Soldiers." *Time*. Time Inc. 29 June 2015.

"DREAM Act Congressional Legislative History," *University of Houston*. University of Houston Law School. 2017.

Dudden, Faye E. *Fighting Chance: The Struggle Over Woman Suffrage and Black Suffrage in Reconstruction America*. New York: Oxford UP, 2011.

Dunn, Rob. "The Top Ten Daily Consequences of Having Evolved." *Smithsonian*. Smithsonian Institution. 19 Nov. 2010.

Eckerson, Helen F. "Immigration and National Origins." *The Annals of the American Academy of Political and Social Science*. Vol. 367, The New Immigration (1966), pp. 4–14.

"Ellis Island History," The Statue of *Liberty—Ellis Island Foundation, Inc.*

Embury-Dennis, Tom. "Trump's environment chief Scott Pruitt suggests climate change could be good for humanity." *Independent*. Independent News and Media. 8 Feb. 2018.

"The Emergency Farm Labor Supply Program 1943–1947 (The Bracero Program) Agreement." *OPB*. Oregon Public Broadcasting. The Oregon Experience Archive. 2018.

"Emergency Quota Law 1921." *University of Washington-Bothell Library*. Sixty-Seventh Congress; 19 May 1921.

Eschner, Kat. "How President William McKinley's Assassination Led to the Modern Secret Service." *Smithsonian*. Smithsonian Institution. 14 Sept. 2017.

Evans, Rob, and David Hencke. "US felt ban on Graham Greene 'tarnished its image.'" *The Guardian*. Guardian News and Media. 21 Sept. 2003.

Ewing, Walter A., and Daniel E. Martínez. "The Criminalization of Immigration in the United States." *American Immigration Council*. Special Report. July 2015.

"Fact Sheet: The Secure Fence Act of 2006." *Georgewbush-White House*. White House. Oct. 26, 2006.

Flanagin, Jake. "9/11 forever changed the concept of immigration in the US." *Quartz*. Quartz Media LLC [US]11 Sept. 2015.

Flanagin, Jake. "For the last time, the American Civil War was not about states' rights." *Quartz*. Atlantic Media. 8 Apr. 2015.

Flores, Antonio. "How the U.S. Hispanic population is changing." *Pew Research Center*. Pew Research. 18 Sept. 2017.

Flores, Esteban. "Walls of Separation." *HIR*. Harvard International Review. 27 July 2017.

Frank, Jason, and Isaac Kramnick. "What 'Hamilton' Forgets About Hamilton." *New York Times*. New York Times, Co. 10 June 2016.

"Freedom Day." *New York Times*. New York Time, Co. 19 Oct. 1986.

Frej, Willa. "How U.S. Immigration Policy Has Changed Since 9/11." *Huff Post*. Huffington Post. 9 Sept. 2016.

Fried, Amy. "Government public opinion research and the Japanese-American internment." *BDN*. Bangor Daily News. Pollways. 29 Dec. 2011.

Friedersdorf, Conor. "The Obama Administration's Drone-Strike Dissembling." *The Atlantic*. Atlantic Monthly Group. 14 Mar. 2016.

Friedman, Uri. "What Is a Nativist?" *The Atlantic*. Atlantic Monthly Group. 11 Apr. 2017.

Fuchs, Chris. "150 Years Ago, Chinese Railroad Workers Staged the Era's Largest Labor Strike." *NBC News*. NBC Universal. 21 June 2017.

Fussell, Elizabeth. "Warmth of the Welcome: Attitudes towards Immigrants and Immigration Policy." *Annual Review of Sociology*. July 2014, Vol. 40, pp. 479–498. PDF.

Galarza, Ernesto. "Strangers in our Fields." Washington, DC: U.S. Section Joint United States–Mexico Trade Union Committee. 1956.

Gandhi, Lakshmi. "A History Of Indentured Labor Gives 'Coolie' Its Sting." *NPR*. National Public Radio. 25 Nov. 2013.

Garcia, Juanita. "Migratory Labor. Hearings before Subcommittee on Labor and Labor-Management Relations." 82nd Congress, 2nd Session. *Digital History*. University of Houston. 2016.

Garcia, Maria Cristina. *Seeking Refuge: Central American Migration to Mexico, the United States, and Canada*. U of California P, 2006.

"German U-Boat Reaches Baltimore, Having Crossed Atlantic in 16 Days; Has Letter from Kaiser to Wilson." *New York Times*. New York Times, Co. 10 July 1916.

Gjelten, Tom. *A Nation of Nations: A Great American Immigration Story*. New York: Simon & Schuster, 2015 pp. 119–121.

Golden, Ian, Geoffrey Cameron, and Meera Balarajan, *Exceptional People*: *How Migration Shaped Our World and Will Define Our Future*. Princeton UP, 2011, p. 58.

Goldhill, Olivia. "Astronauts report an 'overview effect' from the awe of space travel—and you can replicate it here on Earth." *Quartz*. Quartz Media. 6 Sept. 2015.

Gomez, Alan. "There are 3.6M 'DREAMers'—a number far greater than commonly known." *USA Today*. USA Today. 18 Jan. 2018.

Gonzales, Manuel G. *Mexicanos: A History of Mexicans in the United States*. Bloomington, IN: Indiana UP, 2009.

"Good Fences, Good Neighbors: Public Opinion on Border Security." *Roper Center*. Cornell University. 2015.

Goyette, Braden. "How Racism Created America's Chinatowns." *Huffington Post*. Huffington Post. 6 Dec. 2017.

Grant, Madison. *The Passing of the Great Race: Or, the Racial Basis of European History*. New York: Charles Scribner's Sons, 1918, p. 193.

Grant, Melissa Gira. "When Prostitution Wasn't a Crime: The

Fascinating History of Sex Work in America." *Alternet*. Alternet. 18 Feb. 2013.

"The Great Depression (1929–1939)." *George Washington University*. The Eleanor Roosevelt Papers Project. Department of History. 2016.

Greenberg, David. "Anarchy in the U.S.: A century of fighting the man" *Slate*. Slate Group. 28 Apr. 2000.

Greenberg, Jon. "Ben Shapiro says a majority of Muslims are radicals." *Politifact*. Punditfact. 5 Nov. 2014.

Grizzard, Frank E. Jr., and D. Boyd Smith. *Jamestown Colony: A Political, Social, and Cultural History*. Santa Barbara, CA: AB-CLIO, Mar. 2007.

Gugliotta, Guy. "New Estimate Raises Civil War Death Toll." *New York Times*. 2 Apr. 2012.

"Guns." *Gallup News*. Gallup, Inc. 2018.

Guthman, Edwin. "Underground Railroad, 1980's Style." *New York Times*. New York Times, Co. 25 Sept. 1988.

Gutiérrez, Ramón. "George W. Bush and Mexican Immigration Policy." Cairn. *Revue Française D'Études Américaines*. Vol. 113, No. 3 (2007), pp. 70–76.

Gzesh, Susan. "Central Americans and Asylum Policy in the Reagan Era." *MPI*. Migration Policy Institute. 1 Apr. 2006.

Hardman, John. "The Great Depression and the New Deal." *EDGE*. Ethics of Development in a Global Environment. Stanford University. 26 July 1999.

Harte, Bret. "The Heathen Chinee" (formerly "Plain Language from Truthful James."). The Overland Monthly Magazine. (Sept. 1879). *Mark Twain Library*. University of Virginia.

Ha, Thu-Huong. "The story behind the Statue of Liberty's unexpected transformation into a beacon for refugees and immigrants." *Quartz*. Quartz Media LLC. 1 Feb. 2017.

"Have We a Dusky Peril?" *Puget Sound American*. 16 Sept. 1906.

"Henderson v. Mayor of City of New York." *FindLaw*. Thomson Reuters. 2018.

Hernandez, Kelly Lytle. "The Crimes and Consequences of Illegal Immigration: A Cross-Border Examination of Operation Wetback, 1943 to 1954." *The Western Historical Quarterly*. Vol. 37, No. 4 (Winter, 2006).

Heumer, Michael. "Is There a Right to Immigrate." *Social Theory and Practice*. Vol. 36, No. 3 (2010), pp. 429–61.

Higham, John. *Strangers in the Land: Patterns of American Nativism, 1860–1925*. New Brunswick, NJ: Rutgers UP, 1955.

Higham, John. *Strangers in the Land: Patterns of American Nativism, 1860–1925*. New Brunswick, NJ: Rutgers UP, 2002, pp. 505–559.

Hing, Bill Ong. *Defining America Through Immigration Policy*. Philadelphia, PA: Temple UP, 2012. p. 21.

Hingston, Sandy. "Bullets and Bigots: Remembering Philadelphia's 1844 Anti-Catholic Riots." *Philadelphia*. News & Opinion. 17 Dec. 2015.

Hira, Ron. "New Data Show How Firms Like Infosys and Tata Abuse the H-1B Program." *EPI*. Economic Policy Institute. Working Economics Blog. 19 Feb. 2015.

"Historical Record: 1614 Treaty." *Charlescity*. Natives in the Landscape. Charles City County. 2006.

Hollender, Jeffrey, and David Levine. "Huffpo: The Harms of Regulation Phobia." American Sustainable Business Council, *Huffington Post*. Huffington Post. 2 June 2011.

Holmes, Steven A. "Legislation Eases Limits on Aliens." *New York Times*. New York Times, Co. 2 Feb. 1990.

"How to tell Japs from the Chinese." *Life Magazine*. 22 Dec. 1941, p. 81.

"Illinois DREAM Act Signed by Governor Quinn." *HuffPost*. Huffington Post. 2 Oct. 2011.

"Immigration." *Gallup*. Gallup News. 2017.

"Immigration Act of 1917." *University of Washington-Bothell Library*. Sixty-Fourth Congress. Sess. II. Chapters 27–29. 1917.

"The Immigration Act of 1924." *U.S. Department of State*. Office of the Historian. 2017.

"Immigration and the Great War." *NPS*. National Park Service. 2017.

"The Immigration and Nationality Act of 1952 (The McCarran-Walter Act)." *U.S. Department of State*. Office of the Historian. Milestones. 2017.

"Immigration Timeline." *Liberty Ellis Foundation*. The Statue of Liberty—Ellis Island Foundation, Inc. 2017.

"In First Month, Views of Trump Are Already Strongly Felt, Deeply Polarized." *Pew Research Center*. 16 Feb. 2017.

Ingraham, Christopher. "The riches 1 percent now owns more of the country's wealth than at any time in the past 50 years." *The Washington Post*. Washington Post Co. 6 Dec. 2017.

"INS Records for 1930s Mexican Repatriations." *USCIS*. U.S. Citizenship and Immigration Services. Department of Homeland Security. 3 Mar. 2014.

"Is Trump A Racist?" *Rasmussen Reports*. Rasmussen Reports, LLC. 18 Jan. 2018.

James, Mike. "Trump seeks $18 billion to extend border wall over 10 years." *USA Today*. USA Today. 6 Jan. 2018.

Johnson, Jenna and Abigail Hauslohner. "'I think Islam hates us': A timeline of Trump's comments about Islam and Muslims." *The Washington Post*. Washington Post Co. 20 May 2017.

Johnson, Kevin R. "The Forgotten Repatriation of Persons of Mexican Ancestry and Lesson for the War on Terror." *Pace Law Review*. Vol. 26, Iss. 1. Digital Commons. Sept. 2005.

Johnson, Lyndon B. "Immigration and Nationality Act of 1965." Full Remarks. 2 Oct. 1965. *LBJ Library*.

Jones, Jeffrey M. "Americans Again Opposed to Taking in Refugees." *Gallup*. Gallup News. 23 Nov. 2015.

Joshi, Anu. "Donald Trump's Border Wall—An Annotated Timeline." *Huffington Post*. Huffington Post. 1 Mar. 2017.

"Judging the Impact: A Post 9/11 America." *NPR*. National Public Radio. 16 July 2004.

Jue, Stanton. "Anson Burlingame, an American Diplomat." *UNC*. American Diplomacy. University of North Carolina, Chapel Hill. September 2011.

Kammer, Jerry. "The Hart-Celler Immigration Act of 1965." *CIS*. Center for Immigration Studies. 30 Sept. 2015.

Kang, Jerry. "Denying Prejudice: Internment, Redress, and Denial." *USLA Law Review*. Vol. 51, No 933. 2004.

Kang, S. Deborah. *The INS on the Line: Making Immigration Law on the US–Mexico Border, 1917–1954*. New York: Oxford UP, 2017 pp. 140–142.

Kelly, Amita. "FACT CHECK: Have Immigrants Lowered Wages For Blue-Collar American Workers?" *NPR*. National Public Radio. 4 Aug. 2017.

Kelly, Gary, Christine Bold, and Joad Raymond, Eds. *The Oxford History of Popular Print Culture: Volume Six: US Popular Print Culture 1860–1920*. New York: Oxford UP, 2012.

Kershner, Isabel. "Trump Cites Israel's 'Wall' as Model. The Analogy Is Iffy." *New York Times*. New York Times co. 27 Jan. 2017.

Kilgannon, Corey, and Joseph Goldstein. "Sayfullo Saipov, the Suspect in the New York Terror Attack, and His Past." *New York Times*. New York Times, Co. 31 Oct. 2017.

Kimmel, Lauren. "Does the Dakota Access Pipeline Violate Treaty Law?" *Michigan Journal of International Law*. Vol. 38, 17 Nov. 2016.

Kirby, Jen. "Trump blasts 'Diversity Visa Lottery Program,' after NYC terror attack." *VOX*. Vox Media. 1 Nov. 2017.

Kishi, Katayoun. "Assaults against Muslims in U.S. surpass 2001 level." *Pew Research*. Pew Research Center. 15 Nov. 2017.

Koslowski, Rey. "The Evolution of Border Controls as a Mechanism to Prevent Illegal Immigration." *MPI*. Migration Policy Institute. Reports. Feb. 2011.

Kramer, Paul A. "The Case of the 22 Lewd Chinese Women." *Slate*. The Slate Group. 23 Apr. 2012.

"Kristallnacht." *Holocaust Encyclopedia*. United States Holocaust Memorial Museum. 2018.

Labrador, Rocio Cara, and Danielle Renwick. "Central America's Violent Northern Triangle." *CFR*. Council on Foreign Relations. 18 Jan. 2018.

LaCasse, Alexander. "How many Muslim extremists are there? Just the facts, please." *CSMonitor*. The Christian Science Monitor. 13 Jan. 2015.

Laws of the State of New-York, Relating particularly to the City of New-York. New York: Gould and Banks, 1833, pp. 567–68.

Lazarus, Emma. "The New Colossus" (2 Nov. 1883), *NPS*. National Park Service. Statue of Liberty. 31 Jan. 2018.

Lee, Jonathan H.X. *Chinese Americans: The History and Culture of a People*. Santa Barbara, CA: ABC–CLIO. 2015.

Leiken, Robert S. "War On Terror: Mexico More Critical Than Ever for U.S." *Brookings*. Brookings Institution. 24 Mar. 2002.

LeMay, Michael C., and Elliott Robert Barkan. *U.S. Immigration and Naturalization Laws and Issues: A Documentary History*. Westport, CT: Greenwood P, 1999.

Lincoln, Abraham. "Speech to Germans at Cincinnati, Ohio." In Smith, Steven B. ed. *The Writings of Abraham Lincoln*. New Haven, CT: Yale UP, 2012.

"Lincoln on the Know-Nothing Party." August 24, 1844: Letter to

Joshua F. Speed. *NPS*. National Park Service. 10 Apr. 2015.

Lind, Dara. "How many immigrants have DACA, really? We finally have one answer—just as they start to lose it." Vox. 6 Oct 2017.

———. "Operation Wetback, the 1950s immigration policy Donald Trump loves, explained." *VOX*. Vox Media. 11 Nov. 2015.

———. "Why historians are fighting about 'No Irish Need Apply' signs—and why it matters." *VOX*. Vox Media. 4 Aug. 2015.

Lipka, Michael. "Muslims and Islam: Key findings in the U.S. and around the world." *Pew Research Center*. Pew Research. Facttank. 9 Aug. 2017.

Liptak, Adam. "Trump's Latest Travel Ban Suffers Blow From a Second Appeals Court." *New York Times*. New York Times Co. 15 Feb. 2018.

Lister, Tim. "Today's refugees follow path of Hungarians who fled Soviets in 1956." *CNN*. CNN World. 7 Sept. 2015.

Loveland, Ian D. *Constitutional Law*. New York: Routledge, 2000.

"Low-Skilled Immigrants." *IGM Chicago*. IGM Forum. 10 Dec. 2013.

Lynch, Grace Hwang. "Chinese Laborers Built Sonoma's Wineries. Racist Neighbors Drove Them Out." *NPR*. National Public Radio. 13 July 2017.

MacMedan, Dan. "U.S. urged to apologize for 1930s deportations." *USA Today*. Gannet Co, Inc. 5 Apr. 2006.

Madden, Mary, and Lee Rainie. "Americans' Attitudes About Privacy, Security and Surveillance." *Pew Research*. Pew Research Center. Internet and Technology. May 20, 2015. Web. 3 Nov. 2017.

Magness, Phillip W. "Alexander Hamilton as Immigrant: Musical Mythology Meets Federalist Reality." *Independent Review*. The Independent Institute, Vol. 21, No. 4, Spring 2017.

Manseau, Peter. "A forgotten History of Anti-Sikh Violence in the Early-20th-Century Pacific Northwest." *Slate*. Slate Group.

"Married Women's Property Laws." *Library of Congress*. American Women. 2018.

Marsh, Clay. "Opioid Addiction Isn't The Disease; It's The Symptom." Well-Being. *Thrive Global*. Huffington Post.9 Aug. 2017.

Martin, Philip. "Braceros: History, Compensation." *Rural Migration News*. University of California–Davis. Vol. 12, No. 2. Apr. 2006.

Martin, Philip L., Michael Fix, and Edward J. Taylor. *The New Rural Poverty: Agriculture & Immigration in California*. Washington, DC: The Urban Institute P, 2006 p. 12.

McCarthy, Joseph. "'Enemies from Within' Speech Delivered in Wheeling, West Virginia (1950)." *Digital History Project*. University of Houston.

McElroy, John Harmon. "Understanding the First Amendment's Religion Clauses." *ISI*. Intercollegiate Review. Intercollegiate Studies Institute. Spring 2011.

McGreevy, Patrick, and Anthony York. "Brown signs California Dream Act." *Los Angeles Times*. Los Angeles Times. 9 Oct. 2011.

McManus, Doyle. "To avoid a Manchester-type bombing on American soil, integrate Muslims." *Los Angeles Times*. Los Angeles Times. 24 May 2017.

Mehlman, Ken. "Hispanic outreach crucial to GOP." *Politico*. Political Inc. 1 May 2007.

"Memorandum from William J. Hopkins, 20 June 1952." *Truman Library and Museum*. University of Missouri. 2018.

Menn, Joseph. "Distrustful U.S. allies force spy agency to back down in encryption fight." *Reuters*. Thomson Reuters. Sept. 21, 2017. Web. 3 Nov. 2017.

Michener, James A. *The Bridge at Andau*. New York: Random House, 2014.

Miller, Greg, Vitkovskaya, Julie, and Reuben Fischer-Baum. "'This deal will make me look terrible': Full transcripts of Trump's calls with Mexico and Australia." *The Washington Post*. Washington Post Co. 3 Aug. 2017.

"*Minor v. Happersett.*" *Cornell*. Cornell Law School. Supreme Court. LII. 2018.

Mirrer, Louise. "As American as the Haitian Revolution." *Huffington Post*. Huffington Post. 17 Jan. 2018.

Mitter, Rana. "Forgotten ally? China's unsung role in World War II." *CNN*. CNN. 31 Aug. 2015.

"Mob Drives out Hindus." *New York Times*. New York Times, Co. 6 Sept. 1907.

Mohamed, Besheer. "A new estimate of the U.S. Muslim population." *Pew Research*. Pew Research Center.6 Jan. 2016.

Montero, David. "There is a renewed push to remove the McCarran name in Nevada." *Los Angeles Times*. Tronc Publishing. 27 Mar. 2017.

"Monthly Harvard-Harris Poll: January 2018 Re-Field." *Harvardharris Poll*. Harvard University Center for American Political Studies. Jan. 2018.

Moses, Paul. "Irish-Americans: Remember from whence you came." *CNN*. CNN. 16 Mar. 2017.

Munro, Neil. "USA Today: Amnesty Debate Is About 3.6 Million 'Dreamers,' not Just 800,000 DACA Illegals." *Freerepublic*. 20 Jan. 2018.

Naurath, Nicole. "Most Muslim Americans See No Justification for Violence." *Gallup News*. Gallup. 2 Aug. 2011.

Neiwert, David. "Home Is Where the Hate Is." *The Investigative Fund*. The Nation Institute. 22 June 2017.

Newport, Frank. "American Say Reagan Is the Greatest U.S. President." *Gallup*. Gallup News. 18 Feb. 2011.

———. "Historical Review: Americans' Views on Refugees Coming to U.S." *Gallup*. Gallup News. 19 Nov. 2015.

Nowrastex, Alex. "More Family-Based Immigrants in Australia & Canada than in the United States." *CATO*. Cato at Liberty. 11 Apr.

2017.

O'Keefe, Ed, David Weigel, and Paul Kane. "Nancy Pelosi's filibuster-style speech tops eight hours in bid to force immigration votes." *Washington Post*. Washington Post Co. 7 Feb. 2018.

O'Leary, Anna Ochoa. *Undocumented Immigrants in the United States: An Encyclopedia of Their Experience.*2014. Santa Barbara, CA: Greenwood P, 2014.

Olivas, Michael A. "The Story of *Plyler v. Doe*." *UH*. University of Houston Law Center. 2004.

Olmstead, Kenneth and Aaron Smith. "Americans and Cybersecurity." *Pew Research*. Pew Research Center. Jan. 26, 2017. Web. 4 Nov. 2017.

O'Neil, Tim. "A look back—Irish immigrants fight back in 1854 nativist riots." *St. Louis Post Dispatch*. STL Today. 8 Aug. 2010.

Orchowski, Margaret Sands. *The Law that Changed the Face of America: The Immigration and Nationality Act of 1965*. New York: Rowman & Littlefield, 2015.

"Origins of the Federal Immigration Service." *USCIS*. U.S. Citizenship and Immigration Services, Department of Homeland Security. 4 Feb. 2016.

"Orrenius, Pia M., and Madeline Zavodny. "A Comparison of the U.S. and Canadian Immigration Systems." *NAS*. National Academies of Science. 22 Sept. 2014.

O'Toole, James. *The Faithful: A History of Catholics in America*. Cambridge, MA: Harvard UP, 2009, p. 89.

Paine, Thomas. "Thoughts on the Present State of American Affairs." *Common Sense*. Independence Hall Association. 2018.

"The Partisan Divide on Political Values Grows Even Wider," *Pew Research*. 5 Oct. 2017.

Peralta, Eyder. "It Came Up In The Debate: Here Are 3 Things To Know About 'Operation Wetback.'" *NPR*. National Public Radio. 11

Nov. 2015.

Perlroth, Nicole, Larson, Jeff, and Scott Shane. "N.S.A. Able to Foil Basic Safeguards of Privacy on Web." *New York Times*. New York Times Company. Sept. 5, 2013. Web. 29 Oct. 2017.

Peters, Gerhard. "Presidential Job Approval Ratings Following the First 100 Days." *The American Presidency Project*. U of California. 2017.

Pfaelzer, Jean. *Driven Out: The Forgotten War Against Chinese Americans*. Berkeley, CA: U of California P, 2008.

Pipes, Daniel. "The Muslims are Coming! The Muslims are Coming!" *National Review*. 19 Nov. 1990.

Plumer, Brad. "Congress tried to fix immigration back in 1986. Why did it fail?" *Washington Post*. Washington Post, Co. 30 Jan. 2013.

"Plyler v. Doe." *Cornell Law School*. LII. Supreme Court. 2017.

"Plyler v. Doe." *US Courts*. Administrative Office of the US Courts. 2017.

Preston, Julia. "Immigrants Aren't Taking Americans' Jobs, New Study Finds." *New York Times*. New York Times, Co. 21 Sept. 2016.

"Public Remains Conflicted Over Islam." *Pew Research*. Pew Research Center. 24 Aug. 2010.

"Public Trust in Government: 1958–2017." *Pew Research*. Pew Research Center. 3 May 2017.

Purdy, Jedediah. "Environmentalism's Racist History." *New Yorker*. Condé Nast. 13 Aug. 2015.

"Racism & Exclusion." *National Park Service*. Manzanar National Historic Site. 2016.

Rashke, Richard. "The Horrible Laws that Blocked Jews from the US after World War 2 but Let Nazis in." *History News Network*. George Washington University. 20 Nov. 2016.

Raviv, Shaun. "If People Could Immigrate Anywhere, Would Poverty Be Eliminated?" *The Atlantic*. Atlantic Monthly Group. 26 Apr.

2013.

Reagan, Ronald. "Statement on United States Immigration and Refugee Policy." 30 July 1981. *The American Presidency Project*. U of California. 2018.

"The Recommendations of the President's Commission on Migratory Labor." U.S. Department of Labor. Apr. 1952. *UC-Berkeley Library*. Digital Collection. 2018.

"Refugee Act of 1980." *National Archives Foundation*. National Archives Foundation. 2018.

"Religious Landscape Study." *Pew Research*. Pew Research Center. 2018.

"Remarks by the President on Immigration." *Obama White House*. Office of the Press Secretary. 15 June 2012.

"Remembering California's 'Repatriation Program.'" *NPR*. National Public Radio. 2 Jan. 2006.

Reston, Maeve, and Gabe Ramirez. "How Trump's deportation plan failed 62 years ago." *CNN*. CNN. 19 Jan. 2016.

Richardson, Mark. *Robert Frost in Context*. New York, Cambridge UP, 2014.

Riley, Jason L. *Let Them In: The Case for Open Borders*. New York: Gotham Books, 2008.

Rizzo, Salvador. "Trump's claim that immigrants bring 'tremendous crime' is still wrong." *The Washington Post*. Washington Post, Co. 18 Jan. 2018.

Robert Siegel and Selena Simmons-Duffin. "How Did We Get To 11 Million Unauthorized Immigrants?" *NPR*. National Public Radio. 7 Mar. 2017.

Roberts, Sam. "Story of the First Through Ellis Island Is Rewritten." *New York Times*. New York Times Co. 14 Sept. 2006.

Rodriguez, Nicole. "Trump's Border Wall Was a $2.6 Million Hit on San Diego Taxpayers." *Newsweek*. Newsweek, LLC.19 Jan. 2018.

Rollo, David. "Gerald of Wales' 'Topographia Hibernica': Sex and the Irish Nation." *The Romantic Review*. Vol. 86, No. 2. March 1995.

Romero, Anthony D. "School Is For Everyone: Celebrating *Plyler v. Doe*." *ACLU*. American Civil Liberties Union. 11 July 2012.

Roosevelt, Franklin D. "Message to Congress on Repeal of the Chinese Exclusion Law." 11 Oct. 1943. *The American Presidency Project*. University of California, Santa Barbara.

Roosevelt, Theodore. *A Square Deal*. Allendale, NJ: The Allendale Press, 1906.

Rosenbaum, Ron. "The Shocking Savagery of America's Early History." *Smithsonian*. Smithsonian Institution. 21 Feb. 2013.

Ruiz, Vicki L. *From Out of the Shadows: Mexican Women in Twentieth-Century America*. New York: Oxford UP, 1998.

Sanchez, George J. *Becoming Mexican American: Ethnicity, Culture, and Identity in Chicanos Los Angeles, 1900–1945*. New York: Oxford UP, 1993.

Saphier, Jon. *High Expectations Teaching: How We Persuade Students to Believe and Act on "Smart Is Something You Can Get"*. Thousand Oaks, CA: Corwin, 2017.

Schilling, Vincent. "The True Story of Pocahontas: Historical Myths Versus Sad Reality." *Indian Country*. Indian Country Media Network. 8 Sept. 2017.

Schmitt, Eric, and Linda Qiu. "Fact Check: The Trump Administration's Arguments for a Border Wall." *New York Times*. New York Times co. 27 Apr. 2017.

Shanks, Cheryl Lynne. *Immigration and the Politics of American Sovereignty, 1890–1990*. Ann Arbor, MI: U of Michigan P, 2009.

Shear, Michael D. "How Washington Reached the Brink of a Shutdown." *New York Times*. New York Times, Co. 19 Jan. 2018.

"'Shut the Door': A Senator Speaks for Immigration Restriction." *George Mason University*. History Matters. 3 Jan. 2017.

Singh, Minal. "A Chinaman's chance: The immigrant's journey—Eric Liu on race, immigration, and citizenship." *Asian Weekly*. 30 Jan. 2015.

Smith, Daniel Scott. "The Demographic History of Colonial New England." *Journal of Economic History*, Cambridge UP Vol. 32, No. 1, Mar. 1972: pp. 165–83.

Sondhaus, Lawrence. *World War I: The Global Revolution*. New York: Cambridge UP, 2011.

"Soong Mei-Ling, 'Addresses To The House Of Representatives And To The Senate,' February 18, 1943." *USC*. University of Southern California. USC US–China Institute. 1943.

"State of Hawai'i and Ismael Elshickh Vs. Donald J. Trump, Et Al—Order." *ACLU*. American Civil Liberties Union. 2018.

"Statements from the Debate on Indian Removal." *Columbia University*.

Steckelberg, Aaron, Chris Alcantara, and Tracy Jan. "A look at Trump's border wall prototypes." *The Washington Post*. Washington Post Company. 31 Oct. 2017.

"The Strange Case of the Chinese Laundry." *Thirteen*. Freedom: A History of the U.S. PBS. 2002.

Suls, Rob. "Most Americans continue to oppose U.S. border wall, doubt Mexico would pay for it." *Pew Research*. Pew Research Center. 24 Feb. 2017.

Suro, Roberto. "America's Views of Immigration: The Evidence from Public Opinion Surveys." *Migration Policy Institute*. Transatlantic Council on Migration. May 2009.

Swanson, Ana. "Opening up borders: An idea economists tend to love and politicians detest." *Washington Post*. Washington Post, Co. 14 Oct. 2016

Swift, Art. "Gallup Vault: WWII-Era Support for Japanese Internment." *Gallup News*. Gallup Vault. Aug. 31, 2016.

"Takao Ozawa v. US." (1922) *FindLaw*. Thomson Reuters. US Supreme Court. 2016.

Tan, Avianne. "Without immigrants, the US economy would be a 'disaster,' experts say." *ABC News*. ABC. 16 Feb. 2017.

Taylor, Frank J. "The People Nobody Wants." *Saturday Evening Post*. Saturday Evening Post Society. 9 May 1942.

Tchen, John Kuo Wei. *New York before Chinatown: Orientalism and the Shaping of American Culture: 1776–1882*. Baltimore, MD: The John Hopkins UP, 1999.

Tharoor, Ishaan. "What Americans thought of Jewish refugees on the eve of World War II." *Washington Post*. Washington Post, Co. 17 Nov. 2015.

"There Are 3.6M 'Dreamers'—A Number Far Greater Than Commonly Known." *AMREN*. American Renaissance. 19 Jan. 2018.

"'This Is About Basic Decency.' Obama Rips Trump Over DACA Decision," *Time*. Time Inc. 5 Sept. 2017.

Tichenor, Daniel J. *Dividing Lines: The Politics of Immigration Control in America*. Princeton, NJ: Princeton UP, 2002.

Tiezzi, Shannon. "When the US and China Were Allies." *The Diplomat*. The Diplomat. 21 Aug. 2015.

Tomsen, Jaqueline. "Trump waives dozens of environmental rules to speed up construction of border wall." *The Hill*. Capitol Hill Publishing Group. 22 Jan. 2018.

Torres, Nicole. "The H-1B Visa Debate, Explained." *HBR*. Harvard Business Review. 4 May 2017.

"Transcript of the Chinese Exclusion Act (1882)." *Our Documents*. The U.S. National Archives. 2018.

"Treaty With the Delawares: 1778." *Yale Law School*. Lillian Goldman Law Library.

"The Trial." *University at Buffalo Libraries*. Pan-American Exposition of 1901. 2018.

Truman, Harry S. "Statement and Directive by the President on Immigration to the United states of Certain Displaced Persons and Refugees in Europe." 22 Dec. 1945. *Truman Library & Museum*. University of Missouri. 2018.

———. "Statement by the President Upon Signing Bill Amending the Displaced Persons Act." 16 June 1950. *Truman Library and Museum*. University of Missouri. 2018.

———. "Statement by the President Upon Signing the Displaced Persons Act." 25 June 1948. *The American Presidency Project*. University of California. 2018.

———. "Veto of Bill To Revise the Laws Relating to Immigration, Naturalization, and Nationality." 25 June 1952. *Truman Library & Museum*. University of Missouri. 2018.

Trump, Donald. "Remarks by President Trump in Joint Address to Congress." *White House*. Trump White House. 28 Feb. 2017.

"U.S. Immigration Station, Angel Island." *NPS*. National Park Service. 2018.

"U.S. Rel. Turner v. Williams. (1904)" *FindLaw*. Thompson Reuters. 2018.

"U.S. v. Bhagat Singh Thind." *FindLaw*. Thompson Reuters. US Supreme Court. 2016.

Valverde, Miriam. "A look at the data on domestic terrorism and who's behind it." *Politifact*. Politifact, LLC. 16 Aug. 2017.

———. "Timeline: DACA, the Trump administration and a government shutdown." *Politifact*. Politifact. 22 Jan. 2018.

———. "Will a border wall stop drugs from coming into the United States?" *Politifact*. Politifact. 26 Oct. 2017.

"Voters Say Islamic Leaders Should Do More to Promote Peace," *Rasmussen Reports*. Rasmussen Reports, LLC. 30 May 2017.

Wade, Lisa. "US Schools are Teaching Our Children that Native Americans are Dead." *PS Mag*. Pacific Standard. Dec 3, 2014.

Wang, Amy B. "'Brave and selfless' Oregon stabbing victims hailed as heroes for standing up to racist rants." *The Washington Post*. Washington Post, Co. 28 May 2017.

Wang, Hansi Lo. "Broken Promises On Display At Native American Treaties Exhibit." *NPR*. National Public Radio. 18 Jan. 2015.

———. "Chinese-American Descendants Uncover Forged Family Histories." *NPR*. National Public Radio. 17 Dec. 2013.

Waters, Mary C., and Marisa Gerstein Pineau (Eds.). "The Integration of Immigrants into American Society." *NAP*. National Academies Press. 2015.

Waxman, Olivia B. "Ellis Island's Busiest Day Ever Was 110 Years Ago. Here's Why." *Time*. Time Inc. 17 Apr. 2017.

Weber, Mark. "The Japanese camps in California." *Journal of Historical Review*. Vol. 2, Iss. 1. p. 50, 1981.

Weiner, Rachel. "Pete Hoekstra's China ad provokes accusations of racism." *The Washington Post*. Washington Post co. 6 Feb. 2012.

Weissmann, Jordan. "U.S. Income Inequality: It's Worse Today Than It Was in 1774." *The Atlantic*. Atlantic Monthly Group. 19 Sept. 2012.

Westcott, Lucy. "What History Tells Us About Building A Wall To Solve A Problem." *Newsweek*. Newsweek, LLC. 14 Oct. 2015.

"What is Genocide?" *USHMM*. United States Holocaust Memorial Museum. Holocaust Encyclopedia. 2017.

White, Steven. "Many Americans support Trump's immigration order. Many Americans backed Japanese internment camps, too." *The Washington Post*. Washington Post, Co. 2 Feb. 2017.

Wilkerson, Miranda E., and Salmons, Joseph. "Linguistic Marginalities: Becoming American without Learning English." *Journal of Transnational American Studies*. 2012.

Wills, Matthew. "The Curious History of Ellis Island." *Jstor Daily*. ITHAKA. 1 Jan. 2017.

Wilson, Reid. "Texas officials warn of immigrants with terrorist ties crossing southern border." *Washington Post*. Washington Post, Co. 26 Feb. 2015.

Wolfensberger, Don. "Woodrow Wilson, Congress and Anti-Immigrant Sentiment in America: An Introductory Essay." *Wilson Center*. Woodrow Wilson International Center for Scholars. 12 Mar. 2007.

Wong, Julia Carrie. "Trump's border wall: prototypes loom large, but where are the protesters?" *The Guardian*. Guardian News and Media. 29 Jan. 2018.

Woollacott, Martin. "The Boat People." *The Guardian*. Guardian News and Media. 3 Dec. 1977.

Wu, Jean Yu-Wen Shen, and Thomas Chen. *Asian American Studies Now*. New Brunswick, NJ: Rutgers UP, 2010 p. 605.

"The XYZ Affair and the Quasi-War with France, 1798–1800." *Office of the Historian*. U.S. Department of State. 2016.

Ye Hee Lee, Michelle. "Do 80 percent of Americans oppose sanctuary cities?" *The Washington Post*. Washington Post, Co. 28 Mar. 2017.

Younge, Gary. "Mexicans expelled in 30s ask for justice." *The Guardian*. Guardian News and Media. 16 July 2003.

Zahra, Tara. *The Great Departure: Mass Migration from Eastern Europe and the Making of the Free World*. New York: W.W. Norton & Company, 2016.

Index